T0181938

Communications
in Computer and Information Science　　1910

Rationale
The CCIS series is devoted to the publication of proceedings of computer science conferences. Its aim is to efficiently disseminate original research results in informatics in printed and electronic form. While the focus is on publication of peer-reviewed full papers presenting mature work, inclusion of reviewed short papers reporting on work in progress is welcome, too. Besides globally relevant meetings with internationally representative program committees guaranteeing a strict peer-reviewing and paper selection process, conferences run by societies or of high regional or national relevance are also considered for publication.

Topics
The topical scope of CCIS spans the entire spectrum of informatics ranging from foundational topics in the theory of computing to information and communications science and technology and a broad variety of interdisciplinary application fields.

Information for Volume Editors and Authors
Publication in CCIS is free of charge. No royalties are paid, however, we offer registered conference participants temporary free access to the online version of the conference proceedings on SpringerLink (http://link.springer.com) by means of an http referrer from the conference website and/or a number of complimentary printed copies, as specified in the official acceptance email of the event.

CCIS proceedings can be published in time for distribution at conferences or as post-proceedings, and delivered in the form of printed books and/or electronically as USBs and/or e-content licenses for accessing proceedings at SpringerLink. Furthermore, CCIS proceedings are included in the CCIS electronic book series hosted in the SpringerLink digital library at http://link.springer.com/bookseries/7899. Conferences publishing in CCIS are allowed to use Online Conference Service (OCS) for managing the whole proceedings lifecycle (from submission and reviewing to preparing for publication) free of charge.

Publication process
The language of publication is exclusively English. Authors publishing in CCIS have to sign the Springer CCIS copyright transfer form, however, they are free to use their material published in CCIS for substantially changed, more elaborate subsequent publications elsewhere. For the preparation of the camera-ready papers/files, authors have to strictly adhere to the Springer CCIS Authors' Instructions and are strongly encouraged to use the CCIS LaTeX style files or templates.

Abstracting/Indexing
CCIS is abstracted/indexed in DBLP, Google Scholar, EI-Compendex, Mathematical Reviews, SCImago, Scopus. CCIS volumes are also submitted for the inclusion in ISI Proceedings.

How to start
To start the evaluation of your proposal for inclusion in the CCIS series, please send an e-mail to ccis@springer.com.

Wang Yongtian · Wu Lifang

Editors

Image and Graphics Technologies and Applications

18th Chinese Conference, IGTA 2023
Beijing, China, August 17–19, 2023
Revised Selected Papers

 Springer

Editors
Wang Yongtian
Beijing Institute of Technology
Beijing, China

Wu Lifang
Beijing University of Technology
Beijing, China

ISSN 1865-0929   ISSN 1865-0937 (electronic)
Communications in Computer and Information Science
ISBN 978-981-99-7548-8   ISBN 978-981-99-7549-5 (eBook)
https://doi.org/10.1007/978-981-99-7549-5

This Springer imprint is published by the registered company Springer Nature Singapore Pte Ltd.
The registered company address is: 152 Beach Road, #21-01/04 Gateway East, Singapore 189721, Singapore

Paper in this product is recyclable.

Preface

We were honored to organize the 18th Image and Graphics Technology and Application Conference (IGTA 2023). The conference was sponsored by Beijing Society of Image and Graphics and was organized by Beijing University of Technology. The conference was held at Beijing Friendship Hotel from Aug 17 to 19, 2023.

IGTA is a professional conference and an important forum for image processing, computer graphics, and related topics, including but not limited to image analysis and understanding, computer vision and pattern recognition, data mining, virtual reality and augmented reality, and image technology applications. The theme of IGTA 2023 was "Images, Graphics, and Large Models". This year, we received submissions from different countries and regions and the selection criterion was competitive. At least two reviewers reviewed each submission. After careful evaluation, 27% of submissions (35 manuscripts) were selected for oral or poster presentations.

The keynote speech, invited talks, and oral presentations of IGTA 2023 reflected the latest progress in the field of images and graphics. We believe that these provide a valuable reference for scientists and engineers with relevant interests.

As the conference chairs, we would like to thank our committee members and staff for all the hard work they have done for this conference under unprecedented difficulties. Thanks go to all the authors for their contributions and all the reviewers for their valuable suggestions. Finally, I would also like to thank our host, professors, and students from the Beijing University of Technology for their tremendous support. We hope to see you face to face at IGTA 2024!

April 2023

Wang Yongtian
Wu Lifang

Organization

General Conference Chairs

Wang Yongtian   Beijing Institute of Technology, China
Wu Lifang   Beijing University of Technology, China

Organizing Chairs

Liu Yue   Beijing Institute of Technology, China
Liu Yongjin   Tsinghua University, China
Ma Nan   Beijing University of Technology, China
Yang Zhen   Beijing University of Technology, China
Zhang Man   Beijing University of Posts and
                       Telecommunications, China
Hu Yongli   Beijing University of Technology, China

Executive and Coordination Committee

Duan Haibin   Beihang University, China
Huang Hua   Beijing Normal University, China
Huang Qingming   University of Chinese Academy of Sciences,
                       China
Ma Huimin   University of Science and Technology Beijing,
                       China
Ji Xiangyang   Tsinghua University, China
Liu Chenglin   Institute of Automation, Chinese Academy of
                       Sciences, China
Peng Yuxin   Peking University, China
Yang Weijun   First Research Institute of the Ministry of Public
                       Security of P.R.C., China
Zhao Yao   Beijing Jiaotong University, China

Program Committee Chairs

He Ran (PC Chair)	Institute of Automation Chinese Academy of Sciences, China
Wu Zhongke	Beijing Normal University, China
Ma Zhanyu	Beijing University of Post and Telecommunications, China
Song Weitao	Beijing Institute of Technology, China
Gu Ke	Beijing University of Technology, China
Yin Xucheng	
Si Pengbo	Beijing University of Technology, China

Research Committee Chairs

Zhang Fengjun	Software Institute of the Chinese Academy of Sciences, China
Li Haisheng	Beijing Technology and Business University, China
Li Xueming	Beijing University of Post and Telecommunications, China
Dong Jing	Institute of Automation Chinese Academy of Sciences, China
Liang Xiaohui	Beihang University, China
Yang Jian	Beijing Institute of Technology, China

Publicity and Exhibition Committee Chairs

Yuan Xiaoru	Peking University, China
Yan Jun	Journal of Image and Graphics, China
Yang Lei	Communication University of China, China
Lu Feng	Beihang University, China
Yan Jianzhuo	Beijing University of Technology, China
Feng Jinchao	Beijing University of Technology, China
Wang Xingce	Beijing Normal University, China

Web Publicity Chairs

Jia Maokun	Beijing University of Technology, China
Zhang Haopeng	Beihang University, China
Jian Meng	Beijing University of Technology, China

Program Committee Members

Jeremy M. Wolfe	Harvard Medical School, USA
Takafumi Taketomi	NAIST, Japan
Henry Been-Lirn Duh	La Trobe University, Australia
Youngho Lee	Mokpo National University, South Korea
Huang Yiping	Taiwan University, China
Nobuchika Sakata	Osaka University, Japan
Seokhee Jeon	Kyung Hee University, Korea
Cao Weiqun	Beijing Forestry University, China
Di Kaichang	Aerospace Information Research Institute, Chinese Academy of Sciences, China
Gan Fuping	Ministry of Land and Resources of the People's Republic of China, China
Jiang Yan	Beijing Institute of Fashion Technology, China
Li Xueyou	National Surveying and Mapping Engineering Technology Research Center, China
Zhao Huijie	Beijing University of Aeronautics and Astronautics, China
Chen Yi	Beijing Technology and Business University, China
Lv Ke	University of Chinese Academy of Sciences, China
Ma Siwei	Peking University, China
Cheng Mingzhi	Beijing Institute of Technology, China
Li Qingyuan	Chinese Academy of Surveying & Mapping, China
Liu Liang	Beijing University of Posts and Telecommunications, China
Sun Yankui	Tsinghua University, China
Wang Yahui	Beijing University of Graphic Communication, China
Wang Yiding	North China University of Technology, China
Yang Cheng	Communication University of China, China
Wang Shengjin	Tsinghua University, China
Zhao Yao	Beijing Jiaotong University, China
Yao Guoqiang	Beijing Film Academy, China
Yuan Jiazheng	Beijing Union University, China
Zhang Aiwu	Capital Normal University, China
Fan Jingfan	Beijing Institute of Technology, China
Han Xiangdi	Journal of Image and Graphics, China
Huang Gao	Tsinghua University, China

Huang Huaibo	Institute of Automation, Chinese Academy of Sciences, China
Huang Yetao	Beijing Fengjing Technology Co., Ltd, China
Li Feng	Qian Xuesen Laboratory CAST, China
Li Sheng	Peking University, China
Li Xirong	Renmin University of China, China
Meng Bo	First Research Institute of the Ministry of Public Security of P.R.C., China
Ren Lifeng	Global saile (Beijing) Technology Co., Ltd, China
Sang Xinzhu	Beijing University of Posts and Telecommunications, China
Shi Xiaogang	Beijing Xiaolong Technology Co., Ltd, China
Song Yong	Beijing Institute of Technology, China
Tan Li	Beijing Technology and Business University, China
Tian Yun	Beijing Normal University, China
Tian Zheng	Beijing Chaori 3D Technology Co., Ltd, China
Wang Miao	Beijing University of Aeronautics and Astronautics, China
Wang Wei	Institute of Automation, Chinese Academy of Sciences, China
Wang Chunshui	Beijing Film Academy, China
Weng Dongdong	Beijing Institute of Technology, China
Zang Xiaojun	Beijing Sweet Technology Co., Ltd, China
Zhang Man	Beijing University of Posts and Telecommunications, China
Zhao Jian	Academy of Military Sciences, China

Contents

Visualization and Visual Analysis

Virtual Reality and Human-Computer Interaction

Applications of Image and Graphics

xiv   Contents

Image Processing and Enhancement Techniques

Underwater Image Enhancement and Restoration Techniques: A Comprehensive Review, Challenges, and Future Trends

Mingjie Wang, Fengquan Lan, Zezhao Su, and Weiling Chen[✉]

Fujian Key Lab for Intelligent Processing and Wireless Transmission of Media Information,
Fuzhou University, Fuzhou 350108, China
{221127190,221127157,041802220,weiling.chen}@fzu.edu.cn

Abstract. Underwater optical images serve as crucial carriers and representations of ocean information. They play a vital role in the field of marine exploration. However, the quality of images captured by underwater cameras often falls short of the expected standards due to the complex underwater environment. This limitation significantly hampers the application and advancement of intelligent underwater image processing systems. Consequently, underwater image enhancement and restoration have been attracting extensive research efforts. In this paper, we review the degradation mechanisms and imaging models of underwater images, and summarize the challenges associated with underwater image enhancement and restoration. Meanwhile, we provide a comprehensive overview of the research progress in underwater optical image enhancement and restoration, and introduces the publicly available underwater image datasets and commonly-used quality evaluation metrics. Through extensive and systematic experiments, the superiority and limitations of underwater image enhancement and restoration methods are further explored. Finally, this review discusses the existing issues in this field and prospects future research directions. It is hoped that this paper will provide valuable references for future studies and contribute to the advancement of research in this domain.

Keywords: Underwater image enhancement · Underwater image restoration · Image quality assessment · Underwater optical imaging · Object detection

1 Introduction

In recent years, the rapid advancement of economic has led to escalating pressures in the exploitation and utilization of terrestrial space and resources. Consequently, an increasing number of researchers have turned their attention to the enigmatic underwater world. The processing of underwater images plays a pivotal role in a wide range of domains, including ocean resource development, environmental monitoring, and security defense. Nevertheless, underwater imagery exhibits entirely different characteristics compared to atmospheric imagery. Influenced by the unique physical and chemical properties of the underwater environment, underwater images frequently encounter challenges such as blurred details, reduced contrast, and color distortions. The progress of underwater computer vision applications relies on the quality of the acquired images. Hence, it is crucial to design algorithms capable of enhancing and restoring underwater images in various complex environments.

Recently, researchers worldwide have conducted extensive investigations into underwater image processing and visual technologies, with several scholars providing reviews of the field's current progress. Han et al. [1] provided an overview of underwater image dehazing and color restoration algorithms, but did not introduce the relevant datasets and quality evaluation metrics. Wang et al. [2] discussed traditional methods for underwater image enhancement and restoration, but did not comprehensively review data-driven approaches. In contrast to the aforementioned studies, this paper presents the following significant contributions: First, we conduct a comprehensive examination of the challenges and recent advancements in the field of underwater image enhancement and restoration. Second, we sort out the publicly available underwater image datasets and commonly-utilized quality evaluation metrics. And then we implement the quantitative and qualitative experimental analyses of classical algorithms. Third, we innovatively explore the interplay between low-level underwater image enhancement and downstream high-level vison tasks. Finally, the paper concludes by providing a forward-looking perspective on the future trends in underwater image enhancement and restoration techniques.

2   Underwater Image Enhancement and Restoration

Underwater image enhancement and restoration techniques assume a crucial role in optimizing the overall quality of underwater images. This section provides an introductory overview of underwater imaging model and various types of image quality degradation. Furthermore, clear taxonomies are used to offer a systematic review of existing classical algorithms employed for underwater image enhancement and restoration. Figure 1 visually illustrates the classification of underwater image enhancement and restoration schemes.

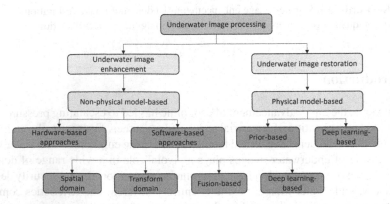

Fig. 1. Classification of algorithms for underwater image enhancement and restoration.

2.1 Challenges of Underwater Imaging

The underwater imagery data represents a vital source of optical information within the marine realm. Nevertheless, the field of underwater imaging confronts a range of severe challenges owing to the inherent complexity of the underwater environment. Gaining profound insights into the characteristics of underwater optical imaging models holds immense potential in facilitating the exploration and formulation of robust and efficacious strategies for optimizing the quality of underwater images. Commonly, methods for underwater image restoration are constructed upon the foundation of the classical Jaffe-McGlamery model or its variations. Figure 2 visually presents the underwater optical imaging process and the wavelength-dependent attenuation of light during underwater propagation. During the process of underwater imaging, notable degradation factors can be succinctly outlined as follows:

1) The absorption and scattering coefficients of light at different wavelengths vary underwater. This fact results in a prevalent and pronounced color cast attribute in underwater images, primarily manifesting as a blue-green tone.
2) Light scattering phenomena are commonly present in underwater environments, leading to image degradation such as blurring, fogging, and reduced contrast.
3) With increasing underwater depth, natural light intensity undergoes significant attenuation. To address this, artificial light sources are often employed to facilitate illumination during deep-sea photography. However, this practice introduces noticeable disparities in the distribution of brightness within underwater images.

To sum up, underwater optical images encounter a series of complex degradation factors, leading to impaired visual quality and restricting their usability in subsequent machine vision tasks.

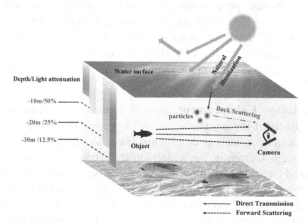

Fig. 2. Schematic diagram of underwater optical imaging and light attenuation.

2.2 Underwater Image Enhancement

Underwater image enhancement techniques are typically non-physical model-based approaches, aiming to enhance the visual quality of low-quality images by directly manipulating pixel values. These methods generally neglect prior knowledge of optical imaging parameters in water and primarily concentrate on improving contrast, sharpness, and color rendition to ensure the enhanced images are more confirm to the human visual perception. Underwater image enhancement methods are commonly classified into two categories: hardware-based methods and software-based methods.

2.2.1 Hardware-Based Approaches

Early investigations in the field of underwater image quality improvement mainly concentrated on upgrading hardware-based imaging devices. Schechner et al. [3] proposed a polarization-based algorithm, which effectively removed the effects of light scattering to a certain extent. However, it is unsuitable for images obtained underwater with artificial illumination. Treibitz et al. [4] developed a non-scanning recovery method based on active polarization imaging. It is beneficial to yield significant enhancement in the visibility of degraded images, and is capable of working with the simple and compact hardware. Liu et al. [5] used a self-built range-gated imaging system to construct a scattering model and proposed an optimal pulse with a gate control coordination strategy.

However, these hardware-dependent approaches commonly exhibit limitations such as low efficiency and high costs associated with frequent updates, impeding their capacity to address the multifaceted challenges inherent in diverse underwater environments.

2.2.2 Software-Based Approaches

With the maturation and progression of image processing and computer vision technologies, researchers have increasingly redirected their focus towards software-based methodologies. Underwater image enhancement and restoration algorithms are employed to ameliorate the quality of underwater images, thus enabling the resultant processed images to align with human visual perception characteristics and meet the demands of high-level machine vision tasks.

Spatial-Domain Image Enhancement. Spatial domain image enhancement directly manipulates the pixels of the image, adjusting the grayscale values of the red, green, and blue color channels, as well as employing grayscale mapping to modify the color hierarchy of the image. Currently, the widely-utilized spatial domain techniques can be broadly categorized into contrast enhancement methods and color correction methods.

High-contrast images tend to have both rich grayscale details and high dynamic range. Zuiderveld et al. [6]. Proposed Contrast Limited Adaptive Histogram Equalization (CLAHE), which applied constraints to the local contrast of an image, achieving simultaneous contrast enhancement and noise reduction. Huang et al. [7] presented a relative global histogram stretching (RGHS) method for shallow-water image enhancement. Although histogram equalization and its variant algorithms generally achieve relatively good enhancement results for regular images, they may not be fully applicable to underwater scenes. These algorithms insufficiently consider the inherent characteristics of the underwater environment, leading to significant artifacts and amplified noise when applied to underwater images, especially in low-light conditions, the images are more susceptible to color distortion.

Due to the selective attenuation of light in the underwater environment, underwater images frequently suffer from significant color deviations. To tackle aforementioned problems, Henke et al. [8] proposed a novel feature-based color constancy hypothesis. Based on this hypothesis, an algorithm utilized for removing the color cast of images captured underwater was given. Inspired by the Multi-Scale Retinex with Color Restoration (MSRCR) framework proposed in [9], Liu et al. [10] presented a two-stage method. Initially, the MSRCR joint guided filtering method was given for dehazing, and then the white balance fusion global guided image filtering (G-GIF) technology was proposed aiming at enhancing the edge details and correcting the color of underwater images.

Transform-Domain Image Enhancement. Unlike the spatial-domain approaches, transform-domain image enhancement methods generally transform the spatial domain image to the corresponding domain for processing by applying the Fourier transform, Laplacian pyramid, wavelet transform, and other techniques [11]. In the frequency domain, the low frequency components of an image normally represent the smooth background region and texture information, whereas the high frequency components correspond to the edge region where the pixel values change dramatically. The quality of the image can be improved effectively by amplifying the frequency component of interest and suppressing the frequency component of disinterest, simultaneously.

Wavelet transform is usually employed in underwater image enhancement, Srikanth et al. [12] developed a representation of the energy functionals for the approximation and the detailed coefficients of the underwater image. In order to adjust the contrast and correct the color cast, the detailed coefficients and the approximation coefficients of RGB components were modified meticulously. Iqbal et al. [13] introduced an underwater image enhancement approach utilizing Laplacian decomposition. The image was divided into the low-frequency and high-frequency sub-bands by Laplacian transform. The low-frequency image was dehazed and normalized for white balancing while amplifying the high-frequency sub-band for maintaining the edge details. Subsequently, the enhanced image was obtained from fusing the two processed images.

Fusion-Based Image Enhancement. Considering that use single feature to design an underwater image enhancement method may not give full play to the advantages of the features, several algorithms based on fusion have been extensively studied and applied to underwater image enhancement one after another. The fusion images can reflect multi-dimensional details from the source images, enabling a comprehensive representation of the scenes that satisfies the requirements of both human observers and computer vision systems.

Ancuti et al. [14] developed a strategy to improve the visual quality of underwater images and videos by multi-scale fusion. The specific operation of this technique can be summarized as follows. Firstly, the proposed approach took the color-corrected and contrast-enhanced versions of the original underwater image/video frame as the input. Then, four fusion weights were defined in accordance with the contrast, salience and exposedness of the two input images, which aimed to improve the visibility of the degraded target scene. Finally, the multi-scale fusion method was employed for obtaining the final enhanced result with the aim of overcoming the demerits of artifacts and undesirable halos brought by linear fusion. Analogously, Muniraj et al. [15] proposed a method for underwater image perceptual enhancement via a combination of color constancy framework and dehazing. Chang et al. [16] introduced a color-contrast complementary framework consisting of two steps, i.e., adaptive color perception balance and attentive weighted fusion.

Deep Learning-Based Image Enhancement. With the substantial advances in deep learning, a variety of learning-based methods have been broadly exploited in vision tasks and demonstrated excellent performance.

As a convolutional neural network (CNN) is capable to learn robust image representation on various vision tasks, numerous novel CNN-based algorithms are developed for underwater image enhancement. Perez et al. [17] took the lead to make a groundbreaking attempt. In the same year, Wang et al. [18] subsequently presented an end-to-end CNN-based framework (UIE-Net) containing two subnets employed for color correction and haze removal, which was applicable to cross-scene applications. Li et al. [19] established a large-scale underwater image enhancement pseudo-reference dataset referred to as UIEBD. Meanwhile, motivated by the multi-scale fusion strategy, the authors designed a gated fusion network trained on the constructed UIEBD. Wang et al. [20] proposed a novel UIEC^2-Net that creatively incorporated both HSV color space and RGB color space in one simple CNN framework, which played a guiding role in the subsequent investigations of underwater image color correction. Moreover, the coarse-to-fine strategy has drawn considerable attention in low-level vision tasks recently and attained impressive performance. Inspired by it, Cai et al. [21] conducted a coarse-to-fine scheme that utilizes three different cascaded subnetworks to progressively improve underwater image degradation.

Generative Adversarial Networks (GANs) represent a type of novel network structure designed to generate desired outputs through adversarial learning between a generative model and a discriminator model. The data-driven training approach of GANs is particularly well-suited for addressing the issue of underwater image degradation caused by multiple factors. Consequently, GAN models have gained significant traction in the field of underwater image enhancement and restoration. Fabbri et al. [22] applied a CycleGAN [23] to synthesize a diversity of paired training data, and then utilized these pairs to correct color deviation in a supervised manner. All of the aforementioned algorithms utilize sufficient synthetic data to train their networks and obtain decent performance. Nevertheless, the significant domain discrepancies between the synthetic and real-world data are generally not taken into consideration by these methods, resulting in the undesirable artifacts and color distortions on diverse real-world underwater images. To address this issue, a novel two-stage domain adaptation network for enhancing underwater images was developed in [24], which improved both the robustness and generalization capabilities of the network.

Deep learning has undoubtedly demonstrated its significance in underwater image enhancement. However, most mainstream algorithms are computationally expensive and memory intensive, hindering their deployment in practical applications. To overcome this challenge, Li et al. [25] proposed a lightweight CNN-based model that directly reconstructs the clear underwater images in place of estimating parameters of underwater imaging model. This method can be extended to underwater video frame-by-frame enhancement efficiently. Similarly, Naik et al. [26] unveiled a novel shallow neural network known as Shallow-UWnet that requires less memory and computational costs while achieving comparable performance to state-of-the-art algorithms. Islam et al. [27] presented a fully-convolutional GAN-based model, which met the demand for real-time underwater image enhancement. Jiang et al. [28] introduced an innovative recursive strategy for model and parameter reuse, enabling the design of a lightweight model based on Laplacian image pyramids.

2.3 Underwater Image Restoration

The restoration of underwater images can be regarded as an inverse process of underwater imaging, which typically employs prior knowledge and optical properties of underwater imaging to implement degraded image reconstruction. Currently, underwater image restoration methods primarily encompass prior-based approaches and deep learning-based approaches. In this section, we conduct a systematic review of classical restoration schemes.

2.3.1 Prior-Based Image Restoration

Prior-based underwater image restoration methods typically rely on various prior knowledge or assumptions to deduce the crucial parameters of the established degradation model, facilitating the restoration of underwater imagery.

In 2011, He et al. [29] proposed an image prior - dark channel prior (DCP), subsequently, the DCP-based strategies have been widely applied to efficiently remove haze from a single atmospheric image [30]. Images captured underwater are commonly affected by the suspended particles in waterbody, similar to the effect of thick fog in atmosphere, hence the standard DCP scheme is also adopted to restore the degraded underwater images. In reference [31], Chao et al. directly employed the DCP scheme for underwater image dehazing. For refining the DCP-based parameter estimation, Akkaynak et al. [32] designed a Sea-thru framework by combining with the revised image information model (IFM) and transmission map, whereby the distance-dependent attenuation coefficients are obtained via estimating the spatially varying illuminant. Regrettably, the DCP-based schemes mentioned above cannot apply to the restoration of underwater images with multiple types of distortion, and they struggled to demonstrate significant superiority. This is due to their inadequate consideration of the specific transformation discrepancies between in-air and underwater scenes, especially concerning the scene depth-dependent and wavelength-dependent light attenuation. In light of these challenges, a series of priors specifically targeting the optical imaging properties of underwater scenes has been developed.

Taking the viewpoint that the blue and green channels are the principal source of underwater visual information into account, an underwater DCP (UDCP) restoration algorithm was proposed in [33], whereby the DCP was adopted exclusively for the blue and green color channels to recover the color properties of underwater images. Despite the improved performance in estimating transmission map, the restored images still fall short of desired quality, as UDCP neglected the information from the red channel under any circumstance. Galdran et al. [34] designed a simple yet robust red channel prior-based approach (RDCP) for recovering the visibility loss and improving the color distortion. By exploiting hierarchical searching technique and innovative scoring formula, a generalized UDCP was proposed in [35] to obtain more robust back-scattered light estimation and transmission estimation. However, due to the inherent limitations of DCP, partial images recovered by the above methods still exhibit incorrect or unreal colors.

Carlevaris-Bianco et al. [36] presented a novel maximum intensity prior (MIP), it was an innovative exploration of the strong attenuation difference between the varying color channels of underwater images for estimating transmission map. Correspondingly, the MIP was adopted in [37] to estimate the background light. Considering the multiple spectral profiles of different waterbodies, Berman et al. [38] proposed a scheme to handle wavelength-dependent attenuation. The image restoration process was simplified to one procedure of single image dehazing via estimating the attenuation ratios of the blue-green and blue-red channels. Given that the methods based on DCP or MIP are likely to be invalidated by the changeable lighting conditions in underwater images, Peng et al. [39] exploited both light absorption and image blurriness to estimate more accurate scene depth, background light, and transmission map. Song et al. [40] explored an effective scene depth estimation framework on the basis of underwater light attenuation prior (ULAP), which can smoothly estimate the background light and the transmission maps to restore the true scene radiance.

2.3.2 Deep Learning-Based Image Restoration

Deep learning has made remarkable advancements in modeling complex nonlinear systems due to the rapid development of artificial intelligence and computer vision technology. Consequently, the innovative combination of underwater physical models with deep learning techniques has received growing research attention over recent years. Numerous studies showed that the deep neural network-based underwater image restoration schemes can accurately estimate the background light and transmission map.

Benefiting from the knowledge of underwater imaging, Li et al. [41] designed an unsupervised GAN for synthesizing realistic underwater-like images from in-air image and depth maps. Then a color calibration network was employed to correct color deviations utilizing these generated data. Li et al. [42] proposed a deep underwater image restoration framework Ucolor. The proposed network can be roughly divided into two subnetwork, multi-color space encoder coupled with channel attention and medium transmission-guided decoder. More particularly, the encoder part enables the varied feature representations from multi-color space and adaptively highlights the most discriminative information while the decoder part is responsible for enhancing the response of network towards quality-degraded regions. Based on physical model and causal intervention, a two-stage GAN-based framework was investigated in [43] for restoring the underwater low-quality images in real time. Notably, the majority of existing deep learning-based algorithms rely upon synthetic paired data to train a deep neural network for underwater image recovery, which may be subject to the domain shift issue. In view of this challenge, Fu et al. [44] provided a new research perspective for underwater image restoration, designing an effective self-supervised framework with the homology constraint.

Mitigating the limited availability of restoration methods based on deep learning is of great significance. It is worth considering the combination of deep learning with suitable underwater physical models or traditional restoration methods, which can contribute to achieving underwater image restoration applicable to different underwater environments with promising prospects.

3   Underwater Image Datasets and Quality Metrics

Underwater image datasets play a crucial role in data-driven visual tasks, providing valuable references and support for objective quality assessment and visual enhancement of underwater images. Furthermore, establishing a comprehensive underwater image quality evaluation framework will strongly promote innovative advancements in underwater image enhancement and restoration algorithms.

Table 1. A summary of underwater image datasets.

Dataset	Year	Images	Scenes	Resolution	MOS
Port Royal [41]	2015	18091	Natural and artificial structures	1360 × 1024	N
SQUID [38]	2018	57 pairs	Coral reefs, rocks, shipwrecks	5474 × 3653	N
UIEBD [19]	2019	890	Marine environment and marine life	Variable	N
RUIE [45]	2019	About 4000	Scallops, sea urchins and sea cucumbers	400 × 300	N
EUVP [27]	2020	1449	Marine environment and marine life	Variable	N
UFO-120 [46]	2020	1620	Marine environment and marine life	640 × 480	N
DUO [47]	2021	7782	Scallops, sea urchins, Sea cucumbers and starfishes	Variable	N
UIDEF [16]	2023	9200	Coral reefs, rocks, and starfishes	Variable	N

However, underwater image acquisition is challenging and costly due to environmental and equipment constraints, resulting in a scarcity of comprehensive and large-scale underwater image datasets. Existing datasets suffer from limitations such as limited diversity in target scenes, fewer category groupings, and a lack of extensive subjective experiments. This section summarizes a series of publicly available datasets used in underwater image enhancement and recovery algorithm research, as presented in Table 1. Moreover, it is worth noting that the existing image quality assessment (IQA) methods are primarily tailored for atmospheric color images and lack of reliability for assessing the quality of enhanced underwater images. To fill this gap, several objective quality evaluation metrics have been developed for underwater images, as illustrated in Table 2. Among them, the following three quality metrics are widely used in the field. UCIQE [48] is a no-reference quality assessment metric designed based on the chromaticity, contrast, and saturation in the CIELab color space of underwater images. UIQM [49], inspired by the human visual system, combines underwater image contrast measurement (UIConM), underwater image chromaticity measurement (UICM), and underwater image sharpness measurement (UISM) to evaluate different attributes of underwater images. On the other hand, the CCF metric [50] takes inspiration from the principles of underwater imaging and utilizes a weighted fusion of color, fog density, and contrast metrics to provide a comprehensive quality evaluation.

Table 2. The image quality metrics used for underwater image quality evaluations.

Metrics	Year	Evaluation criterion	Prefer	Deep learning-based/No-reference
UCIQE [48]	2015	Chroma, contrast, saturation	↑	×/√
UIQM [49]	2016	Contrast, sharpness, colorfulness	↑	×/√
CCF [50]	2018	Colorfulness, fog density	↑	×/√
UIF [51]	2022	Naturalness, sharpness, structure	↑	×/ ×
NUIQ [52]	2022	Brightness, chroma	↑	√/√

4   Experiments and Analysis

The performance of varying algorithms is discussed from both subjective and objective perspectives in this section, followed by an analysis and outlook on the semantic-aware ability of these enhancement and restoration algorithms in further high-level vision tasks.

Dataset and Implementation Details. In order to perform comprehensive and systematic experiments, various underwater enhancement and restoration methods are selected for assessment. Typical methods include traditional enhancement schemes (e.g., CLAHE [6], Fusion [14], RGHS [7]), traditional restoration methods (e.g., UDCP [33], ULAP [40], IBLA [39]), and data-driven approaches (e.g., UWCNN [25], FUnIE-GAN [27], Shallow-UWnet [26], USUIR [44]). The UIEBD dataset comprises a total of 890 authentic underwater images, providing comprehensive representation of the diversity in real underwater scenes. It is commonly employed for evaluating the performance of underwater image enhancement and restoration algorithms. To ensure the diversity of the test set, we select 60 challenging images from the UIEBD dataset, covering various distortion types such as blue-green color cast, reduced contrast, non-uniform illumination, and turbidity. Additionally, each distortion type includes images with different levels of distortion. Then, the challenging underwater object detection dataset UDD is utilized to explore the relationship between the improvement of underwater image quality and the high-level vision tasks.

To ensure fairness in both qualitative and quantitative evaluations, all training and testing are carried out on a Windows 11 PC with an NVIDIA 3060 GPU. The experiments are conducted using Python 3.7 and Matlab 2021b.

Results on Qualitative and Quantitative Evaluations. The visual comparisons of various algorithms are successively conducted on the Test U-C60 dataset, as illustrated in Fig. 3. It can be observed that the USUIR algorithm achieves satisfactory visual results, effectively coping with the diversity of underwater degraded images. Among the traditional algorithms, Fusion and RGHS demonstrate relatively strong universality and flexible applicability to different types of underwater images, while UDCP and IBLA tend to cause over-enhancement and over-saturation. Moreover, almost all algorithms still exhibit limited enhancement effects on turbidity images.

Since Test U-C60 set is lack of corresponding reference images, the performance of algorithms is assessed in terms of UCIQE, UIQM and CCF. The comparison results are summarized in Table 3, where the highest score is indicated in bold, and the second highest scores are underlined. We observe that not all objective evaluation results align with subjective human perception. To be specific, UDCP achieves the highest scores of UCIQE and CCF metrics; however, subjective assessments reveal recurrent issues of excessive color enhancement and blurring in the images processed by UDCP. This phenomenon can be attributed to the fact that UCIQE and CCF metrics primarily emphasize the chromaticity and saturation of the enhanced images, while UIQM additionally considers the sharpness characteristics. This discrepancy in evaluation criteria is a key factor leading to UDCP's lowest score in the CCF metric.

Application to High-Level Vision Tasks. As depicted in Fig. 4. It is visually evident that the results of IQA metrics are not linearly correlated with the accuracy of the object detection. Compared to the original degraded images, the enhanced images show improvement in the evaluation metric scores to some extent, but do not achieve superior detection accuracy. Therefore, the practical effects of underwater image enhancement and restoration on object detection and other computer vision applications deserve further in-depth research. The selection and design of effective image enhancement and restoration methods based on the specific requirements of advanced visual tasks are of paramount importance and significance.

Table 3. Quantitative comparisons of all methods by underwater image quality metrics.

Methods	Test U-C60		
	UCIQE	UIQM	CCF
Raw	0.366	1.950	20.829
CLAHE [6]	0.402	2.492	20.494
Fusion [14]	0.478	2.475	26.652
RGHS [7]	0.483	2.112	32.669
UDCP [33]	**0.501**	1.305	**33.613**
IBLA [40]	0.461	1.935	30.941
ULAP [39]	0.456	1.659	30.128
UWCNN [25]	0.328	2.222	15.255
FUnIE-GAN [26]	0.413	**2.506**	18.338
Shallow-UWnet [27]	0.341	2.123	16.824
USUIR [44]	0.438	2.494	21.384

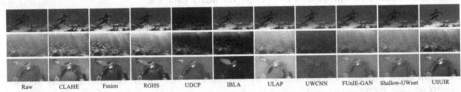

Raw   CLAHE   Fusion   RGHS   UDCP   IBLA   ULAP   UWCNN   FUnIE-GAN   Shallow-UWnet   USUIR

Fig. 3. Visual comparisons of different methods performed on the challenging images of Test U-C60 dataset.

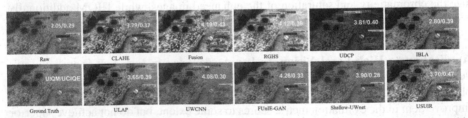

Fig. 4. Application examples of different methods on the object detection task in the real-world UDD dataset. (UIQM↑UCIQE↑)

5   Opportunities and Future Trends

For future research endeavors in the field of underwater image enhancement and restoration, improvements and innovations are needed in several aspects:

1) Existing approaches tend to consume substantial computational resources and cannot be deployed in detection devices with limited processing capacity. Therefore, it is imperative to design lightweight networks for resource-limited scenarios.

2) It is an urgent and meaningful need to study algorithms that can adapt to diverse underwater environments and dynamically adjust based on different degradation types of underwater images. Further exploration of the application of self-supervised and unsupervised strategies in enhancing algorithm adaptability is also warranted.
3) Data-driven algorithms often overlook the disparities between real and synthetic data, hindering their effective generalization to real-world underwater applications. Domain adaptation techniques offer a promising solution to this challenge, providing a new direction for improving underwater image quality in the future.
4) Existing objective quality metrics and the detection accuracy in underwater object detection are not linearly correlated, thus failing to provide effective guidance for downstream advanced tasks. Therefore, further research into utility-oriented quality assessment methods is highly warranted.
5) Existing methods mostly focus on improving the perceive quality of underwater images, neglecting the underlying connection between enhancement tasks and high-level vision tasks. Investigating the utilization of multitask learning paradigms to integrate underwater image enhancement and restoration techniques and advanced vision tasks represents a research avenue worthy of exploration.

Addressing these research aspects will undoubtedly contribute to the advancement of underwater image enhancement and restoration, ultimately facilitating the development of more effective and practical solutions in this field.

6 Conclusion

This review summarizes the current research status of underwater optical image enhancement and restoration techniques. A brief exposition of the underwater optical imaging model is firstly presented to facilitate a better understanding and analysis of the diverse causes of underwater image degradation. Subsequently, existing methods are systematically classified and discussed, followed by a concise introduction of publicly available underwater image datasets and quality evaluation approaches. Furthermore, we conduct comprehensive evaluations and comparisons of the classical methods, and then sort out the opportunities and future trends. This extensive survey of the state-of-the-art schemes provides guidance for future research and would be valuable for newly interested researchers.

Acknowledgments. This work was supported by the Natural Science Foundation of Fujian Province under Grant 2022J05117.

References

1. Han, M., Lyu, Z., Qiu, T., et al.: A review on intelligence dehazing and color restoration for underwater images. IEEE Trans. Syst. Man Cybern. Syst. **50**(5), 1820–1832 (2020)
2. Wang, Y., Song, W., Fortino, G., et al.: An experimental-based review of image enhancement and image restoration methods for underwater imaging. IEEE Access **7**, 140233–140251 (2019)

3. Schechner, Y.Y., Karpel, N.: Recovery of underwater visibility and structure by polarization analysis. IEEE J. Ocean. Eng. **30**(3), 570–587 (2005)
4. Treibitz, T., Schechner, Y.Y.: Active polarization descattering. IEEE Trans. Pattern Anal. Mach. Intell. **31**(3), 385–399 (2009)
5. Liu, W., Li, Q., Hao, G., et al.: Experimental study on underwater range-gated imaging system pulse and gate control coordination strategy. In: Proceedings of the SPIE, Beijing, China (2018)
6. Zuiderveld, K.: Contrast limited adaptive histogram equalization. Graph. Gems. 474–485 (1994)
7. Huang, D., Wang, Y., Song, W., Sequeira, J., Mavromatis, S.: Shallow-water image enhancement using relative global histogram stretching based on adaptive parameter acquisition. In: Schoeffmann, K., et al. (eds.) MMM 2018. LNCS, vol. 10704, pp. 453–465. Springer, Cham (2018). https://doi.org/10.1007/978-3-319-73603-7_37
8. Henke, B., Vahl, M., Zhou, Z.: Removing Color cast of underwater images through non-constant color constancy hypothesis. In: 8th International Symposium on Image and Signal Processing and Analysis (ISPA), Trieste, Italy, pp. 20–24 (2013)
9. Jobson, D.J., Rahman, Z., Woodell, G.A.: A multiscale retinex for bridging the gap between color images and the human observation of scenes. IEEE Trans. Image Process. **6**(7), 965–976 (1997)
10. Liu, K., Li, X.: De-hazing and enhancement method for underwater and low-light images. Multimed Tools Appl. **80**(13), 19421–19439 (2021)
11. Agaian, S.S., Panetta, K., Grigoryan, A.M.: Transform-based image enhancement algorithms with performance measure. IEEE Trans. Image Process. **10**(3), 367–382 (2001)
12. Vasamsetti, S., Mittal, N., Neelapu, B.C., et al.: Wavelet based perspective on variational enhancement technique for underwater imagery. Ocean Eng. **141**, 88–100 (2017)
13. Iqbal, M., Riaz, M.M., Sohaib Ali, S., et al.: Underwater image enhancement using laplace decomposition. IEEE Geosci. Remote Sens. Lett. **19**, 1–5 (2022)
14. Ancuti, C., Ancuti, C.O., Haber, T., et al.: Enhancing underwater images and videos by fusion. In: 2012 IEEE Conference on Computer Vision and Pattern Recognition, Providence, RI, USA, pp. 81–88 (2012)
15. Muniraj, M., Dhandapani, V.: Underwater image enhancement by combining color constancy and dehazing based on depth estimation. Neurocomputing **460**, 211–230 (2021)
16. Chang, L., Song, H., Li, M., et al.: UIDEF: a real-world underwater image dataset and a color-contrast complementary image enhancement framework. ISPRS-J. Photogramm. Remote. Sens. **196**, 415 (2023)
17. Perez, J., Attanasio, A.C., Nechyporenko, N., Sanz, P.J.: A deep learning approach for underwater image enhancement. In: Ferrández Vicente, J.M., Álvarez-Sánchez, J.R., de la Paz López, F., Toledo Moreo, J., Adeli, H. (eds.) IWINAC 2017. LNCS, vol. 10338, pp. 183–192. Springer, Cham (2017). https://doi.org/10.1007/978-3-319-59773-7_19
18. Wang, Y., Cao, J., Wang, Z.: A deep CNN method for underwater image enhancement. In: 2017 IEEE International Conference on Image Processing (ICIP), Beijing, China, pp. 1382–1386 (2017)
19. Li, C., Guo, C., Ren, W., et al.: An underwater image enhancement benchmark dataset and beyond. IEEE Trans. Image Process. **29**, 4376–4389 (2020)
20. Wang, Y., Guo, J., Gao, H., et al.: UIEC^2-net: CNN-based underwater image enhancement using two color space. Signal Process.: Image Commun. **96**, Art. no. 116250 (2021)
21. Cai, X., Jiang, N., Chen, W., et al.: CURE-Net: a cascaded deep network for underwater image enhancement. IEEE J. Ocean. Eng. (2023). https://doi.org/10.1109/JOE.2023.3245760
22. Fabbri, C.M., Islam, J., Sattar, J.: Enhancing underwater imagery using generative adversarial networks. In: 2018 IEEE International Conference on Robotics and Automation (ICRA), Brisbane, QLD, Australia, pp. 7159–7165 (2018)

23. Zhu, J. -Y., Park, T., Isola, P., et al.: Unpaired image-to-image translation using cycle-consistent adversarial networks. In: 2017 IEEE International Conference on Computer Vision (ICCV), Venice, Italy, pp. 2242–2251 (2017)
24. Wang, Z., Shen, L., Xu, M., et al.: Domain adaptation for underwater image enhancement. IEEE Trans. Image Process. **32**, 1442–1457 (2023)
25. Li, C., Anwar, S., Porikli, F.: Underwater scene prior inspired deep underwater image and video enhancement. Pattern Recognit. **98**, Art no. 107038 (2020)
26. Naik, A., Swarnakar, A., Mittal, K.: Shallow-UWnet: compressed model for underwater image enhancement. arXiv preprint arXiv:2101.02073 (2021)
27. Islam, M.J., Xia, Y., Sattar, J.: Fast underwater image enhancement for improved visual perception. IEEE Robot. Autom. Lett. **5**(2), 3227–3234 (2020)
28. Jiang, N., Chen, W., Lin, Y., et al.: Underwater image enhancement with lightweight cascaded network. IEEE Trans. Multimed. **24**, 4301–4313 (2022)
29. He, K., Sun, J., Tang, X.: Single image haze removal using dark channel prior. IEEE Trans. Pattern Anal. Mach. Intell. **33**(12), 2341–2353 (2011)
30. Parihar, A.S., Gupta, Y.K., Singodia, Y., et al.: A comparative study of image Dehazing algorithms. In: International Conference on Communication and Electronics Systems, Coimbatore, India, pp. 766–771 (2020)
31. Chao, L., Wang, M.: Removal of water scattering. In: 2nd International Conference on Computer Engineering and Technology, Chengdu, V2-35–V2-39 (2010)
32. Akkaynak, D., Treibitz, T.: Sea-Thru: a method for removing water from underwater images. In: 2019 IEEE/CVF Conference on Computer Vision and Pat-tern Recognition (CVPR), Long Beach, CA, USA, pp. 1682–1691 (2019)
33. Drews, P., Nascimento, E., Moraes, F., et al.: Transmission estimation in underwater single images. In: Proceedings of the IEEE International Conference on Computer Vision, Sydney, Australia, pp. 825–830 (2013)
34. Galdran, A., Pardo, D., Picón, A., et al.: Automatic red channel underwater image restoration. J. Vis. Commun. Image Represent. **26**, 132–145 (2015)
35. Liang, Z., Ding, X., Wang, Y., et al.: GUDCP: generalization of underwater dark channel prior for underwater image restoration. IEEE Trans. Circ. Syst. Video Technol. **32**(7), 4879–4884 (2022)
36. Carlevaris-Bianco, N., Mohan, A., Eustice, R.M.: Initial results in underwater single image dehazing. In: OCEANS-MTS/IEEE Seattle, Seattle, WA, USA, pp. 1–8 (2010)
37. Zhao, X., Jin, T., Qu, S.: Deriving inherent optical properties from background color and underwater image enhancement. Ocean Eng. **94**, 163–172 (2015)
38. Berman, D., Levy, D., Avidan, S., et al.: Underwater single image color restoration using haze-lines and a new quantitative dataset. IEEE Trans. Pattern Anal. Mach. Intell. **43**, 2822–2837 (2021)
39. Peng, Y.-T., Cosman, P.C.: Underwater image restoration based on image blurriness and light absorption. IEEE Trans. Image Process. **26**(4), 1579–1594 (2017)
40. Song, W., Wang, Y., Huang, D., Tjondronegoro, D.: A rapid scene depth estimation model based on underwater light attenuation prior for underwater image restoration. In: Hong, R., Cheng, W.-H., Yamasaki, T., Wang, M., Ngo, C.-W. (eds.) PCM 2018. LNCS, vol. 11164, pp. 678–688. Springer, Cham (2018). https://doi.org/10.1007/978-3-030-00776-8_62
41. Li, J., Skinner, K.A., Eustice, R.M.: WaterGAN: unsupervised generative network to enable real-time color correction of monocular underwater images. IEEE Robot. Autom. Lett. **3**(1), 387–394 (2018)
42. Li, C., Anwar, S., Hou, J., et al.: Underwater image enhancement via medium transmission-guided multi-color space embedding. IEEE Trans. Image Process. **30**, 4985–5000 (2021)
43. Hao, J., Yang, H., Hou, X., et al.: Two-stage underwater image restoration algorithm based on physical model and causal intervention. IEEE Signal Processing Lett. **30**, 120–124 (2023)

44. Fu, Z., Lin, H., Yang, Y., et al.: Unsupervised underwater image restoration: from a homology perspective. In: Proceedings of the AAAI Conference on Artificial Intelligence, vol. 36, no. 1, pp. 643-651 (2022)
45. Liu, R., Fan, X., Zhu, M.: Real-world underwater enhancement: challenges, benchmarks, and solutions under natural light. IEEE Trans. Circuits Syst. Video Technol. **30**(12), 4861–4875 (2020)
46. Islam, M. J., Luo, P., Sattar, J.: Simultaneous enhancement and super-resolution of underwater imagery for improved visual perception. arXiv preprint arXiv:2002.01155 (2020)
47. Liu, C., Li, H., Wang, S., et al.: A dataset and benchmark of underwater object detection for robot picking. IEEE International Conference on Multimedia & Expo Workshops (ICMEW), pp. 1–6 (2021)
48. Yang, M., Sowmya, A.: An underwater color image quality evaluation metric. IEEE Trans. Image Process. **24**(12), 6062–6071 (2015)
49. Panetta, K., Gao, C., Agaian, S.: Human-visual-system-inspired underwater image quality measures. IEEE J. Ocean. Eng. **41**(3), 541–551 (2016)
50. Wang, Y., Li, N., Li, Z., et al.: An imaging-inspired no-reference underwater color image quality assessment metric. Comput. Electr. Eng. **70**, 904–913 (2018)
51. Zheng, Y., Chen, W., Lin, R., et al.: UIF: an objective quality assessment for underwater image enhancement. IEEE Trans. Image Process. **31**, 5456–5468 (2022)
52. Jiang, Q., Gu, Y., Li, C., et al.: Underwater image enhancement quality evaluation: benchmark dataset and objective metric. IEEE Trans. Circ. Syst. Video Technol. **32**(9), 5959–5974 (2022)

A Self-supervised Learning Reconstruction Algorithm with an Encoder-Decoder Architecture for Diffuse Optical Tomography

Yaxuan Li[1,2], Chengpu Wei[1,2], Wenqian Zhang[1,2], Zhe Li[1,2], Zhonghua Sun[1,2], Kebin Jia[1,2], and Jinchao Feng[1,2(✉)]

[1] Beijing Key Laboratory of Computational Intelligence and Intelligent System, Faculty of Information Technology, Beijing University of Technology, Beijing 100124, China
fengjc@bjut.edu.cn
[2] Beijing Laboratory of Advanced Information Networks, Beijing 100124, China

Abstract. Diffuse optical tomography (DOT) is an emerging non-invasive optical imaging technique, which has a promising application in breast cancer detection and diagnosis. However, the conventional image reconstruction algorithm in DOT is time-consuming and easy to error when recovering the distribution of optical parameters within the complete tissue. In this paper, we present an end-to-end reconstruction algorithm for DOT based on a deep convolutional encoder-decoder architecture, which consists of a data processing part and a convolutional encoder-decoder net. Its effectiveness was evaluated using simulation data. The results show that the overall quality of our method is significantly improved compared with the traditional algorithm based on the FEM method, the single inclusion deviation is reduced by 150% compared with the traditional algorithm, the standard deviation is reduced by 50%; multiple inclusions deviation is reduced by 100% and the standard deviation by 38.7%.

Keywords: Diffusion optical tomography (DOT) · Image reconstruction · NIRFAST · Deep learning · Self-supervised learning · Convolutional neural network

1 Introduction

According to the Global Cancer Report 2020 published by the World Health Organization-International Cancer Research Agency, global cancer incidence is increasing year by year, and the number of cancer patients worldwide may increase by more than 60% over the next two decades; and by more than 80% in LMICs countries [1]. Among them, breast cancer is the main cause of cancer death in women the Over 2.1 million additional breast cancer patients worldwide in 2018, and over 627,000 people have died from breast cancer.

The examination is effective for breast cancer and can increase the therapeutic effect. Therefore, accurate screening and symptomatic treatment are effective methods to improve the efficacy of breast cancer treatment. At present, clinical testing mainly relies on modern medical imaging technology, such as breast X-ray photography, ultrasonic detection, MRI and PET, etc. After detecting an abnormality, the pathological examination is often used to give the final diagnosis. However, the above four detection methods have various problems. For example, breast X-ray photography and PET can lead to radiation causing cancer; the MRI has a high cost, and people with metal in their bodies are prohibited from screening.

Diffuse optical tomography (DOT) is an attractive optical imaging technique because it is non-invasive, fast, relatively inexpensive, and poses no risk of ionizing radiation compared to clinical X-ray, ultrasound, and MRI. DOT use near-infrared light to illustrate the breast and measures the functional characteristics of breast lesions. Normal tissue and diseased tissue have different absorption and scattering effects on NIR light. Using this feature, DOT can achieve the purpose of detection by reconstructing the optical parameters of the tissue. Over the years, many clinical studies have demonstrated the ability of the DOT technique to distinguish tumor properties [2–7] and help doctors judge treatment outcomes [8–10].

However, the image quality of NIRST tends to be poor due to light scattering in biological tissue, which limits its clinical application in breast imaging. To improve the imaging contrast and simplify the imaging process of DOT, a time-resolved diffuser-assisted diffusion optical imaging method was developed, which adds diffusion plates between the light source and the measured tissue body [11]. Medhi et al. proposed an improved experimental device using a camera unit instead of a fiber-connected detector and changed the imitation from fixed to rotating, thus solving the discomfort of the inverse problem in the DOT method [12].

In recent years, deep learning has attracted increasing attention in DOT. Yoo et al. proposed a deep learning model for learning nonlinear photon scattering physics, aiming to reverse the Lippman-Schwinge integral equation using convolution small framework mathematical theory to improve the reconstruction quality [13]. An end-to-end deep learning model (FDU-Net) is developed for fast 3D DOT reconstruction [14], which consists of a fully connected layer, a convolutional encoder-decoder, and a U-net. Compared with the traditional algorithm, the reconstruction speed is improved by more than 4 times, and the reconstruction quality is significantly better than the traditional algorithm. However, this deep-learning-based method was required to be trained on labeled datasets. Nevertheless, it is impossible to obtain labeled datasets in practical applications.

To overcome this problem, we design a deep encoder-decoder architecture for DOT reconstruction based on self-supervised learning. It takes the acquired optical signals as network input and directly outputs the image of the absorption coefficient with high quality. It was trained on a dataset without manual labeling, and generated entirely by open-source software, NIRFAST [15] using MATLAB.

2 Method

2.1 Light Propagation Model

In the field of biology optics, there are many models developed for the study of light propagation, the commonly used models include the Monte-Carlo model [16–18], radiative transfer equation (RTE) model and diffusion equation (DE) [19]. DE is a first-order approximation of RTE, and it is easy to implement. Therefore, we used DE to model light propagation in this paper. DE is given by [20]

$$-\nabla \cdot \kappa(r)\nabla\Phi(r) + \mu_a(r)\Phi(r) = q_0(r) \tag{1}$$

where μ_a and μ_s' are absorption and reduced scattering coefficients, respectively $q_0(r)$ is an isotropic source term, $\Phi(r)$ is the photon fluence rate at position r (the intensity of outgoing light), $\kappa = 1/3(\mu_a + \mu_s')$ is the diffusion coefficient.

Due to the irregularity of the tissues, the finite element method (FEM) is often used to solve the diffusion equation. The matrix form of DE in the FEM framework is given by [20]

$$(K(\kappa) + C\mu_a + \frac{1}{2A}F)\Phi = q_0 \tag{2}$$

where the matrices $K(\kappa)$, $C\mu_a$ and F is given by

$$K_{ij} = \int_\Omega \kappa(r)\nabla u_i(r) \cdot \nabla u_j(r)\mathrm{d}^n r \tag{3}$$

$$C_{ij} = \int_\Omega \mu_a(r)u_i(r)u_j(r)\mathrm{d}^n r \tag{4}$$

$$F_{ij} = \oint_{\partial\Omega} u_i(r)u_j(r)\mathrm{d}^{n-1} r \tag{5}$$

and the source vector q_0 has terms

$$q_{0_i} = \int_\Omega u_i(r)q_0(r)\mathrm{d}^n r \tag{6}$$

the A can be derived from Fresnel's law:

$$A = \frac{2/(1-R_0) - 1 + |\cos\theta_c|^3}{1 - |\cos\theta_c|^2} \tag{7}$$

where $\theta_c = \arcsin(n_{AIR}/n_1)$, the angle at which total internal reflection occurs for photons moving from region Ω with RI n_1 to air with RI n_{AIR}, and $R_0 = (n_1/n_{AIR} - 1)^2/(n_1/n_{AIR} + 1)^2$.

Here, we use NIRFAST to solve the DE.

2.2 Deep Convolutional Encoder-Decoder Architecture

To aim of DOT is to recover the distribution of optical properties from boundary measurements. Instead of using traditional regularization in reconstruction, we develop a deep learning algorithm for DOT reconstruction. In general, the network is trained under supervised learning. However, manual-annotation data is required. To avoid this, a self-supervised based reconstruction algorithm is designed for DOT, as shown in Fig. 1. It can be trained with label-free data. The Forward process of the DOT is shown in Fig. 2.

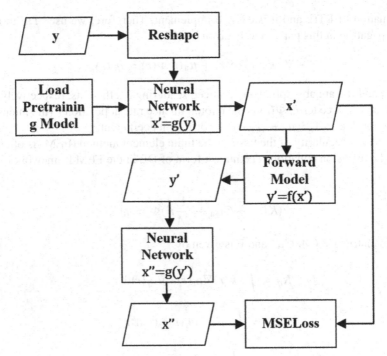

Fig. 1. The flowchart of self-supervised DOT reconstruction. y is the acquired boundary measurements; x' is the predicted optical properties given y by a neural network; y' is the calculated measurements with the predicted x', x'' is the recovered optical coefficients with y' by a neural network

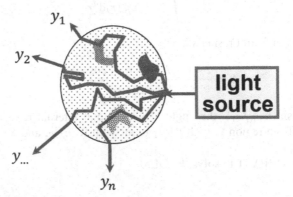

Fig. 2. Forward process of the DOT. The y_1 to y_n is the light emitted in different directions after scattering.

We assume that x represents the true distribution of optical parameters and y represents the measured intensity of outgoing light. To recover the distribution of optical properties, it would be ideal to minimize the difference between the acquired measurements y and the predicted measurements y'. However, the DE is solved by NIRFAST using MATLAB, which is divorced from Python interpreter. Therefore, we try to minimize the difference between the predicted x' with acquired measurements y and the predicted x'' with predicted measurements y'.

It has three steps. The first step is to obtain the predicted x' from acquired measurements y, which is given by:

$$x' = g(y) \tag{8}$$

where x' is the recovered optical coefficients by a neural network g. The second step is to infer y' from x', which can be described as:

$$y' = f(x') \tag{9}$$

where f is the forward model, x is the optical coefficients to be reconstructed, y is acquired measurements.

The third step is to infer x'' from y', which can be described as:

$$x'' = g(y') \tag{10}$$

where f is the forward model, x is the optical coefficients to be reconstructed, y is acquired measurements.

The Mean-square error (MSE) function is used as our loss function, which is given by:

$$Loss(x'', x') = \frac{1}{n}\sum(x'' - x')^2 = \frac{1}{n}\sum(f(g(y)) - g(y))^2 \tag{11}$$

In this paper, the neural network used has an encoder-decoder architecture, as shown in Fig. 3.

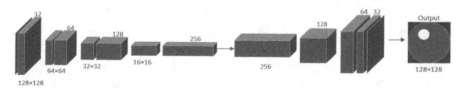

Fig. 3. The structure of the Encoder-Decoder network. The left side shows the down-sampling section, the input is $128 \times 128 \times 1$ and the output is $16 \times 16 \times 256$; the right side shows the up-sampling section, the input is $16 \times 16 \times 256$, and the size of eventual optical image is $128 \times 128 \times 1$.

The encoder-decoder net is composed of an encoder and a decoder. The encoder contains four convolution blocks and three down-sampling layers, each block containing two convolution layers with a kernel size of 3×3 and step size of 1. In down-sampling. To avoid the information loss caused by maximum/minimum/average pooling, the quality of the reconstruction results eventually decreases, we used a convolution layer with a convolution kernel size 3×3 and step size 2 to achieve down-sampling, to ensure the quality of results. In up-sampling, we did not use interpolation, but instead used transposed convolution with convolution kernel size 3×3 and step size 2. This has the benefit of making the results more accurate. All the convolutional layers of the network use LeakyReLU as the activation function.

3   Results

3.1   Dataset

The dataset we used was created by NIRFAST. We used a circular phantom with a radius of 50mm to synthesize the dataset. The value of its absorption coefficient was $0.01mm^{-1}$. Sixteen light sources and sixteen detectors were used, as illustrated in Fig. 4. An inclusion with different sizes was added into different positions of the phantom, as shown in Fig. 5. The absorption coefficients of inclusions were $0.02mm^{-1}$.

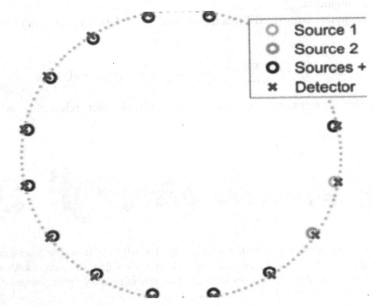

Fig. 4. The layout of the sources and detectors. The small circles represent the sources, The crosses represent the Detectors.

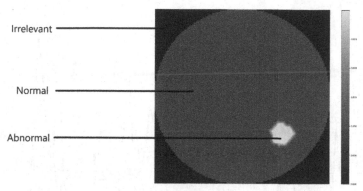

Fig. 5. Ground-truth. The blue region is the normal region, its absorption coefficient is 0.01 mm^{-1}, the yellow region is inclusion with an absorption coefficient higher than 0.02 mm^{-1}. (Color figure online)

3.2 Reconstruction Results

The result of the Encoder-Decoder-based reconstruction algorithm on the single anomaly regions mesh is illustrated in Fig. 6. The results of Encoder-Decoder-based reconstruction are better. The boundary of the abnormal region is clear and the noise in the normal region is very low. Furthermore, traditional algorithm have a misdescription of the parameters of the normal region, which did not occur in our method.

The reconstruction loss is illustrated in Fig. 7, which clearly shows the advantages of our method. The single loss and the average loss are both lower than the traditional DOT method, and our method outperformed than traditional algorithm in over 95 percent of the cases.

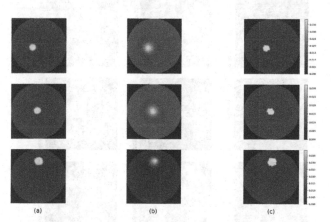

Fig. 6. Ground-truth and recovered absorption coefficients. (a) reconstruction result of the self-supervised training model, (b) reconstruction result of the traditional algorithm, (c) label.

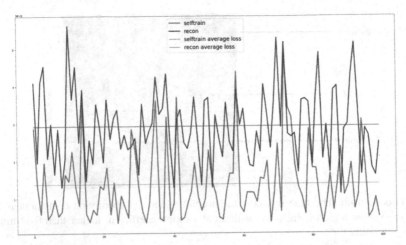

Fig. 7. The loss between reconstruction results and label. The curve is the single loss, there are 100 data. The straight line is the average loss. The red line is our method, the blue line is the traditional algorithm. (Color figure online)

The result of the Encoder-Decoder-based reconstruction algorithm on the Multiple inclusion is illustrated in Fig. 8. The contrast between the two method in Fig. 8 is even more obvious. For the adjacent abnormal regions, our method can accurately reconstruct them, but the traditional algorithm directly ignores one of them. When handling the abnormal regions in which both the diffusion coefficient and area are relatively small, the traditional algorithm is not reconstructed.

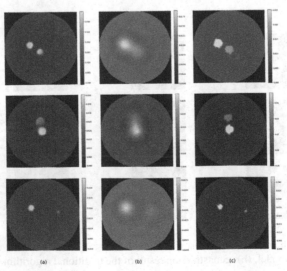

Fig. 8. Ground-truth and recovered absorption coefficients. (a) reconstruction result of the self-supervised training model, (b) reconstruction result of the traditional algorithm, (c) label.

The reconstruction loss is illustrated in Fig. 9, as the case of single anomaly regions, our method still take the lead.

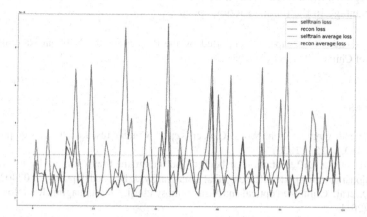

Fig. 9. The loss between reconstruction results and label. The curve is a single loss, there are 100 data. The straight line is the average loss. The blue line is our method, the red line is the traditional algorithm.

Our method not only has better intuitive effects but also has a great improvement at the data level. Table 1 shows the reconstruction deviation and speed for the two methods. Both the deviation in the single anomalous region and those in the multiple anomalous regions are significantly reduced, our method reduces the deviation by at least 100%, and also far exceeds the traditional algorithm in the stability of the reconstruction results. The imaging speed improvement of deep learning algorithms is even more impressive, with our method imaging once 24 times faster compared to traditional algorithm.

Table 1. Reconstruction deviation and time used.

	Single inclusion		Multiple inclusions		Time
	Average	Deviation	Average	Deviation	
Traditional	0.026	0.07	0.03	0.07	2.4 s
Ours	0.01	0.05	0.016	0.05	0.11 s

4 Conclusions

Since traditional DOT reconstruction algorithms have poor quality and slow speed, we designed a reconstruction algorithm based on deep learning and self-supervised training. It uses the forward model in NIRFAST and the neural network to automatically generate labels.

The results of the experiment show that our method has a better reconstruction image than the traditional algorithm, especially when reconstructing the mesh with multiple abnormal regions, the advantage is more obvious. Furthermore, our method has an over 20-fold advantage in the reconstruction speed.

Acknowledgments. This paper is supported by the Project for the National Natural Science Foundation of China (82171992, 62105010).

References

1. World Health Organization. World Cancer Report. Cancer research for cancer prevention. Lyon WHO, p. 253 (2020)
2. Choe, R., et al.: Differentiation of benign and malignant breast tumors by in-vivo three-dimensional parallel-plate diffuse optical tomography. J. Biomed. Opt. **14**(2), 024020 (2009)
3. Fang, Q., et al.: Combined optical and X-ray tomosynthesis breast imaging. Radiology **258**(1), 89–97 (2011)
4. Mastanduno, M.A., et al.: MR-guided near-infrared spectral tomography increases diagnostic performance of breast MRI. Clin. Cancer Res. **21**(17), 3906–3912 (2015)
5. Chae, E.Y., et al.: Development of digital breast tomosynthesis and diffuse optical tomography fusion imaging for breast cancer detection. Sci. Rep. **10**(1), 13127 (2020)
6. Feng, J., et al.: Addition of T2-guided optical tomography improves non-contrast breast magnetic resonance imaging diagnosis. Breast Cancer Res. **19**(1), 117 (2017)
7. Zhu, Q., et al.: Assessment of functional differences in malignant and benign breast lesions and improvement of diagnostic accuracy by using US-guided diffuse optical tomography in conjunction with conventional US. Radiology **280**(2), 387–397 (2016)
8. Choe, R., et al.: Diffuse optical tomography of breast cancer during neoadjuvant chemotherapy: a case study with comparison to MRI. Med. Phys. **32**(4), 1128–1139 (2005)
9. Sajjadi, A.Y., et al.: Normalization of compression-induced hemodynamics in patients responding to neoadjuvant chemotherapy monitored by dynamic tomographic optical breast imaging (DTOBI). Biomed. Opt. Express **8**(2), 555–569 (2017)
10. Tromberg, B.J., et al.: Predicting responses to neoadjuvant chemotherapy in breast cancer: ACRIN 6691 trial of diffuse optical spectroscopic imaging (DOSI). Cancer Res. **76**(20), 5933–5944 (2016)
11. Chuang, C.-C., et al.: Diffuser-aided time-domain diffuse optical imaging. In: 2014 International Symposium on Computer, Consumer and Control, Raleigh American, p. 929 (2014)
12. Medhi, B., Kandhirodan, R.: Image sensor based diffuse optical tomographic system. In: 2019 International Conference on Signal Processing and Communication (ICSPC-2019), Coimbatore, India, p. 209 (2019)
13. Yoo, J., Heo, D., Kim, H., Wahab, A., et al.: Deep learning diffuse optical tomography. IEEE Trans. Med. Imaging **39**(4), 877–887 (2020)
14. Deng, B., et al.: FDU-net: deep learning-based threedimensional diffuse optical image reconstruction. IEEE Trans. Med. Imaging (2023)
15. Dehghani, H., Eames, M.E., Yalavarthy, P.K., et al.: Near infrared optical tomography using NIRFAST: algorithm for numerical model and image reconstruction. Commun. Numer. Methods Eng. **25**(6), 711–732 (2008)
16. Kumar, Y.P., Vasu, R.M.: Reconstruction of optical properties of low-scattering tissue using derivative estimated through perturbation Monte-Carlo method. J. Biomed. Opt. **9**(5), 1002–1012 (2004)

17. Heiskala, J., Kotilahti, K., Nissila, I.: An application of perturbation Monte Carlo in optical tomography. In: Proceedings of the 27th Annual International Conference of the IEEE Engineering in Medicine and Biology Society (2005)
18. Heiskala, J., Pollari, M., Metsaranta, M., et al.: Probabilistic atlas can improve re-construction from optical imaging of the neonatal brain. Opt. Express **17**(17), 14977–14992 (2009)
19. Boas, D.A.: Diffuse photon probes of structural and dynamical properties of turbid media: theory and biomedical applications. University of Pennsylvania, Philadelphia (1996)
20. Nisa, W., et al.: Continuous wave diffuse optical tomography for imaging defect in agricultural. In: 2018 2nd Borneo International Conference on Applied Mathematics and Engineering (BICAME), Balikpapan, Indonesia, p. 123 (2018)

TSR-Net: A Two-Step Reconstruction Approach for Cherenkov-Excited Luminescence Scanned Tomography

Wenqian Zhang[1,2], Jinchao Feng[1,2(✉)], Zhe Li[1,2], Zhonghua Sun[1,2], and Kebin Jia[1,2]

[1] Beijing Key Laboratory of Computational Intelligence and Intelligent System, Faculty of Information Technology, Beijing University of Technology, Beijing 100124, China
fengjc@bjut.edu.cn
[2] Beijing Laboratory of Advanced Information Networks, Beijing 100124, China

Abstract. Cherenkov-excited luminescence scanned tomography (CELST) can recover a high-resolution 3D distribution of luminescent sources within tissue. However, reconstructing the distribution of the quantum field from boundary measurements is a typical ill-posed problem. In this work, we propose a novel two-step reconstruction network (TSR-Net) based on a fusion mechanism, that integrates two encoder-decoder networks (ED-Net) using a concatenation block. Firstly, an ED-Net is trained to learn the CT structural features of tissues with the measured data. Then, the trained ED-Net is fixed and cascaded by another ED-Net for a second-step training to predict the 3D distributions. Numerical simulations reveal that the proposed approach can not only accurately reconstruct the intensity values of the luminescent sources, but also achieve a reconstruction resolution of 1mm with low target-background contrast. Furthermore, the well-trained network is still effective in the reconstruction of tissues with different shapes, which indicates an excellent generalization ability of the algorithm.

Keywords: Cherenkov-excited luminescence scanned imaging · tomography · feature fusion · generalization ability

1 Introduction

Cherenkov-excited luminescence scanned tomography (CELST) is a new molecular imaging modality, which can *invivo* monitor biological characteristics of tumors during radiology therapy [1, 2]. Cherenkov radiation is induced utilizing sheet-shaped megavolt (MV) x-ray or electron beams generated by a medical linear accelerator (LINAC), and when the luminescence is emitted by Cherenkov radiation, this secondary emission can be captured by a time-domain gated intensified charge-coupled device (ICCD) camera [3–5]. However, CELSI imaging fails to truly reflect in-depth and quantitative information of luminescent sources. As a result, the tomographic techniques of CELSI (CELST) have been further developed, which can provide a 3D internal distribution of the luminescent probe from the captured surface image [6]. Owing to its high specificity and strong sensitivity, CELST has the unique advantages of high spatial resolution and deep imaging depth [5, 6].

W. Yongtian and W. Lifang (Eds.): IGTA 2023, CCIS 1910, pp. 30–41, 2023.
https://doi.org/10.1007/978-981-99-7549-5_3

However, since the photon undergoes multiple scattering events before reaching the surface and a small amount of available measurements, the CELST reconstruction is a severely ill-posed problem. Regularization is a universal method to alleviate the ill-posedness, such as Tikhonov regularization [6], sparse-promoting regularization (L_1 and L_p) [7–9], and total variation (TV) constraints [10]. However, regularization-based algorithms usually require multiple iterations, which results in a large computational burden in the inverse problem. In addition, the reconstructed image tends to be over-smoothed and artifacts might be introduced.

Completely different from these traditional methods, deep learning (DL) has been increasingly used for image reconstruction in optical tomography [11–14]. For instance, Zhang et al. proposed a 3D-En-Decoder framework to reconstruct the fluorescent sources and achieved higher quality imaging at a much faster reconstruction speed than the conventional iteration-based regularization methods [14]. Furthermore, recent studies have demonstrated the efficiency of the two-step DNN strategy in solving the problems of coherent scattering [15, 16] and computational imaging [17], and that yields better results than one-step training. However, these deep learning methods achieve success under the training of sufficient data pairs (surface measurements and their corresponding ground truths) [18, 19], while these ground truths are often unavailable, especially in live animal imaging studies. In addition, for CELST, end-to-end training is particularly helpful when the measurements acquired on the tissue same as the training datasets but fail on other tissues [20], therefore, the application of a well-trained reconstruction model to other tissues imaging is a leap of faith.

In this study, a two-step training reconstruction network (TSR-Net) in image reconstruction is proposed for CELST reconstruction. The first step (step 1) trains a 3D encoder-decoder network (ED-Net) to develop a mapping model between the surface measurements and the CT structural images. Then, the parameters trained in step 1 are fixed and concatenated with another encoder-decoder module for the second step (step 2) training, to approximate the imaging model between measurements and the 3D distribution of luminescent sources. Simulation experiments show that compared with the 3D encoder-decoder network (ED-Net), our proposed scheme has outstanding performance in quantum field recovery especially in the generalization ability test.

2 Methods

The performance of CELST reconstruction mainly depends on two critical issues: the forward problem modeling and the inverse problem solving.

2.1 Forward Problem

The forward problem in CELST is to detect the escaped photons from the body surface, which can be modeled with the following coupled diffusion equations [6, 21]:

$$\begin{cases} -\nabla D_x(\mathbf{r})\nabla \Phi_x(\mathbf{r}) + \mu_{ax}(\mathbf{r})\Phi_x(\mathbf{r}) = S(\mathbf{r}) \\ -\nabla D_m(\mathbf{r})\nabla \Phi_m(\mathbf{r}) + \mu_{am}(\mathbf{r})\Phi_m(\mathbf{r}) = \Phi_x(\mathbf{r})\eta\mu_{af}(\mathbf{r}) \end{cases} (r \in \Omega) \qquad (1)$$

where the subscripts x and m denote the excitation and emission processes, respectively. $\Phi_{x,m}(r)$ are the excitation and emission fields at position r in the imaging domain Ω, $S(r)$ denotes the Cherenkov excitation source term at position r induced by sheet-shaped LINAC beams, $D_{x,m}(r) = 1/3(\mu_{ax,am}(r) + \mu'_{sx,sm}(r))$ denotes the diffusion coefficient; $\mu_{ax,am}(r)$ and $\mu'_{sx,sm}(r)$ are the absorption and reduced scattering coefficients, respectively; η is the fluorophore's quantum efficiency, and $\eta\mu_{af}(r)$ to be reconstructed is the unknown distribution of the luminescence yield [3].

Considering there is refraction on the surface of the tissue in contact with the air, the Robin-type boundary condition is adapted [22, 23]. Based on the finite element method (FEM) [24], the relationship between the detected surface fluorescence signals y and the unknown distribution of luminescence yield u can be obtained by discretizing Eq. (1):

$$y = f(u) \tag{2}$$

where $f(\cdot)$ represents the forward model.

2.2 Inverse Problem

Since the CELST reconstruction is ill-posed and under-conditioned, the distribution u cannot be obtained by directly inverting Eq. (2). In general, the inverse problem is reformulated into the following optimization problem based on regularization theory [6, 7]:

$$\hat{u} = \arg\min_u \frac{1}{2}\|Au - y*\|_2^2 + \lambda\|u\|_2^2 \tag{3}$$

where λ is a regularization parameter which is used to balance the weight between the data fitting term $\|Au - y^*\|_2^2$ and the regularization term $\|u\|_2^2$. The distribution of quantum field can be obtained by optimizing Eq. (3). The optimization problem usually requires several iterations. In addition, the regularization parameters need to be appropriately selected.

Unlike the traditional methods, CELST reconstruction based on deep learning aims to directly establish a mapping model between the surface fluorescence signals and the interior luminescent sources. Following deep learning methodology, the CELST reconstruction can be formulated as:

$$\hat{u} = g(y^*) \tag{4}$$

where $g(\cdot)$ denotes the reconstruction network, which maps the acquired boundary measurements y^* to the reconstructed distribution of the luminescence yield $\hat{u}$.

2.3 Two-Step Reconstruction Algorithm

In this work, the whole inverse problem is decoupled into two sub-problems with the two-step training strategy, we enforce the first step to obtain the features of tissue shapes and the second step to learn the 3D distribution of quantum field. The two-step reconstruction framework can be described by:

$$\hat{u} = g_1(y^*) \oplus g_2(y^*) \tag{5}$$

where $g_1(\cdot)$ means the mapping model between the measurement data and the shapes of tissues (as the background) in step 1, $g_2(\cdot)$ is the mapping between the measurement data and the luminescent sources (as the targets), $\oplus$ represents the fusion operation of features in corresponding layers, which significantly mitigate the ill-posedness of the inverse problem by concatenating the low-level and high-level features extract from step 1 and step 2, respectively.

During the network training process, the parameters can be updated iteratively by minimizing the mean square error (MSE) between $\hat{u}$ and u.

$$MSE = \frac{1}{N} \sum_{i=1}^{N} \left\| u_i^* - \hat{u}_i \right\|^2 \tag{6}$$

where N is the number of training samples.

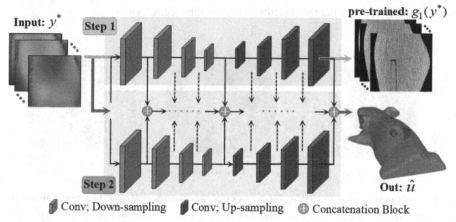

Fig. 1. The framework of the developed TSR-Net. Step 1 is training the ED-Net and step 2 is training a fusion network concatenated with the fixed pre-trained ED-Net.

In our approach, the 3D distributions of luminescent sources are reconstructed from the acquired surface signals guided by predicted micro-CT images through end-to-end training with simulated datasets. Figure 1 shows the TSR-Net architecture, which can be described in the following steps:

Step 1. The surface fluorescence signals y^* are fed into the encoder-decoder network (ED-Net) and mapped into the micro-CT images of tissues. The encoder module contains 4 convolution blocks and 4 down-sampling layers. Every convolution block is composed of two convolution layers, and each has a kernel size of 3×3 with a stride of 1. For down-sampling operations, a convolution of size 3×3 with a stride of 2 was adopted to reduce information loss. In the decoder network, a transposed convolution with a kernel of 3×3 and stride of 2 in up-sampling layers [25]. In addition, we use leaky rectified linear units (ReLU) as the activation function to intensify the network in each convolutional layer. The batch normalization (BN) technique is used to accelerate the learning process [26]. The decoder module contains 4 convolution blocks and 4 up-sampling layers. Corresponding to the encoder module, transposed convolutions with the kernel of $2 \times 2 \times 2$ and stride of 2 are used for up-sampling operations in the decoder network.

Step 2. The weights of this trained ED-Net in step 1 are fixed and concatenated with another untrained encoder-decoder module for second-step training to effectively improve the reconstruction quality of the results predicted with one-step training. The two encoder-decoder networks are concatenated with a fusion mechanism containing an error feedback module, which allows the model to have a self-correcting procedure [27]. The schema enables the networks to preserve the high-resolution components by learning various up and down-sampling operators and generating deeper features to exactly reconstruct the distribution of luminescent yield.

Overall, the mapping model between the measured data and the micro-CT image learned in step 1 provides the structural priors to guide the 3D reconstruction in step 2. The low-level and high-level features from two ED-Net modules are correspondingly fused to finally reconstruct the distribution of luminescence yield.

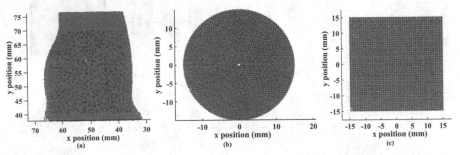

Fig. 2. The illustration of the 3D-phantom and the correspondent source-detector configuration used in the experiments. (a) the mouse phantom; (b) the cylinder phantom and (c) the slab phantom.

3 Results

To demonstrate the effectiveness of the proposed algorithm, numerical simulation experiments were carried out to discuss the performance of the TSR-Net. To synthesize the forward data, the mouse phantom (XFM-2, PerkinElmer Health Sciences), cylinder phantom, and slab phantom were used. Detectors were placed at the top surface of the phantoms to mimic the acquired fluorescence signals, as presented in Fig. 2. The forward data for each phantom were generated with the open-source software NIRFAST [21, 28]. The absorption coefficient μ_a and reduced scattering coefficient μ'_s for wavelength excitation and emission were set the same as [2, 12]. For training step 1, the forward data was generated with the mouse phantom, cylinder phantom and slab phantom by changing the number and the diameter of fluorescent targets, as well as the optical parameters, the CT images were simulated with the binary images of the phantoms. A total of 2400 samples were finally generated, including 1800 samples for training, and 600 samples for validation. For training step 2, the forward data was generated with only the mouse phantom. A total of 1600 samples were finally generated, including 1200 samples for training, and 400 samples for validation. All the forward data was simulated with 1% Gaussian noise added. Note that testing datasets were additionally created, such that the testing dataset was never been used in network training.

For comparative purposes, reconstruction with an encoder-decoder network (ED-Net) was also applied to execute reconstruction experiments on the above data. The mean squared error (MSE), peak signal-to-noise ratio (PSNR), and structural similarity (SSIM) were used as metrics to quantitatively analyze the reconstruction performance. The reconstruction network was implemented in Python 3.8 with PyTorch [29], and the Adam optimizer [30] was used to train for 500 epochs with the learning rate of 10^{-4}, and the batch size of 16. All computations were run on a 64-bit PC, having an Intel Core i7–9700 CPU at 3.00 GHz with 32 GB RAM and two NVIDIA GeForce RTX 3090 graphic cards.

3.1 Reconstruction Depth Test

A single target with a diameter of 6 mm was placed at different depths inside the mouse phantom to evaluate the performance of the proposed TSR-Net. The target-to-background contrast of quantum field was 3:1.

Some visual results for the two methods and quantitative analysis at different depths are shown in Fig. 3, respectively. Ground truths were shown in 3D rendered and 2D axial images (Fig. 3(a)), where the small yellow circles in 2D images represent the actual positions of the target. Figure 3(b)–(c) are the reconstructed images by ED-Net

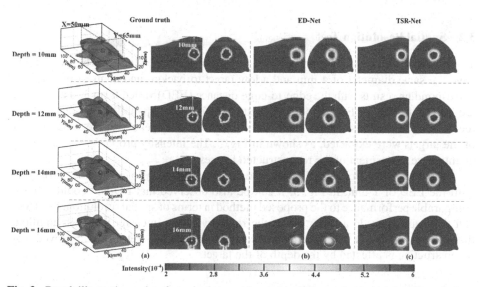

Fig. 3. Result illustrations when for a single target located in different depths. (a) the 3D rendering of the ground-truth images, the corresponding 2D cross-section, and (b)–(c) the reconstructed results by ED-Net, TSR-Net.

and TSR-Net with varied depths from 10 to 16 mm. It can be seen from Fig. 3(b) that some artifacts are presented in the reconstruction results of ED-Net, which reflects the performance of TSR-Net for artifact removal. Furthermore, when the depth is 16 mm, ED-Net fails to recover the intensity, whole closer intensity to the ground-truth images can be reconstructed by TSR-Net.

Table 1 shows the quantitative results with the increased depth. From Table 2, we can see that superior performance is obtained by TSR-Net. Compared with ED-Net, the average PSNR, and SSIM are improved more than 3.3% and 1.9%, respectively; and MSE is reduced more than 21.5%. Overall, TSR-Net yields better than ED-Net results as the depth increases.

Table 1. Quantitative comparisons of reconstruction results using ED-Net and TSR-Net with varied depths.

Depth(mm)	Metric					
	MSE		PSNR (dB)		SSIM	
	ED-Net	TSR-Net	ED-Net	TSR-Net	ED-Net	TSR-Net
10	4.3×10^{-6}	3.3×10^{-6}	33.5	34.2	0.94	0.95
12	7.4×10^{-6}	5.2×10^{-6}	31.6	32.5	0.93	0.94
14	1.1×10^{-5}	8.4×10^{-6}	29.9	30.8	0.90	0.92
16	2.6×10^{-5}	1.9×10^{-5}	27.8	29.4	0.86	0.89

3.2 Spatial Resolution Test

The spatial resolution of the proposed algorithm was also evaluated. The two targets have the same diameter of 4 mm and a low target-to-background contrast of 2:1. The corresponding results with the edge-to-edge distance (EED) varied from 3 mm to 0 mm are shown in Fig. 4. Furthermore, to better compare the spatial resolution of these reconstruction methods, line profiles of the reconstructed images across the central height of the targets were extracted, as shown in Fig. 5. The intensity profiles provide a more quantitative assessment of the reconstructed images.

From Fig. 4, ED-Net and TSR-Net have the same capability to resolve the two targets with the EED of 1 mm. In Fig. 5, it can be also observed that ED-Net could achieve comparable performance to the proposed method in terms of spatial resolution, but TSR-Net does appear to do a better job in the recovery of the intensity value. In addition, the intensity values of the two targets reconstructed by TSR-Net in Fig. 5 proved that reconstruction is affected by the depth of the target.

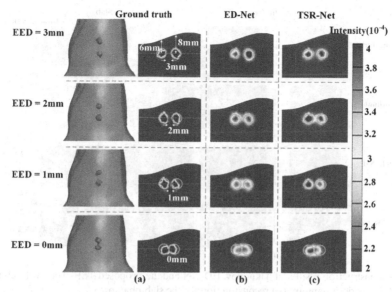

Fig. 4. Result illustrations for the EEDs decrease from 3 to 1 mm. (a-c) are the ground truths and results reconstructed by ED-Net and TSR-Net.

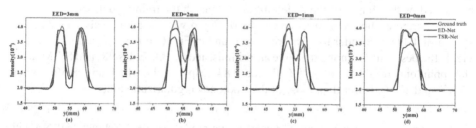

Fig. 5. Intensity profiles corresponding to different EEDs along the y-axis direction in the cross-sections (*green dotted line in Fig. 4(a)*). (Color figure online)

3.3 Generalization Ability Test

Simulations with different phantoms were conducted to test the generalization ability of the two DL methods, using the well-trained network on the dataset of mouse phantom. Representative results methods with phantoms of cylinder and slab were shown in Fig. 6, in which a single target with the diameter of 5 mm was set in the depth of 8 mm and 10 mm, respectively. The target-to-background contrast is 2:1. In addition, we also presented the results with the iterative algorithm Tikhonov regularization [6] to better demonstrate the generalization ability of the proposed method.

From Fig. 6, it can be clearly seen that over-smoothed images were obtained by Tikhonov regularization, indicating that the target shapes could not be recovered. The reconstruction results under different phantoms proved that the ED-Net methods failed in the target location and shape recovery. By contrast, the TSR-Net method has achieved the best performance in terms of quantum fields and localization accuracy. However,

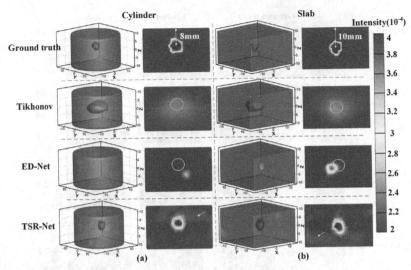

Fig. 6. Reconstruction results of Tikhonov, ED-Net and the proposed TSR-Net. (a) Reconstruction for the cylinder phantom; (b) reconstruction for the slab phantom.

artifacts were introduced in the cylinder and slab phantoms reconstructions, which may be caused by the shapes of the phantoms do not match the training dataset.

Furthermore, the reconstruction results of Fig. 6 were quantitatively calculated as shown in Table 2. Similar to what we have found in Fig. 6, it is revealed that TSR-Net yields the best results among the three algorithms, and the MSE, PSNR, and SSIM in the slab phantom are 3.8×10^{-5}, 25.6 dB and 0.84, respectively, which are 98.5% higher, 75.3% and 47.4% lower than those of the Tikhonov regularization method.

Table 2. Quantitative comparisons of reconstruction results using ED-Net and TSR-Net with varied phantoms.

Methods	Phantoms					
	Cylinder			Slab		
	MSE	PSNR(dB)	SSIM	MSE	PSNR(dB)	SSIM
Tikhonov	3.7×10^{-3}	14.0	0.53	2.5×10^{-3}	14.6	0.57
ED-Net	7.4×10^{-3}	12.7	0.48	2.4×10^{-3}	15.2	0.60
TSR-Net	4.2×10^{-5}	24.9	0.82	3.8×10^{-5}	25.6	0.84

4   Discussion and Conclusions

When it comes to CELST reconstruction, iteration-based methods are usually time-consuming. It takes about 1.2 h for Tikhonov regularization algorithm to reconstruct the 3D distribution of the luminescence yield. By contrast, the iterative process is replaced by an end-to-end mapping model using DL-based reconstruction in this study, so as a result the computational time can be reduced to a few seconds once the network parameters are well-trained.

As seen in Fig. 3 and Fig. 4, the ED-Net method could obtain comparable performance to TSR-Net for the mouse phantom reconstruction, where the forward data matched with the training datasets. Furthermore, it was observed that TSR-Net yields relatively better image quality compared with the ED-Net method, as presented in Fig. 6. Since the model mismatch will lead to inaccurate image reconstruction and therefore affects the DL prediction, the ED-Net failed to recover the quantum fields and localization of the luminescence sources, and then results in the lowest SSIM value for the cylinder phantom reconstruction. By comparison, Tikhonov achieved better positioning accuracy but failed in intensity recovery.

Besides, for the TSR-Net method, the training datasets used in step 1 and step 2 are different: The forward data generated with 3 different phantoms and the micro-CT images are used for step 1 training, which may be easy to obtain in clinical practice; another set of forward data and the ground truths of the mouse phantom are used in step 2. The network parameters well-trained in step 2 with the mouse phantom are effective to reconstruct cylinder and slab phantoms, such that the requirement of the corresponding ground-truth images could be alleviated.

In conclusion, an end-to-end image reconstruction algorithm for CELST is developed by a two-step reconstruction network (TSR-Net), in which the reconstruction is decoupled into two steps: Step 1 for CT structural image reconstruction, step 2 for the 3D distribution of the quantum field reconstruction. Numerical simulations are conducted to validate the performance of TSR-Net. In contrast with the direct reconstruction using the encoder-decoder network (ED-Net), the two-step reconstruction network (TSR-Net) can yield closer locations and intensities of the targets to the actual ones, and appears with significant generalization ability. However, it is an issue that remains to be addressed the artifacts will be introduced when the phantoms do not match with the training datasets. In future work, it should be expected that denoising approaches could be incorporated to improve the generalizability of the model.

Acknowledgments. This paper is supported by the Project for the National Natural Science Foundation of China (82171992, 62105010).

References

1. Ruggiero, A., Holland, J.P., Lewis, J.S.: Cerenkov luminescence imaging of medical isotopes. J. Nucl. Med. **51**(7), 1123–1130 (2010)
2. Pogue, B.W., et al.: Map of in vivo oxygen pressure with submillimeter resolution and nanomolar sensitivity enabled by cherenkov-exited luminescence scanned imaging. Nat. Biomed. Eng. **2**(4), 254–264 (2018)
3. Brůža, P., Lin, H., Vinogradov, S.A., Jarvis, L.A., Gladstone, D.J., Pogue, B.W.: Light sheet luminescence imaging with Cherenkov excitation in thick scattering media. Opt. Lett. **41**(13), 2986–2989 (2016)
4. Tanha, K., Pashazadeh, A.M., Pogue, B.W.: Review of biomedical Čerenkov luminescence imaging applications. Opt. Express **6**(8), 3053–3065 (2015)

5. Lin, H., et al.: Comparison of Cherenkov excited fluorescence and phosphorescence molecular sensing from tissue with external beam irradiation. Phys. Med. Biol. **61**(10), 3955–3968 (2016)
6. Feng, J., Bruza, P., Dehghani, H., Davis, S.C., Pogue, B.W.: Cherenkov-excited luminescence sheet imaging (CELSI) tomographic reconstruction. In: Proceedings of SPIE, vol. 10049, p. 1004912 (2017)
7. Shi, J., Liu, F., Zhang, G., Luo, J., Bai, J.: Enhanced spatial resolution in fluorescence molecular tomography using restarted L1-regularized nonlinear conjugate gradient algorithm. J. Biomed. Opt. **19**(4), 046018 (2014)
8. Zhao, L., Yang, H., Cong, W., Wang, G., Intes, X.: LP regularization for early gate fluorescence molecular tomography. Opt. Lett. **39**(14), 4156–4159 (2014)
9. Shi, J., Zhang, B., Liu, F., Luo, J., Bai, J.: Efficient L1 regularization based reconstruction for fluorescent molecular tomography using restarted nonlinear conjugate gradient. Opt. Lett. **38**(18), 3696–3699 (2012)
10. Lu, W., Duan, J., Miguel, D.O., Herve, L., Styles, L.B.: Graph- and finite element-based total variation models for the inverse problem in diffuse optical tomography. Biomed. Opt. Express **10**(6), 2684–2707 (2019)
11. Feng, J., et al.: Deep-learning based image reconstruction for MRI-guided near-infrared spectral tomography. Optica **9**, 264–267 (2022)
12. Zhang, W., et al.: Selfrec-net: self-supervised deep learning approach for the reconstruction of cherenkov-excited luminescence scanned tomography. Biomed. Opt. Express **14**, 783–798 (2023)
13. Yoo, J., et al.: Deep learning diffuse optical tomography. IEEE Trans. Med. Imaging **39**(4), 877–887 (2020)
14. Guo, L., Liu, F., Cai, C., Liu, J., Zhang, G.: 3D deep encoder-decoder network for fluorescence molecular tomography. Opt. Lett. **44**(8), 1892–1895 (2019)
15. Liao, M., Zheng, S., Lu, D., Situ, G., Peng, X.: Real-time imaging through moving scattering layers via a two-step deep learning strategy. In: Proceedings of SPIE, vol. 11351, p. 113510V (2020)
16. Zhu, S., Guo, E., Gu, J., Bai, L., Han, J.: Imaging through unknown scattering media based on physics-informed learning. Photonics Res. **9**(5), B210–B219 (2021)
17. Shang, R., Hoffer-Hawlik, K., Wang, F., Situ, G., Luke, G.P.: Two-step training deep learning framework for computational imaging without physics priors. Opt. Express **29**, 15239–15254 (2021)
18. Belthangady, C., Royer, L.A.: Applications, promises, and pitfalls of deep learning for fluorescence image reconstruction. Nat. Methods **16**(12), 1215–1225 (2019)
19. Weigert, M., et al.: Content-aware image restoration: pushing the limits of fluorescence microscopy. Nat. Methods **15**(12), 1090–1097 (2018)
20. Shimobaba, T., et al.: Computational ghost imaging using deep learning. Opt. Commun. **413**, 147–151 (2018)
21. Dehghani, H., et al.: Near infrared optical tomography using NIRFAST: algorithm for numerical model and image reconstruction. Commun. Num. Methods Eng. **25**(6), 711–732 (2009)
22. Soubret, A., Ripoll, J., Ntziachristos, V.: Accuracy of fluorescent tomography in the presence of heterogeneities: study of the normalized born ratio. IEEE Trans. Med. Imaging **24**(10), 1377–1386 (2005)
23. Arridge, S.R.: Optical tomography in medical imaging. Inverse Probl. **15**(2), 41–93 (1999)
24. Cong, A.X., Wang, G.: A finite-element-based reconstruction Method for 3D fluorescence tomography. Opt. Express **13**(24), 9847–9857 (2005)

25. Ding, X., Guo, Y., Ding, G., Han, J.: ACNet: strengthening the kernel skeletons for powerful CNN via asymmetric convolution blocks. In: 2019 IEEE International Conference on Computer Vision, ICCV, Seoul, pp. 1911–1920 (2019)
26. Çiçek, Ö., Abdulkadir, A., Lienkamp, S., Brox, T., Ronneberger, O.: 3D U-net: learning dense volumetric segmentation from sparse annotation. In: Ourselin, S., Joskowicz, L., Sabuncu, M., Unal, G., Wells, W. (eds.) MICCAI 2016. LNCS, vol. 9901, pp. 424–432. Springer, Cham (2016). https://doi.org/10.1007/978-3-319-46723-8_49
27. Haris, M., Shakhnarovich, G., Ukita, N.: Deep back-projection networks for super-resolution. In: 2018 IEEE/CVF Conference on Computer Vision and Pattern Recognition, CVPR, Salt Lake City, pp. 1664–1673 (2018)
28. Jermyn, M., et al.: Fast segmentation and high-quality three-dimensional volume mesh creation from medical images for diffuse optical tomography. J. Biomed. Opt. 18(8), 086007 (2013)
29. Paszke, A., et al.: Automatic differentiation in PyTorch. In: Advances in Neural Information Processing Systems (NIPS), Long Beach (2017)
30. Kingma, D.P., Ba, J.: Adam: a method for stochastic optimization. arXiv:1412.6980 (2014)

A Method for Enhancing the Quality of Compressed Videos Based on 2D Convolution and Aggregating Spatio-Temporal Information

Pengyu Liu[1]([✉]), Pengcheng Jin[1], Shanji Chen[2], Weiwei Huang[1], and Sirong Wang[1]

[1] Beijing Laboratory of Advanced Information Networks, Beijing Key Laboratory of
Computational Intelligence and Intelligent System, Beijing University of Technology,
Beijing 100124, China
liupengyu@bjut.edu.cn
[2] School of Physics and Electronic Information Engineering, Qinghai Nationalities University,
Xining 810007, Qinghai, China

Abstract. Existing block-based video coding frameworks are often affected by the quantization step size and motion compensation accuracy, resulting in the loss of high-frequency information and compression artifacts. Especially in the case of limited coding resources, the blurring of content edges and obvious compression distortion will have a negative impact on the subjective quality of the video. Therefore, there is an urgent need to build a quality enhancement method to improve the compressed video quality at the receiving end under the same coding resources. This paper proposes a compression video quality enhancement method based on 2D convolution that aggregates spatial and temporal information. Based on the objective facts of analyzing the spatiotemporal correlation and video quality fluctuation, this method constructs a multi-frame input mechanism consisting of the current frame to be enhanced and its adjacent frames; furthermore, it efficiently extracts and integrates the temporal and spatial information features of the input video sequence by utilizing the excellent feature extraction and fusion capabilities of the encoder-decoder structure, achieving implicit alignment. On this basis, an attention mechanism is integrated to more accurately locate and extract key information in the video, thereby more accurately restoring the detail information in the video and improving the performance of the model. In public benchmark tests, our method achieved average ΔPSNR gains of 0.801 dB, 0.796 dB, 0.792 dB, and 0.714 dB on 18 video test sequences with QP = 22, 27, 32, and 37, respectively, outperforming other methods. Compared with the state-of-the-art algorithms, our method achieved speed improvements of 13.2%, 10.5%, and 6.2% for processing videos with resolutions of 832×480, 1080×720, and 1920×1080, respectively. The above results show that our method can improve the compressed video quality at the receiving end under the same coding resources and outperforms other methods in terms of performance.

Keywords: compressed video · quality enhancement · deep learning

Supported by The National Key Research and Development Program of China (2018YFF01010100), The Beijing Natural Science Foundation (4212001), Key R&D and Transformation Program of Qinghai Province (2022-QY-205).

1 Introduction

With the explosive growth of high-quality video data on the Internet, video compression plays an important role in efficient video transmission with limited bandwidth. However, due to the use of block-based video coding frameworks in existing video coding methods, compression artifacts are inevitably generated, which may seriously reduce the Quality of Experience (QoE) of videos, especially at low bit rates [1, 2]. The distortion in low-quality compressed videos often reduces the performance of subsequent visual tasks (such as recognition, detection, and tracking) in low-bandwidth applications [3]. Therefore, research on video quality enhancement (VQE) is crucial. In order to improve the quality of compressed videos, researchers have conducted a lot of work in the past few years. For example, [4] proposed a four-layer convolutional neural network called ARCNN, which was successfully applied to single-frame images to improve the quality of compressed images. Zhang et al. proposed a denoising CNN (DnCNN) [5], which uses a residual learning strategy for image denoising and deblocking. However, these methods only independently enhance single frames and cannot utilize the relevant information of adjacent frames in the video sequence. Zhang et al. proposed an even deeper network RNAN [6] with residual non-local attention mechanism to capture long-range dependencies between pixels and set up a new state-of-the-art of image quality enhancement. These methods tend to apply large CNNs to capture discriminative features within an image, resulting in a large amount of computations and parameters.Furthermore, [7] proposed a non-local Kalman network, which recursively enhances the current frame to be enhanced by utilizing the time-related information from the previously reconstructed frames. Yang et al. [8] proposed a multi-frame quality enhancement (MFQE 1.0, Multi-Frame CNN) method that uses temporal information to enhance VQE. Specifically, this method uses high-quality frames in compressed videos as reference frames and uses a new multi-frame CNN (Multi-Frame CNN) to improve the quality of adjacent low-quality target frames. Recently, the upgraded version MFQE 2.0 [9] further improved the efficiency of MF-CNN and achieved state-of-the-art performance. In [10], a spatiotemporal deformable fusion (STDF) module was proposed to aggregate spatiotemporal information to enhance video quality. Currently, video compression enhancement methods usually utilize display alignment techniques such as optical flow or implicit alignment techniques like 3D convolution to fuse spatio-temporal information of videos, aiming to better utilize the temporal correlation information of compressed videos. For instance, MFQE2.0 estimates the motion information between video frames by calculating the optical flow after pre-searching high-quality frames around the current frame, and then fuses the spatio-temporal information. However, any errors in optical flow calculation can introduce new artifacts around the image structure in the aligned adjacent frames, which may degrade the image quality and worsen the effect of subsequent video enhancement tasks. Moreover, accurate optical flow estimation can lead to worrying processing speed of the model. 3D convolution is widely used in implicit alignment methods, but the significant increase in the number of 3D convolution parameters results in high model computational complexity and memory consumption, and may also lead to overfitting. These drawbacks limit the performance and scalability of 3D convolution in practical applications. In contrast, 2D convolution has lower parameter volume and computational complexity, thus having advantages in processing speed and memory consumption. In the case of multi-frame input, 2D convolution can achieve implicit alignment through channel concatenation, thereby maintaining high image quality while reducing computational complexity and memory consumption. Therefore, based on the analysis of the unet structure and attention mechanism, this paper proposes a new multi-frame spatio-temporal information fusion 2D convolution compressed video enhancement network model. Specifically, this paper inputs the current frame to be enhanced and its adjacent 3 frames through channel concatenation into the unet structure combined with the attention mechanism for enhancement. The unet network can efficiently extract and fuse the time-related information and spatial information features of the input video sequence by virtue of its encoder-decoder structure. At the same time, the integration of the attention mechanism in the model can more accurately locate and extract key information in the video, thereby more accurately restoring the detail information in the video and improving the performance of the model. Compared with other compressed video enhancement methods, the model proposed in this paper has a more efficient processing speed and better subjective and objective compressed video enhancement effects.

2 Related Work

2.1 Unet

Unet consists of an encoder that gradually reduces the size of feature maps and a decoder that gradually increases the size of feature maps. It can capture multi-scale contextual information through hierarchical feature extraction. In addition, it strengthens the image reconstruction process and preserves edge and detail information by establishing skip connections between the encoder and decoder. Due to its superior feature extraction and fusion capabilities, as well as its ability to fuse with different feature extraction blocks to improve performance and generalization, it has been widely used in visual tasks such as image denoising.

2.2 Attention Mechanisms

In the field of deep learning, attention mechanism modules have become a popular research direction. Attention mechanism modules can help deep learning models better process input information, thereby improving the performance of the model. In natural language processing tasks, attention mechanism modules have been widely used in machine translation, text classification, question answering systems, and other tasks. Among them, neural machine translation models based on attention mechanisms have become one of the mainstream methods in the field of machine translation. In addition, attention mechanisms have also been applied in image recognition, speech recognition, and other fields. In the field of video enhancement, by introducing attention mechanisms, specific regions in the video can be automatically selected and enhanced, thereby improving the quality and visual effects of the video. For example, in video super-resolution reconstruction, attention mechanisms can be used to select the regions that need to be reconstructed to improve the reconstruction effect. In video denoising, attention mechanisms can help the model better focus on the noisy regions, thereby improving the denoising effect. The application of attention mechanisms in the field of video enhancement has brought new opportunities and challenges for the development of video processing technology.

3 The Proposed Approach

3.1 Method Proposal

[13] indicates that there is a correlation between pixels within a video frame, while [9] observes a high degree of similarity between frames within a short period of a video sequence. When the distance between two frames is within 10 frames, the average correlation coefficient value is greater than 0.75. It is also found that there are significant quality fluctuations in compressed videos, and the average distance between two adjacent high-quality frames is less than 7 frames. These results suggest that the current frame to be enhanced contains sufficient spatial and temporal related information within its adjacent 3 frames. The Unet network, with its encoder-decoder structure, can efficiently extract and fuse the temporal and spatial feature information of the input video sequence. Meanwhile, the incorporation of the attention mechanism in the model can more accurately locate and extract key information in the video, thereby more accurately restoring the detail information in the video and improving the performance of the model. Based on the above, this paper inputs the current frame to be enhanced and its adjacent 3 frames into the Unet structure combined with the attention mechanism for enhancement processing through channel concatenation.

3.2 Framework

Figure 1 shows the overall framework of our method in this paper. Given a compressed video that generates compression artifacts and distortion, our method aims to remove these artifacts and improve the video quality accordingly. Specifically, at time t_0, we enhance each current frame $I_{t_0}^{LQ} \in R^{H \times W}$ separately. To fully utilize temporal information, we use the three adjacent frames before and after the current frame $I_{t_0}^{LQ}$ as references to help improve the quality of each target frame. The enhanced solution $\hat{I}_{t_0}^{HQ}$ can be represented as:

$$\tilde{I}_{t_0}^{HQ} = F_\theta \left(\left\{ I_{t_0-3}^{LQ}, I_{t_0-2}^{LQ}, I_{t_0-1}^{LQ}, I_{t_0}^{LQ}, I_{t_0+1}^{LQ}, I_{t_0+2}^{LQ}, I_{t_0+3}^{LQ} \right\} \right) \tag{1}$$

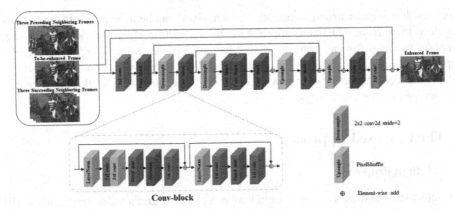

Fig. 1. Overview of the proposed framework for compressed video quality enhancement.

3.3 Conv-block Module

In order to increase the receptive field and extract more informative features, while achieving a balance between complexity and performance, we designed the following conv-block module structure, which consists of two levels. The first level contains a normalization layer, a convolutional layer, a gating structure [14], and a channel attention [15] structure. The input feature map first passes through the normalization layer, then through 1×1 and 3×3 convolutional layers before entering the gating unit, then through the channel attention layer, and finally through a 1×1 convolutional layer to output the feature map, which is then added to the initial feature map as input to the second level. The second level contains a normalization layer, a convolutional layer, and a gating structure: the feature map passes through the normalization layer, then through a 1×1 convolutional layer, then through the gating unit, and finally through a 1×1 convolutional layer to output the feature map, which is then added to the input feature map of the second level as the final output.

Gated units:

$$Gated(X, f, g, \sigma) = f(X) \odot \sigma(g(X)) \tag{2}$$

where X represents the feature map, f and g are linear transformers, which are used to transform the input data. σ is a non-linear activation function such as Sigmoid, which is used to introduce non-linearity into the data being processed. The symbol $\odot$ denotes element-wise multiplication, which means each element in the first matrix is multiplied by the corresponding element in the second matrix.

Channel Attention:

$$Attention(X) = X * \sigma(W_2 \max(0, W_1 pool(X))) \tag{3}$$

where X represents the feature map. The term 'pool' denotes the global average pooling operation, which is used to aggregate spatial information into channels, reducing the spatial dimensions while retaining the depth. The symbol σ represents a non-linear activation function such as Sigmoid, which is used to introduce non-linearity into the data being processed. W_1 and W_2 are fully connected layers, which are used to transform the input data, with a ReLU (Rectified Linear Unit) activation function in between to introduce non-linearity and improve the learning capability of the model. The symbol $*$ denotes a channel-wise convolution operation, which means the convolution is performed independently on each input channel.

4 Experiments

4.1 Experimental Setup

The proposed method is based on the PyTorch framework. For training, we randomly crop 64 × 64 patches from both the original videos and their corresponding compressed videos as training samples. Data augmentation (rotation or flipping) is further applied to better utilize these training samples. We use the Adam optimizer [16] to train all models with $\beta_1 = 0.9$, $\beta_2 = 0.999$, $\epsilon = 10^{-8}$, , batch size of 16, initial learning rate of 5e-4, which remains constant throughout the entire training process. We train four models from scratch for four QPs, respectively. For evaluation, similar to previous works, we only apply quality enhancement on the Y channel (luminance component) in the YUV/YCbCr space. We use the delta peak signal-to-noise ratio (ΔPSNR) and the delta structural similarity (ΔSSIM) [17] to evaluate the quality enhancement performance, which measures the improvement of the enhanced video relative to the compressed video. We also evaluate the complexity of the quality enhancement method from the perspective of parameters and computational cost.

4.2 Dataset

To train the proposed models, the database by Guan et al. [9] is used. The database consists of 130 uncompressed videos, selected from datasets of Xiph.org [18] and VQEG [19], with 106 videos used for training and the rest are for validation. For testing, the proposed models are evaluated on 18 standard test videos [20], which are collected from JCT-VC and widely used for video quality assessment. All the above videos are compressed by HM 16.5 in LDP mode with four different QPs, namely 22, 27, 32, and 37.

4.3 Comparison to State-of-the-Arts

Quantitative Results. We compared our proposed method with state-of-the-art single-frame/multi-frame video quality enhancement methods, including AR-CNN [4], RNAN [6], MFQE 2.0 [9] and STDF [10]. For fair comparison, all image quality enhancement methods were retrained on our training set. Tables 1 and 2 give quantitative results for accuracy and model complexity, respectively. It can be observed that in the 18 test videos, our method consistently outperforms all compared methods in terms of average ΔPSNR and ΔSSIM. In addition, Table 1 shows the detailed PSNR and SSIM gains after enhancement for the tested video sequences at QP 37.

Table 1. Overall Comparison for ΔPSNR(dB) and ΔSSIM($\times 10^{-2}$) Over Test Sequences at Four QPS.

QP	Video Sequence		ARCNN [4]	RNAN [6]	MFQE2.0 [9]	STDF-R3 [10]	Proposed
			PSNR/SSIM	PSNR/SSIM	PSNR/SSIM	PSNR/SSIM	PSNR/SSIM
37	Class A	Traffic	0.27/0.50	0.40/0.86	0.59/1.02	0.65/1.04	0.73/1.26
		PeopleOnstreet	0.37/0.76	0.74/1.30	0.92/1.57	1.18/1.82	1.32/2.12
	Class B	Kimono	0.20/0.59	0.33/0.98	0.55/1.18	0.77/1.47	0.91/1.59
		ParkScene	0.14/0.44	0.20/0.77	0.46/1.23	0.54/1.32	0.57/1.49
		Cactus	0.20/0.41	0.35/0.76	0.50/1.00	0.70/1.23	0.69/1.27
		BQTerrace	0.23/0.43	0.42/0.84	0.40/0.67	0.58/0.93	0.58/1.02
		BasketballDrive	0.23/0.51	0.43/0.92	0.47/0.83	0.66/1.07	0.72/1.22
	Class C	RaceHorse	0.23/0.49	0.39/0.99	0.39/0.80	0.48/1.09	0.40/1.09
		BQMall	0.28/0.69	0.45/1.15	0.62/1.20	0.90/1.61	0.93/1.83
		Partyscene	0.14/0.52	0.30/0.98	0.36/1.18	0.60/1.60	0.57/1.93
		BasketballDrill	0.23/0.48	0.50/1.07	0.58/1.20	0.70/1.26	0.69/1.50
	Class D	RaceHorses	0.26/0.59	0.42/1.02	0.59/1.43	0.73/1.75	0.69/1.81
		BQSquare	0.21/0.30	0.32/0.63	0.34/0.65	0.91/1.13	0.95/1.43
		BlowingBubbles	0.16/0.46	0.31/1.08	0.53/1.70	0.68/1.96	0.72/2.31
		BasketballPass	0.26/0.63	0.46/1.08	0.73/1.55	0.95/1.82	1.01/2.17
	Class E	FourPeople	0.40/0.56	0.70/0.97	0.73/0.95	0.92/1.07	1.06/1.30
		Johnny	0.24/0.21	0.56/0.88	0.60/0.68	0.69/0.73	0.80/0.92
		KristenAndSara	0.41/0.47	0.63/0.80	0.75/0.85	0.94/0.89	1.09/1.03
	Average		0.25/0.50	0.44/0.95	0.56/1.09	0.75/1.32	**0.801/1.52**
32	Average		0.19/0.17	0.41/0.62	0.52/0.68	0.73/0.87	**0.796/1.03**
27	Average		0.16/0.09	-/-	0.49/0.42	0.67/0.53	**0.792/0.71**
22	Average		0.13/0.04	-/-	0.46/0.27	0.57/0.30	**0.714/0.43**

From Table 2, it can be seen that the proposed method has a faster processing speed and comparable number of parameters compared to other methods. We note that our model only uses a total of 6 frames (3 preceding and 3 succeeding frames) as references and inputs them into the model to utilize temporal information, instead of using high-quality neighboring frames like MFQE 2.0 [9], which saves the computational cost of searching for these high-quality frames in advance. Moreover, our method does not

Table 2. Quantitative results of speed (FPS) and amount of parameters. Results of speed are measured on Nvidia GeForce GTX 1080Ti GPU.

	ProcessingSpeed (/fps)			Param (K)
	832 × 480	1080 × 720	1920 × 1080	
RNAN [6]	–	–	–	8957
MFQE1.0 [8]	3.8	1.6	0.7	1788
MFQE2.0 [9]	8.4	3.7	1.6	255
STDF-R3 [10]	9.1	3.8	1.6	365
Ours	12.5	5.9	2.4	480

require the early fusion of temporal and spatial information like STDF-R3 [10], which speeds up the processing.

Qualitative Results. Figure 2 provides the qualitative results on 4 test videos. It can be seen that compressed frames are seriously distorted by various compression artifacts (e.g., ringing in Kimono and blurring in FourPeople). Although image quality enhancement methods can effectively reduce these artifacts, the resulting frames often become overly blurred and lack details. On the other hand, video quality enhancement methods achieve better enhancement results with the help of reference frames. Compared with MFQE 2.0 [9], our model better restores structural details.

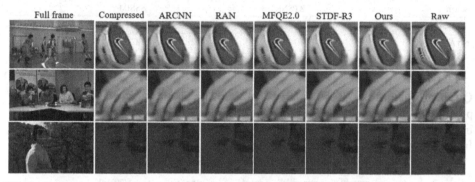

Fig. 2. Subjective quality performance on BasketballDrive at QP = 37, Foupeople at QP = 37 and Kimmono at QP = 37.

4.4 Analysis and Discussions

Effectis of Utilizing Temporal Information. To validate the effectiveness of our model in utilizing temporal information in video sequences, we conducted experiments under the same conditions using different numbers of frames as input. The results are shown in Table 3, where all methods utilizing reference frames outperform the single-frame baseline, demonstrating the effectiveness of our model in utilizing temporal information. Moreover, as the number of utilized reference frames increases, the PSNR of the enhanced videos by our method also increases.

Table 3. The enhancement effect and model parameter quantity under different numbers of input frames.

Number of input frames	ΔPSNR/dB	Parameters
1	0.492	476587
3	0.710	477759
5	0.782	478931
7	0.801	480103

Effectiveness of Channel Attention. To verify the effectiveness of the attention module, we train the proposed model with and without channel attention under the same experimental setup. The model with the best validation results after 300k training iterations is selected. Table 4 shows the PSNR/SSIM improvement results of the two models on the validation data. As shown in the second row of the table, the model without attention fusion strategy has a significant decrease in PSNR, indicating the effectiveness of the designed conv-block module for restoration performance.

Table 4. Ablation study on Attention.

Scheme	ΔPSNR/dB	ΔSSIM
Ours	0.801	1.52
No Attention	0.760	1.33

Quality Fluctuation. It is observed that dramatic quality fluctuation exists in compressed video [9], which may severely break temporal consistency and degrade QoE. To investigate how our method can help with this, we plot PSNR curves of 2 sequences (i.e. frames 50 to 100 of the *BQSquare* video and frames 100 and 150 of the *PartyScene* video)

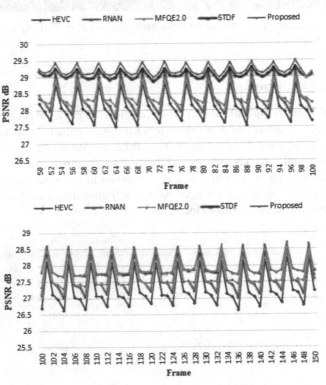

Fig. 3. PSNR curves of 2 test sequences at QP 37. Top: BQSquare. Bottom: PartyScene.

in Fig. 3. As can be seen, Our model can effectively enhance most low-quality frames, alleviate quality fluctuations, and achieve better performance than other comparative methods.

5 Conclusion

Based on the objective facts of analyzing the spatiotemporal correlation of videos and the quality fluctuations of videos, this paper constructs a multi-frame input mechanism consisting of the current frame to be enhanced and its adjacent frames before and after. Furthermore, a network model based on the Unet encoder-decoder structure is constructed to efficiently extract and fuse temporal and spatial information features of the input video sequence. On this basis, the attention mechanism is incorporated to more accurately locate and extract key information in the video, thereby more accurately restoring the detail information in the video and improving the performance of the model. The proposed model has the fastest model processing speed compared to other methods and achieves the best compressed video enhancement effect on benchmark databases. A large number of experimental results show that our method significantly improves the quality of compressed videos and outperforms other state-of-the-art methods.

References

1. Seshadrinathan, K., Soundararajan, R., Bovik, A.C.: Study of subjective and objective quality assessment of video. IEEE Trans. Image Process. **19**(6), 1427–1441 (2010)
2. Tan, T.K., Weerakkody, R., Mrak, M.: Video quality evaluation methodology and verification testing of HEVC compression performance. IEEE Trans. Circ. Syst. Video Technol. **26**(1), 76–90 (2016)
3. Galteri, L., Seidenari, L., Bertini, M.: Deep generative adversarial compression artifact removal. In: Proceedings of the IEEE International Conference on Computer Vision (2017)
4. Dong, C., Deng, Y., Loy, C.C.: Compression artifacts reduction by a deep convolutional network. In: Proceedings of the IEEE International Conference on Computer Vision (2015)
5. Zhang, K., Zuo, W., Chen, Y.: Beyond a Gaussian denoiser: residual learning of deep CNN for image denoising. IEEE Trans. Image Process. **26**(7), 3142–3155 (2017)
6. Zhang, Y., Li, K., Li, K.: Residual non-local attention networks for image restoration. arXiv preprint arXiv:1903.10082 (2019)
7. Lu, G., Zhang, X., Ouyang, W.: Deep non-local kalman network for video compression artifact reduction. IEEE Trans. Image Process. **29**, 1725–1737 (2019)
8. Yang, R., Xu, M., Wang, Z.: Multi-frame quality enhancement for compressed video. In: Proceedings of the IEEE Conference on Computer Vision and Pattern Recognition (2018)
9. Guan, Z., Xing, Q., Xu, M.: MFQE 2.0: a new approach for multi-frame quality enhancement on compressed video. IEEE Trans. Pattern Anal. Mach. Intell. **43**(3), 949–963 (2019)
10. Deng, J., Wang, L., Pu, S.: Spatio-temporal deformable convolution for compressed video quality enhancement. In: Proceedings of the AAAI Conference on Artificial Intelligence, vol. 34, no. 07, pp. 10696–10703 (2020)
11. Ronneberger, O., Fischer, P., Brox, T.: U-net: convolutional networks for biomedical image segmentation. In: Navab, N., Hornegger, J., Wells, W., Frangi, A. (eds.) MICCAI 2015, Part III. LNCS, vol. 9351, pp. 234–241. Springer, Cham (2015). https://doi.org/10.1007/978-3-319-24574-4_28

12. Knudsen, E.I.: Fundamental components of attention. Annu. Rev. Neurosci. **30**, 57–78 (2007)
13. Habibi, A., Wintz, P.: Image coding by linear transformation and block quantization. IEEE Trans. Commun. Technol. **19**, 50–62 (1971)
14. Dauphin, Y.N., Fan, A., Auli, Grangier, D.M.: Language modeling with gated convolutional networks. In: International Conference on Machine Learning, pp. 933–941 (2017)
15. Hu, J., Shen, L., Sun, G.: Squeeze-and-excitation networks. In: Proceedings of the IEEE Conference on Computer Vision and Pattern Recognition, pp. 7132–7141 (2018)
16. Kingma, D.P., Ba, J. Adam: a method for stochastic optimization. arXiv preprint arXiv:1412. 6980 (2014)
17. Wang, Z., Bovik, A.C., Sheikh, H.R.: Image quality assessment: from error visibility to structural similarity. IEEE Trans. Image Process. **13**(4), 600–612 (2004)
18. Xiph.org. Xiph.org video test media (derf's collection). https://media.xiph.org/video/derf/
19. VQEG. Vqeg video datasets and organizations. https://www.its.bldrdoc.gov/vqeg/video-dat asets-and-organizations.aspx
20. Ohm, J.R., Sullivan, G.J., Schwarz, H.: Comparison of the coding efficiency of video coding standards—including high efficiency video coding (HEVC). IEEE Trans. Circ. Syst. Video Technol. **22**(12), 1669–1684 (2012)

Multimedia-Based Informal Learning in Museum Using Augmented Reality

Mengze Zhao, Shining Ma, Yue Liu, and Weitao Song[✉]

Beijing Engineering Research Center of Mixed Reality and Advanced Display, School of Optics and Photonics, Beijing Institute of Technology, Beijing, China
swt@bit.edu.cn

Abstract. Many studies have demonstrated that augmented reality (AR) learning environments could effectively enhance learning efficiency in formal education compared to real learning environments. Furthermore, multimedia learning in AR has been shown to significantly improve learning performance and reduce cognitive load. However, few studies have explored the impact of AR environments on cognitive load and learning performance in informal learning, such as museum education. This study aims to fill this gap and investigate the impact of the relationship between the visual and auditory channels on knowledge acquisition and cognitive load in AR, as quantified by various indicators including heart rate variability, knowledge questionnaire score, user preference, and NASA-TLX. The results of within-group experiments suggested that the combination of visual and auditory information can substantially improve learning performance and reduce the task load compared to single-channel information delivery.

Keywords: Museum Education · Informal learning · Augmented Reality · Cognitive Load

1 Introduction

As an important informal learning environment, museums provide an opportunity for the public to visit the exhibited collections and informally acquire relevant knowledge [1–3]. In addition, with the development of various display technology, many museums have shifted their focal points from pure exhibitions to interactive experiences designed for educational goals. In most traditional museums, the explanation text of each item is always printed on a small label located next to the corresponding item, which increases the input intensity and reduces the learning efficiency. At the same time, these traditional museums become less attractive to younger generations [4].

Augmented reality (AR) technology which enables the fusion of the virtual scene and real environment could present the contextualized information about the exhibit as an overlay of the museum cabinet. As it can enrich the environment with various forms of learning information, such as digital text, image, audio, and video, AR technology has expanded its application area to tourism, education, and entertainment [5, 6]. Many studies have demonstrated that the use of AR can enhance learning efficiency and user motivation in formal education [7, 8].

However, aimed at informal learning in museums, the application of AR has hardly been investigated. It is still unclear how to design the virtual presentation content to optimize learning performance. To fill this gap, this study focused on the optimization of exhibition mode in AR and investigated the impact of information media, the number of input channels, and temporal synchronization on learning performance, as quantified by cognitive load, task load, user preference, and acquired knowledge.

2   Related Work

2.1   Cognitive Theory of Multimedia Learning in AR

In 1999, Mayer and Moreno proposed the cognitive theory of multimedia learning (CTML) [9] on the presumptions that there are two channels for learning: auditory and visual. Twelve principles constitute CTML. For example, the modality principle of this theory states that "people can learn more deeply from pictures and spoken words than that from pictures and printed words". Many studies have adopted this theory to guide the design of AR application systems. Lai has developed an AR-based educational learning system based on the proximity principle of Mayer's multimedia learning theory and confirmed the effectiveness of the system in improving learning performance and reducing cognitive load [10]. However, Krüger has not obtained the expected results using the AR system in compliance with the principle of spatial continuity and the principle of consistency [11]. The conveyance mode principle in the CTML suggests that the use of two or more modes of information delivery to present material can prevent cognitive overload and contribute to a better learning outcome [9]. Previous studies have found that AR with multimedia input leads to better performance in reducing cognitive load [12].

2.2   AR in Museum Learning

Many studies have suggested that the use of AR in informal learning creates a more engaging experience and enhances the educational function of the museum by offering considerable advantages in information capacity and interaction diversity [1, 13, 14]. In addition, AR technology enables museums to make virtual exhibitions without encroaching on physical space, which solves the problem of limited museum space [15, 16]. Consequently, AR is increasingly being used to aid informal learning in science, art, and history museums [17].

However, as previously described, most studies stopped at the comparison between AR and other multimedia formats, and did not investigate the optimization of AR systems under the guidance of well-accepted multimedia learning theories. At the same time, as most visitors keep relaxed during the visit (unlike formal learning scenarios), the impact of AR systems on cognitive load and learning effects in this scenario is still unclear. Further investigation of AR systems designed for museum exhibitions is needed in informal learning scenarios.

3   Method

3.1   Environment Scenario

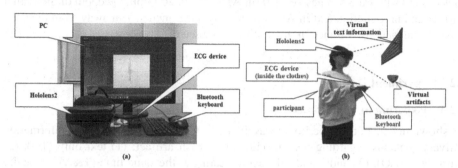

Fig. 1. Experimental set-up. (a) equipment used in the experiment. (b) real environment during the study.

Equipment. The experiment used the Microsoft HoloLens2, an optical see-through head-mounted-display (OST HMD) device with a field of view of $43° \times 29°$. The display resolution is 2048×1080 per eye. The application for this experiment was developed using Unity3D (version 2021.3). Also, an ECG device has been used to calculate task load, which has been shown in Fig. 1(a). Before the formal experiment for each participant, the HoloLens2 underwent a calibration procedure to determine the user's gaze direction and actual pupillary distance, serving as a reference for calculating the horizontal displacement between binocular images.

Real Environment. The experiment was conducted in a distraction-free room with a size of $3 \text{ m} \times 3 \text{ m}$. Participants stood during the experiment and were allowed to walk freely around the room. The virtual scenes in AR were presented against the white wall in the room to simulate the exhibition scene in the museum and enhance the visual contrast. To comply with the museum lighting standard, ambient lighting has a correlated color temperature (CCT) of 3000 K and an illuminance of around 300 lx. Before the formal experiment, a pilot test was conducted to confirm that the interior lighting condition could provide a comfortable lighting environment, and enable users to view the virtual artifact clearly.

Artifact Database. We have selected 24 ceramic artifacts that shared common shapes and exhibited similar sizes from the collection of the Palace Museum. The chosen artifacts were then subjected to precise modeling in 3ds Max 2014, ensuring the faithful replication of their shape, size, and surface texture. These modeling efforts were guided by the comprehensive information and imagery provided on the official website, enabling the creation of an accurate 1:1 scale representation. Subsequently, Unity3D was utilized to import these models along with their corresponding texture images.

For each artifact, we have prepared a brief introduction including the name, dynasty, size, appearance, and key features. The structure of the introduction kept consistent among 24 artifacts. In the virtual environment, the introduction text was added to the blank space right above the corresponding artifact. The length of each line was kept at around 36 characters with a font size of 59.4 *pt*. To maximize the visual contrast and legibility of the introduction text, the white text was presented against the black background with transparency set to 0 (in AR) [21]. In addition, the depth of the virtual artifact and introduction text in AR was initially positioned at 1 m away from the user, close to the viewing distance in the traditional museum.

3.2   Experiment Design

3.2.1   Experiment Conditions

As shown in Fig. 2., the experiment was divided into six sessions varying in information delivery methods regarding the introduction of each artifact: (1) text only (TO), (2) audio only (AO), (3) audio and full text appearing at the same time (T&A), (4) audio and text in subtitle format (sentence by sentence) appearing synchronously (SBS-T&A), (5) audio and text in subtitle format with the text appearing 2 s faster than audio (SBS-FT&A), (6) audio and text in subtitle format with the text appearing 2 s slower than audio (SBS-ST&A). Sessions TO and AO vary in input media. Sessions TO, AO, and T&A have different numbers of input channels. Sessions T&A and SBS-T&A have the same information capacity but different text information densities. Sessions SBS-T&A, SBS-FT&A, and SBS-ST&A have the same input format but differ in the temporal synchronization between the audio speech and subtitle-style text.

For each session, the participants were required to view four randomly selected artifacts from a database of artifacts. To avoid confusion, only one artifact was displayed at a time, with participants utilizing a Bluetooth keyboard to control the switching process. As previously mentioned, an introductory text accompanied each artifact, positioned above it. The audio file accompanying the text was generated using Microsoft Azure's text-to-speech service. To prevent any potential bias stemming from repetitive exposure, the 24 artifacts were divided into six groups through a random allocation process and each artifact was assigned to only one session.

3.2.2   The Measurement of Cognitive Load

During the visit in the AR-based virtual museum, two objective and two subjective assessment methods were adopted for the evaluation of the cognitive load and learning performance in the informal learning of these historical artifacts. These methods were introduced in detail as follows:

Objective Method:
Knowledge questionnaire score. After the informal learning for four artifacts in each session, the participant was required to answer 12 multiple-choice questions. Each artifact presented during the session corresponded to three specific questions, aligning with key details outlined in the artifact introduction. The questionnaire employed a four-choice format for each question, including one correct answer, two incorrect answers, and one option denoted as 'unknown'. A correctly answered question earned four points, while an

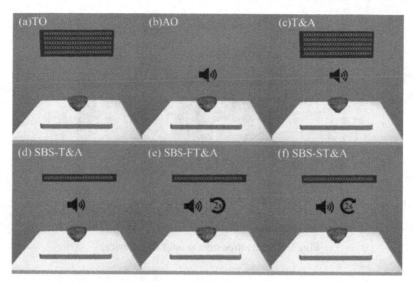

Fig. 2. The visual field of the participant when performing the informal learning experiment. Note that the audio symbol and the 2 s fast/slow symbol are used to indicate the difference among six sessions, but not presented in AR. (a) Text only (TO). (b) Audio only (AO). (c) Audio and full text (A&O). (d) Audio and subtitle-style text with synchronous relationship. (e) Audio and subtitle-style text with the text appearing 2 s faster than audio (SBS-FT&A), (f) Audio and subtitle-style text with the text appearing 2 s slower than audio (SBS-ST&A).

incorrectly answered question carried zero points. The final score served as a metric for evaluating the extent of knowledge acquired through the informal learning experience.

Heart rate variability (HRV). Several studies have indicated that HRV can be used as an indicator of cognitive load. In this study, the standard deviation of the NN interval (SDNN) was chosen as the estimation metric of HRV. As shown in Fig. 3, a small, portable, wireless electrocardiogram (ECG) device was used to collect the HRV data, and the ECG signals were transmitted wirelessly in real-time to a computer during the experiment. Prior to the experiment, a pilot study was conducted to validate the effectiveness of this ECG system in measuring HRV as an indicator of cognitive load.

Subjective Method:
Task load. It was assessed using the NASA-TLX [18] questionnaire, a widely recognized multidimensional scale utilized in the field of human-computer interaction. This questionnaire encompasses six evaluation dimensions: mental demand, physical demand, temporal demand, own performance, effort, and frustration. The NASA-TLX questionnaire consists of two steps: the first one is to evaluate the factors that affect the workload of a specific task; the second one is to rate the impact of each factor on the specific task. The final score was calculated by weighted averaging the score of each dimension.

User Preference: Upon completion of all experiment sessions, each participant was requested to rank six information delivery methods based on their preference [19]. Participants were instructed to assign a ranking score ranging from 1 to 6 to indicate their

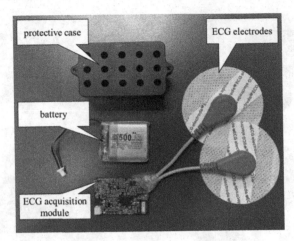

Fig. 3. The electrocardiogram (ECG) device.

order of preference, with "1" representing the most preferred method and "6" indicating the least preferred method.

3.3 Experiment Procedure

At the beginning of the experiment, the participants were given a brief introduction of the experimental procedure. Then they were asked to sign a consent form and complete a short survey. Before the formal experiment, a series of visual tests were conducted for each participant to check their visual acuity, hearing, etc. Subsequently, the participants were instructed to wear the HoloLens2 and perform the eye adaptation and calibration procedure. Next, the participants had seven minutes to get familiar with the AR environment and interaction operations. Once they felt comfortable with the environment, they could notify the experimenter that they were ready to begin the experiment. Then they were instructed to wear a wireless ECG device which recorded the ECG signals during the whole experiment. Afterwards the official experiment procedure started.

Each participant was required to spend three minutes viewing the four cultural relics in each group. Note that the participants could freely walk around the room when performing the task. Within the three minutes, participants were free to choose which cultural relic to view based on their preference. They could control the appearance, disappearance, and switching of the cultural relics along with the corresponding information (text and audio) using the keyboard.

After the informal learning of each session, the participants were asked to complete the NASA-TLX questionnaire and the knowledge questionnaire. Before the start of the next session, the participants were given a five-minute rest to relax and release the pressure from the previous workload. After finishing three sessions, the participants took a half-hour break before continuing the experiment. The order of six sessions was randomized for each participant. Upon completing the experiment, the participants were asked to rank the six sessions according to their personal preferences.

3.4 Participant

A total of 13 participants, aged between 22 and 27 years old (Mean = 24.00, SD = 1.68), were recruited from the Beijing Institute of Technology. They all had normal or corrected normal vision and normal hearing. And they have no difficulties with head movements (which we examined prior to the experiment). Four participants had previous experience with VR, but none of them could be considered regular users (daily or weekly). Four participants had previous experience with AR in the past 3–6 months, but none were frequent users.

4   Result

The Shapiro-Wilk test was employed to assess the normality of collected data. If the data conformed to a normal distribution and met the assumption of the equality of variances, one-way ANOVA was adopted to perform the statistic test, followed by Student's t-test for post-hoc analysis. For non-normally distributed data, the Kruskal-Wallis test was used, which was followed by the Wilcoxon signed-rank test for post-hoc comparison [20].

4.1   Task Load

The task load was quantified by the NASA-TLX questionnaire score. The average NASA-TLX scores over all the participants for six information delivery methods were plotted in Fig. 3(a), where the error bar represents the corresponding standard deviation. It could be found that the task load for TO is higher than that of AO, indicating that the text information results in a higher task load than the audio one. The task load of AO is similar to that of T&A and SBS-T&A. As for the comparison among SBS-T&A, SBS-FT&A, and SBS-ST&A, the task load of SBS-T&A is lower than the other two, indicating that the temporal mismatch between audio and subtitle-format text leads to a slight increment of task load. However, as confirmed by the ANOVA test, the impact of the information delivery method on task load is insignificant, and there are no significant differences found in the pairwise comparisons ($p > 0.05$). It could be found that the task load of each participant is relatively low (<18). The insignificant difference between the six sessions could be due to the lack of psychological pressure and the low difficulty of tasks.

4.2   Cognitive Load

The cognitive load was characterized by the heart rate variability which was estimated by SDNN. The average SDNN values for six different delivery methods were summarized in Fig. 3(b). It could be observed that the cognitive load of TO is higher than that of AO, indicating that text information brings more cognitive load than audio. The cognitive loads of T&A and SBS-T&A are higher than that of TO and AO, suggesting a positive effect of the number of input channels on the cognitive load. Additionally, for the three sessions with the same information format, the cognitive load of SBS-T&A is higher than the other two. It could be concluded that the temporal mismatch between audio and subtitle-format text could decrease the cognitive load. As the cognitive load may reflect the amount of knowledge occupying the memory of each participant, the asynchronous presentation of speech and text disrupts the participant's memory, consequently decreasing the cognitive load. However, it is important to note that no significant impact of the delivery method on cognitive load is observed using the Kruskal-Wallis test ($p > 0.05$). Pairwise comparisons do not reveal any significant differences among the delivery methods ($p > 0.05$) (Fig. 4).

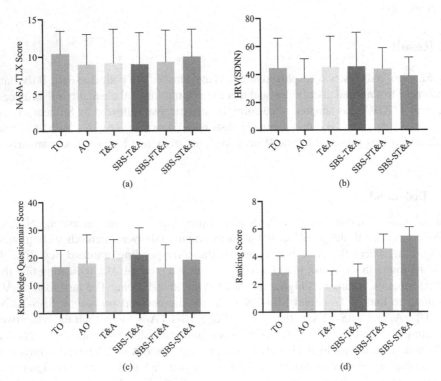

Fig. 4. The summary of the average assessment indicators (error bar represents the standard deviation) for six delivery methods. (a) Task load. (b) Cognitive load. (c) Acquired knowledge. (e) User preference.

4.3 Acquired Knowledge

The acquired knowledge was assessed by the knowledge questionnaire score. A higher score means that more knowledge was acquired by the participant during the informing learning, corresponding to better learning performance. Regarding different input channels, it can be observed that the knowledge score of AO is higher than that of TO, consistent with the modality principle in CTML. The knowledge scores of T&A and SBS-T&A are higher than that of TO and AO, suggesting the positive influence of multimedia input on learning performance. Regarding the comparison among SBS-T&A,

SBS-FT&A, and SBS-ST&A, the knowledge score of SBS-T&A is higher than the other two, indicating the importance of maintaining coherence between audio and visual elements for optimal learning outcomes. However, it is noteworthy that no significant impact of the delivery method on acquired knowledge is found. Pairwise comparisons using the ANOVA test do not reveal any significant differences ($p > 0.05$) among the delivery methods in terms of knowledge acquisition.

4.4 User Preference

The preference score averaged over all the participants was used to evaluate the general preference of the information delivery method in AR, a lower score indicating a higher preference. In the comparison between text and audio, the preference score of TO mode is smaller than that of AO, but there is no significant difference between the two modes as confirmed by the Wilcoxon signed-rank test ($p > 0.05$).

In addition, it could be found that the mean preference value of the T&A is smaller than that of the TO and AO where the information is presented through a single channel. The Kruskal-Wallis test reveals a significant difference between the three sessions ($p < 0.05$). Post hoc comparisons demonstrate a significant difference between TO and T&A ($p < 0.05$), AO and T&A ($p < 0.05$). This indicates that multimedia input with the combination of text and audio can effectively enhance participants' preferences compared to the single channel.

Regarding the temporal relationship between text and audio, the mean preference of the SBS-T&A mode is significantly lower than that of SBS-FT&A ($p < 0.05$) and SBS-ST&A ($p < 0.05$), as confirmed by post hoc comparisons of the Wilcoxon signed-rank test. That means the temporal mismatch between text and audio can negatively influence user experience. Additionally, SBS-FT&A has a significantly lower preference score than SBS-ST&A ($p < 0.05$), suggesting that presenting text faster than audio is more acceptable for users than presenting text slower than audio.

Among the six delivery methods, T&A and SBS-T&A are the firstly and secondly preferred ones with the highest knowledge score. Overall, all the participants selected one of them as the first or second preference. It can be inferred that temporal mismatch between multimedia channels is more unacceptable for participants than the absence of one information channel.

5 Discussion

There are still some factors that can potentially bias the collected subjective or objective data. Before the formal experiment, each participant was informed that they need to finish a knowledge questionnaire after the learning session. Although the experimenter repeatedly emphasized the importance to keep a relaxing learning mode, the competitive mindsets of most participants led to a test-taking mentality, which prevented them from observing the artifacts in the same way as a regular museum visit. Therefore, most of them experienced educational formal learning, instead of informal learning during the experiment. This tendency could bias the obtained multi-dimensional scores.

Although we have made our best to control the information capacity and question difficulty for different artifacts, it is possible that the participants could have different levels of interest regarding different types of information and they may focus on different aspects of memory retention. Therefore, it is almost impossible to ensure a 100% consistency in information capacity and question difficulty between these artifacts, which could become another bias factor in the evaluation of learning performance and task load.

In this study, four participants have used AR in the past few months, while the rest of them are naive participants without any prior experience with AR. Various studies have reported a notable difference in subjective evaluation between experienced and naïve participants. For example, Hopkinson found that experienced participants tend to give more consistent estimations within or between participants compared to native participants. To check the impact of prior experience on user experience, the Wilcoxon signed-rank test was conducted by comparing the two groups of participants. It has been found that there is a significant difference in cognitive load between experienced and naive participants ($p < 0.05$), but not for the other three measurement metrics (task load, acquired knowledge, and user preference) ($p > 0.05$).

6 Conclusions and Future Work

This study investigated the effect of the information delivery method on learning performance and user experience. Although the statistical analysis results did not show significant differences in task load, cognitive load, and acquired knowledge between the six methods, we still observed some obvious trends with reasonable explanations. Aimed for the application design of AR museum, T&A and SBS-T&A with synchronized multimedia signals are the most appropriate choices with the optimized learning performance and the most preferred user experience, indicating the importance of multi-channel information delivery in informal learning.

The findings of this study offer valuable theoretical guidance and practical implications for the design of AR museums. In the future, the investigation of user experience in AR museums will be extended to encompass various types of exhibits and different real-world environments varying in background and illumination conditions, to develop a more comprehensive solution for optimizing the user experience and performance of informal learning in AR museum settings.

References

1. de Rijcke, S., Beaulieu, A.: Image as interface: consequences for users of museum knowledge. Libr. Trends **59**, 663–685 (2011). https://doi.org/10.1353/lib.2011.0020
2. Guzin, O.A., Yildirim, R.G., Ellez, A.M.: An alternative educational method in early childhood: Museum education. Educ. Res. Rev. **12**, 688–694 (2017). https://doi.org/10.5897/ERR 2017.3145
3. Xanthoudaki, M.: Is it always worth the trip? The contribution of museum and gallery educational programmes to classroom art education. Camb. J. Educ. **28**, 181–195 (1998). https://doi.org/10.1080/0305764980280204

4. Crowley, K., Pierroux, P., Knutson, K.: Informal learning in museums. In: Sawyer, R.K. (ed.) The Cambridge Handbook of the Learning Sciences, pp. 461–478. Cambridge University Press (2014)

5. Azuma, R.T.: A survey of augmented reality. Presence Teleoper. Virtual Environ. **6**, 355–385 (1997). https://doi.org/10.1162/pres.1997.6.4.355

6. Fanini, B., Pagano, A., Pietroni, E., Ferdani, D., Demetrescu, E., Palombini, A.: Augmented reality for cultural heritage. In: Nee, A.Y.C., Ong, S.K. (eds.) Springer Handbook of Augmented Reality, pp. 391–411. Springer, Cham (2023). https://doi.org/10.1007/978-3-030-67822-7_16

7. Chiu, J.L., DeJaegher, C.J., Chao, J.: The effects of augmented virtual science laboratories on middle school students' understanding of gas properties. Comput. Educ. **85**, 59–73 (2015). https://doi.org/10.1016/j.compedu.2015.02.007

8. Di Serio, Á., Ibáñez, M.B., Kloos, C.D.: Impact of an augmented reality system on students' motivation for a visual art course. Comput. Educ. **68**, 586–596 (2013). https://doi.org/10.1016/j.compedu.2012.03.002

9. Mayer, R.: Multimedia Learning. Cambridge University Press, Cambridge (2020)

10. Lai, A.-F., Chen, C.-H., Lee, G.-Y.: An augmented reality-based learning approach to enhancing students' science reading performances from the perspective of the cognitive load theory: augmented reality-based science learning. Br. J. Educ. Technol. **50**, 232–247 (2019). https://doi.org/10.1111/bjet.12716

11. Krüger, J.M., Bodemer, D.: Application and investigation of multimedia design principles in augmented reality learning environments. Information **13**, 74 (2022). https://doi.org/10.3390/info13020074

12. İbili, E.: Effect of augmented reality environments on cognitive load: pedagogical effect, instructional design, motivation and interaction interfaces. IJPE. **15**, 42–57 (2019). https://doi.org/10.29329/ijpe.2019.212.4

13. Jung, T., tom Dieck, M.C., Lee, H., Chung, N.: Effects of virtual reality and augmented reality on visitor experiences in museum. In: Inversini, A., Schegg, R. (eds.) Information and Communication Technologies in Tourism 2016, pp. 621–635. Springer, Cham (2016). https://doi.org/10.1007/978-3-319-28231 2_45

14. González Vargas, J.C., Fabregat, R., Carrillo-Ramos, A., Jové, T.: Survey: using augmented reality to improve learning motivation in cultural heritage studies. Appl. Sci. **10**, 897 (2020). https://doi.org/10.3390/app10030897

15. Choudary, O., Charvillat, V., Grigoras, R., Gurdjos, P.: MARCH: mobile augmented reality for cultural heritage. In: Proceedings of the 17th ACM International Conference on Multimedia, pp. 1023–1024. ACM, Beijing (2009)

16. Wojciechowski, R., Walczak, K., White, M., Cellary, W.: Building virtual and augmented reality museum exhibitions. In: Proceedings of the Ninth International Conference on 3D Web Technology, pp. 135–144. ACM, Monterey (2004)

17. Zhou, Y., Chen, J., Wang, M.: A meta-analytic review on incorporating virtual and augmented reality in museum learning. Educ. Res. Rev. **36**, 100454 (2022). https://doi.org/10.1016/j.edurev.2022.100454

18. Hart, S.G., Staveland, L.E.: Development of NASA-TLX (task load index): results of empirical and theoretical research. In: Advances in Psychology, pp. 139–183. Elsevier (1988)

19. Bernard, M.L., Chaparro, B.S., Mills, M.M., Halcomb, C.G.: Comparing the effects of text size and format on the readability of computer-displayed times new roman and arial text. Int. J. Hum Comput Stud. **59**, 823–835 (2003). https://doi.org/10.1016/S1071-5819(03)00121-6

20. Tomczak, M., Tomczak, E.: The need to report effect size estimates revisited. An overview of some recommended measures of effect size. Trends Sport Sci. **1** (2014)

21. Falk, J., Eksvard, S., Schenkman, B., Andren, B., Brunnstrom, K.: Legibility and readability in augmented reality. In: 2021 13th International Conference on Quality of Multimedia Experience (QoMEX), pp. 231–236. IEEE, Montreal (2021)

Machine Vision and 3D Reconstruction

MAIM-VO: A Robust Visual Odometry with Mixed MLP for Weak Textured Environment

Zhiwei Shen[1,2(✉)] and Bin Kong[1,3,4(✉)]

[1] Institute of Intelligent Machines, Chinese Academy of Sciences, Hefei 230031, China
shenzw@mail.ustc.edu.cn, bkong@iim.ac.cn
[2] University of Science and Technology of China, Hefei 230026, China
[3] Anhui Engineering Laboratory for Intelligent Driving Technology and Application,
Hefei 230088, China
[4] Innovation Research Institute of Robotics and Intelligent Manufacturing (Hefei), Chinese
Academy of Sciences, Hefei 230088, China

Abstract. Visual localization is a critical technology for visual SLAM systems, which determines the relative position and motion trajectory by tracking feature points. In recent years, deep learning has been widely applied to the field of visual localization. The method based on deep learning is capable of surpassing the limitations of traditional manual feature extraction methods and achieving high-precision visual localization in complex scenes, thus realizing the goal of lifelong SLAM. The MLP model has characteristics such as flexibility and adaptability. The Mixer-WMLP achieves token information exchange between spatial positions by evenly dividing the feature map into non-overlapping windows, which makes the Mixer-WMLP approach a global receptive field. Compared to CNNs and Transformers, Mixer MLPs have higher computational efficiency and robustness. In this paper, we utilize the Mixer MLP structure to design a deep learning-based visual odometry system called MAIM-VO. Even in complex scenes with low texture areas, high-quality matching can be achieved. After obtaining the matching point pairs, the camera pose is solved in an optimized way by minimizing the reprojection error of the feature points. Multiple datasets and experiments in real-world environments have demonstrated that MIAM-VO exhibits higher robustness and relative localization accuracy compared to currently popular visual SLAM systems.

Keywords: Receptive field · Life SLAM · Visual Odometry · Mixer MLP

1 Introduction

Visual sensors provide rich environmental texture information through capturing images of the environment, making visual simultaneous localization and mapping (SLAM) an important task for mobile robot navigation and AR/VR. Currently, feature-based SLAM algorithms are widely applied in industries and military fields due to their high performance and computation efficiency. However, these feature-based matching methods heavily rely on the description of key points. Extracted feature points are not stable enough due to various factors such as low texture, lighting changes, viewpoint changes, and motion blur, making it impossible to complete the positioning task. Handcrafted features such as SIFT [1], SURF [2], and ORB [3] are unable to extract reliable key points for matching in areas with low texture or motion blur. In fact, these extreme environments are challenging for any visual SLAM method. With the development of computer computing power, deep learning-based feature extraction and matching methods have gradually replaced manual methods and become standard methods in research and practical applications. By replacing manually crafted features with deep features, the robustness of visual SLAM systems can be improved. Superpoint first proposed a end-to-end deep network that can simultaneously detect key points in images and generate descriptors, giving them better consistency and playing an important role in visual SLAM. GCN [5] adopts recursive neural networks to predict the position and description of keypoints and applies them to camera motion estimation. Although these deep learning-based methods have better performance than traditional methods in complex environments, there is still significant room for improvement when dealing with highly degraded scenes. Recently, some works [6, 7] have proposed to predict pixel-level matching of images directly using Transformer [8]. LoFTR [7] uses a transformer [8] with self-attention and cross-attention mechanisms to construct an detector-free feature matching model that can produce high-quality dense matches even in areas with low texture, motion blur, or repetitive patterns. However, due to the quadratic computational complexity of Transformers, LoFTR has higher requirements for both computing performance and memory. Compared with Transformer, MLP [9] models have become a better choice in the field of computer vision due to their superior processing capabilities, computing efficiency, and lower complexity. MAIM [10] reduces the calculation memory and time required for image matching by building a Mixer MLP structure called Mixer-WMLP, and can extract dense matching in complex environments.

In this paper, we introduce the MAIM-VO visual odometry method, which is based on a detector-free image matching using the Mixer MLP structure. Due to the proposed method being able to generate stable feature matching between two images, we have obtained more robust pose estimation results. Firstly, two consecutive frames are input into the image matching network to generate a large number of matching point pairs. Then, the visual odometry system uses non-linear optimization to reduce the reprojection error and iteratively obtain the best pose estimation between the two frames. In the second section, we discuss the research on visual odometry and feature matching. The third section introduce the system structure and derivation of the relevant formulas of MAIM-VO visual odometry. In the fourth section, MAIM-VO is extensively evaluated on multiple datasets and in real-world environments.

2   Related Work

Visual SLAM (Simultaneous Localization and Mapping) uses cameras as the primary sensor to establish spatial relationships with the surrounding environment. By estimating the camera motion between keyframes from a sequence of images or videos captured by a camera with a given internal parameter, the environmental map can be established. Visual front-end is a technique that uses image data collected by sensors to estimate the position and orientation relationship between key frames, also known as visual odometry. The technology can be roughly divided into two methods: feature-based and direct-based. The direct method estimates image motion by photometric changes, while the indirect method relies on image feature extraction and matching for motion estimation. LSD-SLAM [11] is a direct monocular method that can generate semi-dense consistent maps of large-scale scenes. Sparse direct visual odometry (DSO) [12] omits the smoothness used in other direct methods and uniformly samples pixels throughout the entire image. MonoSLAM [13] is the first real-time monocular visual SLAM system based on the Extended Kalman Filter (EKF) algorithm, which tracks sparsely distributed feature points at the front end. PTAM [14], on the other hand, is the first algorithm to separate tracking and mapping threads to achieve better performance. ORB-SLAM [15] is a representative visual SLAM system that uses the ORB [3] features and integrates tracking, local mapping, and loop closing to accomplish its tasks through three different threads. The VINS [16] system uses a visual-inertial fusion SLAM approach, with a sparse direct visual odometry that only calculates feature points without descriptors. This is achieved through the use of optical flow to track the motion of feature points, thereby reducing the time required for descriptor calculations and matching.

With the development of deep learning in computer vision tasks, learning-based feature extraction and matching methods have achieved better performance in handling complex scenes. SuperPoint [4] builds on the foundation of MagicPoint [17] and further improves keypoint detection and description performance by using homography matrices for self-supervised training. SuperGlue [18] is a matching method based on deep learning. Unlike traditional feature matching methods, SuperGlue uses graph neural networks to learn the matching relationship between two sets of key points with descriptors, thereby improving matching accuracy and robustness. However, even with perfect descriptions, the performance and stability of matching can be affected if repeatable key points cannot be detected. Recently, researchers have proposed some detector-free feature matching methods. NCNet [19] achieves direct learning of dense correspondences through an end-to-end approach. It constructs a 4D cost volume to enumerate all possible matches between images, and uses 4D convolutions to regularize the cost volume and enforce local consensus among all matches. LoFTR uses Transformer as its core architecture, extracting local features directly from the original image and performing matching. The Transformer has a global perspective, allowing LoFTR to produce high-quality dense matches even in complex environments with weak textures. However, the computational complexity of Transformer also exhibits quadratic growth, requiring a significant amount of time and computational memory. In MAIM [10], feature maps are divided into windows, and a Mixer MLP model called Mixer-WMLP is constructed to exchange token information between spatial and channel positions. This approach has the advantage of achieving nearly global vision, while significantly reducing time and computational costs compared to Transformers. Thanks to the development of feature matching methods based on deep learning, the visual SLAM system has made significant improvements. DS-SLAM [20] uses semantic segmentation networks to filter features on moving objects, achieving better positioning accuracy in highly dynamic environments. In GCN-SLAM [5], the neural network called GCNv2 is used to generate key points and binary descriptors, which replace the ORB features used in ORB-SLAM2 [20]. TRVO [21] uses LoFTR for visual odometry. With the Transformer structure introduced by the LoFTR network, it is able to effectively utilize the global information within the images. TRVO offers accurate feature matching results in challenging environments, such as low-texture and varying illumination in indoor scenes, or changes in perspective due to camera movements. This ensures smooth camera pose estimation. However, using the LoFTR network to obtain feature matching results is time-consuming and cannot guarantee real-time performance, which reduces the practicality of the entire visual odometry. To further improve the efficiency of the algorithm, this paper designs MAIM-VO, which uses the Mixer MLP model Mixer-WMLP with a view close to global, and then applies nonlinear optimization methods to obtain the pose estimation results of each frame by minimizing the reprojection error. At the same time, the network model is also able to provide accurate matching and tracking in complex scenarios, further enhancing the practicality of the visual odometry system.

3 Method

3.1 System Architecture

The visual odometry framework proposed in this article is shown in Fig. 1. The front-end structure of the ORB-SLAM2 system is similar. The system processes the two frames collected by the camera sensor each time, that is, the last frame and the current frame, using the MAIM network to obtain feature matching results. The MAIM method comes from our recent research work, serving as the front-end matching component in visual odometry [10]. The Mixer-WMLP uses window partitioning to divide tensors between specified window sizes. Coarse-level feature maps are partitioned from (N, H, W, C) to (num_windows, window_size, window_size, C). N represents the number of feature maps, H, W, and C represent the height, width, and number of channels of the tensor, num_windows represents the number of windows, and window_size represents the size of each window. Then, after passing through two MLP modules, information from different spatial positions is fused to form Nc spatial mixture layer and channel mixture layer. At the Coarse Level, a feature map with dimensions of 1/8(H x W) x C is input into the Mixer-WMLP model and passed to the matching module. The matching model uses a differentiable matching layer to match the transformed features into a confidence matrix P_c. Then, based on the confidence threshold and mutual nearest neighbor, we select matching items from P_c to obtain a coarse-level matching prediction M_C. The network will assign a score to each pair of matched points, selecting those pairs with a score higher than a preset threshold. Using the depth image, it will then calculate the 3D coordinate positions of these selected point pairs in the spatial domain. Then, based on the optimization results of the previous frame, the spatial coordinate positions (the spatial positions when the camera captured the first frame image) of these matched point pairs relative to the origin of the world coordinate system are generated, and these positions are re-projected into the current frame. By optimizing the reprojection error, the relative pose relationship between the previous frame and the current frame can be obtained. In order to improve the optimization efficiency, it is assumed that the camera maintains a constant velocity in a short period of time. In the first optimization iteration, the velocity of the previous frame is integrated as the initial value of the current frame position. The entire process continues and a complete visual odometry can be obtained.

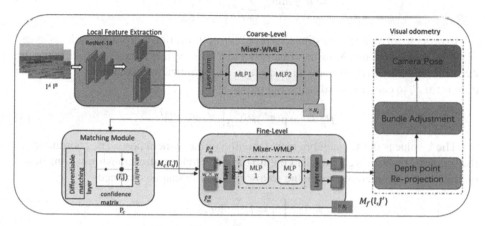

Fig. 1. Visual Odometry Framework

In the problem of camera pose estimation, if only the matched point pairs, i.e., 2D-2D point pairs, in two images are known, at least 8 pairs of points are required to compute the camera's relative motion using the epipolar geometry method, and there exist initialization, pure rotation, and scaling issues. If the 3D position of one feature point in two images is known, i.e., the 3D-2D point correspondence, the camera pose can be estimated using the PnP algorithm. At least three point correspondences are needed to estimate the camera motion. Therefore, we use data from RGB-D cameras as the source for our system design and experiments. If the 3D positions of n feature points are known, a non-linear least squares problem can be directly constructed to obtain the relative camera motion between two images by minimizing the reprojection error. This linear optimization problem can be easily solved using optimization libraries such as g2o and Ceres. Considering a set P that contains n 3D points and their projections in an image, our goal is to calculate the camera pose T, consisting of a rotation matrix R and a translation vector t. The spatial coordinates of a certain three-dimensional point are $P_i = [X_i, Y_i, Z_i]^T$,

Its pixel coordinates projected in the image are $Q_i = [u_i, v_i]^T$. Then the relationship between the pixel position and the 3D point position satisfies the following equation:

$$Z_i \, P_{uv} = Z_i \begin{bmatrix} u_i \\ v_i \\ 1 \end{bmatrix} = \begin{bmatrix} f_x & 0 & c_x \\ 0 & f_y & c_y \\ 0 & 0 & 1 \end{bmatrix} (RP_i + T) \tag{1}$$

The equation includes the intrinsic parameter matrix K of the camera and the homogeneous coordinate representation P_{uv} of u. However, due to the unknown camera pose, there is an error on both sides of the Eq. (1). To solve this, we add up all the errors of n feature points and construct a least squares problem (2). When the error is minimized, we can find the optimal pose estimation.

$$T^* = arg \min_{T} \frac{1}{2} \sum_{i=1}^{n} \left\| Q_i - \frac{1}{Z_i} KTP_i \right\|_2^2 \tag{2}$$

In order to solve the pose estimation problem, optimization algorithms such as Gauss-Newton and Levenburg-Marquardt can be used. However, it is necessary to know the derivatives of the error terms with respect to the optimization variables. Now, we can transform P_i to camera coordinates and obtain P_i'.

$$P_i' = (\exp(\xi^\wedge)P_i)_{1:3}[X_i', Y_i', Z_i']^T \tag{3}$$

The ξ value is the Lie algebra representation of the camera pose. The coordinates in the formula are homogeneous, and the first three are taken after transformation. Based on the camera projection model, the following formula can be obtained:

$$\begin{cases} u = f_x \frac{X_i'}{Z_i} + c_x \\ v = f_y \frac{Y_i'}{Z_i'} + c_y \end{cases} \tag{4}$$

When calculating the error, we calculate the difference between the coordinate value calculated by the above formula and the actual pixel value measured in the image. The Jacobian matrix is obtained by applying the chain rule and multiplying pairwise, which is used to calculate the motion information between adjacent images.

3.2 Mixer-WMLP Architecture

The Mixer-WMLP network model is derived from the MAIM [10], which enables linear computational complexity while maintaining a global field of view, making it suitable for visual odometry applications. We briefly introduce the design of the Mixer-WMLP network structure. The Mixer-WMLP evenly distributes the extracted feature maps into non-overlapping window arrays. By controlling the window-based computation region, the computational complexity of this method is linearly related to the sequence length N, reducing the computational cost of the network. Unlike traditional convolution, spatial and channel domains are operated separately. The former allows communication between different spatial markers operated on the same channel, while treating each column as input. The latter allows communication between different channels. The input feature map is defined as H × W × C, and the window size is M. There are H/M × W/M windows in total. Substituting this into Eq. (5), we obtain the computational complexity shown in Eq. (6). Clearly, the computational complexity is reduced from (N^2) to (N). α is the unfolding factor for the first MLP node, while C represents the feature dimension (Fig. 2).

The inferential formula for calculating complexity is as follows:

$$\Omega(WMLP) = 2\alpha(HW)^2 C \tag{5}$$

$$\Omega(WMLP) = \Omega\left(\frac{H}{M} \times \frac{W}{M}\left(M^2\right)^2 C\right) = 2\alpha(HW)M^2 C \tag{6}$$

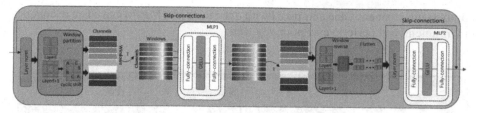

Fig. 2. The Mixer-WMLP structure with linear window global domain

Multiplying H and W results in sequence N. With Eq. (6), it can be seen that Mixer-WMLP is linearly correlated with sequence N, reducing the computational complexity. The window size is represented by M. Mixer-WMLP employs matrix transposition and MLP to perceive global information.

4   Experiments

In this section, we conducted a series of experiments to evaluate our proposed MAIM-VO system. We used multiple datasets and complex scene data for the evaluation. We compared the localization accuracy of MAIM-VO with ORB-SLAM2, DXSLAM, and TRVO. The following methods are all performed on a PC running Ubuntu Linux, equipped with an RTX 2080Ti GPU. The RTX 2080Ti has 11 GB of GDDR6 VRAM with a speed of 14Gbps. The CPU is Intel Xeon Silver 4210.

4.1   Feature Matching

In the first experiment, we compared the performance of ORB feature, SIFT feature, feature matching network combining Superpoint and SuperGlue, and MAIM feature matching in terms of feature matching. The image data used in this study were extracted from the Megadepth dataset [22], the RobotCar dataset [23], the TUM RGB-D dataset [24], and our own dataset obtained by our intelligent driving vehicle equipped with stereolabs ZED cameras. Intelligent driving vehicles are equipped with stereolabs ZED MINI cameras for image acquisition and transmission. We have selected five complex scene data sets for comparison. We selected data from the Megadepth dataset with large viewpoint changes, data from the RobotCar dataset with lighting variations, and two sets of data with weak texture environments from the TUM RGB-D dataset. We also included data from complex outdoor road environments collected through autonomous driving vehicles. For ORB features and SIFT, given a pair of images, generate key points and descriptors for each image, then match them based on the Hamming distance between the descriptors, and further filter the correct matching results using the RANSAC algorithm. For the network that combines Superpoint and SuperGlue, we use the confidence scores generated by the network to filter out outliers. We show the qualitative results in Fig. 3(a)–3(e). ORB and SIFT features are sparse and have low matching accuracy, and cannot generate matching pairs in the data of Fig. 3(e). The features learned by Superpoint and SuperGlue generate sparse matches in weak-textured environments but have higher matching accuracy. The MAIM network can generate dense and accurate matches in

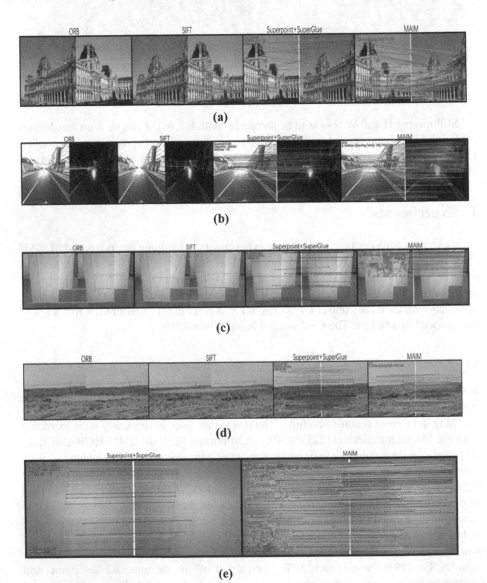

complex environments, and compared with other methods, MAIM can adapt to complex environments and perform exceptionally well.

Fig. 3. (a) Viewpoint variation comparison in Megadepth dataset. (b) Comparison of lighting variations in the RobotCar-Seasons dataset. (c) Comparison of weak texture environments in the TUM-RGBD dataset. (d) Comparison of Weak Textured Environments in Sampling Data of Intelligent Driving Vehicles. (e) Extreme weak texture environments in TUM-RGBD dataset (where ORB and SIFT fail to extract feature points)

4.2 Localization on TUM RGB-D Dataset

In order to evaluate the localization accuracy of our proposed visual odometry, we conducted visual localization experiments on the widely-used SLAM benchmark dataset TUM RGB-D. It provides various data sequences with precise ground truth trajectories. In this experiment, we selected handheld SLAM, robotics, and structure and texture categories, consisting of 11, 1, and 8 sub-sequences respectively. The experiment was conducted on a PC equipped with an RTX 2080Ti GPU and Intel Xeon Silver 4210 CPU.

ORB-SLAM2, DXSLAM, SuperVO, TRVO and our method were tested. Among them, we define SuperVO a visual odometry designed to solve the camera poses in an optimal way by minimizing the feature point reprojection error with Superpoint as the detection end and SuperGlue as the matching end as an effect comparison.

We compared the positioning accuracy of these five systems at different sequences. Figure 4, Fig. 5 shows the curves of Relative Distance Error (RDE) and Mean Distance Error (MDE) plotted by evo tool. Due to space limitation, we randomly selected six sets of sequences for display. Figure 6 shows the error curves of two deformations of MAIM-VO and SuperVO in the freiburg1_floor sequence of TUM RGB-D, respectively, for the visual odometry composed of Superpoint with SuperGlue and FLANN. Figure 7 shows the error curves of MAIM-VO with SuperVO on the sequence freiburg2_large_no_loop sequence. There is a small difference between the results of MAIM-VO and SuperVO methods as can be seen in Fig. 6 and Fig. 7, which can be confirmed in Table 1. Table 1 shows the performance of the five systems in all the tested sequences. We use the relative positional error to evaluate the localization accuracy. Since SuperVO, TRVO and MAIM-VO are only a visual odometer, which is equivalent to the front-end of the visual SLAM system, there will be some cumulative error in the positional estimation, while the back-end optimization, loop detection and repositioning modules in ORB-SLAM2 and DXSLAM will reduce to some extent the cumulative error, resulting in lower absolute positional error. Therefore, in order to make the comparison as fair as possible, we choose Relative Pose Error (RPE) as the evaluation criterion. From the table, we can see that MAIM-VO has the lowest Relative Pose Error in most sequences.

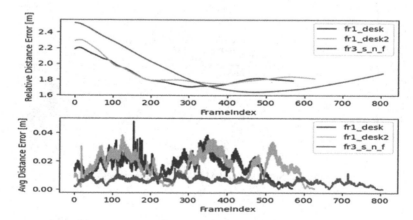

Fig. 4. Error curves on fr1_desk, fr1_desk2, fr3_s_n_f sequences

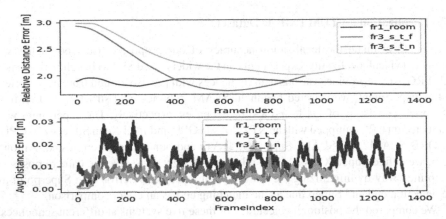

Fig. 5. Error curves on fr1_room, fr3_s_t_f, fr3_s_t_n sequences

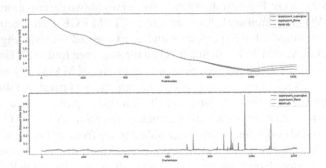

Fig. 6. SuperVO (Superpoint+SuperGlue/Superpoint+flann) and MAIM-VO error curves

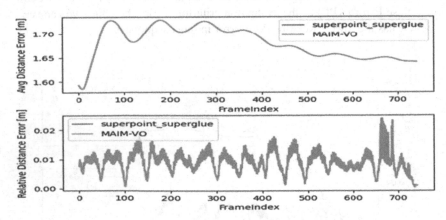

Fig. 7. SuperVO and MAIM-VO error curves

Table 1. Mean relative pose error calculated by evo.

Dataset	EVO_RPE				
	ORB-SLAM2	DXSLAM	SuperVO	TRVO	MAIM-VO
fr1_360	0.240654	0.013515	0.009547	0.012753	**0.008944**
fr1_desk	0.014376	0.016301	0.016339	0.012022	0.016297
fr1_desk2	0.015431	0.016248	0.015279	0.012817	0.015775
fr1_floor	0.006921	0.005871	0.110557	0.007212	0.010776
fr1_room	0.013139	0.011891	0.117436	0.010296	0.117424
fr2_360_h	0.017897	0.013530	0.005849	0.021250	**0.005849**
fr2_360_k	0.014510	0.013143	0.011811	0.016878	**0.011804**
fr2_desk	0.006578	0.007624	0.008839	0.006971	0.008990
fr2_l_n_l	0.017060	0.018296	0.020364	0.026593	0.020364
fr2_l_w_l	0.020013	0.015282	0.135425	0.022142	**0.126924**
fr3_l_o_h	0.007284	0.007479	0.134372	0.007094	0.133362
fr2_p_360	0.023103	0.026169	0.009559	0.022892	**0.008580**
fr3_n_n_f	0.028068	-	-	0.023827	**0.006606**
fr3_n_n_n_w	-	-	-	0.027900	**0.010930**
fr3_n_t_f	0.030258	0.028255	0.010416	0.022806	**0.009685**
fr3_n_t_n_w	0.014841	0.014618	0.008213	0.014105	**0.008211**
fr3_s_n_f	0.010663	-	0.006327	0.007317	**0.005625**
fr3_s_n_n	0.019516	-	0.004226	0.009913	**0.003993**
fr3_s_t_f	0.012829	0.012706	0.008453	0.010329	**0.006475**
fr3_s_t_n	0.012155	0.011895	0.008285	0.009827	**0.004771**

. '-' means the algorithm fail to track all the frames

5 Conclusions

In this paper, we propose MAIM-VO, a visual odometry method based on a Mixer MLP model. MAIM-VO obtains feature matches between images from the matching method constructed by the Mixer-WMLP network, and estimates the camera pose by minimizing the reprojection error using a nonlinear optimization method. A Mixer MLP structure is used, which can utilize the global information of the image and has high computational efficiency. Our experiments show that the MAIM-VO system gives pose estimates with lower relative pose errors and is more robust in challenging environments such as low texture, large viewpoint or illumination changes, while handcrafted and CNN-based methods often do not work well in such cases. However, the running memory and time of MAIM-VO are still not optimistic in terms of application, and the detector-free matching method is used, which makes it impossible to perform operations such as back-end optimization, loop detection and relocation. These are the obvious shortcomings of MAIM-VO, which will be the focus of our future work.

Acknowledgments. This work was supported by the Institute of Robotics and Intelligent Manufacturing Innovation, Chinese Academy of Sciences (Grant number: C2021002).

References

1. Lowe, D.G.: Distinctive image features from scale-invariant keypoints. Int. J. Comput. Vis. **60**(2), 91–110 (2004)
2. Bay, H., Ess, A., Tuytelaars, T., et al.: Speeded-up robust features (SURF). Comput. Vis. Image Underst. **110**(3), 346–359 (2008)
3. Rublee, E., Rabaud, V., Konolige, K., Bradski, G.: ORB: an efficient alternative to SIFT or SURF. In: 2011 International Conference on Computer Vision, pp. 2564–2571 (2011)
4. DeTone, D., Malisiewicz, T., Rabinovich, A.: Superpoint: self-supervised interest point detection and description. In: Proceedings of the IEEE Conference on Computer Vision and Pattern Recognition Workshops, pp. 224–236 (2018)
5. Tang, J., Ericson, L., Folkesson, J., et al.: GCNv2: efficient correspondence prediction for real-time SLAM. IEEE Robot. Autom. Lett. **4**(4), 3505–3512 (2019)
6. Jiang, W., Trulls, E., Hosang, J., et al.: Cotr: correspondence transformer for matching across images. In: Proceedings of the IEEE/CVF International Conference on Computer Vision, pp. 6207–6217 (2021)
7. Sun, J., Shen, Z., Wang, Y., et al.: LoFTR: detector-free local feature matching with transformers. In: Proceedings of the IEEE/CVF Conference on Computer Vision and Pattern Recognition, pp. 8922–8931 (2021)
8. Vaswani, A., Shazeer, N., Parmar, N., et al.: Attention is all you need. In: Advances in Neural Information Processing Systems, vol. 30 (2017)
9. Tolstikhin, I.O., et al.: MLP-mixer: an all-MLP architecture for vision. Neural Inf. Process. Syst. **34**, 24261–24272 (2021)
10. Shen, Z., Kong, B., Dong, X.: MAIM: a mixer MLP architecture for image matching. Vis. Comput. (2023)
11. Engel, J., Schöps, T., Cremers, D.: LSD-SLAM: large-scale direct monocular SLAM. In: Fleet, D., Pajdla, T., Schiele, B., Tuytelaars, T. (eds.) ECCV 2014. LNCS, vol. 8690, pp. 834–849. Springer, Cham (2014). https://doi.org/10.1007/978-3-319-10605-2_54
12. Engel, J., Koltun, V., Cremers, D.: Direct sparse odometry. IEEE Trans. Pattern Anal. Mach. Intell. **40**(3), 611–625 (2017)
13. Davison, A.J., Reid, I.D., Molton, N.D., Stasse, O.: MonoSLAM: real-time single camera SLAM. IEEE Trans. Pattern Anal. Mach. Intell. **29**(6), 1052–1067 (2007). https://doi.org/10.1109/TPAMI.2007.1049
14. Kameda, Y.: Parallel tracking and mapping for small AR workspaces (PTAM) Augmented Reality. J. Instit. Image Inf. Telev. Eng. **66**(1), 45–51 (2012). https://doi.org/10.3169/itej.66.45
15. Campos, C., Elvira, R., Rodríguez, J.J.G., Montiel, J.M., Tardós, J.D.: ORB-SLAM3: an accurate open-source library for visual, visual–inertial, and multimap SLAM. IEEE Trans. Robot. **37**(6), 1874–1890 (2021)
16. Qin, T., Li, P., Shen, S.: VINS-Mono: a robust and versatile monocular visual-inertial state estimator. IEEE Trans. Robot. **34**(4), 1004–1020 (2018)

17. DeTone, D., Malisiewicz, T., Rabinovich, A.: Toward geometric deep SLAM. arXiv:1707. 07410 (2017)
18. Sarlin, P.-E., DeTone, D., Malisiewicz, T., Rabinovich, A.: Superglue: learning feature matching with graph neural networks. In: Proceedings of the IEEE/CVF Conference on Computer Vision and Pattern Recognition (CVPR), pp. 4938–4947 (2020)
19. Rocco, I., Cimpoi, M., Arandjelović, R., et al.: Neighbourhood consensus networks. In: Advances in Neural Information Processing Systems, vol. 31 (2018)
20. Yu, C., Liu, Z., Liu, X.J., et al.: DS-SLAM: a semantic visual SLAM towards dynamic environments. In: 2018 IEEE/RSJ International Conference on Intelligent Robots and Systems (IROS), pp. 1168–1174. IEEE (2018)
21. Gao, Y., Zhao, L.: TRVO: a robust visual odometry with deep features. In: The 7th International Workshop on Advanced Computational Intelligence and Intelligent Informatics (IWACIII) (2021)
22. Li, Z., Snavely, N.: MegaDepth: learning single-view depth prediction from internet photos. In: 2018 IEEE/CVF Conference on Computer Vision and Pattern Recognition, pp. 2041–2050 (2018)
23. Maddern, W.P., Pascoe, G., Linegar, C., Newman, P.: 1 year, 1000 km: the Oxford RobotCar dataset. Int. J. Robot. Res. **36**, 15–23 (2017)
24. Schubert, D., Goll, T., Demmel, N., et al.: The TUM VI Benchmark for Evaluating Visual-Inertial Odometry. IEEE (2018)

Visual SLAM Algorithm Based on Target Detection and Direct Geometric Constraints in Dynamic Environments

Jun Lin, Zhengyong Feng[✉], and Jialiang Tang

School of Electronic Information Engineering, China West Normal University,
Nanchong 637002, China
{Jun.Lin,Zhengyong.Feng,Jialiang.Tang}@cwnu.edu.com

Abstract. To enhance the localization accuracy and robustness of the visual SLAM algorithm in dynamic environments, this paper proposes a methodology that relies on target detection and direct geometric constraints. The algorithm first obtains static feature points and possible dynamic feature points of the current frame using a YOLOV7 target detection network. It then judges the real dynamic target using the geometric change relationship between the edges connecting the feature points of two adjacent frames. Based on the motion information of the dynamic target in past frames, the potential dynamic targets of the current frame are again examined, all feature points in the dynamic target frame are removed. Comparative experiments on the TUM dataset show that the proposed algorithm reduces the absolute trajectory error by an average of 94.69% compared to ORB-SLAM2. It outperforms mainstream dynamic vision SLAM schemes such as Dyna-SLAM and DS_SLAM in terms of localization accuracy.

Keywords: SLAM · Target Detection · Dynamic Environments · Geometric Constraints

1 Introduction

Simultaneous Localization and Mapping (SLAM) refers to an intelligent body to construct a map of the environment and estimate its own pose during motion by relying on its own sensors, all without priori information about the surroundings [1]. It is a technique used in various fields, including robotics and autonomous driving. In recent years, with the development of computer vision technology, Visual SLAM (VSLAM) technology utilizing cameras as the main sensor has been widely studied and applied with the advantages of low cost, easy installation, and extensive information acquisition capabilities. Many excellent VSLAM algorithms have emerged, such as Vins-mono [2], ORB-SLAM2/3 [3, 4].

Most current VSLAM schemes are renowned for high efficiency and robustness, but it is typically achieved under the assumption of static environments [2–4]. However, the dynamic objects, such as people, animals, and moving vehicles, are inevitable in practical application scenarios. The VSLAM algorithm introduces a large number of dynamic errors by treating dynamic features on dynamic objects as static features. It results in a significant reduction or even failure of its localization accuracy, so improving the accuracy and robustness of the VSLAM algorithm in dynamic environments becomes the key to practical applications.

To enhance the localization accuracy and robustness of the visual SLAM algorithm in dynamic environments, and ensure the real-time performance of the algorithm. This paper proposes a methodology that relies on target detection and direct geometric constraints. Our contribution is summarized as follows:

1) By utilizing the geometric constraint relationship of edges connecting adjacent frames of feature points, we developed a dynamic target discrimination method, which is integrated with a YOLOV7 [5] target detection network with fast detection speed and high accuracy. This approach effectively eliminates the errors resulting from the inaccurate initial camera pose solution, while successfully rejecting all the features situated on dynamic targets and ensuring the real-time performance of the system.
2) We designed a multi-frame target tracking module to address the issue of performing dynamic discrimination when matching features on dynamic targets are missing.
3) Ablation and comparison experiments were conducted on the TUM dataset to verify the effectiveness and robustness of the proposed methodology.

2 Related Works

Recent research studies have proposed various solutions to overcome the influence of dynamic objects in the environment on the VSLAM algorithm. These proposed solutions can be classified into two main categories, depending on whether the initial camera pose is calculated before determining the dynamic features: indirect geometric constraint methods and direct geometric constraint methods [6].

2.1 Indirect Geometric Constraint Method

Indirect geometric constraint method involves calculating the initial camera pose and then identifying and rejecting dynamic features through geometric constraint relationships. Sun et al. [7] utilized the Random Sampling Consensus (RANSAC) method to calculate the single response matrix between two adjacent frames and then determined dynamic feature points using reprojection error. Fu et al. [8] obtained the initial camera pose using an IMU and filtered dynamic feature points based on motion consistency detection. However, these methods are highly sensitive to noise and lack robustness in complex scenes. The emergence of deep learning has introduced new techniques to address these issues. Dyna-SLAM [9] utilizes a combination of Mask R-CNN [10] and multi-view geometry to filter all dynamic feature points. DS-SLAM [11] employs Seg-Net [12] for semantic segmentation and motion consistency detection to obtain dynamic regions in the environment. YOLO-SLAM [13] improves upon the YOLOv3 [14] network and combines depth information for dynamic feature identification to improve real-time performance. DGS-SLAM [15] enhances semantic key frame selection strategy and combines reprojection error and spatial correlation residuals for identify dynamic targets. Nevertheless, in the aforementioned method, the challenge presented by the interdependence between resolving the camera pose and recognizing dynamic features can be compared to the classic "chicken and egg" problem [16]. This often results in significant errors when the initial camera pose is inaccurately estimated.

2.2 Direct Geometric Constraint Method

The direct geometric constraint method skips the initial camera pose estimation step and utilizes a priori semantic information or geometric constraints to directly identify and reject dynamic features. Sheng et al. [17] utilized the Mask R-CNN algorithm to segment highly dynamic targets in the environment and determine the dynamic regions based on four neighborhoods of pixel points. Soares et al. [18] directly identified people as the primary dynamic targets in indoor settings and rejected them. It leads to the erroneous rejection of static regions and an under-rejection of dynamic regions. Dai et al. [19] used the Delaunay algorithm [20] to connect feature points into multiple triangles. They then compared corresponding edges in two adjacent frames to remove dynamic edges, leading to multiple connected domains with consistent internal motion. Smaller connected domains were filtered out based on the assumption that the largest region in space is static. Yang et al. [21] calculated the proportion of dynamic edges among all edges connected to a feature point, identifying points with a dynamic edge proportion higher than 60% as dynamic feature points. These methods improve algorithm accuracy, but they still struggle to accurately reject dynamic features within dynamic regions. The difference between the two methods is illustrated in Fig. 1.

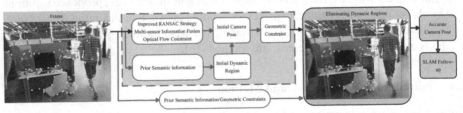

Fig. 1. Difference between the processes of direct and indirect geometric constraint methods.

3   Method

3.1   System Overview

ORB-SLAM2 served as the fundamental framework and was further enhanced in this paper. As illustrated in Fig. 2, both feature extraction and YOLOv7 target detection threads analyze the input images and obtain the matching feature points and potential dynamic target frames of the current frame. The dynamic targets are then identified via direct geometric constraints, combined with feature points of the previous frame. Considering that direct geometric constraint may fail in the absence of correct matching features, the algorithm integrates a multi-frame dynamic target tracking algorithm by leveraging motion probability of potential dynamic targets in past frames to re-determine potential dynamic targets. Prior to positional estimation and map construction, all dynamic features are eliminated in the constant velocity motion model tracking. Additionally, high dynamic targets, such as people, are directly excluded in the reference keyframe tracking session, the map points generated in dynamic object frames are excluded in the keyframe generation process as well. The remaining local map building threads and loopback detection threads remain unchanged.

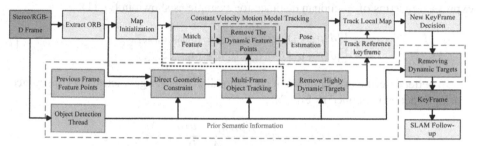

Fig. 2. Improved SLAM system framework.

3.2 Dynamic Feature Detection Based on Target Detection and Direct Geometric Constraints

In the VSLAM systems, the time interval Δt between input images is exceptionally brief, resulting in minimal projection distortion caused by the camera pose change between two adjacent frames. The geometric relationship between static feature points in an unknown environment docs not change significantly, but the relationship between dynamic and static feature points alters dramatically in the presence of dynamic objects. Geometric changes between matching feature points in two adjacent frames enable the detection of dynamic feature points.

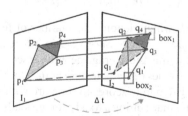

Fig. 3. Schematic diagram of the geometric constraint model.

As shown in Fig. 3, suppose two adjacent frames I_1, I_2 have 4 pairs of matching feature points, and box_1, box_2 in I_2 are potential dynamic target boxes obtained by YOLOv7 target detection thread. The feature points q_2, q_3 in image I_2 are outside

box_1 and box_2, which can be directly determined as static feature points. The feature points q_2', q_4 are inside box_1, box_2 respectively, assuming that the object in box_2 has moved while the object in box_1 is stationary. The feature point q_1' is the feature point q_1 following the object movement. From these matching feature points, two sets of corresponding triangles can be constructed between two frames respectively: $\triangle p_1 p_2 p_3$ and $\triangle q_1' q_2 q_3$, $\triangle p_2 p_3 p_4$ and $\triangle q_2 q_3 q_4$. . Then the corresponding edge variation between two static vertices between two adjacent frames will be in a small range. However, the corresponding edge variation between a dynamic vertex and a static vertex will be beyond this range, the corresponding edge changes between (q_2, q_3) and (q_1', q_2) can be expressed in terms of Euclidean distance for example as shown in Eq. (1).

$$\begin{cases} |d(p_2, p_3) - d(q_2, q_3)| \in (d_{\min}, d_{\max}) \\ |d(p_2, p_1) - d(q_2, q_1')| \notin (d_{\min}, d_{\max}) \end{cases}. \tag{1}$$

To better describe this variation of corresponding edges, a geometrically constrained scoring function is defined as Eq. (2).

$$q_g(i, j) = \exp(|\frac{d(p_i, p_j) - d(q_i, q_j)}{A(i, j)}|). \tag{2}$$

$A(i, j)$ represents the average distance between two feature points, as shown in Eq. (3).

$$A(i, j) = [d(p_i - p_j) - d(q_i - p_j)]/2. \tag{3}$$

To determine whether a feature point q_x in box_i is a dynamic feature point, connect the point q_i with each static feature point q_x outside the box and obtain its average dynamic geometric constraint score $Score\_dynamic$. Then connect the point q_i with another randomly selected static feature point q_j outside the box to obtain its average static geometric constraint score $Score\_static$, as shown in Eq. (4).

$$\begin{cases} Score\_dynamic = \dfrac{\sum\limits_{i=0}^{M} q_g(x, j)}{M} \\ Score\_static = \dfrac{\sum\limits_{i=0}^{M} q_g(i, j)}{M} \end{cases}. \tag{4}$$

Equation (4) contains M, which denotes the number of feature points within static regions. When $Score\_dynamic$ exceeds $Score\_static$, point q_x can be identified as a dynamic feature point. Calculating the average geometric score minimizes chance errors that may be induced by mismatches of static feature points due to camera motion between adjacent frames. By utilizing dynamic scores to compare with static scores to determine dynamic feature points, rather than setting a fixed geometrically constrained score threshold manually. There is no misclassification due to the variable nature of dynamic scores between frames.

$$Score\_box_i = \frac{\sum\limits_{x=0}^{count_i} W_i^x}{count_i}. \tag{5}$$

In Eq. (5), $count_i$ is the total number of feature points in box_i. W_i^x is the dynamic identifier of feature point q_x within box_i, as shown in Eq. (6).

$$W_i^x = \begin{cases} 1 & Score\_dynamic > Score\_static \\ 0 & else \end{cases}. \tag{6}$$

When the box_i is larger, the total number of feature points in the box tends to be larger, which may contain more static feature points belonging to the background, resulting in a small $Score\_box_i$. When the box_i is smaller, the total number of feature points in the box is usually smaller, and even a small number of feature points misclassified as dynamic due to mis-matching will lead to a larger $Score\_box_i$. Therefore, the dynamic judgment threshold is set according to the number of total feature points in box_i, as shown in Eq. (7).

$$box_i\_\theta_{th} = \alpha * count_i \beta. \tag{7}$$

In Eq. (7), $box_i\_\theta_{th}$ is the dynamic determination threshold of box_i. α and β are dynamic threshold factors, $\alpha = 1.553$ and $\beta = -0.588$ respectively. If $Score\_box_i$ is greater than $box_i\_\theta_{th}$, then box_i is determined as the dynamic target box.

3.3 Multi-frame Dynamic Target Tracking Based on Target Detection

ORB-SLAM2 uses map point projection from the previous frame to the current frame in the constant velocity motion model to swiftly locate matching feature points. However, this dynamic target determination method may fail to deliver results when matching feature points on dynamic objects are not obtainable due to the significant motion change of objects in dynamic environments. Therefore, this paper proposes a multi-frame dynamic target tracking method based on target detection. If a potential dynamic target cannot be classified as dynamic in the current frame, its dynamic score in the previous consecutive frames is evaluated to render dynamic judgments again. If a dynamic target obtains a higher dynamic score in the current frame, its dynamic score in previous frames will be updated. The codes for the detailed multi-frame dynamic target tracking method are shown in font Courier.

Algorithm 1: Multi-frame object tracking algorithm

Input: Dynamic weights of y targets from the previous x
frames: dynamists[x][y].wt.
Dynamic weight of the z target for the current frame:
dynaObj[z].wt
Output: List of corrected dynamic target indexes for the
current frame: dynaBoxs

```
1: for i ← 0 to dynaObj.size() do
2:    if dynaObj[i].wt > 0.5 and dynaList[0][i].wt < 0.1
3:       dynaList[0][i].wt ←+ dynaObj[i].wt * 0.3
4:    else if dynaList[0][i].wt > 0.3
5:       dynaObj[i].flag ← ture
6:       Dynaboxs ← dynaObj[i]
7:       dynaObj[i].wt← dynaObj[i].wt+dynaList[0][i].wt*0.5
8:    else
9:       for j ← to dynaList.size() do
10:         DynaScore ← DynaScore + dynaList[j][i].wt * i/10
11:      end for
12:      if DynaScore > Dynamic target threshold
13:         dynaObj[i].flag ← ture
14:         Dynaboxs ← dynaObj[i]
15: end for
```

3.4 Saliency Map Reconstruction and Supervision Strategy

After obtaining all dynamic target frames in the current frame using the above dynamic feature detection algorithm and multi-frame dynamic target tracking algorithm in the constant velocity motion model, all feature points in the frames corresponding to map points are deleted, leaving the set of valid static feature points X with the corresponding set of map points P. The camera pose T_{cw}^* is optimized using the minimized reprojection error solution PnP, as shown in Eq. (8).

$$T_{cw}^* = \arg\min \frac{1}{2} \sum_{x_i \in x, P_i \in P}^{n} \|x_i - \pi(T_{cw}P_i)\|^2. \tag{8}$$

Equation (8) involves x_i, which references a feature point on the current frame; P_i is a 3D map point corresponding to the feature point; and π is the projection equation. In addition to constant velocity motion model tracking, dynamic feature points are eliminated from reference keyframe tracking and keyframe generation. Dynamic feature judgment is less reliable with reference keyframe tracking, which is used less frequently and runs only when constant velocity motion model tracking fails. Therefore, highly dynamic targets are eliminated directly. During the keyframe generation session, points on dynamic targets that are not 3D-based are regenerated into map points and added to the local map. This approach can result in a significant tracking error in the local map. Thus, regenerated dynamic map points are excluded to prevent this problem.

4 Experiments

To verify the validity and robustness of the proposed algorithm, this paper conducted three experiments using four dynamic sequences from the TUM dataset. These experiments include dynamic target detection and multi-frame tracking, dynamic feature rejection and ablation, and performance comparison of the improved SLAM algorithm. The dataset comprises four canonical camera motion types, namely "halfsphere", "rpy", "xyz" and "static", that represent camera motion along hemispheric trajectory, yaw-pitch-roll axis, xyz axis, and basic camera fixation, respectively. The computer configuration used for the experiments was Intel i10-1090k CPU, NVIDIA RTX 3080 = GPU and ubuntu 18.04 operating system. All experiments were tested 5 times and averaged.

4.1 Dynamic Target Detection and Multi-Frame Tracking Experiments

In this section, experiments are conducted on the fr3_walking_xyz sequence of the TUM dataset. The purpose of it is to verify the effectiveness of the dynamic feature detection algorithm and the multi-frame dynamic target tracking algorithm proposed in this paper. As shown in Fig. 4, (a) shows the distribution of matching feature points extracted by the original algorithm, and (b) shows the experimental results of the dynamic feature detection algorithm based on target detection and direct geometric constraints.

(a) Matching feature points extracted by the original algorithm

(b) Dynamic feature detection results

Fig. 4. Dynamic feature detection experimental results. (Color figure online)

The green and blue points in Fig. 4(a) are the feature points inside and outside the potential dynamic target box respectively. The red points in (b) indicate the feature points that are determined as dynamic by the algorithm, the white and red boxes indicate the targets that are determined as static and dynamic by the algorithm respectively. The comparison of the first column of images in (a) and (b) shows that the algorithm can accurately detect dynamic feature points and determine dynamic targets. The chair pushed by a person is also judged as a dynamic target in the second column, indicating that the algorithm can detect the forced moving target. The third column of images shows that the algorithm can also correctly determine the dynamic target when the human body is moving locally. In summary, the comparative analysis shows that the dynamic detection algorithm in this paper can better detect all the targets that are really moving.

As shown in Fig. 5, (a) is a set of continuous images without multi-frame target tracking, and (b) is the result of the corresponding image after multi-frame dynamic target tracking based on target detection.

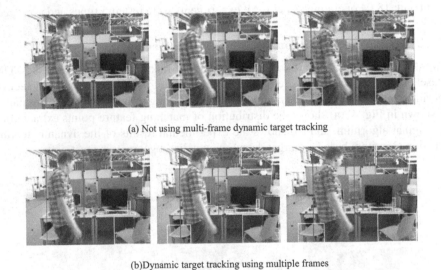

(a) Not using multi-frame dynamic target tracking

(b)Dynamic target tracking using multiple frames

Fig. 5. Experimental results of multi-frame dynamic target tracking algorithm.

In the three frames of Fig. 5(a), frames 1 and 3 can determine the human is dynamic target. However, the direct geometric constraint dynamic detection algorithm fails in frame 2. This is due to the human surface is not correctly matched with the feature points, which does not affect the positional optimization in the constant velocity motion model tracking. But affects the local map tracking by mapping the points on the human surface, which are not 3Dized as map points in the key frame generation. As shown in Fig. 5(b), the multi-frame dynamic target tracking algorithm corrects the dynamic target judgments. In the cases of missing matching points, blurred images and high target dynamics, the dynamic target judgments result to compensate for the shortcomings of the dynamic target detection algorithm that cannot correctly determine dynamic objects.

4.2 Dynamic Feature Rejection Ablation Experiment

In this section, we perform ablation experiments on the proposed dynamic feature point rejection method. For clarity, the method that directly rejects all feature points in the target frame where the "person" is detected by YOLO-V7 is denoted as "Y-SLAM". The dynamic feature detection method that uses only target-based detection and direct geometric constraints is denoted as "YG-SLAM". Finally, the method that employs a combination of dynamic feature detection and multi-frame dynamic tracking is referred to as "YGD-SLAM". The Absolute Trajectory Error (ATE), the most commonly used in VSLAM validation, was adopted as the evaluation index. Five consecutive experimental data collections were conducted for each data set, which including Root Mean Square Error (RMSE) and Standard Deviation (SD). The mean value of the experiment was taken as the final data sample. The results of the experiments are presented in Table 1.

Table 1. Absolute trajectory error of each algorithm on the dataset (unit: m).

Sequences	ORB-SLAM2		Y-SLAM		YG-SLAM		YGD-SLAM		Improvements against ORB-SLAM2	
	RMSE	SD	RMSE	SD	RMSE	SD	RMSE	SD	RMSE (%)	SD (%)
fr3_w_xyz	0.7521	0.3759	0.0138	0.0074	0.0131	**0.0060**	**0.0127**	**0.0060**	98.31	98.40
fr3_w_static	0.3900	0.1602	0.0102	0.0053	0.0071	0.0035	**0.0061**	**0.0029**	98.44	98.19
fr3_w_rpy	0.8705	0.4520	0.1169	0.0881	0.0381	0.0213	**0.0321**	**0.0187**	96.31	95.86
fr3_w_half	0.4863	0.2290	0.0369	0.0187	0.0264	0.0130	**0.0249**	**0.0122**	85.73	94.67

The experimental optimal results are shown in bold in Table 1. Analyzing the data in Table 1, we can observe that although the localization accuracy of "Y-SLAM" has improved compared to that of "ORB-SLAM2", it is still inferior to that of "YG-SLAM". This suggests that the "YG-SLAM" algorithm is capable of identifying moving targets such as people and pushed chairs, which leads to better rough camera pose in constant velocity motion model segments. The accuracy of the "YGD-SLAM" algorithm is even better than that of the "YG-SLAM" algorithm, indicating that multi-frame dynamic tracking based on target detection improves the algorithm's correct discrimination rate for dynamic objects, thereby achieving better results. So, the ablation experimental results verify the effectiveness of the algorithm in this paper.

Figure 6 provides a comparison of the trajectories of ORB-SLAM2 and the proposed algorithm across four different sequences. In this figure, the true trajectory is depicted in black, while the blue trajectory represents the fitted trajectory of both ORB-SLAM2 and the proposed algorithm. The differences between the fitted trajectory and the true trajectory are illustrated in red. As seen in Fig. 6, the proposed algorithm's trajectory has a good fit with the true trajectory. While, the original ORB-SLAM2 algorithm has significant drift.

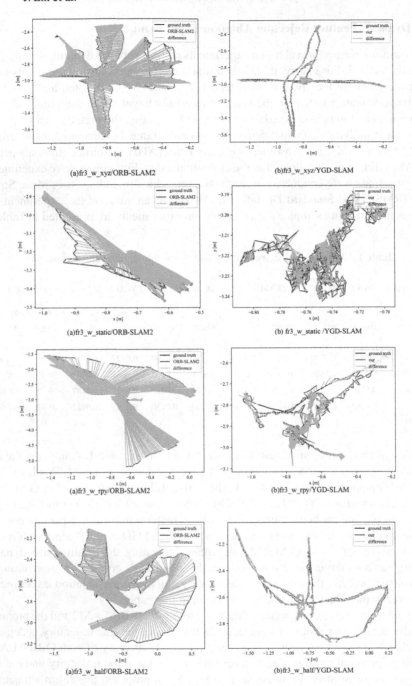

Fig. 6. Comparison of the trajectories of the algorithms on each dataset (Color figure online)

4.3 Improved SLAM Algorithm Performance Comparison Experiment

This section provides a comparison of the proposed method with existing SLAM algorithms for dynamic scenes. The direct geometric constraint algorithm, MGC-VSLAM [19], is currently the most effective method that does not rely on neural networks. Indirect geometric constraint methods that use neural networks in recent literature include SOLO-SLAM [22], DGS-SLAM [15] and YOLO-SLAM [11]. Additionally, Dyna-SLAM [7] and DS-SLAM [9] are classical and commonly used algorithms for comparison. Tables 2, 3 and 4 present the RMSE values for the absolute trajectory error, relative translation and relative rotational trajectory error of each algorithm.

Table 2. RMSE comparison of the absolute errors of each algorithm on the data set (unit: m).

Sequences	Dyna-SLAM	DS-SLAM	MGC-VSLAM	SOLO-SLAM	DGS-SLAM	YOLO-SLAM	Our
fr3_w_xyz	0.0164	0.0247	*0.0144*	0.0187	0.0156	0.0146	**0.0127**
fr3_w_static	0.0064	0.0081	0.0071	0.0104	**0.0059**	0.0073	*0.0061*
fr3_w_rpy	0.0357	0.4442	0.1326	0.1194	**0.0301**	0.2164	*0.0321*
fr3_w_half	*0.0250*	0.0303	0.0253	0.0276	0.0259	0.0283	**0.0249**

Table 3. RMSE comparison of relative translational trajectory errors on the dataset for each algorithm (unit: m/frame).

Sequences	Dyna-SLAM	DS-SLAM	MGC-VSLAM	SOLO-SLAM	DGS-SLAM	YOLO-SLAM	Our
fr3_w_xyz	0.0235	0.0333	*0.0190*	0.0200	0.0228	0.0194	**0.0099**
fr3_w_static	0.0102	0.0102	*0.0087*	0.0117	0.0101	0.0094	**0.0057**
fr3_w_rpy	*0.0415*	0.1503	0.1234	0.0452	0.0432	0.0933	**0.0192**
fr3_w_half	0.0394	0.0297	0.0251	*0.0214*	0.0366	0.0268	**0.0119**

Table 4. RMSE comparison of relative rotational trajectory errors on the dataset for each algorithm (unit: °/frame).

Sequences	Dyna-SLAM	DS-SLAM	MGC-VSLAM	SOLO-SLAM	DGS-SLAM	YOLO-SLAM	Our
fr3_w_xyz	0.6212	0.8266	0.6011	–	0.6425	*0.5984*	**0.2888**
fr3_w_static	0.2659	0.2690	*0.2483*	–	0.2639	0.2623	**0.1682**
fr3_w_rpy	*0.8788*	3.0042	2.2798	–	0.9213	1.8238	**0.4798**
fr3_w_half	0.8839	0.8142	0.7539	–	0.8848	*0.7534*	**0.3848**

In Tables 2, 3 and 4, the optimal experiment results are shown in bold, with the suboptimal solutions displayed in italics. Tables 2, 3 and 4 shows that this paper's ATE index achieves optimal performance on "xyz" and "half" sequences, with suboptimal performance on "static" and "rpy" sequences. The suboptimal results on the "static" sequence are attributed to the retention of some dynamic feature points during map initialization. This creates some false matches due to the relatively fixed camera. On the other hand, the suboptimal results on the "rpy" sequence are due to partially missed target detection during violent camera rotation. Meanwhile, the algorithm's relative translation and rotation trajectory error metrics achieve optimal values across all four sequences. In summary, the proposed algorithm demonstrates good accuracy and robustness in dynamic environments.

In practical applications, time cost is also an important index to evaluate the quality of SLAM systems. The time consumption of different SLAM systems is shown in Table 5.

Table 5. Comparison of real-time performance of each algorithm on the dataset

Systems	Average processing time per frame (/ms)	Hardware platform
ORB-SLAM2	36.37	Intel i10-1090k NVIDIA-RTX-3080 GPU
Dyna-SLAM	499.39	AMD 5900HX NVIDIA-GTX3070 GPU
DS-SLAM	76.46	Intel i7 P4000 GPU
SOLO-SLAM	67.00	Intel i7-12700H NVIDIA-3070TI GPU
DGS-SLAM	38.53	AMD 5900HX NVIDIA-GTX3070 GPU
YOLO-SLAM	696.09	Intel Core i5-4288U CPU
Our	33.98	Intel i10-1090k NVIDIA-RTX-3080 GPU

The data presented in Table 5 is obtained from experiments except for ORB-SLAM2 and the algorithm data in this paper, which are sourced from literature. Furthermore, the YOLOV7 target recognition network selected for this paper was embedded into the SLAM system in parallel with multi-threading, resulting in an average time per frame of 33.98ms with GPU acceleration. The comparison table highlights the strong real-time performance of the proposed algorithm.

5   Conclusion

In this paper, we propose a dynamic feature detection method based on ORB-SLAM2 with target detection and direct geometric constraints. Our algorithm utilizes multi-frame image information to track and judge dynamic targets, while also rejecting dynamic features during constant velocity motion model tracking, reference keyframe tracking and keyframe generation. Through experimentation using the TUM dynamic dataset, we conclude that our proposed algorithm outperforms the original ORB-SLAM2 algorithm. Compared with the original ORB-SLAM2 algorithm, the RMSE of ATE metrics on the four datasets is reduced by 94.69% on average. The robustness, accuracy and stability of the algorithm are also improved compared with the existing SLAM algorithm in dynamic environment.

Many of the current algorithms used to construct maps only provide sparse point cloud maps. Unfortunately, these types of maps do not provide the level of detail required for advanced applications, such as robot navigation. Therefore, our focus for future research will be on developing target detection networks and constructing multi-level semantic maps capable of handling dynamic environments.

Acknowledgements. This research was supported by the Project of China West Normal University under Grant 17YC046.

References

1. Huang, S.D., Dissanayake, G.: A critique of current developments in simultaneous localization and mapping. Int. J. Adv. Robot. Syst. **13**(5) (2016)
2. Qin, T., Li, P., Shen, S.: VINS-mono: a robust and versatile monocular visual-inertial state estimator. IEEE Trans. Robot. **34**(4), 1004–1020 (2018)
3. Mur-Artal, R., Tardós, J.D.: ORB-SLAM2: an open-source SLAM system for monocular, stereo, and RGB-D cameras. IEEE Trans. Robot. **33**(5), 1255–1262 (2017). https://doi.org/10.1109/TRO.2017.2705103
4. Campos, C., Elvira, R., Rodríguez, J.J.G., et al.: ORBSLAM3: an accurate open-source library for visual, visual–inertial, and multimap SLAM. J. IEEE Trans. Robot. **37**(6), 1874–1890 (2021)
5. Wang, C.Y., Bochkovskiy, A., Liao, H.Y.M.: YOLOv7: trainable bag-of-freebies sets new state-of-the-art for real-time object detectors. arXiv preprint arXiv:2207.02696 (2022)
6. Wang, K., Yao, X., Huang, Y., et al.: Review of visual SLAM in dynamic environment. J. Robot. **43**(6), 715–732 (2021)
7. Sun, Y., Liu, M., Meng, M.Q.H.: Improving RGB-D SLAM in dynamic environments: a motion removal approach. Robot. Auton. Syst. **89**, 110–122 (2017). https://doi.org/10.1016/j.robot.2016.11.012
8. Fu, D., Xia, H., Qiao, Y.: Monocular visual-inertial navigation for dynamic environment. Remote Sens. **13**(9), 1610 (2021). https://doi.org/10.3390/rs13091610
9. Bescos, B., Fácil, J.M., Civera, J., et al.: DynaSLAM: tracking, mapping, and inpainting in dynamic scenes. J. IEEE Robot. Autom. Lett. **3**(4), 4076–4083 (2018)
10. He, K., Gkioxari, G., Dollár, P., et al.: Mask RCNN. In: The IEEE International Conference on Computer Vision, Venice, Italy, pp. 2980–2988 (2017)
11. Yu, C., Liu, Z., Liu, X., et al.: DS-SLAM: a semantic visual SLAM towards dynamic environments. In: IEEE/RSJ International Conference on Intelligent Robots and Systems (IROS), Madrid, Spain, pp. 1168–1174 (2018)
12. Badrinarayanan, V., Kendall, A., Cipolla, R.: SegNet: a deep convolutional encoder-decoder architecture for image segmentation. IEEE Trans. Pattern Anal. Mach. Intell. **39**(12), 2481–2495 (2017). https://doi.org/10.1109/TPAMI.2016.2644615
13. Wu, W., Guo, L., Gao, H., et al.: YOLO-SLAM: a semantic SLAM system towards dynamic environment with geometric constraint. J. Neural Comput. Appl. **34**(8), 6011–6026 (2021)
14. Redmon, J., Divvala, S., Girshick, R., et al.: You only look once: unified, real-time object detection. In: IEEE Conference on Computer Vision and Pattern Recognition, Piscataway, USA. IEEE (2016)
15. Yan, L., Hu, X., Zhao, L., et al.: DGS-SLAM: a fast and robust RGBD SLAM in dynamic environments combined by geometric and semantic information. J. Remote Sens. **14**(3), 795–819 (2022)
16. Saputra, M.R.U., Markham, A., Trigoni, N.: Visual SLAM and structure from motion in dynamic environments: a survey. ACM Comput. Surv. **51**(2), 1–36 (2018). https://doi.org/10.1145/3177853
17. Sheng, C., Pan, S.G., Gao, W.: Dynamic-DSO: direct sparse odometry using objects semantic information for dynamic environments. Appl. Sci. **10**(4), 1467 (2020). https://doi.org/10.3390/app10041467

18. Soares, J.C.V., Gattass, M., Meggiolaro, M.A.: Visual SLAM in human populated environments: exploring the trade-off between accuracy and speed of YOLO and mask R-CNN. In: 19thInternational Conference on Advanced Robotics, Piscataway, USA. IEEE (2019)
19. Dai, W.C., Zhang, Y., Li, P., et al.: RGB-D SLAM in dynamic environments using point correlations. IEEE Trans. Pattern Anal. Mach. Intell. **44**, 373–389 (2020)
20. Barber, B.C., Dobkin, P.D., Huhdanpaa, H.: The Quickhull algorithm for convex hulls. ACM Trans. Math. Softw. **22**(4), 469–483 (1996). https://doi.org/10.1145/235815.235821
21. Yang, S.Q., Fan, G.H., Bai, L.L., et al.: MGC-VSLAM: a meshingbased and geometric constraint VSLAM for dynamic indoor environments. IEEE Access **8**, 81007–81021 (2020)
22. Sun, L., Wei, J., Su, S., et al.: SOLO-SLAM: a parallel semantic SLAM algorithm for dynamic scenes. Sensors **22**(18), 6977 (2022)

3D Shape Similarity Measurement Based on Scale Invariant Functional Maps

Ning Wang[1,2,3] and Dan Zhang[1,2,3(✉)]

[1] Computer College of Qinghai Normal University,
Xining 81017, People's Republic of China
`danz@mail.bnu.edu.cn`
[2] State Key Lab of Tibetan Intelligent Information Processing and Application
(Co-established by Province and Ministry), Xining 81017, People's Republic of China
[3] Academy of Plateau Science and Sustainability,
Xining 81017, People's Republic of China

Abstract. In recent years, the research focus on shape analysis has centered around the similarity and consistency of 3D models. The matching results derived from this analysis have broad applications in various fields, including shape retrieval and symmetry detection. Shape similarity measurement primarily encompasses feature extraction and distance calculation, with the challenge of effectively handling the non-rigid transformation of shapes. However, most existing shape similarity measurement methods neglect the scale invariance of shapes during feature extraction, rendering them unsuitable for the current task. In this paper, we propose the construction of a 3D signature called AvgSI, which is based on scale-invariant functional maps. AvgSI is a shape descriptor that leverages Laplace-Beltrami operators to efficiently extract geometric and topological information from 3D models. It is capable of extracting high-level features from multiple characteristics. By combining AvgSI with the scale-invariant BCICP (bijective and continuous Iterative Closest Point), we establish an effective pipeline for measuring the similarity of 3D models. This is achieved by calculating the correlation coefficient distance between the AvgSI values of the 3D shapes. Through comprehensive comparisons with the initial BCICP, our proposed method demonstrates stronger scale invariance, topological robustness, and isometric invariance. Results from a series of experiments validate the suitability of our framework for measuring the similarity of 3D models.

Keywords: 3D shape similarity · shape feature · scale invariance · BCICP · Laplace-Beltrami operator

1 Introduction

Notions of similarity and correspondence between 3D models are central to many tasks in geometry processing, computer vision, and computer graphics, which are used in many fields, including statistical shape analysis [1], shape segmentation [2], deformation transfer [3], and more. Therefore, 3D shape similarity measurement in shape processing has played a basic work. Shape similarity measurement primarily involves feature extraction and distance calculation. During feature extraction, it is essential to maintain isometric invariance, scale invariance, and topological robustness. Additionally, the features should possess a strong ability to describe details and effectively differentiate shape differences. Distance calculation necessitates the availability of a corresponding point set (CPS) between two shapes, enabling the computation of distances between sampled points' features. However, existing methods for shape similarity calculation fail to adequately fulfill the aforementioned requirements. To address this, we propose the definition of AvgSI descriptors for shape feature extraction based on functional maps. These descriptors maintain various invariant characteristics, particularly scale, and isometric invariance. Furthermore, we introduce a three-dimensional similarity measurement framework for shape similarity calculation, leveraging the AvgSI descriptors. Experimental results demonstrate the effectiveness of our framework in achieving reliable shape similarity measurements.

1.1 Related Works

For two given shapes, shape matching can be expressed as a problem of obtaining the correspondence between vertices on two shapes, which can be divided into rigid and non-rigid matching problems according to the shape type. Rigid matching refers to rigid transformations such as rotation, translation, and scale scaling between shapes that maintain Euclidean space. The corresponding non-rigid shape matching means that there are not only rigid transformations between shapes, but also non-rigid transformations that will cause shape topological changes, etc., and a certain degree of rigid transformation may lead to non-rigid deformation of shapes, such as human shapes, animal shapes, etc. This section mainly introduces several classic 3D non-rigid shape matching.

(1) **Based on Point methods**: In the shape matching, the matching between shape pairs is usually found by looking for the mapping between pairs of shapes that maintain the structure, and this matching result preserves the intrinsic distance between pairs of points on the shape. One major advancement in point-based shape matching algorithms is the development of robust and efficient feature descriptors. Feature descriptors capture distinctive geometric properties of individual points, allowing for effective shape matching and recognition. Various descriptors have been proposed, such as the Scale-Invariant Feature Transform (SIFT) [4] for 3D point clouds, Fast Point Feature Histograms (FPFH) [5], and Signature of Histograms of Orientations (SHOT) [6]. These descriptors extract local geometric information, such as surface normals, curvatures, or local shape contexts, enabling accurate and discriminative shape matching.

(2) **Based on the spectral analysis method**: In recent years, the shape descriptor based on the Laplace-Beltrami operator is called the spectral shape descriptor, which has been widely used in shape matching and analysis, that is, the Laplace-Beltrami operator constructed on the surface of the grid shape, and the geometric structure generated by the eigenvalue λ_i

and the eigenvector φ_i of LBO [7] is used, and then the spectral characteristics of the shape are scaled and calculated, and the shape is mapped from the Euclidean space to the low-spectral space for subsequent matching and similarity calculations. Reuter et al. Ovsjanikov et al. [8] constructed a new global point signature (GPS) by adding the use of feature vectors to ShapeDNA. GPS is also independent of other external spatial information, and similarly only feature values and feature vectors defined on the shape grid are used for calculations. Sun et al. [9] proposed heat kernel signature (HKS), which have multi-scale properties and can be changed by adjusting the time t to describe the local or global features of the shape. Based on HKS, Bronstein et al. [10] improved HKS and proposed a scale-invariant heat kernel signature (SIHKS). SIHKS has all the benefits of HKS, plus scaling immutability. Aubry et al. [11] proposed the wave kernel signature (WKS), WKS is free for time parameters, and its biggest advantage is that the use of band-pass filters can clearly separate different frequency sets in shape. Li et al. [12] added scale invariance to WKS, called scale-invariant wave kernel signature (SIWKS).

(3) **Based on functional maps methods**: Ovsjanikov et al. [13] proposed the concept of functional maps to apply to non-rigid shape matching, functional maps is a new mapping representation between pairs of shapes, the key to this method is that it does not need to establish point-to-point correspondence, but puts the corresponding real-valued function in the map. Kovnatsky et al. [14] assumed as input a set of corresponding functions that could be derived from point-by-point landmarks or area correspondences, and then estimated functional maps matrix that allowed real-valued functions to be passed between two shapes and then converted into point-by-point mappings. Furthermore, since the resulting maps may not be continuous or bijective, Huang and Ovsjanikov [15] propose several strong regularizers to promote certain desirable properties to improve bipolarization by accompanying regularization.

(4) **Based on deep learning methods**: the emergence of deep learning has had a profound impact on 3D shape matching based on point methods [16–18]. Convolutional Neural Networks (CNNs) [19] have been successfully applied to point clouds, enabling end-to-end learning of shape descriptors and matching functions. PointNet [16] and its variants are notable examples that directly process unordered point sets while capturing local and global information. These deep learning-based approaches have shown remarkable performance in shape matching tasks, surpassing traditional handcrafted feature descriptors in many cases. But this method requires a large number of training samples and is time-consuming for 3D shape matching.

1.2   Contribution

HKS is multiscale, determined by the time parameter t, and the point describes the local or global properties of the shape. WKS is free on time parameters, and when non-rigid shape matching is selected under different energy levels, when the number of energy levels increases, WKS can more accurately express the local characteristics of the shape, but too large energy levels will increase the global characteristics of WKS unable to depict the shape, indirectly increasing more calculation errors. Based on the method of feature fusion, we introduce SIHKS and SIWKS, both of which have the characteristics of scale invariance, isometric invariance and topological robustness, etc. Therefore, our research contributions are as follows:

- We propose a new shape descriptor AvgSI based on scale invariant functional maps using multi-feature fusion in deep learning, the feature descriptors used include SIHKS and SIWKS, and high-level features extracted from multiple shape feature descriptors are proposed. The AvgSI can not only handle complex topological structures of 3D models, but also is robust to scale transformation and approximate isometric transformation of 3D shapes.
- We propose our pipeline using scale invariant BCICP. our proposed method is less affected by scale changes compared to BCICP and can effectively measure the similarity of 3D models. We validate the effectiveness of our proposed method with a large number of experiments based on the SHREC 2010 and the TOSCA database.

Figure 1 schematically shows the framework for 3D shape similarity measurement based on scale invariant functional maps. The specific five steps of the pipeline are as follows: A. Input 3D models. This paper deals with triangle mesh models including the effective geometric information and topology; B. Calculate feature. We calculate the eigenvalues λ_i and eigenfunctions ϕ_i of the Laplace Beltrami operator (LBO) of 3D shapes. Then, we calculate the AvgSI of 3D shapes; C. Calculate map. Based on the AvgSI, we use the functional maps to obtain the CPS of a pair of 3D shapes; D. Calculate similarity. Based on the AvgSI values of CPS, we define a similarity measurement by using the correlation coefficient distance which is removed the differences in the dimensions of different variables during the calculation process.

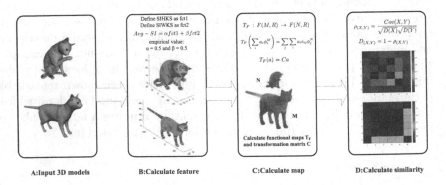

A:Input 3D models   B:Calculate feature   C:Calculate map   D:Calculate similarity

Fig. 1. The pipeline of 3D shape similarity measurement based on scale invariant functional maps.

The rest of this article is organized below. In Sect. 2, we introduce the fundamentals of our proposed method. In Sect. 3, we provide the AvgSI in detail and construct a similarity measurement for 3D shapes. In Sect. 4, we present the results of our experiment and analyze the results. Finally, we draw conclusions regarding our study in Sect. 5.

2 Fundamentals

In this section, we first introduce the definition of the Laplace-Bertalami operator and its discretization and spectral factorization forms, and then introduce scaling invariant wave kernel signature and scaling invariant heat kernel signature.

2.1 Laplace-Beltrami Operator

The Laplace Bertalami operator is a generalization of the Laplace operator on Riemannian manifolds and is an important operator in spectral analysis. The Laplace operator is a second-order differential operator acting on the smooth function f in Euclidean space, described as the divergence of the gradient of f. The Laplace operator for any second-order differentiable function is defined as:

$$\Delta f = \nabla \cdot \nabla f = \nabla^2 f = \frac{\partial^2 f}{\partial x^2} + \frac{\partial^2 f}{\partial y^2} + \frac{\partial^2 f}{\partial z^2} \tag{1}$$

According to the definition of gradients and divergence of Riemannian manifolds, if g is the metric tensor on the manifold and G is the determinant of the matrix g^{ij}, then the LB operator of the function f in the local coordinate system is expressed as [20]:

$$\Delta f = \nabla \cdot \nabla f = \frac{1}{\sqrt{G}} \sum_{i,j=1}^{n} g^{ij} \frac{\partial}{\partial x^i} (\sqrt{G} g^{ij} \frac{\partial f}{\partial x^j}) \tag{2}$$

In non-rigid 3D shape matching, the researcher needs to calculate the LB operator value for each vertex on the discrete mesh. If the function f is defined on a triangular mesh with the number of vertices n, the discrete LB operator of the function at the vertex v_i of the mesh can be defined as:

$$LB(f(v_i)) = \sum_{j=1}^{n} \omega_{ij}(f(v_i) - f(v_j)) \tag{3}$$

When calculating the LB operator for point v_i, consider all vertices in the mesh. For a vertex v_i on the mesh, if only the energy of the surrounding triangular patches is summed, and then its partial derivatives are calculated and the homogeneous terms are combined, the value of the discrete LB operator corresponding to that point is obtained:

$$LB(f(v_i)) = \frac{1}{2} \sum_{v_j \in Neigh(v_i)} (cot\alpha_j + cot\beta_j) \cdot |f(v_i) - f(v_j)| \tag{4}$$

where α_j and β_j represent the diagonals on both sides of the edge e_{ij} connecting v_i and v_j, respectively, and $Neigh(v_i)$ represents the set of vertices adjacent to vertex v_i. LB operator defined on a fully bounded compact manifold with symmetry and non-negativity. If the LB operator is spectratically decomposed (or feature decomposed) into the form of a matrix product of eigenvalues and eigenvectors, the LB operator spectral decomposition on the manifold can be obtained: $\Delta M \varphi_i = \lambda_i \varphi_i$, λ_i is the $i - th$ eigenvalue, φ_i is the eigenvector corresponding to the $i - th$ eigenvalue.

2.2 Scaling Invariant Wave Kernel Signature (SIWKS)

Since the WKS can capture the intrinsic characteristics of the shape and is very stable under shape perturbation, this makes it very suitable for analyzing complex shapes, but the significant disadvantage of WKS is the sensitivity to scale transformations. For a given shape S and its scaled form $S' = \beta S$, the new eigenvalues and eigenfunctions will satisfy $\lambda' = \beta^2 \lambda$ and $\phi' = \beta \phi$. Associating S' signature WKS' with S signature WKS, Eq. (5) can be further written as:

$$\begin{cases} WKS'(x,\cdot) : R \to R; \\ WKS'(x, e_N) = \beta^2 \cdot WKS(x, e_N) \end{cases} \tag{5}$$

In order to overcome the problem that WKS is sensitive to scale transformation, Li et al. [12] adopts the idea of eigenvalue normalization method to construct the Scale Invariant Wave Kernel Signature (SIWKS). To achieve scale invariance, we need to consider how to remove the scale factor β^2 from Eq. (6). First, given a compact Riemannian manifold M and a point $x(x \in M)$, When represented by base $\{\phi_k\}_{k=1}^{\infty}$, it corresponds to a vector of rescaling coefficients near x indicating the function. Finally, scale invariance is the motivation of this paper to scale WKS with eigenvalue normalization. The Scale Invariant Wave Kernel Signature (SIWKS) at the point $x(x \in M)$ can be expressed as:

$$\begin{cases} SIWKS(x,\cdot) : R \to R; \\ SIWKS(x, e_N) = C_e \sum_k \frac{\phi_k^2(x)}{\lambda_k} e^{\frac{-(e_N - \log \lambda_k)^2}{2\sigma^2}}, C_e = (\sum_k e^{\frac{-(e_N - \log \lambda_k)^2}{2\sigma^2}})^{-1} \end{cases} \tag{6}$$

2.3 Scaling Invariant Heat Kernel Signature (SIHKS)

According to the theory of heat diffusion, it is assumed that there is an initial heat source $\mu_0(x)$ at each point on the shape, and heat diffusion is carried out on the surface of shape M with time t. Spectral decomposition of heat kernel, if the heat kernel is confined to the time domain, the heat kernel signature as:

$$h_t(x, x) = \sum_{i=0}^{\infty} e^{-\lambda_i t} \varphi_i(x)^2 \tag{7}$$

HKS has multi-scale characteristics, and can change the local or global characteristics of the shape by adjusting the time t. After the improvement of HKS,

Bronstein et al. [10] proposed scale-invariant heat kernel signature (SIHKS). The descriptor adopts logarithmic sampling and Fourier transform, which eliminates the scaling factor before and after the scaling of a pair of shapes, and adds the characteristics of invariant scaling on the original HKS. First, let the scaling factor be β, and for shape M, the shape after scaling is $M' = \beta M$. Referring to the HKS definition, the scaled eigenvalues and eigenvectors satisfy $\lambda' = \beta^2 \lambda$, $\varphi' = \beta \varphi$, then after scaling, the spectral decomposition form of $HKS(x)$ at a point x on shape M' can be written as:

$$h'_t(x, x) = \sum_{i=0}^{\infty} e^{-\lambda_i t \beta^2} \varphi_i(x)^2 \beta^2 \tag{8}$$

Secondly, under the proportional transformation, $h'_t(x, x) = \beta^2 h_t(x, x)$, the heat kernel function on the time domain is logarithmically sampled, and the time $t = \alpha^\tau$, the new function equation is $h_\tau(x, x) = h(x, \alpha^\tau)$. At this point, the effect of β^2 caused by the scaling transformation translates into a time shift of $h'_\tau = \beta^2 h_{\tau+s}$, where $s = \alpha \log_a \beta$. Finally, take the logarithm of h to eliminate the effect of β^2: $\dot{h}_\tau = \dot{h}_{\tau+s}$, then $\dot{h}_\tau = \log_{h_{\tau+1}} - \log_{h_\tau}$ Then perform a Fourier transform on $\dot{h}_\tau$ to transfer the translation transformation of the time domain to the complex domain:

$$H'(\omega) = H'(\omega) e^{2\pi \omega s} \tag{9}$$

Taking the Fourier mold on both sides yields: $|H'(\omega)| = |H(\omega)|$. The heat kernel signature before and after shape scaling is only offset on the timeline, and SIHKS has scale transformation invariance. The scaling invariant heat kernel signature is approximated by:

$$SIHKS(p_i, \tau) \approx \sum_{i=0}^{k} e^{-\lambda_i \alpha^\tau} \varphi_i(x)^2 \tag{10}$$

where p_i is the point of three-dimensional mesh M and α^τ is the time sampling logarithmically of the heat signature at each shape point p_i.

3   Feature and Similarty Measurement

In this section, we construct a new feature descriptor AvgSI, then we calculate the functional maps of a pair of 3D models based on the constructed feature AvgSI and scale invariant BCICP, and finally measure the similarity between this pair of 3D models.

3.1   AvgSI

Among the previously mentioned shape descriptors, HKS is mainly transmitted by low frequencies, which can well describe the local geometric information of the shape, and has strong robustness to weaken the influence of local noise.

The biggest advantage of WKS is that the use of band-pass filters can clearly separate different frequency sets in shape, and allows access to high-frequency information, thereby increasing the exact matching ability of operators, in addition, WKS has multi-scale characteristics by selecting different energy scales. Based on HKS and WKS, the researchers made improvements and proposed two new shape descriptors, SIHKS and SIWKS, which have all the advantages of HKS and WKS, but also have scale invariance, which is ideal for constructing features.

Based on the idea of feature fusion in deep learning, we propose a shape matching method of scale invariant functional maps, extract advanced features from multiple shape feature descriptors, and construct a new feature based on the two shape descriptors of SIHKS and SIWKS: AvgSI. First we need to calculate the value of the shape's SIHKS and define it as $fct1$, then calculate the value of the shape's SIWKS, define it as $fct2$, and finally let

$$AvgSI = \alpha fct1 + \beta fct2 \tag{11}$$

where $\alpha + \beta = 1$. These two parameters α and β can be selected experimentally. Through a large number of experiments, for the values of α and β, we obtained that the experimental values is $\alpha = 0.5$ and $\beta = 0.5$, when $\alpha = 0.5$ and $\beta = 0.5$ the resulting map is smoother and the coverage of the map is higher. The new features we construct have the advantages of SIHKS and SIWKS, and have better performance when measuring the similarity of 3D models.

3.2   Invariance of AvgSI

The feature of our construction, AvgSI, has good performance under various deformations, and it has the following characteristics:

Sampling Robustness: For shape M, if the vertices of the triangular mesh model of M are sampled, including upsampling and downsampling, the values of AvgSI of the shape before and after sampling remain unchanged.

Scale Invariance: AvgSI has scale invariance. For a given shape S and its scaled form $S' = \beta S$, the new eigenvalues and eigenfunctions will satisfy $\lambda' = \beta^2 \lambda$ and $\phi' = \beta \phi$. AvgSI can eliminate the effect of β^2 caused by scaling transformations. Therefore, if we calculate AvgSI before and after the shape scale change separately, this value remains unchanged.

Isometric Invariance: AvgSI has isometric invariance. A transformation between surfaces that is isometric if it keeps the length of any curve on the surface constant. Since the LBO is an intrinsic operator of a shape with robustness and stability, if we calculate the AvgSI before and after the isometric shape change separately, this value remains the same.

Topological Robustness: When the shape is topologically transformed, noise is likely to occur. Since the wave diffusion distance and heat diffusion distance are less sensitive to topological changes, AvgSI has good robustness to topological noise of shapes.

3.3 Scale Invariant BCICP

After constructing a new feature, we introduce the constructed feature into the scale invariant BCICP framework. Let's first introduce the Iterative Closest Point (ICP) algorithm, ICP is a point cloud matching algorithm. The idea is to minimize the distance between two sets of points by rotating and translating. The ICP algorithm, proposed by Besl et al. [21], uses the quaternion method to solve the rotation matrix. The ICP algorithm is essentially an optimal registration method based on least squares method. The algorithm repeatedly selects the corresponding relationship point pairs, and calculates the optimal rigid body transformation until the convergence accuracy requirements of correct registration are met. Ren et al. [22] made improvements based on ICP and proposed Bijective and Continuous ICP (BCICP). BCICP is a method that uses the functional maps framework to efficiently calculate directional and approximately continuous correspondence between non-rigid shapes, with the goal of finding continuous, almost continuous, and dual point mappings along the direction. This approach significantly extends the iteration nearest point (ICP) refinement proposed in the original functional maps pipeline. The method is based on iteratively recalculating the point-to-point map from its functional counterpart, simply by searching for the nearest neighbor in the spectral domain and updating the functional maps by projecting to the nearest orthogonal matrix. The result is that by updating the mapping in the spectral and spatial domains, we can obtain a significant improvement in the final overall mapping quality, especially to promote continuity without sacrificing computational efficiency.

In our paper, we replace the WKS operator in the initial BCICP with the AvgSI operator, increasing the scaling invariance of the initial BCICP. Scale invariance BCICP takes two functional maps C_{12} and C_{21} between shapes S_1 and S_2 as input, then initializes them and alternates between computing the two point-by-point maps, refines them using the steps described below, and recalculates the induced functional maps. The point-wise map from S_1 to S_2 (each with n_1 and n_2 vertices) is represented in two ways: (1) A vector $T_{12} \in R^{n_1}$, where the i-th vertex of shape S_1 is mapped to the $T_{12}(i)$ vertex of shape S_2. We use this phrase in algorithm descriptions. (2) As a matrix $\pi_{12} \in R^{n_1 n_2}$, where $_{12}(i, T_{12}(i)) = 1, \forall i = 1, \ldots, n_1$, the remaining items are 0.

3.4 Calculate Functional Maps

Based on constructed features and BCICP calculates the functional maps between a pair of 3D models. Let $T : M \rightarrow N$ be a bijective mapping between manifolds M and N (continuous or discrete). T then induces natural transformations of derived quantities, such as functions on M. Given a scalar function $f : M \rightarrow R$, then we get the corresponding function $g : N \rightarrow R$ by composition, such as $g = f \circ T^1$. Let us denote this inductive transformation by $T_F : F(M, R) \rightarrow F(N, R)$, where we denote the general space of real-valued functions by $F(\cdot, R)$. We call T_F the functional representation of the mapping T. Now suppose that the function space of M is equipped with a basis such that any function $f : M \to R$ can be expressed as a linear combination of the basis functions $f = \sum_i a_i \phi_i^M$. Furthermore, if N is equipped with a set of basis functions $\{\phi_j^N\}$, then $T_F(\phi_i)^M = \sum_j c_{ij} \phi_j^N$ and

$$T_F(f) = \sum_i a_i \sum_j c_{ij} \phi_j^N = \sum_j \sum_i a_i c_{ij} \phi_j^N \tag{12}$$

The map T_F can be expressed as a matrix C s.t. and for any function f represented as a vector with coefficients a, then $T_F(a) = Ca$. This annotation, combined with the previous two, indicates that matrix C fully encodes the original map T. In our paper, we obtain the initial corresponding point set(CPS) between a pair of 3D shapes using the scale invariant BCICP, as shown in Fig. 4. Then, we can measure the 3D shape similarity by calculating the distance between AvgSI defined on the shapes CPS.

3.5　3D Models Similarity Measurement

In this paper, after calculating the functional maps between a pair of 3D models, we use the correlation coefficient distance as the similarity measurement, which can effectively measure the similarity of the 3D model. For two manifolds M and N in three-dimensional space, $AvgSI(x_M)$ and $AvgSI(x_N)$ are the corresponding point set(CPS) calculated using scale-invariant BCICP on manifolds M and N, the correlation coefficient between them is defined as:

$$\rho(M, N) = \frac{Cov(AvgSI(x_{Mi}), AvgSI(x_{Ni}))}{\sqrt{D(AvgSI(x_{Mi}))}\sqrt{D(AvgSI(x_{Ni}))}} \tag{13}$$

where $AvgSI(x_{Mi})$ and $AvgSI(x_{Ni})$ represent the corresponding point i on shapes M and N, D is the variance, $\sqrt{D}$ is the standard deviation, $Cov(AvgSI(x_{Mi}), AvgSI(x_{Ni}))$ is called the covariance of the random variable $AvgSI(x_{Mi})$ and $AvgSI(x_{Ni})$, and the quotient of the covariance and standard deviation between two variables is called the correlation coefficient. Let's continue to refine the definition of the correlation coefficient in detail:

$$\rho(M, N) = \frac{E((AvgSI(x_{Mi}) - \mu_{AvgSI(x_{Mi})}), (AvgSI(x_{Ni}) - \mu_{AvgSI(x_{Ni})}))}{\sqrt{\sum_{i=1}^{n}(AvgSI(x_{Mi}) - \mu_{AvgSI(x_{Mi})})^2}\sqrt{\sum_{i=1}^{n}(AvgSI(x_{Ni}) - \mu_{AvgSI(x_{Ni})})^2}} \tag{14}$$

where E is the mathematical expectation, μ_{AvgSI} is the mean AvgSI of the 3D models, and n is the number of points of the M and N CPS. The definition of the correlation coefficient distance is:

$$D_{(M,N)} = 1 - \rho_{(M,N)} \tag{15}$$

The correlation coefficient distance is defined according to the correlation, and the larger the value, the farther the distance.

4   Experiments and Analysis

In this section, we will present the results of the experiment and analyze the results. We used the TOSCA dataset [23] and SHREC 2010 dataset [24], which provides a large number of 3D shapes for non-rigid deformed shape analysis.

4.1   Comparison with Other Descriptors

We also use HKS, WKS, SIHKS, SIWKS, and our proposed AvgSI to describe the same shape, Fig. 2 shows that compared to the other four spectral descriptors, using AvgSI can clearly separate different frequency sets on the shape, it can better describe the geometric information of the 3D model, can handle more details of the 3D model, and has strong robustness to weaken the effect of local noise, which is ideal for 3D shape similarity measurement.

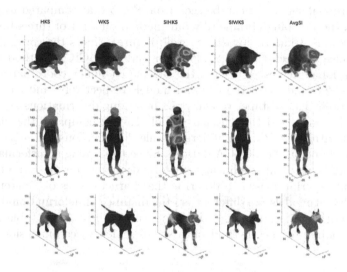

Fig. 2. The models describing by using HKS, WKS, SIHKS, SIWKS and AvgSI.

4.2   Robutness of the AvgSI

We did experiments on the SHREC 2010 dataset and compared scaling invariance, noise, sampling and topology robustness of AvgSI in Fig. 3, and we can see that the features AvgSI has scaling invariance, sampling, topology and robustness, which can describe more details of 3D models and has good performance for measuring the similarity of 3D models. We have conducted several experiments on the TOSCA dataset, and compared the maps generated by the combination of three features WKS, HKS, AvgSI with ICP and BCICP methods, respectively. In terms of isometric invariance and scale invariance of 3D shape, it can be seen from Fig. 4 that the results produced by the combination of WKS, HKS,

AvgSI and BCICP are more accurate, but compared with WKS and HKS, the features proposed by us combined with BCICP have stronger scale invariance and isometric invariance, and the resulting mapping is smoother and more accurate. In addition, our method achieves the best global accuracy while preserving local details. Table 1 shows the coverage of three features WKS, HKS, AvgSI combined with ICP and BCICP. It can be seen that the method of combining BCICP with our proposed feature AvgSI has the largest coverage, which indicates that the mapping quality generated by our method achieving comparable or better quality.

4.3   The Similarity Results Based on the AvgSI

We use the correlation coefficient distance as the similarity measurement, which can effectively measure the similarity of the 3D model. Figure 5 shows the correlation coefficient distance between the AvgSI operator and the BCICP method on three-dimensional shapes. It can be seen from Fig. 5 that compared to the original BCICP, the mapping obtained by our method on a set of three-dimensional shapes maintains isometric invariance well. Figure 6 shows the correlation coefficient distance between the AvgSI operator and the BCICP method on scaled three-dimensional shapes. We scale the 3D model under coordinates to 0.5x, 0.25x, 0.75x, 2x, and 3x of the original model, respectively, and calculate the correlation coefficient distance of two pairs of scaling deformations according to the 5 scaled models and the original model. Table 2 compares the distance of our method with BCICP under different scale deformations of the same three-dimensional shape on the TOSCA dataset. Since the scaling transformation performed in the experiment is a linear transformation, and our descriptor AvgSI is a nonlinear descriptor used to describe the characteristics of different scaling models, different models are different, so the distance of deformation 4 is higher than that of other deformations. As can be seen from Fig. 6 and Table 2 that the mapping obtained by our method on a set of scaled three-dimensional shapes

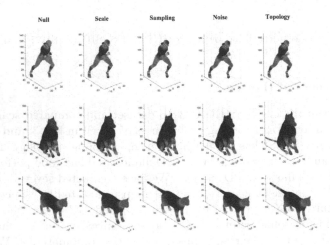

Fig. 3. Visual diagram of the different deformation models describing by AvgSI.

Fig. 4. Comparison of scale invariance of HKS, WKS and AvgSI.

Table 1. Coverage of HKS, WKS and AvgSI and ICP, BCICP, SI-BCICP

Methods	WKS+ICP	HKS+ICP	AvgSI+ICP	WKS+BCICP	HKC+BCICP	AvgSI+SI-BCICP
Coverage	4.66%	4.08%	4.4%	83.92%	88.84%	90.56%

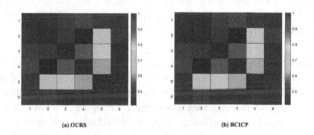

Fig. 5. Visual thermodynamic diagram of the model similarity results using OURS and BCICP on three-dimensional shapes.

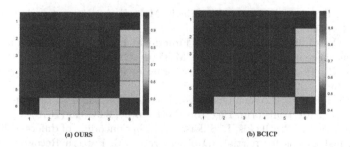

Fig. 6. Visual thermodynamic diagram of the model similarity results using OURS and BCICP on scaled three-dimensional shapes.

Table 2. The distance of the model under different scale deformations of the same three-dimensional shape using our method and BCICP.

Methods	Deformation1	Deformation2	Deformation3	Deformation4	Deformation5	Average
OURS	0.6208	0.6127	0.6167	0.9870	0.6304	**0.6935**
BCICP	0.6577	0.6519	0.6550	0.9931	0.6636	0.7243

generates a smaller distance than the BCICP method, which indicates that our method obtains a higher degree of similarity. These visual thermodynamic diagrams shown that AvgSI has scale invariance and sampling robustness.

5   Conclusion

In this paper, we define an effective shape descriptor AvgSI based on scale invariant functional maps, introduces the feature descriptor we define into the scale invariant BCICP framework, and provides a method for 3D model similarity measurement. This method performs well in the similarity measurement of 3D models, which is the basis for shape classification, shape segmentation and shape retrieval. We have carried out a large number of experiments, and the experimental results based on SHREC 2010 and TOSCA dataset show that AvgSI has isometric and scaling invariance, topology, sampling, and robustness. Our method can produce similar or better quality on a wide range of shape matching problems, and the results obtained are more accurate, and the similarity of 3D models can be effectively and accurately measured.

Acknowledgements. This work was supported in part by the Natural Science Youth Foundation of Qinghai Province(No. 2023-ZJ-947Q); National Natural Science Foundation of China (Grant Nos. 62102213); Independent project fund of the state key lab of the Tibetan Intelligent Information Processing and Application (Co-established by the province and the ministry) (Grant Nos. 2022-SKL-014); Young and middle-aged scientific research fund of Qinghai Normal University (Grant Nos. kjqn 2021004).

References

1. Bogo, F., Romero, J., Loper, M., Black, M.J.: Faust: dataset and evaluation for 3D mesh registration (2014)
2. Huang, Q., Guibas, L., Wang, F.: Functional map networks for analyzing and exploring large shape collections. ACM Trans. Graph. **33**, 1–11 (2014)
3. Sumner, R., Popovic, J.: Deformation transfer for triangle meshes. ACM Trans. Graph. **23**(3), 399–405 (2004)
4. Soyel, H., Demirel, H.: Facial expression recognition based on discriminative scale invariant feature transform. Electron. Lett. **46**(5), 343–345 (2010)
5. Savelonas, M.A., Pratikakis, I., Sfikas, K.: Fisher encoding of differential fast point feature histograms for partial 3D object retrieval. Pattern Recogn. **55**, 114–124 (2016)
6. Zhen, M., Wang, W., Wang, R.: Signature of unique angles Histograms for 3D data description. In: 2015 IEEE International Conference on Multimedia & Expo Workshops (ICMEW), pp. 1–6. IEEE (2015)

7. Fan, D., Liu, Y., He, Y.: Recent progress in the Laplace-Beltrami operator and its applications to digital geometry processing. J. Comput.-Aided Des. Comput. Graph. **27**(4), 559–569 (2015)

8. Ovsjanikov, M., Sun, J., Guibas, L.: Global intrinsic symmetries of shapes. In: Proceedings of the Symposium on Geometry Processing, pp. 1341–1348. Eurographics Association (2008)

9. Sun, J., Ovsjanikov, M., Guibas, L.: A concise and provably informative multi-scale signature based on heat diffusion. Comput. Graph. Forum **28**(5), 1383–1392 (2009)

10. Bronstein, M.M., Kokkinos, I.: Scale-invariant heat kernel signatures for non-rigid shape recognition. In: 2010 IEEE Computer Society Conference on Computer Vision and Pattern Recognition (2010)

11. Aubry, M., Schlickewei, U., Cremers, D.: The wave kernel signature: a quantum mechanical approach to shape analysis. In: IEEE International Conference on Computer Vision Workshops (2011)

12. Li, H., Sun, L., Wu, X., Cai, Q.: Scale-invariant wave kernel signature for non-rigid 3D shape retrieval. In: 2018 IEEE International Conference on Big Data and Smart Computing (BigComp) (2018)

13. Ovsjanikov, M., Ben-Chen, M., Solomon, J., Butscher, A., Guibas, L.: Functional maps: a flexible representation of maps between shapes. ACM Trans. Graph. **31**(4CD), 1–11 (2012)

14. Kovnatsky, A., Bronstein, M.M., Bronstein, A.M., Glashoff, K., Kimmel, R.: Coupled quasi-harmonic bases. Comput. Graph. Forum **32**(2pt4), 439–448 (2013)

15. Huang, R., Ovsjanikov, M.: Adjoint map representation for shape analysis and matching. Comput. Graph. Forum **36**(5), 151–163 (2017)

16. Qi, C.R., Su, H., Mo, K., Guibas, L.J.: Pointnet: Deep learning on point sets for 3d classification and segmentation. IEEE (2017)

17. Qi, C.R., Yi, L., Su, H., Guibas, L.J.: PointNet++: Deep Hierarchical Feature Learning on Point Sets in a Metric Space (2017)

18. Zhou, W., Jiang, X., Liu, Y.H.: Mvpointnet: Multi-view network for 3d object based on point cloud. IEEE Sensors J PP(99), 11 (2019)

19. Zhang, L., Zhu, G., Shen, P., et al.: Learning spatiotemporal features using 3DCNN and convolutional LSTM for gesture recognition. In: Proceedings of the IEEE International Conference on Computer Vision Workshops, pp. 3120–3128 (2017)

20. Rustamov, R.M.: Laplace-Beltrami eigenfunctions for deformation invariant shape representation. In: Proceedings of the Fifth Eurographics Symposium on Geometry Processing, Barcelona, Spain, 4–6 July 2007 (2007)

21. Besl, P.J., Mckay, H.D.: A method for registration of 3-D shapes. IEEE Trans. Pattern Anal. Mach. Intell. **14**(2), 239–256 (1992)

22. Ren, J., Poulenard, A., Wonka, P., Ovsjanikov, M.: Continuous and orientation-preserving correspondences via functional maps. ACM Trans. Graph. **37**(6), 1–16 (2018)

23. Bronstein, A.M., Bronstein, M.M., Kimmel, R.: Numerical Geometry of Non-Rigid Shapes. MCS, Springer, New York (2009). https://doi.org/10.1007/978-0-387-73301-2

24. Bronstein, A.M., Bronstein, M.M., Castellani, U., Falcidieno, B., Ovsjanikov, M.: SHREC 2010: robust large-scale shape retrieval benchmark. ProcDOR (2010)

Visualization Research on Industry and Spatial Distribution of Industrial Heritage in New China

E. Senni and Huaping Shen[✉]

School of Design and Art, Beijing University of Technology, Beijing 100081, China
18204895596@163.com

Abstract. Aiming at the spatial distribution and industrial distribution characteristics of industrial heritage built after 1949 in China, using visual analysis methods such as kernel density analysis diagram, point distribution diagram, pie chart, and chord diagram, a macroscopic analysis of the industrial heritage of New China is carried out from the perspectives of overall and regional research. The results show that the industrial heritage of New China is mainly distributed in central and south-western China as well as in the north-east. Spatially, it is characterised by macro-uniformity and micro-agglomeration; in terms of industrial characteristics, the industrial heritage industry types in the border areas are dominated by a single heavy industry, while those in the inland areas are more abundant. In addition, nearly half of the industrial heritage of science and technology is located in south-west China, and the industrial heritage of transportation is mainly located in east and central China. Finally, the future development of China's industrial heritage conservation and reuse is reflected upon and foreseen.

Keywords: Industrial Heritage · New China · Visualization Research

1 Introduction

The concept of "Industrial Heritage" was first introduced in 1978 at the Third International Conference on the Preservation of Industrial Monuments. In 2003, the International Committee for the Conservation of Industrial Heritage (TICCIH) drafted and submitted to the International Council on Monuments and Sites (ICOMOS) and finally published by UNESCO. The Haute-Tal Charter, published by UNESCO, finally elaborated and defined the definition, scope and typology of industrial heritage, which became an important part of the world cultural heritage. On the International Day of Monuments and Sites on 18 April 2006, China held the first China Industrial Heritage Conservation Forum and adopted the "Wuxi Recommendations", which set out the responsibilities, approaches and plans for the conservation of China's industrial heritage and opened the door to industrial heritage conservation at the national level [1]. The promulgation of the "National Measures for the Management of Industrial Heritage" in July 2022 means that the management of industrial heritage in China has formally stepped into a comprehensive, systematic and integrated stage, and for the first time, a comprehensive value assessment system and conservation and reuse path for industrial heritage has been established [2].

W. Yongtian and W. Lifang (Eds.): IGTA 2023, CCIS 1910, pp. 110–121, 2023.
https://doi.org/10.1007/978-981-99-7549-5_9

China's industrial development began with the Westernization Movement, while the real turnaround and take-off of China's industrialisation began after the establishment of People's Republic of China in 1949 [3]. Many industrial factories and mines from the early days of the founding of the country have witnessed the course of China's industrialisation and urban development, and have good locational value in today's cities, so the industrial heritage of New China has a closer relationship with contemporary society and urban development, and it carries the industrial spirit and national collective The industrial spirit and national collective memory genes it carries can enhance people's identity and strengthen their cultural confidence. Since 2016 China has been mapping its industrial heritage and establishing a list of industrial heritage. In the course of China's current industrial transformation, many young but important industrial heritage, like those of the Third-Line Construction period factories and mines, have been severely damaged. Therefore, Sort out and analyze the spatial distribution and industry type characteristics of New China's industrial heritage from a macro perspective, conduct targeted research on New China's industrial heritage, has great reference significance to the protection, development, management of China's industrial heritage, urban planning of china and jointly build the new pattern of "Belt and Road" regional economy.

The industrial heritage of the post-statehood period mainly includes the "156 Projects" of the First and Second Five-Year Plan periods, as well as the industries of the Third-Line Construction period. The 156 Projects was built with the assistance of the former Soviet Union and China's own construction, established the initial foundation for China's industrialization [4]. The subsequent Third-Line Construction had a special context of the times, when industries from coastal areas and frontier cities were relocated inland and in the mountainous regions of the central and western parts of the country to form a strategic large rear economic region centred on the construction of national defence undertakings. It can be said that the Third-Line Construction improved the unbalanced industrial layout of China's early years, laid the foundation for industry in the west [5] and led to a number of new industrial cities such as Panzhihua, Liupanshui, Shiyan and Jinchang, providing the basic conditions for the economic development of central and western China.In order to introduce the historical background of the new China's industrial heritage in more detail (1950s–1960s), the article sorts out the timeline of social and economic development in the early days of the founding of the new China (Fig. 1).

The People's Republic of China is established.

1949

China transitioned from New Democracy to Socialism, formulated the first five-year plan for the development of our national economy, and implemented it. The Soviet Union aided China in the construction of "156 Project".

1953

The Soviet government tore up the agreement on new national defense technology signed by China and the Soviet Union, and the Soviet aid to industrialization construction ended.

1959

1952

The Recovery of The National Economy has achieved great success. The total output value of industry and agriculture was 81 billion yuan, an increase of 77.5% over 1949.

1958

From 1958 to 1960, the "Great Leap Forward" movement occurred in China, which had a certain negative impact on China's economy and industrialization. Seriously disrupted the proportional relationship of the national economy and the proportional relationship between various departments within the industry.

In order to get rid of the difficulties brought about by the three-year "Great Leap Forward", China entered a period of national economic adjustment from 1961 to 1965.

1961

China set off the "Cultural Revolution", so due to the "Cultural Revolution" and "Third-Line Construction", it had an impact on the development of China's industrial economy.

1966

1964

Due to the international situation at that time, China began to deploy and practice the "Third-Line Construction" project.

1965

The production capacity of emerging industries such as petroleum, chemical industry, electronics and nuclear industry has developed significantly, and China has preliminarily established an industrial system with a considerable production scale and a certain level of technology.

Fig. 1. The development of the industrial economy of the People's Republic of China

2 Data and Sources for the Study

In order to summarise the spatial layout and characteristics of the industrial heritage of the New China in a more realistic and reliable manner, the industrial heritage list used in this paper will be selected and analysed from a number of industrial heritage lists released by various national ministries. At present, the published industrial heritage lists in China are: 1. the "China's 20th Century Architectural Heritage" (2016, 2017, 2018) issued by the Chinese Cultural Relics Association and the Chinese Institute of Architecture; 2. the "The Protection List of Industrial Heritage in China" (2018, 2019) issued by the Chinese Association of Science; 3. a total of five batches of the "National Industrial Heritage List" (2017, 2018, 2019, 2020, 2021) issued by the Ministry of Industry and Information Technology; 4. "List of National Key Cultural Relics Protection Units" issued by the Ministry of Culture and Tourism and the State Administration of Cultural Heritage; 5. "The List of Industrial Cultural Heritage of Central Enterprises" issued by the State-owned Assets Supervision and Administration Commission; 6. "The National Mine Park" issued by the Ministry of Natural Resources; 7. "The National Industrial Tourism Demonstration Base" issued by the Ministry of Culture and Tourism.

After comparing and analysing the above lists, it was found that "the List of National Key Cultural Heritage Protection Units" involved a total of 106 heritage sites, "the National Industrial Heritage List" contained 197 heritage sites in 5 batches, and "the List of China's Industrial Heritage Protection issued" contained 200 heritage sites in 2 batches, which has the advantages of a large number base, covering a wide range of industries and including a comprehensive range of industrial heritage. Therefore, this paper takes the above three cultural heritage lists as the main research target, and after combining the three cultural heritage lists, eliminating the duplicate items, and adding three industrial architectural heritage items from "the China 20th Century Architectural Heritage", we finally get a total of 418 heritage sites. Some of the industrial heritage sites cover industrial buildings built over a long period of time, and some of these sites were built before the founding of the People's Republic of China, while others were built afterwards, such as the Wanshan Mercury Mine, the Dezhou Machine Tool Factory, the Dushanzi Oil Refinery and the Gutianxi Hydroelectric Power Plant, etc.; there are also some industrial heritage sites that were built in the modern era but were heavily rebuilt and reconstructed after the founding of the People's Republic of China, such as the Benxihu Iron and Steel Works and the Anshan Iron and Steel Works, which were part of the 156 construction projects. Therefore, this study considers this type of industrial heritage as the industrial heritage of New China. Based on the above criteria, the 417 industrial heritage items include 144 New China industrial heritage items.

This paper presents a visual analysis of the spatial distribution and industrial type characteristics of the industrial heritage within the above-mentioned study area, from both an overall and a regional perspective.

Nowadays, the visualization research related to the analysis of industrial heritage characteristics is relatively mature and has relatively standardized analysis methods. For example, the kernel density analysis and point distribution analysis of the spatial distribution of industrial heritage based on ArcGIS [6–9]; the provincial distribution analysis of industrial heritage [7, 10]; Spatial distribution centre of gravity and standard deviation ellipse analysis about industrial heritage by period [7, 9, 10]; Analysis of the impact of natural and geographical factors such as river factors, elevation factors, climate factors on the distribution of industrial heritage [7, 10]; analysis of the impact of transportation factors such as railways on the distribution of industrial heritage [7, 10], and inductive analysis of industrial heritage industry types [6, 7], etc.

The research object of this study is the industrial heritage after the founding of the People's Republic of China, and its construction period is concentrated in the 50s–60s, so no research on the temporal and spatial distribution is carried out. The purpose of this study is to summarize the characteristics of industrial heritage for the reuse of industrial heritage. Therefore, it is not the purpose to study the natural factors, traffic factors and other factors that affect the distribution characteristics of industrial heritage. Furthermore, this paper sets up a regional analysis based on the Administrative Region of the People's Republic of China, so it is redundant to carry out provincial distribution analysis.

Therefore, this paper chooses the visual analysis methods such as kernel density analysis, point distribution, pie chart, and chord diagram to study and analyze the spatial distribution characteristics and industry characteristics of the industrial heritage in New China.

3   Comprehensive Analysis of the Spatial Distribution of Industrial Heritage in New China

Understanding the macro characteristics of the industrial heritage of New China is of great significance to the management and conservation of the industrial heritage of New China. Therefore, this paper conducts a kernel density analysis and industrial distribution analysis study of New China's industrial heritage. Due to the characteristics of the research methodology, among the 144 New Chinese industrial heritage items covered in this paper, four railway-type linear heritage items will be removed, treat the remaining 140 industrial heritages as point data, and conduct spatial and industry distribution research on them.

3.1   Kernel Density Analysis

In statistics, kernel density estimation (KDE) is the application of kernel smoothing for probability density estimation, i.e., a non-parametric method to estimate the probability density function of a random variable based on kernels as weights [11]. In geography, kernel density analysis can express the Spatial Agglomeration of event. Kernel density analysis is well placed to break down administrative boundaries and obtain more objective results for spatial distribution characterisation.

Nuclear density estimates are publicly available as

$$p\,(x) = \frac{1}{N} \sum_{k=1}^{N} \frac{1}{h} K\left(\frac{x - x_k}{h}\right)$$

where K denotes the kernel function; N is the number of industrial heritage of; and h is the threshold value of the search radius distance; x_k denotes $k(k = 1, 2, \ldots, N)$

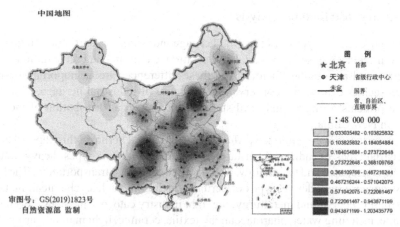

Fig. 2. Analysis of the nuclear density of industrial heritage in the New China

The kernel density was analysed using Kernel Density in the Spatial Analyst Tools in ArcGIS software (Fig. 2).

The average observation distance between the industrial heritage of New China is 97488.9516 m, the expected average distance is 166871.9726 m, therefore, its nearest neighbor ratio R = 0.584214 < 1 can be calculated, it shows that the spatial distribution type of new China's industrial heritage is a cohesive type. It can be seen from Fig. 4 that the industrial heritage of New China has two high-density core areas, which are located in the Beijing-Tianjin-Hebei Urban Agglomeration and the eastern part of Sichuan; three sub-density core areas are in the eastern area of Yunnan; The province's Yangtze River basin area; the border area of Shanxi and Henan provinces. Generally speaking, these gathering areas are distributed in the southeastern half of my country, within the Hu Huanyong line[1].

At the same time, due to the algorithmic feature of planar KDE, a smooth density surface of spatial point events in a two-dimensional geographic space is generated [12]. In some cases, distortions that do not meet the purpose of the experiment will appear. For example, in this study, the highly concentrated industrial heritage of the New China in Beijing caused a certain distortion in the Beijing-Tianjin-Hebei Urban Agglomeration in the nuclear density analysis map of the industrial heritage of New China, that is, the high nuclear density value spread to the surrounding area of Beijing.

---

[1] The Heihe–Tengchong Line (simplified Chinese: 黑河–腾冲线; traditional Chinese: 黑河–騰衝線; pinyin: Heihe–Tengchong xian), also called the Aihui-Tengchong Line (and internationally as the Hu line), is an imaginary line that divides the area of China into two parts with contrasting population densities. It stretches from the city of Heihe in northeast to Tengchong in south, diagonally across China. The eastern portion, area shown in red in the map, is further subdivided into north and south halves. As of 2015, 94% of China's population live east of the line, in an area that is 43% of China's total, whereas 57% of the Chinese territory is west of the line has but only 6% of the country's population.

3.2 Industry Distribution Analysis

The differences in the types of industrial heritage industries make it more obvious that there are differences in scale, material composition, environmental remediation, corporate culture and many other factors. And these differences are an important basis for practices such as evaluation, conservation and reuse of industrial heritage. This paper therefore presents a macro-analytical study of the industrial distribution of industrial heritage in New China.

Based on the above-mentioned differences in industrial heritage, this paper classifies the industrial types of industrial heritage in New China into six types: heavy industry, light industry, science and technology, water conservancy, and transportation. The heavy industry category includes six types of heritage, including nuclear, chemical, manufacturing, mining, energy and metallurgy; the light industry category includes eleven types of heritage, including water, pharmaceutical, textile, ceramic, light manufacturing, food, telecommunications, film and fertiliser; the transportation category includes three types of heritage, including bridges and railway stations;

A scatterplot is a commonly used visualization tool for displaying and comparing numerical values. Therefore, This paper uses the point data distribution chart in ArcGIS to conduct a comparative study on the distribution of new China's industrial heritage of different industry types.

As can be seen from Fig. 3, the industrial heritage of the heavy industry category is the most widely distributed and the most numerous in the industrial distribution of industrial heritage in New China. In descending order is the industrial heritage of the light industry category, which is significantly less distributed in the border areas of Tibet, Xinjiang, Qinghai, Inner Mongolia and Heilongjiang compared to the industrial heritage of the heavy industry category. The industrial heritage of military, aerospace and scientific research industries is mainly located in: 1) sparsely populated areas such as the Third Line and Northwest China; 2) Beijing and nearby areas; 3) areas near Jiangsu, Zhejiang and Shanghai. The industrial heritage of the water Conservancy category is mainly distributed in central and eastern China, with some correlation to the Yangtze and Yellow River basins. Among the 144 New China's industrial heritage items covered in this study, two railway stations are included, namely Beijing Station in Beijing and Shaoshan Station in Shaoshan City. The industrial heritage of the bridge category is mainly located in the Yangtze River basin in Sichuan, Chongqing, Hubei, Anhui and Zhejiang, as well as in Yunnan.

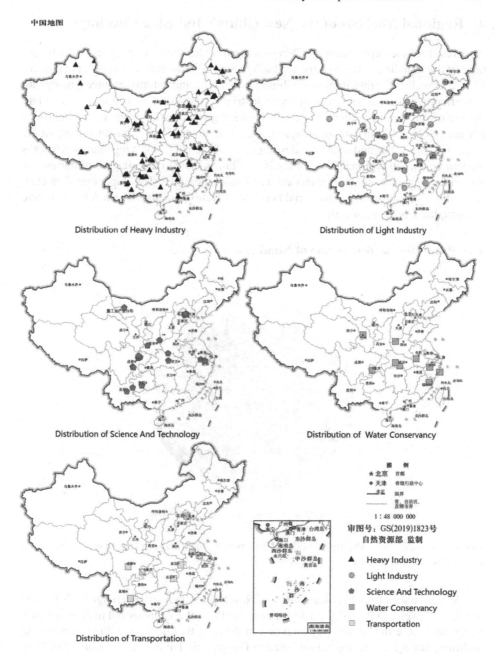

Fig. 3. Distribution of industrial heritage industries in the New China

4   Regional Analysis of the New China's Industrial Heritage

As a result of the deployment of China's industrial development policies at the beginning of the founding of the country, the background of industrial development in modern China, as well as the distribution of China's population and natural resources, many factors affecting the characteristics of the industrial heritage of New China have a certain degree of territoriality. Therefore, a sub-regional generalization study of the industrial heritage of New China is of great significance in summarizing its characteristics. At the same time, the urban and industrial development of each of China's regional provinces is uneven, and a sub-regional study of the New China's industrial heritage is important for the implementation of local conservation and reuse measures. This paper therefore classifies the distribution of the industrial heritage of New China into Seven Administrative Geographic Divisions in China.

4.1   Proportional Distribution of Numbers

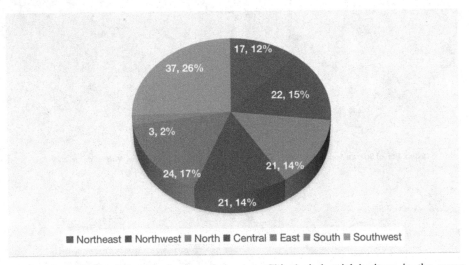

Fig. 4. Pie analysis of the distribution of the new China's industrial heritage in the seven administrative geographical divisions

As can be seen from Fig. 4, a quarter of New China's industrial heritage is distributed in the southwest, so it is of great significance to the cause of industrial heritage conservation and reuse in China to pay attention to the industrial heritage in the southwest. In addition, among the Seven Administrative Geographic Divisions, the number of New China's industrial heritage distributed in the southwest, northwest and northeast regions exceeds that of northern, eastern and central China. Therefore, the current situation of industrial and urban development in southwest, northwest and northeast China should be fully analyzed to guide the local practice of industrial heritage conservation and reuse, and avoid copying the cases of industrial heritage reuse in relatively more economically developed regions such as east and central China.

4.2 Distribution of Industry Types

In order to analyse more specifically the regional characteristics of the industrial heritage of New China, this paper analyses the industrial types of the New China's industrial heritage in the Seven Administrative Geographic Divisions of China. Sankey diagrams give emphasis to the size and direction offlows within a system, and because of their broad utility have beenapplied in many geographic or human-environment research con-texts [13]. In this study, the area to which the industrial heritage belongs and the type of industry form two attributes in this system. The Sankey diagram is used to analyze the mutual flow of these two attributes, to understand the relationship between the distribution area and the type of industrial heritage in New China.

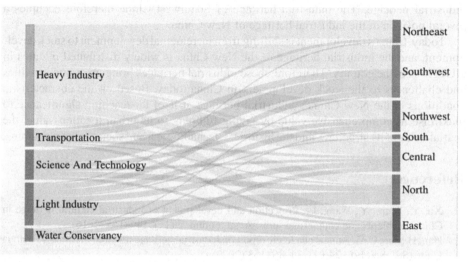

Fig. 5. Sankey diagrams of industrial heritage industries in the seven administrative geographical regions

As can be seen from Fig. 5, the industrial heritage in the Northeast is very homogeneous in terms of industrial heritage, with the majority being of the heavy industry type. Therefore, exploring how to reuse and develop the industrial heritage of the heavy industry category on a large scale, so as to promote the urban and industrial development of the northeast region, is an important issue in the industrial heritage protection in China today. In addition, the southwest region is home to half of China's technological industrial heritage. Therefore, it is important for the industrial heritage protection in the southwest region to explore how to develop industrial heritage of high technological and historical value, so that its values can be fully reflected and thus contribute to the development of culture and society in China, is worth to get attention in the protection of industrial heritage in Southwest China.

5 Conclusions and Insights

The visualisation study reveals that the industrial heritage of New China accounts for one-third of China's total industrial heritage. In contrast to the coastal tendency of the distribution of China's modern industrial heritage, the industrial heritage of New China is mainly distributed in the central, south-western and north-eastern parts of the country, with a spatial distribution characterised by macro-uniformity and micro-agglomeration. The industrial heritage of heavy industry is the most numerous and widely distributed type of industrial heritage in New China. Compared to the single industrial type of industrial heritage in the frontier regions, the industrial heritage in central and eastern China is richer in industrial types. In addition, Southwest China is home to a quarter of New China's industrial heritage and, moreover, gathers half of China's technological industrial heritage. The industrial heritage of Southwest China therefore occupies a pivotal position in the industrial heritage of New China.

Today, China's development is shifting from incremental development to stock development, and the industrial heritage of the New China is widely distributed in cities in all regions of the country. Therefore, these industrial heritages bring great opportunities and challenges to the stock development in China today. Based on the characteristic conditions of the New China's industrial heritage, it is of far-reaching significance to maximise its comprehensive value by giving full play to its urban location value, the spatial value of its structures and the historical, technological and social value it contains.

References

1. Xu, Y., Wang, Y., Wang, L.: Protection and development of industrial cultural heritage in China: problems and countermeasures. Acad. Forum **39**(11), 149–155 (2016)
2. Han, H., Sun, C.Y.: Annual academic report on industrial heritage research in China. J. Beihua Univ. (Soc. Sci. Ed.) **24**(01), 74–86+153 (2023)
3. Xu, S.: The significance of the industrial heritage of the third line construction: the perception of institutional value based on the meaning of political economy. Southeast Cult. (01), 6–11 (2020)
4. Dong, Z.K.: On the establishment of "156 items". Stud. Chin. Econ. Hist. (04), 95–109 (1999)
5. Xu, T.: The construction of the third line - the forerunner of the great development of western China. J. Southwest Inst. Nationalities (Philos. Soc. Sci. Ed.) (10), 4–6 (2002)
6. Zhao, Y.: Spatial distribution characteristics and influencing factors of industrial heritage in China. Archit. Cult. (09), 88–91 (2020)
7. Zeng, C., Liu, P., Liu, B., Huang, X., Cao, Y.: Temporal and spatial distribution characteristics and influencing factors of industrial heritage in China: a case study of the four batches of industrial heritage lists. Trop. Geogr. **42**(05), 740–750 (2022)
8. Cui, W., Wang, Z., Xu, B.: Spatial structure and determinants of world industrial heritages. Econ. Geogr. **37**(06), 198–205 (2017)
9. Zhang, J., Sun, H., Xu, S., Aoki, N.: Analysis of the spatial and temporal distribution and reuse of urban industrial heritage: the case of Tianjin, China. Land **11**(12), 2273 (2022). https://doi.org/10.3390/land11122273
10. Zhao, Q., Li, H.: Research on the spatial differentiation characteristics and formation mechanism of national industrial heritage. Urban Issues (11), 54–64 (2022)

11. Wikipedia contributors. Kernel density estimation. In Wikipedia, The Free Encyclopedia (2023). https://en.wikipedia.org/w/index.php?title=Kernel_density_estimation&oldid=1136297214. Accessed 27 Apr 2023
12. Xie, Z., Yan, J.: Kernel Density Estimation of traffic accidents in a network space. Comput. Environ. Urban Syst. **32**, 396–406 (2008)
13. Cuba, N.: Research note: Sankey diagrams for visualizing land cover dynamics. Landscape Urban Plan. **139**, 163–167 (2015)
14. Liu, B., Feng, Z.: Urban Industrial Land Renewal and Industrial Heritage Protection. China Construction Industry Press, Beijing (2009)
15. Wusih propose-pay attention to the protection of industrial heritage during the period of rapid economic development. ArchiCreation (08), 195–196 (2006)
16. Liu, B., Li, K.: A review of three important historical periods in China's industrial development. Beijing Plan. Rev. (01), 8–12 (2011)
17. Xv, S., Lai, S., Liu, J., Aoki, N.: A research on historical stages of urban industrial development in China. Architects' J. (06), 40–47 (2017)
18. Dong, Z., Wu, J.: The Founding Stone of China's Industry (156 Construction Studies 1950–2000). Guangdong Economic Publishing House (2004)
19. Yang, P., Yang, R.: Research on the protection of industrial building heritage of 156 projects during the "1st five year plan" period. Beijing Plan. Rev. (01), 13–17 (2011)
20. Dong, Z.: The establishment of "156 items". Res. Chin. Econ. Hist. (04), 95–109 (1999)
21. Gu, B., Li, W.: Study on the construction of industrial heritage corridor in the third line of Southwest China. Sichuan Archit. Sci. Res. **40**(03), 265–268 (2014)
22. Chen, D.: The third line construction: the closest industrial heritage. Party Gov. Forum (02), 84 (2007)
23. Han, F., Tong, Y.: Industrial heritage protection and tourism utilization in Northeast China. Econ. Geogr. **30**(01), 135–138+161 (2010)
24. Zhou, D., Liu, J.: City memories and cultural heritage—Chinese workers' village under the protection of industrial heritage. Nationalities Res. Qinghai **23**(02), 1–5 (2012)
25. Yao, Y., Zhang, L.: Population migration and social and economic development in Xinjiang from the beginning of the People's Republic of China to the "cultural revolution". Lantai World (13), 33–34 (2013)
26. Jiang, T.: Modern enlightenment from population changes and urban and rural population structure in modern China. Strategy Manag. (04), 69–75 (1994)
27. Shi, Y.: The enlightenment of modern industrialization in Hubei Province. Centurial Trip (07), 30–31 (2003)
28. Iqbal, N., Akbar, S.H., Van Cleempoel, K.: Identification of industrial heritage and a theoretical framework for an industrial heritage inventory system in Pakistan. Sustainability **14**, 5797 (2022)

Image/Video Big Data Analysis and Understanding

SCGTS: Semantic Content Guiding Teacher-Student Network for Group Activity Recognition

Zeyu Xi, Ge Shi, Lifang Wu[✉], and Xuefen Li

Faculty of Information Technology, Beijing University of Technology, Beijing 100124, China
xi961226@163.com

Abstract. Group activity recognition refers to the process of comprehending the activity performed by multi-person in a video. However, most methods need pre-defined individual labels during training or testing, which is impractical and lacks intelligence. Moreover, they only consider visual features and ignore corresponding semantic information. To address these issues, a Semantic Content Guiding Teacher-Student (SCGTS) network is developed. SCGTS depends neither on pre-defined individual labels nor on any detection methods. It utilizes a large-scale language model as the teacher network to extract content features from textual descriptions of labels. The semantic content features are then used to supervise the training of the baseline network which serves as the student network. In this way, the student network is enforced to mimic the teacher network to extract visual features with semantic information. Experiments on 2 challenging benchmarks, including Volleyball and NBA, demonstrate SCGTS outperforms the baseline network and achieves the leading performance.

Keywords: Group activity recognition · Semantic content guiding · Teacher-student network

1 Introduction

Group activity recognition (GAR) is an important task in the field of video understanding. This task is used to comprehend what a collective of people are doing in a video. GAR has been widely used in many fields, including safety monitoring, sports competitions and social media. Compared to traditional action recognition which primarily focuses on comprehending individual actions [1–5], GAR is a more challenging task as it demands further comprehending interactions among the actors. Hence, it's very important for GAR to precisely identify the coordinates of the individual actor and model the relation among the actors.

To tackle the challenges and difficulties of GAR, most existing methods in fully supervised setting require pre-defined individuals' bounding boxes by using off-the-shelf detectors for training and testing [6–11]. These methods extract visual features from individuals' bounding boxes and model the spatial and temporal relationships

W. Yongtian and W. Lifang (Eds.): IGTA 2023, CCIS 1910, pp. 125–140, 2023.
https://doi.org/10.1007/978-981-99-7549-5_10

between them by using graph convolution or Transformer [12]. Although these methods achieve advanced recognition performance, they require accurate and heavy manual labels during training and testing, which is impractical and unintelligent. Furthermore, the generalization of these methods is weak. It is very necessary to develop the methods based on the weakly supervised learning.

Methods based on weakly supervised learning have also been developed rapidly in recent years. Li et al. [13] use the LSTM [14] model to generate a caption for each frame. The set of captions is then used to predict group activity. This method is computationally complex and requires a tedious reasoning process. Zhang et al. [15] exploit individual action labels to estimate bounding boxes of actors at inference. This method still needs numerous real ground-truth bounding boxes in the training phase. Yan et al. [16] investigate GAR in weakly supervised setting which only provides video-level labels for each video clip. They use the off-the-shelf detector to generate individuals' bounding boxes instead of annotated boxes. But the detector may provide misleading proposal regions when facing similar objects and occlusion. Kim et al. [17] propose the Detector-free method with the Transformer model in weakly supervised setting. They put learnable tokens as input to the encoder so that each of them learns to localize partial contexts of a group activity. The group activity is estimated by modelling relationships among partial contexts. However, this method lacks textual semantic information, which can be viewed as complementary to visual information.

Inspired by people's ability to infer group activities from textual descriptions, we propose the Semantic Content Guiding Teacher-Student (SCGTS) network for GAR. And the baseline model is Detector-free. The first step is to collect relevant professional English explanations of NBA and Volleyball datasets' labels from professional sports platforms[1,2]. The explanations are highly relevant to the content of the video clip. A large-scale pre-training model BERT [18] is used to extract text content features. Since the BERT model is trained on a large-scale corpus database (such as Wikipedia[3]), it is directly served as a teacher network without any fine tuning. Detector-free serves as a student network. During training, textual features are used to supervise student network's training. The student network is enforced to mimic the teacher network to extract visual features with semantic information. The student network directly obtains the representation of group activity feature with semantic information according to the input video clip at inference.

We evaluate SCGTS on 2 datasets, Volleyball [9] and NBA [16]. SCGTS achieves the leading performance on 2 benchmarks in the weakly supervised setting. The contributions of this paper are as follows.

1. A large-scale pre-trained language model BERT is used to extract text features to help the model consider the corresponding semantic information.
2. A teacher-student network framework is proposed. Through a simple knowledge distillation method, the student network is forced to mimic the teacher network to extract the visual features with semantic information. The model does not consider more individual labels, which reduces more computation and manual annotations.

---

[1] https://jr.nba.com.

[2] https://www.fivb.com/en/volleyball.

[3] https://en.wikipedia.org/wiki/main_page.

3. On the two benchmarks, the proposed method outperforms the baseline network and achieve the leading performance. It even outperforms some GAR models which is based fully supervised learning.

2 Related Works

In this section, we will briefly review 3 related topics: 1) group activity recognition, 2) large-scale language model, 3) knowledge distillation.

2.1 Group Activity Recognition

Group activity recognition (GAR) is an important tasks in video understanding [19]. The methods of GAR can be roughly divided into 2 categories: hand-crafted feature based and deep learning feature based methods [20].

For hand-crafted feature based method, researchers utilize hand-crafted features to model the relationships between individuals and describe the group activity. Lan et al. [21] consider the contextual information such as actor-actor interaction and actor-group interaction into the group activity understanding system. Yan et al. [22] propose a cardinality kernel to model cardinality relations and count instance labels in a video. Shu et al. [23] and Amer et al. [24] design an AND-OR graph to model group activities. However, these methods heavily rely on prior knowledge and have the weak generalization ability.

For deep learning feature based method, researchers model group activity using deep learning methods. LSTM-based methods [7, 8, 25] use the CNN to extract individual visual features, which are then fed into LSTM to capture individual temporal-dynamic features. Graph-based methods [16, 27, 28] extract visual features from individual bounding boxes. These features are then represented as nodes in a graph. And edges are defined as the relationships between nodes. Transformer-based methods [7, 9, 10, 29] use Transformer model to embed spatiotemporal relational contexts. However, the above methods rely too much on the quality of the annotations and the performance of the detector. Detector-free [17] in weakly supervised setting depends neither on predefined individual labels nor on any off-the-shell detectors. Hence, we use this method as the baseline network and let it serve as a student network.

2.2 Large-Scale Pre-training Language Model

In recent years, large-scale pre-trained language models have become a popular research direction in natural language processing. These models are pre-trained on large-scale corpus, and can learn rich language knowledge.

Currently, the most representative large-scale pre-trained language models include GPT, BERT [18] and XLNet [30]. GPT uses self-regressive language model for pre-training and can generate coherent natural language text. BERT and XLNet use a combination of masked language model and self-regressive language model for pre-training, and can learn more comprehensive language knowledge. BERT is trained on the large corpora, such as Wikipedia, and can generate text features related to knowledge about sports. Unlike traditional self-regressive language models, BERT uses a bidirectional language model to better understand the meaning and semantics of words in text. We utilize BERT to extract the textual features of labels' descriptions. And the textual features are then used to supervise student network's learning.

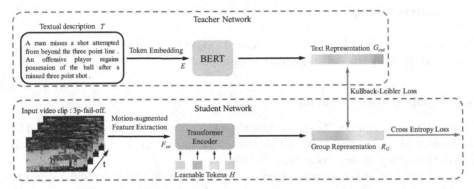

Fig. 1. SCGTS framework structure.

2.3 Knowledge Distillation

Hinton et al. [31] first propose the concept of "Knowledge distillation", which aims to improve model performance and reduce computation cost by transferring knowledge from a complex model to a simpler model. A large pre-trained model is typically used as the "teacher network", and its knowledge is transferred to a smaller model as the "student network".

Hao et al. [32] propose a spatiotemporal distilled dense-connectivity network for video action recognition to explore interactions between appearance and motion streams. Wu et al. [33] propose a multi-teacher knowledge distillation framework for compressed video action recognition to let student network learn more comprehensive and better knowledge. Feng et al. [34] propose a structural knowledge distillation scheme for skeleton-based action recognition to improve recognition model's robustness and minimize the accuracy degradations. However, the above methods only consider the visual features and ignore the semantic features. Tang et al. [35] explore the knowledge in 2 different domains (semantic domain and appearance domain) for GAR. But this method still relies on predefined individual labels. Different from [35], the SCGTS we proposed doesn't depend on individual labels. From the perspective of content guidance, the student network is enforced to mimic the teacher network to extract the group activity feature representation with semantic information.

3 Semantic Content Guiding Teacher-Student Network

The details of semantic content guiding teacher-student network (SCGTS) will be described in this section. As shown in Fig. 1, the proposed SCGTS mainly includes 2 parts: The upper branch is BERT network, which serves as teacher network. The lower branch is baseline network, which serves as student network. The textual features extracted by the teacher network serve as transfer knowledge to guide the student network's learning. In this way, student network is enforced to mimic the teacher network to extract the group activity video features with corresponding semantic information.

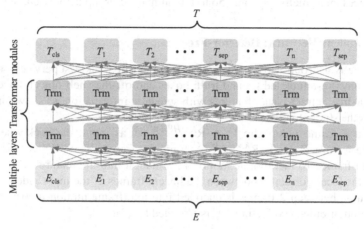

Fig. 2. BERT framework structure.

3.1 The Teacher Network: BERT

BERT is a language representation model whose full name is "Bidirectional encoder representations from transformer". The goal of BERT is to obtain textual feature representations containing rich semantic information through large-scale corpus training. BERT is a network with multiple Transformer modules. The Transformer module is composed of an encoder and a decoder, and the BERT only uses the encoder part of the Transformer. Each layer of the encoder consists of two parts: self-attention mechanism and feed-forward neural network. The BERT model utilizes the deep bidirectional representation of textual descriptions learned from the encoder. BERT consists of an input layer, an encoding layer and an output layer.

As shown in Fig. 2, $E\{E_{cls}, E_1, E_2, \ldots, E_{sep}, \ldots E_n, E_{sep}\}$ represents the embedded representation of the textual description T, which corresponds to the label. The encoding layer is composed of multiple stacked Transformer modules, and "Trm" represents the Transformer module. $T\{T_{cls}, T_1, T_2, \ldots, T_{sep}, \ldots T_n, T_{sep}\}$ represents the generated the word vector feature. Each element in E corresponds to each element in T. Special markers are added to the input text. Token "[CLS]" represents the classification of the sentence. Token "[SEP]" represents the end of the sentence and the interval between 2 sentences. Token "[CLS]" is located at the beginning of the sentence, its corresponding final hidden state will represent the global features of the input text, denoted as $G_{cls} \in R^{1 \times 256}$. We need to obtain the global feature representation of the textual description as the transfer knowledge to guide the learning of the student network. The text feature G_{out} is obtained by (1):

$$G_{out} = W_{fc}F_{bert}(E) \tag{1}$$

where $F_{bert}(\cdot)$ represents BERT network. And $W_{fc} \in \mathrm{R}^{256 \times N}$ represents the linear layer, which reduces the dimension from 256 to the number of group activity class N.

3.2 The Student Network: Detector-Free

Detector-free is a group activity recognition method in weakly supervised setting. It disregards any pre-annotated ground truth boxes and off-the-shelf object detectors. To let Detector-free extract visual features with semantic information, as shown in Fig. 1, it serves as the student network.

Given a K-frame video clip $V \in \mathrm{R}^{K \times H^0 \times W^0 \times 3}$ as input, the backbone ResNet extracts the feature $F_{video} \in \mathrm{R}^{K \times H \times W \times C}$ frame by frame. $H^0 \times W^0 \times 3$ is the size of the input frame. To incorporate motion information into the features, Detector-free calculates the local correlation between 2 adjacent frames of the input video clip. And the correlation between 2 frames is encoded into interframe motion information M^k. Then the motion-enhanced feature F_{en}^k is obtained by (2):

$$F_{en}^k = F_{video}^k + M^k \tag{2}$$

Given the motion-enhanced feature $F_{en} \in \mathrm{R}^{K \times H \times W \times C}$ for K frames and a set of L learned tokens $H = \{h_i\}_{i=1}^L$, the encoder of Transformer module outputs the group activity representation R_G.

$$R_G = W_V(F_{encoder}(F_{en}, H)) \tag{3}$$

where $W_V \in \mathrm{R}^{256 \times N}$ represents the linear layer, which reduces the dimension from 256 to the number of group activity class N. And $F_{encoder}(\cdot)$ represents the encoder module.

3.3 Semantic Guiding Knowledge Distillation

As far as we know, people can easily infer a certain group activity from a set of textual descriptions. Moreover, the baseline network (Detector-free) simply considers the visual features and ignores the textual semantic features, which can be viewed as complementary to visual information.

To incorporate the semantic information into visual features, we don't simply combine text features and visual features. The network is enhanced to extract the visual features with semantic information by using the method of knowledge distillation. This method allows the network to learn how to extract semantic information with minimum computational cost.

We use Kullback-Leibler (KL) and Cross Entropy (CE) loss as the supervision to train the student network. The KL loss is defined as:

$$L_{kl} = \sum_i P_G(\log(P_G) - \log(Q_R))$$

$$= \sum_i \delta\left(\frac{G_{out}}{\tau}\right)\left(\log\left(\delta\left(\frac{G_{out}}{\tau}\right)\right) - \log\left(\delta\left(\frac{R_G}{\tau}\right)\right)\right) \tag{4}$$

where P_G represents probability distribution of the text feature's each dimension. Q_R represents probability distribution of the visual feature's each dimension. $\delta(\cdot)$ is the Softmax function. Temperature τ is set to 3. And i represents the index of dimension.

The CE loss is defined as:

$$L_{ce} = -\sum_j R_G \cdot \log(Y) \tag{5}$$

where j represents the index of dimension and Y represents the ground truth label.

The total loss function is defined as:

$$L = \lambda L_{kl} + (1 - \lambda)L_{ce} \tag{6}$$

where λ represents the weights of KL and CE loss. In the whole model training, we set a larger weight of KL loss to enhance semantic features' influence on visual features. λ is set to 0.6. The network can learn how to extract visual features with semantic information on 2 kinds of constrains.

4 Experiments

To verify the performance of the proposed method, SCGTS is evaluated on 2 challenging datasets, including Volleyball [9] and NBA [16]. It is also compared with the state-of-the-art weakly supervised GAR and fully supervised GAR methods. And we further conduct the ablation experiments and provide the visualizations to verify the effectiveness of the proposed SCGTS.

4.1 Datasets

Volleyball Dataset. Volleyball is one of the most commonly used group activity recognition datasets. It has 3493 video clips for training and 1337 video clips for testing. Each video clip has 41 frames. The middle frame is labeled with one of 8 group activity labels. Players in each frame are labeled with their corresponding bounding boxes and action labels. However, in weakly supervised setting, the action labels are no longer used. Multi-class Classification Accuracy (MVA) and Merged MCA are adopted for evaluation during the experiments. Like SAM [16] and Detector-free [17], we merge the classes right set and right pass into right pass-set, and left set and left pass into left pass-set for a fair comparison. In addition, to extract textual features that fit the video contents and group activity labels, we search for relevant descriptions from the professional sport platform. The Volleyball group activity labels and corresponding textual descriptions are shown in Table 1.

NBA Dataset. NBA is a large-scale dataset that contains 7624 video clips for training and 1548 video clips for testing. It is the only dataset for GAR in weakly supervised setting. Each video clip is only labeled with one of 9 group activity labels. None of individual labels such as bounding boxes and action labels are provided. Each video clip has 72 frames. So, the dataset requires the method that captures long-term temporal dynamics. NBA is further a challenging dataset due to fast motion, camera view change, occlusion, similar objects and appearance deformation in each video clip. Multi-class Classification Accuracy (MCA) and Mean Per Class Accuracy (MPCA) are adopted for evaluation during the experiments. We search for relevant descriptions of labels from the professional sport platform. The NBA group activity labels and corresponding textual descriptions are shown in Table 2.

Table 1. Volleyball dataset group activity labels and corresponding textual descriptions.

Labels	Textual descriptions of the labels
r_set	Back set performed by the second setter who is positioned on the right side of the volleyball court
r_spike	Powerful attacking action performed by the opposite hitter positioned on the right side of the volleyball court
r_pass	Cross-court passing action initiated by the libero or outside hitter positioned on the right side of the volleyball court
r_winpoint	Players on the right side of the court celebrate together
l_set	Back set performed by the second setter who is positioned on the left side of the volleyball court
l_spike	Powerful attacking action performed by the opposite hitter positioned on the left side of the volleyball court
l_pass	Cross-court passing action initiated by the libero or outside hitter positioned on the left side of the volleyball court
l_winpoint	Players on the left side of the court celebrate together

4.2 Implementation Details

Sampling Strategy. T frames are sampled by using segment-based method [36]. Each frame size is 720 × 1280. Concretely, T is set to 5 in Volleyball dataset and T is set to 18 in NBA dataset.

Hyperparameters. The proposed SCGTS's teacher network is BERT$_{BASE}$. The number of layers in BERT is 12 and the hidden size is 512. The number of self-attention heads is 12. And the student network is the baseline network which is called Detector-free. We stack 6 Transformer encoder layers with 4 attention heads and 256 channels for the NBA dataset, and 2 Transformer encoder layers with 2 attention heads and 256 channels for the Volleyball dataset.

Training. The optimization is ADAM [37] with $\beta_1 = 0.9$, $\beta_2 = 0.999$, and $\varepsilon = 1e-8$. There are 40 training epochs in total. When performing training in the first 5 epochs, the warmup learning rate of $5e-5$ is used to train the student network for Volleyball dataset and NBA dataset. From the 6th epoch of training, the student network is trained with learning rate decayed from $5e - 5$ to $5e - 7$. Since BERT model has been pre-trained on large-scale datasets, it can extract a large amount of rich semantic knowledge. And the size of the group activity recognition dataset and textual descriptions are not enough to fine tune the BERT model. Therefore, in training phase, the output of teacher network is directly used as the supervision information to train the student network. The proposed SCGTS is implemented with Python 3.9 and PyTorch 1.12 and is performed on a server with a Nvidia 3090ti GPU and a 12th Gen Intel (R) Core (TM) i9-12900k × 24 CPU.

Table 2. NBA dataset group activity labels and corresponding textual descriptions.

Labels	Textual descriptions of the labels
2p-succ	A man makes a shot attempted from inside of the three point line
2p-fail.-off	A man misses a shot attempted from inside of the three point line. An offensive player regains possession of the ball after a missed two point shot
2p-fail.-def	A man misses a shot attempted from inside of the three point line. A defensive player gains possession of the ball after an offensive player misses two-point shot
2p-layup-succ	A man makes a shot which is a two point shot attempt made by leaping from below, laying the ball up near the basket, and using one hand to bounce it off the backboard and into the basket
2p-layup-fail.-off	A man misses a shot which is a two point shot attempt made by leaping from below, laying the ball up near the basket, and using one hand to bounce it off the backboard and into the basket. An offensive player regains possession of the ball after a missed layup shot
2p-layup-fail.-def	A man misses a shot which is a two point shot attempt made by leaping from below, laying the ball up near the basket, and using one hand to bounce it off the backboard and into the basket. A defensive player gains possession of the ball after an offensive player misses layup shot
3p-succ	A man makes a shot attempted from beyond the three point line
3p-fail.-off	A man misses a shot attempted from beyond the three point line. An offensive player regains possession of the ball after a missed three point shot
3p-fail.-def	A man misses a shot attempted from beyond the three point line. A defensive player gains possession of the ball after an offensive player misses three point shot

4.3 Comparison with the State-of-the-Art Methods

Volleyball Dataset. The proposed SCGTS is compared with the state-of-the-art methods in 2 settings: fully supervised setting and weakly supervised setting. Note that these methods only use the RGB inputs for a fair comparison. As shown in Table 3, SCGTS has the best results in weakly supervised setting methods. Compared with Detector-free (baseline network), SCGTS improves the score by 0.6 for MCA and 0.4 for merged MCA. Compared with SAM, SCGTS improves the score by 4.8 for MCA and 1.7 for merged MCA. SCGTS even outperforms some advanced methods in fully supervised setting. Compared with SACRF, SCGTS improves the score by 0.4 for MCA and 2.1 for merged MCA. All of these results demonstrate that our method is competitive. And with the help of textual supervision, the performance of the baseline is improved.

Table 3. Comparison with the state-of-the-art methods on the Volleyball dataset. Numbers in **bold** indicate the best performance and underlined ones are the second best.

Method	Backbone	MCA	Merged MCA
Fully supervised			
ARG [11]	ResNet-18	91.1	95.1
HigCIN [27]	ResNet-18	91.4	-
AT [7]	ResNet-18	90.0	94.0
SACRF [29]	ResNet-18	90.7	92.7
DIN [28]	ResNet-18	93.1	**95.6**
SPTS [35]	DCNN	89.3	-
TCE+STBiP [10]	VGG-16	**94.1**	-
GroupFormer [9]	Inception-v3	**94.1**	-
Weakly supervised			
ARG [11]	ResNet-18	87.4	92.9
AT [7]	ResNet-18	84.3	89.6
SACRF [29]	ResNet-18	83.3	86.1
DIN [28]	ResNet-18	86.5	93.1
SAM [16]	ResNet-18	86.3	93.1
Detector-free [17]	ResNet-18	90.5	94.4
Ours	ResNet-18	**91.1**	**94.8**

NBA Dataset. We compare the proposed SCGTS with the advanced methods in fully supervised setting and weakly supervised setting. Their backbones are ResNet-18 and they only use the RGB frames as input for a fair comparison. Table 4 summarizes the results. The proposed SCGTS outperforms all the methods. Specifically, SCGTS outperforms Detector-free by 0.6 and 0.4 for the MCA score and MPCA score, respectively. Compared with SAM, SCGTS improves the score by 22.1 for MCA and 19.9 for MPCA. These results indicate even though NBA is a challenging dataset due to fast motion, camera view change and occlusion in each video clip. SCGTS can still better cope with these challenges.

Table 4. Comparison with the state-of-the-art methods on the NBA dataset. Numbers in **bold** indicate the best performance and underlined ones are the second best.

Method	MCA	MPCA
TSM [38]	66.6	60.3
VideoSwin [39]	64.3	60.6
ARG [11]	59.0	56.8
SACRF [29]	56.3	52.8
DIN [28]	61.6	56.0
SAM [16]	54.3	51.5
Detector-free [17]	75.8	71.2
Ours	**76.4**	**71.4**

4.4 Ablation Studies

The main innovation of SCGTS is that textual features serve as supervised information to guide student network's training. To study its effectiveness, comparative ablation experiments are carried out on Volleyball. The MCA score and Merged MCA score are used to evaluate the method's performance. Table 5 summarizes the effect of this approach. Baseline is the Detector-free. SCGTS's teacher network is BERT model. And its student network is Detector-free model.

Table 5. Ablation on teacher network guiding training strategy. Numbers in **bold** indicate the best performance.

Model	MCA	Merged MCA
Baseline	90.5	94.4
Baseline+BERT	**91.1**	**94.8**

When choosing the loss function, we also conduct the corresponding ablation experiments. The loss function is designed with multi-task learning. The Cross Entropy (CE) loss of the student network is fixed. The loss function between teacher network and student network needs to choose with corresponding experiments. Candidate loss functions are L1 loss, L2 loss, Smooth L1 loss (S_L1), Cosine similarity (CS) Loss and Kullback-Leibler (KL) loss. Temperature τ is set to 3 in KL loss. In the experiments, we assume that the weight of both candidate loss and CE loss is 1. As shown in Table 6, the addition of different loss functions makes network have different performance on Volleyball. It can be seen from the table that the MCA score and Merged MCA score of SCGTS with KL Loss is higher than other methods and the addition of other loss functions actually reduce the network performance.

Table 6. Different loss functions and performance comparison on Volleyball. Numbers in **bold** indicate the best performance.

Model	MCA	Merged MCA
SCGTS (L1 Loss)	90.8	94.4
SCGTS (L2 Loss)	88.7	89.0
SCGTS (S_L1 Loss)	90.5	92.3
SCGTS (CS Loss)	84.5	87.2
SCGTS (KL Loss)	**90.9**	**94.6**

Since it is the multi-task learning, the value of weight λ between KL loss and CE loss needs to be selected by experiments. To highlight the effect of teacher network on student network, KL loss should be weighted more heavily than CE loss. Therefore, in the experiment, alpha goes from 0.6 to 0.9 increases gradually in unit of 0.1. As shown in Table 7, the different weight settings of the KL loss make network have different performance on Volleyball. The performance of network is the best when λ is set to 0.6. And the MCA score and the merged MCA score are 91.1 and 94.8, respectively.

Table 7. Different weight settings and performance comparison on Volleyball. Numbers in **bold** indicate the best performance.

Model	MCA	Merged MCA
KL loss ($\lambda = 0.6$)	**91.1**	**94.8**
KL loss ($\lambda = 0.7$)	91.0	94.3
KL loss ($\lambda = 0.8$)	90.1	92.6
KL loss ($\lambda = 0.9$)	90.0	94.6

4.5 Visual Analysis

Figure 3 shows the t-SNE visualization for embedding the video representation learned by baseline method and our method on Volleyball dataset and NBA dataset. Specifically, the group activity representations of video clips are projected on the validation set of Volleyball dataset and NBA dataset into 2-dimensional space using t-SNE. It can be seen that the video-level representations learned by SCGTS are better separated.

Figure 4 presents the comparison of confusion matrices on the baseline method and our method. For baseline method, "right set" is sometimes confused with the activity "right pass", and "2p-succ." is likely to be misclassified as "2p-layup-succ.". This is because in volleyball game, the appearance of activity set and activity pass are visually very similar, which is easy to be confused. In basketball game, 2 point shot and 2 point layup shot is belongs to 2 point shot. But the textual descriptions of these activities are not

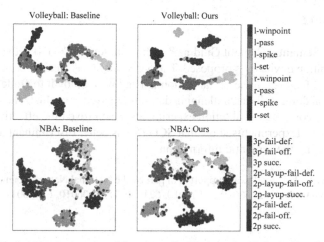

Fig. 3. T-SNE visualization results of feature embedding on the Volleyball and NBA datasets.

the same. When applying our method, we clearly find that this phenomenon is alleviated. This is because semantic differences help the model better distinguish between actions which look similar. These visualization results indicate our SCGTS method is more effective for group activity recognition. Moreover, extracting the visual features with semantic information leads to better discriminate group activities.

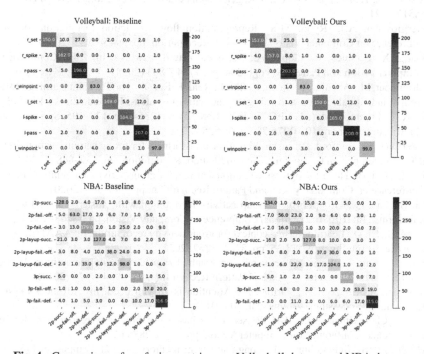

Fig. 4. Comparison of confusion matrices on Volleyball dataset and NBA dataset.

5 Conclusion

In this paper, a Semantic Content Guiding Teacher-Student (SCGTS) network for group activity recognition in videos is proposed. The proposed SCGTS explores the knowledge of global textual features in the semantic domain and we employ it to guide the learning process in visual domain. Two challenging datasets are used to evaluate the performance of SCGTS. The comparative ablation experiments have proved the effectiveness of the proposed method. Experiments show that SCGTS has better discriminant ability due to further considering the semantic information.

Acknowledgment. This work was supported in part by the National Natural Science Foundation of China under Grant NO. 62236010, 61976010, 62106011, 62106010, 62176011.

References

1. Fan, L., Huang, W.: Identification of common molecular subsequences. In: IEEE Conference on Computer Vision and Pattern Recognition, pp. 6016–6025 (2001)
2. Girdhar, R., Carreira, J.: Video action transformer network. In: IEEE Conference on Computer Vision and Pattern Recognition, pp. 244–253 (2019)
3. Kwon, H., Kim, M., Kwak, S., Cho, M.: Motionsqueeze: neural motion feature learning for video understanding. In: Vedaldi, A., Bischof, H., Brox, T., Frahm, J.-M. (eds.) ECCV 2020. LNCS, vol. 12361, pp. 345–362. Springer, Cham (2020). https://doi.org/10.1007/978-3-030-58517-4_21
4. Piergiovanni, A.J., Ryoo, M.S.: Representation flow for action recognition. In: IEEE Conference on Computer Vision and Pattern Recognition, pp. 9945–9953 (2019)
5. Wang, X., Girshick, R., Gupta, A.: Non-local neural networks. In: IEEE Conference on Computer Vision and Pattern Recognition, pp. 7794–7803 (2018)
6. Ehsanpour, M., Abedin, A., Saleh, F., Shi, J., Reid, I., Rezatofighi, H.: Joint learning of social groups, individuals action and sub-group activities in videos. In: Vedaldi, A., Bischof, H., Brox, T., Frahm, J.-M. (eds.) ECCV 2020. LNCS, vol. 12354, pp. 177–195. Springer, Cham (2020). https://doi.org/10.1007/978-3-030-58545-7_11
7. Gavrilyuk, K., Sanford, R., Javan, M.: Actor-transformers for group activity recognition. In: IEEE Conference on Computer Vision and Pattern Recognition, pp. 839–848 (2020)
8. Hu, G., Cui, B., He, Y.: Progressive relation learning for group activity recognition. In: IEEE Conference on Computer Vision and Pattern Recognition, pp. 980–989 (2020)
9. Li, S., Cao, Q.: GroupFormer: group activity recognition with clustered spatial-temporal transformer. In: IEEE International Conference on Computer Vision, pp. 13668–13677 (2021)
10. Yuan, H., Ni, D.: Learning visual context for group activity recognition. In: AAAI Conference on Artificial Intelligence, vol.35, pp. 3261–3269 (2021)
11. Wu, J., Wang, L.: Learning actor relation graphs for group activity recognition. In: IEEE Conference on Computer Vision and Pattern Recognition, pp. 9964–9974 (2019)
12. Vaswani, A., Shazeer, N., Parmar, N.: Attention is all you need. In: Advances in Neural Information Processing Systems, vol. 30 (2017)
13. Li, X., Choo Chuah, M.: SBGAR: semantics based group activity recognition. In: IEEE International Conference on Computer Vision, pp. 2876–2885 (2017)
14. Hochreiter, S., Schmidhuber, J.: Long short-term memory. Neural Comput. **9**, 1735–1780 (1997)

15. Zhang, P., Tang, Y.: Fast collective activity recognition under weak supervision. IEEE Trans. Image Process. **29**, 29–43 (2019)

16. Yan, R., Xie, L., Tang, J., Shu, X., Tian, Q.: Social adaptive module for weakly-supervised group activity recognition. In: Vedaldi, A., Bischof, H., Brox, T., Frahm, J.-M. (eds.) ECCV 2020. LNCS, vol. 12353, pp. 208–224. Springer, Cham (2020). https://doi.org/10.1007/978-3-030-58598-3_13

17. Kim, D., Lee, J.: Detector-free weakly supervised group activity recognition. In: IEEE Conference on Computer Vision and Pattern Recognition, pp. 20083–20093 (2022)

18. Devlin, J., Chang, M.W.: BERT: pre-training of deep bidirectional transformers for language understanding. arXiv:1810.04805 (2018)

19. Wu, L., Lang, X., Xiang, Y.: Active spatial positions based hierarchical relation inference for group activity recognition. IEEE Trans. Circuits Syst. Video Technol. **33**(6), 2839–2851 (2023). https://doi.org/10.1109/TCSVT.2022.3228731

20. Wu, L., Wang, Q., Jian, M.: A comprehensive review of group activity recognition in videos. Int. J. Autom. Comput. **18**, 334–350 (2021)

21. Lan, T., Wang, Y., Yang, W.: Discriminative latent models for recognizing contextual group activities. IEEE Trans. Pattern Anal. Mach. Intell. **34**, 1549–1562 (2011)

22. Hajimirsadeghi, H., Yan, W., Vahdat, A.: Visual recognition by counting instances: a multi-instance cardinality potential kernel. In: IEEE Conference on Computer Vision and Pattern Recognition, pp. 2596–2605 (2015)

23. Shu, T., Xie, D., Rothrock, B.: Joint inference of groups, events and human roles in aerial videos. In: IEEE Conference on Computer Vision and Pattern Recognition, pp. 4576–4584 (2015)

24. Amer, M.R., Xie, D., Zhao, M., Todorovic, S., Zhu, S.-C.: Cost-sensitive top-down/bottom-up inference for multiscale activity recognition. In: Fitzgibbon, A., Lazebnik, S., Perona, P., Sato, Y., Schmid, C. (eds.) ECCV 2012. LNCS, vol. 7575, pp. 187–200. Springer, Heidelberg (2012). https://doi.org/10.1007/978-3-642-33765-9_14

25. Shu, T., Todorovic, S., Zhu, S.C.: CERN: confidence-energy recurrent network for group activity recognition. In: IEEE Conference on Computer Vision and Pattern Recognition, pp. 5523–5531 (2017)

26. Wang, M., Ni, B., Yang, X.: Recurrent modeling of interaction context for collective activity recognition. In: IEEE Conference on Computer Vision and Pattern Recognition, pp. 3048–3056 (2017)

27. Yan, R., Xie, L., Tang, J.: HiGCIN: hierarchical graph-based cross inference network for group activity recognition. IEEE Trans. Pattern Anal. Mach. Intell. (2020)

28. Yuan, H., Ni, D., Wang, M.: Spatio-temporal dynamic inference network for group activity recognition. In: IEEE Conference on Computer Vision and Pattern Recognition, pp. 7476–7485 (2021)

29. Pramono, R.R.A., Chen, Y.T., Fang, W.H.: Empowering relational network by self-attention augmented conditional random fields for group activity recognition. In: Vedaldi, A., Bischof, H., Brox, T., Frahm, J.-M. (eds.) ECCV 2020. LNCS, vol. 12346, pp. 71–90. Springer, Cham (2020). https://doi.org/10.1007/978-3-030-58452-8_5

30. Yang, Z., Dai, Z., Yang, Y.: XLNet: generalized autoregressive pretraining for language understanding. In: Advances in Neural Information Processing Systems, vol. 32 (2019)

31. Hinton, G., Vinyals, O., Dean, J.: Distilling the knowledge in a neural network. arXiv:1503.02531 (2015)

32. Hao, W., Zhang, Z.: Spatiotemporal distilled dense-connectivity network for video action recognition. Pattern Recogn. **92**, 13–23 (2019)

33. Wu, M.C., Chiu, C.T.: Multi-teacher knowledge distillation for compressed video action recognition based on deep learning. J. Syst. Archit. **103**, 101695 (2020). https://doi.org/10.1016/j.sysarc.2019.101695

34. Bian, C., Feng, W., Wan, L.: Structural knowledge distillation for efficient skeleton-based action recognition. IEEE Trans. Image Process. **30**, 2963–2976 (2021)
35. Tang, Y., Wang, Z., Li, P.: Mining semantics-preserving attention for group activity recognition. In: 26th ACM International Conference on Multimedia, pp. 1283–1291 (2018)
36. Wang, L., Xiong, Y., Wang, Z.: Temporal segment networks: towards good practices for deep action recognition. In: Leibe, B., Matas, J., Sebe, N., Welling, M. (eds.) ECCV 2016. LNCS, vol. 9912, pp. 20–36. Springer, Cham (2016). https://doi.org/10.1007/978-3-319-46484-8_2
37. Kingma, D.P., Ba, J.: Adam: a method for stochastic optimization. arXiv:1412.6980 (2014)
38. Lin, J., Gan, C., Han, S.: TSM: temporal shift module for efficient video understanding. In: IEEE International Conference on Computer Vision, pp. 7083–9093 (2019)
39. Lin, Z., Ning, J., Cao, Y.: Video swin transformer. In: IEEE Conference on Computer Vision and Pattern Recognition, pp. 3202–3211 (2022)

Infrared Small Target Detection Based on Prior Weighed Sparse Decomposition

Dongning Yang[1,2,3], Haopeng Zhang[1,2,3]($\boxtimes$) (iD), Fengying Xie[1,2,3], and Zhiguo Jiang[1,2,3]

[1] Department of Aerospace Information Engineering (Image Processing Center), School of Astronautics, Beihang University, Beijing 102206, China
{yangdongning,zhanghaopeng,xfy_73,jiangzg}@buaa.edu.cn
[2] Beijing Key Laboratory of Digital Media, Beijing 102206, China
[3] Key Laboratory of Spacecraft Design Optimization and Dynamic Simulation Technologies, Ministry of Education, Beijing 102206, China

Abstract. Infrared small target detection is a critical topic and research focus in target detection. Compared to visible light and radar detection, infrared imaging-based detection can effectively avoid illumination limitations and potential exposure risks. However, detecting small infrared targets with complex backgrounds and significant noise is challenging, and existing algorithms often have low detection rates, high false alarm rates, long calculation times, and unsatisfactory performance. To address these issues, we proposes an infrared small target detection algorithm based on sparse representation. The algorithm enhances target sparsity through multi-scale contrast saliency mapping and global gray value fusion, leveraging the low rank of the background. We evaluate the proposed method on SIRST dataset and compare its performance with traditional and recent algorithms. The results demonstrate the superiority of our algorithm in terms of detection rate, false alarm rate, and calculation time.

Keywords: Infrared image · Small target detection · Sparse decomposition

1 Introduction

Detection systems today can be categorized into three types based on the detection method and image type obtained: visible light detection, radar system detection, and infrared imaging detection [7]. Visible light detection is limited to daytime due to lighting constraints, while radar system detection carries potential risks in military applications, as it requires active emission of electromagnetic waves [18]. Infrared detection, based on imaging, effectively overcomes the limitations of the two aforementioned methods and possesses strong penetration

© The Author(s), under exclusive license to Springer Nature Singapore Pte Ltd. 2024
W. Yongtian and W. Lifang (Eds.): IGTA 2023, CCIS 1910, pp. 141–153, 2024.
https://doi.org/10.1007/978-981-99-7549-5_11

capabilities, reducing external interferences such as smog and cloud cover [7,18]. These features make infrared detection an efficient alternative or supplement to visible light and radar detection systems. Due to the characteristics and the limitations of conditions in practical applications, the detection of infrared small targets has difficulties [12]. Infrared small targets are difficult to detect due to their small size and low energy, which makes it challenging to extract features such as texture and shape. Additionally, the lack of color features in grayscale infrared images makes it difficult to use conventional image-based target detection methods. And the low signal-to-noise ratio and the presence of pulse noise further increase the false alarm rate in the detection of small infrared targets. And the complex background in infrared images, including buildings and other structures, requires algorithms with higher robustness.

In this paper, we present a novel approach for infrared small target detection using sparse decomposition. The detection of small targets in infrared images poses significant challenges due to the low contrast and complex background. Our algorithm addresses these challenges by constructing a prior weight map using a fusion of local multi-scale contrast maps and global grayscale. The weight map enhances the sparsity of the infrared small target and the low rank of the background in infrared images.

To validate the feasibility and effectiveness of our proposed algorithm, we compared its performance with several state-of-the-art infrared small target detection algorithms, including those based on the human vision system, deep learning, and sparse representation. We evaluated and compared the algorithms using several performance metrics, such as detection rate, false alarm rate, background suppression factor, and signal-to-clutter ratio gain.

Moreover, we analyzed the advantages and disadvantages of various methods and provided potential reasons for their performance. Our results demonstrate that our proposed algorithm outperforms the other methods in terms of both performance and computational efficiency.

The contributions of our work are as follows:

(1) We propose a novel approach to calculate a prior weight map based on the fusion of multiscale contrast and global grayscale before sparse decomposition. This approach improves the performance of infrared small target detection by better exploiting the underlying sparsity and low-rank structure of infrared images.
(2) We evaluate our proposed algorithm on the SIRST dataset, and the results show that our algorithm achieves superior performance compared to existing state-of-the-art methods.
(3) We provide a comprehensive analysis of the advantages and limitations of various methods, which can serve as a useful reference for future research in the field of infrared small target detection.

2 Related Work

The current mainstream methods for detecting infrared small targets based on a single frame image typically relies on some assumptions about the target and background to build a model and design an algorithm. Adopting more general and effective assumptions can improve the algorithm's robustness.

2.1 Methods Based on Human Visual System

The Human Visual System (HVS) is a highly evolved information processing system that is critical to human perception. Several infrared small target detection algorithms based on HVS have been proposed, such as a classic image saliency detection method by Itti et al. [18] and the local gradient and contrast method by Xiong Bin et al. [13], which use grayscale contrast to detect small targets due to the lack of color information in infrared images. These methods enhance the overall performance of the detection models by incorporating the visual process of the human eye.

2.2 Methods Based on Deep Learning

In recent years, deep learning technology has been widely applied in infrared small target detection. Hyper-Net [8] combines shallow and deep network features into a hyper feature space to maintain information integrity of small targets. SSD [10] is a regression-based target detection algorithm that extracts features from different scale feature maps to improve the detection rate. The RSSD network [6] uses rainbow concatenation to fuse feature maps of different layers, increasing the number of feature maps and enhancing the connection between them to improve performance.

2.3 Methods Based on Sparse Decomposition

Target detection algorithm based on sparse characteristics regards the image as a linear combination of three parts, namely the background f_B, target f_T, and noise parts f_N. Gao et al. proposed a method based on low-rank matrix sparse decomposition that utilizes patch images to enhance spatial correlation [4]. Since then, various techniques have been proposed to further improve detection performance. For example, Wang et al. used full variable regularization and principal component tracking [11], Dai et al. introduced the concept of singular value partial sum into patch images [1], and Zhang et al. developed the Non-Convex Rank Approximation Minimization (NRAM) method based on non-convex low-rank optimization [14]. He et al. extended the concept of single subspace to multi-subspace and proposed a method based on low-rank sparse representation [17], while Zhang et al. constructed a tensor to extend the original space to a 3D tensor space and improved the use of spatial correlation through the Reweighted Infrared Patch-Tensor (RIPT) method [16].

3   Method

We uses the partial sums of tensor kernel norms as a proxy for the low-rankness of tensor images [15]. For the first time, we added the concept of a prior weight map to the optimization function. This reduces the influence of edges on the detection results to a certain extent and decreases the false alarm rate. To improve the performance of small target detection, we used an algorithm that fuses a local multi-scale contrast map with the global grayscale to obtain the prior weight map (Fig. 1).

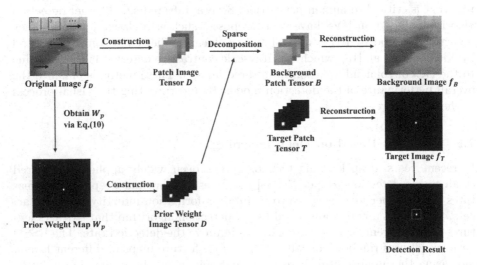

Fig. 1. The Whole Flowchart of Our Method

3.1   Construction of Image Tensor

Infrared small target detection based on tensor models transforms the original method of unfolding each image into columns and synthesizing a patch image into directly stacking the images obtained by sliding in the direction perpendicular to the image plane, resulting in a three-dimensional tensor. The construction method is illustrated in Fig. 2.

During the construction of the tensor, the patches, such as clouds, in the infrared image still exhibit spatial correlation in the three-dimensional tensor space. Therefore, the background in any slice of the three-dimensional tensor still satisfies low rank. Furthermore, since the target appears continuously in the adjacent sliding images, the constructed tensor still satisfies the continuity of the target in the three-dimensional space when the selected sliding step size is appropriate. Since the target exhibits sparsity in the original image, the objects obtained in image tensors are still sparse.

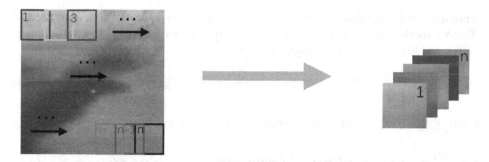

Fig. 2. Construction of Image Tensor. Image patches are transformed into a $k \times k \times n$ tensor, where $k \times k$ is the size of image patch and n is the amount of image patches.

3.2   Sparse Decomposition in Tensor Space

In the tensor space we constructed, assumptions can be made about the noise that for some $\delta > 0$, there is $||N||_F \leq \delta$, which can be rewritten as:

$$||\mathcal{D} - \mathcal{B} - \mathcal{T}||_F \leq \delta \tag{1}$$

where $\mathcal{D}, \mathcal{B}, \mathcal{T}, \mathcal{N} \in R^{m \times n \times k}$ represents input patch tensor, background patch tensor, target patch tensor, noise patch tensor respectively. $||.||_F$ represents Frobenius norm. We can separate $\mathcal{D}$ from $\mathcal{T}$ by solving the following tensor robust principal component analysis (TRPCA) problem:

$$\min_{\mathcal{B},\mathcal{T}} rank(\mathcal{B}) + \lambda||\mathcal{T}||_0, s.t. \mathcal{D} = \mathcal{B} + \mathcal{T} \tag{2}$$

where $||.||_0$ represents l_0 norm.

3.3   Representation of Tensor Sparsity

In RIPT [16], the low-rank of the background tensor is represented by the Sum of Nuclear Norms (SNN), which is defined as:

$$SNN = \sum_i ||X_{(i)}||_* \tag{3}$$

where $||.||_*$ represents the nuclear norm, that is, the sum of the singular values of the matrix. SNN is used as alternatives to hard-to-compute tensor kernel norms. But SNN has limitations, and the obtained solutions are often not optimal, which means using SNN as Representation of tensor sparsity causes false alarm [15].

The Tensor Nuclear Norm (TNN) is derived from t-SVD and has been shown to have better performance than the Singular Nuclear Norm (SNN). However, as larger singular values correspond to image details and should be assigned smaller weights, it is not reasonable for SNN and TNN to process each singular value in the same way. To address this issue, it is more appropriate to use non-convex relaxation with unequal weights. We extend the Partial Sum of Singular Values (PSSV) method proposed by Zuo et al. [19] to tensors, and use the Partial Sum of Tensor Nuclear Norms instead of TNN.

$$||X||_{PSTNN} = \sum_{i=1}^{n_i} ||\overline{X}^{(i)}||_{p=N} \tag{4}$$

where $||.||_{p=N}$ represents partial sum of singular value.

3.4   Construction of Prior Weight Map

The PSTNN algorithm proposed in [15] employs local priors based on angular strength functions, which only consider the local gradient features to obtain the local prior weight tensor. However, this method neglects the global positional relationship of pixels, which may result in target shrinkage in the presence of complex bright backgrounds. Additionally, this method tends to identify many regions in the local structure prior weight map as targets, leading to higher false alarm rates.

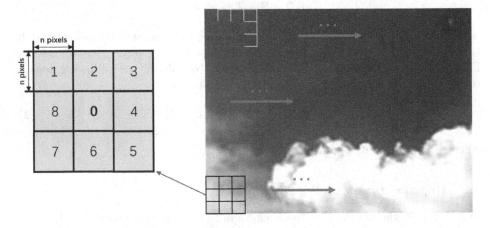

Fig. 3. Acquisition of local contrast

In our algorithm, we utilize a fusion of multi-scale contrast map and global gray scale to obtain a prior weight map, as depicted in Fig. 3. Firstly, we employ a 3 × 3 sliding frame to number the 9 units of the sliding frame in an infrared image. The central unit is used for calculating the contrast, but it is crucial to include the small target in this unit as much as possible. Additionally, the size of this unit should not be too much larger than the small target so that the background can be suppressed more accurately. The local contrast of the center pixel can be calculated by:

$$C_{(x,y)}^i = [(\frac{L_n}{G_i})exp(\frac{L_n}{G_i}) - 1] \tag{5}$$

where $i = 1, 2, ..., 8$ represents the numbered sliding frame. (x, y) is the center of area 0, and A_i is the set of pixel values in area i. The parameter G_i represents the mean of the largest m_2 elements in A_i, which can effectively reduce the impact of impulse noise in the neighborhood on contrast detection. To distinguish the target and the edge area, we take the minimum value in $C^i_{(x,y)}$ as the local contrast of the pixel. Then, the visual saliency map can be calculated as:

$$C_{(x,y)} = (C_{min} - 1) \times G_0 \tag{6}$$

where $C_{(x,y)}$ is LCM of center pixel(x, y), G_0 is the mean of the largest m_1 elements, which can reduce false alarm in center area.

Because using only a fixed scale of contrast cannot achieve good detection results for all sizes of infrared small targets, so we use the maximum value of the contrast of different L scales as the final contrast of the pixel.

$$SM_{(x,y)} = C_{m(x,y)} = max(C_{l_i(x,y)}), i = 1, 2, ..., L \tag{7}$$

To avoid losing target in complex backgrounds such as buildings, we fuse the LCM with the global gray value(which represents the information of background) by:

$$W_p(x, y) = \begin{cases} 0.3 \times D_{(x,y)}, & SM_{(x,y)} < 0 \\ 0.5 \times D_{(x,y)}, & 0 < SM_{(x,y)} < \mu \\ 1 \times D_{(x,y)}, & \mu < SM_{(x,y)} < \mu + 2\sigma \\ 1.5 \times D_{(x,y)}, & \mu + 2\sigma < SM_{(x,y)} < \mu + 4\sigma \\ 1.8 \times D_{(x,y)}, & \mu + 4\sigma < SM_{(x,y)} < \mu + 6\sigma \\ 5 \times D_{(x,y)}, & SM_{(x,y)} > \mu + 6\sigma \end{cases} \tag{8}$$

where $W_p(x, y)$ is the prior weight map, $D_{(x,y)}$ is the gray value of the original infrared image at (x, y) coefficient in (16) are determined experimentally. μ is the mean value of the significance contrast, and σ is the standard deviation of the significance contrast.

3.5 Optimization Problem Construction and Solution

After using l_1 norm to relax non-smooth and discrete l_0 norm, the small target detection problem with prior weight map can be written as:

$$\min_{\mathcal{B},\mathcal{T}} ||\mathcal{B}||_{PSTNN} + \lambda ||\mathcal{T} \otimes \mathcal{W}_{rec}||_1, s.t. \mathcal{D} = \mathcal{B} + \mathcal{T} \tag{9}$$

where $\otimes$ represents hadamard product, $\mathcal{W}_{rec}$ is the reciprocal of the tensor constructed by W_p. Using alternating direction method of multipliers(ADMM) to solve (17), the augmented Lagrangian is:

$$L_\mu(\mathcal{B}, \mathcal{T}, \mathcal{W}, \mathcal{Y}) = ||\mathcal{B}||_{PSTNN} + \lambda ||\mathcal{T} \otimes \mathcal{W}_1 +, < \mathcal{Y}, \mathcal{B} + \mathcal{T} - \mathcal{D} > + \frac{\mu}{2}||\mathcal{B} + \mathcal{T} - \mathcal{D}||_F^2 \tag{10}$$

$arg\,min_{\mathcal{B},\mathcal{T},\mathcal{W},\mathcal{Y}}\,L_\mu(\mathcal{B},\mathcal{T},\mathcal{W},\mathcal{Y})$ can be divided into several small questions, in which $\mathcal{B},\mathcal{T}$ can be updated in the $k+1$-th step by:

$$\mathcal{T}^{k+1} = arg\,\min_{\mathcal{T}}\,||\mathcal{T}\otimes\mathcal{W}^k||_1 + \frac{\mu^k}{2}||\mathcal{B}^k + \mathcal{T} - \mathcal{D} + \frac{Y^k}{\mu^k}||_F^2 \qquad (11)$$

$$\mathcal{B}^{k+1} = arg\,\min_{\mathcal{B}}\,||\mathcal{B}||_{PSTNN} + \frac{\mu^k}{2}||\mathcal{B} + \mathcal{T}^{k+1} - \mathcal{D} + \frac{Y^k}{\mu^k}||_F^2 \qquad (12)$$

(19) can be solved by:

$$\mathcal{T}^{k+1} = S_{\frac{\lambda\mathcal{W}^k}{\mu^k}}(\mathcal{D} - \mathcal{B}^{k+1} - \frac{\mathcal{Y}^k}{\mu^k}) \qquad (13)$$

and (20) can be solved in fourier domain. After getting $\mathcal{T}$, small targets can be reconstructed from $\mathcal{T}$.

4   Experiment and Results

4.1   Dataset and Experiment Setup

We use SIRST infrared small target detection dataset [2], which has 427 real scene infrared images, and in each image, there are different number of small targets ranging from 1 to 6. Both simple backgrounds like cloud and complicated backgrounds like buildings are included in it.

We choose six different algorithms as baselines, including Top-Hat [3], LCM [5], IPI [4], NRAM [14], PSTNN [15], DNA-net [9]. Top-Hat transform is an algorithm that uses morphological operators to process images and detect targets by enhancing targets and suppressing backgrounds. It is a classic traditional method algorithm with fast calculation speed and generally higher robustness than other traditional methods. LCM obtains the probability that each pixel is a small target by calculating the saliency contrast map. Furthermore, the threshold value processing is performed on the saliency contrast map to obtain the position of the possible small target, and the position corresponding to the original image is the final detection result. IPI is the most original detection algorithm based on matrix sparse low-rank decomposition. NRAM is a relatively new weak target detection algorithm based on single subspace sparse decomposition proposed in 2018. It has better performance and is more representative among similar algorithms. DNA-net is a deep learning detection algorithm based on the attention mechanism proposed in 2021. Due to its timeliness and algorithm results, it is representative in this field based on deep learning. For our method, we set λ to $0.6/\sqrt{max(n_1,n_2)*n_3}$ [15] to balance the weight of the two constraints.

4.2   Evaluation Metrics

For a comprehensive comparison with the aforementioned state-of-the-art approaches, we uses several typical metrics including the signal-to-clutter ratio gain(SCRG), the background supression factor(BSF), and the detection rate P_d and false-alarm rate F_a. These evaluation metrics reveal the ability in target enhancement, background suppression, and target detection. SCRG is defined as:

$$SCRG = \frac{SCR_{out}}{SCR_{in}} \qquad (14)$$

and $SCR = \frac{|\mu_t - \mu_b|}{\sigma_b}$, where μ_t is the average grayscale of the target area, and μ_b, σ_b represents the average pixel value and the standard deviation of the surrounding local neighborhood region, respectively. The larger the value of SCRG, the better the algorithm can suppress the background clutter, and the performance of the algorithm to separate the target is better. BSF is defined as:

$$BSF = \frac{\sigma_{in}}{\sigma_{out}} \qquad (15)$$

In general, the larger the value of BSF, the better the algorithm can suppress the background when the target and the background are mixed, and separate the target more completely.

4.3   Visual Comparison with Baselines

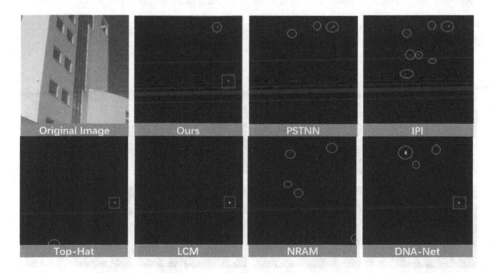

Fig. 4. Results of the different approaches in complex background

The results obtained by all the tested methods are displayed in Fig. 4, Fig. 5, Fig. 6.

Figure 4 shows the results in detecting in complex background, edges of the building and windows in original image can be regarded as target by almost all the algorithms because they have similar feature. Our algorithm and LCM has better performance in such task, because they both suppress the edge and noise in complex backgrounds, which reduces the false alarm rate and improves the detection rate.

Figure 5 shows the results in a bright background. In this case, both the contrast of target and background and the sparsity of target are suppressed by bright background. Our method avoid miss detection and false alarm using multi scale contrast and shows the best performance in this case.

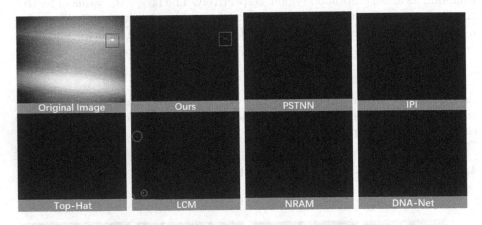

Fig. 5. Results of the different approaches in a bright background

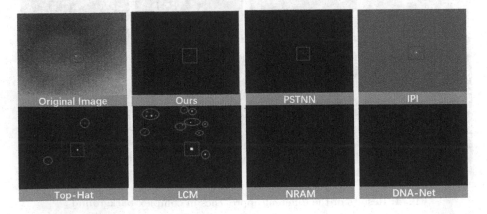

Fig. 6. Results of the different approaches in images heavily polluted by noise

Figure 6 shows the result in images heavily polluted by noise. Algorithms based on sparse decomposition have better performance than others. Traditional methods like LCM and Top-Hat cause severe false alarm in this case.

4.4   Quantitative Evaluation

Table 1 shows the quantitative results of all the methods. Results are adaptively thresholded before calculating P_d and P_f. In the comparison of all algorithms, our algorithm shows the best performance in terms of detection rate and false alarm rate. In the comparison of the BSF and the SCRG, which are two indicators to distinguish whether the shape of the small target can be well preserved, our algorithm is still in an advantageous position. Among them, the shape of the small target is lost in the morphological operation in Top-Hat. And because the calculation of the contrast of LCM is based on a square template, the detected target shape is also close to the square. For detection methods based on sparse decomposition such as IPI, NRAM, and PSTNN, since the edges of small objects cannot be ignored when the object has a certain shape, the small objects detected often have the defect of excessive shrinkage. Our method can distinguish the edge from the background of the small target, resulting in the shape of the detection result being similar to the shape of the real target.

Table 1. Quantitative Evaluation of All Method. Among them, the numbers in bold represent the optimal indicators, and the numbers with underlines represent the suboptimal indicators

	Top-Hat	LCM	IPI	NRAM	PSTNN	DNA-net	ours
P_d	92.7%	88.4%	93.1%	88.6%	91.8%	91.5%	**93.5%**
P_f	20.2%	13.4%	18.5%	10.1%	16.7%	11.9%	**9.9%**
BSF	0.5509	0.2982	0.5344	**0.7457**	0.5351	0.2916	0.5602
SCRG	0.8010	0.5930	0.6754	0.6439	0.8634	**0.9967**	0.8782
Time/s	**0.04**	7.71	10.36	5.57	0.54	6.54	4.75

For calculation time, traditional methods such as Top-Hat perform better. Our method increases the overall detection time significantly due to the increase of the iterative contrast process pixel by pixel. Although our method takes a long time to calculate, it is still relatively short compared to other method. And this can be alleviated by changing the template size, or changing the number of contrast scales. With some prior knowledge about the size of small objects, the computation time of multiscale contrast can be greatly reduced.

5   Conclusion

In this work, we presented a novel approach for detecting small targets in infrared images based on sparse decomposition. Our proposed method leverages a prior weight map that combines multiscale contrast and global grayscale information to enhance target visibility and suppress background clutter. We evaluated our approach against several state-of-the-art methods, and our experimental results demonstrate that our algorithm outperforms existing methods in detecting small objects in infrared imagery. These promising findings suggest that our approach could be valuable for various practical applications, such as surveillance, target recognition, and object tracking. Further research may explore ways to enhance the robustness and efficiency of our algorithm for real-time applications in complex environments.

Acknowledgments. This work was supported by the Fundamental Research Funds for the Central Universities.

References

1. Dai, Y., Wu, Y., Song, Y., Guo, J.: Non-negative infrared patch-image model: robust target-background separation via partial sum minimization of singular values. Infrared Phys. Technol. **81**, 182–194 (2017)
2. Dai, Y., Wu, Y., Zhou, F., Barnard, K.: Asymmetric contextual modulation for infrared small target detection. In: Proceedings of the IEEE/CVF Winter Conference on Applications of Computer Vision, pp. 950–959 (2021)
3. Deshpande, S.D., Er, M.H., Venkateswarlu, R., Chan, P.: Max-mean and max-median filters for detection of small targets. In: Signal and Data Processing of Small Targets 1999, vol. 3809, pp. 74–83. SPIE (1999)
4. Gao, C., Meng, D., Yang, Y., Wang, Y., Zhou, X., Hauptmann, A.G.: Infrared patch-image model for small target detection in a single image. IEEE Trans. Image Process. **22**(12), 4996–5009 (2013)
5. Han, J., et al.: Infrared small target detection based on the weighted strengthened local contrast measure. IEEE Geosci. Remote Sens. Lett. **18**(9), 1670–1674 (2020)
6. Jeong, J., Park, H., Kwak, N.: Enhancement of SSD by concatenating feature maps for object detection. arXiv preprint arXiv:1705.09587 (2017)
7. Jinhui, H., et al.: Infrared dim and small target detection: a review. Infrared Laser Eng. **51**(1), 20210393-1 (2022)
8. Kong, T., Yao, A., Chen, Y., Sun, F.: HyperNet: towards accurate region proposal generation and joint object detection. In: Proceedings of the IEEE Conference on Computer Vision and Pattern Recognition, pp. 845–853 (2016)
9. Li, B., et al.: Dense nested attention network for infrared small target detection. IEEE Trans. Image Process. **32**, 1745–1758 (2022)
10. Liu, W., et al.: SSD: single shot multibox detector. In: Leibe, B., Matas, J., Sebe, N., Welling, M. (eds.) ECCV 2016. LNCS, vol. 9905, pp. 21–37. Springer, Cham (2016). https://doi.org/10.1007/978-3-319-46448-0_2
11. Wang, X., Peng, Z., Kong, D., Zhang, P., He, Y.: Infrared dim target detection based on total variation regularization and principal component pursuit. Image Vis. Comput. **63**, 1–9 (2017)
12. Xia, C., Chen, S., Zhang, X., Chen, Z., Pan, Z.: Infrared small target detection via dynamic image structure evolution. IEEE Trans. Geosci. Remote Sens. **60**(3), 1–18 (2022)
13. Xiong, B., Huang, X., Wang, M.: Local gradient field feature contrast measure for infrared small target detection. IEEE Geosci. Remote Sens. Lett. **18**(3), 553–557 (2020)

14. Zhang, L., Peng, L., Zhang, T., Cao, S., Peng, Z.: Infrared small target detection via non-convex rank approximation minimization joint l 2, 1 norm. Remote Sens. **10**(11), 1821 (2018)
15. Zhang, L., Peng, Z.: Infrared small target detection based on partial sum of the tensor nuclear norm. Remote Sens. **11**(4), 382 (2019)
16. Zhang, T., Peng, Z., Wu, H., He, Y., Li, C., Yang, C.: Infrared small target detection via self-regularized weighted sparse model. Neurocomputing **420**, 124–148 (2021)
17. Zhang, T., Wu, H., Liu, Y., Peng, L., Yang, C., Peng, Z.: Infrared small target detection based on non-convex optimization with Lp-norm constraint. Remote Sens. **11**(5), 559 (2019)
18. Zhao, M., Li, W., Li, L., Hu, J., Ma, P., Tao, R.: Single-frame infrared small-target detection: a survey. IEEE Geosci. Remote Sens. Mag. **10**(2), 87–119 (2022)
19. Zuo, W., Lin, Z.: A generalized accelerated proximal gradient approach for total-variation-based image restoration. IEEE Trans. Image Process. **20**(10), 2748–2759 (2011)

CPML: Category Probability Mask Learning for Fine-Grained Visual Classification

Shangzhi Teng[✉], Changwang Mei, Xindong You, and Xueqiang Lyu

Beijing Key Laboratory of Internet Culture Digital Dissemination, Beijing Information Science and Technology University, Beijing 100101, China
{tengshangzhi,2021020593,youxindong,lxq}@bistu.edu.cn

Abstract. Fine-Grained Visual classification (FGVC) is a fundamental problem in computer vision. FGVC is determined by subtle appearance difference of local parts, which thus inspires many part-based methods. Different from attention-based methods and other part-based methods, we propose a novel Category Probability Mask Learning (CPML) module to discover nuanced local differences and mitigate cluttered backgrounds. Meanwhile, the CPML is a simple and efficient module, which can be applied to both convolution neural networks and vision transformers to enhance the ability of feature representation. In addition, we utilize a Category Consistency Loss (CCL) to promote the robustness and discrimination of learned backbone deep features. It is worth mentioning that we only use global branch at test stage because the global feature is already regularized by the part features with CPML and CCL in training steps. Compared with current state-of-the-art methods, our methods achieve promising performance on three widely used FGVC datasets.

Keywords: fine-grained visual classification · soft attention · consistent learning · computer vision

1 Introduction

Fine-grained visual classification (FGVC) aims to distinguish fine-grained classes under the same coarse class labels, such as bird species [1], brands of cars [2], and models of aircrafts [3], etc. The challenges of the FGVC task are mainly due to the subtle inter-class difference and large intra-class variance. For example, it is difficult to distinguish chipping sparrow from clay colored sparrow caused by highly similar sub-categories, but it can be identified by some subtle local differences between them. To achieve better fine-grained classification performance, it is necessary to enable the network to extract unique local area features of objects while ignoring the clutter background features of objects.

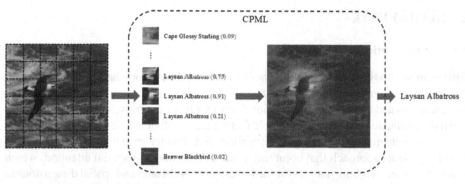

Fig. 1. Illustration of our CPML to identify bird category.

Current approaches of FGVC can be summarized into two categories. (1) Local feature learning with unsupervised mechanism [4–6]. With the feature map generated by the backbone network, the features with high response values are extracted as the local feature representation. They fuse the global and local information to improve the classification accuracy. (2) Additional annotation information, such as part-level bounding boxes, semantic masks, and text descriptions, which can be used to enhance the feature representation ability [7–9]. The model complexity and annotation cost of these methods are too expensive, which limits the flexibility and versatility of practical applications in FGVC. Explicitly extracting local features either requires extra key point annotations or labeled bounding boxes.

To alleviate the expensive data annotation and differentiate visually similar categories, we propose an attention-based method to learn discriminative features. This proposed method is inspired by semantic segmentation. Semantic segmentation networks require pixel-by-pixel category labeling information of the object regions during training which is different from our method. Our method does not require additional pixel-level category annotation of the object regions. As shown in Fig. 1, our CPML extracts features and performs category prediction for each region on the image, and then the final prediction result is obtained by mask learning. Our contributions can be summarized as follows:

(1) We propose a novel category probability mask learning (CPML) module to mitigate cluttered backgrounds and discover nuanced local differences.
(2) Our CPML is a lightweight plug-in module and can be readily inserted into any backbone to enhance the ability of feature representation, e.g., ResNet, DenseNet, ViT.
(3) Compared to current attention methods, our proposed method has the state-of-the-art performance on the FGVC datasets.

2 Related Work

2.1 Soft Attention

Attention methods can be divided into soft attention [10–15] and hard attention [16–18]. For hard attention, each value of the attention map is 1 or 0. It chooses the important local features and discard the other region features. On the contrary, soft attention usually learn the probability values on the whole feature map. Soft attention methods are mainly divided into channel attention, spatial attention, and channel-spatial attention. Woo et al. [19] propose an approach that combines channel attention and spatial attention, which learns different weighting factors for the feature map in channel and spatial dimensions to improve the feature representation. Qin et al. [14] perform frequency analysis of different channels of the feature map to obtain more channel information. ECANet [15] proposes to use one-dimensional convolutional layers to reduce the number of parameters and computational complexity.

Inspired by the above works, in this paper, we propose a soft attention approach to make the network focus on discriminative regions and ignore the interference of backgrounds.

2.2 Consistent Learning

Consistent learning not only prevents overfitting of the network, but also improves the robustness of the network. Zhang et al. [20] let two different models learn from each other. Meanwhile, the Kullback-Leibler (KL) function is used as a consistency loss method to make the features more robust. Xu et al. [21] propose a Grad-CAM-guided channel spatial attention module, which uses Kullback-Leibler (KL) to learn Grad-CAM [22] by generating a prediction vector consistent with the attention weight vector in the backbone network.

In this paper, we introduce a category consistency loss (CCL) to supervise and constrain the attention weights, which improves the robustness and discriminative power of the learned backbone depth features.

3 Proposed Method

In this section, we will introduce the proposed CPML module in detail. We obtain a category probability mask (CPM) from each position of the feature map. Introduce Category Consistency Loss (CCL) to help CPM learn better global and local features.

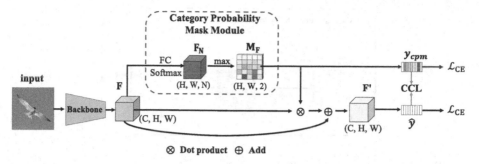

Fig. 2. Illustration of the proposed category probability mask learning (CPML) network. Put the images into the backbone network to generate the feature map F. Then, input F to the category probability mask module generates the category prediction vector y_{cpm}. Category consistency loss (CCL) is used for y_{cpm} and $\hat{y}$ to improve the robustness and discriminative power of the learned backbone depth features.

3.1   Category Probability Mask

Considering that each feature point on the feature map can be mapped to the corresponding region of the input image. Therefore, it is essential to maximize the use of the feature map information. As show in Fig. 2, we classify each feature point on the feature map to obtain $F_N \in R^{C \times H \times W}$. Specifically, the feature map $F \in R^{C \times H \times W}$ is classified to obtain $F_N \in R^{H \times W \times N}$, followed by the FC layer and the Softmax function, where C, H, W, and N denote channel, height, width, and class number, respectively. $M_F \in R^{H \times W \times 2}$ is obtained by taking the maximum value for the dimension N of F_N. The number 2 denotes the classification prediction maximum in CPM and the class corresponding to that value.

As show in Fig. 3(b) and (c). Each position of the matrix M_F represents the part regions $\{R_1, R_2, ..., R_n\}$ of the input image, where n = H × W. Specifically, the predicted value of the part region classification is denoted as the confidence score as $S(R_i) \in R^{HW \times 1}$. The part region prediction class is denoted as $C(R_i) \in R^{HW \times 1}$, where i = 0, 1, ..., n−1. M_F contains two matrices $S(R_i)$ and $C(R_i)$.

$$(S(R_i), C(R_i)) = M_F = Max(F_N) \tag{1}$$

where Max(·) records the channel-wise maximum value and the corresponding channel index, and then store them in each of the two matrices $S(R_i)$ and $C(R_i)$.

Then iterate through each region R_i and add up $S(R_i)$ of the same prediction categories. A classification probability mask is finally obtained as follows:

$$C_{class}^j = \sum_0^{n-1} P(j, C(R_i)) \times S(R_i) \tag{2}$$

$$P(j, C(R_i)) = \begin{cases} 1, & C(R_i) = j \\ 0, & C(R_i) \neq j \end{cases} \tag{3}$$

where $C_{class}^j \in R^{HW \times 1}$ is a zero vector initially. It is used to judge whether the class j is equal to the region $C(R_i)$ and accumulate $S(R_i)$ of equal class regions.

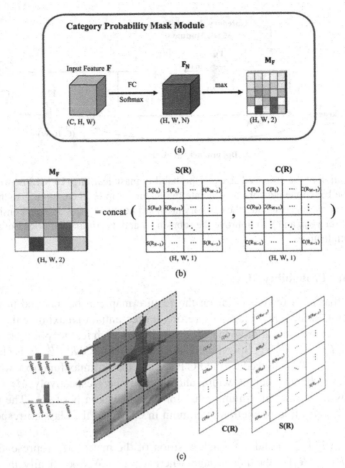

Fig. 3. (a) The details of Category Probability Mask Module. After the input feature map F passes through the classification layer, a Softmax function is performed to obtain a feature map F_N with a channel number of N. Then the CPM as M_F is obtained by taking the maximum value of the channel dimension. (b) Each M_F consists of 2 matrices of H × W concatenated. They represent the part region classification confidence scores S(R) and the part region prediction categories C(R), respectively. (c) Illustration of the input image mapped to the category prediction matrix M_F, where S(R) is the confidence matrix as well as C(R) is the prediction category matrix.

Furthermore, we normalize C_{class}^j as follows:

$$y_{cpm} = f\left(C_{class}^0, C_{class}^1, ..., C_{class}^{N-1}\right) \qquad (4)$$

where $f(\cdot)$ denotes $L1 - norm(\cdot)$ and $y_{cpm} \in R^N$ denotes the prediction vector of CPM.

To enhance the features in important regions while suppressing the background region features, we multiply the CPM as attention weights by the original feature map to obtain a new feature map $F' \in R^{C \times H \times W}$. In this way, the network is prompted to dynamically adjust the CPM value to improve the network's representation of discriminative regions of the input image.

$$\hat{y} = FC(GAP(F + F \times S(R))) \tag{5}$$

where $GAP(\cdot)$ denotes global average pooling and $FC(\cdot)$ denotes linear classification layer, $\hat{y} \in R^N$ denotes the prediction vector.

3.2 Category Consistency Loss

To make the generated category probability vectors y_{cpm} consistent with the category prediction vectors $\hat{y}$ generated by the backbone network. We introduce Category Consistency Loss ($\mathcal{L}_{CCL}$), which performs as a symmetrical Kullback-Leibler (KL) divergence between y_{cpm} and $\hat{y}$, as in Eq. 6. The category prediction vector y_{cpm} generated by CPM maximizes the feature representation of discriminative regions. These local feature needs to be interacted with the global feature with CCL. The CPM implicitly learns the values of class predictions through the classification loss and CCL generated by y_{cpm}. These values are used as attention weights to discover subtle local differences from feature maps.

$$\mathcal{L}_{CCL} = \tfrac{1}{2}\left(KL\left(\hat{y}\|y_{cpm}\right) + KL\left(y_{cpm}\|\hat{y}\right)\right) \tag{6}$$

where $KL(x\|y)$ is the KL divergence from x to y.

Moreover, as we use the original cross-entropy (CE) loss $\mathcal{L}_{CE}$ for y_{cpm} and $\hat{y}$ to train the model as well, the final loss function of the whole network can be defined as:

$$Loss = \mathcal{L}_{CE}\left(\hat{y}, y\right) + \mathcal{L}_{CE}\left(y_{cpm}, y\right) + \lambda \mathcal{L}_{CCL} \tag{7}$$

where λ is a hyper-parameter.

During inference, we only use y_{cpm} to conduct our inference.

4 Experiments

4.1 Experimental Setup

Datasets. To evaluate the proposed CPML, we conduct extensive experiments on three datasets, including CUB-200-2011 (CUB) [1], FGVC-Aircrafts (Air) [3] and Stanford Cars (Car) [2]. CUB-200-2011 is a bird species dataset, which contains 200 bird subclasses. FGVC-Aircrafts dataset contains 100 aircraft categories. Stanford Cars dataset contains 196 vehicle brands. We do not use any bounding box or part annotations in all our experiments. CUB-200-2011 is split into 5994 images for training and 5794 images for testing, FGVC-Aircrafts is split into 6667 images for training and 3333 images for testing, Stanford Cars is split into 8144 images for training and 8041 images for testing.

Implementation Details. We conducted extensive experiments to verify the performance of CPML on different backbone networks (ResNet-50 [27], DenseNet-161 [28], MobileNetV3-small [29], ViT [30], and Swin Transformer [31]).

For ResNet-50, DenseNet-161 and MobileNetV3-small backbone networks, the size of the input image is resized to 448 × 448. For Swin-T and ViT backbone networks, the size of the input image is resized to 224 × 224. In training phrase, data augmentation is performed with Random Crop and Random Horizontal Flip. During training, the learning rate is set to 0.025 with the cosine decay. The weight decay is set to 0.0005 and the optimizer choose SGD. The batch size is set to 64. For the CNN, a total of 128 epochs are trained. For the ViT and Swin Transformer, a total of 50 epochs are trained.

All experiments are completed on a single Nvidia A40, and the Pytorch toolbox is used as the main implementation substrate.

Table 1. Comparison results on three different FGVC datasets.

Method	Backbone	Accuracy (%)		
		CUB-200-2011	FGVC-Aircrafts	Stanford Cars
API-Net [23]	Resnet-50	87.7	93.0	94.8
DF-GMM [24]	Resnet-50	88.8	**93.8**	94.8
PMG [25]	Resnet-50	89.6	93.4	95.1
GGAM-Loss [21]	Resnet-50	88.45	93.42	94.41
Baseline	Resnet-50	85.15	91.05	93.09
CPML	Resnet-50	87.70 (+2.55)	93.12 (+2.07)	94.21 (+1.12)
CPML_PMG	Resnet-50	**89.90 (+4.75)**	93.60 (2.55)	**95.20 (+2.11)**
PC [26]	DenseNet-161	86.87	89.24	92.86
Baseline	DenseNet-161	85.30	93.40	94.44
CPML	DenseNet-161	**88.60 (+3.30)**	**93.90 (+0.50)**	**94.84 (+0.40)**
Baseline	MobileNetV3-small	76.70	85.20	84.86
CPML	MobileNetV3-small	**78.30 (+1.60)**	**86.30 (+1.10)**	**87.48 (+2.60)**

Table 2. Performance of Vit and Swin-T on the CUB-200-2011 dataset.

Dataset	Method	Model	
		ViT	Swin-T
CUB-200–2011	Baseline	84.8%	81.1%
	CPML	**86.9%**	**85.0%**

4.2 Results

Comparison With Recent Works. This part compares CPML against recent works. For fair comparison, we conduct extensive experiment with different backbone. As shown in Table 1, our CPML exhibits competitive performance with a series of state-of-the-art accuracy with different backbone networks. We further have tested our CPML with PMG [25] model, which performs better than PMG. Comparative experiments show that our CPML makes the network focus on discriminative regions by using a soft attention approach with category masks.

Moreover, we apply CPML to the ViT and Swin Transformer-Tiny, respectively. The pre-training dataset for ViT and Swin-T are ImageNet-1K. The input image size for training is 224 × 224. As shown in Table 2, the improvement in CUB-200-2011 is 2.1% and 3.9%, respectively.

As we can capture in the Table 1 and Table 2, sufficient experiments have demonstrated that our CPML module can be applied to convolutional neural networks and visual converters. Besides, our CPML module is simple and effective. As shown in Table 3 and Table 4, the performance of our CPML outperforms SENet and CBAM on CUB, Air and Car datasets. Meanwhile, the number of parameters and FLOPs of CPML is less than CBAM. Compared to current attention methods, our CPML has the state-of-the-art performance on the three FGVC datasets.

Table 3. Evaluations and comparisons to attention methods.

Method	Accuracy (%)		
	CUB-200-2011	FGVC-Aircrafts	Stanford Cars
Baseline	85.15	91.05	93.09
+ SENet [32]	86.78	91.37	93.10
+ CBAM [19]	86.99	91.91	93.35
CPML	**87.70**	**93.12**	**94.21**

Ablation Studies. The experiments are conducted to compare the values of the hyperparameter λ in CCL, where the range of λ is from 0.2 to 3. Since the value of λ represents the importance of category consistency. As shown in Fig. 4, our CPML achieves the best accuracy with $\lambda = 2$ on the CUB and Air tasks. Meanwhile, the best accuracy is achieved on Car with $\lambda = 0.25$.

We conduct ablation studies to understand different components in our proposed CPML. In Table 5, we can find that without the CCL, the CPM model only achieves a limited performance gain. The combination of CPM and CCL achieves the best performance. This indicates that, the performance gains of CPML are come from the combinatorial usage of the CPM and CCL.

Moreover, we conducted comparative experiments on the category consistency loss function. As shown in Table 6, we find the best performance obtained using the KL loss function being a 2.55% performance improvement.

Table 4. Comparisons between baseline model, CBAM model and CPML model in training parameters, flops and model performance.

Dataset	Resnet-50	Parameters (M)	FLOPs (G)	Accuracy (%)
CUB	Baseline	23.92	4.132	85.15
	CBAM	26.84	4.160	86.99
	CPML	24.32	4.152	**87.70**
Air	Baseline	23.71	4.132	91.09
	CBAM	26.64	4.159	91.91
	CPML	23.92	4.142	**93.12**
Car	Baseline	23.75	4.132	93.09
	CBAM	26.84	4.160	93.35
	CPML	24.31	4.152	**94.21**

Table 5. The accuracy by gradually adding each component in the Resnet-50 backbone network.

Component	Accuracy (%)
Baseline	85.15
Baseline + CPM	85.72
Baseline + CPM + CCL	**87.70**

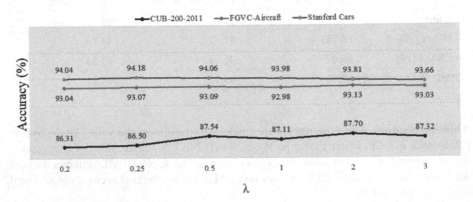

Fig. 4. Comparative experiment of λ.

To further evaluate the performance of KL Loss, we conduct three ways of KL calculation methods based on y_{cpm} and $\hat{y}$. The experimental results are summarized in Table 7, where $KL(\hat{y}\|y_{cpm}) + KL(y_{cpm}\|\hat{y})$ outperforms the $KL(\hat{y}\|y_{cpm})$ and $KL(y_{cpm}\|\hat{y})$. Therefore, we choose the $KL(\hat{y}\|y_{cpm}) + KL(y_{cpm}\|\hat{y})$ as our final KL Loss.

Table 6. The accuracy of choosing different consistency loss functions on CUB-200–2011 dataset.

CCL	L_1 Loss	L_2 Loss	Cosine Loss	KL Loss
Accuracy (%)	86.50	85.83	85.91	**87.70**

Table 7. Comparative experiment of KL loss. $\hat{y}$ denotes the prediction vector generated by the backbone network. y_{cpm} denotes the prediction vector generated by the CPM.

KL Loss	Accuracy (%)
$KL\left(\hat{y} \| y_{cpm}\right)$	87.12
$KL\left(y_{cpm} \| \hat{y}\right)$	87.11
$KL\left(\hat{y} \| y_{cpm}\right) + KL\left(y_{cpm} \| \hat{y}\right)$	**87.70**

Visualization Experiments. Figure 5 shows the response of feature maps in the ResNet-50 backbone, which indicates the focused regions by the learned neural network. It could be observed that, the activated regions of our CPML contain more discriminative details, than the ones of the baseline model. And CPML is effective in capturing discriminative cues from fine-grained object. The visualization experiments confirm that the introduction of CPML enables better feature representation learning over multiple discriminative regions compared to the original backbone, which is crucial for FGVC.

Compared with CBAM, which is weighted to consider only local range information, CPML is not only able to learn local information, but also to learn global information by using CCL. To better explain the improvement of our method, Fig. 6 shows the visualization of different attentional mechanism models, which were generated by the Grad-CAM. The baseline cannot clearly focus on the right region of the object. With the addition of Channel attention, Spatial attention and CBAM, the models tend to pay attention on the beak and the neck of the bird, which are discriminative parts. However, the regions of attention focused on by the above attention methods are distracted by the background around the object, which distracts part of the attention. Our CPML not only better focuses attention on discriminative regions, but also effectively eliminates the negative effects of background.

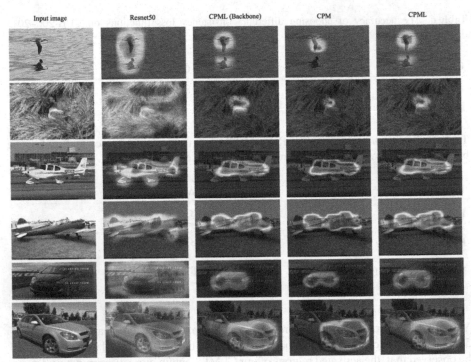

Fig. 5. Visualization Experiments of attention map. The first column shows the input image. The second column shows the attention map of the baseline model of Resnet-50. As shown in Fig. 2, CPML (Backbone) denotes F, CPM denotes F_N, and CPML denotes F'. The red color stands for high attention. (Color figure online)

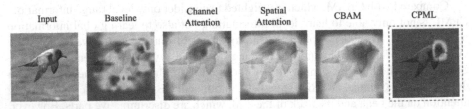

Fig. 6. Visualization of the different attention mechanism models. The first column represents the original image. The following four columns show visualization results of the baseline, the channel attention, the spatial attention, and the CBAM, respectively. The red box indicates the visualization result of our proposed method. (Color figure online)

5 Conclusion

In this paper, we propose a novel Category Probability Mask Learning (CPML) module to mitigate cluttered backgrounds and discover subtle local differences. We creatively implement a direct optimization for the attention map, which enhances the regional attention for fine-grained visual classification. Extensive experiments have verified the superior performance of our CPML on various FGVC tasks. In addition, CPML exhibits strong interpretability and competitive performance in the localization of discriminative regions.

The effectiveness of the proposed CPML reveals the critical role of regional category predictive attention in FGVC, which provide an enlightening reference for future research.

Acknowledgments. This work was supported in part by The National Natural Science Foundation of China (62202061;62171043); Beijing Natural Science Foundation (4232025); R&D Program of Beijing Municipal Education Commission (KM202311232002); Scientific Research Project of National Language Commission (ZDI145-10).

References

1. Wah, C., Branson, S., Welinder, P., et al.: The Caltech-UCSD birds-200-2011 dataset (2011)
2. Krause, J., Stark, M., Deng, J., et al.: 3D object representations for fine-grained categorization. In: Proceedings of the IEEE International Conference on Computer Vision Workshops, pp. 554–561 (2013)
3. Maji, S., Rahtu, E., Kannala, J., et al.: Fine-grained visual classification of aircraft. arXiv preprint arXiv:1306.5151 (2013)
4. Liu, C., Xie, H., Zha, Z.J., et al.: Filtration and distillation: enhancing region attention for fine-grained visual categorization. In: Proceedings of the AAAI Conference on Artificial Intelligence, vol. 34, no. 07, pp. 11555–11562 (2020)
5. Zheng, H., Fu, J., Mei, T., et al.: Learning multi-attention convolutional neural network for fine-grained image recognition. In: Proceedings of the IEEE International Conference on Computer Vision, pp. 5209–5217 (2017)
6. Yang, X., Wang, Y., Chen, K., et al.: Fine-grained object classification via self-supervised pose alignment. In: Proceedings of the IEEE/CVF Conference on Computer Vision and Pattern Recognition, pp. 7399–7408 (2022)
7. Wei, X.S., Xie, C.W., Wu, J., et al.: Mask-CNN: localizing parts and selecting descriptors for fine-grained bird species categorization. Pattern Recogn. **76**, 704–714 (2018)
8. Zhang, H., Cao, X., Wang, R.: Audio visual attribute discovery for fine-grained object recognition. In: Proceedings of the AAAI Conference on Artificial Intelligence, vol. 32, no. 1 (2018)
9. Xu, H., Qi, G., Li, J., et al.: Fine-grained image classification by visual-semantic embedding. In: IJCAI, pp. 1043–1049 (2018)
10. Chen, B., Deng, W., Hu, J. Mixed high-order attention network for person re-identification. In Proceedings of the IEEE/CVF International Conference on Computer Vision, pp. 371–381 (2019)
11. Zhang, Z., Lan, C., Zeng, W., et al.: Relation-aware global attention for person re-identification. In: Proceedings of the IEEE/CVF Conference on Computer Vision and Pattern Recognition, pp. 3186–3195 (2020)
12. Chen, Y., Dai, X., Liu, M., et al.: Dynamic convolution: attention over convolution kernels. In: Proceedings of the IEEE/CVF Conference on Computer Vision and Pattern Recognition, pp. 11030–11039 (2020)
13. Hou, Q., Zhou, D., Feng, J.: Coordinate attention for efficient mobile network design. In: Proceedings of the IEEE/CVF Conference on Computer Vision and Pattern Recognition, pp. 13713–13722 (2021)

14. Qin, Z., Zhang, P., Wu, F., et al.: Fcanet: frequency channel attention networks. In: Proceedings of the IEEE/CVF International Conference on Computer Vision, pp. 783–792 (2021)
15. Wang, Q., Wu, B., Zhu, P., et al.: ECA-Net: efficient channel attention for deep convolutional neural networks. In: Proceedings of the IEEE/CVF Conference on Computer Vision and Pattern Recognition, pp. 11534–11542 (2020)
16. Dai, J., Qi, H., Xiong, Y., et al.: Deformable convolutional networks. In: Proceedings of the IEEE International Conference on Computer Vision, pp. 764–773 (2017)
17. Sun, Y., Zheng, L., Yang, Y., et al.: Beyond part models: person retrieval with refined part pooling (and a strong convolutional baseline). In: Proceedings of the European Conference on Computer Vision (ECCV), pp. 480–496 (2018)
18. Papadopoulos, A., Korus, P., Memon, N.: Hard-attention for scalable image classification. Adv. Neural. Inf. Process. Syst. **34**, 14694–14707 (2021)
19. Woo, S., Park, J., Lee, J.Y., et al.: CBAM: convolutional block attention module. In: Proceedings of the European Conference on Computer Vision (ECCV), pp. 3–19 (2018)
20. Zhang, Y., Xiang, T., Hospedales, T.M., et al.: Deep mutual learning. In: Proceedings of the IEEE Conference on Computer Vision and Pattern Recognition, pp. 4320–4328 (2018)
21. Xu, S., Chang, D., Xie, J., et al.: Grad-CAM guided channel-spatial attention module for fine-grained visual classification. In: 2021 IEEE 31st International Workshop on Machine Learning for Signal Processing (MLSP), pp. 1–6. IEEE (2021)
22. Selvaraju, R.R., Cogswell, M., Das, A., et al.: Grad-cam: Visual explanations from deep networks via gradient-based localization. In: Proceedings of the IEEE International Conference on Computer Vision, pp. 618–626 (2017)
23. Zhuang, P., Wang, Y., Qiao, Y.: Learning attentive pairwise interaction for fine-grained classification. In: Proceedings of the AAAI Conference on Artificial Intelligence, vol. 34, no. 07, pp. 13130–13137 (2020)
24. Wang, Z., Wang, S., Yang, S., et al.: Weakly supervised fine-grained image classification via Guassian mixture model oriented discriminative learning. In: Proceedings of the IEEE/CVF Conference on Computer Vision and Pattern Recognition, pp. 9749–9758 (2020)
25. Du, R., Chang, D., Bhunia, A.K., et al.: Fine-grained visual classification via progressive multi-granularity training of jigsaw patches. In: Vedaldi, A., Bischof, H., Brox, T., Frahm, J.M. (eds.) Computer Vision–ECCV 2020, pp. 153–168. Springer, Cham (2020). https://doi.org/10.1007/978-3-030-58565-5_10
26. Dubey, A., Gupta, O., Guo, P., et al.: Pairwise confusion for fine-grained visual classification. In: Proceedings of the European Conference on Computer Vision (ECCV), pp. 70–86 (2018)
27. He, K., Zhang, X., Ren, S., et al.: Deep residual learning for image recognition. In: Proceedings of the IEEE Conference on Computer Vision and Pattern Recognition, pp. 770–778 (2016)
28. Huang, G., Liu, Z., Van Der Maaten, L., et al.: Densely connected convolutional networks. In: Proceedings of the IEEE Conference on Computer Vision and Pattern Recognition, pp. 4700–4708 (2017)
29. Howard, A., Sandler, M., Chu, G., et al.: Searching for mobilenetv3. In: Proceedings of the IEEE/CVF International Conference on Computer Vision, pp. 1314–1324 (2019)
30. Dosovitskiy, A., Beyer, L., Kolesnikov, A., et al.: An image is worth 16x16 words: transformers for image recognition at scale. arXiv preprint arXiv:2010.11929 (2020)
31. Liu, Z., Lin, Y., Cao, Y., et al.: Swin transformer: hierarchical vision transformer using shifted windows. In: Proceedings of the IEEE/CVF International Conference on Computer Vision, pp. 10012–10022 (2021)
32. Hu, J., Shen, L., Sun, G.: Squeeze-and-excitation networks. In: Proceedings of the IEEE Conference on Computer Vision and Pattern Recognition, pp. 7132–7141 (2018)

DPFMN: Dual-Path Feature Match Network for RGB-D and RGB-T Salient Object Detection

Xinyu Wen, Zhengyong Feng[✉], Jun Lin, and Xiaomei Xiao

School of Electronic Information Engineering, China West Normal University,
Nanchong 637002, China
{XinyuWen,ZhengyongFeng,JunLin,XiaomeiXiao}@cwnu.edu.com

Abstract. Feature match is a hot research topic in salient object detection, because the information definition is complex and it is difficult to explore an effective match strategy. In this paper, we propose a Dual-Path Feature Match Network (DPFMN) to enhance the cross-modal and global-local match efficiency. Specifically, in the cross-modal match, we propose the Auxiliary-enhanced Module (AEM) to excavate the auxiliary information. In the global-local match, we propose the Capsule Correlation Module (CCM) to store information hierarchically in the sub-capsules, which can enhance the correlation from global to local features. Also, we design the Guided Fusion Module (GFM) to integrate global-local features in a distributed manner to ensure information integrity. Considering the quality and detail of the saliency map, we introduce the Saliency Reconstruct Module (SRM) for progressive image reconstruction to avoid the unstable reconstruction information caused by too large gradients. The method proves its effectiveness through a fair comparison with 12 RGB-D and 7 RGB-T networks on 8 public datasets.

Keywords: RGB-D Salient Object Detection · RGB-T Salient Object Detection · Feature Matching · Capsule Network · Feature Integrity · Saliency Map Reconstruction

1 Introduction

The Salient Object Detection (SOD) task aims to mimic the human eye's observation behavior by capturing the most interesting objects in the observation range and separating them from other irrelevant backgrounds. SOD is now widely used in several computer vision fields such as object tracking [1], image retrieval [2], and defect detection [4]. The information in some RGB maps causes the network to fail to capture salient objects, which affects the detection results. With the popularity and application of smart hardware devices, some auxiliary maps (e.g., depth maps and thermal maps) more explicitly demonstrate their value in computer vision. Therefore, some studies [5–7] have used auxiliary maps to initially localize objects as a way to reduce the difficulty of SOD tasks.

However, not all the information in the auxiliary maps is valid. Some auxiliary map acquired in complex environments can also be affected by irrelevant and noisy information, thus causing detection errors. Meanwhile, most of the salient object detection tasks use the convolutional neural network (CNNs) [8–10] to process images. Although this approach achieves a efficient form of human-computer interaction, the features dependency varies, it is difficult for CNNs to accurately screen and process important features, which will lead to the loss of information and the exploitation of irrelevant information. Until today, this problems are still at the pain point of research.

In recent years, due to the expansion of the application field of dual-path networks [37], more and more methods have adopted this method of design. Therefore, we propose a dual-path feature matching network (DPFMN) to address above problems. We categorize a series of negative relationships between RGB map and auxiliary map as the modal information mismatch problem, and focus on mining more effective auxiliary information. As for the dynamicized feature loss of CNNs, we classify it as a global-local feature matching problem, and design capsule correlation module and guided fusion module to achieve global-local feature correlation and fusion. Finally, in order to improve the efficiency of saliency map reconstruction, we introduce the saliency reconstruct module. DPFMN is validated to achieve effective migration between RGB-D and RGB-T tasks.

Our contribution is summarized as follows:

1. We propose a Dual-Path Feature Matching Network (DPFMN) to address cross-modal and global-local matching problems, and ensure the integrity of salient features.
2. We design an Auxiliary-enhanced Module (AEM) to excavating the auxiliary information and improving cross-modal matching confidence. Meanwhile, we propose Capsule Correlation Module (CCM) and Guided Fusion Module (GFM) to enhance global-local information correlation and fusion. Considering the reconstruction efficiency and information integrity, we introduce the Saliency Reconstruct Module (SRM).
3. In comparison with 12 RGB-D and 7 RGB-T methods in 8 public datasets, we demonstrate the effectiveness and migration capability of the DPFMN.

2 Related Works

2.1 RGB-D Salient Object Detection

Early RGB-D salient object detection tasks were performed by traditional manual extraction of object features, which exploited the depth information in the depth map to explore part of the valid information to enhance the ability to detect salient objects in complex scenes, such as appearance attributes, boundary information, surface normals, etc. In the traditional manual era, several research works have proposed effective traditional RGB-D methods such as contrast, center-surround, center or boundary a priori, etc. Lang et al.[11] introduced a depth prior and modeled the correlation between depth and saliency maps using a hybrid Gaussian model. The work of Ciptadi et al.[12] focused on modeling the interaction between RGB maps and depth maps regarding layout and shape features, and used it as an early RGB-D model. Although these methods increase the diversity of RGB-D tasks to a certain extent, they limited detection performance.

After, some research works have proposed methods combined with convolutional neural networks (CNNs) and achieved positive detection results. Ji et al. [5] introduction into CNNs proposes a new saliency framework that allows more efficient use of edges, depth, and saliency. Zhai et al. [7] designed a simple and efficient cascade refinement network, which achieves excellent performance using CNNs. Most of the current methods incorporate CNNs, whose flexible processing capability of salient features better solves the problems left by traditional methods.

2.2 RGB-T Salient Object Detection

Similar to RGBD salient object detection, RGBT salient object detection mainly uses one RGB map and one thermal map to detect the object. In the early stage, some methods mainly use machine learning to extract object features. When deep learning emerged in the field of vision, some methods started to investigate RGB-T methods combined with deep neural networks. MIDD [13] proposed a dual decoder to achieve multimodal global contextual interaction, which enhanced the application scope of the network. APNet [14] constructed an iterative adversarial learning approach to generate and discriminate feature information, gradually refining the features at multiple scales. OSRNet [15] was developed by early fusion of RGB and thermal maps to obtain complementary information and refine feature information using a single-stream semantic guidance strategy. LSNet [16] uses MobileNet to replace the backbone to achieve network lightweight and proposes a boundary-boosting algorithm to reduce the information collapse of features. As the application of Vision Transformer increases, some methods start to adopt Vision Transformer to enhance the detection performance. SSNet [17] uses scribble-supervised for detection and proposes a prediction module to alleviate the ambiguity of boundaries. Currently, RGB-T task still have some inherent problems, such as the emergence of detection performance bottlenecks and the mismatch of new modal information in task migration.

3   Method

Figure 1 shows the general framework structure of the Dual-Path Feature Match Network (DPFMN) proposed in this paper. It mainly contains the following four parts: feature extraction and cross-modal feature match, feature diversity enhancement and dimension reduction, global-local feature match and fusion, and saliency map reconstruction.

3.1   Feature Extraction and Cross-modal Matching

Since Pyramid Vision Transformer (PVT) [18] can capture long-distance dependent global contextual information more efficiently, this paper uses PVT to extract multi-scale features. The dimensions of the input map are $\mathbb{R}^{3 \times H \times W}$ and $\mathbb{R}^{1 \times H \times W}$. Maps entering the PVT will be segmented into several small patches and formed into multi-scale feature maps with spatial dimensions of $\mathbb{R}^{64 \times H/4 \times W/4}$, $\mathbb{R}^{128 \times H/8 \times W/8}$, $\mathbb{R}^{320 \times H/16 \times W/16}$, and $\mathbb{R}^{512 \times H/32 \times W/32}$ using a progressive shrinkage strategy. Since the spatial shrinkage attention (SRA) in the progressive shrinkage strategy reduces the spatial scale of key

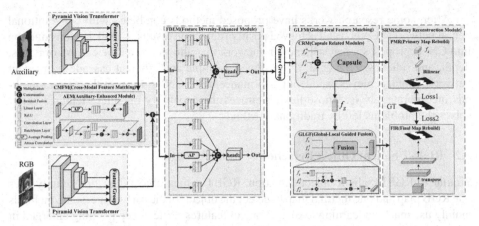

Fig. 1. The overall architecture of the network in this paper.

(K) and value (V), this reduces the network computation to a large extent. The RGB features and auxiliary features extracted by PVT are denoted as $\{R_1, R_2, R_3, R_4\}$ and $\{A_1, A_2, A_3, A_4\}$, respectively.

Due to equipment or algorithm limitations, some auxiliary maps are affected by irrelevant and noisy information. Inspired by previous studies [7], a cross-modal feature matching (CMFM) strategy is proposed in this paper. The strategy is mainly divided into two parts: Auxiliary-Enhanced Module (AEM) and residual feature fusion. The AEM is mainly divided into Channel Processing Units (F_{cpu}) and Spatial Processing Units (F_{spu}), as expressed below

$$x_i = F_{spu}(F_{cpu}(A_i)). \tag{1}$$

$$F_{cpu}(a) = f \otimes (F_{LS}[F_{SP}(a)]). \tag{2}$$

$$F_{spu}(a) = F_{CP}(a) \otimes F_{BC}[C(F_{BC}[F_{CP}(a)], F_{BC_2}[F_{CP}(a)])]. \tag{3}$$

where $F_{SP}(\cdot)$ and $F_{CP}(\cdot)$ denote spatial and channel pooling respectively, $F_{LS}(\cdot)$ denote Linear $\rightarrow$ ReLU $\rightarrow$ Linear $\rightarrow$ Sigmoid, $F_{BC}(\cdot)$ and $F_{BC_2}(\cdot)$ denote convolution blocks and atrous convolution blocks with dilation of 2, $\otimes$ denote element-wise multiplication. The features x_i processed by the auxiliary-enhanced module will be residually fused with the RGB features R_i of the same level to improve the stability of modal feature match $C(\cdot)$ denote concatenation,

$$f_i = R_i \otimes x_i \oplus R_i. \tag{4}$$

where $\oplus$ denotes the matrix addition operation.

3.2 Feature Diversity Enhancement and Dimension Reduction

Since the hybrid features (f_1, f_2, f_3, f_4) have single information by themselves, which may reduce the learning efficiency of the network. And the number of channels in each

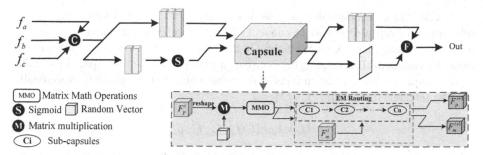

Fig. 2. The architecture of the Capsule Correlation Module.

layer feature is different, which will increase the computational difficulty. Therefore, this paper combines RFB [19] and ASPP [20] to design a Feature Diversity-Enhanced Moudle (FDEM), which can increase the feature diversity and motivate the network to learn more information. The module consists of the atrous convolution group and head. For the features $[f_1, f_2, f_3]$ we choose the atrous convolution blocks with dilation rate combination (1, 3, 5, 7) to expand the receptive field and integrate them to obtain the diverse features $[f_d^1, f_d^2, f_d^3]$, the head (F_{head}) is used to enhance the diverse expressions, and the structure of the head is as follows

$$F_{head}(a) = R(0.1 \otimes F_{BC}(a) + F_{BC}[F_{BC}(a)]). \tag{5}$$

Since the feature f_4 contains more global concept information, we choose a more sparse dilation rate combination (1, 6, 12, 18) of the atrous convolution block for diverse feature extraction, and use the $F_{BC}(\cdot)$ as the head to obtain the diverse feature f_d^4. To simplify the calculation, the feature channel are adjusted to 64.

3.3 Global-Local Feature Match and Fusion

Due to the disadvantages of the dynamic feature loss of CNNs, some local information will be regarded as irrelevant and abandoned. As shown in Fig. 2, inspired by the capsule network [21, 22], we embed a Capsule Correlation Module.

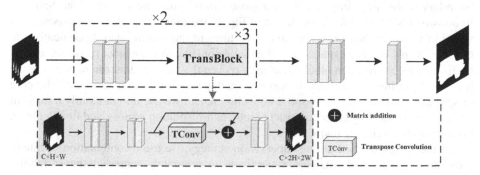

Fig. 3. The architecture of the Saliency Reconstruction Module.

(CCM) in the decode fusion process, which aims to use the global-local feature correlation of the capsule network to connect all kinds of relevant information. Second, to make the capsule network more efficient in handling effective global-local feature relations, we restrict the EM Routing between capsules to a limited defined space by simulating the sequence of information transfer from the subject to the secondary. Specifically, we first integrate features $[f_d^2, f_d^3, f_d^4]$

$$f_c = F_{BC}[C(f_d^2, f_d^3, f_d^4)]. \tag{6}$$

which will continue the pre-processing by double branch, and obtain the initial pose matrix M_0 and the proposal matrix m_0. Note that the M_0 are used to model the global-local attributes, while the m_0 are used to determine whether the global-local attributes belong to the object. The M_0 undergoes a series of matrix transformations in the main capsule and randomly obtains an uncertain capsule vote, which will be passed to the first level sub-capsule to assist in the computation of the updated pose matrix M_1 and proposal matrix m_1 and stored in that level capsule. The M_1 and m_0 will continue to iterate through the next level capsule for computation and storage. Passing in the above way, the final relationship from global to local is established and fixed by capsules at all levels, the global-local matched features f_m and information screening matrix f_s are obtained, which will residual fused

$$f_g = [F_{CP}(f_s)] \otimes f_m \oplus f_m. \tag{7}$$

Before performing global-local guided fusion, f_g is reconstructed to initial saliency map S_1.

The role of the Guided Fusion Module (GFM) is to integrate global-local information in a distributed manner to avoid information loss in the final fusion stage. We use the tight connection of global-local information in feature f_g to guide features $[f_d^1, f_d^2]$ to learn and fuse local information, respectively, to obtain better local feature representation, and then integrate them to complement the missing information.

3.4 Saliency Map Reconstruction and Supervision Strategy

Considering the saliency map reconstruction process, such as detail preservation and boundary sharpening, inspired by Transpose Convolution, we introduce the Saliency Reconstruct Module (SRM), as shown in Fig. 3, the module combines transpose convolution to reconstruct the resolution of features in the feature map. Specifically, the module mainly includes spatial and channel reconstruction. Channel reconstruction is performed by convolution blocks gradually reduce the channel dimension, avoiding the loss of object information due to too large a dimension reduction gradient. The core of spatial reconstruction is transpose convolution, and we use it to randomly transform the vectors so that they are reconstructed into high-resolution vectors, and finally obtain high-resolution saliency maps S_2.

In the design of the training supervision strategy, we use a combination of binary cross-entropy loss and IoU loss supervision to accurately represent the variability between Ground Truth and Saliency Map, while supervising the learning process of the network with constraints and guidance. The specific expression of the supervised strategy is as follows

$$\mathcal{L}_1 = \mathcal{L}_{bce}(S, GT). \tag{8}$$

$$\mathcal{L}_2 = \mathcal{L}_{IoU}(S, GT). \tag{9}$$

$$\mathcal{L}_{all} = \mathcal{L}_1 + \mathcal{L}_2. \tag{10}$$

where $\mathcal{L}_{bce}(\cdot)$ denotes the binary cross-entropy loss function, $\mathcal{L}_{IoU}(\cdot)$ denotes the IoU loss function, $\mathcal{L}_{all}(\cdot)$ denotes the total loss function, S denotes the saliency map S_1 and S_2.

4 Experiments

4.1 Datasets and Parameter Settings

We will use 8 datasets for method comparison, namely RGB-D datasets (NJU2K [23], NLPR [24], SIP [6], SSD [25], STERE [26]) and RGB-T datasets (VT821 [27], VT1000 [28], VT5000 [29]). NJU2K contains 1985 pairs RGB-D images obtained from the network, movies, and camera. NLPR consists of 1000 pairs of RGB-D images, the main types of outdoor and indoor objects. SIP consists of 929 pairs of high-resolution images. SSD consists of 80 pairs of images from 3 stereoscopic movies. 1250 stereoscopic images are collected in STERE. VT821 contains 821 pairs of images, but there are quality differences between heatmaps. VT1000 contains 1000 pairs of RGB-T images in a minimalist style with good information matching between the two modalities. The VT5000 dataset contains 5000 pairs of RGB-T maps from 11 challenging scenarios.

In the RGB-D task, inspired by the training approach of BBSNet [7], 1485 pairs from NJU2K and 700 pairs of from NLPR are input to the network for training and learning, while the test set includes the remaining images from NJU2K and NLPR, and other datasets. In the RGB-T task, 2500 pairs of RGB-T images in VT5000 are used for network training, and the remaining RGB-T images in VT5000 and other datasets are used for testing.

During training, we use the Adam optimizer for model optimization, setting the initial learning rate to 1e-5 and decreasing it by a factor of 10 every 60 rounds. To prevent overfitting of the data, we performed preprocessing operations, such as cropping and flipping. The PVT in the network was pretrained by ImageNet, the epoch was 200 and batch size was 8.

4.2 Evaluation Metrics

In this paper, 5 mainstream evaluation metrics will be used to compare with other methods, which are S-measure(S_α), F-measure(F_β), E-measure(E_ξ), mean absolute error (M), and precision-recall curve. S-measure (S_α) is used to evaluate the structural similarity between the detection region S_γ and the object S_o, which can be expressed as

$$S_\alpha = \alpha * S_o + (1 - \alpha) * S_\gamma. \tag{11}$$

where α is the equilibrium parameter, usually 0.5. F-measure(F_β) is the summed average of precision and recall weighting, which can be expressed as

$$F_\beta = (1 + \beta^2)[(P * R)/(\beta^2 P + R)]. \tag{12}$$

to enhance accuracy, β^2 is usually set to a constant value of 0.3. E-measure(E_ξ) is used to obtain the image level statistics and its local pixel-matching information, which can be expressed as

$$E_\xi = [1/(W \times H)] \sum_{i=1}^{W} \sum_{j=1}^{H} \xi(i,j). \tag{13}$$

where $\xi(\cdot)$ represents the augmented diagonal matrix. MAE indicates the mean of the absolute error between the predicted salient object area and ground truth. Precision-Recall Curve is a visual representation of the variability between the prediction region and the ground truth, which can visually represent the saliency prediction performance of the network.

Table 1. Metrics comparison results of our method with 12 RGB-D methods, the best indicators is red, blue, and green. "↑" and "↓" is the excellent trend of the values.

Dataset	Metric	CNN-based								Transformer-based				
		CoNet	D3Net	BBSNet	UC-Net	BiANet	DCF	MaD	SPSN	TriTransNet	CAVER	AFNet	CIPT	Ours
NJU2K	$S_a\uparrow$	.894	.895	.926	.897	.904	.912	.921	.912	.919	.927	.926	.926	.933
	$F_\beta\uparrow$	.895	.889	.927	.896	.908	.915	.903	.912	.926	.932	.928	.930	.937
	$E_\xi\uparrow$	.934	.932	.957	.939	.941	.950	.930	.943	.955	.956	.958	.959	.961
	$M\downarrow$	.046	.047	.033	.041	.047	.036	.037	.033	.030	.028	.032	.028	.027
NLPR	$S_a\uparrow$	.908	.905	.930	.920	.927	.926	.933	.926	.929	.930	.936	.936	.940
	$F_\beta\uparrow$	.887	.885	.912	.901	.921	.912	.901	.914	.921	.923	.925	.930	.932
	$E_\xi\uparrow$	.945	.946	.961	.954	.962	.963	.955	.962	.964	.961	.968	.970	.970
	$M\downarrow$	.031	.034	.024	.025	.024	.021	.022	.022	.021	.023	.020	.017	.017
SSD	$S_a\uparrow$	.862	.882	.877	.864	.870	.842	.872	-	.866	.887	.897	-	.879
	$F_\beta\uparrow$	.859	.859	.873	.863	.870	.841	.850	-	.870	.876	.885	-	.870
	$E_\xi\uparrow$	.907	.919	.907	.905	.907	.883	.907	-	.905	.932	.943	-	.919
	$M\downarrow$	.071	.044	.065	.067	.052	.075	.045	-	.066	.037	.038	-	.043
SIP	$S_a\uparrow$	.858	.864	.887	.875	.884	.876	.884	.890	.886	.895	.896	.902	.904
	$F_\beta\uparrow$	.867	.862	.895	.879	.895	.884	.877	.896	.899	.909	.909	.922	.920
	$E_\xi\uparrow$	.913	.910	.928	.919	.928	.922	.920	.936	.930	.935	.939	.946	.941
	$M\downarrow$	.063	.063	.052	.051	.051	.052	.051	.042	.043	.043	.043	.035	.039
STERE	$S_a\uparrow$	.905	.899	.912	.904	.904	.902	.910	.906	.909	.917	.918	.920	.926
	$F_\beta\uparrow$	.900	.891	.908	.898	.908	.900	.892	.898	.911	.918	.918	.922	.925
	$E_\xi\uparrow$	.945	.938	.946	.942	.944	.943	.939	.942	.952	.951	.957	.960	.957
	$M\downarrow$	.036	.046	.037	.038	.042	.038	.037	.035	.034	.032	.034	.029	.030

4.3 Experimental Comparison and Analysis of Results

The DPFMN will be compared with RGB-D methods (CoNet [5], D3Net [6], BBSNet [7], UC-Net [8], BiANet [9], DCF [10], MaD [3], SPSN [30], TriTransNet [31], CAVER

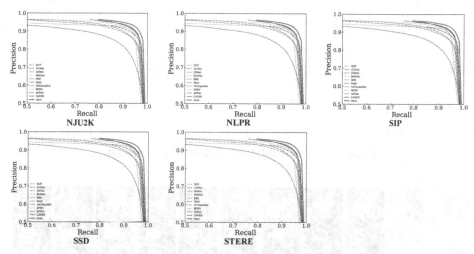

Fig. 4. Precision-Recall Curve of RGB-D SOD methods

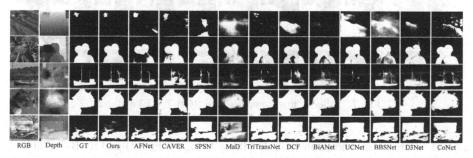

Fig. 5. Saliency map comparison of RGB-D SOD methods

Table 2. Metrics comparison results of our method with 7 RGB-T methods, the best indicators is red, blue, and green. "↑" and "↓" is the excellent trend of the values.

Methods	VT821				VT1000				VT5000			
	$S_\alpha\uparrow$	$F_\beta\uparrow$	$E_\xi\uparrow$	$M\downarrow$	$S_\alpha\uparrow$	$F_\beta\uparrow$	$E_\xi\uparrow$	$M\downarrow$	$S_\alpha\uparrow$	$F_\beta\uparrow$	$E_\xi\uparrow$	$M\downarrow$
MIDD	.871	.851	.918	.045	.915	.913	.957	.027	.867	.849	.920	.043
APNet	.867	.818	.908	.034	.920	.885	.938	.021	.875	.822	.914	.034
MM	.875	.850	.921	.040	.917	.912	.954	.027	.864	.834	.912	.043
OSR	.875	.839	.916	.043	.926	.920	.960	.022	.875	.848	.918	.040
MIA-DPD	.844	.831	.902	.070	.924	.928	.964	.025	.878	.865	.929	.040
LSNet	.879	.842	.919	.032	.926	.913	.962	.025	.877	.834	.923	.040
SS	.895	.875	.934	.027	.925	.914	.949	.020	.877	.858	.913	.033
Ours	.899	.871	.927	.034	.939	.935	.974	.021	.908	.881	.949	.032

[32], and AFNet [33], CIPT [34]) and RGB-T methods (MIDD [13], APNet [14], MM [35], OSRNet [15], MIA-DPD [36], LSNet [16], SS [17]), the assessments obtained

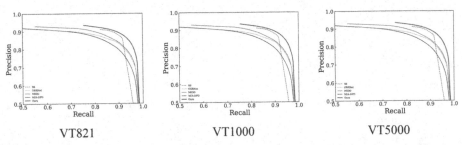

VT821   VT1000   VT5000

Fig. 6. Precision-Recall Curve of RGB-T SOD methods

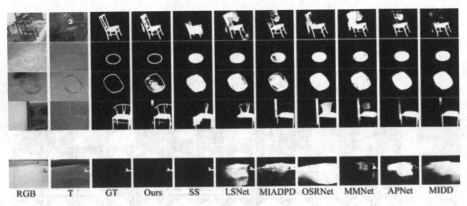

RGB   T   GT   Ours   SS   LSNet   MIADPD   OSRNet   MMNet   APNet   MIDD

Fig. 7. Saliency map comparison of RGB-T SOD methods

after comparison are shown in RGB-D (Table 1, Fig. 4, Fig. 5) and RGB-T (Table 2, Fig. 6, Fig. 7).

Evaluation of Metrics. As seen from Table 1 and Table 2, DPFMN is higher than other SOTA methods in all 3 evaluation metrics of NJU2K, NLPR, and VT5000. As seen from Fig. 4 and Fig. 6, our method outperforms other methods in the P-R curve.

Saliency Map Comparison. The visual comparison results is in Fig. 5 and Fig. 7. In the simple scenes, the saliency map obtained by our method will be more complete. In the complex scenes, the saliency map obtained by our method is better than most methods regarding shape integrity and boundary separation. In the case of the auxiliary map, results obtained by some of the other methods may show some missing or blurred boundaries of the salient objects, while our method not only detects the salient objects more completely, but also separates the boundaries of the objects more clearly. In the case of small object detection, our method can accurately detect the location of the small object.

Table 3. Ablation study of various modules on NJU2K and NLPR

Methods	NJU2K				NLPR			
	$S_\alpha\uparrow$	$F_\beta\uparrow$	$E_\xi\uparrow$	$M\downarrow$	$S_\alpha\uparrow$	$F_\beta\uparrow$	$E_\xi\uparrow$	$M\downarrow$
w/o AEM	.929	.933	.958	.029	.892	.906	.931	.048
w/o FDEM	.930	.933	.957	.028	.896	.911	.936	.042
w/o CCM	.932	.937	.961	.028	.896	.910	.934	.042
w/o GFM	.929	.931	.958	.028	.893	.910	.936	.043
w/o SRM	.929	.932	.958	.029	.896	.911	.936	.044
base	**.933**	**.938**	**.961**	**.027**	**.904**	**.920**	**.941**	**.039**

4.4 Ablation Analysis

To demonstrate the effectiveness of the modules, we will set up a series of ablation experiments, and this part of the experiments will be performed on NJU2K and NLPR. The results are shown in Tab. 3, Fig. 8, Fig. 9, w/o means remove the module.

RGB   Depth   GT   Base   w/o AEM

Fig. 8. Visual comparison of AEM ablation experiments

The Effectiveness of Cross-Modal Feature Matching Strategy. The core of cross-modal feature matching is the auxiliary-enhanced module (AEM). From the metrics evaluation results, it can be seen that the feature enhancement operation of AEM on the auxiliary features significantly improves the overall performance of the network. The Fig. 8 shows that the auxiliary features lacking the AEM processing process cannot be effectively matched with RGB features, thus cannot effectively detect detecting the salient object.

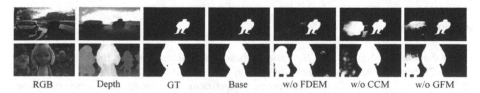

RGB   Depth   GT   Base   w/o FDEM   w/o CCM   w/o GFM

Fig. 9. Visual comparison of FDEM, CCM, and GFM ablation experiments

The Effectiveness of Feature Diversity Enhancement Module (FDEM). From the metrics evaluation of the ablation experiments, it is known that FDES improves the performance of the network. The Fig. 9 shows that without the feature diversity learning of this strategy, the network will lack the ability to recognize some irrelevant features, which will lead to various irrelevant salient objects in the saliency map.

The Effectiveness of Global-Local Feature Match. To verify the effectiveness of the global-local feature match strategy proposed in this paper, we ablated the capsule correlation module (CCM) and the guided fusion module (GFM), respectively. From the evaluation metrics, it is seen that both CCM and GFM have positive effects on the detection of the network, with the SIP dataset being the most obvious. Figure 9 shows the comparison of saliency maps, the lack of both CCM and GFM causes the network to fail to detect the salient objects accurately.

The Effectiveness of Saliency Reconstruct Module. Saliency Reconstruct Module (SRM) aims to prevent information loss due to large gradients of dimensional changes during saliency reconstruction. We directly replace the SRM with conv 1×1 and bilinear interpolation layer. From the evaluation of the metrics, it can be seen that the SRM is more effective in improving network performance.

5 Conclusion

In this paper, we propose a DPFMN to handle feature match problems. In cross-modal feature match, we propose an Auxiliary-enhanced Module (AEM) to excavating the auxiliary information. In global-local feature matching, we propose Capsule Correlation Module (CCM) to realize the correlation between global-local features, and design Guided Fusion Module (GFM) to reduce the feature fusion loss rate. In the saliency map reconstruction, we introduce the Saliency Reconstruct Module (SRM) to ensure information stability. The effectiveness of our method is demonstrated in the comparison of 5 RGB-D and 3 RGB-T public datasets. In the future, we will reflect on and improve the unsatisfactory detection effect of some tasks, and continue to explore feature matching problems, and expand the scope of migration.

Acknowledgements. This research was supported by the Project of China West Normal University under Grant 17YC046.

References

1. Mahadevan, V., Vasconcelos, N.: Saliency-based discriminant tracking. In: IEEE Conference on Computer Vision and Pattern Recognition, pp. 1007–1013. IEEE (2009)
2. Jang, Y,K., Cho, N.I.: Generalized product quantization network for semi-supervised image retrieval. In: IEEE Conference on Computer Vision and Pattern Recognition, pp. 3420–3429. IEEE (2020)
3. Song, M., Song, W., Yang, G., Chen, C.: Improving RGB-D salient object detection via modality-aware decoder. J. IEEE Trans. Image Process. **31**, 6124–6138 (2022)

4. Huang, Y., Qiu, C., Yuan, K.: Surface defect saliency of magnetic tile. J. Vis. Comput. **36**, 85–96 (2020)

5. Ji, W., Li, J., Zhang, M., Piao, Y., Lu, H.: Accurate RGB-D salient object detection via collaborative learning. In: Vedaldi, A., Bischof, H., Brox, T., Frahm, J.-M. (eds.) ECCV 2020. LNCS, vol. 12363, pp. 52–69. Springer, Cham (2020). https://doi.org/10.1007/978-3-030-58523-5_4

6. Fan, D.P., Lin, Z., Zhang, Z., Zhu, M., Cheng, M.M.: Rethinking RGB-D salient object detection: models, data sets, and large-scale benchmarks. J. IEEE Trans. Neural Netw. Learn. Syst. **32**(5), 2075–2089 (2020)

7. Zhai, Y., et al.: Bifurcated backbone strategy for RGB-D salient object detection. J. IEEE Trans. Image Process. **30**, 8727–8742 (2021)

8. Zhang, J., et al.: UC-Net: uncertainty inspired RGB-D saliency detection via conditional variational autoencoders. In: IEEE Conference on Computer Vision and Pattern Recognition, pp. 8582–8591. IEEE (2020)

9. Zhang, Z., Lin, Z., Xu, J., Jin, W.D., Lu, S.P., Fan, D.P.: Bilateral attention network for RGB-D salient object detection. J. IEEE Trans. Image Process. **30**, 1949–1961 (2021)

10. Ji, W., et al.: Calibrated RGB-D salient object detection. In: IEEE Conference on Computer Vision and Pattern Recognition, pp. 9471–9481. IEEE (2021)

11. Lang, C., Nguyen, T.V., Katti, H., Yadati, K., Kankanhalli, M., Yan, S.: Depth matters: Influence of depth cues on visual saliency. In: 12th European Conference on Computer Vision, pp. 101–115 (2012)

12. Ciptadi, A., Hermans, T., Rehg, J.: An in depth view of saliency. In: British Machine Vision Conference (2013)

13. Tu, Z., Li, Z., Li, C., Lang, Y., Tang, J.: Multi-interactive dual-decoder for RGB-thermal salient object detection. J. IEEE Trans. Image Process. **30**, 5678–5691 (2021)

14. Zhou, W., Zhu, Y., Lei, J., Wan, J., Yu, L.: APNet: adversarial learning assistance and perceived importance fusion network for all-day RGB-T salient object detection. J. IEEE Trans. Emerg. Top. Comput. Intell. **6**(4), 957–968 (2021)

15. Huo, F., Zhu, X., Zhang, Q., Liu, Z., Yu, W.: Real-time one-stream semantic-guided refinement network for RGB-Thermal salient object detection. J. IEEE Trans. Instrum. Meas. **71**, 1–12 (2022)

16. Zhou, W., Zhu, Y., Lei, J., Yang, R., Yu, L.: LSNet: Lightweight spatial boosting network for detecting salient objects in RGB-thermal images. J. IEEE Trans. Image Process. **32**, 1329–1340 (2023)

17. Liu, Z., Huang, X., Zhang, G., Fang, X., Wang, L., Tang, B.: Scribble-Supervised RGB-T Salient Object Detection. arXiv preprint arXiv:2303.09733 (2023)

18. Wang, W., et al.: Pyramid vision transformer: a versatile backbone for dense prediction without convolutions. In: Proceedings of the IEEE/CVF International Conference on Computer Vision, pp. 568–578 (2021)

19. Liu, S., Huang, D.: Receptive field block net for accurate and fast object detection. In: Proceedings of the European Conference on Computer Vision, pp. 385–400 (2018)

20. Chen, L.C., Papandreou, G., Schroff, F., Adam, H.: Rethinking atrous convolution for semantic image segmentation. arXiv preprint arXiv:1706.05587 (2017)

21. Hinton, G.E., Sabour, S., Frosst, N.: Matrix capsules with EM routing. In: International Conference on Learning Representations (2018)

22. Sabour, S., Frosst, N., Hinton, G.E.: Dynamic routing between capsules. In: Advances in Neural Information Processing Systems (2017)

23. Ju, R., Ge, L., Geng, W., Ren, T., Wu, G.: Depth saliency based on anisotropic center-surround difference. In: IEEE International Conference on Image Processing, pp. 1115–1119 (2014)

24. Peng, H., Li, B., Xiong, W., Hu, W., Ji, R.: RGBD salient object detection: a benchmark and algorithms. In: The 13th European Conference on Computer Vision, pp. 92–109 (2014)

25. Zhu, C., Li, G.: A three-pathway psychobiological framework of salient object detection using stereoscopic technology. In: IEEE International Conference on Computer Vision Workshops, pp. 3008–3014 (2017)

26. Niu, Y., Geng, Y., Li, X., Liu, F.: Leveraging stereopsis for saliency analysis. In: IEEE Conference on Computer Vision and Pattern Recognition, pp. 454–461 (2012)

27. Wang, G., Li, C., Ma, Y., Zheng, A., Tang, J., Luo, B.: RGB-T saliency detection benchmark: dataset, baselines, analysis and a novel approach. In: 13th Conference on Image and Graphics Technologies and Applications, pp. 359–369 (2018)

28. Tu, Z., Xia, T., Li, C., Wang, X., Ma, Y., Tang, J.: RGB-T image saliency detection via collaborative graph learning. J. IEEE Trans. Multimedia $22(1)$, 160–173 (2019)

29. Tu, Z., Ma, Y., Li, Z., Li, C., Xu, J., Liu, Y.: RGBT salient object detection: a large-scale dataset and benchmark. IEEE Trans. Multimedia (2022)

30. Lee, M., Park, C., Cho, S., Lee, S.: Spsn: Superpixel prototype sampling network for rgb-d salient object detection. In: Avidan, S., Brostow, G., Cissé, M., Farinella, G.M., Hassner, T. (eds.) Computer Vision – ECCV 2022, vol. 13689, pp. 630–647. Springer, Cham (2022). https://doi.org/10.1007/978-3-031-19818-2_36

31. Liu, Z., Wang, Y., Tu, Z., Xiao, Y., Tang, B.: TriTransNet: RGB-D salient object detection with a triplet transformer embedding network. In: The 29th ACM International Conference on Multimedia, pp. 4481–4490 (2021)

32. Pang, Y., Zhao, X., Zhang, L., Lu, H.: CAVER: cross-modal view-mixed transformer for bi-modal salient object detection. J. IEEE Trans. Image Process. (2023)

33. Chen, T., Xiao, J., Hu, X., Zhang, G., Wang, S.: Adaptive fusion network for RGB-D salient object detection. J. Neurocomput. 522, 152–164 (2023)

34. Wu, J., Hao, F., Liang, W., Xu, J.: Transformer fusion and pixel-level contrastive learning for RGB-D salient object detection. J. IEEE Trans. Multimedia (2023)

35. Gao, W., Liao, G., Ma, S., Li, G., Liang, Y., Lin, W.: Unified information fusion network for multi-modal RGB-D and RGB-T salient object detection. J. IEEE Trans. Circ. Syst. Video Technol. $32(4)$, 2091–2106 (2021)

36. Liang, Y., Qin, G., Sun, M., Qin, J., Yan, J., Zhang, Z.: Multi-modal interactive attention and dual progressive decoding network for RGB-D/T salient object detection. J. Neurocomput. 490, 132–145 (2022)

37. Gu, K., Xia, Z., Qiao, J., Lin, W.: Deep dual-channel neural network for image-based smoke detection. J. IEEE Trans. Multimed. $22(2)$, 311–323 (2020)

A Optical Flow-Based Fight Behavior Detection Method for Campus Scene

Shu Yang[✉], Yali Li, and Shengjin Wang

Department of Electronic Engineering, Tsinghua University, Beijing 100084, China
yangshu91@mail.tsinghua.edu.cn

Abstract. Campuses contain a large number of facilities that must all
be monitored to ensure security. However, most of the existing video
surveillance needs to be watched by people, and it is impossible to realize
the automatic early warning of some dangerous situations. In this paper,
a video-based action detection method is proposed for high-frequency
student fight on campus, which uses an optical flow algorithm to perform
coarse positioning of the area where fight actions may occur and uses
the transformer network to identify the action category of the region
of interest. In addition, this paper builds a dataset of fight recognition
in middle school campuses for model training, validation and testing.
The experimental results show that the method proposed in this paper
can locate fight actions relatively accurately and provide real-time early
warning.

Keywords: Action recognition · Fight detection · Optical flow · Video
swin transformer

1 Introduction

With the rapid development of big data computing technology and Internet
of Things technology in China, smart campuses are an inevitable trend in the
development of digital campus construction. At present, the "smart campus"
system refers to quickly processing data information such as professional course
teaching and students' daily lives and storing the processed data content in the
background database to meet leadership management decision-making, teachers'
teaching and students' needs [1]. Among these data, surveillance data occupy a
large amount of storage space; however, these unstructured video data have not
been effectively utilized. Due to the lack of effective algorithms, these surveillance
videos are only used as the basis for determining responsibility after an incident
and cannot provide timely early warning when an incident occurs. Therefore,
for a truly *smart* campus system, video analysis algorithms that can accurately
analyze the monitored content and warn of possible dangers are very important.

On campuses, especially middle school campuses, student fights are a dangerous behavior that occurs frequently and can cause a certain degree of physical

Supported by China Postdoctoral Science Foundation (Grant No. 2022M721893).

and mental harm to students. If timely reminders can be given at the early stages of conflict, further escalation and more serious harm can be avoided. However, fights are characterized by uncertain times, uncertain locations, variable numbers of participants, complex movements and strong diversity, so there is a lack of effective and generalized fight recognition algorithms. This paper proposes a fight detection method for smart campuses, and the main contributions include the following:

1. A fight detection method based on optical flow is proposed, which realizes the coarse precision positioning of the area where the fight may occur by detecting the fast-moving region.
2. A fight dataset in the middle school campus was established, and a transformer network was trained on the public dataset and this dataset so that the model could identify the fight action in the campus scene.

2   Related Work

Action recognition [2–4] refers to the identification of a video clip that contains only a single action, and the model is trained with video clips with category labels to classify actions in unknown short videos. Temporal action detection [5–7] aims to identify long, untrimmed videos, each of which often contains multiple instances of actions in multiple categories. The task needs to provide not only the categories of actions contained in the video but also the time when each instance of action occurred. In the fields of surveillance, video retrieval and human-computer interaction, action recognition and detection are of great significance.

The existing action recognition and detection methods are based on object detection, skeletons, and spatiotemporal feature extraction. The method based on object detection [8–12] is to locate and identify people and objects in the scene to provide clues for the classification of actions. For example, in the action of *playing basketball*, key information such as basketball court, basketball, and players is more likely to appear, while in the action of *drinking*, bottles or cups need to appear. However, in video surveillance systems, the scene captured by the same camera is usually fixed, and even people and objects do not change much, making it difficult to distinguish the different actions that appear in the video. The skeleton-based method [13–22] first performs human detection and key point extraction and then distinguishes different actions, such as running, walking, falling, jumping, etc., by tracking body posture and movement patterns. These methods have two disadvantages. On the one hand, when the monitoring scene has a large flow of people, such as railway stations, supermarkets, and campuses, the key points will not be accurately detected due to a large amount of occlusion, which seriously affects the final action classification. On the other hand, in complex actions with variable body postures and movement patterns, such as fight, errors or missed detection often occur.

The method based on spatiotemporal feature extraction adopts a two-branch [6,23–26] or single-branch [27–29] deep neural network to extract static scene features and dynamic temporal features at the same time. These methods can adapt to a variety of shooting angles and shooting distances and have strong generalization ability. This paper focuses on the action of fight in campus scenes from the perspective of practical application. Considering the fact that the body movement in the fight is faster than normal activity, an optical flow-based method is used to locate the region of interest with coarse accuracy, thereby reducing the computational amount of the subsequent feature extraction model. In addition, this paper uses a large-scale general fight dataset and a small-scale campus scene fight dataset to train a video transformer to extract the spatiotemporal features of fight.

3   Our Approach

The proposed fight detection framework is shown in Fig. 1, which consists of four modules: a preprocessing module, a region of interest (ROI) detection module, a feature extraction module and a classification module. First, the input video is sliced for a certain duration in the preprocessing module. Second, these video clips are fed into the ROI detection module, the motion region is located based on the optical flow algorithm, and the video area that may have dangerous action is cropped. Again, the extracted spatial features and temporal features of the cropped video are performed. Finally, the presence of fight in this region is classified based on the extracted features.

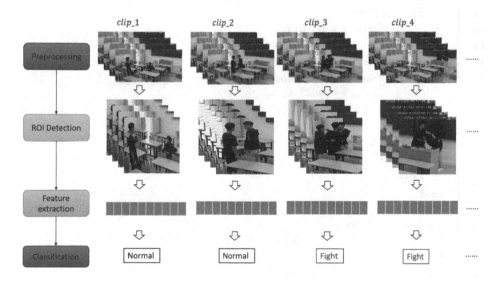

Fig. 1. The proposed fight detection framework.

3.1   ROI Detection Based on Optical Flow

In surveillance video, especially in indoor scenes, most of the background is static, while dangerous actions, such as fight, often manifest as strenuous exercise. Therefore, the detection of moving areas helps to focus the attention of the feature extraction model on these areas that are more likely to exhibit dangerous actions, thereby improving the accuracy of classification. In this paper, a motion region detection method based on optical flow is proposed, as shown in Algorithm 1.

Algorithm 1: ROI detection based on optical flow

Input: video clip $\{I_t\}, t \in (1, T)$
Output: $BBox$, ROI clip $\{I_t^r\}, t \in (1, T)$
1 Initialization: $X_{min} \leftarrow width, Y_{min} \leftarrow height, X_{max} \leftarrow 0, Y_{max} \leftarrow 0$
2 **begin**
3 | **for** $t \in (1, T-1)$ **do**
4 | | Calculate the optical flow of (I_t, I_{t+1}) based on Equation 1
5 | | Convert the optical flow to polar coordinates and into RGB space
6 | | **for** *each pixel* (r, g, b) *in the optical flow image* **do**
7 | | | $gray = 0.299r + 0.578g + 0.114b$
8 | | | $binary = gray > \alpha?255 : 0$
9 | | **end**
10 | | Draw contours C for the binary image
11 | | **for** $c \in C$ **do**
12 | | | **if** $Area(c) > \beta$ **then**
13 | | | | Calculate the bounding box (x_1, y_1, x_2, y_2) of c
14 | | | | $X_{min} \leftarrow min(X_{min}, x_1)$
15 | | | | $Y_{min} \leftarrow min(Y_{min}, y_1)$
16 | | | | $X_{max} \leftarrow max(X_{max}, x_2)$
17 | | | | $Y_{max} \leftarrow max(Y_{max}, y_2)$
18 | | | **else**
19 | | | | Pass
20 | | | **end**
21 | | **end**
22 | **end**
23 | $BBbox \leftarrow (X_{min}, Y_{min}, X_{max}, Y_{max})$
24 | **for** $t \in (1, T)$ **do**
25 | | $I_t^r \leftarrow I_t[Y_{min} : Y_{max}, X_{min} : X_{max}]$
26 | **end**
27 | **return** $BBbox, \{I_t^r\}, t \in (1, T)$
28 **end**

Given T video frames, the optical flow of all points is first obtained based on two adjacent video frames, and the Lucas-Kanade [30] optical flow algorithm is used here. This method calculates the movement of each pixel position between two frames under three assumptions: constant brightness (that is, the gray value of the target pixel in the scene does not change with the tracking of the frame), time continuity (that is, the change in time does not cause a drastic change in the position of the pixel), and spatial consistency (that is, adjacent points on the same surface in the scene have similar motion). Therefore, it can be assumed that within a window of size $n = m \times m$, the optical flow is calculated as follows:

$$\begin{bmatrix} u \\ v \end{bmatrix} = \begin{bmatrix} \sum_{i=1}^{n} \nabla_{xi}^2 & \sum_{i=1}^{n} \nabla_{xi} \nabla_{yi} \\ \sum_{i=1}^{n} \nabla_{xi} \nabla_{yi} & \sum_{i=1}^{n} \nabla_{yi}^2 \end{bmatrix}^{-1} \begin{bmatrix} -\sum_{i=1}^{n} \nabla_{xi} \nabla_{ti} \\ -\sum_{i=1}^{n} \nabla_{yi} \nabla_{ti} \end{bmatrix} \tag{1}$$

where u and v represent the speed of movement in two directions (x direction and y direction). ∇_x, ∇_y and ∇_t represent gradients of brightness on the three axes.

Then, the Cartesian coordinates of the optical flow image are converted to polar coordinates, normalized and converted into RGB space, as shown in Fig. 2(b), which is a visualization of the optical flow using color images. Next, the RGB image is grayscale and binarized with threshold α to obtain pixels with relatively fast moving speed, and the contour calculation and the external rectangle calculation are performed on these areas. As shown in Fig. 2(c), two rectangular areas are obtained after removing the noise region with threshold β. Finally, after T frames are calculated, all regions are merged by counting the maximum and minimum values of the coordinates in all rectangular regions to avoid the loss of critical regions caused by inaccurate estimation. As shown in Fig. 2(d), the resulting cropped video preserves the motion region over the entire time domain.

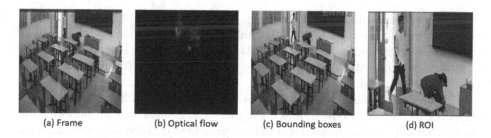

| (a) Frame | (b) Optical flow | (c) Bounding boxes | (d) ROI |

Fig. 2. The (a) input, (b)(c) intermediate results, and (d) output of the proposed ROI detection method.

3.2 Action Recognition Based on Swin Transformer

In the video feature extraction and classification stage, traditional methods usually use 2D CNN-RNN [31, 32] or 3D CNN [5, 25, 28, 29]. This paper uses a transformer network that is more suitable for processing sequence information. Compared with 3D CNNs, transformers have low computational complexity, and compared with RNNs, transformers can realize parallel computing and use positional coding to solve the problem of loss of timing information.

A multi-stage transformer [33] is adopted, as shown in Fig. 3. Compared with text, the resolution of images and videos is large, the scale of visual instances varies greatly, and multi-scale feature learning cannot be achieved using traditional visual transformers, such as ViT [34]. Therefore, [33] introduces a hierarchical construction method of CNN into the transformer, that is, through multiple stages, the number of tokens decreases, and the sensory field of each token becomes increasingly larger. This method reduces the amount of computation by decreasing the number of tokens and calculating the window transformer. At the same time, considering that pixels that are closer in the distance between the spatial and temporal domains will be more correlated, the network adopts a local self-attention structure.

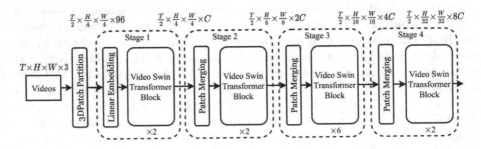

Fig. 3. The network architecture of the video swin transformer [33].

In the training phase, each video clip is evenly sampled in the time domain, and a 32-frame slice with a resolution of 224×224 is obtained as the input of the feature extraction model. Then, a 3D sliding window with a size of $8 \times 7 \times 7$ is used to sample with a time domain step of 2, and a 3D token with a size of $16 \times 56 \times 56$ is obtained.

In the verification and testing phase, each video clip is first divided into 4 segments in the time domain, and 3 samples of 224×224 size are performed in the spatial domain to obtain 4×3 video slices, that is, 12 videos with different viewing angles. Then, the trained feature extraction model and classifier are used to classify these 12 slices, and the average of the 12 obtained predictions is used as the final prediction result of the video sample.

4   Experiments

4.1   Datasets and Settings

The experiment uses two datasets, which are described in detail as follows:

Five-Fight Dataset: It consists of 5 public datasets containing a total of 3,000+ violent and nonviolent video clips ranging in length from 2 s to 5 s. Sources of this dataset include sports games, movies, public surveillance, and indoor interpretations, some of which contain both violent and nonviolent samples, as shown in Fig. 4. In this paper, refer to the settings in [35], 80% of the two categories are randomly selected for the training of the transformer network, and the remaining 20% are utilized for validation.

Fig. 4. Sample examples of the Five-fight dataset.

School-Fight Dataset: This is our self-collected campus fight dataset, using the monitoring perspective in the classroom, where students perform learning, talking, fighting and other behaviors. As shown in Fig. 5, the dataset has fixed backgrounds and people, so the classification task is more dependent on temporal features and more challenging. In the training and verification phase of the transformer network, the video is cut into 858 clips for 2 s to 3 s and divided into two categories: "fight" and "normal". During the testing phase of the entire algorithm, the input is a long video of more than 10 s, and the training and validation slices are not included in the testing video.

Settings: The feature extraction model uses a Swin-T [33] pre-trained on the Kinetics-400 dataset [4], and the classification layer is randomly initialized. Eight TITAN XP GPUs are used for training, and the batch size is set to 8. The model first performs 50 epochs of iterative optimization on the Five-fight dataset and then 30 epochs on the School-fight dataset.

4.2   Results

Table 1 shows the sample distribution of the training and validation sets. Figure 6 shows the confusion matrix on the two validation sets. The experimental results show that the accuracy of the model reaches more than 96% on the verification set of the two datasets. In particular, in the campus scene, all the fight samples are detected, and the missed detection rate is 0.

Table 2 shows the accuracy of our model and existing fight detection tool PaddleDetection [35] on the validation set. The PaddleDetection tool uses the

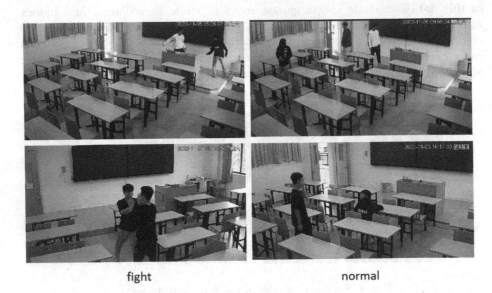

fight   normal

Fig. 5. Sample examples of our School-fight dataset. The faces have been blurred.

Table 1. Sample distributions of two fight datasets.

Dataset	number of training samples	number of val samples
Five-fight	3,080	770
School-fight	739	119

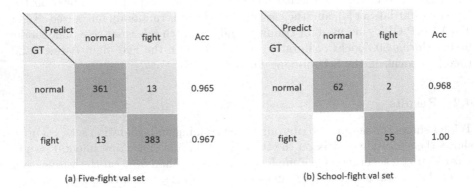

(a) Five-fight val set   (b) School-fight val set

Fig. 6. Confusion matrix for validation sets.

ResNet50 model based on Simple Semi-supervised Label Distillation (SSLD) to extract frame features, and uses the VideoMix [36] data enhancement method to train the classification model. Experimental results show that the swin transformer-based model in our method can extract spatial and temporal domain features and outperform the CNN-based model without additional optimization tricks.

Table 2. Performance on validation sets.

Method	Five-fight	School-fight
PaddleDetection [35]	88.01%	–
Ours	96.62%	98.32%

In the testing phase, predictions are made every 2 s for long, untrimmed videos in School-fight, including ROI detection and fight prediction for the 2-second video clips. The experimental results are shown in Fig. 7. At the beginning of the video, the two classmates are learning, which includes some conversation and physical contact, and the model predicts these behaviors as "normal", indicating that the algorithm can recognize normal physical contact without misjudging it as a fight. A third person then approached and got into an altercation with one of them, the conflict escalated and a fight occurred, at which point the prediction turned out to be "Fight" and a red alert signal was issued. Then, the other person joins the fight, and the model still predicts "Fight", indicating that the algorithm can identify more than two participants in the fight. In terms of computational efficiency, for each 2-second test clip, the running time of the ROI detection algorithm based on optical flow is approximately 1.3 s, and the prediction time of feature extraction and classification is approximately 0.45 s, indicating that the algorithm can realize real-time warning of fight behavior.

Figure 8 shows the test results in other scenarios. The results show that the method proposed in this paper can effectively detect fighting behaviors in various shooting angles, scenes, and the number of participants, and has good generalization.

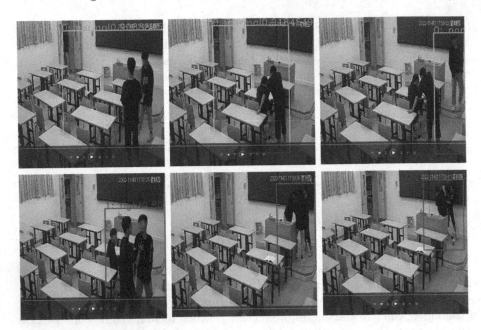

Fig. 7. The results of fight detection on untrimmed long videos. The faces have been blurred.

Fig. 8. Tested in multiple scenes. Videos are from the Internet, and the faces have been blurred.

5   Conclusion

In this paper, a fight detection method based on optical flow is proposed, and a school fight dataset in middle school campus scenes is established for training and testing the transformer network. Experimental results show that the proposed algorithm can effectively identify the fight of different positions in the picture and different numbers of participants.

References

1. Xu, Y.: Research on the design of smart campus system based on big data and internet of things. China Computer and Communication (2019)
2. Kuehne, H., Jhuang, H., Garrote, E., Poggio, T., Serre, T.: HMDB: a large video database for human motion recognition. In: Proceedings of the International Conference on Computer Vision (ICCV) (2011)
3. Soomro, K., Zamir, A.R., Shah, M.: Ucf101: a dataset of 101 human actions classes from videos in the wild. Computer Science (2012)
4. Kay, W., Carreira, J., Simonyan, K., Zhang, B., Zisserman, A.: The kinetics human action video dataset (2017)
5. Xu, H., Das, A., Saenko, K.: R-c3d: region convolutional 3d network for temporal activity detection. In: 2017 IEEE International Conference on Computer Vision (ICCV), pp.5794–5803 (2017)
6. Chao, Y.W., Vijayanarasimhan, S., Seybold, B., Ross, D.A., Deng, J., Sukthankar, R.: Rethinking the faster R-CNN architecture for temporal action localization. In: 2018 IEEE/CVF Conference on Computer Vision and Pattern Recognition (CVPR), pp. 1130–1139 (2018)
7. Long, F., Yao, T., Qiu, Z., Tian, X., Luo, J., Mei, T.: Gaussian temporal awareness networks for action localization. In: 2019 IEEE/CVF Conference on Computer Vision and Pattern Recognition (CVPR), pp. 344–353 (2019)
8. Wang, H., Kläser, A., Schmid, C., Liu, C.L.: Dense trajectories and motion boundary descriptors for action recognition. Int. J. Comput. Vis. **103**(1), 60–79 (2013)
9. Wang, H., Schmid, C.: Action recognition with improved trajectories. In: 2013 IEEE International Conference on Computer Vision (2014)
10. Akila, K., Chitrakala, S.: Discriminative human action recognition using hoi descriptor and key poses. In: 2014 International Conference on Science Engineering and Management Research, pp. 1–6 (2014)
11. Wang, X., Chen, D., Feng, H., Yang, T., Bo, H.U.: Action recognition based on object detection and dense trajectories. J. Fudan Univ. (Nat. Sci.) (2016)
12. Min, J., Kasturi, R.: Activity recognition based on multiple motion trajectories. In: Proceedings of the 17th International Conference on Pattern Recognition 2004, ICPR 2004 (2004)
13. Vemulapalli, R., Arrate, F., Chellappa, R.: Human action recognition by representing 3d skeletons as points in a lie group. In: 2014 IEEE Conference on Computer Vision and Pattern Recognition, pp. 588–595 (2014)
14. Wang, H., et al.: Understanding the robustness of skeleton-based action recognition under adversarial attack. In: 2021 IEEE/CVF Conference on Computer Vision and Pattern Recognition (CVPR), pp. 14651–14660 (2021)
15. Devanne, M., Wannous, H., Berretti, S., Pala, P., Daoudi, M., Del Bimbo, A.: 3-d human action recognition by shape analysis of motion trajectories on Riemannian manifold. IEEE Trans. Cybern. **45**(7), 1340–1352 (2015)
16. Du, Y., Wang, W., Wang, L.: Hierarchical recurrent neural network for skeleton based action recognition. In: 2015 IEEE Conference on Computer Vision and Pattern Recognition (CVPR), pp. 1110–1118 (2015)

17. Zhang, P., Lan, C., Xing, J., Zeng, W., Xue, J., Zheng, N.: View adaptive neural networks for high performance skeleton-based human action recognition. IEEE Trans. Pattern Anal. Mach. Intell. **41**(8), 1963–1978 (2019)
18. Shi, L., Zhang, Y., Cheng, J., Lu, H.: Skeleton-based action recognition with directed graph neural networks. In: 2019 IEEE/CVF Conference on Computer Vision and Pattern Recognition (CVPR), pp. 7904–7913 (2019)
19. Cheng, K., Zhang, Y., He, X., Chen, W., Cheng, J., Lu, H.: Skeleton-based action recognition with shift graph convolutional network. In: 2020 IEEE/CVF Conference on Computer Vision and Pattern Recognition (CVPR), pp. 180–189 (2020)
20. Liu, Z., Zhang, H., Chen, Z., Wang, Z., Ouyang, W.: Disentangling and unifying graph convolutions for skeleton-based action recognition. In: 2020 IEEE/CVF Conference on Computer Vision and Pattern Recognition (CVPR), pp. 140–149 (2020)
21. Zhang, X., Xu, C., Tao, D.: Context aware graph convolution for skeleton-based action recognition. In: 2020 IEEE/CVF Conference on Computer Vision and Pattern Recognition (CVPR), pp. 14321–14330 (2020)
22. Zhang, P., Lan, C., Zeng, W., Xing, J., Xue, J., Zheng, N.: Semantics-guided neural networks for efficient skeleton-based human action recognition. In: 2020 IEEE/CVF Conference on Computer Vision and Pattern Recognition (CVPR), pp. 1109–1118 (2020)
23. Simonyan, K., Zisserman, A.: Two-stream convolutional networks for action recognition in videos. In: Advances in Neural Information Processing Systems, vol. 1 (2014)
24. Feichtenhofer, C., Pinz, A., Zisserman, A.: Convolutional two-stream network fusion for video action recognition. In: 2016 IEEE Conference on Computer Vision and Pattern Recognition (CVPR), pp. 1933–1941 (2016)
25. Carreira, J., Zisserman, A: Quo vadis, action recognition? a new model and the kinetics dataset. In: 2017 IEEE Conference on Computer Vision and Pattern Recognition (CVPR), pp. 4724–4733 (2017)
26. Feichtenhofer, C., Fan, H., Malik, J., He, K.: Slowfast networks for video recognition. In: 2019 IEEE/CVF International Conference on Computer Vision (ICCV), pp. 6201–6210 (2019)
27. Graham, W.T., Fergus, R., Lecun, Y., Bregler, C.: Convolutional learning of spatio-temporal features. In: European Conference on Computer Vision (2010)
28. Tran, D., Bourdev, L., Fergus, R., Torresani, L., Paluri, M.: Learning spatiotemporal features with 3d convolutional networks. In: 2015 IEEE International Conference on Computer Vision (ICCV), pp. 4489–4497 (2015)
29. Qiu, Z., Yao, T., Mei, T.: Learning spatio-temporal representation with pseudo-3d residual networks. In: 2017 IEEE International Conference on Computer Vision (ICCV), pp. 5534–5542 (2017)
30. Lucas, B.D.: Generalized Image Matching by the Method of Differences. Carnegie Mellon University (1985)
31. Sharma, S., Kiros, R., Salakhutdinov, R.: Action recognition using visual attention (2015)
32. Dai, C., Liu, X., Lai, J.: Human action recognition using two-stream attention based LSTM networks. Appl. Soft Comput. **86**, 105820 (2020)
33. Liu, Z., et al.: Video swin transformer. In: 2022 IEEE/CVF Conference on Computer Vision and Pattern Recognition (CVPR), pp. 3192–3201 (2022)
34. Dosovitskiy, A., et al.: An image is worth 16x16 words: transformers for image recognition at scale. In: International Conference on Learning Representations (2021)

35. Authors, P.: Paddledetection, object detection and instance segmentation toolkit based on paddlepaddle. https://github.com/PaddlePaddle/PaddleDetection (2019)
36. Yun, S., Oh, S.J., Heo, B., Han, D., Kim, J.: Videomix: Rethinking data augmentation for video classification (2020)

Attention-Guided Neural Network for Face Mask Detection

Bowen Zhang, Shuyi Li, Zhuming Wang, and Lifang Wu[✉]

Faculty of Information Technology, Beijing University of Technology, Beijing 100124, China
{syli2022,lfwu}@bjut.edu.cn

Abstract. With the outbreak of COVID-19 and various influenza diseases, it is necessary to wear masks properly in crowded public places to prevent the spread of the virus. Therefore, detecting mask-wearing efficiently and accurately is essential for people's physical health and safety. In this paper, we present a novel one-stage mask detection method, named attention-guided neural network (AGNN) that can efficiently detect non-mask-wearing faces in public. Specifically, we started with YOLOv5 as a baseline and integrated the coordinate attention mechanism module into YOLOv5 to guide the holistic model for improving the ability of feature extraction. Furthermore, we explored utilizing the focal loss to solve the problem of class imbalance. The experiment is conducted on the face mask detection dataset of real-life scenes with twenty different categories. Experimental results demonstrate that the proposed AGNN method achieves higher precision and recall than the original YOLOv5 in multi-classification mask detection.

Keywords: Attention mechanism · Face mask detection · One-stage detector · Focal Loss

1 Introduction

COVID-19-infected pneumonia is easily transmitted by droplets or aerosols [1]. Maintaining social distance is the key to controlling the COVID-19 pandemic, which can prevent droplet transmission of the virus. In recent years, it has been proven that the effectiveness of masks in preventing virus transmission is approximately 68% and can reach 91% [2]. Therefore, to avoid the direct spread of infectious diseases, wearing a mask is very important for the health and safety of individuals and the public. Therefore, efficiently detecting whether personnel are wearing masks correctly has become an important issue. Compared to the traditional manual way of mask detection, the deep learning-based mask detection algorithm can significantly improve efficiency and reduce the risk of cross-infection.

In general, the mask detection task is treated as a downstream task of object detection. Existing deep learning-based object detection algorithms are mainly divided into two categories: the one-stage detection algorithm and the two-stage detection algorithm. Among them, the representative two-stage algorithm is the regions with convolutional neural networks (R-CNN) [3]. In the first stage, region proposal, the R-CNN algorithm

W. Yongtian and W. Lifang (Eds.): IGTA 2023, CCIS 1910, pp. 194–207, 2023.
https://doi.org/10.1007/978-981-99-7549-5_15

divided the candidate regions where the target might appear in the input image. Then, in the second stage, the R-CNN used the CNN network to classify and regress each candidate region to detect the target. The classical one-stage algorithm is represented by the You Only Look Once (YOLO) algorithm [4]. YOLO used the CNN network to extract the features of the input image and explored the regression method to generate detection information. Following this, targets are located and classified according to the extracted position coordinates and category probability. It can be observed that the two-stage detection algorithm has high accuracy but slow speed, while the one-stage detection algorithm has fast speed but low accuracy. Due to the high real-time requirement of the mask detection task, using the YOLO series algorithm to detect face mask-wearing is becoming increasingly popular. Moreover, compared with other YOLO series, YOLOv5 has the advantages of high detection efficiency, easy reproduction, and better accuracy [5]. Thus, in this paper, we developed a novel mask detection algorithm based on the YOLOv5 framework to accurately detect face masks.

In recent years, various face mask detection methods have been proposed and widely developed in real-life application scenarios [6]. For example, Sethi et al. [7] present a deep learning-based face mask detection technique that efficiently detects non-mask faces and enables real-time detection in public scenes. Subsequently, Wang et al. [8] proposed a two-stage approach to detect wearing masks using hybrid machine learning techniques. Experimental results on a self-built wearing-mask database demonstrated the effectiveness of the proposed methods in simple and complex scenes. However, most face mask detection methods are generally regarded as a binary classification problem of whether a mask is being worn or not. In real-life scenarios, the way of mask-wearing is various and different, which can greatly affect the effectiveness of the mask in protecting against viruses [7]. For instance, wearing a mask under the nose or the mouth belongs to incorrect mask-wearing behavior. Nevertheless, the simple binary classification cannot distinguish the above non-mask-wearing behaviors. Therefore, this article treats the face mask detection task as a multi-classification task in real-life scenes.

To solve this problem, we present an attention-guided neural network (AGNN) for multi-classification face mask detection. In the proposed AGNN, we focus on investigating the effectiveness of an attention mechanism to improve detection accuracy and the significance of a focal loss to solve the problem of class imbalance. Specifically, we first integrated the coordinate attention mechanism module into YOLOv5 to improve the feature extraction capability. Further, we replaced the binary cross-entropy loss using the focal loss to solve the problem of class imbalance. We performed the experiments on a self-built face mask detection dataset under real-life scenes. The dataset covers various public areas such as residential areas, factories, crowded markets, bus stops, etc. Experimental results show that the proposed AGNN achieves better accuracy than the original YOLOv5.

The contributions of our work can be summarized as follows:

(1) We proposed a novel attention-guided neural network (AGNN) based on YOLOv5 for multi-classification mask detection in public scenes. The proposed AGNN model utilized the coordinate attention module to guide the whole network to accurately detect the mask features from video streams.

(2) We explored to use of the focal loss to replace the standard binary cross-entropy loss to address the class imbalance. This loss helps in better localizing the real target in the case of various anchor boxes falling in the background area.

(3) We evaluated the proposed AGNN under the public real-life scenes. Experimental results show that our proposed method has a superior detection performance compared to the original YOLOv5 framework. More importantly, the computational complexity of the proposed model was not significantly increased.

2 Related Work

2.1 YOLO Algorithm

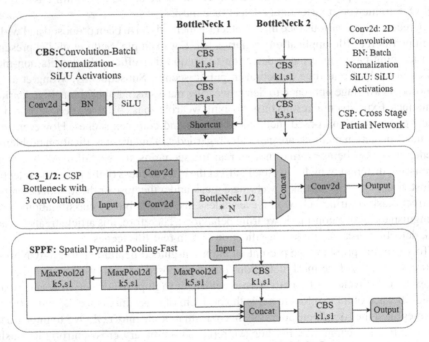

Fig. 1. Modules in the backbone of YOLOv5.

As one of the most popular target detection algorithms, YOLO has solved the trade-off between speed and accuracy in detecting objects [9]. However, YOLO does not detect small targets well, and the YOLO model without the previous frames results in low detection accuracy. To address this problem, YOLOv2 [10] used the Darknet to optimize the network and added the initialized anchor boxes to reduce the difficulty of box prediction. It still has the problems of the single feature map, difficulty in detecting small targets, and insufficient depth of neural network layers. For this reason, YOLOv3 incorporated the residual network and the feature fusion methods, as well as used the Darknet-53 optimized network structure [11]. YOLOv3 has the advantage of high speed, high versatility, and low background false detection rate. Unfortunately, YOLOv3 suffers from low model recall and difficulty in handling occluded images and target-dense images. YOLOv4 [12] was published with an architecture divided into three main parts: the backbone for feature extraction, the neck for feature aggregation, and the head for localization and classification decisions.

The structure of YOLOv5 is similar to YOLOv4. The main included modules of YOLOv5 as shown in Fig. 1. The convolution-batch normalization-SiLU activations block (CBS) and the cross-stage partial network (CSP) bottleneck with three convolutions (C3) block are used for feature extraction. The spatial pyramid pooling-fast (SPPF) block made use of the fusion of different pools to obtain the fused features of the different receptive fields. Meanwhile, YOLOv5 improves the auto-learning of bounding box anchors and introduces the mosaic data augmentation technique. Compared with other series of YOLO, YOLOv5 has accurate target localization and fast convergence speed, achieving a high correct classification rate and low training time cost [13].

2.2 Attention Mechanism

The principle of the attention mechanism is similar to the way humans acquire information from images. The attention mechanism model extracts all features in an image and then quickly captures the detailed information for the region of interest. This makes the model sensitive to the valid features in the image and suppresses the invalid features.

As one of the most commonly used attention modules, the squeeze-and-excitation (SE) attention [14] has primordially been applied to lightweight models. However, it generally neglects the positional information, which is significant for the generation of spatially selective attention maps [15]. Subsequently, the convolutional block attention module (CBAM) [16] tries to exploit the positional information by global pooling on channels [17]. However, this approach only obtains local information and cannot extract long-range relationships. In this paper, the coordinate attention (CA) module [18] is introduced to improve the original YOLOv5 model by avoiding the problems of the above-mentioned attention mechanism.

3 Proposed Method

In this section, we propose a novel target detection algorithm, called attention-guided neural network (AGNN), for multi-classification face mask detection. The overall framework of the proposed AGNN model is illustrated in Fig. 2.

As shown in Fig. 2, the main blocks of the proposed AGNN are summarized in four parts: the input for image preprocessing, the backbone for feature extraction, the neck for feature aggregation, and the head for category detection.

1) Input: Given the training images, the input part is mainly for image preprocessing, such as data augmentation, image normalization, and other operations. AGNN preprocesses input images mainly using mosaic data augmentation and adaptive image scaling.

2) Backbone: As shown in Fig. 2, the CBS block and the C3 block are used multiple times for feature extraction in the backbone. AGNN utilizes the CA module to represent different features. In this way, the network can fully extract the semantic features of masks and faces in the image [19]. In the CA module, the extracted features are weighted and fused to reduce information loss. The SPPF block enhances the ability of the model to detect objects of different sizes by enriching the feature map information.

3) Neck: The neck part is used to adjust the features extracted by the backbone to better match the requirements of the head. Due to the large size of the features output by the backbone, it cannot be used directly for object detection and classification. To integrate the semantic features of different levels and localize the target more accurately. AGNN performs a weighted features fusion of different dimensions through the neck network combined with feature pyramid networks (FPN) [20] and path aggregation network (PAN) [21].

4) Head: The output of the head part is the bounding box coordinates and category labels. YOLOv5 calculated the position loss of the bounding box by the CIOU loss [22] and the class loss by the binary cross-entropy loss. AGNN uses the focal loss instead of the binary cross-entropy loss to improve the focus of the model on hard-to-classify targets. In this way, AGNN can locate the positions of mask and face targets quickly and accurately, which improves the accuracy of face mask detection. To filter the predicted bounding boxes, the non-maximum suppression algorithm (NMS) [23] was used. The remaining bounding boxes and their categories are output after removing the predicted bounding boxes with high local coincidence or low confidence.

3.1   Backbone of AGNN

As shown in Fig. 2, the AGNN model includes the base backbone module of YOLOv5 and the CA module. The base backbone module of YOLOv5 is used to extract the features of three different sizes in the input image through five convolutions and four residual networks. The extracted features of the smallest size are fed to the CA module for further feature extraction. The detailed basis backbone module for YOLOv5 can be found in Sect. 2.1.

In the CA module, the input features are initially averaged in both horizontal and vertical directions by the block. The features are aggregated in both spatial directions to produce a pair of feature maps that are sensitive to directionality. Secondly, the module uses the concatenate operation to merge the two feature maps. The convolution operation is performed in the spatial dimension to compress the channels. The vertical and horizontal spatial information is subsequently encoded using batch normalization (BN) and the sigmoid function. Thirdly, the CA module conducts a convolution operation to split the features and adjust the number of channels to match that of the input feature vector. Finally, The normalization weighting is conducted, and the extracted features are subsequently generated [24].

In contrast to the attention module of SE, which solely considers encoding of inter-channel information. The CA module also incorporates positional information encoding. A pair of maps along the horizontal and vertical directions are applied to the input features

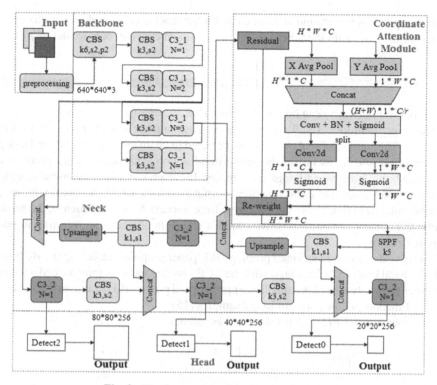

Fig. 2. The framework of the proposed AGNN

simultaneously. These two transformations also enable our attention block to effectively capture long-range dependencies in one spatial direction while preserving precise positional information in the other spatial direction [18]. This encoding process enables the model to accurately localize the object of interest through channel attention, which helps the overall model to better identify the target. It also enriches the expressiveness capability of the model by giving higher weights to the output features.

The CA module is flexible and lightweight enough to be simply embedded into the core architecture of a network. It can be used as a pre-trained model for multiple tasks with good performance improvement.

3.2 Loss Function

The category prediction loss is to determine whether the object in the anchor box is the real target (positive sample) or the background (negative sample). In the original YOLOv5, the binary cross-entropy (BCE) loss is used to calculate the category prediction loss. The BCE loss of $CE(p, y)$ can be calculated as follows:

$$CE(p, y) = \begin{cases} -log(p), & if \ y = 1 \\ -log(1 - p), & otherwise \end{cases} \tag{1}$$

where y represents the ground-truth class and p denotes the estimated probability of the model for the class with the label $y = 1$. For notational convenience, we define p_t as:

$$p_t = \begin{cases} p, & \textit{if } y = 1 \\ 1 - p, & \textit{otherwise} \end{cases} \tag{2}$$

In this way, $CE(p, y)$ can be rewritten as $CE(p, y) = CE(p_t) = -\log(p_t)$.

However, the model of YOLOv5 generates a large number of anchor boxes to localize the target. The number of real targets to be detected in an image is very small and a large number of anchor boxes fall in the background region. This leads to the problem of non-equilibrium positive and negative samples. In the presence of class imbalance, the negative samples dominate the function computation loss, while the small number of positive samples and difficult samples have little impact. As a consequence, the model barely learns the features of positive samples and difficult samples, resulting in poor detection results.

To solve the above-mentioned problem, this paper proposed replacing the BCE loss with the focal loss [25]. Compared with the BCE loss, the focal loss introduced a weight coefficient α to solve the class imbalance problem and proposed a parameter γ to reshape the loss function to down-weight easy examples [15].

The focal loss of $FL(p, y)$ is calculated as follows:

$$FL(p, y) = \begin{cases} -\alpha(1 - p)^\gamma \log(p), & \textit{if } y = 1 \\ -(1 - \alpha)p^\gamma \log(1 - p), & \textit{otherwise} \end{cases} \tag{3}$$

where α is the weight coefficient to balance the importance of positive and negative samples. When α is greater than 0.5, the weight of the positive sample is greater than that of the negative sample. In this way, the sensitivity of the model to positive samples can be improved. In general, the parameter α is equal to 0.75, the model achieves the best result. Same as the above-mentioned $CE(p_t)$, $FL(p, y)$ can be rewritten as $FL(p, y) = FL(p_t) = -(1- p_t)^\gamma \log(p_t)$.

In Eq. (3), the parameter γ represents the degree of model focus on hard-to-classify samples. Figure 3 illustrates the effect of parameter γ on loss [25]. The BCE loss can be seen as the blue (top) curve in Fig. 3. Setting $\gamma > 0$ reduces the relative loss for well-classified examples ($p_t > 0.5$), putting more focus on hard, misclassified examples, and as γ is increased the effect of the modulating factor is likewise increased (we found $\gamma = 1.5$ to work best in our experiments). The proposed focal loss enables training highly accurate dense object detectors in the presence of vast numbers of easy background examples [26].

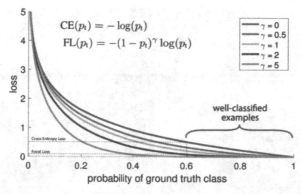

$$CE(p_t) = -\log(p_t)$$

$$FL(p_t) = -(1 - p_t)^\gamma \log(p_t)$$

Fig. 3. Effect of parameter γ on loss

4 Experiment and Analysis

We use the original YOLOv5 model as the baseline experiment. Then, we replace the BCE loss with the focal loss. We set parameter γ as 1.5 and parameter α as 0.75. Finally, we add the CA block in the YOLOv5 framework. All experiments are implemented in Python. The simulation experiments are run on the Extreme Mart platform with an Nvidia Tesla T4-16 GB GPU. We use images with size 640 × 640 pixels, batch size equal to 32, hyperparameter configuration file use hyp.scratch-low, and train the model for 100 epochs.

4.1 Dataset

To verify the performance of the proposed algorithm, we conduct the experiments on a self-built Face Mask Detection dataset from the Extreme Mart platform [27]. The face mask dataset includes 50,068 images in total, and there are 39,938 images in the training dataset and 10,130 images in the test dataset. The dataset images include a variety of real-life scenes such as kitchens, residential areas, factories, and hospitals. All of which are camera surveillance images 3–5 m from the ground. There are both single-target face mask detection images and multiple-target face mask detection images in the dataset. Some example images are shown in Fig. 4.

This face mask detection dataset categorizes over 20 classes, including the detection of masks worn on the front, side, and back. For front faces, there are four types of front faces and three types of face masks labeled: front wearing face, front no wearing face, front under nose wearing face, front under mouth wearing face, mask front wearing, mask front under nose wearing, mask front under mouth wearing. For the side faces, the face and mask types are similar to the front types above. The side and back faces are labeled mainly for the back face where the mask band is visible. When the mask band can be seen, the mask is considered to be worn. The last four types are labeled on the back of the head, the straps, the front unknown, and the side unknown.

By labeling the dataset in multiple categories, the model can detect the specific behavior of wearing the mask incorrectly. The discriminative power of the model is increased and the practical application value of the model is improved.

Fig. 4. Some example images in the face mask detection dataset.

4.2 Performance Metrics

To evaluate the performance of the proposed model, in the experiments, we compared the precision, recall, and F-score results. The precision is the ratio of correct prediction boxes to all prediction boxes and is used to measure the ability of the model to accurately find the correct prediction box. The recall is the proportion of correct prediction boxes to all real boxes and is used to measure the ability of the model to recall the real boxes. The precision and the recall are defined as follows:

$$Precision = \frac{True\ Positive(TP)}{True\ Positive(TP) + False\ Positive(FP)} \tag{4}$$

$$Recall = \frac{True\ Positive(TP)}{True\ Positive(TP) + False\ Negative(FN)} \tag{5}$$

where TP denotes the prediction box overlaps with the real target box, and the prediction category is the same as the real category. TN represents the background that does not contain a real target box and is not model-checked. FP is the prediction box that does not detect the real target, that is, the background is mistaken for the target. FN is the real target that is not detected.

Obviously, the higher the precision and recall, the better the performance of the model. In real-life large-scale datasets, these two above-mentioned indicators are often mutually restricted. The F-score, which combines precision and recall, is proposed as an evaluation metric for fair validation of models. The F-score can be represented as follows:

$$F - score = \frac{2 * precision * recall}{precision + recall} \tag{6}$$

The value of the F-score ranges from 0 to 1, with higher values indicating better performance of the detector.

4.3 Experimental Result

To verify the effectiveness of the proposed algorithm, we conducted three sets of quantitative evaluation experiments separately.

First, we compared the proposed algorithm with the original YOLOv5 algorithm and the YOLOv5 algorithm with focal loss. The average precision, recall, and F-score results for the twenty classes of different algorithms are shown in Table 1. From Table 1, we can see that the proposed algorithm consistently achieves the best precision, recall, and F-score. Specifically, in comparison to the original YOLOv5, the proposed algorithm improves precision by 1.1%, recall by 2.27%, and F-value by 1.82%, respectively. This result indicates that the attention mechanism module can help improve the detection performance. Further over, it is worth noting that the performance of the YOLOv5 with focal loss algorithm outperforms the original YOLOv5. The precision and recall improved by 0.51% and 0.7%, and the F-score improved by 0.63%. This result validates the effectiveness of the focal loss.

Second, we compared the number of parameters of the proposed algorithm with the other two algorithms. As reported in Table 1, the proposed algorithm increases the number of model parameters by 25k, which is only 0.36% of the total number of model parameters. By adding the attention layer, the model adds only a small number of parameters but obtains an obvious improvement in detection accuracy.

Third, we reported the detection results for each category in this face mask dataset, which are listed in Table 2. From Table 2, it can be found that the detection performance of the model on the front face and mask is better than those on the sides, and the detection performance on the face is better than those on the mask. The precision, recall, and F-score of the front and side unknown class are equal to 0. This is mainly because the number of samples in these two categories is too small compared to the other categories.

Table 1. Experimental results of comparison between the proposed AGNN, the original YOLOv5, and the YOLOv5 with focal loss.

Algorithm	Parameter	Precision	Recall	F-score
YOLOv5	7074k	0.8293	0.6748	0.7441
YOLOv5 + Focal loss	7074k	0.8344	0.6818	0.7504
The Proposed AGNN	7099k	**0.8403**	**0.6975**	**0.7623**

Table 2. Experimental results of each category.

Category	Number of samples	Precision	Recall	F-score
back_head	2988	0.8538	0.8149	0.8339
front_no_wear	2236	0.8651	0.8117	0.8376
front_under_mouth_wear	2774	0.8686	0.9102	0.8889
front_under_nose_wear	2985	0.8741	0.8881	0.881
front_unknown	98	0	0	0
front_wear	4061	0.8987	0.8254	0.8605
mask_front_under_mouth_wear	2774	0.8811	0.7509	0.8108
mask_front_under_nose_wear	2985	0.9065	0.8221	0.8623
mask_front_wear	4061	0.9245	0.7387	0.8212
mask_side_under_mouth_wear	1957	0.8111	0.463	0.5895
mask_side_under_nose_wear	1888	0.8372	0.4793	0.6096
mask_side_wear	2751	0.8794	0.4453	0.5912
side_back_head_no_wear	908	0.6996	0.5925	0.6416
side_back_head_wear	2978	0.787	0.7923	0.7755
side_no_wear	1759	0.7484	0.7271	0.7376
side_under_mouth_wear	1957	0.7466	0.8431	0.7919
side_under_nose_wear	1888	0.7289	0.8061	0.7656
side_unknown	164	0	0	0
side_wear	2751	0.7891	0.7452	0.7665
strap	13415	0.8397	0.542	0.6588

4.4 Visual Result

Figure 5 indicates the visual results of face mask detection in real-life scenes. The green boxes represent the true boxes and the red boxes denote the predicted boxes of the model. From Fig. 5, we can see that the predicted boxes basically overlap with the true boxes. Moreover, the category of the predicted boxes is correct in the case of both close and distant face mask detection cases. This verifies that our proposed model can be well adapted to the task of face mask detection in complex real-life scenarios.

Fig. 5. Examples of visual results in real-life scenes.

5 Conclusion

In this paper, we proposed a novel attention-guided neural network (AGNN) based on YOLOv5 for face mask detection. In the proposed AGNN model, the BCE loss in the original YOLOv5 is replaced by the focal loss that helps in better localizing the real target to solve the problem of class imbalance. Furthermore, we integrated the coordinate attention module into the backbone of YOLOv5 to improve detection accuracy. Experimental results on the real-life scenes show that our proposed model achieves a 1.8% improvement in F-score over the original YOLOv5, but only a 0.36% increase in parameters. Additionally, it is noted from the results that the proposed AGNN has a low recall rate for the side-mask targets. Hence, in further work, we will focus on solving the problem of side-mask detection to improve the detection performance. Furthermore, we will explore applying effective image enhancement techniques to balance the number of different categories.

References

1. Centers for Disease Control and Prevention (CDC): Interim Infection Prevention and Control Reccommendations for patients with suspected or confirmed Coronavirus Disease 2019 (COVID-19) in Healthcare settings. https://www.cdc.gov/coronavirus/2019-nconv/hcp/infection-control-recommendations.html. Accessed Feb 2022
2. World Health Organization (WHO): Coronavirus disease (COVID-19) pandemic. Accessed Feb 2022. https://www.who.int/emergencies/diseases/novel-coronavirus-2019. Accessed Feb 2022
3. Girshick, R., Donahue, J., Darrell, T., Malik, J.: Rich feature hierarchies for accurate object detection and semantic segmentation. In: 2014 IEEE Conference on Computer Vision and Pattern Recognition, pp. 580–587 (2014)
4. Redmon, J., Divvala, S., Girshick, R., Farhadi, A.: You only look once: unified, real-time object detection. In: 2016 IEEE Conference on Computer Vision and Pattern Recognition (CVPR), pp. 779–788 (2016)

5. Zhang, X., Fan, H., Zhu, H., Huang, X., Wu, T., Zhou, H.: Improvement of YOLOV5 model based on the structure of multiscale domain adaptive network for crowdscape. In: 2021 IEEE 7th International Conference on Cloud Computing and Intelligent Systems (CCIS), pp. 171–175 (2021)
6. Wang, B., Zheng, J., Chen, C.L.P.: A survey on masked facial detection methods and datasets for fighting against COVID-19. IEEE Trans. Artif. Intell. **3**, 323–343 (2022)
7. Sethi, S., Kathuria, M., Kaushik, T.: Face mask detection using deep learning: an approach to reduce risk of coronavirus spread. J. Biomed. Inform. **120**, 103848 (2021)
8. Wang, B., Zhao, Y., Chen, C.L.P.: Hybrid transfer learning and broad learning system for wearing mask detection in the COVID-19 Era. IEEE Trans. Instrum. Meas. **70**, 1–12 (2021)
9. Wang, Y., Pan, L.: YOLOV5s-Face face detection algorithm. In: 2022 China Automation Congress (CAC), pp. 1107–1112 (2022)
10. Redmon, J., Farhadi, A.: YOLO9000: better, faster, stronger. In: 2017 IEEE Conference on Computer Vision and Pattern Recognition (CVPR), 6517–6525 (2017)
11. Redmon, J., Farhadi, A.: YOLOv3: An Incremental Improvement. ArXiv (2018)
12. Bochkovskiy, A., Wang, C.-Y., Liao, H.: YOLOv4: Optimal Speed and Accuracy of Object Detection. ArXiv (2020)
13. Sudars, K., et al.: YOLOv5 deep neural network for quince and raspberry detection on RGB images. In: 2022 Workshop on Microwave Theory and Techniques in Wireless Communications (MTTW), pp. 19–22 (2022)
14. Hu, J., Shen, L., Albanie, S., Sun, G., Wu, E.: Squeeze-and-excitation networks. IEEE Trans. Pattern Anal. Mach. Intell. **42**, 2011–2023 (2020)
15. Lao, M., Guo, Y., Liu, Y., Lew, M.S.: A language prior based focal loss for visual question answering. In: 2021 IEEE International Conference on Multimedia and Expo (ICME), pp. 1–6 (2021)
16. Woo, S., Park, J., Lee, J.-Y., Kweon, I.S.: CBAM: Convolutional Block Attention Module (2018)
17. Li, Y., Cheng, R., Zhang, C., Chen, M., Ma, J., Shi, X.: Sign language letters recognition model based on improved YOLOv5. In: 2022 9th International Conference on Digital Home (ICDH), pp. 188–193 (2022)
18. Hou, Q., Zhou, D., Feng, J.: Coordinate attention for efficient mobile network design. In: 2021 IEEE/CVF Conference on Computer Vision and Pattern Recognition (CVPR), pp. 13708–13717 (2021)
19. Chen, J., Wei, Y., Zhou, Y.: Dense crowd detection algorithm for YOLOv5 based on coordinate attention mechanism. In: 2022 2nd International Conference on Algorithms, High Performance Computing and Artificial Intelligence (AHPCAI), pp. 187–190 (2022)
20. Lin, T.-Y., Dollar, P., Girshick, R., He, K., Hariharan, B., Belongie, S.: Feature pyramid networks for object detection. In: 2017 IEEE Conference on Computer Vision and Pattern Recognition (CVPR), pp. 936–944 (2017)
21. Liu, S., Qi, L., Qin, H., Shi, J., Jia, J.: Path aggregation network for instance segmentation. In: 2018 IEEE/CVF Conference on Computer Vision and Pattern Recognition, pp. 8759–8768 (2018)
22. Zheng, Z., Wang, P., Liu, W., Li, J., Ye, R., Ren, D.: Distance-IoU loss: faster and better learning for bounding box regression. In: Proceedings of the AAAI Conference on Artificial Intelligence, pp. 12993–13000 (2020)
23. Neubeck, A., Van Gool, L.: Efficient non-maximum suppression. In: 18th International Conference on Pattern Recognition (ICPR 2006), pp. 850–855 (2006)
24. Liu, R., Cui, B., Fang, X., Guo, B., Ma, Y., An, J.: Super-resolution of GF-1 multispectral wide field of view images via a very deep residual coordinate attention network. IEEE Geosci. Remote Sens. Lett. **19**, 1–5 (2022)

25. Lin, T.-Y., Goyal, P., Girshick, R., He, K., Dollar, P.: Focal loss for dense object detection. IEEE Trans. Pattern Anal. Mach. Intell. **42**, 318–327 (2020)
26. Cheng, Z., Chai, S.: A cyber intrusion detection method based on focal loss neural network. In: 2020 39th Chinese Control Conference (CCC), pp. 7379–7383 (2020)
27. Extreme Mart platform. https://cvmart.net

Double-Stream Network for Clothes-Changing Person Re-identification Based on Clothes Related Feature Suppression and Attention Mechanism

Dingyi Wang and Haishun Du[✉]

School of Artificial Intelligence, Henan University, Zhengzhou, Henan, China
104754201214@henu.edu.cn, jddhs@vip.henu.edu.cn

Abstract. The standard person re-identification task has a basic assumption that pedestrians will not change their clothes. However, in a more realistic and challenging scenario for clothes-changing person re-identification, this assumption does not hold, resulting in the failure of most mainstream methods in this scenario. To this end, a double-stream network for clothes-changing person re-identification based on clothes related feature suppression and attention mechanism is proposed. Firstly, the network is composed of a clothes feature stream and a pedestrian feature stream. By using attention modules on the two streams, salient clothes features and pedestrian features are extracted respectively. Then, the clothes related feature suppression module is used in the pedestrian feature stream to force it to learn clothes unrelated features. Finally, the triplet loss and cross entropy loss are used to supervise the training of the network. The ablation experiment shows that each module effectively improves the performance of the model. A large number of experiments on the PRCC and VC-Clothes datasets have been conducted in order to assess the proposed model. The experimental results show that the accuracy of mAP and Rank-1 is improved compared with other representative methods.

Keywords: Deep Learning · Clothes-Changing Person re-identification · Clothes Related Feature Suppression Module · Computer Vision

1 Introduction

With the advancement and use of monitoring technology in recent years, ineffective manual retrieval has gradually given way to automatic retrieval of specific pedestrians from a large amount of monitoring data using intelligent algorithms. Person Re- identification (Re-ID), a crucial component of intelligent monitoring technology, has grown in popularity as a research area. The majority of existing Re-ID techniques over-rely on clothes-related features like clothes color and style because they assume that pedestrians won't change their clothes. However, pedestrians often change clothes during a long term, so in the real world, clothes related features are frequently unreliable in real-world scenarios. Therefore, the secret to increasing the precision of clothes-changing Re-ID is learning clothes unrelated features, such as hairstyle, face, gait, and body shape.

© The Author(s), under exclusive license to Springer Nature Singapore Pte Ltd. 2023
W. Yongtian and W. Lifang (Eds.): IGTA 2023, CCIS 1910, pp. 208–219, 2023.
https://doi.org/10.1007/978-981-99-7549-5_16

Scholars have done a lot of research and suggested a lot of good solutions to the clothes-changing Re-ID. These methods can be separated into RGB modal-based and multi-modal-based methods.

Methods Based on RGB Modality

Zhang et al. [1] proposed an AutoEncoder framework that can extract pedestrian pose and appearance features from RGB images, and over time, generate clothes unrelated pedestrian gait features based on a pose feature set of LSTM networks. Zheng et al. [2] proposed a joint discriminative and generative learning framework that combines feature learning and data generation end-to-end to learn the appearance and structural features. Gu et al. [3] proposed a clothes-based adversarial loss, which can punish the network when learning clothes related features, thus forcing the network to learn clothes unrelated features.

Methods Based on Multiple Modalities

Hong et al. [4] proposed a fine-grained shape appearance mutual learning framework, which is based on RGB, human posture, and pedestrian silhouette modalities. Under the guidance of identity, the framework learns fine-grained discriminative silhouettes, and then extracts fine-grained shape features through a multi-branches network of specific poses, thereby learning clothes unrelated features. Xin et al. [5] proposed the GI-ReID framework, which is based on RGB and pedestrian silhouette modalities. Through image re-identification streams and auxiliary gait re-identification streams, this framework learns clothes unrelated biological motion features. Qian et al. [6] proposed a method based on RGB and human pose modalities, which eliminates unreliable clothes features and learns pedestrian body shape information through shape embedding modules and fabric elimination shape extraction modules. Yang et al. [7] proposed a method based on the modal of human contour sketches, which introduces a spatial polar coordinate transformation layer in convolutional neural networks to learn reliable discriminative human contour sketch features in polar coordinate space. In addition, this method further improves the performance of the model by extracting more fine-grained discriminative angle features through angle specific extractors. Chen et al. [8] proposed a method 3DSL based on RGB, pose, silhouette and 3D modalities. This method uses 3D body reconstruction as an auxiliary task and regularization to directly extract 3D shape discriminant features from 2D images.

However, the majority of the aforementioned techniques call for the use of auxiliary networks such as pre-trained pose estimation, human semantic segmentation, and other models, which increases the computational complexity of the models. In order to achieve this, we created a double-stream network for clothes-changing person re-identification based on clothes related feature suppression and attention mechanism(CRFS-Net). The network specifically consists of a pedestrian feature stream and a clothes related feature stream. We created a spatial attention module and a channel attention module to improve the dual stream network's capacity to extract pertinent features. Additionally, we created a module to prevent the propagation of clothes related features in pedestrian feature stream using the spatial attention weights in clothes related feature stream. This forces pedestrian feature stream to learn clothes unrelated features instead.

2 Proposed Method

2.1 Framework of Network

Figure 1 shows CRFS-Net's structure. Double stream structure can help researchers achieve better results [9, 10], Therefore, CRFS-Net also adopts a double stream structure. From Fig. 1, it can be seen that the network consists of a clothes feature stream and a pedestrian feature stream. We use ResNet-50 as the backbone network for each stream and set the last stride of the fourth convolutional block to 1. We added a channel attention module (CAM) and a spatial attention module (SAM) after each convolutional block in the clothes feature stream to extract salient clothes features. In the pedestrian feature stream, the output feature map of each convolutional block needs to first go through the clothes related feature suppression module (CRFSM), and then undergo CAM and SAM processing to extract clothes unrelated pedestrian salient features. In the training phase, the feature maps of the two streams will be processed by GeMpooling to get the corresponding feature vectors to calculate the cross entropy loss and triplet loss. In the testing phase, we use the features extracted from the pedestrian feature stream as the final pedestrian features. It should be noted that we use clothes label to calculate the loss function in the clothes feature stream, so as to supervise its extraction of clothes related features, and use pedestrian label to calculate the loss function in the pedestrian feature stream, so as to supervise its extraction of pedestrian features.

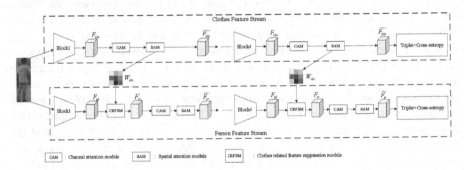

Fig. 1. Structure of CRFS-Net

2.2 Attention Module

The spatial attention mechanism can reduce the interference of invalid information and enhance the expression of salient discriminative features in the spatial dimension by introducing a small number of trainable parameters, thereby guiding the network to extract richer and more robust pedestrian features. This article improves the traditional spatial attention module and proposes a multi-granularity spatial attention module (SAM). Figure 2 shows its specific structure.

Assuming the input feature map is $X \in R^{C \times H \times W}$, first divide it evenly along the channel dimension into 4 blocks to obtain p_1, p_2, p_3 and p_4. Then, take any 2 blocks from these 4 blocks and concatenate them along the channel dimension. There are a total of 6 cases to obtain $p_{12}, p_{13}, p_{14}p_{23}, p_{24}$ and p_{34}. Then, take any three of these four blocks and concatenate them along the channel dimension, in a total of four cases to obtain p_{123}, p_{124}, p_{134} and p_{234}. Subsequently, 10 local feature maps were encoded using 10 1×1 convolutional layers, BN layers, and ReLu layers to reduce their channels to 1. Finally, the encoded feature maps were added and passed through a sigmoid layer to obtain the spatial attention weight A_s.

After obtaining the spatial attention feature map A_s, we first use the tensor broadcasting mechanism to expand the A_s size to $C \times H \times W$, denoted as $\widetilde{A_s}$, and then fuse $\widetilde{A_s}$ with the original feature X by element-wise multiplication to obtain the final output $F \in R^{C \times H \times W}$.

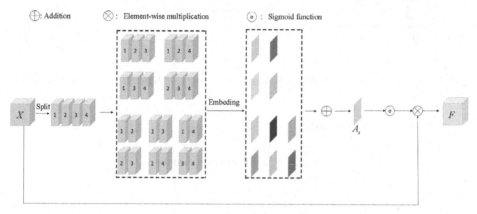

Fig. 2. Spatial Attention Module

This article also built a channel attention module (CAM) based on local and global salient features, and Fig. 3 displays its specific structure, in order to further improve the network's capacity to mine and exploit pedestrian salient signals in the channel dimension. Based on the spatial attention module, this module further extracts richer pedestrian information by learning a channel attention weight that is consistent with the channel dimension of the input feature map.

From Fig. 3, it can be seen that the module consists of a global branch and a local branch. Assuming the input feature map is $X \in R^{C \times H \times W}$, in the local branch, first divide it evenly into 4 blocks along the channel dimension to obtain p_1, p_2, p_3, and p_4. Then, these four blocks are pooled through four GeMpooling to obtain corresponding vectors, and these vectors are concatenated along the channel dimension to obtain a local feature vector v_1. In the global branch, the feature map is directly pooled through a GeM to obtain the global based feature vector v_2. Then, v_1 and v_2 are added to obtain v_3, which passes through two fully connected layers and one sigmoid layer to obtain the channel attention weight A_c. The above operation can be formulated as:

$$\begin{cases} v_1 = [GeM(p_1); GeM(p_2); GeM(p_3); GeM(p_4)] \\ v_2 = GeM(X) \\ A_c = \sigma(\mathbf{W}_2\mathbf{W}_1(v_1 + v_2)) \end{cases} \quad (1)$$

Among them, [;] represents the concatenation operation along the channel, $\sigma(.)$ represents the sigmoid function, $\mathbf{W}_1 \in \mathbf{R}^{\frac{C}{16} \times C}$ and $\mathbf{W}_2 \in R^{C \times \frac{C}{16}}$ represent the parameters of the fully connected layer, and $GeM(\cdot)$ represents GeMpooling.

After obtaining the channel attention feature map A_c, we first use the tensor broadcasting mechanism to expand the A_c size to $C \times H \times W$, denoted as $\tilde{A}_c$, and then multiply $\tilde{A}_c$ with the corresponding elements of the original feature X to obtain the final output $F \in R^{C \times H \times W}$.

It should be pointed out that we connect SAM in series after CAM in the network, forming an Attention Module (AM).

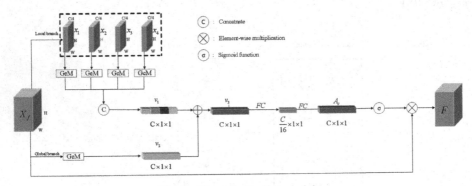

Fig. 3. Channel attention module

2.3 Clothes Related Feature Suppression Module

In order to suppress the propagation of clothes related features in pedestrian feature streams, we designed a clothes related feature suppression module (CRFSM). As shown in Fig. 4, the input of this module is the attention weight W_{clo} of SAM in the clothes feature stream and the feature map F_{id} in the pedestrian feature stream. Firstly, W_{clo} needs to be processed through a threshold function $T(\cdot)$ to obtain $\widetilde{W_{clo}}$. The threshold function can be formulated as:

$$\widetilde{W_{i,j}} = \begin{cases} W_{i,j} & if W_{i,j} > n \\ 0 & otherwise \end{cases} \tag{2}$$

In the formula, $W_{i,j}$ represents the element in W_{clo}, $\widetilde{W_{i,j}}$ represents the elements in $\widetilde{W_{clo}}$, n is the threshold value and is a hyperparameter, this paper sets it to 0.9.

Furthermore, we fuse W_{clo} and F_{id} by element-wise multiplication s to obtain the clothes related feature F_c in F_{id}; Then, we subtract the corresponding elements of F_{id} and F_c to obtain clothes unrelated pedestrian features. The above operation can be formulated as:

$$\begin{cases} \widetilde{W_{clo}} = T(W_{clo}) \\ F_{ir} = F_{id} - F_{id} \odot \widetilde{W_{clo}} \end{cases} \tag{3}$$

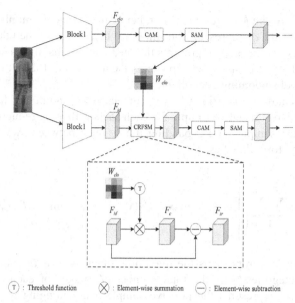

(T) : Threshold function   (X) : Element-wise summation   (—) : Element-wise subtraction

Fig. 4. Clothes related feature suppression module

In summary, CRFSM can utilize the spatial attention weights in clothes feature stream to suppress the propagation of clothes related features in pedestrian feature stream, thereby helping the network extract clothes unrelated pedestrian features.

2.4 Loss Function

This research employs cross-entropy loss function and triplet loss function combination for training to aid the model in extracting more robust and plentiful features. Cross entropy loss and triplet loss training together can improve network monitoring and stop the network from overfitting. Both of these two types of losses are computed using the extracted pedestrian features and clothes related features from the model. The loss function can be formulated as:

$$L = L_{cls} + L_{tri} \tag{4}$$

where, L_{cls} and L_{tri} represent cross entropy loss and triplet loss respectively.

Cross entropy loss: classification loss is more sensitive to the feature scale, so the network uses label smooth cross entropy loss function. Before calculating the cross entropy loss, we used the full connection layer and BatchNorm layer to reduce the dimension of pedestrian features and clothes related features and obtain the corresponding prediction probability. Cross entropy loss can be formulated as:

$$L_{cls} = -\sum_{n=1}^{N}\sum_{k=1}^{K} q_k^n \log(p_k^n) \quad \begin{cases} q_k^n = \frac{\varepsilon}{K} & y^n \neq k \\ q_k^n = 1 - \varepsilon\frac{K-1}{K} & y^n = k \end{cases} \tag{5}$$

In the formula, N and K represent the number of images and the number of categories per batch, respectively. q_k^n represents the smoothed label value of the nth image in each batch that belongs to class k. p_k^n represents the prediction probability that the nth image in each batch belongs to class k, y^n represents the true label of the nth image in each batch, ε is the label smoothing coefficient.

Triplet loss: Hard sample triplet loss is calculated by finding the farthest positive sample and the nearest negative sample for each anchor, thereby reducing the distance between intra class samples and expanding the distance between inter class samples. Triplet loss can be formulated as:

$$
L_{BH-Triplet} = \sum_{i=1}^{P} \sum_{a=1}^{M} \left[m + \max_{p=1,2,...,M} D(x_a^i, x_p^i) - \min_{\substack{j=1,2,...,P \\ n=1,2,...,M \\ j \neq i}} D(x_a^i, x_n^j) \right]_{+} \tag{6}
$$

In the formula, $[x]_+$ represents the maximum function, P is the number of pedestrian (clothes) categories, M is the total number of images of each class of pedestrian (clothes), $x_a^i x_p^i$ represents the positive sample pair belonging to the i-th pedestrian (clothes), $x_a^i x_n^j$ represents negative sample pairs belonging to different pedestrians (clothes), $D(\cdot)$ represents the distance between sample pairs, m is the threshold

3 Experiment

3.1 Experimental details

The model proposed in this article is implemented through the deep learning framework Pytorch. The GPU used is the Nvidia Rtx-3090. During the training phase, the input image size is adjusted to 384×192, and use random erasure, horizontal flipping, and random cropping for data augmentation. During the training process, the batch size is set to 32 and the number of iterations is set to 60. We used the Adam optimizer for optimization and set the initial learning rate to 3.5, which decreased tenfold in the 20th and 30th cycles, respectively. To verify the performance of our model, we conducted experiments on two benchmark datasets for Re-id, PRCC [7] and VC-Clothes [11], using mAP and Rank-1 as evaluation indicators.

3.2 Datasets

The PRCC dataset was captured indoors using three cameras. The same pedestrian is wearing the same clothes under camera A and camera B, while the clothes under camera C is different from A and B. This dataset contains a total of 33698 pedestrian images and 221 pedestrian IDs. The training set contains 17896 pedestrian images and 150 pedestrian IDs, and the library contains 3384 pedestrian images and 71 pedestrian IDs. To simulate practical applications, this dataset provides two query methods: same clothes (SC) and cross clothes (CC). SC query includes 3873 pedestrian images and 71 pedestrian IDs, while CC query includes 3543 pedestrian images and 71 pedestrian IDs.

The VC-Clothes dataset was captured using four virtual cameras in the 3D game GTA-5. This dataset contains 19060 pedestrian images and 512 pedestrian IDs, with each pedestrian has 1 to 3 sets of clothes. The same pedestrian is wearing the same clothes under camera 2 and camera 3, so literature [4, 6] sets a subset of cameras 2 and 3 as SC query. In addition, these methods also set a subset of cameras 3 and 4 as CC query. Our experimental setup is consistent with these methods.

3.3 Comparison with State-of-the-Art Methods

Table 1. Performance (%) comparisons between CRFS-Net and current advanced methods on PRCC

Method	Modality	PRCC			
		SC		CC	
		Rank-1	mAP	Rank-1	mAP
HACNN [12]	RGB	82.5	–	21.8	–
IANet [13]	RGB	99.4	98.3	46.3	45.9
PCB [14]	RGB	99.8	97.0	41.8	38.7
MGN [15]	RGB	99.5	98.4	33.8	35.9
HPM [16]	RGB	99.4	96.9	40.4	37.2
SketchNet [17]	Sketch	64.6	–	17.9	–
GI-ReID [5]	RGB + silhouettes	80.0	–	33.3	–
SPT + ASE [7]	Sketch	64.2	–	34.4	–
RCSANet [18]	RGB	100	97.2	50.2	48.6
3DSL [8]	RGB + pose + silhouettes + 3D	–	–	51.3	–
CRFS-Net	RGB	**100**	**98.6**	**54.4**	**52.8**

Experimental results on the PRCC dataset: From Table 1, it can be seen that the SC query of CRFS-Net achieved 100% Rank-1 accuracy and 98.6% mAP accuracy, significantly outperforming traditional methods such as HACNN, IANet, and PCB. When compared with the advanced Re-ID methods SPT + ASE and GI-ReID for changing clothes pedestrians, CRFS-Net's Rank-1 has significantly improved by 35.8% and 20.0%, respectively. Although the Rank-1 accuracy of CRFS-Net is same as RCSANet, the mAP accuracy is 1.4% higher. In CC query, CRFS-Net achieved 54.4% Rank-1 accuracy and 52.8% mAP accuracy, significantly improving performance compared to traditional methods such as HACNN, IANet, and PCB. When compared with the advanced Re-ID methods RCSANet and 3DSL for clothes-changing Re-ID, CRFS-Net's Rank-1 has improved by 4.2% and 3.1%, respectively. The above comparison results indicate that CRFS-Net has reached advanced level.

The evaluation results of the VC-Clothes dataset: From Table 2, it can be seen that CRFS-Net achieved 90.8% Rank-1 accuracy and 82.0% mAP accuracy in the General

Table 2. Performance (%) comparisons between CRFS-Net and current advanced methods on VC-Clothes

Method	General (all cams)		SC (cam2&cam3)		CC (cam3&cam4)	
	Rank-1	mAP	Rank-1	mAP	Rank-1	mAP
MDLA[19]	88.9	76.8	94.3	93.9	59.2	60.8
PCB[14]	87.7	74.6	94.7	94.3	62.0	62.2
Part-aligned[20]	90.5	79.7	93.9	93.4	69.4	67.3
FSAM[4]	–	–	94.7	94.8	78.6	78.9
CRFS-Net	**90.8**	**82.0**	**95.3**	**94.4**	**79.3**	**71.4**

query. When compared with MDLA, PCB, and Part aligned, CRFS-Net's Rank-1 has improved by 1.9%, 3.1%, and 0.3%, respectively. CRFS-Net achieved 95.3% Rank-1 accuracy and 94.4% mAP accuracy in SC query. When compared with MDLA, PCB, Part-aligned, and FSAM, CRFS-Net's Rank-1 accuracy has improved by 1.0%, 0.6%, 1.4%, and 0.6%, respectively. CRFS-Net achieved 79.3% Rank-1 accuracy and 71.4% mAP accuracy in CC query. When compared with MDLA, PCB, Part aligned, and FSAM, CRFS-Net's Rank-1 accuracy has improved by 20.1%, 17.3%, 9.9%, and 0.7%, respectively. The above comparison results indicate that CRFS-Net is superior to most existing methods.

3.4 Ablation Studies

This article conducted ablation experiments on the PRCC dataset to evaluate the performance of CRFSM and AM. As shown in Table 3, When compared with CRFS-Net, the Rank-1 accuracy of CRFS-Net without CRFSM decreased by 5.1%, while the Rank-1 accuracy of CRFS-Net without CRFSM and AM decreased by 8.6%. This phenomenon proves that both CRFSM and AM can increase the discriminative power of pedestrian final features.

Table 3. Ablation Study on PRCC Dataset

	Rank-1(%)	mAP(%)
CRFS-Net	54.4	52.8
CRFS-Net without CRFSM	49.3	47.8
CRFS-Net without CRFSM and AM	45.8	46.8

3.5 Hyperparameter Studies

In order to study the impact of hyperparameter n in CAFSM on model performance, we conducted experiments on the PRCC dataset, and the experimental results are shown in Fig. 5. From Fig. 5, it can be seen that the model performs best when n is 0.9, while the model performs worst when n is 0.1 and 0.2. Therefore, we set the hyperparameter n in CRFSM to 0.9.

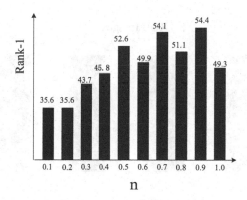

Fig. 5. Hyper parameter experimental results on PRCC dataset

3.6 Visualization studies

In order to demonstrate the effectiveness of CRFSM more intuitively, as shown in Fig. 6, we visualized the pedestrian feature maps extracted by CRFS-Net and CRFS-Net without CRFSM on the PRCC dataset, respectively. From Fig. 6, it can be seen that the pedestrian feature maps extracted by CRFS-Net focus more on clothes unrelated shoulder, facial, and contour features than the feature maps extracted by CRFS-Net without CRFSM, thereby increasing the matching evidence for clothes-changing Re-ID.

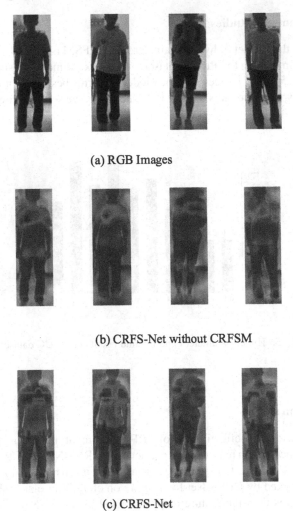

(a) RGB Images

(b) CRFS-Net without CRFSM

(c) CRFS-Net

Fig. 6. Visualization results on PRCC dataset

4   Conclusion

This paper proposes a double-stream network based on clothes related feature suppression and attention mechanism for clothes-changing Re-ID. By utilizing the attention module and clothes related feature suppression module, CRFS-Net obtains more rich and robust clothes unrelated features, thereby alleviating the impact of pedestrian clothes change on model recognition accuracy to a certain extent. The accuracy of CRFS-Net for clothes-changing Re-ID has achieved the present advanced level, according to a large number of testing findings on the PRCC and VC-Clothes datasets.

References

1. Zhang, Z., et al.: Gait recognition via disentangled representation learning. In: CVPR (2019)
2. Zheng, Z., Yang, X., Yu, Z., Zheng, L., Yang, Y., Kautz, J.: Joint discriminative and generative learning for person re-identification. In: CVPR (2019)
3. Gu, X., Chang, H., Ma, B., Bai, S., Shan, S., Chen, X.: Clothes-changing person re-identification with RGB modality only. In: CVPR (2022)
4. Hong, P., Wu, T., Wu, A., Han, X., Zheng, W.S.: Fine-grained shape-appearance mutual learning for cloth-changing person re-identification. In: CVPR (2021)
5. Jin, X., et al.: Cloth-changing person reidentification from a single image with gait prediction and regularization. arXiv preprint arXiv:2103.15537 (2021)
6. Qian, X., et al.: Long-term cloth-changing person re-identification. In: ACCV (2020)
7. Yang, Q., Ancong, W., Zheng, W.-S.: Person reidentification by contour sketch under moderate clothing change. TPAMI 43(6), 2029–2046 (2021)
8. Chen, J., et al.: Learning 3d shape feature for texture-insensitive person re-identification. In: CVPR (2021)
9. Gu, K., Xia, Z., Qiao, J., et al.: Deep dual-channel neural network for image-based smoke detection. IEEE Trans. Multimed. 22(2), 311–323 (2019). https://doi.org/10.1109/TMM. 2019.2929009
10. Gu, K., et al.: Pm 2.5 monitoring: use information abundance measurement and wide and deep learning. IEEE Trans. Neural Netw. Learn. Syst. 2, 4278–4290 (2021). https://doi.org/ 10.1109/TNNLS.2021.3105394
11. Wan, F., Wu, Y., Qian, X., Chen, Y., Fu, Y.: When person re-identification meets changing clothes. In: CVPR Workshop (2020)
12. Li, W., Zhu, X., Gong, S.: Harmonious attention network for person re-identification. In: CVPR (2018)
13. Hou, R., Ma, B., Chang, H., Gu, X., Shan, S., Chen, X.: Interaction-and-aggregation network for person re-identification. In: CVPR (2019)
14. Sun, Y., Zheng, L., Yang, Y., Tian, Q., Wang, S.: Beyond part models: person retrieval with refined part pooling (and a strong convolutional baseline). In: Ferrari, V., Hebert, M., Sminchisescu, C., Weiss, Y. (eds.) ECCV 2018. LNCS, vol. 11208, pp. 501–518. Springer, Cham (2018). https://doi.org/10.1007/978-3-030-01225-0_30
15. Wang, G., Yuan, Y., Chen, X., Li, J., Zhou, X.: Learning discriminative features with multiple granularities for person re-identification. In: Proceedings of the 26th ACM International Conference on Multimedia, pp. 274–282 (2018)
16. Fu, Y., et al.: Horizontal pyramid matching for person re-identification. Proc. AAAI Conf. Artif. Intell. (AAAI) 33(01), 8295–8302 (2019)
17. Simonyan, K., Zisserman, A.: Very deep convolutional networks for largescale image recognition. In: International Conference on Learning Representations (ICLR) (2015)
18. Huang, Y., Wu, Q., Xu, J., Zhong, Y., Zhang, Z.: Clothing status awareness for long-term person re-identification. In: ICCV (2021)
19. Qian, X., Fu, Y., Jiang, Y.G., Xiang, T., Xue, X.: Multi-scale deep learning architectures for person re-identification. In: ICCV (2017)
20. Suh, Y., Wang, J., Tang, S., Mei, T., Lee, K.M.: Part-aligned bilinear representations for person re-identification. In: ECCV (2018)

Semantic Guided Attention for Weakly Supervised Group Activity Recognition

Tingting Liu, Ye Xiang, Lifang Wu$^{(\boxtimes)}$, and Ge Shi

Faculty of Information Technology, Beijing University of Technology, Beijing 100124, China
liutingting@emails.bjut.edu.cn, {xiangye,lfwu,shige}@bjut.edu.cn

Abstract. The objective of group activity recognition is to identify behaviors performed by multiple individuals within a given scene. However, current weakly supervised approaches often rely on object detectors or use self-attention mechanisms. The former approach is susceptible to background clutter and entails high computational costs, while the latter method learns weights from the input video and assigns them to key targets which is not reliable enough to find the key person. To address these limitations, we present a novel weakly supervised framework. Our proposed framework eliminates the need for ground-truth bounding boxes or object detectors. Meanwhile, it incorporates the semantics of individual action labels to replace self-attention to guide the learning process, enabling the extraction of more sophisticated semantic features relevant to activity. This approach also explores the interactions to promote group activity classification. Experimental results demonstrate that our method achieves state-of-the-art performances on both volleyball and collective datasets.

Keywords: group activity recognition · semantic attention · weakly supervised learning · video analysis

1 Introduction

Group activity recognition (GAR) involves identifying collective activities performed by multiple individuals in a video. It plays a crucial role in video understanding [1–3] and finds applications in areas like surveillance, sports video analysis, and social behavior understanding. Unlike conventional action recognition that focuses on individual actions [2, 5–10], GAR requires modeling complex scenes with multiple people, posing challenges in actor localization and modeling their spatio-temporal relationships.

In recent years, deep learning-based methods [11–18] have shown promising performance in video-based GAR. These methods extract features for each person using bounding boxes supervised by individual action labels. They explore relations among individuals and fuse person-level features into group-level representations for classification. However, these approaches heavily rely on extensive annotations, particularly bounding boxes during reasoning.

To address these issues, some weakly supervised GAR (WSGAR) methods [19, 20] that rely on object detectors to locate actors have been proposed. This approach eliminates the need for bounding boxes during both training and inference. Instead, it generates actor box proposals using a detector pre-trained on an external dataset and learns to refine and filter out irrelevant proposals. However, relying on detectors introduces certain drawbacks. These include susceptibility to occlusion and background clutter, which often results in inaccurate detections. Additionally, detector-based methods demand higher computational and memory requirements. In a recent study by Dongkeun Kim et al. [21] a detector-free model based on Transformers was proposed as an alternative to address these limitations. This model replaces the detector component with a self-attention mechanism. However, the lack of supervision or guidance in their "self-attention" scheme raises concerns about its physical explanation and precise localization abilities.

In order to enhance the performance and interpretability of WSGAR models, it is essential to consider more complex information that captures effective relationships. In team sports, specific group activities reflect the execution and implementation of tactics, which involves correlations and distributions of corresponding individual actions. For instance, in volleyball matches, the "r-spike" activity includes a "spiking" player, some "waiting" players, and some "blocking" players. Furthermore, there is a small probability for "spiking" and "setting" actions to exist in the same scene, and a r-spike activity will never involve a "setting" player. This provides powerful clues or distinguishing r-spike activity from other activities such as r-set. This valuable information can enhance video understanding and has been validated in subsequent experiments.

In this paper, we propose a novel approach to address the challenges encountered in weakly supervised group activity recognition (WSGAR). We aim to alleviate the heavy reliance on extensive annotations and object detectors by introducing a semantic attention model. Instead, our method harnesses the power of semantic action labels associated with group activities to guide the learning process. Instead of using self-attention alone, we incorporate a semantic attention module that exploits the semantics of action labels, effectively guiding the model's focus towards relevant semantic regions. To further enhance our model's understanding of complex relationships, we introduce a graph propagation mechanism that leverages statistical label co-occurrence. Additionally, we integrate a motion information module inspired by recent advancements in video representation architectures. This module captures motion cues by embedding local correlations between feature maps of adjacent frames.

We evaluate our proposed approach on two benchmark datasets, namely the Volleyball dataset and the Collective Activity Dataset, to assess its performance. The experimental results showcase the state-of-the-art capabilities of our framework within the weakly supervised learning setting.

The contributions of our work can be summarized as follows:

1. We introduce a novel semantic attention model for WSGAR that does not rely on ground-truth bounding boxes or object detectors. This eliminates the need for extensive manual annotation and costly detection mechanisms, making our approach more practical and efficient.
2. We develop a semantic attention module that incorporates action label semantics to guide the learning of more sophisticated label-specific features.

3. Through extensive experiments on the two widely used benchmark datasets, we demonstrate that our proposed method achieves state-of-the-art performance. Also, our solution even outperforms early GAR models that depend on stronger supervision than ours (Fig. 1).

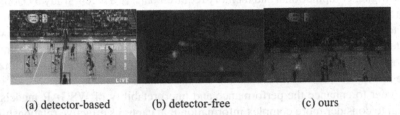

(a) detector-based   (b) detector-free   (c) ours

Fig. 1. Comparison of different visual tokens for group activity recognition under a weakly-supervised setting. The detector-based method (a) generates a large number of proposals, including irrelevant entities such as spectators, passers-by, and judges. Meanwhile, the framework based on transformer (b) [21] captures key information in each frame but lacks guidance, leading to the extraction of messy information such as letter patterns in the background and passing pedestrians by some tokens. In contrast, our proposed method accurately extracts relevant features for different individual behaviors, improving the overall accuracy of group activity recognition. (c) shows the activation graph corresponding to the individual behavior "spiking"

2 Related Work

2.1 Group Activity Recognition

In the early stages of group activity recognition, traditional methods [22–27] such as hidden Markov models, Bayesian networks, graphical models, and conditional random fields were commonly used to model hierarchical structural relationships within group activities. However, with the emergence of deep learning in computer vision, researchers began incorporating deep learning techniques with graph models, relationship networks, and other approaches to capture the hierarchical relationship structures in multi-person scenes GAR [16, 28–31]. For instance, Ibrahim et al. [11] proposed a two-stage deep model that utilizes LSTM networks to capture the action dynamics of each actor and aggregate individual-level representations. Li et al. introduced an SBGAR scheme [32] that generates captions for each frame and aggregates them to predict the group activity class. Tang Y et al. [28] developed a knowledge distillation model that employs semantically preserved attention to automatically identify key characters in the scene while discarding irrelevant characters. Moreover, Tianshan et al. proposed a bidirectional mapping method to integrate information from both visual and semantic domains, leveraging multimodal data for recognition. Some of these approaches even leverage higher-level semantic domain information to enhance classification, yielding promising results. However, these models require action-level supervision for training and testing, necessitating time-consuming annotation efforts and exhibiting sensitivity to changes in the number of characters per frame.

2.2 Weakly Supervised Group Activity Recognition

To address the challenges associated with weakly supervised group activity recognition, recent efforts have focused on reducing the need for extensive supervision during model training. For example, Rui Yan et al. [19] constructed a dense relation graph based on proposals generated by a third-party pedestrian detector and learned to crop the graph. However, this approach incurs redundant computational costs in the first step and does not allow for end-to-end training. Peizhen Zhang et al. [20] proposed an end-to-end framework that jointly trained actor detection and weakly supervised collective activity reasoning by sharing convolutional layers. Nevertheless, this approach still relies on action proposals for model training and does not accurately remove irrelevant individuals from the group activity. To overcome these limitations, Donkeum Kim et al. [21] proposed a transformer-based method that adaptively searches for ROI using a series of learnable tokens. However, due to the lack of supervision, this approach can only achieve rough localization of regions.

3 Approach

The motivation of this work is to leverage high-level semantic domain information to guide the exploration of the appearance domain information. Given a video clip, we begin by employing a backbone network, along with a motion information computing module, to extract features for each video frame. Our approach involves two key modules: the semantic attention module and the semantic interaction module. In the semantic attention module, we incorporate the semantics of individual actions to guide the learning process, focusing on extracting semantic-aware features that are relevant to the specific action label. The semantic interaction module utilizes the co-occurrence matrix of individual action labels extracted from the training sets to construct a graph. This graph associates the individual label-based features and facilitates the exploration of semantic interactions. Finally, the results will be aggregated into group-level representations while capturing the spatio-temporal context. During training, our model is optimized using the cross-entropy loss function. Figure 2 illustrates a detailed pipeline of our framework.

3.1 Motion Feature Extraction Module

Given a video clip of T frames, denoted as $X_{video} \in R^{T \times H' \times W' \times 3}$, we first use an ImageNet pretrained ResNet [33] backbone to extracts features $F_{video} \in R^{T \times H \times W \times C}$. Inspired by recent advancements in motion feature learning [7], we incorporate the local correlation computation from FlowNet which enables us to incorporate motion information into the backbone network.

To compute the correlation scores for a spatial position x between two adjacent feature maps, we employ 1×1 convolution to reduce the channel dimension of the feature to C'. Then, we apply the function S to compute the correlation scores as follows:

$$S : \left\langle F^{(t)}, F^{(t+1)} \right\rangle \to S^{(t)} \in R^{H \times W \times P \times P}. \tag{1}$$

224   T. Liu et al.

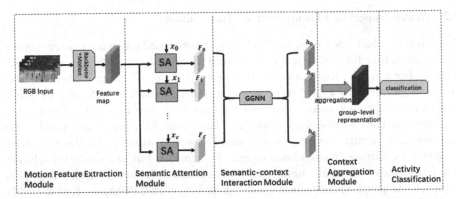

Fig. 2. Illustration of our framework: Given a video clip, a CNN backbone incorporating a motion feature computation module extracts a feature map. At each frame, the semantic attention module (SA) extracts semantic-aware features, $x_0, \cdots\cdots x_c$ represent the semantic words of action labels. The semantic interaction (SI) module utilizes the co-occurrence matrix of individual action labels to construct a graph that associates the individual label-based features and facilitates the exploration of semantic interactions. Then, the results are aggregated into group-level representations while capturing the spatio-temporal context. Finally, the results are fed into the classifier.

where

$$\left(S^{(t)}\right)_{(x,p)} = \left\langle \left(F^{(t)}\right)_{(X)}, \left(F^{(t+1)}\right)_{(X+P)}\right\rangle. \tag{2}$$

$x \in [0, H-1] \times [0, W-1]$, $p \in [-l, l]^2$. Here, $\left(S^{(t)}\right)_{(x,p)}$ represents the dot product similarity of displaced vectors between adjacent frames $F^{(t)}$ and $F^{(t+1)}$. We set the parameter l to limit the maximum displacement, resulting in the correlation scores computed only within a local neighborhood of size $p = 2l + 1$. The correlation map $S^{(t)}$ reveals the motion at each location of $F^{(t)}$ in the form of $P \times P$ local correlation map. We then use 1×1 convolution to reshape the local correlation tensor $S^{(t)} \in R^{H \times W \times P \times P}$ into motion feature $M^{(t)} \in R^{H \times W \times C}$. These motion features are inserted into the backbone using a residual connection:

$$F'^{(t)} = F^{(t)} + M^{(t)}. \tag{3}$$

3.2 Semantic Attention Module (SA)

The module aims to learn semantic-aware feature guided by the semantics of individual action labels. We now provide a detailed description of the semantic attention mechanism.

For each action label c, the framework extracts a d_s-dimensional semantic-embedding vector using a pre-trained Word2vec [35] model: word2vec-google-news-300.

$$L_c = f_w(x_c). \tag{4}$$

where x_c represents the semantic word of action label c. Next, we use semantic attention mechanism added semantic vector to guide the model to pay more attention to semantically related areas, enable the learning of label-specific features. Specifically, a bilinear pooling method [36] is introduced in order to better fuse the feature of different modes. For each position (w, h) in feature map of each frame $F'^{(t)}$, we apply the following operations:

$$\tilde{F}'^{(t)}_{c,wh} = P^T \left(\tan\left(\left(\widetilde{U^T F'^{(t)}_{wh}} \right) \odot \left(V^T L_c \right) \right) \right) + b. \tag{5}$$

Here $\tan(\cdot)$ represents the hyperbolic tangent function, $U \in R^{N \times d_1}$, $V \in R^{d_s \times d_1}$, $P \in R^{d_1 \times d_2}$, and $b \in R^{d_2}$ are learnable parameters, and $\odot$ denotes the element-wise multiplication. The dimensions d_1 and d_2 correspond to the semantic embeddings and output features, respectively. Next, an attention function is used to calculate the attention coefficients for each position:

$$\tilde{a}_{c,wh} = f_a \left(\tilde{F}'^{(t)}_{c,wh} \right). \tag{6}$$

The value of this function represents the importance of the feature vector at this location relative to the overall feature map. $f_a(\cdot)$ is an attentional function implemented by a fully connected network layer. To ensure comparability, the coefficients are normalized over all locations using a softmax function:

$$a_{c,wh} = \frac{exp(\tilde{a}_{c,wh})}{\sum_{w',h'} exp(\tilde{a}_{c,w'h'})}. \tag{7}$$

Finally, a weighted average pooling is applied over all positions:

$$F_c^{(t)} = \sum_{w,h} a_{c,wh} F_{c,wh}^{(t)}. \tag{8}$$

This process is repeated for each individual action label, resulting in feature maps associated with all labels at all time $\{F_0, F_1, \ldots, F_{c-1}\}$.

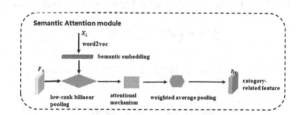

Fig. 3. Detailed architectures of the semantic attention module.

3.3 Semantic-Context Interaction Module (SI)

We propose to construct a graph to correlate these feature maps based on the statistical label co-occurrence and introduce a graph neural network to propagate messages through the graph to explore their interactions. The details are described as follows.

Semantic-Context Graph Construction. The initial node attributes of the graph are the feature maps corresponding to specific action labels, while the edges are defined based on the co-occurrence between corresponding action labels. The graph can be represented as $G = \{V, A\}$. To be specific, if our dataset covers C action labels, $V = \{v_0, v_1, \ldots, v_{c-1}\}$ with element v_c denoting the feature map corresponding to action label c and element A can be represented as $\{a_{00}, a_{01}, \ldots, a_{0(c-1)}, \ldots, a_{(c-1)(c-1)}\}$ where $a_{cc'}$ denotes the probability of the existence of an individual belonging to action c in the presence of an individual belonging to action c'. Figure 3 shows the co-occurrence matrix of individual labels in the volleyball dataset, from which it can be seen that there is a significant contribution relationship between individual actions.

Relation Reference. We adopt a gated recurrent update mechanism [37–40] to propagate messages through the graph and explore the interactions among the semantic-aware features. In each parameter update, each node receives and sends information from neighboring nodes. Specifically, at time step t each node $V_c \in V$ have a hidden state h_c^t. We initialize the node feature at time step $t = 0$ with the feature associated with corresponding label from semantic attention module.

$$h_c^0 = f_c. \tag{10}$$

At time step t, the attribute of node is updated by aggregating the representations of neighboring nodes

$$a_c^t = \left[\sum_{c'} (a_{cc'}) h_c^{t-1}, \sum_{c'} (a_{c'c}) h_c^{t-1} \right]. \tag{11}$$

In this way, the framework encourages message propagation if node c' has a high correlation with node c, and suppresses propagation otherwise. It propagates messages through the graph and explores node interactions guided by the prior knowledge of statistical label co-occurrence to refine features. The hidden state is updated based on the aggregated feature a_c^t and its hidden state at previous timestep h_c^{t-1} using a gated mechanism. The basic recurrence of the gated recurrent unit is as follows:

$$z_c^t = \sigma \left(W^z a_c^t + U^z h_c^{t-1} \right). \tag{12}$$

$$r_c^t = \sigma \left(W^r a_c^t + U^r h_c^{t-1} \right). \tag{13}$$

$$\widetilde{h_c^t} = \tanh \left(W a_c^t + U \left(r_c^t \odot h_c^{t-1} \right) \right). \tag{14}$$

$$h_c^t = \left(1 - z_c^t \right) \odot h_c^{t-1} + z_c^t \odot h_c^t. \tag{15}$$

Here, $\sigma(\cdot)$ is the logistic sigmoid function, $tanh(\cdot)$ is the hyperbolic tangent function, $\odot$ represents element-wise multiplication. The evolved semantic node embeddings, generated after t layers in the graph, can carry contextualized messages from other nodes. The final hidden states are $H = \{h_0^T, h_1^T, \ldots, h_{C-1}^T\}$ (Fig. 4).

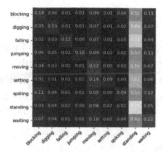

Fig. 4. Action label co-occurrence Matrix on volleyball datasets.

3.4 Context Aggregation Module (CA)

To enhance the representational ability of features, after acquiring features with semantic information $H \in R^{T \times C \times D}$, we incorporate contextual relationships among actors in both temporal and spatial dimensions. These aggregated features are then used to derive the final group-level representation $G \in R^D$. The module consists of two steps: modeling the temporal evolution of feature embeddings for the same label and deducing interactions between individuals of different action labels using multiple self-attention mechanisms. Here is a detailed explanation of the process:

Temporal Context Aggregation. Firstly, we aggregate the feature maps corresponding to the same action label across different frames. Along the temporal dimension T, we employ a series of 1D convolution layers followed by ReLU [41] activation to progressively aggregate features. The result obtained by the final operation of *AvgPooling* can be formulated as $H' \in R^{C \times D}$. By sharing parameters across these networks in real-time, our model effectively captures the dynamic temporal context of actors.

Spatial Context Aggregation. Next, we normalize the feature maps and apply a single layer of multihead self-attention to capture spatial interactions between individuals. The output of this operation is further processed by applying *AvgPooling* operation is applied in C dimension to obtain the group-level representation $G \in R^D$.

By integrating both temporal and spatial context aggregation, our model captures comprehensive contextual information and produces a robust group-level representation G suitable for subsequent recognition tasks.

4 Experiments

4.1 Datasets

The Volleyball Dataset (VD) consists of 55 videos capturing a volleyball game, containing a total of 4,830 clips. The dataset is split into 3,493 training clips and 1,337 testing clips. Each clip is annotated with eight group activity labels, which include actions like spiking, setting, passing, and winpoint on both the left and right courts. Additionally, there are nine individual action labels, such as waiting, setting, digging, failing, spiking, standing, jumping, moving, and blocking. In the WSGAR setting, models, including ours, solely rely on the group activity labels while disregarding the more detailed and fine-grained annotations.

The Collective Activity Dataset (CAD) comprises 44 video sequences, with sequence lengths varying from 190 frames to 1800 frames. We utilize 32 videos for training and 12 videos for testing. The dataset encompasses five group activity labels: crossing, walking, queuing, talking, and waiting. Additionally, the individual action labels consist of six categories, including NA, crossing, walking, queuing, talking, and waiting.

4.2 Implementation Details

Sampling Strategy. For both datasets, we employ the segment-based sampling technique [10] to extract T frames, which are then resized to 720×1280. Specifically, we set T = 5 for VD and T = 3 for the CAD.

Hyperparameters. Our model adopts a ResNet-18 [33] backbone pretrained on ImageNet. The motion feature extraction module utilizes a 1×1 convolution operation to reduce the channel dimension to $C'' = 64$. Considering that the number of motion layers is inserted too early, the local correlation cannot be calculated. For VD, we insert motion feature module after the 4th block and the local neighborhood size is set to 11, while for the CAD, it is insert after 3rd and the local neighborhood size is set to 5. The time step of the GGNN is set to 3. In the context aggregation module, we use two 1D convolutional layers with a kernel size of 3 and zero-padding for the Volleyball dataset, and three layers for the Collective Activity Dataset. For the multi-head self-attention (MHSA) aggregation, a single layer with 256 channels is used for both datasets, with 2 heads for the Volleyball dataset and 4 heads for the CAD.

Training. We optimize our model using the ADAM optimizer [42] with $\beta_1 = 0.9$, $\beta_2 = 0.999$, $\epsilon = 1e - 8$ for a total of 60 epochs. The weight decay is set to $1e - 3$. The initial learning rate is set to $1e - 6$ with a linear warmup to $9e - 5$ for 5 epochs for VD and $9e - 6$ for 5 epochs for CAD, and linearly decayed after the 6th epoch. We use a mini-batch of size 2 on VD and 4 on CAD.

4.3 Comparison with the State-of-the-Art Methods

Volleyball Dataset. In the case of the Volleyball Dataset, we conducted a comprehensive comparison of our model with state-of-the-art methods in both fully supervised and weakly supervised settings. The fully supervised approach necessitates the utilization of individual bounding boxes and individual action labels for both training and testing. Conversely, the weakly supervised approach requires only partial or no individual-level labels. To ensure a fair comparison, we present the results of the previous method [16, 17, 28, 43, 47, 48] that exclusively utilized RGB inputs, as reported in the original paper [18, 44–46], as well as the reproduced results obtained by employing ResNet-18 as the backbone. Table 2 showcases the outcomes achieved by the previous method under both full and weak supervision. Notably, our method exhibits significant superiority over all models in the weakly supervised setting, with an impressive margin of 1.0% in terms of MCA. Furthermore, our approach outperforms some recent fully supervised models [17, 18, 28, 43–45] and achieves highly competitive results.

Collective Activity Dataset. Similar to the Volleyball Dataset, we conducted a thorough evaluation of different approaches on the Collective Activity Dataset, considering both fully supervised and weakly supervised settings, as presented in Table 2. Specifically, our approach outperforms the majority of weakly supervised methods, falling slightly behind HIGCIN [43]. However, it is worth noting that HIGCIN [43] leverages all available supervised annotations except for the action labels. In contrast, our method is the first to achieve competitive performance on the Collective Activity Dataset without utilizing any individual-level annotations during both training and testing. Although our performance may be lower than that of most fully supervised approaches, it is important to note that these methods rely on individual bounding boxes during testing, which is often impractical. Moreover, some of these approaches [44, 48, 50] even employ computationally expensive backbone networks to obtain separate spatio-temporal representations. In comparison, our approach remains feasible and effective (Table 1).

Table 1. Comparison with the state-of-the-art methods on the Volleyball dataset. '-' indicates that the result is not provided, and the ' +' indicate result is copied directly from SAM [19].

Method	Backbone	MCA (VD)
Fully supervised		
SSU [17]	Inception-v3	89.9
StageNet [28]	VGG-16	89.3
ARG [18]	ResNet-18	91.1
CRM [16]	I3D	92.1
HIGCIN [43]	ResNet-18	91.4
AT [44]	ResNet-18	90.0
SACRF [45]	ResNet-18	90.7
TCE+STBiP [47]	VGG-16	94.1
GroupFormer [48]	Inception-v3	94.1
Weakly supervised		
ARG [18]	ResNet-18	87.4
AT [44]	ResNet-18	84.3
SACRF [45]	ResNet-18	83.3
DIN [46]	ResNet-18	86.5
SAM [19]	ResNet-18	86.3
Detector-free [21]	ResNet-18	90.5
Ours	ResNet-18	**91.47**

4.4 Ablation Studies

We conducted a series of ablation experiments on the Volleyball Dataset to assess the effectiveness of our method. As our approach is built upon the ResNet-18 backbone, augmented with a motion information computing module that has previously demonstrated its utility in group activity recognition tasks in [21], our baseline model consists of ResNet-18, the motion computing layer, global pooling, and a linear classifier. If the context aggregation module is not used, the feature graph is globally pooled to obtain group representation. To evaluate the impact of semantic attention graph learning on group activity recognition, we compared our proposed framework against this baseline. These experiments were specifically conducted on the Volleyball Dataset, and the corresponding results are presented in the table.

Table 2. Comparison with the state-of-the-art methods on the Collective Activity Dataset. 'AL' denotes action label. 'Bbox' denotes bounding boxes.

Method	Backbone	train		test	MCA
		AL	Bbox	Bbox	
Fully supervised					
StagNet [28]	Vgg16	Yes	Yes	Yes	89.1
ARG [18]	Vgg16	Yes	Yes	Yes	90.1
ARG [18]	ResNet-18	Yes	Yes	Yes	91.0
GAIM [49]	ResNet-18	Yes	Yes	Yes	90.6
Ehsanpour et al. [50]	I3D	Yes	Yes	Yes	89.4
AT [44]	I3D	Yes	Yes	Yes	90.8
GroupFormer [48]	Inception-v3	Yes	Yes	Yes	93.6
Weakly supervised					
HIGCIN [43]	ResNet-18	No	Yes	Yes	92.5
CRM [16]	I3D	Yes	Yes	No	83.4
SBGAR [32]	Inception-v3	Yes	No	No	83.7
Zhang et al. [50]	ZFNet	No	Yes	No	83.8
Wu et al. [51]	Inception-v3	No	Yes	No	85.0
Ours	ResNet-18	No	No	No	**86.54**

Contribution of Proposed Modules:
The results presented in Table 3 demonstrate the consistent performance improvements achieved by our proposed modules in two key evaluation metrics. The semantic attention module notably enhanced the Mean Class Accuracy (MCA) from 85.99% to 87.33% and the Mean Per-Class Accuracy (MPCA) from 86.73% to 87.64%. This indicates that our semantic attention module is more effective in identifying semantic regions.

Table 3. Contributions of the proposed modules.

Model	MCA	MPCA
Base model	85.99	86.73
Base model + SA	87.33	87.64
Base model + SA + SD	88.03	88.30
Base model + SA + CA	89.46	89.41
Base model + SA + SD + CA	91.47	91.75

Furthermore, the semantic interaction module further boosted the MCA from 87.33% to 88.03% and the MPCA from 87.64% to 88.30%. This highlights the utility of leveraging label co-occurrence knowledge in the dataset to enhance the model's understanding of individual interactions and promote improved classification performance. Moreover, the context aggregation module resulted in substantial gains, increasing the MCA from 89.46 to 91.47 and the MPCA from 89.41 to 91.75. This indicates that the aggregation method we employed successfully captures both temporal and spatial contextual information.

Overall, the results emphasize the effectiveness of our proposed modules in enhancing the model's performance across various measurement aspects, including semantic understanding, interaction modeling, and context aggregation.

Figure 5 presents the confusion matrices for VD and CAD, illustrating the efficacy of our method in distinguishing left and right activities within videos. Remarkably, our approach achieves classification accuracies exceeding 90% for all activities on VD, with the exception of left pass. On CAD, the accuracy for the "waiting" category is relatively lower due to the frequent confusion between crossing and waiting actions.

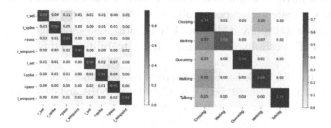

Fig. 5. Confusion matrices on the VD and CAD

4.5 Qualitative Analysis

Figure 6 depicts the visualization of attention obtained from the semantic attention module on VD, showcasing the effectiveness of our approach. The attention mechanism captures features corresponding to individual labels with motion information, such as "spiking," "setting," "falling," "jumping," "blocking," and "digging," highlighting

Fig. 6. Visualization of the feature map obtained from the semantic attention module, and the individual actions corresponding to these graphs are "setting", "falling", "digging", "spiking", "jumping", and "blocking".

their relevance to group behavior recognition. Conversely, static individual labels like "waiting" and "standing" receive less attention.

5 Conclusion

We propose a novel semantic attention model for weakly supervised group behavior recognition, eliminating the need for individual annotations and target detectors. Our method accurately captures subactions crucial for group behavior classification through a semantic attention mechanism. By leveraging both the co-occurrence matrix and graph convolution, we explore the relationships between individuals and perform effective aggregation. Our approach achieves state-of-the-art performance on two weakly supervised benchmarks, surpassing several models relying on higher levels of supervision. These results demonstrate our effective utilization of semantic information and tag co-occurrence knowledge to guide model learning, providing valuable insights for the future of group behavior recognition. In future work, we aim to enhance the information encoded in the semantic vector, potentially incorporating scene semantics or other contextual information to capture additional key features. Our ongoing efforts will further improve the model's performance and expand its capabilities in this exciting field.

Acknowledgments. This work has been supported by the National Natural Science Foundation of China under Grants No. 62106011, 62336010, 61976010, and 62106010. We gratefully acknowledge their financial support, which has enabled us to conduct this research.

References

1. Wang, L., Li, W., Li, W., Van Gool, L.: Appearance-and-relation networks for video classification. In: CVPR, pp. 1430–1439 (2018)
2. Simonyan, K., Zisserman, A.: Two-stream convolutional networks for action recognition in videos. In: NIPS, pp. 568–576 (2014)
3. Gan, C., Wang, N., Yang, Y., Yeung, D.-Y., Hauptmann, A.G.: DevNet: a deep event network for multimedia event detection and evidence recounting. In: CVPR, pp. 2568–2577 (2015)

4. Carreira, J., Zisserman, A.: Quo vadis, action recognition? A new model and the kinetics dataset. In: Proceedings of the IEEE Conference on Computer Vision and Pattern Recognition (CVPR) (2017)
5. Fan, L., Huang, W., Gan, C., Ermon, S., Gong, B., Huang, J.: End-to-end learning of motion representation for video understanding. In: Proceedings of the IEEE Conference on Computer Vision and Pattern Recognition (CVPR) (2018)
6. Girdhar, R., Carreira, J., Doersch, C., Zisserman, A.: Video action transformer network. In: Proceedings of the IEEE Conference on Computer Vision and Pattern Recognition (CVPR), pp. 244–253 (2019)
7. Kwon, H., Kim, M., Kwak, S., Cho, M.: MotionSqueeze: neural motion feature learning for video understanding. In: Vedaldi, A., Bischof, H., Brox, T., Frahm, J.-M. (eds.) ECCV 2020. LNCS, vol. 12361, pp. 345–362. Springer, Cham (2020). https://doi.org/10.1007/978-3-030-58517-4_21
8. Lin, J., Gan, C., Han, S.: TSM: temporal shift module for efficient video understanding. In: Proceedings of the IEEE International Conference on Computer Vision (ICCV), pp. 7083–7093 (2019)
9. Piergiovanni, A.J., Ryoo, M.S.: Representation flow for action recognition. In: Proceedings of the IEEE Conference on Computer Vision and Pattern Recognition (CVPR), pp. 9945–9953 (2019)
10. Wang, L., Xiong, Y., Zhe Wang, Yu., Qiao, D.L., Tang, X., Gool, L.: Temporal segment networks: towards good practices for deep action recognition. In: Leibe, B., Matas, J., Sebe, N., Welling, M. (eds.) ECCV 2016. LNCS, vol. 9912, pp. 20–36. Springer, Cham (2016). https://doi.org/10.1007/978-3-319-46484-8_2
11. Ibrahim, M.S., Muralidharan, S., Deng, Z., Vahdat, A., Mori, G.: A hierarchical deep temporal model for group activity recognition. In: CVPR (2016)
12. Tang, Y., Wang, Z., Li, P., Lu, J., Yang, M., Zhou, J.: Mining semantics-preserving attention for group activity recognition. In: ACM MM (2018)
13. Tang, J., Shu, X., Yan, R., Zhang, L.: Coherence constrained graph LSTM for group activity recognition. TPAMI 44(2), 636–647 (2019)
14. Shu, T., Todorovic, S., Zhu, S.C.: CERN: confidence-energy recurrent network for group activity recognition. In: CVPR (2017)
15. Wang, M., Ni, B., Yang, X.: Recurrent modeling of interaction context for collective activity recognition. In: CVPR (2017)
16. Azar, S.M., Atigh, M.G., Nickabadi, A., Alahi, A.: Convolutional relational machine for group activity recognition. In: CVPR (2019)
17. Bagautdinov, T., Alahi, A., Fleuret, F., Fua, P., Savarese, S.: Social scene understanding: end-to-end multi-person action localization and collective activity recognition. In: CVPR (2017)
18. Wu, J., Wang, L., Wang, L., Guo, J., Wu, G.: Learning actor relation graphs for group activity recognition. In: CVPR (2019)
19. Yan, R., Xie, L., Tang, J., Shu, X., Tian, Qi.: Social adaptive module for weakly-supervised group activity recognition. In: Vedaldi, A., Bischof, H., Brox, T., Frahm, J.-M. (eds.) Computer Vision – ECCV 2020: 16th European Conference, Glasgow, UK, August 23–28, 2020, Proceedings, Part VIII, pp. 208–224. Springer, Cham (2020). https://doi.org/10.1007/978-3-030-58598-3_13
20. Zhang, P., Tang, Y., Hu, J.-F., Zheng, W.-S.: Fast collective activity recognition under weak supervision. IEEE Trans. Image Process. 29, 29–43 (2019)
21. Kim, D., Lee, J., Cho, M., Kwak, S.: Detector-free weakly supervised group activity recognition. In: Proceedings of the IEEE/CVF Conference on Computer Vision and Pattern Recognition, pp. 20083–20093 (2022)

22. Zhang, D., Daniel, G.P., Bengio, S., et al.: Modeling individual and group actions in meetings: a two-layer HMM framework. In: Proceedings of the CVPR Workshops, p. 117 (2004)
23. Dai, P., Di, H., Dong, L., et al.: Group interaction analysis in dynamic context. IEEE Trans. Syst. Man Cybern. **38**(1), 275–282 (2008)
24. Lan, T., Wang, Y., Yang, W., et al.: Beyond actions: discriminative models for contextual group activities. In: Proceedings of the NIPS, pp. 1216−1224 (2010)
25. Kaneko, T., Shimosaka, M., Odashima, S., et al.: Consistent collective activity recognition with fully connected CRFs. In: Proceedings of the ICPR, pp. 2792−2795 (2012)
26. Amer, M.R., Todorovic, S., Fern, A., et al.: Monte Carlo tree search for scheduling activity recognition. In: Proceedings of the ICCV, pp. 1353−1360 (2013)
27. Amer, M.R., Lei, P., Todorovic, S.: HiRF: hierarchical random field for collective activity recognition in videos. In: Fleet, D., Pajdla, T., Schiele, B., Tuytelaars, T. (eds.) ECCV 2014. LNCS, vol. 8694, pp. 572–585. Springer, Cham (2014). https://doi.org/10.1007/978-3-319-10599-4_37
28. Qi, M., Qin, J., Li, A., Wang, Y., Luo, J., Gool, L.: StagNet: an attentive semantic RNN for group activity recognition. In: Ferrari, V., Hebert, M., Sminchisescu, C., Weiss, Y. (eds.) ECCV 2018. LNCS, vol. 11214, pp. 104–120. Springer, Cham (2018). https://doi.org/10.1007/978-3-030-01249-6_7
29. Ibrahim, M.S., Mori, G.: Hierarchical relational networks for group activity recognition and retrieval. In: Ferrari, V., Hebert, M., Sminchisescu, C., Weiss, Y. (eds.) Computer Vision – ECCV 2018: 15th European Conference, Munich, Germany, September 8–14, 2018, Proceedings, Part III, pp. 742–758. Springer, Cham (2018). https://doi.org/10.1007/978-3-030-01219-9_44
30. Hu, G., Cui, B., He, Y., et al.: Progressive relation learning for group activity recognition. In: Proceedings of the CVPR, pp. 977−986 (2020)
31. Xu, D., Fu, H., Wu, L., et al.: Group activity recognition by using effective multiple modality relation representation with temporalspatial attention. IEEE Access **8**, 65689–65698 (2020)
32. Li, X., Chuah, M.C.: SBGAR: semantics based group activity recognition. In: 2017 IEEE International Conference on Computer Vision (ICCV), pp. 2895–2904 (2017). https://doi.org/10.1109/ICCV.2017.313
33. He, K., Zhang, X., Ren, S., Sun, J.: Deep residual learning for image recognition. In: Proceedings of the IEEE Conference on Computer Vision and Pattern Recognition (CVPR), pp. 770–778 (2016)
34. Sun, D., Yang, X., Liu, M.-Y., Kautz, J.: PWC-Net: CNNs for optical flow using pyramid, warping, and cost volume. In: Proceedings of the IEEE Conference on Computer Vision and Pattern Recognition (CVPR), pp. 8934–8943 (2018)
35. Mikolov, T., Sutskever, I., Chen, K., Corrado, G.S., Dean, J.: Distributed representations of words and phrases and their compositionality. In: NeurIPS, pp. 3111–3119 (2013)
36. Kim,J.-H., On, K.-W., Lim, W., Kim, J., Ha, J.-W., Zhang, B.-T.: Hadamard product for low-rank bilinear pooling. arXiv preprint arXiv:1610.04325 (2016)
37. Li, Y., Tarlow, D., Brockschmidt, M., Zemel, R.: Gated graph sequence neural networks. arXiv preprint arXiv:1511.05493 (2015)
38. Chen, T., Lin, L., Chen, R., Wu, Y., Luo, X.: Knowledge-embedded representation learning for fine-grained image recognition. In: Proceedings of International Joint Conference on Artificial Intelligence (IJCAI), pp. 627–634 (2018)
39. Wang, Z., Chen, T., Ren, J., Yu, W., Cheng, H., Lin, L.: Deep reasoning with knowledge graph for social relationship understanding. In: Proceedings of International Joint Conference on Artificial Intelligence (IJCAI), pp. 2021–2018 (2018)
40. Chen, T., Yu, W., Chen, R., Lin, L.: Knowledge-embedded routing network for scene graph generation. In: Proceedings of IEEE Conference on Computer Vision and Pattern Recognition (CVPR) (2019)

41. Nair, V., Hinton, G.E.: Rectified linear units improve restricted Boltzmann machines. In: Proceedings of the International Conference on Machine Learning (ICML) (2010)
42. Kingma, D.P., Ba, J.: Adam: a method for stochastic optimization. In: Proceedings of the International Conference on Learning Representations (ICLR) (2015)
43. Yan, R., Xie, L., Tang, J., Shu, X., Tian, Q.: Higcin: hierarchical graph-based cross inference network for group activity recognition. IEEE Trans. Pattern Anal. Mach. Intell. (TPAMI) **45**(6), 6955–6968 (2020)
44. Gavrilyuk, K., Sanford, R., Javan, M., Snoek, C.G.M.: Actor-transformers for group activity recognition. In: Proceedings of the IEEE Conference on Computer Vision and Pattern Recognition (CVPR), pp. 839–848 (2020)
45. Pramono, R.R.A., Chen, Y.T., Fang, W.H.: Empowering relational network by self-attention augmented conditional random fields for group activity recognition. In: Vedaldi, A., Bischof, H., Brox, T., Frahm, J.-M. (eds.) Computer Vision – ECCV 2020: 16th European Conference, Glasgow, UK, August 23–28, 2020, Proceedings, Part I, pp. 71–90. Springer, Cham (2020). https://doi.org/10.1007/978-3-030-58452-8_5
46. Yuan, H., Ni, D., Wang, M.: Spatio-temporal dynamic inference network for group activity recognition. In: Proceedings of the IEEE International Conference on Computer Vision (ICCV), pp. 7476–7485 (2021)
47. Yuan, H., Ni, D.: Learning visual context for group activity recognition. In: Proceedings of the AAAI Conference on Artificial Intelligence (AAAI), vol. 35, pp. 3261–3269 (2021)
48. Li, S., et al.: GroupFormer: group activity recognition with clustered spatial-temporal transformer. In Proceedings of the IEEE International Conference on Computer Vision (ICCV), pages 13668–13677, 2021
49. Lu, L., Lu, Y., Yu, R., Di, H., Zhang, L., Wang, S.: GAIM: graph attention interaction model for collective activity recognition. IEEE Trans. Multimedia **22**(2), 524–539 (2019)
50. Ehsanpour, M., Abedin, A., Saleh, F., Shi, J., Reid, I., Rezatofighi, H.: Joint learning of social groups, individuals action and sub-group activities in videos. In: Vedaldi, A., Bischof, H., Brox, T., Frahm, J.-M. (eds.) ECCV 2020. LNCS, vol. 12354, pp. 177–195. Springer, Cham (2020). https://doi.org/10.1007/978-3-030-58545-7_11
51. Wu, J., Lang, X., Xiang, Y., Chen, C., Li, Z., Wang, Z.: Active spatial positions based hierarchical relation inference for group activity recognition. IEEE Trans. Circ. Syst. Video Technol. **33**(6), 2839–2851 (2023). https://doi.org/10.1109/TCSVT.2022.3228731

Computer Graphics

Research on Contrast Calculation Method for Color Image

Jing Qian[1,2,3](✉), Bin Kong[1,3,4], Jing Yang[3,5], and Can Wang[1]

[1] Hefei Institutes of Physical Science, Chinese Academy of Sciences, Hefei 230031, China
qjjq@mail.ustc.edu.cn
[2] University of Science and Technology of China, Hefei 230026, China
[3] Peng Cheng Laboratory, Shenzhen 518053, China
[4] Anhui Key Laboratory of Biomimetic Sensing and Advanced Robot Technology, Hefei 230031, China
[5] School of Artificial Intelligence and Big Data, Hefei University, Hefei 230031, China

Abstract. Contrast is one of the commonly used indicators for evaluating image quality and is related to color information. However, the traditional contrast calculation method only reflects the clarity of the image by counting the distribution probability of the gray difference between adjacent pixels in the region, which lacks consideration of the chrominance information. We propose a contrast calculation method considering the perceptual color difference in color images. First, we obtain each pixel's hue and saturation information from the HSV color space. And the luminance information of each pixel is obtained while retaining the color contrast information of the original image. Then, the contrast of a color image is obtained by counting the number of adjacent pixels whose color difference exceeds the threshold and calculating the sum of color differences. Experiment results show that our method is less affected by the uniform color patches than other methods. It can effectively reflect the relationship between the contrast values of different images and reduce the information loss of color contrast. In addition, for different color images, the magnitude of the contrast value obtained by our method is consistent with the trend of human visual judgment.

Keywords: Image processing · image quality · image color analysis · contrast measures · perceptual contrast

1 Introduction

In the common image quality assessment indicator, contrast is one of the most relevant characteristics of visual signals [1]. It has been widely used in related high-tech fields such as aerospace, medical bioengineering, robot vision, military security [2–7]. However, Although the vision research has been developed for many years, there is still no calculation method of contrast that can perfectly simulate the contrast judgment of color images by the human eyes. Therefore, research on the contrast calculation method of color images is still a valuable topic, we hope this work can provide a new idea for the contrast calculation for color images.

W. Yongtian and W. Lifang (Eds.): IGTA 2023, CCIS 1910, pp. 239–253, 2023.
https://doi.org/10.1007/978-981-99-7549-5_18

Color image is composed of luminance information and chrominance information. Chrominance is a color property that contains hue information and saturation information. Both luminance and chrominance will affect the contrast judgment of the observer [8–10]. And the judgment of contrast information is also affected by the perceptual cognition of the observer. However, most of the existing methods do not fully consider the information of perceptual color difference, which is brought by the visual characteristics of the human eyes [11]. Based on this consideration, this paper proposes a contrast calculation method that considers the perceptual color difference. First, we use the hue and saturation information of the HSV (hue, saturation, value) color space as the chrominance information of each image pixel. And the luminance information of the image is obtained by calculating the RGB decolorization parameter, which retains the image's contrast information. Finally, the contrast is calculated by counting the quantity information and perceptual color difference information of the pixels whose color difference exceeds the threshold between adjacent pixels.

The traditional contrast calculation method for color image usually converts the color image to gray image first, then calculates the gray difference between each pixel and its adjacent pixels to reflect the administrative levels and clarity of the image, like the method in literature [17]. However, this will ignore the color difference information of some color images and cannot express the objective color contrast relationship. For example, we design a special synthetic images (see Fig. 1) to illustrate the problem of the traditional method [4].

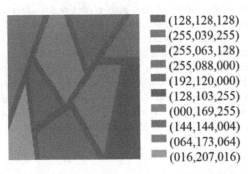

(128,128,128)
(255,039,255)
(255,063,128)
(255,088,000)
(192,120,000)
(128,103,255)
(000,169,255)
(144,144,004)
(064,173,064)
(016,207,016)

Fig. 1. The synthetic image with different colors, but its gray values calculated by the traditional gray scale conversion method are all 128, this causes the gray difference to be 0.

Figure 1 is an image composed of pure color regions. From the perspective of human vision, the image has obvious color differences between different regions, but its traditional contrast value is zero, this is because after transforming it from RGB to grayscale, all pixels have the same value of 128, which means the gray difference is zero.

In order to obtain more accurate contrast information, it is necessary to change the calculation method of luminance information and consider the color information.

The rest of the paper is organized as follows: In Sect. 2, we give a brief review of the related works. In Sect. 3, we describe our method in detail. In Sect. 4, we show the experiment results and compare them with other methods. Finally, the conclusions and future works are presented in Sect. 5.

2 Related Work

With the development of visual information processing and analysis, contrast, as one of the first and widely investigated psycho-visual aspects in vision research [12], has been widely used in medical imaging, image quality evaluation, visual signal analysis and other work. Regarding how to define and use contrast, researchers have proposed many calculation methods based on different principles and applications. According to the time sequence and the different research fields, we divide these methods into two categories: the early definition of optical contrast and the definition of digital contrast for computers. Here we briefly review the two types of methods in the following.

In the early stages of measuring and defining contrast, to quantify this purely psychophysical measure, the scientists used the most intuitive measure, using optical experiments, to calculate the relative luminance difference between the target and the background.

In 1834, Weber et al. [13] pioneered the measurement and definition of visual contrast. In their experiment, the region with an incremental luminance of ΔL is set in the background with a uniform luminance of L, the value of ΔL is changed continuously so that the difference region is just visible. The value of ΔL is recorded, the relationship between the incremental luminance ΔL and the background luminance L is studied. The contrast defined by this experimental model is generally called Weber-Fechner contrast.

In 1943, Moon-Spencer et al. [14] proposed the definition of optical contrast in a non-uniform luminance setting, as opposed to the uniform luminance setting set by the Weber-Fechner contrast method [13]. This method first uses the Holladay principle [15]. That is, any non-uniform background can be replaced by another uniform luminance that produces the same perceptual effect and divides the background around the target with different luminance into near and far surrounding areas with uniform luminance. Then, the luminance adaptation information of the background is obtained according to the contribution ratio of the two regions to the target. Finally, the luminance contrast information is calculated using the scale constant obtained from the psycho-visual test and Hecht's law [16] experiment.

As early as the 1950s, people began to use computers to process digital image information. Subsequently, digital image processing has become a new subject. In order to facilitate the processing and analysis of acquired digital images, researchers have proposed many different definition methods of contrast.

In 1973, Haralick et al. proposed a contrast calculation method based on the Gray Level Co-occurrence Matrix (GLCM) [17], which can obtain the average local variation information of pixels. But there are significant errors when there are large uniform or nearly uniform color patches in the image.

In 1990, Moulden et al., based on the grayscale information of the image, proposed six definition methods (SD contrast, SDLG contrast, SAM contrast, SALGM contrast, SAW contrast and SALGW contrast) for analyzing the grayscale random dot image [18]. These definitions have advantages over other traditional measures, such as the Weber contrasts [13], because they consider more factors that affect the contrast.

In 2002, Bex and Makous introduced a relatively simple global contrast metric for natural images called RMS contrast [24]. RMS contrast measurement method is based on the standard deviation of image brightness. This measure has been proven to be a reliable predictor of human contrast detection thresholds in natural scenes.

In 2020, Yelmanov et al. proposed a method to quantify the overall image contrast [19]. They use the contrast information of partial, incomplete integration of the image to better and faster achieve the accuracy and reliability of the rapid assessment of the overall contrast of multi-element images. The core of this method is to calculate the probability density function of the brightness information of each local area in the image relative to the overall image brightness information. It is worth noting that in the literature [19], the author used various contrast definition methods to verify the effectiveness of the proposed method.

Despite the continuing progress made by the vision research community, it is still necessary to study the definition of digital contrast.

3   Method

In this section, we propose a contrast calculation method which considers the color difference. First, the original color image is processed in two independent steps. One step is to obtain the hue and saturation information of each pixel in the HSV color space as the chrominance information through color space conversion; the other step is to obtain the luminance information of each pixel of the image by linear decolorization parameter, which retains the contrast information of the image. Finally, by counting the number and color difference information of the adjacent pixels whose color difference exceeds the threshold, get the contrast value of the color image.

3.1   Chrominance Information Acquisition Based on HSV Color Space

RGB (Red, Green, Blue) color space is common in image processing. However, the sensitivity of human eyes to these three color components is different. In monochrome, human eyes are least sensitive to red and blue and most susceptible to green, so RGB color space is a color space with poor uniformity. Therefore, we chose to obtain the chrominance information of the image through the HSV color space, which is in line with human visual habits.

In 1978, Alvy Ray Smith proposed the HSV color space based on the intuitive nature of color [20]. Compared with RGB color space, HSV color space is closer to human subjective feelings of color information. It can express color information intuitively and conveniently in image processing applications. Therefore, we choose the H (Hue) component and the S (Saturation) component of HSV color space as the chrominance information of each pixel in the image.

The V (Value) component of the HSV color space directly selects the maximum value of the three channels of the original RGB color space. This selection of V components is simple and direct. Still, direct use of the V component to represent luminance information will lose some of the luminance difference information between colors in contrast to numerical calculation. For example, when the value of one channel is large, the color change caused by changing the value of other channels will not get feedback on the luminance information.

3.2 Calculate Luminance Information

In image processing applications, grayscale information is often equivalent to the luminance information of the image [22]. Usually, the process of graying a color image is to combine the values of R, G, B channels of the original image linearly in a certain proportion. As shown in formula (1):

$$\begin{cases} g = R * w_R + G * w_G + B * w_B \\ w_R > 0;\ w_G > 0;\ w_B > 0 \\ w_R + w_G + w_B = 1 \end{cases} \tag{1}$$

Each channel's proportional parameters (w_R, w_G, w_B) shall meet the constraints in formula (1).

The proportional parameter of the traditional grayscale transformation is $w_R = 0.299$, $w_G = 0.587$, $w_B = 0.114$. Traditional grayscale transformation meets the application requirements of most scenarios. However, in some special scenes, the original information of color contrast will be lost after the color image is converted to gray image. As shown in Fig. 2(a) and (b):

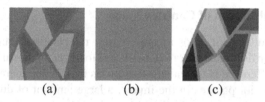

(a)   (b)   (c)

Fig. 2. Display of different graying results (a) Original image; (b) Grayscale result of traditional grayscale transformation; (c) Grayscale result with contrast information

Comparing Fig. 2(a) with Fig. 2(b), significant color difference information is lost in Fig. 2(b). It is not conducive to the objective evaluation of image analysis.

Therefore, we need to calculate each image's scale coefficients of R, G and B channels while retaining the original color contrast information. This calculation is usually intended to minimize the following energy functions (2) to preserve contrast information [21]:

$$\min \sum\nolimits_{x,y} (g_x - g_y - \delta_{x,y})^2 \tag{2}$$

In function (2), g_x and g_y are the gray values for pixel x and pixel y. $\delta_{x,y}$ represents the Euclidean distance in the CIELab color space at point x and point y, which is generally represented by the formula (3):

$$|\delta_{x,y}| = \sqrt{(L_x - L_y)^2 + (a_x - a_y)^2 + (b_x - b_y)^2} \tag{3}$$

In formula (3), L, a and b are the three components of the CIElab color space. In 2012, Lu et al. rewrite function (2) into formula (4) after derivation after derivation [22]:

$$E(g) = -\sum \ln(N_\sigma(\Delta g_{x,y} + \delta_{x,y}) + N_\sigma(\Delta g_{x,y} - \delta_{x,y})) \tag{4}$$

In Formula (4), $\Delta g_{x,y} = g_x - g_y$, it represents the difference between the gray levels of two random points. N_σ means Gaussian function operations. When the value of $E(g)$ is the smallest, the linear proportional parameter (w_R, w_G, w_B) retains the contrast information in the original image to the greatest extent.

Because there are unlimited combinations of (w_R, w_G, w_B) that satisfy the constraint condition (1). Considering that the slight change of coefficients has little influence on the results, Lu et al. [22] propose to discretize the solution space of (w_R, w_G, w_B) in the range of [0,1] with interval 0.1. Thus, only 66 combinations (w_R, w_G, w_B) need to be calculated. Using exhaustion, we can find the proportional parameter (l_R, l_G, l_B), which minimizes the $E(g)$ value and retains the most contrast information from the 66 combinations. By substituting the proportional parameter (l_R, l_G, l_B) into formula (3), we can get the luminance information L of each pixel in the original image.

In calculating (l_R, l_G, l_B), the original high-resolution image can be reduced to a low-resolution image for calculation, reducing time consumption [22].

Figure 2(c) shows the grayscale image obtained by using this method to calculate the scale parameters. We can easily find that the perceptual color difference in the original image is preserved after the grayscale processing.

3.3 Statistical Calculation of Contrast Value

The statistical calculation of color image contrast information obtains the difference information between different colors in the image. However, in the same color connected region, the color difference between adjacent pixels is 0. When there are large uniform or nearly uniform color patches in the image, a large amount of duplicated data with little difference in each region will dilute the information on color difference. Unlike Haralick et al., they chose all adjacent pixels as statistical objects. Our statistical objects are adjacent pixels whose Euclidean distance of color difference exceeds the threshold T. Such selection of statistical targets can reduce the dilution of duplicated data. T refers to the smallest color difference that humans can perceive. The Euclidean distance $F(a, b)$ of color difference between adjacent pixels a and b is calculated by formula (5):

$$
\begin{aligned}
F_A &= S_a * \sin(H_a - H_b) \\
F_B &= S_a * \cos(H_a - H_b) - S_b \\
F_C &= L_a - L_b \\
F(a, b) &= \sqrt{F_A^2 + F_B^2 + F_C^2}
\end{aligned}
\tag{5}
$$

In formula (5), a and b denote two adjacent pixels, H_a and H_b are the hue information, and the value range is $0°$–$360°$; S_a and S_b are the saturation information, the value range is 0–1; L_a and L_b are the luminance information, the value range is 0–1.

Because of the complexity of human vision, it is difficult to get the value of threshold T directly, and we can only make estimates.

The threshold T is calculated in formula (6):

$$
T = \frac{F_{\max}(a, b)}{K}
\tag{6}
$$

In formula (6), $F_{max}(a, b)$ is represented as the theoretical maximum value of the color difference. K indicates the number of bands that human eyes can distinguish.

In order to get the theoretical maximum difference value $F_{max}(a, b)$, we derived formula (6) and obtained formula (7):

$$F(a, b) = \sqrt{S_a^2 + S_b^2 + (L_a - L_b)^2 - 2 * S_a S_b * \cos(H_a - H_b)}$$

$$\leq \sqrt{S_a^2 + S_b^2 + (L_a - L_b)^2 + 2 * S_a S_b} \tag{7}$$

From Formula (7) we can find that when the maximum value is taken in the formula, $|H_a - H_b| = 180°$, and $F(a, b)$ is positively correlated with S_a and S_b. The larger the value of S_a and S_b are, the larger the $F(a, b)$ is. The maximum difference value $F_{max}(a, b)$ can be obtained by comparing all the colors in the color space. Theoretically, the number of colors in the color space is infinite, so comparing and calculating all colors is difficult. Therefore, we use the exhaustive method to calculate the difference information between color $(H, 1, V_a)$ and color $(H + 180°, 1, V_b)$ in HSV space, chosen 1° as the interval of H component, and the value range of H is 0–180°, chosen 0.1 as the interval of V component, and the value range of V is 0–1. Statistics of results by exhaustion, when $H = 120°$, $V_a = V_b = 1$, $F(a, b)$ has a maximum value of 2.236.

The visible spectrum of human eyes is 380 nm–780 nm, and the discrimination thresholds of different wavelengths are different. In the visible spectrum of human beings with normal color vision, the wavelength discrimination threshold of less than 430 nm and more than 650 nm are larger, there only about 3 different color can be distinguished. The wavelength discrimination threshold of other spectral regions is smaller. In 1962, Davson combined anatomical and neurological experiments to plot the mean wavelength discrimination curve from 430 nm to 650 nm [23]. As shown in Fig. 3:

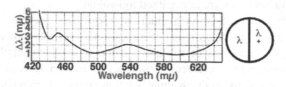

Fig. 3. Mean wavelength discrimination curve. (From Davson [23])

It can be estimated from Fig. 3 that the average discriminant threshold of 430 nm–440 nm is about 4.5 nm, 440 nm–460 nm is about 3 nm, 460 nm–500 nm is about 2 nm, 500 nm–630 nm is about 1.5 nm, and 630 nm–650 nm is about 2.5 nm. Based on the information of the mean wavelength discrimination curve from Fig. 3, We calculated the estimated value of K by using a simple mean:

$$K = \frac{440 - 430}{4.5} + \frac{460 - 440}{3} + \frac{500 - 460}{2} + \frac{630 - 500}{1.5} + \frac{650 - 630}{2.5} + 3 \approx 127 \tag{8}$$

Finally, the contrast information C_0 is obtained by counting the color difference information $\sum\limits_{\forall F(a,b) > T} F(a, b)$ and the quantity information N of the different points. As shown in Formula (9):

$$C_0 = \frac{\sum\limits_{\forall F(a,b)>T} F(a,b)}{N} \qquad (9)$$

In order to facilitate comparison with other methods, we normalize the results in the experiment. It is found that the detection results of natural environment images are rarely close to 1. Most of the calculated results of natural images are in the interval [0,0.1]. This is because most original natural images are composed of a large number of different colors. It is difficult to find an image with few colors and larger color differences. To facilitate users to compare the results of different natural images more intuitively, we provide a method of numerical expansion (10):

$$C = \sqrt{C_0 * (2 - C_0)} \qquad (10)$$

The numerical expansion aims to make the contrast difference more obvious and convenient for comparison and analysis. Formula (10) can expand C_0 values between [0,1], and the numerical size relationship of different C_0 values remains unchanged after expansion.

4 Experiment and Analysis

In order to verify the effectiveness of our method, the proposed method is compared with other methods. The comparison methods we selected were: GLCM [17], RMS [24], SD [18] and AQOC [19]. The experimental images include natural environment images and synthetic images. To facilitate the comparison and analysis between different methods, the results of all the methods are normalized individually.

Because contrast is a subjective evaluation index, there may be significant differences in subjective judgment of contrast of complex natural environment images among different groups (gender, age, race), it is difficult to choose which population to perform subjective evaluation tests. Therefore, in the comparative analysis of natural environment images, we choose the contrast images before and after optimization of the contrast enhancement algorithm [25] as part of the experimental object; In the comparative analysis of experimental images, we designed experimental images which can clearly explain the numerical contrast size as the subjective judgment object for analysis and comparison.

4.1 Comparative Analysis of Natural Environment Images

We experimented with different natural environment images with the size of 640*480 and show some of the results in Fig. 4.

In Fig. 4, The first line is an example of contrast images taken by Dolby Laboratories before and after the use of Dolby Vision (From https://eefocus.com/consumer-electr onics/325413). The left side is a low-contrast image, and the right side is a high-contrast image by using Dolby Vision. The second line and third line are the contrast images

Image	GLCM	RMS	SD	AQOC	Our method	Image	GLCM	RMS	SD	AQOC	Our method
	0.0028	0.013	0.178	0.079	0.192		0.0100	0.024	0.354	0.157	0.303
	0.0151	0.033	0.178	0.072	0.398	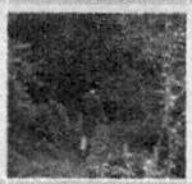	0.0956	0.084	0.374	0.151	0.412
	0.0265	0.045	0.344	0.156	0.358		0.1040	0.090	0.526	0.238	0.425
	0.0017	0.009	0.416	0.176	0.227		0.0367	0.047	0.306	0.121	0.294
	0.0585	0.068	0.590	0.260	0.360	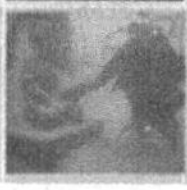	0.0009	0.007	0.171	0.072	0.192

Fig. 4. Experimental results of natural environment images

before and after using the contrast enhancement technique [26]. The left side are the original image without enhancement, and the right side are the resulting image after enhancement. From these contrast images, it can be found that the processed image has better visual effect, and the output results of each method are consistent with visual perception, this means the proposed metric has right correlation with the image quality attribute, contrast in this case. The fourth line and fifth line are examples of natural images. It can be found that after normalization, the numerical results of various methods are smaller. Because the color composition of the natural environment image is complex, and it is difficult to appear the theoretical limit of the contrast method. This is the reason why we added value expansion in Section III. Numerically, when there is a highlighted area in the image, the contrast values are larger (such as the image in the left of the fifth line); when there is some kind of severe color bias in the image, and the visual effect is blurred, the contrast values calculated by the various contrast methods are smaller (such as the image in on the right of the fifth line), this corresponds to the contrast of subjective feelings. It is shown that our method, like other classical methods, can effectively reflect the numerical size relationship between images.

In order to further compare the rationality of the proposed method, we add different degrees of salt & pepper noise, Gaussian blurring and fogging to natural images and obtain degraded images with different degrees. Record the contrast calculation values of different degraded images by comparison methods. As shown in Figs. 5, 6 and 7.

It can be seen from Fig. 5 that after adding salt & pepper noise, the contrast calculation results of each method are increased. This is because salt noise and pepper noise are shown as black and white noise in the image, and the noise itself has a large difference in luminance information from neighboring pixels. Therefore, the more salt & pepper noise added, the higher the image's contrast. In Fig. 5, GLCM is most affected by salt & pepper, while other methods are less affected.

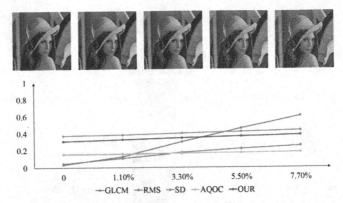

Fig. 5. The contrast of degraded images with different degrees of salt & pepper noise. The ordinate is the calculated value of contrast, and the abscissa is the added amount of salt & pepper noise.

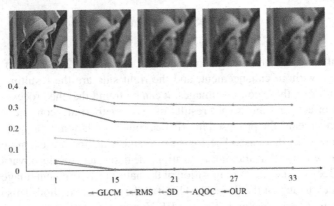

Fig. 6. The contrast of degraded images with Gaussian blurring. The ordinate is the calculated value of contrast, and the abscissa is the convolution kernel of different sizes.

It can be seen from Fig. 6 that after Gaussian blurring, the contrast calculation results of all methods are reduced. This is because Gaussian blur processing will reduce the information difference between pixels and their neighboring pixels. The larger the Gaussian convolution kernel is set, the smaller the image contrast is. In Fig. 6, the effects of Gaussian fuzzy processing on the calculation methods are relatively consistent. This shows that the proposed method, like other classical methods, can correctly reflect the contrast numerical sizes of images.

It can be seen from Fig. 7 that as the number of fogging increases, the scene information in the image gradually becomes blurred, and the contrast calculation results of each method decrease. After several times of fogging, the information in the image is seriously affected, and the color difference is difficult to detect. For example, after four fogging times, the "fortress" in the original image is difficult to distinguish by visual observation. In Fig. 7, the contrast change of the proposed method is the most obvious

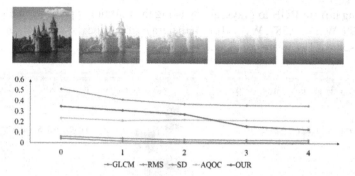

Fig. 7. The contrast of degraded images with different times of fogging. The ordinate is the calculated value of contrast, and the abscissa is the number of fog processing by using the method in literature [26].

with the increased fogging times, the SD method is the second, and the other methods are not obvious.

4.2 Comparative Analysis of Composite Images

In order to analyze and compare the contrast results of different color combinations, we designed some experimental images with different color. The experimental images are shown in Fig. 8:

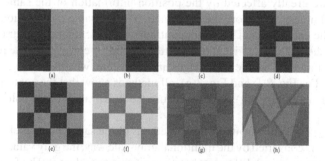

Fig. 8. Synthetic images.

In Fig. 8(a)–(g), each image consists of 16 squares of the same size in solid color. Figure 8(a)–(e) consists of 8 blue (RGB value (0,0,255)) squares and 8 green (RGB value (0,200,0)) squares. In Fig. 8(a)–(e), the number and value of pixels in the five images are the same, and the only difference is the arrangement of the color regions. From the perspective of human vision, the contrast perception of the five images are consistent. Figure 8(f) is staggered combination of 8 squares with RGB values (255,0,255) and 8 squares with RGB values (0,255,0); Fig. 8(g) is staggered combination of 8 squares with RGB values (200,0,200) and 8 squares with RGB values (128,255,0); Fig. 8(h) is a special solid-color combination image. The particularity of this image is that after transforming it from RGB to grayscale by using the traditional proportional parameter: WR = 0.299, WG = 0.587, WB = 0.114, the grayscale values of all pixels are 128. The contrast results of Fig. 8 are counted in Fig. 9:

Image	GLCM	RMS	SD	AQOC	Our method	Image	GLCM	RMS	SD	AQOC	Our method
	0.0042	0.021	0.345	0.345	0.974		0.0084	0.030	0.345	0.345	0.974
	0.0169	0.042	0.345	0.345	0.974		0.0179	0.044	0.345	0.345	0.974
	0.0253	0.052	0.345	0.345	0.974		0.0066	0.026	0.176	0.176	1.000
	0.0019	0.014	0.086	0.086	0.936		0.0000	0.000	0.000	0.000	0.538

Fig. 9. Contrast results of experimental images.

Analysis from the perspective of different image data results for the same method in Fig. 9. The results of the GLCM method and RMS method in Fig. 8(a)–(e) are different, their results are greatly affected by the position information of the same color region in the original image. The more the combination of the same color region, the smaller the value of the calculation. This result contradicts the fact that the contrast perception of the five images in human visual observation should be consistent. The results of SD, AQOC and our method for the five images are consistent, which is more in line with the objective fact. For Fig. 8(f) and Fig. 8(g), all methods show that the contrast of Fig. 8(f) is greater than that of Fig. 8(g). This is because the RGB values of the colors in Fig. 8(g) are smaller.

Analysis of the results from different methods of the same image is shown in Fig. 9. When Fig. 8(h) is converted by the traditional grayscale way, the gray values of each pixel are 128, and the numerical difference between adjacent pixels is 0. The four comparison methods that directly use the traditional gray results as the brightness information all calculate the results of Fig. 8(h) as 0, and the original color contrast information is lost. The luminance information calculation of our method avoids this kind of information loss.

From the comprehensive data in Fig. 9, the results of our method are larger than those of other methods. Because other comparison methods retain a large number of small differences in information invisible to the human eyes, this dilutes the difference information between different colors and makes the contrast result smaller. It is not beneficial to reflect the perceptual differences between different colors. Our method reduces the influence of the imperceptible visual difference on the final result, which helps express the perceptual contrast information of the color image.

To further verify the effectiveness of the method, we use Fig. 8(e) as experimental image models and set the two-component colors of the image to (0, 0, 0) and (ΔP, ΔP, ΔP). The value range of ΔP is 0–255. The contrast values of different methods are recorded by changing the values of ΔP, and the results of each method at different ΔP values are shown in Fig. 10.

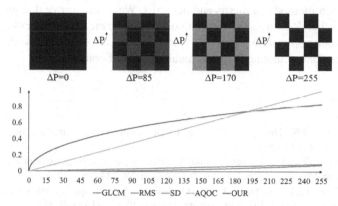

Fig. 10. Contrast values of comparison methods with different ΔP (Use Fig. 8(e) as experimental image models).

It can be seen from Fig. 10 that the contrast value of the AQOC method, SD method and the proposed method are more significant than those of other methods, and the curves of the SD method and AQOC method coincide. The values of all methods increase with the increase of ΔP, which can correctly express the size relationship of contrast.

The color image is a combination of chrominance information and luminance information. Single Luminance information cannot fully tell the difference of color information. The method of SD and AQOC has reached the maximum value of theoretical calculation in the experimental images with only luminance difference; the maximum difference of image contrast recognized by these methods only takes luminance information into account, without chrominance information. Therefore, the method of SD and AQOC are more suitable for pure gray images than color images. After normalization, the results of GLCM and RMS are too small to compare the contrast difference in practical application. Our method can express the contrast relation correctly and be applied to actual contrast difference comparison.

5 Conclusion

Aiming at the problem that the existing contrast calculation methods do not take enough consideration of color difference information. This paper presents a contrast calculation method considering perceptual color differences in color images. Compared with other methods, this method is less affected by the uniform region in the original image, can better preserve the color contrast information and reduce the effect of repeated data. It is more conducive to the expression of color images perceptual contrast information.

Further work is still needed, for example, the calculation ting threshold T is based on the premise of uniform distribution. It could be more reasonable if the wavelength corresponding to color were considered. Reducing computational time is also part of what we need to improve.

For the time being, no definition of contrast exists on which the vision research and visual processing scientific community can agree [8]. According to different principles, each calculation method has merits and demerits. We cannot prove that one method is superior to another. Researchers should choose a suitable method for calculating contrast according to their application scenarios and requirements. We hope our work can provide a new solution for calculating the perceptual contrast of color images.

References

1. Yao, J.C., Shi, J.S., Huang, X.Q., Yang, J.: Definition of color image contrast. J. Yunnan Normal Univ. 49–51 (2006)
2. Li, K., Liu, Y., Wang, Y.T.: Research on the effect of contrast enhancement and illumination condition on 3D visual fatigue. J. Soc. Inf. Display 28, 744–751 (2020)
3. Liu, W., Zhou, F., Lu, T., Duan, J., Qiu, G.: Image defogging quality assessment: real-world database and method. IEEE Trans. Image Process. 30, 176–190 (2021)
4. Qian, J., Kong, B.: Research on global contrast calculation considering color differences. In: Wang, Y., Song, W. (eds.) IGTA 2021. CCIS, vol. 1480, pp. 189–200. Springer, Singapore (2021). https://doi.org/10.1007/978-981-16-7189-0_15
5. Penkelink, G.P.J., Besuijen, J.: Chromaticity contrast, luminance contrast, and legibility of text. J. Soc. Inf. Display 4, 135–144 (1996)
6. Hoffman, D.M., Stepien, N.N., Xiong, W.: The importance of native panel contrast and local dimming density on perceived image quality of high dynamic range displays. J. Soc. Inf. Display 24, 216–228 (2016)
7. Mina, C., Hoffman, D.M.: Efficacy of global dimming backlight and high-contrast liquid crystal panel for high-dynamic-range displays. J. Soc. Inf. Display 25, 283–294 (2017)
8. Beghdadi, A., Qureshi, M.A., Amirshahi, S.A., Chetouani, A., Pedersen, M.: A critical analysis on perceptual contrast and its use in visual information analysis and processing. IEEE Access 8, 156929–156953 (2020)
9. Xue, X., Hao, Z., Ma, L., Wang, Y., Liu, R.: Joint luminance and chrominance learning for underwater image enhancement. IEEE Signal Process. Lett. 28, 818–822 (2021)
10. Ji, S., Jeong, J., Oh, S.H.: Quad-contrast imaging: simultaneous acquisition of four contrast-weighted images (PD-weighted, T2-weighted, PD-FLAIR and T2-FLAIR images) with synthetic T1-weighted image, T1-and T2-maps. IEEE Trans. Med. Imaging 40, 3617–3626 (2021)
11. Mahmoodpour, M., Amirany, A., Moaiyeri, M.H., Jafari, K.: A learning based contrast specific no reference image quality assessment algorithm. In: 2022 International Conference on Machine Vision and Image Processing (MVIP), pp. 1–4 (2022). https://doi.org/10.1109/MVIP53647.2022.9738784
12. Cornsweet, T.N.: Visual perception. In: Academic, pp. 387–389 (1971)
13. Weber, E.H., De, Pulsu., Resorptione, Auditu et Tactu.: Annotationes Anatomicae et Physiologicae, Auctore., Apud CF Koehler, Leipzig, Germany: Prostat Apud CF Koehler (1834)
14. Moon, P., Spencer, D.E.: The specification of foveal adaptation. J. Opt. Soc. Am. 33, 444–456 (1943)

15. Holladay, L.L.: The fundamentals of glare and visibility. J. Opt. Soc. Am. **12**, 271–319 (1926)
16. Hecht, S.: The visual discrimination of intensity and the Weber-fechner law. J. Gen. Physiol. **7**, 235–267 (1924)
17. Haralick, R.M., Shanmugam, K., Dinstein, I.: Textural features for image classification. IEEE Trans. Syst. Man Cybern. 610–621 (1973)
18. Moulden, B., Kingdom, F., Gatley, L.F.: The standard deviation of luminance as a metric for contrast in random-dot images. Perception **19**, 79–101 (1990)
19. Yelmanov, S., Romanyshyn, Y.: A quick no-reference quantification of the overall contrast of an image. In: 2020 IEEE Third International Conference on Data Stream Mining & Processing, pp. 185–190 (2020)
20. Smith, R.A.: Color gamut transform pairs. In: Siggraph 1978: Conference on Computer Graphics & Interactive Techniques, pp. 12–19 (1978)
21. Kim, Y., Jang, C., Demouth, J., Lee, S.: Robust color-to-gray via nonlinear global mapping. ACM Trans. Graph. 1–4 (2009)
22. Lu, C.W., Xu, L., Jia, J.Y.: Real-time contrast preserving decolorizatio. In: SIGGRAPH Asia 2012 Posters, SA 2012 (2012)
23. Davson, H.: Visual Optics and the Optical Space Sense. Visual Optics and the Optical Space Sense, pp. 101–131. Academic Press, USA (1962)
24. Bex, P.J., Makous, W.: Spatial frequency, phase, and the contrast of natural images. J. Opt. Soc. Am. A **19**, 1096–1106 (2002)
25. Kim, J.H., Jang, W.D., Sim, J.Y., Kim, C.S.: Optimized contrast enhancement for real-time image and video dehazing. J. Vis. Commun. Image Represent. **24**, 410–426 (2013)
26. Sun, C.M., Kong, B., He, L.X., Tian, Q.: An algorithm of imaging simulation of fog with different visibility. In: IEEE International Conference on Information and Automation, pp. 1607–1611 (2015)

A Position-Based Dynamics Simulation of Liver Deformation with Ellipsoidal Particles

Xuanlin Long[✉], Yuanyuan Wang, and Jian Yang

School of Optics and Photonics, Beijing Institute of Technology, Beijing, China
xllong0815@gmail.com

Abstract. Virtual liver tumor resection surgery is widely used for training physicians in surgical skills. Establishing a realistic liver deformation model is an important prerequisite for virtual surgery. In this study, we propose a position-based dynamics model using ellipsoidal particles for liver deformation simulation to overcome the low computational efficiency of traditional voxel-sampled position-based dynamics model. Specifically, we segmented the liver and reconstructed its 3D model from medical computed tomography images. Next, we generated ellipsoidal particles at the grid vertices based on center distance constraints. Finally, liver deformation was simulated by solving the shape matching constraints between the particles. The results of simulation experiments showed that our proposed method achieved similar deformation authenticity and reduced computational time compared to the traditionally used voxel-filled particles model. The frame rate of our proposed method achieved 201 frames per second, which satisfies the basic frame rate requirements for real-time display.

Keywords: Position-based dynamics model · Deformation simulation · Ellipsoid particle

1 Introduction

Liver cancer is one of the most lethal malignancies, and the resection of diseased liver segments is an effective and commonly used treatment for liver tumors in clinical practice. According to Couinaud's modern concept of liver anatomy, intact liver segments should be resected to minimize damage to liver function and follow the principles of minimally invasive tumor surgery [1]. Virtual surgery, an important virtual reality technology applied in the medical field, can simulate human tissues, organs, and surgical scenarios, providing repeatable training opportunities and situations for surgeons. As such, it is of great importance for surgeon training.

In virtual surgery, the accuracy of the soft tissue deformation model determines the realism and reliability of the surgical simulation. Currently, two deformation models are widely used in liver deformation simulation: the finite element model and the mass-spring model.

The finite element model [2, 3] discretizes biological tissue into subunits that are interconnected by nodes on the boundary of each unit to form an assembly. The approximation function assumed in each subunit is then used to solve the unknown shape

W. Yongtian and W. Lifang (Eds.): IGTA 2023, CCIS 1910, pp. 254–267, 2023.
https://doi.org/10.1007/978-981-99-7549-5_19

variables in a specific region. The variational principle is used to establish a system of algebraic or differential equations to solve the unknown strain, thus completing the simulation of deformation. Although this model has a high degree of physical realism, it comes at the cost of high computational complexity, which is a major limitation.

The mass-spring model [4, 5] is a deformation model based on elasticity theory. It discretizes the soft tissue model into a series of nodes with masses and connects the masses by springs. When the model is subjected to an external force, the position of the masses will be updated by balancing the external force. This method is simple, easy to implement, and has low computational complexity, making it suitable for situations where the requirement for the accuracy of the simulation model is relatively low.

Both the finite element model and the mass-spring model are built on meshes. However, topology changes in cutting and suturing simulations require the model to remesh frequently, leading to high computational costs and poor haptic performance. To overcome these problems, particle methods, represented by position-based dynamics model, have been gradually applied to deformation simulations. The position-based dynamics model was formally proposed by Müller et al. [7] in 2007 and has since been applied to fabric deformation simulation. Liu et al. [8] used the position dynamics model to perform deformation experiments on rabbits and horses, and the results showed that the position-based dynamics model achieved satisfying modeling performance in computational speed and simulation accuracy. Maciel et al. [9] developed a laparotomy simulation system using the PhysX engine, which contains position-based dynamics model. Due to its unconditional stability, satisfactory frame rate, and simulation accuracy, the position-based dynamics model has been widely used in the deformation simulation of biological soft tissues [10–12].

In the currently used position-based dynamics methods, soft tissues are modeled by generating orbital particles in the center of the voxel after voxelization of the mesh. The number of particles generated by these methods is constrained by the number of input meshes. Therefore, although these methods improve simulation accuracy and speed to some extent, their efficiency and authenticity are still limited by the mesh number and are unable to meet present requirements in clinical applications. To this end, this study proposes a novel simulation method for liver deformation to further improve simulation accuracy and reduce computational cost. Firstly, we extract the 3D model of the liver from medical images and establish the physical deformation model based on ellipsoidal particles at some vertices of the liver mesh model. Then, we establish the collision relationship between the virtual surgical rod and ellipsoidal particles based on the minimum-maximum bounding box. Finally, the position-based dynamics model with constraints of shape-matching is used to simulate the deformation of the liver during the surgical interaction.

2 Methods

Establishing an accurate simulation model of the surgical object is a prerequisite for conducting virtual surgery. Simulation modeling consists of geometric modeling and physical modeling. Geometric modeling is used to simulate the geometric appearance of biological tissues, and physical modeling is used to simulate the kinematic properties of biological tissues, such as the deformation of tissues under the action of external forces. To achieve accurate modeling of the liver, this study implements geometric modeling by segmenting and reconstructing a 3D model of the liver from medical images and physical modeling by the position-based dynamics model with ellipsoidal particles.

2.1 Geometric Modeling of the Liver Based on Computed Tomography Images

In this study, the geometric model of the liver is derived from the open-source medical abdominal computed tomography (CT) dataset 3D-IRACDb, and each of the selected images has 512×512 pixels per slice, a pixel size of 0.57 mm $\times$ 0.57 mm, 129 slices, and a slice thickness of 1.6 mm. The liver region is first segmented semi-automatically using the seeded region growing algorithm [13], and then the segmented region is reconstructed using the Marching Cubes algorithm [14], and finally, a geometric model with 137,762 vertices and 275,356 triangular faces was obtained, as shown in Fig. 1.

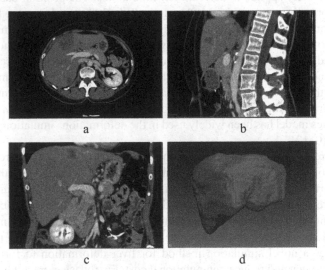

a   b

c   d

Fig. 1. The original abdominal CT image, (a) is a cross-sectional image, (b) is a sagittal image, (c) is a coronal image, and the red area in (a) (b) (c) is the liver area. d is a 3D model of the liver reconstructed by the Marching Cube algorithm [14] (Color figure online).

To investigate the influences of the model mesh number on the deformation simulation, the quadric error metrics (QEM) algorithm [15] was used in this study to geometrically partition the mesh vertices and edges of the model to reduce the complexity of the model, and finally, four geometric models of the liver with different mesh numbers were obtained, as shown in Fig. 2.

2.2 Physical Deformation Modeling Based on Ellipsoidal Particles

To simulate the deformation of soft tissues under the external forces in the surgical simulation, it is necessary to construct physical models of tissues and organs. According to

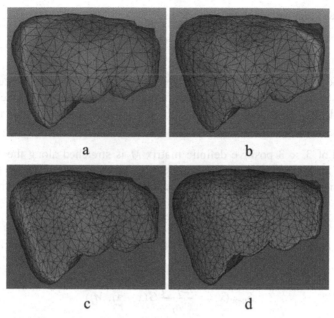

Fig. 2. Liver geometric models with four different mesh numbers.(a) The number of vertices in the liver and the number of triangular faces are 502 and 1000, respectively; (b) The number of vertices in the liver and the number of triangular faces are 752 and 1500, respectively; (c) The number of vertices in the liver and the number of triangular faces are 1302 and 2600, respectively; (d) The number of vertices in the liver and the number of triangular faces are 1802 and 3600, respectively

the biomechanical properties of the target object, a suitable physical model construction method is used to model the fit with more accurate mechanical properties and more realistic deformation and haptic feedback effects of the tissues when the liver is subjected to external forces. In this study, the position- based dynamics method with the ellipsoidal particle is used to physically model the flexible tissue organ of the liver in virtual surgery. First, the ellipsoidal particles are generated at the grid vertices based on the center distance constraint, then the deformation of the liver is simulated by solving the shape matching constraints between the particles, and finally, the collision relationship between the virtual surgery rod and the liver model is established based on the minimum-maximum bounding box.

Ellipsoidal Representation of Surface Particles Based on Center Distance Constraint. In this study, the surface of an object is defined as a scalar field:

$$S(x) = \frac{\sum_j m_j}{\rho_j} G(x - x_j, r_j) \tag{1}$$

where m_j and ρ_j represent the mass and density of particles at the point, respectively. r_j represents the radius of the smooth kernel, and G represents the isotropic smooth kernel function. The G can be calculated as follows:

$$G(R, r) = \frac{\sigma}{r^3} H(\frac{\|R\|}{r})$$ (2)

where σ is the scaling factor, R is the radius vector of the sphere, and H is the symmetric attenuation spline function with finite support. The scalar field $S(x)$ is designed as a normalized density field, and we refer to the equivalence surface of $S(x)$ as a surface consisting of a spherical particle cover.

If a kind of 3×3 positive definite matrix M is stretched along the direction of the radius of the sphere, an ellipsoidal particle is formed and then $G(R,M)$ becomes an anisotropic smooth kernel function, which can be expressed by the following equation

$$G(R, M) = \sigma \det(M) H(\|MR\|)$$ (3)

Through anisotropic smoothing kernel function $G(R,M)$, we can redefine a scalar field:

$$S_{new}(x) = \frac{\sum_j m_j}{\rho_j} G(x - x_j, M_j)$$ (4)

We call the equivalence surface of $S_{new}(x)$ a surface composed of ellipsoidal particle coverings. Different from spherical particles, ellipsoidal particles have a major axis and a minor axis, so it is necessary to determine their major axis direction and major axis radius, that is, to determine the positive definite matrix M. We have applied the weighted version of principal component analysis (WPCA) proposed by Koren and Carmel [16]. Specifically, first, all other particles in the range around a particle $2r_i$ are collected, and these particles form a point cloud. Then, the covariance matrix P of the point cloud relative to this particle and the weighted average $\bar{x}_i$ of all other particles in the range of this particle $2r_i$ are calculated by WPCA. The mathematical expressions are calculated as follows:

$$P = \frac{\sum_i g_{ij}(x_i - \bar{x}_i)g_{ij}(x_i - \bar{x}_i)^T}{\sum_i g_{ij}}$$ (5)

$$\bar{x}_i = \frac{\sum_i g_{ij}x_i}{\sum_i g_{ij}}$$ (6)

In which, gij represents the isotropic smoothing kernel function of particles i and j under the support domain $2ri$.

Then, singular value decomposition (SVD) is performed on the covariance matrix P, and the stretching or shrinking direction of the smooth kernel function is determined according to the feature vector. The formula is as follows:

$$k = R\Sigma R^T$$ (7)

$$\Sigma = diag(\sigma_1, ..., \sigma_n)$$ (8)

where R represents a rotation matrix and $\sum$ represents a diagonal matrix composed of eigenvalues. $\sigma_1, \ldots, \sigma_n$

We take the length L of the oriented bounding box (OBB) contained in a mesh vertex as the radius of the main axis. Finally, the positive definite matrix M can be expressed as:

$$M = \frac{1}{h} L \Sigma^{-1} L^T \tag{9}$$

The traditional position-based dynamics algorithm usually treats the vertices of the mesh as particles or samples the mesh voxel-wise, and then generates particles at the center of the voxel. The limitation is that the algorithm runs inefficiently when the number of mesh vertices and face elements is too large, so in this study, we reduce the computational burden by setting the sampling threshold and generating particles at only some of the mesh vertices. This is done by setting the particle radius r and particle filling rate o in advance, and when the center distance of two particles is not less than $2 \times r \times o$, the particles are generated at the mesh vertices.

Position-Based Dynamics Model with Shape Matching Constraints. The position dynamics model is a heuristic algorithm for simulating the deformation of an object from a Lagrangian perspective. It treats a mesh vertex as a particle with mass and volume, then the whole object becomes a point cloud made of particles. When the whole object is subjected to an external force, the system translates the external force into the amount of velocity and position change of the particle for calculation. A series of constraint functions are added to the system at the beginning of the algorithm, and when the particle position changes during the simulation, the algorithm projects the particle to the appropriate position according to the added constraint functions and updates the velocity value of the particle at the new position.

In this study, the deformation object is the liver, so in the physical modeling, it is necessary to apply a specific constraint function according to the motion characteristics of the liver to improve the simulation performance of liver deformation. Shape matching constraints is a kind of interactive method for deformable objects proposed by Muller et al. [17], which has been demonstrated to have low computational cost, high simulation stability, and authenticity. Therefore, in this study, shape matching constraints are embedded in the framework of position-based dynamics model, and the specific principle is as follows:

The input is assumed to be a group of particles x_i^0 with a mass of m_i, without considering the interaction between particles, only the action of external force and the collision response of each particle with the scene or other objects in the scene are calculated. After each time step, the particle is pulled to the predicted position by an external force. We need to match the original shape x_i^0 with the particle shape at the predicted position x_i, so this method is called shape matching.

The matching problem from the initial particle shape x_i^0 to the predicted particle shape x_i can be described by the following mathematical model: given two sets of point sums m_0 and m_i, find out the rotation matrix R, translation vector t_0 and t, so that the following formula can be minimized:

$$\sum_i w_i(\Delta x_i)^2 = \sum_i w_i(g_i - x_i)^2 \tag{10}$$

Among $g = R(x_i^0 - t_0) + t$, w_i is expressed as the weight of each point to be reasonable physical the best weight is selected as the mass of particles, that is $w = m$. The initial t_0 and t are selected as the centroid of the initial shape and the predicted position shape, that is $t_0 = x_{cm}^0 = \dfrac{\sum_i m_i x_i^0}{\sum_i m_i}$, $t = x_{cm} = \dfrac{\sum_i m_i x_i}{\sum_i m_i}$. Because it is relatively complicated to solve the rotation R and t, the position of the point $q_i = x_i^0 - x_{cm}^0$, $p_i = x_i - x_{cm}$ relative to the center of mass is defined, and the problem of finding the optimal rotation matrix R is simplified to find a linear change L, to minimize $\sum_i m_i(Aq_i - p_i)^2$. By finding the partial derivatives of all the coefficients of L and making the partial derivatives equal to zero, the solution of the equation can be obtained as follows:

$$L = (\sum_i m_i p_i q_i^T)(\sum_i m_i p_i q_i^T)^{-1} = L_{pq}L_{qq} \tag{11}$$

The second term L_{qq} is a symmetric matrix, which only contains scaling but not rotation. Therefore, the matrix containing the rotating part is L_{pq}, and $L_{pq} = RS$ is obtained by polar decomposition, in which symmetric semi-positive definite matrix $S = \sqrt{A_{pq}^T A_{pq}}$ and rotation matrix $R = L_{pq}S^{-1}$. Finally, we can get the target position.

$$g_i = R(x_i^0 - x_{cm}^0) + x_{cm} \tag{12}$$

$$\Delta x_i = g_i - x_i \tag{13}$$

With the target position g_i, the position transformation can be added to the numerical integration to simulate the elastic force of the object, so that it can return to the static state after deformation:

$$v_i(t + h) = v_i(t) + \alpha \frac{\Delta x_i}{h} + \frac{G \times h}{m_i} \tag{14}$$

$$x_i(t + h) = x_i t + v_i(t + h) \times h \tag{15}$$

Among $\alpha \in [0, 1]$ $[0, 1]$, the parameters are used to simulate the stiffness coefficient of the object.

Finally, the liver deformation under external forces is simulated through adding shape-matching constraints to the ellipsoidal particles. The full execution steps of the simulation algorithm, named ellipsoid position-based dynamics, are as shown in Table 1.

In the above algorithm, after applying the corresponding constraints to the target object, it is necessary to select a suitable solver for multiple iterations of the solution, as well as to find a suitable displacement correction amount Δp for the constrained solution target such that the constraints still holds at the position $p + \Delta p$, i.e., it satisfies $C_j(p + \Delta p) = 0$.

Table 1. The execution steps of the ellipsoid position-based dynamics algorithm,

---

Algorithm 1

For all ellipsoidal particles i:

   $x_i = x_i^0$, $v_i = v_i^0$, $w_i = 1/m_i$

End for

Loop

   For all ellipsoidal particles i **do** $v_i \ \leftarrow\ v_i + \Delta t \times G$;

   damp Velocities v_i;

   For all ellipsoidal particles i **do** $p_i \leftarrow xi + \Delta t \times v_i$;

   Loop solver Iterations times

      Project Constraint(C_{ahm}, pi)

   End loop

   For all ellipsoidal particles i **do**:

     $vi \ \leftarrow\ (pi - xi)/\Delta t$

     $xi \ \leftarrow\ pi$

   End for

   Velocities Update($v1, \ldots, vi$)

End loop

The common iterative solution algorithms are the Jacobi iterative algorithm and the Gauss-Seidel iterative algorithm. The Gauss-Seidel iterative method is based on the principle of matrix decomposition and has wide adaptability and fast convergence. The Jacobi iterative method converges relatively slowly but has the advantage of being computationally simple and can be computed in parallel.

Considering that the number of particles involved in deformation calculation is a major factor limiting the efficiency of deformation calculation, therefore, reducing the number of masses is one of the most effective ways to reduce the computational cost of the system. As a result, it is not necessary to calculate the deformation of all the particles in the virtual model, but to set the range of the deformation region according to the parameters, thus in this study, we use the radius of the deformation region to control the number of particles involved in the calculation, so that when the deformation calculation is performed, only the motion state of the particles within the radius of the region is updated, thus reducing the computational burden of the simulation process.

Collision Detection Based on the Min-Max Bounding Box. In virtual surgery, collision detection between object models is very time-consuming. In this study, a method based on a minimum-maximum bounding box is adopted to realize the collision detection between a virtual surgical wand and liver soft tissue, to improve the detection efficiency. The minimum-maximum bounding box is a kind of axially aligned bounding box, which is usually described by six scalars along the coordinate axis. Its geometric description can be expressed by the following formula:

$$S = \{(x, y, z) | ux \le x \le vx, uy \le y \le vy, uz \le z \le vz\} \tag{16}$$

where the vertex coordinates of the model are expressed (x, y, z), ux, uy, uz indicating the minimum value of the vertex on each coordinate axis and vx, vy, vz indicating the maximum value of the vertex on each coordinate axis.

In the virtual surgery simulation, the area interacting with the soft tissue model is usually only the tip of the surgical wand. Therefore, in this study, the collision detection between a virtual surgical wand and soft tissue can be completed only by setting the minimum-maximum bounding box at the tip of the surgical wand.

3 Experimental and Results

In this study, a virtual surgery simulation platform was developed using unity, the open haptics resource package, and the force feedback device Geomagic.The user can use the joystick of the force feedback device to control the movement of the virtual surgical wand on the screen and complete the interactive operation of the virtual liver.

To compare the accuracy of the ellipsoidal and the voxel-filled particle model, three kinds of experiments are carried out. Firstly, the effects of different solver types and the number of iterations on the performance of ellipsoidal particle model-based deformation simulation are investigated; Secondly, the press-back effects of the ellipsoidal particle model and the voxel-filled particle model is qualitatively compared, the corresponding particle total displacements of the two models are quantitatively compared; Finally, the effects of different deformation region radii on the computational efficiency of the ellipsoidal particle model are investigated, and the displayed frame rates of the ellipsoidal particle model are obtained to evaluate the superiority of the ellipsoidal particle-based physical modeling in terms of computational efficiency.

The CPU used in this experiment is Intel(R) Core(TM) i7-8750H CPU 2.2 GHz, the graphics card is NVIDIA GeForce GTX 1050 Ti, and the memory is 16G. The experimental object is the liver model obtained from the real CT images, as mentioned in section II.A, based on which the ellipsoidal particle model and the voxel-filled model of the liver are constructed.

Figure 3 compares the effect of different solver types on the deformation performance of the ellipsoidal particle model. From the figure, it can be observed that the model using the Jacobi iterator produces larger displacements for both the overall and local particles, as shown in Fig. 3(b) green circle while the model using the Gauss-Seidel iterator produces displacements for only the local particles, as shown in Fig. 3(c) green circle. The reason is that the Gauss-Seidel iterator is a serial solver, where all constraints are solved in the order they are created, which has the advantage of reaching convergence faster, but the disadvantage is that the deformation effect is not realistic; whereas the Jacobi iterator is a parallel solver, where all constraints are solved simultaneously and the velocity and position of the particles are adjusted according to the final calculation results, which makes the convergence slower. Therefore, considering the realism of liver deformation simulation, the Jacobi solver is chosen for the ellipsoidal particle model construction in this study.

Table 2 compares the effect of different iteration times on the averaged frame per second (FPS) for a triangular surface number of 1500, a particle radius of 0.1, and a fill rate of 0.5, with the Jacobi iterator. As is observed, the higher the iteration time, the lower

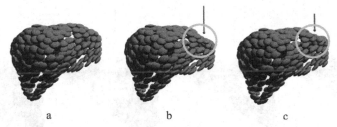

Fig. 3. The simulation performances of pressing the virtual surgical wand (blue part) on the model using different solvers types. (a) is the original model, (b) is the pressed model simulated using the Jacobi iterator, and (c) is the pressed model simulated using the Gauss-Seidel iterator.

Table 2. Effect of different iterations times on the averaged frame rate using the Jacobi iterator

Number of iterations	3	5	10	15
Averaged FPS	184.8	160.1	100.6	40.9

the averaged frame rate, because the more iterations are computed, the more computer memory is used and the more time consuming the modeling process is. However, the influences of the iteration times on the deformation quality are not obvious, therefore, to balance the tradeoff between the deformation quality and the computational cost, we choose the iteration time as 3 in this study.

Figure 4 shows the rebound effect of the model when the virtual surgical wand (blue part) is used to press the liver model (red part) interactively and at the end of the press. From the corresponding deformation results, it can be seen that the ellipsoidal particle model produces surface depression when local force is applied (Fig. 4a), and the surface of the model can rebound after the force is applied (Fig. 4b), which is similar with the voxel-filled particle model (Fig. 4c and d).

Table 3 shows the corresponding particle displacements of these two models under the external forces, and the total force and displacements are synthesized along the x, y, and z directions. As can be seen from Table 3, when the two models are subjected to similar external force, the total displacements of the particles are basically similar, with an error of 0.15 mm. The above results indicate that the simulation accuracy of ellipsoidal particle model is comparable to that of voxel-filled model in simulating the deformation of soft tissues.

Figure 5 shows the influence of different particle fill rates on the physical and geometric models for the triangular surface number of 1500 and the particle radius of 0.1. It can be seen from the figure that there are no obvious differences in the geometric appearance (Fig. 5a and d) and the depression and rebound performances (b and e) between these two models. However, the ellipsoidal particle model has a particle number of 131 and an averaged frame rate of 88.7 FPS for 1 min of the deformation simulation, while the voxel-filled model has a particle number of 378 and an averaged frame rate of 69.2 FPS for 1 min of the deformation simulation, indicating that when achieving similar physical and geometric modeling performance, the ellipsoidal particle model uses less number of

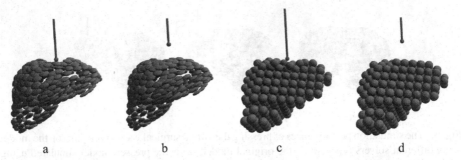

a   b   c   d

Fig. 4. The deformation and rebound of the surface model and voxel model. For both models, the number of triangular surfaces is 1500, the particle radius is 0.1, and the number of particles is 380. (a) shows the depression of the surface model being pressed by the virtual surgical wand (blue part), (b) shows the rebound of the surface model, (c) shows the depression of the voxel model being pressed by the virtual surgical wand (blue part), and (d) shows the rebound of the voxel model (color figure online).

Table3. Comparison of force and displacement values between the ellipsoidal particle model and the voxel-filled model

Model name	x displacement (mm)	y displacement (mm)	z displacement (mm)	x force (N)	y force (N)	z force (N)	Total force (N)	Total displacement(mm)
ellipsoidal	2.82	0.61	−1.4	0.76	0.22	−0.29	0.84	3.21
voxel-filled	2.78	0.59	−1.14	0.73	0.24	−0.34	0.84	3.06

particles for deformation simulation, and thus has higher computational efficiency and higher frame rate for display.

Figure 6 shows the influences of the radius of the deformation region on the averaged frame rate of the deformation simulation for a triangular surface number of 1500, a particle filling rate of 0.5, and a particle radius of 0.1 mm. From the data in the figure, it can be seen that the effect of the radius of the deformation region on the averaged frame rate is almost linear, when the radius of the deformation region is 0.2, i.e., only twice the particle radius, the 1-min averaged frame rate reaches the maximum value, i.e., 104.9 FPS, and when the radius of the deformation region is 1.0, the 1-min averaged frame rate reaches the minimum value, i.e., 27.6 FPS, and as the deformation area radius increases, the averaged frame rate gradually decreases. This is because the radius of the deformation region determines the number of particles involved in the shape matching constraints, and the larger the radius of the deformation region, the more particles are included in the calculation, thus leading to a decrease in the averaged frame rate.

This study also tests the real-time frame rate variation of the ellipsoid-based particle model when it is involved in the deformation calculation over a 1-min time period. The number of vertices of the model is 752, the number of triangular surfaces is 1500, the particle radius is 0.1, the number of particles is 450, and the radius of the deformation region is 0.5. The mean value of the simulation frame rate is 190.5 FPS with a variance of

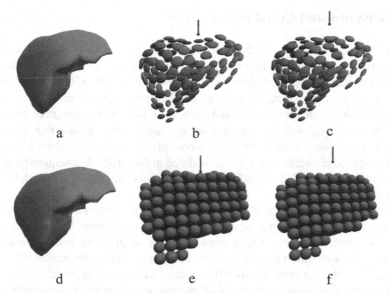

Fig. 5. Comparison of the ellipsoidal particle model and voxel-filled model with a triangular surface number of 1500 and a particle radius of 0.1. (a) is the ellipsoidal particle model after skinning, (b) shows the depression of the ellipsoidal particle model after press with a particle number of 131, (c) shows the rebound of the ellipsoidal particle model with a particle number of 131, (d) is the voxel-filled model after skinning, (e) shows the depression of the voxel-filled model with a particle number of 378, and (f) shows the rebound of the voxel-filled model with a particle number of 378.

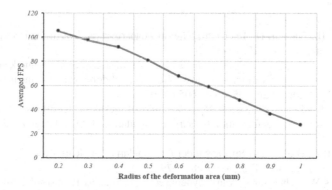

Fig. 6. The averaged FPS in 1 min as a function of the radius of the deformation area.

30, which proves that the method proposed in this study has a great potential in realizing real-time liver virtual simulation.

4 Discussions and Conclusions

Shape-matching-based position dynamics models have been demonstrated to be real-time, accurate, and unconditionally stable, and thus can model organ deformation without complete knowledge of patient-specific tissue properties. A limitation of the proposed method is that it requires parameter tuning for the input mesh, including adjustment of shape region radius, iteration times, and particle fill rate, which also need to take into account the specificity of different patient organs. Another limitation is that although the force feedback device is used for the motion control of the virtual rod, the force feedback effect during model interaction is not considered in this study. Consequently, in future work, we will further design self-adapted force feedback algorithms for the deformation of ellipsoidal particle models.

In this study, we propose an ellipsoidal particle-based position dynamics liver deformation modeling method using medical images as the data input source, and validate the proposed method by building a virtual simulation platform with force feedback equipment. The simulation results show that in terms of the deformation effect, using Jacobi iterator achieves better realism than using Gauss-Seidel iterator. In terms of the authenticity, the simulation accuracy of ellipsoidal particle model is comparable to that of voxel-filled model, with a particle displacement error of 0.15 mm. In terms of the computational efficiency, the simulation speed of the ellipsoidal particle model is 28.2% higher than that of the voxel filling model, which indicate the the proposed ellipsoidal particle-based position dynamics liver deformation model may be a promising tool for real time and high-accuracy deformation simulation of the liver and other soft tissues.

References

1. Descottes, B., Glineur, D., Lachachi, F., et al.: Laparoscopic liver resection of benign liver tumors. J. Surg. Endosc. **17**, 23–30 (2003)
2. Horvat, N., et al.: A finite element implementation of a growth and remodeling model for soft biological tissues: Verification and application to abdominal aortic aneurysms. Comput. Methods Appl. Mech. Eng. **352**, 586–605 (2019)
3. Joldes, G., Bourantas, G., Zwick, B., et al.: Suite of meshless algorithms for accurate computation of soft tissue deformation for surgical simulation. J. Med. Image Anal. **56**, 152–171 (2019)
4. Hammer, P.E., et al.: Mass-Spring Model for Simulation of Heart Valve Tissue Mechanical Behavior. Ann. Biomed. Eng. **39**, 1668–1679 (2011)
5. Mollemans, W., Schutyser, F., Van Cleynenbreugel, J., Suetens, P.: Fast soft tissue deformation with tetrahedral mass spring model for maxillofacial surgery planning systems. In: Barillot, C., Haynor, D.R., Hellier, P. (eds.) MICCAI 2004. LNCS, vol. 3217, pp. 371–379. Springer, Heidelberg (2004). https://doi.org/10.1007/978-3-540-30136-3_46
6. Liu, X., et al.: Deformation of soft tissue and force feedback using the smoothed particle hydrodynamics. J. Comput. Math. Methods Med (2015)
7. Müller, M., Heidelberger, B., Hennix, M., et al.: Position based dynamics. J. Vis. Commun. Image Represent. **18**, 109–118 (2007)
8. Liu, Y., Guan, C., Li, J., et al.: The PBD model based simulation for soft tissue deformation in virtual surgery. J. Phys. Conf. Ser. **1621**, 012043 (2020)

9. Maciel, A., Halic, T., Lu, Z., et al.: Using the PhysX engine for physics-based virtual surgery with force feedback. Int. J. Med. Robot. **5**, 341–353 (2019)
10. Tian, H., et al.: iMSTK-based microwave ablation training system for liver tumors. In: 2022 2nd International Conference on Bioinformatics and Intelligent Computing, in BIC 2022. New York, NY, USA: Association for Computing Machinery, pp. 145–150 (2022)
11. Pan, J., Bai, J., Zhao, X., et al.: Real-time haptic manipulation and cutting of hybrid soft tissue models by extended position-based dynamics. J. Comput. Animat. Virtual Worlds. **26**, 321–335 (2015)
12. Camara, M., Mayer, E., Darzi, A., et al.: Soft tissue deformation for surgical simulation: a position-based dynamics approach. Int. J. Comput. Assist. Radiol. Surg. **11**, 919–928 (2016)
13. Adams, R., Bischof, L.: Seeded region growing. IEEE Trans. Pattern Anal. Mach. Intell. **16**(6), 641–647 (1994)
14. Lorensen, W.E., Cline, H.E.: Marching cubes: a high resolution 3D surface construction algorithm. J. ACM SIGGRAPH Comput. Graph. **21**, 163–169 (1987)
15. Garland, M., Heckbert, P.S.: Surface simplification using quadric error metrics. In: Proceedings of the 24th Annual Conference on Computer Graphics and Interactive Techniques - SIGGRAPH, pp. 209–216 (1997)
16. .Koren, Y., Carmel, L.: Visualization of labeled data using linear transformations. In IEEE Symposium on Information Visualization 2003 (IEEE Cat. No.03TH8714), pp. 121–128 (2003)
17. Müller, M., et al.: Meshless deformations based on shape matching. J. ACM Trans. Graph. **24**, 471–478 (2005)

A Perceptually Uniform Gloss Space for Translucent Materials

Shuo Huang, Hongsong Li$^{(\boxtimes)}$, and Mingyuan Zhang

School of Computer Science, Beijing Institute of Technology, Beijing 100081, China
lihongsong@bit.edu.cn

Abstract. This study proposed a perceptual appearance model for translucent materials, addressing the issue of biased gloss perception by subsurface scattering. We established an empirical model relating the RMS slope first, which is a parameter of the BRDF model, to the measured perceived glossiness with a psychophysical experiment, and created a uniform perceived gloss space for opaque materials. For extending the space to cover the translucent materials, BSSRDF was incorporated to generate rendered objects with a lot of gloss and translucency. A second psychophysical experiment correlated perceived glossiness with both BRDF and BSSRDF, and built an empirical model that predicts the perceived glossiness of translucent materials with diverse surface and volumetric scattering properties. The developed model empowers designers to adjust translucency levels of translucent materials while maintaining perceived glossiness, which is proved by rendered images with various lighting conditions and object shapes. The proposed model provides a valuable tool for industrial design applications.

Keywords: Appearance Modeling · Perceptual BRDF Model · Perceived Glossiness · Perceptual Measurements

1 Introduction

Modeling the human visual system (HVS)'s perception of material appearance is a complex multiplex problem. The CIE175:2006 standard roughly categorizes appearance attributes into four categories: color, gloss, translucency, and texture [1]. It also points out the interference among these four categories of appearance attributes, i.e., the change in one type of appearance attribute will affect the perception of another type. An example of such interference is that the color perception of high-gloss surfaces is usually biased at the highlight areas [2].

In the field of computer graphics, significant progress has been made in the physical modeling of material appearance. Material appearance is presented as the Bidirectional Reflectance Distribution Function (BRDF) [3] for opaque surfaces, and the Bidirectional Subsurface Scattering Reflectance Distribution Function (BSSRDF) [4] for translucent materials. These physical quantities are widely used to describe the appearance of the vast majority of everyday materials. The proposed physical models, implemented with global illumination algorithms such as path tracing, generate highly realistic material appearances and allow fine-tuning of the appearance through model parameters.

The perceptual modeling of material appearance has received more attention in computer graphics and applied perception research in recent years. The main driving force of this research field is to solve the problems encountered by the community of appearance design when applying these physical models [5]. When designers use interactive appearance design tools, they need these tools to provide more intuitive parameters of material appearance, rather than physical parameters. For example, glossiness is more intuitive than surface roughness; metallicity is easier for designers to understand than the index of refraction. In addition, a perceptually uniform space of appearance attribute, where an appearance attribute can be adjusted linearly, is more handy than a nonlinear space. A uniform perceptual space of glossiness or metallicity is analog to CIELAB color space [6], which is used as a perceptually uniform space of color and mimics the nonlinear color response of the human visual system.

In this work, we aim to introduce a perceptually uniform space of glossiness for translucent materials. Although such perceptual space exists for opaque materials, the subsurface scattering of the translucent material bias the glossiness perception with misleading visual cues, and no solution is available to address this issue. We show that it is possible to generate images of a constant perceived glossiness on translucent material surfaces with various surface properties and translucency. The proposed appearance model compensates for the influence of subsurface scattering on the glossiness perception of translucent materials by adjusting the surface RMS slope, which enables the designers of material appearance to obtain constantly perceived glossiness when varying the translucency of target materials.

2   Related Works

Traditionally, the surface gloss was considered as a physical metric and could be measured directly with an instrument such as a gloss meter [7]. However, studies on real samples showed a very poor agreement between the perception of gloss by the HVS and the gloss meter results [8, 9]. In 2006, the CIE proposed a framework [1] for the perceptual measurement of material appearance, formally referring to the metrics related to the perception of the appearance of color, gloss, translucency, and texture as soft metrics.

2.1   Perception and Modeling of Glossiness

Fleming [10] argued that it is difficult for the HVS to perceive glossy surfaces using the inverse optics approach so a pixel-by-pixel approach, such as image statistics, should be considered for perceived glossiness modeling. Motoyoshi et al. [11] concluded that image skewness is highly correlated with glossiness judgments made by the visual system. However, further validation by Anderson and Kim [12], Olkkonen and Brainard [13] showed that a strong correlation among skewness, luminance, and glossiness occurs only in some special cases and is not universal. Subsequent studies have attempted to demonstrate the relationship between weighted combinations of image statistical components and gloss perception. Hunter's [14] definition of six types of gloss (specular gloss, sheen, contrast gloss, absence-of-bloom gloss, distinctness-of-reflected-image/ DOI gloss, and absence-of-surface-texture gloss) has been widely used in a large number of studies.

Marlow and Anderson [15] argued that specular reflectance coverage, DOI gloss, and contrast gloss weighting influence gloss perception judgments. Later, Qi et al. [16] and others also suggested that certain image statistics of specular reflectance correlate with gloss perception, but such methods are still not widely used. With the development of deep learning, some scholars investigated gloss perception using psychophysical methods [17, 18], suggesting that the process of perceiving material appearance by the visual system is very similar to the process of encoding image input by deep neural networks, which may be the operating mechanism of HSV.

Physically based BRDF models control the glossiness of material surfaces in rendered images with physical parameters, but existing physically based metrics fail to predict human judgments of similarity in material appearance [17]. Pellacini et al. [19, 20] related gloss-related physical parameters with perception for the first time through the multidimensional scaling (MDS) method, which embedded BRDF in a low-dimensional perceptual space based on perceived glossiness measurement, and proposed a BRDF model based on the perceptual parameter space. As a follow-up study, Wills et al. [21] extended the range of materials to measure BRDFs using non-metric MDS, showed that there is a correlation between embedding coordinates and gloss measures such as diffuse and contrast gloss, and proposed an interpolation algorithm for perceptual BRDFs based on centroid coordinates that can ensure local perceptual linearity. Toscani et al. [22] conducted another study based on the semantic evaluation of material appearance. They concluded that the perception of achromatic reflections is based on at least three dimensions, i.e., luminance, specular reflectance component, and metallicity. Similarly, Weiqi et al. [23] conducted experiments on the perception of the overall appearance of measured metallic materials, referring to [24], and defined a 4D continuous parametric perceptual space using the NMDS method and Gaussian process regression models. Our work can be considered an extension of these approaches and aim to provide a perceptual BRDF model for translucent materials.

2.2 Perception and Modeling of Translucency

Predicting perceived transparency from images is more challenging. Fleming et al. [25] and Chadwick et al. [26] showed that because the physics of subsurface scattering is very complex, the inverse optics approach is also difficult to explain the perception of translucency. Similar conclusions are drawn in the study of Motoyoshi et al. [27], who proposed that the contrast and sharpness of specular highlights and non-specular parts of a surface provide powerful information for judging perceived transparency and translucency. In a recent study, Kiyokawa et al. [28] extracted specular regions from samples [20] and calculated the correlation coefficients between anisotropy ratio, sharpness, coverage, RMS, and perceived transparency separately, suggesting that the visual system may use a limited set of low-level image statistical features to infer translucency. Liao et al. [29] used an unsupervised image generation model to predict the perceived translucency of real objects; the hierarchical potential representation of the model can be used to synthesize images of realistic translucent materials.

2.3   Correlating Perceived Glossiness and Perceived Translucency

Gigilashvili et al. first included translucency as a factor of perceived glossiness [30], arguing that translucent objects with complex shapes are glossier than those which are opaque. Subsequently, Gigilashvili et al. conducted a qualitative and quantitative study of the effect of subsurface scattering on perceived glossiness [31]. They concluded that subsurface transmittance has an impact on perceived glossiness. On the other hand, it has been shown that surface roughness and glossiness bias the perception of translucency [25, 32]. Kiyokawa et al. [28], by analyzing the statistical features of images at each scale level, suggested that the perceived translucency can be derived indirectly from the inference of the specular highlights of the surface to the 3D shape.

In summary, although qualitative studies [28, 30, 31] have demonstrated a correlation between gloss and translucency, the phenomenon of subsurface scattering was not taken into account in currently available models of perceived glossiness. The quantitative relationship between these two important attributes of material appearance perception remains unknown.

In this work, we took two steps to build the perceptual space as shown in Fig. 1. The first step was to create a one-dimensional, perceptually uniform space of glossiness of opaque materials by Experiment 1. Then this space was extended to incorporate subsurface scattering of translucent materials and converted into a two-dimensional perceptual space of glossiness by Experiment 2.

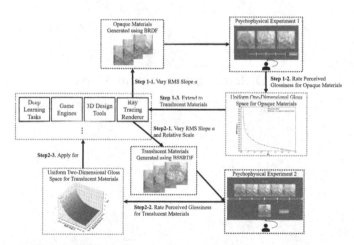

Fig. 1. Flowchart of establishing a uniform gloss space for translucent materials

While the perceived glossiness of translucent materials involves both surface and volumetric scattering of the incident light, and many factors are involved in this complex phenomenon, we make the following assumptions:

1. The perceived glossiness can be considered a one-dimensional, measurable perceptual quantity [17, 18].
2. The perceived glossiness of translucent material can be considered a function of BRDF and BSSRDF.

3. The perceived translucency is considered a one-dimensional and measurable perceptual quantity [29, 31].

3   Perceptually Uniform Space of Glossiness of Opaque Materials

3.1   Stimulus

Experiment 1 was designed to relate BRDF to the perceived glossiness on opaque surfaces. Specifically, the perceived glossiness of sample images with various RMS slopes,
which is a measure of surface roughness, was measured through psychophysical experiments to establish an empirical model correlating the RMS slope with perceived glossiness. Then one-dimensional, perceptually uniform space of glossiness of opaque materials can be established. So, Experiment 1 requires lots of images of opaque objects with
a broad range of perceived glossiness, which were generated by the Mitsuba 3 rendering
system [33].

(a) Different Environment Maps

(b) Different Geometries

Fig. 2. Example images rendered by using different environment maps and geometries

It is well known that the illumination conditions [34], the viewing conditions [35],
and the object shape [13, 18] have their influence on the perceived glossiness. Figure 2
shows examples of such influence.

To obtain consistent measurements of perceived glossiness, we generated several
images with one chosen illumination condition in the form of an environment map,

and with several viewing angles. The environment map is a white-balanced 8192 pixel × 4096 pixel image of a church scene, which was chosen from an environment map database created by Unity Technologies [36]. The environment map has more high-frequency components which can make the specular highlights of the material more pronounced [13]. In addition, the environment map consists of multiple light sources (windows of the church) so that the target object is illuminated from multiple directions, which helps to reveal both the surface and volumetric characteristics of light scattering.

We used Blender [37] to generate a geometry by modulating a sphere with Gaussian random bump mapping [13]. It has been proved that the sharpness of edges (or local curvature) of the geometry influences both perceived glossiness [2] and translucency [38]. Our geometry of the target object was created to augment the perception of glossiness as well as translucency.

We chose the GGX BRDF model for glossiness control and varied the RMS slope α to generate 20 images for the experiment [16, 18–20, 39, 40]. Due to the nonlinear nature of the correlation between the RMS slope α and perceived glossiness, we first generated a series of the RMS slope α varying from 1.0 to 0.01, by the following equation:

$$\alpha = 10^{-0.1*x}, x \in [0, 20] \tag{1}$$

Although these values of RMS slope α will not guarantee the perceived glossiness of the rendering objects increases linearly, it optimizes the distribution of the perceived glossiness of the images. We used Eq. (1) and three randomized viewing directions to generate 60 sample images (Fig. 3).

Fig. 3. Four sample images used in Experiment 1

The other parameters of the GGX model include the diffuse reflectance k_d and the specular reflectance k_s. Indeed, these parameters could also be chosen to vary BRDF or the perceived glossiness of rendered objects [17]. Without losing generality, we simplified the problem by varying only one model parameter, the influence of the other parameters can be incorporated into the proposed model later in the same approach.

3.2 Experiment 1

All the participants were recruited from the campus of the Beijing Institute of Technology, with normal or corrected vision and normal color vision. A total of 19 participants participated in Experiment 1. To ensure consistency between the two experiments, 17 participants from Experiment 1 also participated in Experiment 2, while 7 additional participants were recruited for Experiment 2 to improve the generalizability of the model. The male-to-female ratio in Experiment 1 was 16:3, and the average age was 22; the male-to-female ratio in Experiment 2 was 14:10, and the average age was 23.

A kind of software was built by PsychoPy [41] to guide the participant through the entire experiment. All the participants took the experiment on a calibrated ENZO EV2460 monitor with a resolution of 1920*1080.

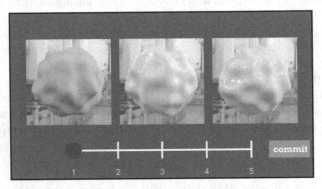

Fig. 4. User interface of experiment 1

We did not explain the definition of glossiness before the experiment to avoid biasing the participants, although HVS interprets glossiness on a surface in various approaches [14]. In this work, the participants were only given a short introduction to the user interface, then the test started. Following the previous works [16–19], the participants were asked to provide their estimation of the perceived glossiness of the central sample images on a 5-point Likert scale (see Fig. 4), by moving the slider at the bottom with discrete values. The experiment had no time limit, and the results could not be changed after the choice was made. The left and right images act as baselines, representing the sample images with the lowest and highest perceived glossiness, respectively.

By setting 1 as the lowest perceived glossiness and 5 as the highest perceived glossiness, we here define a perceptual space of glossiness for this work. Since there is no universal perceptual gloss space available, this proposed space is served as a baseline perceptual space for both opaque and translucent materials.

3.3 Perceptually Uniform Space of Glossiness

The measured perceived glossiness and its corresponding RMS slopes are plotted as black dots in Fig. 5. As the RMS slope increases, the perceived glossiness tends to decrease exponentially (see Fig. 5). We fitted an empirical model of perceived glossiness to measurement data. A nonlinear function of the following form is chosen:

$$G_o = k_1 * c_1^\alpha + c_2, \alpha \in [0, 1] \tag{2}$$

where G_O is the perceived glossiness of opaque materials defined by this work; k_1, c_1, and c_2 are constants determined by fitting the empirical model to the measurement data.

The nonlinear optimization tool of SciPy was used for the data fitting, and the coefficient of determination R^2 was 0.994 for the fitting results. The fitted curve is shown in Fig. 5 as the red line. The corresponding fitting results are $k_1 = 3.691$, $c_1 = 0.001173$, $c_2 = 1.14$.

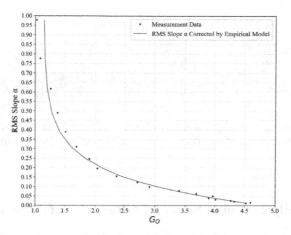

Fig. 5. The measurement data and empirical model of the perceived glossiness

Inversing Eq. (2), we obtain a uniform perceptual gloss space of opaque materials by determining the RMS slopes corresponding to the linearly sampled G_O in the range of $[G_1, G_5]$. The corresponding RMS slope is found by:

$$\alpha = \log_{c1}\left(\frac{G_o - c_2}{k_1}\right), G_o \in [G_1, G_5] \tag{3}$$

The values of five chosen perceived glossiness from G_1 to G_5 and its corresponding RMS slopes are shown in Table 1:

Table 1. The predicted perceived glossiness and its corresponding RMS slope for equal perceptual spacing.

Predicted Perceived Glossiness G_O	RMS slope
1.0 (G_1)	1.000000
2.0 (G_2)	0.204901
3.0 (G_3)	0.102537
4.0 (G_4)	0.042571
5.0 (G_5)	0.000000

The rendered sample images obtained using the above RMS slope values are shown in Fig. 6. The perceived glossiness of the leftmost and rightmost sample images is G_1 and

G_5, representing the roughest and glossiest materials, respectively. From left to right, the perceived glossiness increases linearly and the intervals between sample images are the same in this perceptual space. Then we use this uniform perceptual gloss space as the baseline space for evaluating the influence of subsurface scattering.

Fig. 6. Five material sample images of different RMS slope values with equal perceived glossiness spacing obtained using the modified BRDF were used as baselines for Experiment 2.

4 Perceptually Uniform Space of Glossiness of Translucent Materials

Starting from the uniform perceptual gloss space obtained in the last section, we incorporate the subsurface scattering to evaluate its impact on the perceived glossiness, and obtain a perceptual space of glossiness jointly influenced by BRDF and BSSRDF of translucent materials.

4.1 Stimulus

Experiment 2 used the same illumination, object geometry, and BRDF model for sample image generation. To extend the perceptual space into translucent materials, we also need to simulate a wide range of translucency. Mitsuba 3 Rendering System implemented Jensen's BSSRDF model. We applied a volumetric path tracer as the integrator and participating media to the rendered object, to simulate the volumetric scattering of the translucent materials [4].

Three physical parameters are needed to characterize a homogeneous, translucent volume: the single scattering albedo of media ρ_a, the extinction coefficient σ_t, and the relative scale of medium x_s. x_s is an optional scale factor to correct the extinction parameter σ_t. For the same translucent material, various thickness of the volume leads to various perceived translucency. Therefore, a parameter such as the relative scale of medium x_s is needed to adjust the relative scale of volume thickness and scale of subsurface scattering. Hence, we choose x_s for controlling the translucency of the rendered objects. The relative scale of medium x_s is normalized by the dimension of the rendered object into a range of [0, 1].

As for the relative scale value, we first generated a sufficient number of equally spaced sample images and then filtered them according to the criterion of maximum perceptual difference, obtaining 24 sample images to be measured in Experiment 2.

4.2 Experiment 2

The procedure of Experiment 2 is the same as Experiment 1. Figure 7 shows the experimental interface. We assume that the perceived glossiness of translucent objects is still a one-dimensional soft metric. Thus, analog to Experiment 1, we conducted a rating experiment to measure the perceived glossiness of the sample images and relate various values of relative scale x_s to the measured perceived glossiness. The five sample images (opaque objects) in Fig. 7 were used as baseline images. It is known that the higher the translucency, the greater the gain in perceived glossiness for the same material surface [31]. Therefore, the original range of perceived glossiness may not fully cover the measurement data. To address this issue, we widened the range of perceived glossiness from [1, 5] to [0, 6]. The participants were allowed to provide an estimated glossiness of less than 1 (but no less than 0) or greater than 5 (but no greater than 6). 24 sample images were presented to the participants in random order and each sample was repeated 3 times. Note that the values of the sliders are continuous so the participants were asked to make more precise estimations.

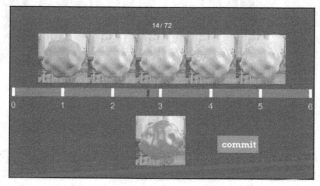

Fig. 7. User interface of Experiment 2. Participants must refer to the five baselines above, with increasing perceived glossiness from left to right, to estimate the perceived glossiness of the sample to be tested.

4.3 Perceived Glossiness vs BRDF and BSSRDF

The results of the rating experiment of Experiment 2 are shown in Fig. 8(a), as the mean and standard deviations of the measured perceived glossiness of the 24 sample images. The x-axis of Fig. 8(a) is the index of sample images. The standard deviation for each sample image is below 1, showing a good agreement in the measurement data among the participants.

The 5 RMS slopes divide the sample images into 5 groups, and the mean perceived glossiness of each group tends to decrease as the RMS slope increases, which is consistent with the results of previous studies [39, 40]. Within each group, the perceived glossiness decreases with increasing relative scale in the first four RMS slope groups, showing how subsurface scattering biases the glossiness perception of HVS. For the group with

RMS slope $\alpha = 1$, there is no significant correlation between the measured perceived glossiness and the relative scale. This is because at RMS slope $\alpha = 1$, the surface is too rough and diffuse to see through, and the distribution of subsurface scattering is blurred completely. HSV is also unable to identify regional characteristics related to gloss in these sample images, such as contrast gloss as well as DOI gloss. Apparently, there is an upper limit of RMS slope (or roughness level) that the subsurface scattering could bias glossiness perception.

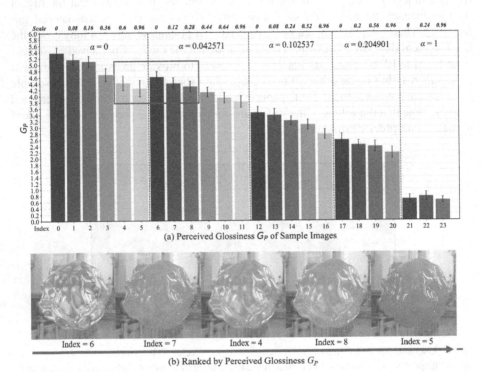

(a) Perceived Glossiness G_P of Sample Images

(b) Ranked by Perceived Glossiness G_P

Fig. 8. (a) Mean perceived glossiness ratings for sample images generated with different RMS slope levels and different values of relative scale, with error bars corresponding to 95% confidence intervals. The RMS slope values of material are different for different groups, increasing from left to right; the relative scale within the group increases from left to right, representing an increasingly opaque material. (b) Taken from the red box of Fig. (a), a typical region: the perceived glossiness of these five materials decreases from left to right, with Sample 6 having a greater RMS slope than Sample 4 and Sample 5.

Figure 8(b) shows the five sample images sorted in descending order of perceived glossiness in the red-boxed area of the bar chart. Although Samples 4 and 5 have a lower RMS slope than Sample 6, the measured perceived glossiness of Sample 4 is lower than that of Sample 6, which has a smaller relative scale or is more transparent. While more light is transmitted through Sample 6, some visual cues such as contrast are enhanced by the transmitted environmental lighting, implying that the degree of transparency provides some gain in perceived glossiness.

It is worth noting that in an image pair comparison experiment of the above sample images, which was carried out after Experiment 2 as supplementary measurements, almost all of the participants spent more time comparing the sample image pairs such as Sample 4 (with lower RMS slope and higher relative scale) and Sample 7 (with higher RMS slope and lower relative scale). Such image pairs have very close perceived glossiness, while there is a significant difference in their corresponding relative scales (*0.12* and *0.6*, respectively), suggesting that subsurface scattering compensates for the less powerful specular reflection components, and vice versa. Sample 4 also has the highest standard deviation of measurement data, implying that HVS has trouble implementing the inverse optics approach and interpreting these image cues.

To correct the perceived glossiness of materials with various relative scale x_s using RMS slope, we constructed a linear perceptual space with RMS slope and relative scale as the independent variables and perceived glossiness as the dependent variable using a nonlinear fitting method. We proposed an empirical correlation among the perceived glossiness, the RMS slope, and the relative scale:

$$G_p = c_3^\alpha * \left(k_2 * (1 - x_s)^{c_4} + c_5\right) + c_6, \quad \begin{cases} \alpha \in [0, 1] \\ x_s \in [0, 1] \end{cases} \tag{4}$$

where G_P is the perceived glossiness of translucent materials; k_2, c_3, c_4, c_5, and c_6 are constants determined by fitting the empirical model to the measurement data. The proposed model is fitted to the measurement data using the nonlinear optimization tool of SciPy, and the coefficient of determination R^2 was 0.994 for the fitting results. The fitting results are $k_2 = 1.041$, $c_3 = 0.011$, $c_4 = 1.595$, $c_5 = 3.619$, and $c_6 = 0.659$.

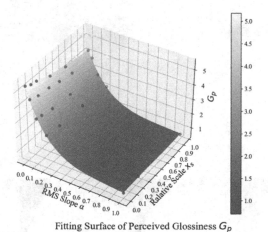

Fitting Surface of Perceived Glossiness G_p

Fig. 9. Perceptual glossiness space fitted by Eq. (4)

The fitted two-dimensional function is shown in Fig. 9, where the red dots are the mean perceived glossiness measured by Experiment 2 and the green curved surface is generated with the fitted model.

Thus, an inverse function of Eq. (4) by introducing x_s to correct the biased perceived glossiness by subsurface scattering, is in Eq. (5):

$$\alpha = \log_{c3}\left(\frac{G_p - c_6}{k_2 * (1 - x_s)^{c4} + c_5}\right), \begin{cases} G_p \in [0, 6] \\ x_s \in [0, 1] \end{cases} \tag{5}$$

One important application of this empirical model is to achieve a constant perceived glossiness while varying the translucency of a target object. To prove the validity of the proposed model, we generated a set of four images by holding the perceived glossiness G_P constant ($G_P = 4$) and varying x_s, as presented in Fig. 10. Thus, for each set of images, although their translucency level varies, the perceived glossiness stays almost unchanged by compensating the subsurface scattering with corresponding RMS slopes.

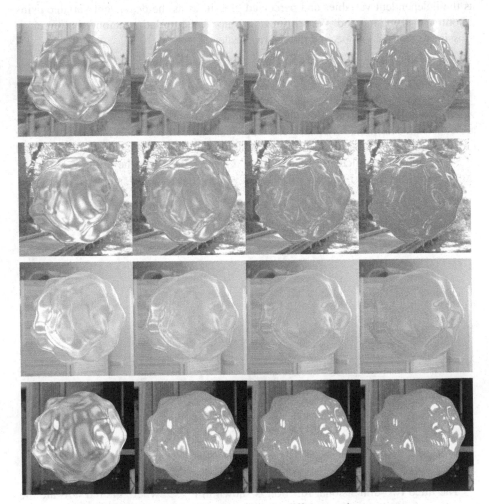

Fig. 10. The materials with $G_P = 4$ under different environment maps

To prove the generality of the proposed model, we used 4 environment maps to generate 4 sets of sample images. Previous work has shown that different lighting environments can affect perceived glossiness. In contrast, our model established a linear gloss perception space that applies to different lighting environments. Similarly, as shown in Fig. 11, although geometry also has an effect on perceived glossiness, our model is still applicable to various geometries.

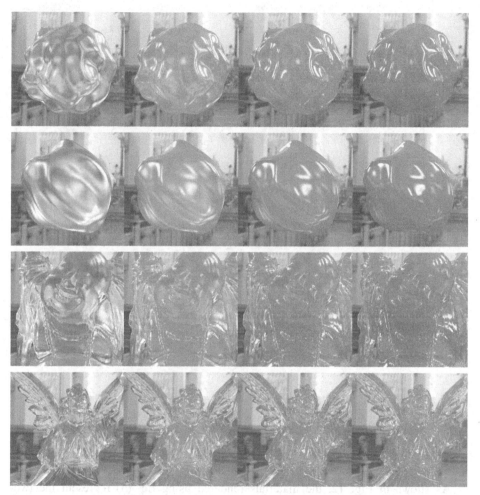

Fig. 11. The materials with $G_P = 4$ using different geometries

There is a general conclusion that the material on the left is more transparent and the material on the right has a smoother surface, yet they have the same perceived glossiness, which we believe can be explained by the following:

(1) Subsurface scattering allows more environmental light to pass through the object, increasing the overall brightness [42], while participants often misinterpret some

of the bright regions produced by the transmission for DOI gloss and tend to overestimate surface gloss;

(2) The lower the roughness, the more obvious the phenomenon of DOI gloss and contrast gloss on the surface of the object, increasing the perceived glossiness.

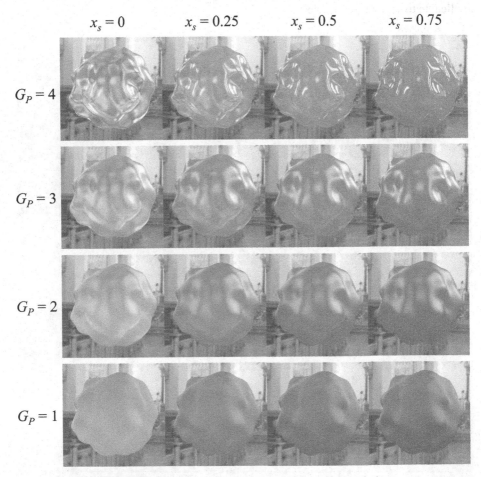

Fig. 12. The materials in two-dimensional uniform perceptual gloss space

As shown in Fig. 12, the materials rendered using Eq. (5) represent the two-dimensional uniform perceptual gloss space that we established. The material in each row has the same G_P.

5 Conclusion and Discussion

In this work, we proposed a quantitative empirical model that correlates perceived glossiness with both BRDF and BSSRDF, for translucent materials with various surface properties. We took two steps: (1) A model of perceived glossiness was proposed based on a classical physical BRDF model which predicts perceived glossiness and provides a linear space of perceived glossiness, assuming that perceived glossiness is a function of a single physical parameter, surface RMS slope. (2) Based on this linear space, image samples with different degrees of translucency and perceived glossiness were generated. An experiment was designed to investigate the correlation of perceived glossiness with BRDF and BSSRDF. As a result, a quantitative model of perceived glossiness was proposed with RMS slope and relative scale as model parameters. Multiple sets of rendered images were presented to validate the proposed model, for more general circumstances including various lighting conditions and object geometries. Thus, the proposed perceptual BRDF model can be used to correct the perceived glossiness of translucent materials in various 3D design software, game engines, renderers, etc. Furthermore, the application of deep learning methods to material perception has shown that the HVS can perceive material appearance by learning some latent patterns in image space [17, 18, 29]. Our experimental framework can be used to generate rendered image datasets with perceptual glossiness, which is useful for deep learning tasks, saving manpower and time costs. As our work is the first one to quantitatively correlate perceived glossiness with BRDF and BSSRDF, some limitations exist. In the future, we will consider recruiting more participants while ensuring that the distribution of gender and age is as even as possible to improve the generalization of the model.

References

1. Junior, E., et al.: CIE 175:2006 A Framework for the Measurement of Visual Appearance (2006)
2. Beck, J., Prazdny, S.: Highlights and the perception of glossiness. Percept. Psychophys. **30**(4), 407–410 (1981)
3. Ramirez, E.: Bidirectional reflectance distribution function. betascript publishing (2010)
4. Jensen, H.W., et al.: A practical model for subsurface light transport. In: Proceedings of the 28th Annual Conference on Computer Graphics and Interactive Techniques, pp. 511–58 (2001)
5. Burley, B., Studios, W.D.A.: Physically-based shading at disney. In: ACM SIGGRAPH, vol. 2012, pp. 1–7 (2012)
6. ISO 12640–3:2022 Graphic technology - Prepress digital data exchange - Part 3: CIELAB standard colour image data (CIELAB/SCID)
7. Leloup, F.B., Obein, G., Pointer, M.R., et al.: Toward the soft metrology of surface gloss: a review. Color. Res. Appl. **39**(6), 559–570 (2014)
8. Baek, Y.S., Kwak, Y., Yang, S.: Visual appearance measurement of surfaces containing pearl flakes. JOSA A **32**(5), 934–942 (2015)
9. Kandi, S.G., Panahi, B., Zoghi, N.: Impact of surface texture from fine to coarse on perceptual and instrumental gloss. Prog. Org. Coat. **171**, 107028 (2022)
10. Fleming, R.W.: Human perception: visual heuristics in the perception of glossiness. Curr. Biol. **22**(20), R865–R866 (2012)
11. Landy, M.S.: A gloss on surface properties. Nature **447**(7141), 158–159 (2007)
12. Kim, J., Anderson, B.L.: Image statistics and the perception of surface gloss and lightness. J. Vis. **10**(9), 3 (2010)
13. Olkkonen, M., Brainard, D.H.: Joint effects of illumination geometry and object shape in the perception of surface reflectance. I-Perception, **2**(9), 1014–1034 (2011)

14. Hunter, R.S.: Methods of determining gloss. NBS Res. Paper RP, **958** (1937)
15. Marlow, P.J., Anderson, B.L.: Generative constraints on image cues for perceived gloss. J. Vis. **13**(14), 2 (2013)
16. Qi, L., Chantler, M.J., Siebert, J.P., et al.: Why do rough surfaces appear glossy? JOSA A **31**(5), 935–943 (2014)
17. Storrs, K.R., Anderson, B.L., Fleming, R.W.: Unsupervised learning predicts human perception and misperception of gloss. Nat. Hum. Behav. **5**(10), 1402–1417 (2021)
18. Serrano, A., Chen, B., Wang, C., et al.: The effect of shape and illumination on material perception: model and applications. ACM Trans. Graph. (TOG) **40**(4), 1–16 (2021)
19. Pellacini, F., Ferwerda, J.A., Greenberg, D.P.: Toward a psychophysically-based light reflection model for image synthesis. In: Proceedings of the 27th Annual Conference on Computer Graphics and Interactive Techniques, pp. 55–64 (2000)
20. Ferwerda, J.A., Pellacini, F., Greenberg, D.P.: Psychophysically based model of surface gloss perception. In: Human Vision and Electronic Imaging vi. SPIE, vol. 4299, pp. 291–301 (2001)
21. Wills, J., Agarwal, S., Kriegman, D., et al.: Toward a perceptual space for gloss. ACM Trans. Graph. (TOG) **28**(4), 1–15 (2009)
22. Toscani, M., Guarnera, D., Guarnera, G.C., et al.: Three perceptual dimensions for specular and diffuse reflection. ACM Trans. Appl. Percept. (TAP) **17**(2), 1–26 (2020)
23. Shi, W., et al.: A low-dimensional perceptual space for intuitive BRDF Editing. In: EGSR 2021-Eurographics Symposium on Rendering-DL-only Track, pp. 1–31 (2021)
24. Lagunas, M., et al.: A similarity measure for material appearance. arXiv preprint arXiv:1905. 01562 (2019)
25. Fleming, R.W., Bülthoff, H.H.: Low-level image cues in the perception of translucent materials. ACM Trans. Appl. Percept. (TAP) **2**(3), 346–382 (2005)
26. Chadwick, A.C., Cox, G., Smithson, H.E., et al.: Beyond scattering and absorption: perceptual unmixing of translucent liquids. J. Vis. **18**(11), 18 (2018)
27. Motoyoshi, I.: Highlight–shading relationship as a cue for the perception of translucent and transparent materials. J. Vis. **10**(9), 6 (2010)
28. Kiyokawa, H., et al.: The perception of translucency from surface gloss. Vis. Res. **205**, 108140 (2023)
29. Liao, C., Sawayama, M., Xiao, B.: Unsupervised learning reveals interpretable latent representations for translucency perception. PLoS Comput. Biol. **19**(2), e1010878 (2023)
30. Gigilashvili, D., et al.: Perceived glossiness: beyond surface properties. In: Color and Imaging Conference. Society for Imaging Science and Technology, vol. 2019. no. 1, pp. 37–42 (2019)
31. Gigilashvili, D., Shi, W., Wang, Z., et al.: The role of subsurface scattering in glossiness perception. ACM Trans. Appl. Percept. (TAP) **18**(3), 1–26 (2021)
32. Gigilashvili, D., et al.: Behavioral investigation of visual appearance assessment. In: Color and Imaging Conference. Society for Imaging Science and Technology, vol. 2018. no. 1, pp. 294–299 (2018)
33. Jakob, W., Speierer, S., Roussel, N., Vicini, D.: DR. JIT: a just-in-time compiler for differentiable rendering. ACM Trans. Graph. (TOG) **41**(4), 1–19 (2022)
34. Adams, W.J., Kucukoglu, G., Landy, M.S., et al.: Naturally glossy: gloss perception, illumination statistics, and tone mapping. J. Vis. **18**(13), 4 (2018)
35. Mao, R., et al.: The effect of motion on the perception of material appearance. In: ACM Symposium on Applied Perception, vol. 2019, pp. 1–9 (2019)
36. Unity. https://assetstore.unity.com/packages/2d/textures-materials/sky/unity-hdri-pack-72511
37. Blender. https://www.blender.org/
38. Xiao, B., Zhao, S., Gkioulekas, I., et al.: Effect of geometric sharpness on translucent material perception. J. Vis. **20**(7), 10 (2020)

39. Qi, L., Chantler, M.J., Siebert, J.P., et al.: The joint effect of mesoscale and microscale RMS slope on perceived gloss. Vis. Res. **115**, 209–217 (2015)
40. Qi, L., et al.: How mesoscale and microscale RMS slope affect perceived gloss. Perception, **41**(3), 375–375 (2012). https://doi.org/10.1068/p7166
41. PsychoPy. https://www.psychopy.org/
42. Marlow, P., Kim, J., Anderson, B.L.: The role of brightness and orientation congruence in the perception of surface gloss. J. Vis. **11**(9), 16 (2011)

X-ray Computed Tomography Reconstruction Algorithm for Refractive Index Gradient

Keliang Liao[1], Qili He[2], Panyun Li[1], Liang Luo[3], and Peiping Zhu[1,2(✉)]

[1] Jinan Hanjiang Opto-Electronics Technology Company Ltd., Jinan, China
zhupp@ihep.ac.cn
[2] Institute of High Energy Physics, Chinese Academy of Sciences, Beijing, China
[3] School of Aerospace Engineering, Tsinghua University, Beijing, China

Abstract. The aim of this research is to reconstruct the 3D X-ray refractive index gradient maps by the proposed vector Radon transform and its inverse, assuming that the small-angle deviation condition is met. Theoretical analyses show that the X-ray beam can be modeled as a streamline with continuous change of direction in a row when measured in one grating period, which allows the extraction of the refraction angle signals. Experimental results show that all the 2D refraction signals of different directions can be acquired by a standard circular scanning procedure, which is typically used in the X-ray differential phase-contrast computed tomography. Furthermore, the 3D refractive index gradient maps that contain the directional density changes, can also be accurately reconstructed.

Keywords: CT reconstruction · Image process · X-ray imaging

1 Introduction

In general, there are two means to reveal the refractive information of samples from the acquired differential phase contrast (DPC) signals. One is to reconstruct the refractive index, and the other is to reconstruct the gradient of the refractive index. Due to its consistency with the classical CT image reconstruction algorithm [1, 2], by far, the first approach has been widely discussed [3–12]. Whereas, only few research interests were attracted onto the second approach [13, 14]. The main reason is the refractive index gradient reconstruction algorithms lack rigorous theoretical foundation for the X-ray DPC imaging. To overcome this difficulty, a new vector Radon and inverse Radon analysis theory has been proposed for the first time in this paper, which takes into account the X-ray beam small angle deviation condition. Based on this new proposed theory, the analytical algorithm for 3D refractive index gradient has been derived strictly.

2 Model and Methodology

The flow chart of the proposed model in this paper can be summarized in Fig. 1. The small angle deviation condition is a crucial process to establish this new theory. In the following section, the detail of each process is presented.

K. Liao and Q. He—Equal contribution.

W. Yongtian and W. Lifang (Eds.): IGTA 2023, CCIS 1910, pp. 286–297, 2023.
https://doi.org/10.1007/978-981-99-7549-5_21

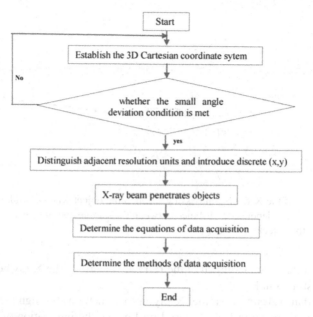

Fig.1. The flow chart of the proposed model in this study.

2.1 Optical Streamline Model

According to the Maxwell's electromagnetic equations, the Helmholtz equation for scalar monochromatic wave in inhomogeneous medium can be derived. Furthermore, both the Eikonal equation and the continuity equation [15] can be obtained. Assuming an infinitely small wavelength, the differential equation of light rays in geometric optics [15, 16] can be expressed as follows:

$$\frac{d}{ds}[\nabla S(\vec{r})] = \frac{d}{ds}[n(\vec{r})\vec{\tau}(\vec{r})] = \nabla n(\vec{r}), \qquad (1)$$

where s is the arc length of the beam, S is the optical path length, $\vec{r}$ is the position vector, $\vec{\tau} = d\vec{r}/ds$ is the unit vector parallel to the tangent of the beam, and $n\vec{\tau}$ is the ray vector, and n is the refractive index of the medium

$$n(\vec{r}) = 1 - \delta(\vec{r}) + i\beta(\vec{r}), \qquad (2)$$

where δ denotes the decrement of the real portion and is related to the beam phase shift, β denotes the imaginary portion and is related to the beam attenuation. Substituting Eq. (2) into Eq. (1), the following results can be obtained:

$$\frac{d}{ds}[\nabla S(\vec{r})] = \frac{d}{ds}\vec{\tau}(\vec{r}) = -\nabla\delta(\vec{r}). \qquad (3)$$

In Eq. (3), both the δ and β are ignored for the middle term, and β is ignored for the last term due to the fact that $\beta \ll \delta \ll 1$, and the ray vector $n\vec{\tau}$ reduced to $\vec{\tau}$ whose

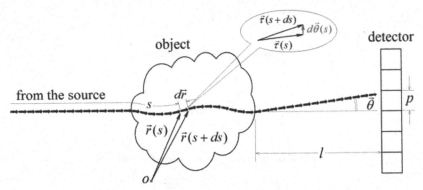

Fig. 2. Illustration of the X-ray beam passing through the object when considering the internal small refractions. The *l* denotes the distance between the sample and the detector, and *p* denotes the dimension of the detector element.

increment is in effect the increment of the refraction angle of the X-ray beam inside the sample, as illustrated in Fig. 2.

Assuming that a group of parallel X-ray beam penetrates through the object with a refractive index n, shown in Fig. 2. Based on Eq. (3), the integration of the refraction index gradient $\nabla\delta$ along a real X-ray beam path (not straight line any longer) is expressed as

$$\nabla S(s) - \nabla S(-\infty) = \vec{\theta}(s) = -\int_{-\infty}^{s} \nabla\delta(\vec{r})ds. \tag{4}$$

The relation between phase and optical path

$$\Phi(s) = \frac{2\pi}{\lambda}S(s) = kS(s) \tag{5}$$

is substituted into Eq. (4), one gets

$$\frac{\nabla\Phi(s) - \nabla\Phi(-\infty)}{-k} = -\vec{\theta}(s) = \int_{-\infty}^{s} \nabla\delta(\vec{r})ds. \tag{6}$$

Alternatively, Eq. (6) can also be rewritten as

$$\frac{\nabla\Phi[s(x,y,z)] - \nabla\Phi(-\infty)}{-k} = -\vec{\theta}[s(x,y,z)] = \int_{-\infty}^{s(x,y,z)} \nabla\delta(x,y,z)ds. \tag{7}$$

Herein, the standard Cartesian coordinate system is selected with the z axis parallel to the incident direction. Due to the inhomogeneous object refractive index distribution, as illustrated in Fig. 2, the exit X-ray beam would be deviated by $\vec{\theta}$ compared to its primary incident direction. However, in the process of experimental data analysis, it is quite difficult to measure the non-zero angular deviations induced by inhomogeneous object. The reason is that the pixel size of the detector is limited. For instance, if $\left|\vec{\theta}\right| < p/l$, the detection system with detector element size of p would be insensitive in probing such tiny beam deviations. In other words, it is difficult for the detector element with finite size to distinguish the refracted X-ray beams from the primary X-ray beams when they are falling within the same resolution unit (suppose the resolution unit size is $2p$). When this happens, essentially, the change of X-ray beam inside the x-y plane should be neglected, the arc length of the beam $s(x, y, z)$ can be reduced to z. In order to distinguish the adjacent resolution units, discrete imaging unit (x, y) according to resolution elements are introduced into the functions of phase gradient and refraction angle, thus Eq. (7) can be simplified as

$$\frac{\nabla \Phi(x, y, z) - \nabla \Phi(-\infty)}{-k} = -\overrightarrow{\theta}(x, y, z) = \int_{-\infty}^{z} \nabla \delta(x, y, z)dz. \tag{8}$$

Please note that since the integration of $\nabla \delta$ is the path integral in front of the detector, (x, y) inside the integral will not be affected by the detector and is still continuous. Therefore, continuity and discreteness coexist in Eq. (8), inside and outside the integral respectively. Once the X-ray beam leaves the object, then $\nabla \delta = 0$. Thus, by letting $z \to \infty$, one gets

$$\overrightarrow{e}_z \frac{\partial \Phi(x, y, \infty)}{\partial z} - \overrightarrow{e}_z \frac{\partial \Phi(-\infty)}{\partial z} = 0, \tag{9}$$

and takes account of the fact

$$\overrightarrow{e}_x \frac{\partial \Phi(-\infty)}{\partial x} + \overrightarrow{e}_y \frac{\partial \Phi(-\infty)}{\partial y} = 0, \tag{10}$$

where $\overrightarrow{e}_x$, $\overrightarrow{e}_y$ and $\overrightarrow{e}_z$ are the unit vector along the x, y and z axis respectively, Eq. (8) can be reduced as

$$\frac{\nabla_\perp \Phi(x, y)}{-k} = -\overrightarrow{\theta}(x, y) = \int_{-\infty}^{\infty} \nabla \delta(x, y, z)dz, \tag{11}$$

where $\nabla_\perp = \overrightarrow{e}_x \partial/\partial x + \overrightarrow{e}_y \partial/\partial y$. Note that $\left| \overrightarrow{\theta}(x, y) \right| < p/l$ is defined as the small angle deviation condition in this work, which solves the contradiction between straight line propagation required by Radon transform and directional change propagation caused by refraction angle. Under this condition, the refraction angle in Eq. (11) is a vector sum (integral) process, as shown in Fig. 3.

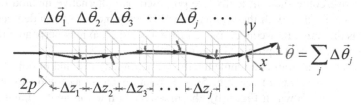

Fig. 3. Diagram of refraction angle formation.

2.2 Vector Reconstruction Algorithm for Refractive Index Gradient

Assuming a parallel X-ray CT imaging geometry with the y axis being the axis of sample rotation, the analytical refractive index gradient $\nabla\delta$ reconstruction algorithm is discussed. Let $y\prime = y$, and $(x\prime, y\prime, z\prime)$ be the object coordinate, as a result, Eq. (11) can be expressed as the Radon transformation of $\nabla\delta$ at the view angle φ between $x\prime$ axis and x axis, namely

$$\frac{\nabla_\perp \Phi(x, y, \varphi)}{-k} = -\vec{\theta}(x, y, \varphi) = \int_{-\infty}^{\infty} \int_{-\infty}^{\infty} \nabla\delta(x', y', z')\hat{\delta}(x'\cos\varphi + z'\sin\varphi - x)dx'dz',$$

(12)

where $\hat{\delta}$ is the Dirac pulse function. Afterwards, applying the inverse Radon operation onto Eq. (12), the $\nabla\delta$ can be readily reconstructed,

$$\nabla\delta(x', y', z') = \vec{e}_{x'}\frac{\partial\delta(x', y', z')}{\partial x'} + \vec{e}_{y'}\frac{\partial\delta(x', y', z')}{\partial y'} + \vec{e}_{z'}\frac{\partial\delta(x', y', z')}{\partial z'} =$$

$$-\int_0^\pi d\varphi \int_{-\infty}^\infty \mathcal{F}_x^{-1}|\rho|\mathcal{F}_x[\theta_x(x, y, \varphi)\vec{e}_x + \theta_y(x, y, \varphi)\vec{e}_y]\hat{\delta}(x'\cos\varphi + z'\sin\varphi - x)dx,$$

(13)

where $\vec{e}_{x'}$, $\vec{e}_{y'}$ and $\vec{e}_{z'}$ are the unit vector along the x', y' and z' axis, respectively; $\theta_x = \partial\Phi/k\partial x$ and $\theta_y = \partial\Phi/k\partial y$ are the component of the refraction angle on the x and y axis, respectively, the operators $\mathcal{F}_x$ and $\mathcal{F}_x^{-1}$ represent the Fourier and inverse Fourier transformation operator along x axis, correspondingly; and variable ρ denotes the frequency counterpart of space variable x.

2.3 DPC Imaging with Inclined Phase and Analyzer Gratings

Despite the explicit reconstruction expression of $\nabla\delta$ shown in Eq. (13), it is still very challenging to apply it on real experimental data analysis. This is because the refraction angle signals along the x axis and y axis are both required to apply into Eq. (13). In practice, the easiest way to obtain the two perpendicular components of refraction angle is to rotate the grating interferometry with respect to the z axis by 90°. Obviously, this may bring inconvenience to the data acquisition and does not meet the fast imaging demand. To overcome such difficulty, we proposed one alternative method to acquire the $\theta_x\vec{e}_x + \theta_y\vec{e}_y$ data with the grating interferometry inclined by ω degrees. In this method, ω is the angle between x'' axis and x axis, and x'' axis is perpendicular to the 1D grating groove, see the proposed grating settings in Fig. 4.

With such special grating alignments, the refraction angle signal of object acquired at ω is equal to $\theta_{x''}(x, y, \varphi)$ see Fig. 5(a). If rotating the object with respect to the y axis by 180°, as shown in Fig. 5(b), the measured refraction angle signal becomes $\theta_{x''}(-x, y, \varphi + \pi)$, which is equal to $\theta_{y''}(x, y, \varphi)$, as shown in Fig. 5(c). As a result, the needed bilateral refraction angle signals along two perpendicular directions can be

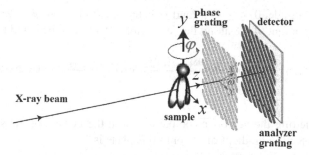

Fig. 4. Illustration of the DPC imaging with inclined phase and analyzer gratings. The variable ω represents the angle between x'' axis and x axis and the x'' axis is parallel to the normal vector of the 1D grating bar.

acquired with continuous object rotation. In all, we have

$$\theta_x(x, y, \varphi) = \frac{\theta_{x''}(x, y, \varphi) - \theta_{y''}(x, y, \varphi)}{2\cos\omega} = \frac{\theta_{x''}(x, y, \varphi) - \theta_{x''}(-x, y, \varphi + \pi)}{2\cos\omega}, \quad (14)$$

$$\theta_y(x, y, \varphi) = \frac{\theta_{x''}(x, y, \varphi) + \theta_{y''}(x, y, \varphi)}{2\sin\omega} = \frac{\theta_{x''}(x, y, \varphi) + \theta_{x''}(-x, y, \varphi + \pi)}{2\sin\omega}. \quad (15)$$

By substituting the Eq. (14) and Eq. (15) back into the Eq. (13), one obtains

$$\nabla\delta(x', y', z') = \overrightarrow{e}_{x'}\frac{\partial\delta(x', y', z')}{\partial x'} + \overrightarrow{e}_{y'}\frac{\partial\delta(x', y', z')}{\partial y'} + \overrightarrow{e}_{z'}\frac{\partial\delta(x', y', z')}{\partial z'}$$

$$= -\int_0^\pi d\varphi \int_{-\infty}^\infty \mathcal{F}_x^{-1}|\rho|\mathcal{F}_x\left[\frac{\theta_{x''}(x, y, \varphi) - \theta_{x''}(-x, y, \varphi + \pi)}{2\cos\omega}\overrightarrow{e}_x + \frac{\theta_{x''}(x, y, \varphi) + \theta_{x''}(-x, y, \varphi + \pi)}{2\sin\omega}\overrightarrow{e}_y\right]$$

$$\hat{\delta}(x'\cos\varphi + z'\sin\varphi - x)dx. \quad (16)$$

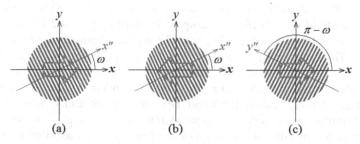

Fig. 5. Scheme of the proposed fast bilateral refraction angle signal acquisition method with the positions of both grating and object: (a) ω, φ; (b) $\omega, \varphi + \pi$; (c)$\pi - \omega, \varphi$. The blue arrow indicates the object.

Assuming a unit vector in the object space.

$$\overrightarrow{e} = \overrightarrow{e}_{x'}\sin\gamma\cos\psi + \overrightarrow{e}_{y'}\cos\gamma + \overrightarrow{e}_{z'}\sin\gamma\sin\psi, \quad (17)$$

where γ is the latitude, $0 \leq \gamma < \pi$, and ψ is the longitude, $0 \leq \psi < 2\pi$. Readily, the 1D projection gradient of $\nabla\delta$ along the $\vec{e}$ vector is derived to be equal to

$$\vec{e}\left[\vec{e} \cdot \nabla\delta(x',y',z')\right] = \vec{e}\left[\sin\gamma\cos\psi\frac{\partial\delta(x',y',z')}{\partial x'} + \cos\gamma\frac{\partial\delta(x',y',z')}{\partial y'} + \sin\gamma\sin\psi\frac{\partial\delta(x',y',z')}{\partial z'}\right]. \tag{18}$$

Moreover, letting the vector $\vec{e}$ be parallel with the normal of the selected plane, then the 2D projection gradient of $\nabla\delta$ onto this plane is

$$\nabla\delta(x',y',z') - \vec{e}\left[\vec{e} \cdot \nabla\delta(x',y',z')\right] = \vec{e}_1\left[\vec{e}_1 \cdot \nabla\delta(x',y',z')\right] + \vec{e}_2\left[\vec{e}_2 \cdot \nabla\delta(x',y',z')\right] =$$
$$\vec{e}_1\left[-\cos\gamma\cos\psi\frac{\partial\delta(x',y',z')}{\partial x'} + \sin\gamma\frac{\partial\delta(x',y',z')}{\partial y'} - \cos\gamma\sin\psi\frac{\partial\delta(x',y',z')}{\partial z'}\right]$$
$$+ \vec{e}_2\left[-\sin\psi\frac{\partial\delta(x',y',z')}{\partial x'} + \cos\psi\frac{\partial\delta(x',y',z')}{\partial z'}\right], \tag{19}$$

where $\vec{e} \perp \vec{e}_1$,

$$\vec{e}_1 = -\vec{e}_{x'}\cos\gamma\cos\psi + \vec{e}_{y'}\sin\gamma - \vec{e}_{z'}\cos\gamma\sin\psi, \tag{20}$$

and

$$\vec{e}_2 = \vec{e} \times \vec{e}_1 = -\vec{e}_{x'}\sin\psi + \vec{e}_{z'}\cos\psi. \tag{21}$$

3 Experimental Validation

3.1 Experimental Setup

Validation experiments were performed on the Talbot interferometer system of the BL13W1 beamline at Shanghai Synchrotron Radiation Facility (SSRF). As shown in Fig. 6, it consists of one 1D phase grating (0.5π shifting, period 2.396 μm) and one 1D absorption grating (period 2.400 μm). The distance between the two gratings is 46.380 mm. The beam energy is 20 keV. The detector pixel size is 6.5 μm. The specimen of a hamster front toe was positioned with its rotation axis along y axis with the grating interferometry inclined by $\omega = 45°$. For this Talbot interferometer on SSRF, the average fringe visibility is about 0.40, and the mean detector readout is around 25,000. The projection images of object were acquired from projection angle 0° to 360° with 0.5° interval. At each projection angle the phase-stepping scan was acquired by translating the absorption grating along the x'' axis with a exposure time of 13 ms in 8 equidistant steps over one grating period. The bilateral refraction angle signals were extracted from two angular intervals: $\theta_{x''}(x,y,\varphi)$ for φ ranges from 0 to π, and $\theta_{x''}(-x,y,\varphi)$ for φ ranges from π to 2π. The programming language used for reconstruction is MATLAB. It takes about 62 s to reconstruct a transverse map, and the COMPUTER CPU is Intel Xeon E5–2667*2.

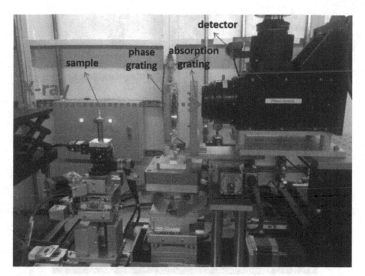

Fig. 6. The experimental setup of the Talbot interferometer system.

3.2 Results

Experimental imaging result of $|\nabla\delta|$ is shown in Fig. 7. The three-dimensional distribution of $|\nabla\delta|$ is presented in the x'-y'-z' Cartesian coordinate system, with x'-z' plane as the transverse plane, x'-y' plane as the coronal plane, and y'-z' plane as the sagittal plane. From this scalar map of $|\nabla\delta|$, the details of the structural information can be obtained, but the directional information about the sample is lost. To reveal the directional information of object, the vector information of $\nabla\delta$ will be discussed in detail in this following section.

In particular, Fig. 8 illustrates two special 1D projection gradients of $\nabla\delta$ in the coronal plane: the $\vec{e}_{y'} \cdot \dfrac{\partial\delta(x',y',z')}{\partial y'}$ is parallel to the hair, and the $\vec{e}_{x'} \cdot \dfrac{\partial\delta(x',y',z')}{\partial x'}$ is perpendicular to the hair. Clearly, the hairs can be easily identified from Fig. 8(b), while hair is almost invisible in Fig. 8(a), which shows the important ability of the proposed vector CT algorithm when compared with the traditional scalar CT algorithms.

In addition, the 2D projection gradient maps of $\nabla\delta$ on the coronal, sagittal, and transverse planes are illustrated in Fig. 9(a) to Fig. 9(c), respectively. In these reconstructed projection maps, the color represents the signal orientation. The gradient variations of the refractive index can be clearly distinguished from the different color and brightness distributions. Figure 9(a) shows the 2D projection gradient in the coronal plane, where $\vec{e} = -\vec{e}_{z'}$, $\vec{e}_1 = \vec{e}_{y'}$, $\vec{e}_2 = \vec{e}_{x'}$. Figure 9(b) shows the 2D projection gradient in the sagittal plane, where $\vec{e} = \vec{e}_{x'}$, $\vec{e}_1 = \vec{e}_{y'}$, $\vec{e}_2 = \vec{e}_{z'}$. Figure 9(c) shows the 2D projection gradient in the transverse plane, where $\vec{e} = \vec{e}_{y'}$, $\vec{e}_1 = \vec{e}_{z'}$, $\vec{e}_2 = \vec{e}_{x'}$. Moreover, the hue saturation value (HSV) color map is used to depict such projection gradient information, including both the absolute signal strength and its angular orientation, into one single image [17]. More specifically, the hue corresponds to the angle; the saturation is set to 1 and the value is defined as the normalized brightness of the directionality in order to fill the span [0, 1], meaning that dark areas in the image correspond

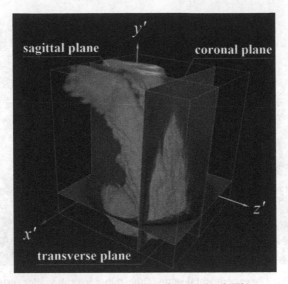

Fig. 7. Experimental imaging result of $|\nabla\delta|$.

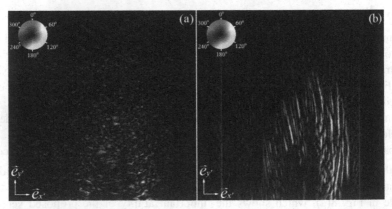

Fig. 8. The image of 1D projection gradient of $\nabla\delta$ on the coronal plane with parallel (a) and perpendicular (b) component, correspondingly.

to areas with no gradient. For instance, the red, yellow, green, cyan, blue, magenta colors correspond to the 0°, 60°, 120°, 180°, 240°, 300° angular direction, respectively.

As a consequence, the line integral process of $\nabla\delta$ in the Radon transform, equals to the 2D vector summation of a collection of the increment of refraction angles along the real X-ray beam propagation path, see Fig. 3 and Eq. (11). However the principle of the inverse Radon transform of $\vec{\theta}$ is to filter these 2D vector summation of each projection direction and back-project them to reconstruct the 3D refractive index gradient $\nabla\delta$, see Eq. (13) or (16). As shown in Fig. 7 to Fig. 9, both the Radon and inverse Radon transforms can be performed on vectors in refraction angle signal based computed vector tomography.

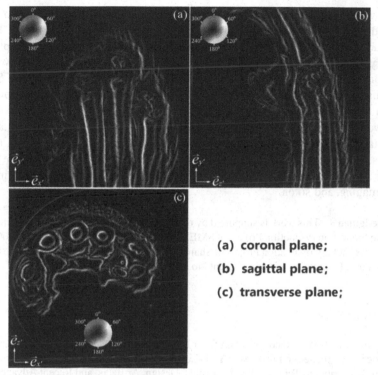

Fig. 9. The 2D projection gradient in the coronal plane (a), the sagittal plane (b) and the axial plane (c).

(a) coronal plane;

(b) sagittal plane;

(c) transverse plane;

3.3 Discussions

Based on the small angle deviation condition, the Radon transform essentially depends on the pixel size of detector. When the pixel element size reduces, the small angle deviation condition approximates to the rigorous straight line propagation condition. In other words, the ideal straight-line propagation condition is the theoretical limit of the small angle deviation condition. Therefore, the deflected X-ray beam induced by the density changes of object is made of two parts: the straight-line component and the streamline component. Obviously, the straight-line component of X-ray beam, which is measured within one resolution unit, meets the requirements of Radon transform. While the streamline component with continuous change of direction, which is measured by the grating period, meets the requirements of extracting the refraction angle signals.

4 Conclusion and Outlook

In this study, the small angle condition was proposed to define the Radon transform of the refractive index gradient. Based on this condition, analytical reconstruction algorithm for the refractive index gradient and the corresponding data acquisition method were developed. In the verification experiment, complete projection data of refractive index gradient were collected by using grating interferometer with inclined degree $\omega = 45°$. Further, the 3D refractive index gradient was reconstructed to verify this new CT image reconstruction theory. Experimental results show two major advantages of this proposed CT theory. First, a standard circular acquisition trajectory typically used in conventional X-ray computed tomography can measure bilateral refraction angle signals. Second, the reconstructed 3D refractive index gradient maps enhance the visualization of the direction of density changes with the flexibility.

Above all, the proposed new reconstruction algorithm has huge promising application scenarios, for example in materials testing of fibrous composites and in medical diagnosis. Besides, the theory and method established in this work can also be applied for other imaging fields, like the neutron imaging, proton imaging, electron imaging, optical imaging, and so on.

Acknowledgments. This work is supported by the Jinan Haiyou Industry Leading Talent Project (2022), the Innovation Promotion Project of SME in Shandong Province(No.2023TSGC0093), the Enterprise Technology Innovation Project of Shandong Province(No.202350100372), the National Natural Science Foundation of China (Grant No. 11535015).

References

1. Herman, G.T.: Image Reconstruction from Projections, the Fundamentals of Computerized Tomography. Academic Press, New York-London (1980)
2. Hsieh, J.: Computed Tomography: Principles, Design, Artifacts, and Recent Advances, SPIE Press monograph. SPIE Press (2003)
3. Huang, Z.-F., et al.: Direct computed tomographic reconstruction for directional-derivative projections of computed tomography of diffraction enhanced imaging. Appl. Phys. Lett. **89**, 041124 (2006)
4. Momose, A., Yashiro, W., Takeda, Y., Suzuki, Y., Hattori, T.: Phase tomography by x-ray talbot interferometry for biological imaging. Jpn. J. Appl. Phys. **45**, 5254–5262 (2006)
5. Pfeiffer, F., Kottler, C., Bunk, O., David, C.: Hard X-ray phase tomography with low-brilliance sources. Phys. Rev. Lett. **98**, 108105 (2007)
6. Chen, G.-H., Qi, Z.: Image reconstruction for fan-beam differential phase contrast computed tomography. Phys. Medicine Biol. **53**, 1015–1025 (2008)
7. Zhang, L., Fang, Q., Huang, Z.:3D reconstruction algorithm for cone-beam differential phase contrast computed tomography. In: 2008 IEEE Nuclear Science Symposium Conference Record, pp. 4193–4197 (2008)
8. Zhu, P., et al.: Low-dose, simple, and fast grating based X-ray phase-contrast imaging. Proc. Natl. Acad. Sci. **107**, 13576–13581 (2010)
9. Rutishauser, S., et al.: A tilted grating interferometer for full vector field differential X-ray phase contrast tomography. Opt. Express **19**, 24890–24896 (2011)
10. Zanette, I., et al.: Trimodal low-dose X-ray tomography. Proc. Natl. Acad. Sci. **109**, 10199–10204 (2012)
11. Wu, Z., et al.: A new method to retrieve phase information for equiangular fan beam differential phase contrast computed tomography. Med. Phys. **40**, 031911 (2013)
12. Li, J., Sun, Y., Zhu, P.: A theoretically exact reconstruction algorithm for helical cone-beam differential phase-contrast computed tomography. Phys. Medicine Biol. **58**, 5421–5432 (2013)
13. Navarrete-Leon, C., et al.: X-ray phase-contrast microtomography of soft tissues using a compact laboratory system with two-directional sensitivity. Optica **10**, 880–887 (2023)

14. He, Q.L., et al.: Accurate reconstruction algorithm for bilateral differential phase signals. Radiat. Detect. Technol. Methods **5**, 474–479 (2021)
15. Paganin, D.M.: Coherent X-ray Optics. Oxford University Press, Oxford (2006)
16. Born, M., Wolf, E.: Principles of Optics: Electromagnetic Theory of Propagation, Interference and Diffraction of Light 7 edn. vol. I. Cambridge University Press, Cambridge (1999)
17. Kagias, M., Wang, Z., Villanueva-Perez, P., Jefimovs, K., Stampanoni, M.: 2D-omnidirectional hard-x-ray scattering sensitivity in a single shot. Phys. Rev. Lett. **116**(9), 093902 (2016)

Visualization and Visual Analysis

Global Temperature Prediction Models Based on ARIMA and LSTM

Yue Yu[1], Yi Xie[1], Zui Tao[2], Hongmei Ju[1], and Meiling Wang[1(✉)]

[1] School of Statistics and Data Science, Beijing Wuzi University, Beijing 101149, China
Blair513131@163.com, 2605186362@qq.com, {juhongmei,
wangmeiling}@bwu.edu.cn
[2] Logistics School, Beijing Wuzi University, Beijing 101149, China
13317054611@163.com

Abstract. Global warming leads to an increase in temperature, which will cause a crisis to the global environment. In this paper, we establish two mathematical models to predict further global temperature based on historical global temperature data. First, after collection and preprocessing of the global temperature data, we build a polynomial regression model with latitude, longitude and time. However, the polynomial regression model is not fit and we find that the data is a nonstationary time series. Therefore, we establish an ARIMA (Auto Regressive Synthetic Moving Average)-based global temperature prediction model and an LSTM (Long and Short-Term Memory)-based global temperature prediction model to predict global monthly temperature. Numerical results show that the ARIMA model performs better than the LSTM model. Based on the results of ARIMA model, the global average temperature will reach 10.53 °C in 2050 and 11.36 °C in 2100.

Keywords: Global Warming · Time Series Forecasting · ARIMA · LSTM
Neural Network

1 Introduction

Climate change is a challenge for humanity as temperatures in many parts of the world have reached record highs, causing catastrophes and placing many countries in a state of emergency. Global warming is related to the natural phenomenon of the Earth's energy absorption and emission system becoming out of balance as the sun changes and the concentration of CO_2 increases. As a result of a series of industrial activities, the system for absorbing and emitting energy is in disequilibrium, leading to an increase in temperature and global warming. In this paper, we focus on predicting global temperature to show the degree of global warming.

The ARIMA (Auto-Regressive Integrated Moving Average) model is a statistical analysis model that uses time series data to future trends. LSTM (Long Short-Term Memory) networks are a type of recurrent neural network capable of learning order dependence in sequence prediction problems. The reasons for our choice of research methodology are as follows. There is almost no research on the analysis and prediction of global temperature using ARIMA and LSTM. At the same time, we compare the accuracy of ARIMA with that of LSTM through the prediction results of global temperature.

In this paper, we aim to find a valid mathematical model to predict global temperature. Based on literature analysis above, we select polynomial regression model, ARIMA model and LSTM neural networks model. Throughout this paper, it assumes that the data collected are true and valid, all global temperatures are terrestrial, and the global temperature is calculated by the average temperature of all cities.

The paper is organized as follows. In Sect. 2, we summarize related work about global temperature prediction. Section 3 builds a regression model in terms of spatial scales, and makes a preliminary analysis of the data. Section 4 introduces the data source, ARIMA model and LSTM model. Section 5 analyzes and forecasts the change of global monthly average temperature with time using ARIMA model and LSTM model, respectively. By comparing the results of the two models, the optimal model is selected and the annual average temperature is predicted according to the optimal model. Finally, Sect. 6 concludes the paper.

2 Related Work

With the increasing impact of global warming on human beings, many domestic experts have also begun to pay attention to global temperature change.

In the time series study, Guoqing Zhang, Pengfei Li, Li Huang and Yaofei Wu conducted the Mann-Kendall mutation test and established the HoltWinters seasonless exponential smoothing model to predict trends in global mean temperature growth over the next 50 years, based on the collected data on global mean temperature distance levels [1]. Shuna Ni, Bo Tang, and Jiahui Cai addressed the characteristics of both trend and fluctuation of global annual mean temperature historical data, and proposed to use the combination of gray system theory and time series analysis to build a GM-ARMA combined model to predict global annual mean temperature [2]. In the work of Zhu and Li, since temperature data are closely related to time, the time series method can be used to analyze and evaluate temperature data [3]. The ARIMA (12,1,5) model is used to predict the global average temperature for the next century (2023–2100) [3].

The global mean annual temperature of the past ten years is predicted by using isometric recursive prediction method. Foreign countries have studied the problem of global warming earlier, and there are more related studies and rich results. Peide Zhang showed that the ARIMA (Auto Regressive Synthetic Moving Average) is one of the most popular linear time series forecasting models of the past 30 years [4]. In the study of neural networks, Yufeng Xue and Chaomei Yang used the Mexican cap wavelet function to analyze the river to study the characteristics of global temperature change in the last hundred years using artificial neural network to predict the global temperature change trend [5]. The results show that the temperature change has different characteristics and sudden change points in different time scales.

Ye Tao and Jinglin Du used random forest to select the meteorological elements highly correlated with temperature as input variables, eliminated the noise in the original meteorological data and reduced the complexity of the network [6]. Their prediction model was established using LSTM (Long and Short-Term Memory) network, and experiments were conducted on the collected multi-element meteorological data. Huiqing Hou considered the atmospheric carbon dioxide emissions over the years, the heat absorption and heat dissipation of the earth, and the ocean surface temperature change. Then the author established a global climate change prediction model based on BP neural network to predict the climate change in the next 25 years [7]. Wu, Yang and Li used a ISSA–LSTM model-based approach for predicting the air quality index (AQI), which consists of three main components: random forest (RF) and mRMR, improved sparrow search algorithm (ISSA), and long short-term memory network (LSTM) [8].

Recently, researches on ANNs (artificial neural networks) forecasting have shown that ANNs are promising methods for linear forecasting. Taylor and Buizza investigated the application of weather ensemble predictions in ANNs to load forecasting from 1 to 10 days in advance [9]. For the issue of global temperature prediction, Yin Zhang et al. used ARIMA model and LSTM model to perform multi-factor regression of global temperature in China [10].

As for other non-global temperature problems, the results of domestic and international studies using ARIMA models and LSTM models are quite remarkable. Sima Siami-Namini, Neda Tavakoli, Akbar Siami Namin investigated that whether the newly developed deep learning-based algorithms for forecasting time series data, such as LSTM, are superior to the traditional algorithms such as ARIMA model, and the results showed that LSTM outperforms ARIMA model [11]. Elsaraiti Meftah, and Adel Merabet aimed to find the most effective predictive model for time series. The result showed that, compared to the ARIMA, using ANNs, recurrent neural networks (RNNs), and LSTM have less errors and higher accuracy in the predictions of wind speed [12].

Based on this recent escalation, the Monkeypox outbreak has become a severe and urgent worldwide public health concern. Long, Tan and Newman aimed to develop an efficient forecasting tool that allows health experts to implement effective prevention policies for Monkeypox. This research utilized five machine learning models, namely, ARIMA, LSTM, Prophet, NeuralProphet, and a stacking model, which forecast the next 7-day trend of Monkeypox cases in the United States [13].

The work of Duan, Gong, Luo and Zhao build a combined model to accurately predict the AQI based on real AQI data from four cities. They used an ARIMA model, a CNN-LSTM model and the Dung Beetle Optimizer algorithm to determine the optimal hyperparameters and check the accuracy of the model [14].Wang used two forecasting models that are proposed in this study, which is the Autoregressive Integrated Moving Average model (ARIMA) compared with Long Short-Term Memory (LSTM), aiming to find a model with higher accuracy of the base station mobile traffic prediction [15].

Summarizing the related research, there is almost no research on the analysis and prediction of global temperature using ARIMA and LSTM. In this paper, we predict global temperature using ARIMA and LSTM and make comparison between the accuracy of ARIMA and that of LSTM.

3 Preliminary Data Analysis

3.1 Data Pre-processing

In this paper, we use the data from Berkeley Earth [16] and preprocess it. The time frame is unified from January 1900 to October 2013. The latitude and longitude of the cities are processed. South latitude and east longitude are assigned positive, and north latitude and west longitude are assigned negative. Since longitude has less influence on temperature [17], based on latitude, we divide the cities into four zones: North Temperate Zone, Northern Tropics, Southern Tropics and South Temperate Zone, with the criteria shown in Table 1.

Table 1. Regional classification criteria

Region	criteria
North Temperate Zone	−66.5 to −23.5
South Temperate Zone	23.5 to 66.5
Northern Tropics	−23.5 to 0
Southern Tropics	0 to 23.5

3.2 Data Analysis

3.2.1 Global Temperature and Time

Based on the four zones obtained above, the regional average temperature trends from January to December in each zone are analyzed separately. Then we get a preliminary understanding of the global temperature.

As shown in Fig. 1, in the long term, global temperatures are on an upward trend and fluctuate up and down on an annual cycle. The annual temperature of the north temperate zone is the lowest in January and the highest in July, with an overall trend of rising and then falling. The annual temperature of the south temperate zone is the lowest in July and the highest in January, with an overall trend of falling to the lowest temperature and then rising. The annual temperature of the northern tropics is the highest in May. And the annual temperature of the southern tropics is the lowest in July. In April and October, the temperature in the north temperate zone is about the same as that in the southern temperate zone. In March and November, the temperature in the northern tropics is approximately the same as that in the southern tropics.

After analysis, we conclude that the temperature in the northern hemisphere tends to rise and then fall throughout the year. And the southern hemisphere shows the opposite trend. The temperature in the southern hemisphere tends to fall and then rise throughout the year. The temperature in the northern and southern hemispheres is basically the same when the sun is directly over the Tropic of Cancer.

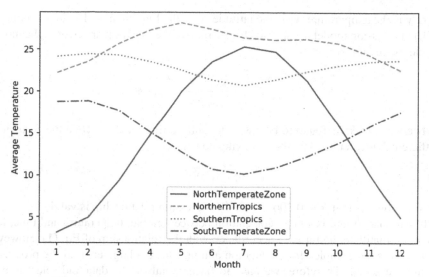

Fig. 1. The temperature curve of the regions varies with the month

3.2.2 Global Temperature and Geographical Location

As shown in Fig. 1, during December to February, temperature is lowest in the north temperate zone and highest in the southern tropics. In July, the temperature in the south temperate zone reaches its lowest value, while the northern tropics is still at their highest temperature. Temperate regions have large fluctuations in temperature throughout the year, while the tropics is in a relatively stable state throughout the year, with their global temperatures above 20 °C.

3.2.3 Global Temperature and Time, Geographical Location

From the preliminary analysis, we obtain the relationship between global temperature and time, and the relationship between global temperature and geographical location. To further determine the conclusion, we take global temperature as the dependent variable. And we take time, longitude, and latitude as the independent variables. The relationship is analyzed below.

First, the known data set is divided into training and validation sets. The training and validation sets are set at 80% and 20%. After training, the multivariate polynomial regression model has a better fit than the multiple linear regression model with a goodness-of-fit of 0.14. The goodness-of-fit of the quadratic polynomial regression model is 0.67 and the goodness-of-fit of the cubic polynomial regression model is 0.82. Therefore, we choose the cubic polynomial regression model and obtain

$$
\begin{aligned}
y = {} & 0.43x_1 + 0.023x_2 - 16.17x_3 - 0.0096x_1^2 + 0.0002x_1x_2 - 0.198x_1x_3 - 0.0002x_2 \\
& + 0.014x_2x_3 + 0.033x_3^2 - 7.51 \times 10^{-6}x_1^3 - 9.71 \times 10^{-6}x_1^2x_2 + 0.00013x_1^2x_3 \\
& + 7.25 \times 10^{-6}x_1x_2^2 - 1.9 \times 10^{-5}x_1x_2x_3 + 0.014x_1x_3^2 - 1.85 \times 10^{-6}x_2^3 \\
& + 1.54 \times 10^{-5}x_2^2x_3 - 0.0011x_2x_3^2 - 0.019x_3^3 + 28.34,
\end{aligned}
$$

$$\tag{1}$$

where y is the temperature, x_1 is the latitude, x_2 is the longitude, and x_3 is the month.

The regression model is validated by the ratio of the mean square error in the model, and the expression is

$$R^2 = 1 - \frac{\sum_n^1 y_{predict_i} - y_{true_i}^2}{\sum_1^n y_{trueMean_i} - y_{true_i}^2}, i \in (1, n). \tag{2}$$

The value of R^2 is found to be 0.82 after substituting the data. Then the correlation coefficient R is calculated by the following equation,

$$R = \sqrt{R^2}. \tag{3}$$

Based on the fact that $R = 0.906 > 0.8$, the regression relationship is valid.

In summary, there is a large correlation between global temperature and time, longitude, and latitude, and it is in accordance with the relationship of Eq. (1). However, this model is too complex for calculation and may have a large error in the process of landing the actual. Therefore, we have to further analyze the data and select a more suitable model.

4 Data Source and Methodology

4.1 Data Source and Data-processing

We use the self-collected global average temperature as a data set and preprocess it [11]. We determine the uncertainty of the values by means and variances and perform descriptive statistics on the uncertainty. When uncertainty is greater than 1, the data is anomalous. Then such anomalous data are excluded, and the rest of the data are considered as valid data. Next, the temperature values of the missing months are supplemented by the values calculated from the average of two adjacent months. The complete data between 1860 and 2013 are finally retained. Figure 2 is a line graph of the global average temperature change between 1860 and 2013.

As shown in Fig. 2, the temperature trend has always been in an upward trend since 1884, which is relatively stable. So the time period chosen for the data in the model is from January 1884 to September 2013. Observing the global temperature line graph, as shown in Fig. 3, the global temperature fluctuates up and down on a yearly cycle.

We resample the data in order to further determine the trend of the average temperature, reduce the amplitude of the vibration of the data and make its linear pattern more obvious. As shown in the Fig. 4, we decompose the time series and calculate the trend term, seasonal term and residual term of the time series.

The vertical axes of the four subplots in Fig. 4 represent the resampled global average temperature and its trend term, seasonal term, and residual term. Trend term is the increasing or decreasing value in the time series. Residual term represents the random variation in the time series. It can be determined that its non-stationary time series has a strong annual seasonal component and an increasing trend over time. In the following, ARIMA model and LSTM model are built to analyze the global average temperature data and predict the future global temperature level, respectively.

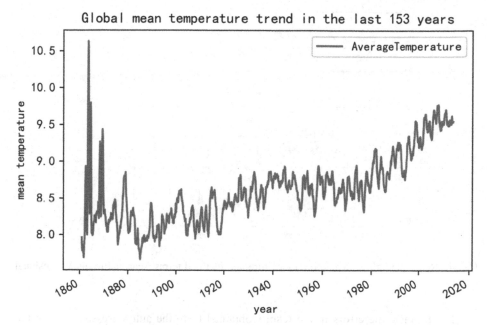

Fig. 2. Global average temperature trend in the last 153 years

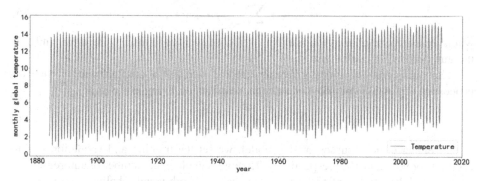

Fig. 3. The global average temperature from 1884 to 2013

4.2 ARIMA

ARIMA model is a regression model, which is one of the methods of time series forecasting analysis. Its autoregressive model expression is

$$y_t = \mu + \sum_{i=1}^{p} \gamma_i y_{t-i} + \varepsilon, \qquad (4)$$

where μ is a constant, p is the order difference, ε is the error, and γ is the autocorrelation coefficient.

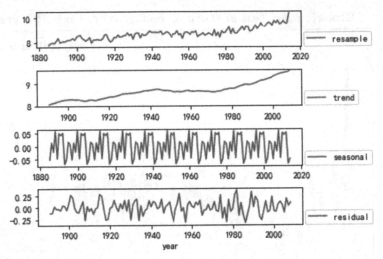

Fig. 4. Resampled global average temperature and its trend terms, seasonal terms and residual terms

To eliminate the errors in the results obtained from the autoregressive model, the following expressions can be used:

$$y_t = \mu + \sum_{i=1}^{q} \beta_i \varepsilon_{t-i} + \varepsilon_t, \tag{5}$$

where μ is a constant, q as the number of sliding average terms ε is the error, and γ is the autocorrelation coefficient.

The autoregressive moving average model requires a combination of the two processes, regression and moving average, with the following expression:

$$y_t = \mu + \sum_{i=1}^{p} \gamma_i y_{t-i} + \sum_{i=1}^{q} \beta_i \varepsilon_{t-i} + \varepsilon_t. \tag{6}$$

To enhance the accuracy of the model, we set the training and validation sets to account for 90% and 10% respectively. Then we calculate the number of autoregressive terms p and the number of sliding average terms q. Both p and q belongs to the model parameters.

4.3 LSTM

LSTM is a special kind of RNNS with additional features to memorize the sequence of data. Through some gates along with a memory line incorporated in a typical LSTM, the memorization of the earlier trend of the data is possible. As shown in Fig. 5, this neural network model can perform regression for long time series [10].

$$\tilde{c}_t = tanh(w_{xc}x_t + w_{ch}x_{t-1} + b_c), \tag{7}$$

$$i_t = \sigma(w_{xi}x_t + w_{hi}h_{t-1} + w_{ci}c_{t-1} + b_c), \tag{8}$$

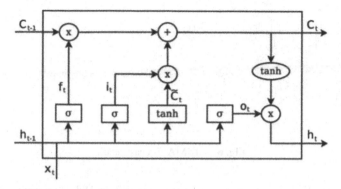

Fig. 5. The structure of LSTM neural network model

$$f_t = \sigma(w_{xf}x_t + w_{hf}h_{t-1} + w_{cf}c_{t-1} + b_f), \tag{9}$$

$$o_t = \sigma(w_{xo}x_t + w_{ho}h_{t-1} + w_{co}c_t + b_o), \tag{10}$$

$$c_t = c_{t-1} \otimes f_t + i_t \otimes \tilde{c}_t, \tag{11}$$

$$h_t = o_t \otimes tanhc_t. \tag{12}$$

In which: $\tilde{c}_t$ denotes the updated state of the memory cell now. i_t, f_t, o_t, c_t and h_t denote the state of the input gate, the forget gate, the output gate, the memory cell, and the output of the hidden layer at time t, respectively. x_i Denotes the input at time t. H_{t-1} and c_{t-1} denote the output of the hidden layer and the memory cell at time $t-1$, respectively. w_{xc} Denote the weight matrices of the memory cell with the input x_i, and w_{ch} denote the weight matrices of the memory cell with the hidden layer. w_{xt}, w_{hi} and w_{ci} denote the weight matrices of the input gate and x_t, the hidden layer, and the memory cell, respectively. w_{xf}, w_{hf} and w_{cf} are the weight matrices of forgetting gate with x_i, output layer, and memory cell, respectively. w_{xo}, w_{ho} and w_{co} are the weight matrices of memory cell with x_i, output layer, and memory cell, respectively. $\otimes$ is the dot product, σ is the Sigmoid activation function, and b_c, b_i, b_f and b_{fo} are for the bias.

5 ARIMA VS LSTM: An Experimental Study of Global Temperature Prediction

5.1 Global Temperature Prediction Based on ARIMA

For the ARIMA (p, d, q) model and the data obtained from the preliminary analysis, we choose the optimal ARIMA $(1, 1, 1)$ model. First, in general, the series can be made smooth by using first-order and second-order differences. First, we choose the difference order d = 1. Then, we adjust the parameters according to the AIC index. The model is most appropriate when the AIC reaches the minimum of negative values. Substituting this temperature data, the ARIMA $(1, 1, 1)$ model is solved to obtain the prediction results of the validation set and compared with the validation set.

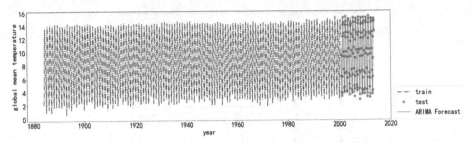

Fig. 6. ARIMA forecast result

As shown in Fig. 6, the results are as follows. Since 1884, the global temperature level has always maintained a steady increase. And the prediction results of its validation set basically overlap with the straight line of the validation set. It shows that the global temperature level in the future will also increase with time. The prediction results of the validation set in the Fig. 6 are basically the same as those of the verification set, which shows that the model is good and can make excellent predictions of global temperature.

With the ARIMA model, we can predict the global average temperature for each month. Substituting the data into the model, we get the annual average temperature in future based on the monthly average temperature in future and visualize the results of prediction.

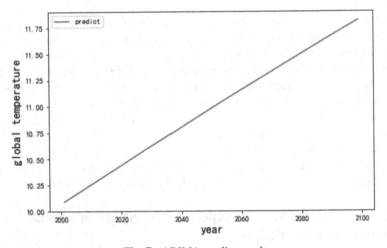

Fig. 7. ARIMA predict result

As shown in Fig. 7, the global average temperature is increasing year by year. The global average temperature will reach 10.53 °C in 2050 and 11.42 °C in 2100.

5.2 Global Temperature Prediction Based on LSTM

To enhance the accuracy of the LSTM model, we now set the training and validation sets to account for 90% and 10%, respectively. We train the LSTM model, where the number of batches size is 200 and the number of neurons in the LSTM layer is 4. The prediction results of the validation set are obtained by substituting the global average temperature data and compared with the true values of the validation set.

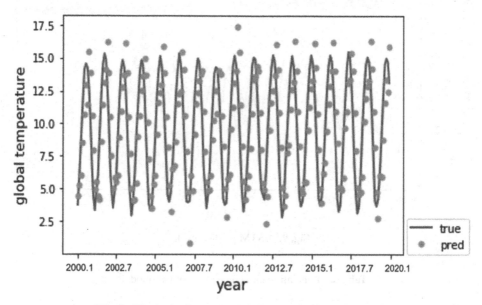

Fig. 8. The real value and prediction result of prediction set

As shown in Fig. 8, the results are as follows. The prediction results of the validation set basically overlap with the trend of the verification set, which shows that the model has a good prediction effect. With the LSTM model, we can predict the global average temperature for each month. Substituting the data into the model, we get the average yearly temperature in the future based on the average monthly temperature in the future and visualize the predicted results.

As shown in Fig. 9, the global average temperature is also increasing. The global average temperature will reach 9.32 °C in 2050 and 10.1 °C in 2100.

5.3 Comparison of Both Global Temperature Prediction Models

Comparing the two global temperature prediction models, RMSE is used to compare the accuracy of the models. RMSE refers to the estimator of the model, which can be used to measure the deviation between the predicted value and the real value. The expression is as follows,

$$RMSE = \sqrt{\frac{1}{n}\sum\nolimits_{k=1}^{n}[S(k) - \overline{S}(k)]^2}.$$ (13)

The RMSE results of ARIMA model and LSTM model are shown in Table 2.

The smaller the RMSE value of the model, the higher the accuracy. Therefore, the ARIMA model is more accurate in the two prediction models.

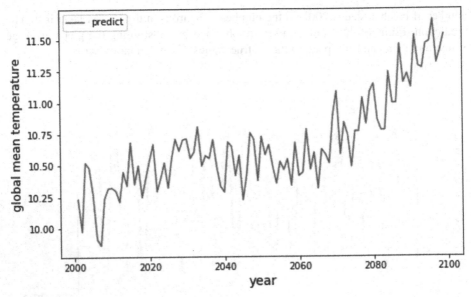

Fig. 9. LSTM predict result

Table 2. Evaluation and comparison of two models

Evaluation index	ARIMA Model	LSTM Model
RMSE	8.439	50.069

This paper speculates that the reason why ARIMA model is better than LSTM may be that the global average temperature data is not very volatile. When the real value fluctuation is not very drastic, the prediction with ARIMA may be more applicable. The neural network LSTM stores data in 'memory nerves', that is, in forgetting gates, input gates, and output gates. The results are not simply averaged, and the predictions may be aggressively biased a bit. The LSTM model may work better when the original data is more volatile.

6   Conclusion

In this paper, we use different methods to study the trend of global average temperature, and use ARIMA model and LSTM model to further analyze the historical data of global average annual temperature. After comparison, the ARIMA model has better prediction effect than the LSTM neural network model. Therefore, the ARIMA model is selected to predict the global average temperature in 2050 and 2100, and the results are very good, which has practical application.

The data selected in this paper all over 100 years. The higher breadth of data not only ensures the rigor of the article, but also eliminates the possibility of inaccurate prediction or classification due to the short time interval. What's more, two models are used in this paper, which are relatively rarely used for global average prediction at home and abroad. In the future, we can apply the two models to temperature prediction in other regions.

In previous studies, using the LSTM model, the prediction results of LSTM model were better compared to ARIMA model. However, in this paper, the prediction effect of ARIMA model is obviously better. We presume the reasons underlying are as follows. The global average temperature data is not very volatile and the principle of ARIMA is sliding average and autoregressive. Therefore, the prediction results are closer to the historical average. And when the real value fluctuation is not very drastic, the prediction by ARIMA may be more applicable. The conclusion can be extended to general data. Further experiments can be conducted in other data with little fluctuation using this conclusion. Also, the two models can be combined in subsequent studies to analyze and predict the global average temperature. Using the ARIMA model, we have predicted the global average annual temperature in 2050 and 2100, and achieved good results. From the available research results, we believe that with the current level of environmental protection, the global average annual temperature will only increase, which will greatly affect people's production and life. We must pay attention to the global warming problem, work together to save energy, develop new energy sources, and make more efforts for sustainable human development.

Acknowledgments. This work was supported by the National Natural Science Foundation of China (Grants No. 61571052) and the innovation and entrepreneurship training program for college students (No. 2023010406013).

References

1. Zhang, G.Q., Li, P.F., Huang, L., Wu, Y.F.: Time series analysis and prediction of global average temperature in the next 50 years. Gansu Sci. Technol. **17**, 72–74 (2008). (in Chinese)
2. Ni, S.N., Tang, B., Cai, J.H.: Global annual mean temperature prediction based on combined GM-ARMA Model. China New Technology and New Products. **12**, 9–10 (2008). (in Chinese)
3. Zhu, L.Y., Li, Q.Q.: Global warming: temperature prediction based on ARIMA. In Proceedings of the 2023 7th International Conference on Innovation in Artificial Intelligence, pp. 121–128(2023)
4. Zhang, G.P.: Time Series Forecasting Using A Hybrid ARIMA and Neural Network Model. Neurocomputing. **50**, 159–175 (2003). (in Chinese)
5. Xue, Y.F., Yang, C.M.: Global temperature change and its trend prediction in the last century. Sichuan Meteorology. **03**, 16–19 (2006). (in Chinese)
6. Tao, Y., Du, J.L.: Long and short-term memory network temperature prediction based on random forest. Comput. Eng. Des. **03**, 737–743 (2019). (in Chinese)
7. Hou, H.Q.: A global climate change prediction model based on BP neural network. Science, Technology, and Innovation. **09**, 10–11 (2021). (in Chinese)
8. Wu, H., Yang, T., Li, H.: Air quality prediction model based on mRMR–RF feature selection and ISSA–LSTM. Sci. Rep. **13**, 12825 (2023)
9. Taylor, J.W., Buizza, R.: Neural network load forecasting with weather ensemble predictions. IEEE Trans. Power Syst. A Publ. Power Eng. Soc. **3**, 626–632 (2002)
10. Wang, Y.H.: Analysis of global temperature prediction based on ARIMA model and LSTM neural network. Sci. Technol. Innovation **35**, 166–170 (2021). (in Chinese)

11. Siami-Namini, S., Tavakoli, N., Siami Namin, A.: A comparison of ARIMA and LSTM in forecasting time series. vol. 10, pp. 1394–1401(2018)
12. Elsaraiti, M., Merabet, A.: A comparative analysis of the ARIMA and LSTM predictive models and their effectiveness for predicting wind speed. Energies **14**, 20 (2021)
13. Long, B., Tan, F., Newman, M.: Forecasting the monkeypox outbreak using ARIMA, prophet, neuralprophet, and LSTM models in the united states. Forecasting. **5**, 127–137 (2023)
14. Duan, J., Gong, Y., Luo, J., Zhao, Z.: Air-quality prediction based on the ARIMA-CNN-LSTM combination model optimized by dung beetle optimizer. Sci. Rep.**13**, 12127 (2023)
15. Wang, Y.: Base station mobile traffic prediction based on ARIMA and LSTM model. In: Ma, M. (ed.) Proceedings of the 4th International Conference on Telecommunications and Communication Engineering. ICTCE 2020. Lecture Notes in Electrical Engineering, vol. 797, pp. 164–175. Springer, Singapore (2022).https://doi.org/10.1007/978-981-16-5692-7_18
16. BERKELEY EARTH, https://berkeleyearth.org/data/
17. Zhang, Y., Yan, K., Liu, Z., Pu, J.B., Zhang, Y.M., Zeng, Y.L.: Spatial and temporal variation of global surface temperature from 1901 to 2018 based on CRU data. J. Capital Normal Univ. (Nat. Sci. Ed.) **06**, 51–68 (2020). (in Chinese)

Virtual Reality and Human-Computer Interaction

Real-Time Image Stitching with Transformers for Complex Traffic Environment

Zhiwei Shen[1,2]([✉]) and Bin Kong[1,3,4]

[1] Institute of Intelligent Machines, Chinese Academy of Sciences, Hefei 230031, China
`shenzw@mail.ustc.edu.cn, bkong@iim.ac.cn`
[2] University of Science and Technology of China, Hefei 230026, China
[3] Anhui Engineering Laboratory for Intelligent Driving Technology and Application, Hefei 230088, China
[4] Innovation Research Institute of Robotics and Intelligent Manufacturing (Hefei), Chinese Academy of Sciences, Hefei 230088, China

Abstract. The existing traditional image stitching methods suffer from accumulating errors in the matching process, which severely limits the final stitching results. Additionally, they cannot find correct correspondences in complex scenes with poor texture, repetitive patterns, and lighting variations. To address these issues, we propose a real-time image stitching method based on the Transformer structure. The self-attention mechanism of the Transformer can dynamically adjust the receptive field based on input content, allowing for effective global information retrieval. Compared to traditional manual and CNN-based deep learning methods, our approach generates dense and high-quality matches even in complex environments. We reduce the complexity of the Transformer model and improve matching speed through knowledge distillation. We use the Kmeans algorithm to optimize point selection for feature point screening and compute the homography matrix value based on the matching result for pixel transformation. After aligning the overlapping regions of the images and averaging them, we apply mask weights obtained from Gaussian fusion of target image layers to achieve the final stitching result. Experimental results demonstrate that our method produces more accurate matches in complex scenes with weak textures compared to traditional and deep learning methods, while also having the shortest matching and stitching times and good stitching results.

Keywords: Image stitching, Transformer · Knowledge distillation · Detector-free

1 Introduction

Weak texture and other complex environments have always been a challenging problem in the field of computer vision. Due to the lack of rich texture information on weakly textured surfaces, the gray-level distribution of pixel neighborhoods is similar, resulting in poor pixel separability. The most popular method for image stitching is currently based on feature points, with commonly used feature extraction methods including SIFT [1] and SURF [2]. However, these methods based on gradient-based feature extraction are no longer applicable in complex traffic environments with weak textures. SuperPoint [3] proposes a self-supervised training method based on homography adaptation, which uses neural networks to learn the mapping relationship between images to be registered and becomes one of the best CNN-based methods. SuperGlue [4] proposes a learning-based local feature matching method, which solves the differentiable optimal transport problem through GNN to construct the loss function. LoFTR [5] uses self-attention and cross-attention transformation layers to find feature point matches in images, while Transformer's [6] global receptive field allows it to detect sparse feature correspondences even in weak texture regions. However, the quadratic complexity of the Transformer network requires a large amount of computing resources for training and inference, making it difficult to adapt to low-end devices with limited computing resources. TRLWAM [7] improves the Transformer structure by introducing a new Vision Transformer attention model, LW-Attention, which limits self-attention calculations to non-overlapping local windows and reduces the computational complexity of each window to linear using the linear dot product of kernel feature maps [8]. It constructs a coarse-to-fine detector-free feature matching method that can extract dense matches in low-texture or repetitive pattern areas in indoor environments, with good computational performance and reduced memory consumption. However, TRLWAM is still insufficient for practical applications on low-end devices with lower computing power.

To address the issue of computational complexity, we employed knowledge distillation [9], which can reduce the computation complexity of complex models while maintaining their accuracy to adapt to devices with lower computing power. Based on this observation, we designed a real-time image stitching method based on Transformer. We compressed the TRLWAM model by retraining it using knowledge distillation and the teacher-student network paradigm, reducing network parameters and model latency while retaining some advantages of the original model. As a result, we obtained a lightweight feature matching model with better real-time performance. After completing the matching, we constructed a real-time image stitching method applicable to complex traffic scenes using homography matrix and Gaussian fusion.

2   Related work

Image stitching is a key and challenging computer vision task that has been well studied in the past few decades. Its purpose is to construct panoramic images with a wider field of view from different images captured from different viewing positions. This technology has a wide range of applications in various fields such as biology [10], medicine [11], autonomous driving [12], and virtual reality (VR) [13]. The mainstream solution for image stitching is feature-based methods, where feature detection is the first step that directly affects the stitching performance. Then, a parameterized image alignment model is established by matching features, which can warp the target image to align with the reference image. Finally, the stitched image can be obtained by assigning pixel values to each pixel in the overlapping region between warped images. Homography transformation is the most commonly used image alignment model, which includes translation, rotation, scaling, and vanishing point transformations, correctly explaining the transformation from one 2D plane to another [14]. Feature-based stitching methods heavily rely on feature detection, so the stitching performance may sharply decrease or even fail in scenes with few features or low resolution. Additionally, [15] has been pointed out that a single homography cannot explain all alignments at different depth levels in practical scenes, which also affects the stitching effect.

With the development of feature matching methods, the problem of extracting features in complex environments with weak textures has been improved. De-Maeztu et al. [16] and Chen [17] proposed an energy function optimization method that improves the accuracy of matching in weak texture regions through smooth constraint terms. However, for large weak texture regions, the registration error rate is still high. Jiang et al. [18] attempted to achieve registration of small weak texture areas through color segmentation, but this method relies on the accuracy of color segmentation and has low accuracy when the weak texture area is large. MagicPoint [19] was the first successful deep learning-based local feature extraction method, which achieved excellent results compared to traditional methods using detector-based manual design methods. Super-Point [3] further improved the performance of keypoint detection and description by using homography matrix for self-supervised training based on MagicPoint [18]. Super-Glue [4] uses graph neural networks to learn the matching relationship between two sets of key points with descriptors, thereby improving the accuracy and robustness of matching. Recently, some detector-free feature matching methods have been proposed. NCNet [19] directly learns dense correspondences in an end-to-end manner by constructing a 4D cost volume to enumerate all possible matches between images. LoFTR [5] uses Transformer as the core architecture to extract local features directly from the original image and perform matching. Transformer [6] has a global view, and even in complex environments such as weak textures, LoFTR can produce high-quality dense matches. However, the computational complexity of Transformer also grows quadratically, requiring a lot of time and computing memory. TRLWAM [7] designed a new Vision Transformer attention model, linear window attention (LW-Attention), to construct a detector-free feature matching method with linear complexity with respect to input sequences, which improves computational efficiency and reduces running time. It can produce dense high-quality matches in complex scenes such as weak textures. However, the computational memory requirements are still difficult to meet for practical applications.

To reduce computational memory while ensuring high-quality matching, current methods mainly include quantization [20], pruning [21], and knowledge distillation [22]. Quantization converts high-precision models into low-precision ones, reducing the number of parameters and computation to speed up the model. This method typically requires a special training process and can only be implemented on high-end GPUs. Pruning reduces model size and computation by removing unnecessary neurons or weights, but it requires more time and computational resources and more manual intervention to accurately evaluate the impact of each parameter. Knowledge distillation improves the performance of small models by transferring knowledge from large models. It reduces the size of the model while maintaining accuracy, enabling faster inference and training. However, knowledge distillation may also lead to decreased model accuracy because the knowledge is transferred to smaller models through an approximation. These methods aim to accelerate the model by reducing its size and computation.

3 Method

3.1 Image Matching TRLWAM

The Transformer's attention mechanism allows it to capture long-term dependencies, making it widely applicable to various visual tasks. However, its quadratic computational complexity is a major obstacle for precise prediction in visual tasks. To address this limitation, TRLWAM [7] introduced a new attention model called Linear Window Attention (LWA) for visual transformers. LWA limits self-attention computation to non-overlapping local windows, represents self-attention as a linear dot product of kernel feature maps, and reduces the computational complexity of each window from quadratic to linear using the constraint properties of matrix multiplication. TRLWAM applies LWA to feature matching and constructs a detector-free coarse-to-fine feature matching method, abbreviated as TRLWAM. At the coarse level, dense pixel-level matching is extracted, and at the fine level, the final matching result is refined through multi-head multi-layer perceptrons. TRLWAM can extract dense matches from low-texture or repetitive pattern areas in indoor environments and has shown good performance on the MegaDepth [23] and HPatches [24] datasets (Fig. 1).

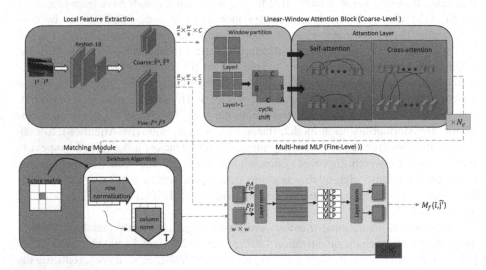

Fig. 1. TRLWAM model structure

3.2 Knowledge Distillation Model

Due to the quadratic complexity of computation and memory requirements per layer, most transformer-based methods require significant computational resources for training and inference. Therefore, it is challenging to make them suitable for running on low-end devices with limited computing resources. To address the high computational complexity, we have improved the transformer structure with a Linear-Window Attention Block

(LWA). However, TRLWAM is still insufficient for real-time performance and running on devices with low computational efficiency. Therefore, we use knowledge distillation to improve computational efficiency while maintaining the advantages of the model. The main idea of this method is to significantly reduce the number of model parameters and transfer knowledge. We only retain the LWA of TRLWAM for coarse feature matching and iteratively select fewer layers in all model blocks (Fig. 2).

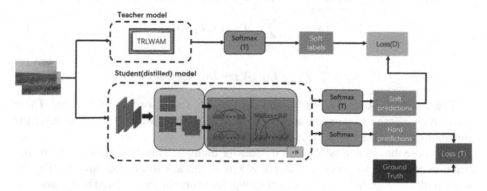

Fig. 2. Knowledge distillation model structure

We constructed a knowledge distillation model for TRLWAM, as shown in the figure, based on the method proposed in [9]. We obtained coarse matching pairs from the TRLWAM pairing. To compute the probability estimate of feature matching, we obtained the score matrix S(i,j) and matching probability P_c from the LWA of TRLWAM. The matrix S(i,j) was used to transfer knowledge from the teacher model to the student model using Kullback-Leibler with soft targets as the global loss function L_D.

$$L_D = \sum P_{stu} \log(\frac{P_{stu}}{P_c}) \tag{1}$$

We use the softmax function with temperature parameter T as shown in Eq. (2). When T = 1, it is the normal softmax calculation. By setting T > 1, we obtain soft softmax. We process the final outputs of both the Teacher model and the Student model using soft softmax. P_{tea} represents the soft target output of the Teacher model, while P_{stu} represents the soft target output of the Student model. Soft targets provide more information compared to unprocessed outputs. The Student model is trained using cross-entropy loss L_D after processing with soft targets.

$$Soft \max(z_i) = \log(\frac{e^{\frac{z_i}{T}}}{\sum_j e^{\frac{z_j}{T}}}) \tag{2}$$

$$P_{stu,i} = \log(\frac{e^{\frac{S_{stu,i}}{T}}}{\sum_j e^{\frac{S_{stu,j}}{T}}}) \tag{3}$$

$$P_{tea,i} = \log\left(\frac{e^{\frac{S_{tea,i}}{T}}}{\sum_j e^{\frac{S_{tea,j}}{T}}}\right) \tag{4}$$

Set parameter T to 5. During training, use L_D decay estimation to select iterations. The optimal increase in entropy value corresponds to better knowledge transfer effects. The complete loss function L of the trained model is a weighted sum of L_D and L_T.

$$L_T = -\sum_{i,j \in M_c^{gt}} P_{tea} \log P_{stu}(i,j) \tag{5}$$

$$L_T = L_D \cdot W_d + L_T \cdot W_t \tag{6}$$

The weight factors, W_d and W_t, are 0.4 and 0.6, respectively, in this paper. These values were chosen to compensate for the relatively small value of L_D and make the contributions of these two parts more equal.

We chose the BlendedMVS [25] dataset for training. This dataset uses a 3D reconstruction algorithm to generate textured 3D mesh models from input images. The 3D mesh model is rendered to each camera viewpoint to obtain the rendered image and corresponding depth map. The BlendedMVS dataset contains 113 scenes, each with 20 to 1000 input images, for a total of 17,818 images. The scenes in the BlendedMVS dataset have various camera trajectories. Non-structured camera trajectories can better model different image capture styles, making the network more capable of reconstructing the real world with better generalization performance.

From the experimental results in Fig. 3, we can see that knowledge distillation reduces the image matching performance of the original TRLWAM method to some extent, but greatly saves computation memory and running time.

3.3 Image Stitching Model

The self-attention mechanism of the Transformer architecture can dynamically adjust the receptive field based on input content to obtain effective global information, providing significant advantages over traditional handcrafted methods and CNN-based deep learning approaches. The TRLWAM method for image matching without detectors can produce dense and high-quality matches in complex traffic scenes with no texture. We reduced the computational complexity of the TRLWAM method and improved its matching speed while retaining the performance advantages of the Transformer algorithm through knowledge distillation. We then used Kmeans to optimize point selection, filtered feature points based on the matching results, calculated the homography matrix value, and implemented pixel transformation and unified coordinates to achieve image alignment and averaging using overlapping regions. The final result was obtained by Gaussian blending of each image layer with mask weights set accordingly. The framework of the stitching model is shown in Fig. 3.

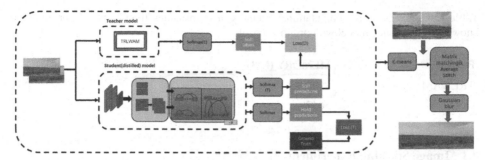

Fig. 3. Image Mosaic model

4 Experiments

TRLWAM can generate dense and accurate matches both indoors and outdoors, thanks to the use of self-attention and cross-attention layers in the transformer. The attention mechanism allows local features to be transformed into context-aware and position-dependent representations, which is crucial for TRLWAM to achieve high-quality matches in complex scenes with low texture on walls and whiteboards.

By establishing a knowledge distillation model, TRLWAM is compressed into a lighter student model while maintaining its accuracy as much as possible. As shown in Fig. 4, the number of points generated by the distilled model is significantly reduced compared to the original model, but the accuracy remains unchanged. Through the comparison data in the stitching experiment in complex scenes below, we can see that the distilled model still has a significant advantage in complex scenes.The following methods are all performed on a PC running Ubuntu Linux, equipped with an RTX 2080Ti GPU. The RTX 2080Ti has 11GB of GDDR6 VRAM with a speed of 14Gbps. The CPU is Intel Xeon Silver 4210.

Fig. 4. Knowledge distillation model matching results

It can be seen from Table 1 that the new model greatly reduces the loss of GPU computing memory and improves computational efficiency. It also has a significant advantage in matching time.

Table 1. Comparison of computational memory and matching time required for training knowledge distillation model with original model.

Process	MEMORY (MB)	Match time
TRLWAM	8192	95
Ours	5647	16

4.1 Image Stitching Experiment

We selected three sets of data for image matching and stitching comparison, including scenes with weak textures (a), unstructured road (b), and repeated patterns (c) in complex traffic scenarios. The data were collected by the visual module of our laboratory's intelligent unmanned vehicles, which are equipped with stereolabs ZED MINI cameras for image acquisition and transmission. All three sets of data were sampled from complex traffic scenarios in the field. We used SIFT and SURF algorithms, commonly used in feature stitching in traditional algorithms, which are still widely used in computer vision tasks. Superpoint and SuperGlue are the most representative feature matching methods based on CNN structures in recent years. Superpoint is used as a feature detector, and SuperGlue is used as a matching backend. For the traditional handcrafted detection algorithms SIFT and SURF, we used brute force matching to find feature points, then used KNN (K-Nearest Neighbor) algorithm to match feature points, and finally set a mask to perform stitching through perspective transformation. For the Superpoint + SuperGlue CNN-based method, we compared it using a similar fusion stitching method to ensure fairness. The selected three sets of data are shown in Fig. 5.

In Fig. 6, we compared the results of traditional handcrafted methods SIFT and SURF with our method. We only kept the results of Superpoint + SuperGlue and our method for comparison. From the experimental results, as observed in Fig. 6(a) and Table 2, it is evident that our method extracts features in approximately the same quantity as the superpoint + superglue algorithm in low-texture environments. However, compared to the Superpoint + SuperGlue method, our approach extracts more matching points on low-texture surfaces while achieving shorter matching and stitching times. The matches extracted by the superpoint + superglue algorithm are primarily concentrated in regions with higher texture complexity, as depicted in Fig. 6(a).

As shown in Fig. 6(b), our method extracts a slightly lower number of matching pairs compared to SIFT in unstructured road environments, but it is still sufficient for subsequent stitching. Furthermore, as indicated by Table 2, we have a clear advantage in terms of processing time.

In the scene with repetitive patterns 6(c), our method demonstrates excellent performance in terms of both the number of extracted features and processing time, giving us a certain advantage. Additionally, we have set the same accuracy threshold for our experiments, which provides a solid foundation for higher matching accuracy in subsequent stitching applications.

Fig.5. Three groups of experimental data: weak texture scene, unstructured road, repeated pattern scene.

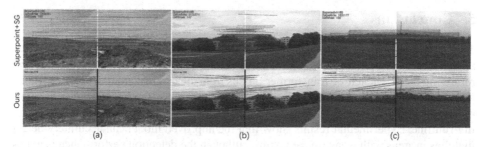

Fig.6. Comparison of matching results between Superpoint + SuperGlue and our method.

4.2 Image Stitching Results

The Stitching results of this method are shown as follows (Fig. 7):

Table 2. Matching and Stitching results of each algorithm.

DATA	Algorithm	Match	Extract	Match ratio	Match time(s)	Stictch time(s)
A	SIFT	3	>2000	0	0.43	*
	SURF	1	>2000	0	0.24	*
	Superpoint	195	654	29	0.15	0.20
	Ours	179	179	100	0.02	0.14
B	SIFT	492	1891	26	0.25	0.76
	SURF	194	656	29	0.18	0.71
	Superpoint	147	312	47	0.08	0.23
	Ours	293	293	100	0.02	0.17
C	SIFT	191	663	28	0.52	1.37
	SURF	144	655	21	0.42	1.30
	Superpoint	100	162	61	0.10	0.22
	Ours	226	226	100	0.02	0.15

    (a)   (b)   (c)

Fig.7. The result of Stitching in complex scenes

5 Conclusions

This article presents a Transformer-based image stitching method applied in complex traffic scenarios. By compressing the TRLWAM model using knowledge distillation and removing precise matching transformer blocks from the original architecture, we significantly reduced the number of top layers and lightweighted the transformers in coarse matching blocks. Our design greatly reduces computational memory while decreasing runtime. Experimental results show that the improved model can accurately detect matches in areas with weak image texture, although the detection performance is not as dense as the original baseline model, real-time performance has improved qualitatively. Compared with traditional manual methods and CNN methods, our approach has certain advantages in complex scenes with weak textures, lighting changes, and repetitive patterns, demonstrating good performance.

Acknowledgments. This work was supported by the Institute of Robotics and Intelligent Manufacturing Innovation, Chinese Academy of Sciences (Grant number: C2021002).

References

1. Lowe, D.G.: Distinctive image features from scale-invariant keypoints. Int. J. Comput. Vision **60**(2), 91–110 (2004)
2. Bay, H., Ess, A., Tuytelaars, T., et al.: Speeded-up robust features (SURF). Comput. Vis. Image Underst. **110**(3), 346–359 (2008)
3. DeTone, D., Malisiewicz, T., Rabinovich, A.: Superpoint: self-supervised interest point detection and description. In: Proceedings of the IEEE Conference on Computer Vision and Pattern Recognition Workshops, pp. 224–236 (2018)
4. Sarlin, P.E., DeTone, D., Malisiewicz, T., Rabinovich, A.: "Superglue: learning feature matching with graph neural networks. In: Proceedings of the IEEE/CVF Conference on Computer Vision and Pattern
5. Sun, J., Shen, Z., Wang, Y., et al.: LoFTR: detector-free local feature matching with transformers.In: Proceedings of the IEEE/CVF Conference on Computer Vision and Pattern Recognition, pp. 8922–8931 (2021)
6. Vaswani, A., Shazeer, N., Parmar, N., et al.: Attention is all you need. In: Advances in Neural Information Processing Systems, vol. 30 (2017)
7. Shen, Z., Kong, B., Dong, X.: Transformer with linear-window attention for feature matching (TRLWAM). IEEE Access (2023)
8. Katharopoulos, A., Vyas, A., Pappas, N., Fleuret, F.:Transformers are RNNs: fast autoregressive transformers with linear attention. In ICML, vol. 3 (2020)
9. Hinton, G., Vinyals, O., Dean, J.: Distilling theknowledge in a neural network (2015)
10. Semenishchev, E., Voronin, V., Marchuk, V., Tolstova, I.: Method for stitching microbial images using a neural network. In: Mobile Multimedia/Image Processing, Security, and Applications 2017, vol. 10221, p. 102210O, International Society for Optics and Photonics (2017)
11. Li, D., He, Q., Liu, C., Yu, H.: Medical image stitching using parallel sift detection and transformation fitting by particle swarm optimization. J. Med. Imaging Health Inf. **7**(6), 1139–1148 (2017)
12. Wang,J., Yu, W., Li, B.: Multi-scenes image stitching based on autonomous driving. In: 2020 IEEE 4th Information Technology, Networking, Electronic and Automation Control Conference (ITNEC), vol. 1, pp. 694–698, IEEE (2020)
13. Li, J., Zhao, Y., Ye, W., Yu, K., Ge, S.: Attentive deep stitching and quality assessment for 360 omnidirectional images. IEEE J. Sel. Top. Signal Process. **14**(1), 209–221 (2019)
14. Nie, L., Lin, C., Liao, K., Liu, M., Zhao, Y.: A view-free image stitching network based on global homography. J. Vis. Commun. Image Representation **73**, 102950 (2020)
15. Nie, L., et al.: Unsupervised deep image stitching: reconstructing stitched features to images. IEEE Trans. Image Process. **30**, 6184–6197 (2021)
16. De-Maeztu, L., Villanueva, A., Cabeza, R.: Near real-time stereo matching using geodesic diffusion. IEEE Trans. Pattern Anal. Mach. Intell. **34**(2), 410–416 (2012)
17. Chen, S.Y., Wang, Z.J.: Acceleration strategies in generalized belief propagation. IEEE Trans. Industr. Inf. **8**(1), 41–48 (2012)
18. Haskins, G., Kruger, U., Yan, P.: Deep learning in medical image registration: a survey. Mach. Vis. Appl. **31**, 1–18 (2019)
19. Rocco, I., et al.: Neighbourhood consensus networks. In: Advances in Neural Information Processing Systems, vol. 31 (2018)
20. Gholami, A., Kim, S., Dong, Z., Yao, Z., Mahoney, M.W., Keutzer, K.:A Survey of quantization methods for efficient neural network inference." ArXiv abs/2103.13630 (2021)
21. Vadera, S., Ameen, S.: Methods for pruning deep neural networks. IEEE Access, 1–1 (2020)
22. Gou, J., et al.: Knowledge distillation: a survey. Int. J. Comput. Vis. **129**, 1–31 (2021)

23. Li, Z., Snavely, N.: MegaDepth: learning single-view depth prediction from internet photos. In: 2018 IEEE/CVF Conference on Computer Vision and Pattern Recognition, pp. 2041–2050 (2018)
24. Balntas, V., Lenc, K., Vedaldi, A., Mikolajczyk, K.: HPatches: a benchmark and evaluation of handcrafted and learned local descriptors. In: CVPR, p. 5 (2017)
25. Yao, Y., et al.: Blendedmvs: a large-scale dataset for generalized multi-view stereo networks (2020)

Research on 3D Visual Perception Quality Metric Based on the Principle of Light Field Image Display

Linkai Lyu[1], Benzhi Yang[2], Wenjun Hou[3,4,5(✉)], Wei Yu[2], and Bing Bai[1]

[1] School of Modern Post (School of Automation), Beijing University of Posts and Telecommunications, No. 10 Xitucheng Road, Beijing 100876, China
[2] China Mobile Research Institute, Beijing 100053, China
[3] School of Digital Media & Design Arts, Beijing University of Posts and Telecommunications, No. 10 Xitucheng Road, Beijing 100876, China
hwj1505@bupt.edu.cn
[4] Beijing Key Laboratory of Network System and Network Culture, No. 10 Xitucheng Road, Beijing 100876, China
[5] Key Laboratory of Interactive Technology and Experience System, Ministry of Culture and Tourism, No. 10 Xitucheng Road, Beijing 100876, China

Abstract. At present, many metrics for 3D visual perception quality of light field images (LFIs) come from studies in the evaluation of traditional stereoscopic display or 2D display. Since these metrics do not take into account the optical display principle of the light field, their correlation with the subjective evaluation of LFIs is often weak. To address this problem, this study designed a new objective evaluation metric for the LFI—Density of perceptible viewpoints (DPV), which reflects the number of perceptible viewpoints at a certain observation angle. The performance differences between DPV and PSNR and SSIM are further compared based on the evaluation experiments of six light field scenes. The results show that the new metric has better correlation than PSNR and SSIM in reflecting the 3D visual perception quality of the human eye for LFI. Finally, a classification of 3D visual experience based on DPV is made in order to apply DPV.

Keywords: Light field image · 3D vision · Density of perceptible viewpoints · Evaluation metric

1 Introduction

Light is an important information carrier in the material world, and the main source of information for humans relies on the visual perception of visible light. Previous studies have shown that the 4D light field function L (u,v,s,t) can fully describe the light perceptible to the human eye through the intersection of two disjoint planes (u,v), (s,t) and light [1, 2]. The light field image (LFI) is a 2D visual representation of the light field function, which records the position and angle information of the light [3]. With the light field display technology, naked-eye 3D display of the LFI can be realized [4], which not only provides people with a more immersive and realistic viewing experience [5], but also has important applications in virtual reality [6], education and training [7], industrial inspection [8] and other fields. Therefore, evaluating the 3D visual perceptual quality of the LFI accurately is important to process light field data more effectively, enhance the visual experience of users, and promote the business applications of light field technology.

In recent years, with the continuous pursuit of 3D vision, light field display technology has made significant progress in the commercial sector. At the same time, a large number of consumer-grade light field display devices have emerged, the most representative of which is the Looking Glass series [9]. In traditional 3D vision evaluation studies, testers are given stereo vision based on the principle of left and right view parallax, which generally has two viewpoints [10]. However, based on the high-dimensional feature data of light-field images, light-field display devices can provide stereoscopic vision with multiple viewpoints, which leads to traditional evaluation metrics that are not fully applicable to the 3D visual perception quality assessment of LFIs. Therefore, there is a gap in metrics research related to 3D visual perceptual quality assessment of LFIs. And relevant research is urgently needed.

Based on the display principle of LFIs in current mainstream light field displays, this study proposes an objective evaluation metric——Density of perceptible viewpoints (DPV), which can be used to evaluate the 3D visual perception quality of LFIs. The calculation of DPV requires the acquisition of two key parameters: (a) the number of viewpoints that can be provided by the LFI, which is obtained from the sub-aperture image of the light field; (b) the view angle (VA) of the LFI device, which is calculated from the refractive metric of the column lens and other parameters.

To verify the validity and advancedness of the DPV metric, this study designs and conducts experiments on 3D visual perceptual quality assessment of LFIs. Using light field display devices to show LFIs, and the subjective evaluation of the "stereoscopic nature" of the LFIs is recorded using a scale to investigate the correlation between DPV and the traditional metrics peak signal-to-noise ratio (PSNR) and structural similarity metric (SSIM) with the subjective 3D visual perception quality. The results show that the DPV metric performs better than traditional metrics in assessing the quality of 3D visual perception of LFIs.

The structure of this paper is arranged as follows: Sect. 2 introduces the current research status of subjective and objective evaluation metrics of LFIs and the problems to be solved; Sect. 3 introduces the principle of the LFI and proposes the DPV metric and its calculation method on this basis; Sect. 4 designs experiments to verify the validity and advancedness of the DPV metric and classifies the 3D visual perception experience level according to DPV; Part 5 presents conclusions and discusses future research directions.

2   The Associated Research

Metrics are the key to assess the quality of 3D visual perception of LFIs. In recent years, with the increasing development of light field technology, many excellent research projects have proposed relevant metrics from different perspectives, including both qualitative and quantitative metrics. The summary of metrics research is shown in Table 1.

Qualitative metrics are often used in subjective quality evaluation experiments to describe the quality of human subjective perception of 3D vision. The paper [11, 12] explained the "naturalness" and "stereo" metrics in detail. The "naturalness" metric describes the comprehensive effect of color, luminance, and contrast of the LFI, while the "stereo" metric describes the effect of parallax conditions on the depth of the objective scene. Meanwhile, the literature [13] considers that "comfort" should be a comprehensive description of the physiological state of eye fatigue and brain neurological fatigue.

Table1. Previous researches of 3D visual perception quality indicators for light field images

Metric Type		References	Metric
Subjective		[11, 12]	Naturalness, three-dimensionality
		[13]	Comfort
Objective	Collection	[16, 17]	Microlens array and detector spacing, adjacent microlens center spacing; Spatial resolution, angular resolution
	Code	[18, 19]	peak signal-to-noise ratio (PSNR), structural similarity metric (SSIM); Light field entropy
	Reconfiguration	[20, 21]	Field of Parallax, Scattered focus, Pixel Consistency
	Rendering	[24, 25]	Minimum sampling, camera resolution, maximum parallax of adjacent views
	Display	[27]	Crosstalk rate, brightness, contrast, color temperature, color gamut

Qualitative metric results are in line with human visual perception characteristics and are more reliable [9], but subjective assessment requires a lot of labor cost and time cost [14]. Therefore, quantitative metrics need to be introduced to simulate human subjective perception of LFIs from an objective perspective using computers. By automatically evaluating the quality of 3D visual perception, we can optimize various LFIs and stereo display systems. Based on the life cycle of "capture-encoding-reconstruction-rendering-display" of LFIs [15], the current research on quantitative metrics can be summarized into five categories.

The first category is the metrics related to LFI acquisition. Literature [16] proposed that due to the need of light field information reconstruction, the two metrics of the spacing between the microlens array plane and the detector plane and the center interval of adjacent microlenses will affect the 3D perception quality of the final LFI; literature [17] suggested that the spatial resolution and angular resolution of the light field acquisition device with multi-sensor capture technology or time-series capture technology will greatly affect the estimation of the depth of the light field and thus the 3D perception quality of the LFI.

The second category is the metrics related to the encoding of LFIs. Some researchers have tried to evaluate the coding of LFIs by using the evaluation metrics of traditional planar image coding, such as PSNR and SSIM [18]. However, the traditional planar image evaluation metric does not take into account that the LFI has higher dimensional feature data, so its evaluation results often do not characterize the coding quality well; to address the above problems, the literature [19] proposed the light field entropy metric based on considering the characteristics of light field 4D structure and optical distortion. By modeling distortion as a random distribution and using KL scatter to measure the offset of the distribution due to coding loss.

The third category is the metrics related to LFI reconstruction. The literature [20] states that the FOP is determined by the angular range of the light captured by the light field camera, which directly affects the observable range of the stereo scene to the human eye. The literature [21] proposes to evaluate the reconstruction effect of LFIs using two quantitative metrics, namely, scatter focus and pixel consistency. The above two metrics are characterized by the gradient value of the refocused image, and the variance value of the pixels within the focused stack image, respectively.

The fourth category is the metrics related to LFI rendering. The classical light field rendering methods are based on resampling and interpolation of rays [22] and geometric information [23]. For the first type of rendering methods, the literature [24, 25] argues that insufficient sampling number leads to ghosting effect in light field rendering. Therefore, the minimum sampling number metric is investigated, and it is proposed that the minimum sampling number varies according to the resolution of the light field camera and the maximum parallax of adjacent views; if the second type of rendering method is adopted, the minimum sampling number required will be greatly reduced [26].

The fifth category is metrics related to LFI display. Since these metrics are closely related to the intrinsic parameters of display devices and cannot be easily linked to LFIs, research on this area is relatively lacking. The literature [27] summarizes key quantitative indicators such as crosstalk rate, brightness, contrast ratio, color temperature, and color gamut for three mainstream light field display technologies, namely, column mirror type, directional backlight type, and liquid crystal raster type, and measures and evaluates them separately.

In summary, the current qualitative assessment metrics about the 3D visual perception quality of LFIs contain three aspects of naturalness, stereo and comfort, and the related research has been relatively mature. The quantitative evaluation metrics are mainly proposed from the computer graphics perspective around the four aspects of LFI acquisition, coding, reconstruction and rendering, while the metrics based on the principle of light field display technology are relatively lacking. Therefore, this study proposes a new metric—DPV.

3   A New Metric-Viewpoint Perception Density

3.1   Light Field Images and Display Devices

The use of time-series capture technology to acquire LFIs is currently the most mature LFI acquisition method, while having the mainstream light field display devices compatible with the image format [28]. The technical principle can be summarized as follows: using a single image sensor like a sensor to capture multiple light field samples from different viewing angles through multiple exposures. Its typical approach is to use a sensor mounted on a mechanical frame to measure the light field at different locations, as shown in Fig. 1.

The working process of acquiring LFIs using the temporal capture technique is shown in Fig. 2. By visualization, the areas shaded in red are the overlapping parts of the camera views at multiple locations, while in some areas at the edges, the camera views do not overlap. Therefore, care should be taken in the acquisition to keep the subject within the overlapping view cones and visible in all views, so that a set of time-series LFIs with good results can be obtained, as shown in Fig. 3.

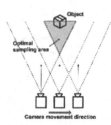

Fig. 1. (left). Light field camera based on time series shooting technology

Fig. 2. (right). Working process of capturing light field images using time series based acquisition technique.

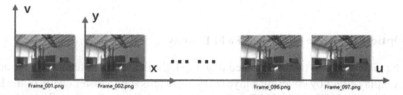

Fig. 3. Light field images captured based on time series technology.

The Looking Glass Portrait is a commercially available light field display with outstanding 3D display capability, enabling multi-view naked eye stereo vision with large free viewing angles. At the same time, it is equipped with an algorithm designed for displaying time-series LFIs, which is capable of resolving and rendering LFIs obtained using time-series capture technology. Therefore, Looking Glass Portrait has become one of the most popular light field display devices, and its key parameters are shown in Table 2.

To display LFIs using Looking Glass Portrait, the original image format needs to be adjusted to meet the requirements of the Quilts standard, an image standard used by the Looking Glass family to enable 3D experiences. The layout format of the LFIs under the Quilts standard is shown in Fig. 4, in which the viewpoint images acquired from left to right during the acquisition process are arranged sequentially according to the rule of "filename_ qs Columns x Rows a AspectRatio.format ", it is generally recommended that the horizontal and vertical dimensions of the Quilts images are the same. Figure 5 presents a Quilts image example.

Table 2. Key parameters of Looking Glass Portrait

Parameter Type	value
Screen size (diagonal)	7.9"
Input resolution	1536 * 2048
Screen ratio (vertical: horizontal: deep)	4: 3: 2
Viewpoints number	45–100
Viewing angle	58°

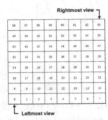

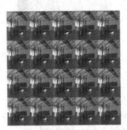

Fig. 4. (left). Layout format for light field images based on Quilts standard.

Fig. 5. (right). Examples of light field images based on Quilts standard.

3.2 Optical Principle of Optical Field Display

Looking Glass Portrait uses integrated imaging light field display technology to achieve stereo display effect by covering a layer of column lens stereo raster on top of the Liquid Crystal Display (LCD) display. The principle is as follows: First, as shown in Fig. 6, the Quilts image is divided into several groups of regularly arranged pixels by software analysis and projected on the LCD display, where each RGB pixel is called a sub-pixel. As shown in Fig. 7, several sub-pixels are grouped together in an array called a parent pixel, and each parent pixel samples one pixel from each viewpoint map of the inner Quilts image in order. Then, based on the column lens grating refraction principle shown in Fig. 8, the column lens grating projects the light from different subpixels in different directions so that only a small portion of each parent pixel can be seen when viewed from any angle. When the light refracted by multiple gratings is summed up, it allows the observer to see only a part of the image with the left eye and another part with the right eye at a certain distance range, thus creating 3D vision. It should be added that the raster is often tilted at an angle, rather than vertically, in order to reduce moiré in the display and to make the pixel transition smoother and reduce visual jumps when changing views.

3.3 Calculation of Viewpoint Perception Density Metric

Light field display technology has the characteristics of multiple viewpoints and large viewing angles. At a certain angle, the number of viewpoints perceivable by the human

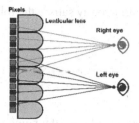

Fig. 6. (left). Sub-pixels presented on the LCD screen are refracted by the column lens.

Fig. 7. (middle). Several sub-pixels on the LCD screen are combined in the form of an array to become the parent pixel.

Fig. 8. (right). Schematic diagram of the refraction principle of a column lens grating.

eye is affected by the input Quilts image and the optical structure of the device, and there exists a variable interval, which may cause differences in the number of images entering the human eye, as well as differences in parallax, thus affecting the quality of 3D visual perception of LFIs. In addition, the number of viewpoints cannot be infinitely large due to technical constraints. Therefore, there is a need to measure the relationship between the number of viewpoints perceived by the human eye and the 3D perceptual experience when viewed at a specific angle. By finding the relationship between the number of viewpoints and the viewing angle under different levels of visual experience, we can provide reference for content production of LFIs and hardware upgrade of light field display devices.

In this study, we propose a new metric—DPV, to evaluate the 3D visual perceptual quality of LFIs, especially the subjective stereoscopic nature, to solve the above problem. The perceptible density of viewpoints is calculated as

$$DPV = \frac{N}{\varphi}. \qquad (1)$$

where N is the number of viewpoint maps in the Quilts image and φ is the viewing angle of the light field display device. However, for marketing and technical leakage prevention considerations, light field display device manufacturers often intentionally exaggerate the number of viewpoints and viewing angles of display devices, and directly use the parameter data provided by the manufacturer, which can cause large measurement errors. Therefore, it is necessary to further calculate the data of N and φ based on reliable parameters.

In order to avoid too few or redundant number of viewpoints affecting the measurement results, a valid range of values for N should be determined in the experience evaluation. According to the light field display principle, the minimum value of N should simultaneously satisfy the following constraints

$$\begin{cases} N_{min} = c * r, N \in N^* \\ w * c \geq W \\ h * r \geq H \\ N_{min} \geq 2 \end{cases} \tag{2}$$

where c and r are the number of columns and rows of the viewpoint map in the Quilts image, respectively, w and h are the horizontal and vertical pixels of a single viewpoint map, respectively, and W and H are the horizontal and vertical input resolutions of the light field display device, respectively. If the minimum value of N does not satisfy the above conditions, the light field display will not produce stereo vision.

The maximum value of N can be obtained by the following calculation,

$$N_{max} = \lfloor r_p * ppL \rfloor. \tag{3}$$

$$r_p = \frac{w_p}{h_p * cot\theta}. \tag{4}$$

$$ppL = \frac{W}{L}. \tag{5}$$

where r_p is the number of rows of subpixels in the parent pixel, and ppl is the average number of subpixels covered by each raster in the horizontal direction. r_p can be calculated from the horizontal and vertical dimensions of subpixels w_p and h_p, as well as the inverse tangent of the angle θ between the raster and the numerical direction. The horizontal and vertical dimensions of the subpixels can be derived from the ratio of the input resolution of the LCD display to its actual size, so it is not repeated. It should be added that if the calculated N_{max} differs significantly from the manufacturer's data, the actual result should be an integer multiple of N_{max}, but should not exceed the manufacturer's data, which indicates that multiple sets of parent pixels are used to display a set of full information when a large number of viewpoints are displayed.

By the above method, a range of values of N can be determined. In the actual evaluation, the DPV experiments can be carried out within this range, and the calculation of φ needs to be derived from the optical parameters of the column lens in the light field display device [29]. The specific method is as

$$\varphi = 2 * arcsin\left[nsin\left(arctan\frac{-w_p(n-1)}{2nR}\right)\right]. \tag{6}$$

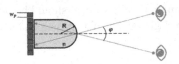

Fig. 9. Schematic diagram of optical parameters and viewing angle of column lens.

where the refractive metric of the column lens is n and the radius of curvature is R. The specific parameter relationships are shown in Fig. 9. After the above method, the results of DPV can be calculated and used in the study of 3D visual perception quality of LFIs.

4   3D Visual Perception Quality Evaluation of Light Field Images

4.1   Preparation of Experimental Data

There exist a large number of publicly available LFI datasets for research use, which mainly include synthetic LFIs, multi-sensor LFIs, time-series based LFIs, and standard/focused LFIs [28]. Since the light field display used in this study is compatible with time-series-based LFIs and the maximum number of viewpoints available is close to 100, the MPI Light Field Archive published by Max Planck Institute is chosen as the experimental data source for this study.

As shown in Fig. 10, three real scenes as well as three LFIs of synthetic scenes are selected from this dataset, covering scene semantic elements such as real/virtual, distant/close, indoor/outdoor, texture, light and shadow, and people/objects. All images are corrected. The zero-difference plane is set so that one third of the scene is in front of the screen, while ensuring that the maximum screen difference between consecutive views is about 1 pixel to avoid blending of visible angles [30].

Fig. 10. Light field image scenes included in the experimental dataset.

In order to obtain better observation and test results, the above selected LFIs are processed into a experimental dataset according to the Quilts display standard adopted by the Looking Glass Portrait light field display, with key parameters shown in Table 3. Figure 11 gives an example of a real scene in the experimental dataset.

Table 3. Key parameters of the experimental dataset

Parameter type	Value
Resolution of the viewpoint map	720 * 720
Number of viewpoint maps	9,14,19,24,29,34,39,44,49,52,56,59,64,69,74,79,84,89,94,96
Number of Quilts images	120 (Each scene has 20 sheets)
Scale of Quilts images	3*3, 4*4, 5*5, 6*6, 7*7, 8*8, 9*9, 10*10 (Insufficient viewpoint map positions are vacated)

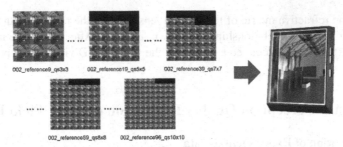

Fig. 11. Example of light field images from the experimental dataset played on looking glass portrait.

4.2 Experiment Methods

The international standards organization has developed the experiment protocol for stereo television images, ITU-R BT.1438, which can be applied in the experiment of this study. In order to obtain the subject's intuition when viewing the LFI, the SSCQE (Single Stimulus Continuous Quality Evaluation) experimental method of the single stimulus experimental method is selected according to the standard experimental protocol. The structure of its material presentation is shown in Fig. 12. In this process, there is no need to refer to the image sequence, only to directly play the LFIs of the experiment to the subject continuously.

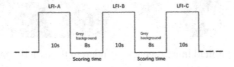

Fig. 12. Presentation method of light field images in experiment datasets.

The playback time of each LFI to be tested lasted 10s, and the test subjects are required to rotate the Looking Glass Portrait to observe it fully, with 5s interval between two test images. During this time, the subject is required to give an evaluation score for the last played LFI, and the rating level is referred to Table 4. To prevent subject fatigue, the length of a single test is controlled to be no more than 30 min.

4.3 Experimental Result Processing

In this experiment, a total of 8 subjects participated, whose ages ranged from 18 to 25 years old, of which 4 subjects are female and 4 are male. By recording the ratings of the eight subjects on the 120 LFIs, the subjective ratings of each LFI in the corresponding DPV conditions in each of the six test scenes could be obtained (Fig. 13). It can be found that in the six test scenes used in the experiment, the subjects' ratings all basically showed an increasing trend as the DPV increased, thus inferring that there is a correlation between the DPV and the 3D visual perceptual quality of the LFIs.

Table 4. Criteria for subjective evaluation of three-dimensionality

Experience level	Scoring criteria	Score
Excellent	DEB (very clear); CDN (very clear); TDE (very obvious)	80–100
Good	DEB (very clear); CDN (clear); TDE (obvious)	60–80
Fair	DEB (clear); CDN (clear); TDE (obvious)	40–60
Poor	DEB (clear); CDN (not clear); TDE (not obvious)	20–40
Bad	DEB (not clear); CDN (not clear); TDE (not obvious)	0–20

Note:DEB refers the depth at the edge of the main body; CDN refers to the contrast between the distant and near scene; TDE refers the three-dimensional effect

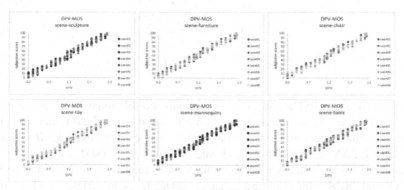

Fig. 13. Schematic diagram of the relationship between DPV and users' subjective scores in the six test scenes.

In order to further investigate the correlation between objective metrics such as DPV and 3D visual perceptual quality, the DPV of all test images and the PSNR and SSIM values of the rightmost and leftmost viewpoint images of each test image are collected. The PSNR and SSIM calculation methods are shown below:

$$PSNR = 10log_{10}\left(\frac{\left(2^{bits} - 1\right)^2}{MSE}\right). \tag{7}$$

$$MSE = \frac{1}{hw}\sum_{i=0}^{h}\sum_{j=0}^{w}\left[X(i,j) - Y(i,j)\right]^2. \tag{8}$$

where *bits* refers to the number of bits per pixel, *MSE* is the maximum mean square error (*h* and *w* in its formula are the horizontal and vertical resolutions of the viewpoint map, respectively), and $X(i,j)$ and $Y(i,j)$ denote the pixel values at the (i,j) coordinates of the leftmost image and the rightmost image, respectively.SSIM mainly considers three key features of the image: Luminance, Contrast and Structure. First, the leftmost image X and the rightmost image Y are chunked, and then SSIM is calculated for the corresponding chunks of the two images

$$SSIM\,(x_i, y_i) = \left[l(x_i, y_i)\right]^\alpha \cdot \left[c(x_i, y_i)\right]^\beta \cdot \left[s(x_i, y_i)\right]^\gamma. \tag{9}$$

where x and y denote the original image blocks and the distorted image blocks corresponding to them, respectively. $\alpha, \beta, \gamma > 0$ is used to adjust the three components of $l(x_i, y_i)$, $c(x_i, y_i)$, and $s(x_i, y_i)$, μ_x and μ_y denote the mean values between x and y, σ_x and σ_y represent the variance of the leftmost and left-right image blocks, σ_{xy} represents the covariance, and C_1, C_2, and C_3 are the constants set to prevent the denominators from being equal.

$$l(x, y) = \frac{2\mu_x\mu_y + C_1}{\mu_x^2 + \mu_y^2 + C_2}. \tag{10}$$

$$c(x, y) = \frac{2\sigma_x\sigma_y + C_2}{\sigma_x^2 + \sigma_y^2 + C_2}. \tag{11}$$

$$s(x, y) = \frac{\sigma_{xy} + C_3}{\sigma_x\sigma_y + C_3}. \tag{12}$$

In the test dataset, PSNR and SSIM have negative correlation with MOS, respectively. In order to facilitate the comparison between different metrics, the original variables are treated as follows: since the most common value range of PSNR is 30 dB–50 dB and SSIM is 0–1, $PSNR* = 50dB - PSNR$ and $SSIM* = 1 - SSIM$ are used instead; in addition, the LFIs with the same DPV conditions in different scenes have different values of PSNR and SSIM values, so the average values are taken as variables and recorded as AVE-PSNR* and AVE-SSIM*, respectively. The MOS scores of the light field images with the same DPV conditions in the six test scenes are linearly fitted with these three metrics as variables (Fig. 14), respectively. The results show that all three metrics reflect to some extent the subjective perception of the quality of 3D visual perception of light field images by the human eye.

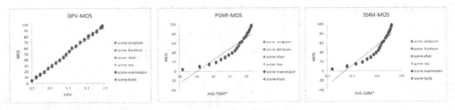

Fig. 14. The relationship between the values of DPV, PSNR, SSIM and MOS, respectively.

4.4 Metric Performance Analysis

As shown in Table 5, the correlation between the objective metric values of DPV, PSNR, and SSIM and the subjective mean score MOS under different DPV conditions is carried out based on the data obtained from the 3D visual perceptual quality evaluation experiments of LFIs. In this study, the Pearson correlation coefficient in statistics is used to measure the correlation between the above indicators and the subjective scores. The results show that the correlation between the new metric DPV proposed in this study and the subjective mean score is higher than that of PSNR (0.931) and SSIM (0.917), reaching 0.988. The above results indicate that the DPV metric with light field display characteristics performs better than the traditional assessment metrics in the task of assessing the quality of 3D visual perception of LFIs.

Table 5. Results of Pearson correlation coefficient

Metric	Pearson correlation coefficient
DPV	0.988**
PSNR(AVE-PSNR*)	0.931**
SSIM(AVE-SSIM*)	0.917**

4.5 Application of Metric

Based on the above metric performance analysis, it is known that there is a significant linear correlation between DPV and the 3D visual perceptual quality of the light field images. Therefore, in the actual production or experience evaluation, the value of DPV can be used to characterize the 3D visual experience of users. Since the user's visual experience is subjective in nature, it is often described as multiple levels. Therefore, according to Table 3 and the regression relationship between DPV and MOS, the MOS scores of the light field images in the six test scenes need to be graded, and then the range of DPV values corresponding to different user experience levels is defined. The correspondence between DPV and user's 3D visual experience levels is shown in Table 6.

Table 6. Correspondence between DPV and 3D visual perception experience level

Experience Level	Bad	Poor	Fair	Good	Excellent
DPV	<0.54	0.54-0.95	0.95-1.36	1.36-1.77	>1.77
Example					

5 Summary

This paper first analyzes the fundamental reasons for the obvious differences between the light field display and the traditional 3D display in terms of both viewpoint number and viewing angle. An objective evaluation metric of 3D visual perception quality based on the optical display principle of LFIs—DPV is proposed. DPV takes the number of viewpoints and viewing angles into consideration, so the metric design is consistent with the characteristics of light field display. In the metric evaluation experiment, it is verified that there is a strong correlation between DPV and users' ratings, thus demonstrating that DPV can better reflect the 3D visual perception quality of LFIs. In addition, by comparing the correlation degree between DPV, PSNR, SSIM and subjective ratings, we found that DPV is have better performance in the task of assessing the 3D visual perceptual quality of LFIs.

The DPV assessment metrics will be further improved in subsequent studies. For example, in this study, it is found that the performance of DPV is not consistent in different scenes, so the DPV metric calculation can be improved based on the content and content semantics of the scene can be considered. Finally, DPV can directly reflect the data volume of LFIs, and exploring the data volume of LFIs under different experience levels is of great research value for remote real-time display of LFIs and assessment of network requirements.

Acknowledgments. This study is funded by Beijing University of Posts and Telecommunications-China Mobile Research Institute Joint Innovation Center.

References

1. Levoy, M., Hanrahan, P.: Light field rendering. In: Proceedings of the 23rd Annual Conference on Computer Graphics and Interactive Techniques (ACM) (1996)
2. Gortler, S., et al.: The lumigraph. In: Proceedings of the 23rd Annual Conference on Computer Graphics and Interactive Techniques (ACM) (1996)
3. Levoy, M.: Light fields and computational imaging. Computer **8**, 46–55 (2006)
4. Xie, Y., Su, X., Zhang, J.: Key properties of antostereoscopic display (in Chinese). Chin. J. Liq. Cryst. Displays **30**, 889–893 (2015)
5. Zhao, P., et al.: DeLFIQE-a low-complexity deep learning-based light field image quality evaluator. IEEE Trans. Instrum. Meas. **70**, 1–11 (2021)
6. Martínez-Corral, M., Javidi, B.: Fundamentals of 3D imaging and displays a tutorial on integral imaging light-field and plenoptic systems. Adv. Opt. Photonics **3**, 512–566 (2018)
7. Hou, W., Bai, B., Yang, B.: Research on the development and business trend of holographic technology under 6G network (in Chinese). Telecommun. Sci. **11**, 1–10 (2021)
8. Marrugo, A., Gao, F., Zhang, S.: State-of-the-art active optical techniques for three-dimensional surface metrology a review. J. Opt. Soc. Am. A **9**, 60–77 (2020)
9. Zhou, J., et al.: Subjective quality analyses of stereoscopic images in 3DTV system. In: Visual Communications & Image Processing (IEEE) (2011)
10. Zou, Z., Qiu, J., Liu, C.: Light-field image quality assessment based on multiple visual feature aggregation (in Chinese). Acta Optica **41**, 1610002 (2021)
11. Zhu, J., et al.: Research on subjective perception evaluation of stereo image quality (in Chinese). J. Ningbo Univ. (NSEE) **1**, 36–41 (2015)
12. Yang, J., Hou, C., Lei, J.: Objective quality evaluation method of stereo image based on human visual characteristics. J. Tianjin Univ. **7**, 623–627 (2009)
13. Stereoscopic Visual Comfort and Its Measurement: a Review. Zou Bochao1,2,3, Liu Yue1,2, and Guo Mei1, 2

14. Wang, X., Kwong, S., Zhang, Y.: Considering binocular spatial sensitivity in stereoscopic image quality assessment. In: Visual Communications and Image Processing (VCIP) (2011)
15. Yin, Y., et al.: Overview of 3D imaging of geometric light field. Chin. J. Lasers **12**, 1209001 (2021)
16. Yuan, S., Li, M., Da, Z.: Calibration method of structure parameter and assembly error of light field camera. Chin. J. Lasers **20**, 2004001 (2021)
17. Zhu, H., Wang, Q., Yu, J.: Light field imaging models calibrations reconstructions and applications. Front. Inf. Technol. Electr. Eng. **9**, 1236–1249 (2017)
18. Viola, I., Rerábek, M., Ebrahimi, T.: Comparison and evaluation of light field image coding approaches. IEEE J. Select. Top. Sign. Process. **7**, 1092–1106 (2017)
19. Hu, S., Guo, B., Wang, J.: Light field entropy: new metric for light field coding objective evaluation. J. Front. Comput. Sci. Technol. **9**, 1466–1474 (2018)
20. Wang, Y., et al.: Selective Light field refocusing for camera arrays using bokeh rendering and super resolution. IEEE Sign. Process. Lett. 1 (2019). https://doi.org/10.1109/LSP.2018.2885213
21. Tao, M., et al.: Depth from combining defocus and correspondence using light-field cameras. In: 2013 IEEE International Conference on Computer Vision. Sydney (IEEE) (2013)
22. Adelson, H., Bergen, J.: The Plenoptic Function and the Elements of Early Vision. MIT Press, USA (1991)
23. McMillan, L., Bishop, G.: Plenoptic modeling: an image-based rendering system. In: Proceedings of the 22nd Annual Conference on Computer Graphics and Interactive Techniques, Los Angeles (ACM) (1995)
24. Chai, J., et al.: Plenoptic sampling. In: Proceedings of the 27th Annual Conference on Computer Graphics and Interactive Techniques SIGGRAPH'00 (ACM) (2000)
25. Lin, Z., Shum, H.: A geometric analysis of light field rendering. Int. J. Comput. Vision **2**, 121–138 (2004)
26. Fang, L., Dai, Q.: Computational light field imaging. Acta Optica Sinica **1**, 0111001 (2020)
27. Xie, Y., et al.: Key properties of autostereoscopic display **5**, 888 (2015). https://doi.org/10.3788/YJYXS20153005.0888
28. Liu, Y., Zhang, L., Ai, H.: Progress and prospect of 3D reconstruction based on light field cameras. Acta Electron. Sinica **7**, 1775–1792 (2022)
29. Wang, J., Ma, T.: Visual area analysis of cylindrical lens raster naked eye 3D display system. Packag. J. **1**, 83–90 (2020)
30. Vamsi, K., et al.: Towards a quality metric for dense light fields. In: Proceedings of the IEEE Conference on Computer Vision and Pattern Recognition (CVPR) (2018)

Nonlinearity Affection Analysis of Spectral Information Reconstruction by Trichromatic Imaging System

Hengrun Chen[1], Yumei Li[1], Shining Ma[1], Xufen Xie[1,2(✉)], Yue Liu[1], and Weitao Song[1]

[1] School of Optoelectronics, Beijing Institute of Technology, Beijing 100081, China
xiexufen11@foxmail.com
[2] Research Institute of Photonics, Dalian Polytechnic University, Dalian 116034, China

Abstract. The nonlinearity of the trichromatic imaging system response affects the accuracy of reconstructed spectral information. In this paper, an experiment was designed to analyze the nonlinearity affection on spectral reconstruction. The TIFF and sRGB PPM format images were obtained by DCraw software as the linear and nonlinear data, and Gamma transform was conducted for linear data to simulate nonlinearity affection. Then, the methods of ordinary least squares (OLS), Wiener filter and principal component analysis (PCA) were used to reconstruct spectrum from linear and nonlinear data. At last, the mean relative difference (MRD) was deduced for the first time. The MRE and color difference were used to evaluate the system response nonlinearity affection on spectrum reconstruction.

Keywords: Trichromatic imaging · nonlinearity response · Spectral reconstruction · Gamma transform

1 Introduction

As an essential attribute of an object, the spectral information describes its internal physical structure and chemical composition which is widely applied in imaging display, color measurement, textile printing, medicine detection and other fields [1–4]. Therefore, the accurate acquisition of spectral information is extremely important, which can be obtained by the spectrophotometer, spectral irradiance meter or imaging system. The imaging spectral measurement systems, including three-channel imaging and multi-channel imaging, have a large imaging field of view for spectral reconstruction, which is a major advantage over the spectrophotometer or spectral irradiance meter. The three-channel imaging system, known as the trichromatic imaging system, is widely used in spectral reconstruction due to its simple structure. There is a mapping function between the imaging system response and the received spectral energy. According to the mapping relationship, the target spectrum can be reconstructed.

However, the spectral reconstruction has some problems including space sampling of the input target, inverse problem modeling and its solution. Most of studies focus on the optimal solution of the problems, such as the selection problem of mapping data pairs [5–10], the study of different constraints and color systems. As for the spectral reconstruction method, various models have been proposed successively, including the least square method (OLS), Wiener filtering method, singular value decomposition (SVD), pseudo-inverse (PI) solution, and so on [1, 2, 12–16]. The regularized estimation method was studied by Heikkinen et al. [17]. The matrix R theory, which plays a significant role in spectral reconstruction methods [18–21], was investigated by Cohen et al., who have also contributed a lot to spectral reconstruction using the method of principal component analysis (PCA) [22]. In the method of PCA, the research of Hardeberg *et al.* showed that more eigenvectors can improve the accuracy of spectral reconstruction [11]. Considering the spectral data redundancy, at least 3 eigenvectors can be used to reconstruct the principal components [23–27], and at most 9 eigenvectors can be adopted to improve the spectral reconstruction accuracy [4]. The problems of input space sampling in spectral reconstruction include the nonlinearity output of imaging system response. For instance, the image output format JPEG, which is common, convenient, and processed by Gamma value, has serious nonlinearity. The Raw format is the original data of the imaging system response and it is linear. Therefore, the influence of linearity or nonlinearity response on the accuracy of spectral information reconstruction should be studied and analyzed.

In this paper, we adopted a trichromatic imaging system to capture target images and obtain the linear and nonlinear response of imaging targets, and used a spectral irra-diance colorimeter to measure the target spectrum. The spectral reconstruction targets were displayed on an LCD screen. Then, the target spectrum information was recon-structed by linear and nonlinear response data of the imaging system. Three methods of OLS (ordinary least squares), Wiener filter method and PCA (principal component analysis) were used to analyze the reconstructed spectral accuracy, respectively. The experimental results indicate that the nonlinear response dada has a serious impact on the reconstruction accuracy by introducing a large error in the spectrum information reconstruction.

2 Mapping Function in Spectrum Information Reconstruction

In the trichromatic imaging system, the response of the three-channel sensor is the function of the received spectral energy, the transmissivity of the filter, and the spectral responsivity of the sensor. When the imaging target is self-luminous, the three-channel response of the imaging system can be represented as

$$\begin{cases} R = Fr\left(\sum_{380}^{780} L(\lambda) \cdot \Omega \cdot A \cdot \tau_r(\lambda)\gamma(\lambda)\Delta\lambda\right) \\ G = Fg\left(\sum_{380}^{780} L(\lambda) \cdot \Omega \cdot A \cdot \tau_g(\lambda)\gamma(\lambda)\Delta\lambda\right) \\ B = Fb\left(\sum_{380}^{780} L(\lambda) \cdot \Omega \cdot A \cdot \tau_b(\lambda)\gamma(\lambda)\Delta\lambda\right) \end{cases}. \tag{1}$$

where R, G and B are the response values of the trichromatic imaging system, $L(\lambda)$ is the spectral radiance of imaging targets, and Ω denotes the solid angle received by the three-channel sensor, and A is the sensor area. $\tau_r(\lambda)$, $\tau_g(\lambda)$ and $\tau_b(\lambda)$ are the transmissivity of the three-channel filters, which are object-independent. $\gamma(\lambda)$ indicates the spectral responsivity of the sensor, which is also object-independent. F_r, F_g and F_b are the transfer functions of the imaging system. The Eq. (1) can be expressed as

$$\mathbf{D_k} = \mathbf{L_k^T} \times \mathbf{T_k} \tag{2}$$

where $\mathbf{D_k} = \begin{bmatrix} R_k & G_k & B_k \end{bmatrix}$ is a row vector and denotes the response value of the trichromatic imaging system. $\mathbf{L_k}$ is a column vector and represents the spectral radiance of the imaging target. $\mathbf{T_k}$ is the mapping matrix from the spectral response to the three-channel response.

According to the mapping function in Eq. (2), the spectral radiance matrix $\mathbf{L_k}$ of imaging targets can be expressed as

$$\mathbf{L_k^T} = \mathbf{D_k} \times \mathbf{F_k} \tag{3}$$

where $\mathbf{F_k}$ is the mapping matrix of spectral radiance reconstruction, and is the inverse matrix of $\mathbf{T_k}$. The matrix $\mathbf{L_k}$ represents the spectral radiance reconstruction information of the trichromatic imaging system.

3   Nonlinearity Affection of System Response

3.1   Error of Reconstructed Spectral Information

The existing methods of spectral information reconstruction for the imaging system are almost based on linearity data. For linearity data the Eq. (3) can be rewritten as

$$\mathbf{L}^T = \mathbf{D} \times \mathbf{F} \tag{4}$$

where $\mathbf{D}$ represents a group of color values of system in device related color space, $\mathbf{F}$ represents the system spectral radiance reconstruction matrix for all color value combination. And $\mathbf{F} = \mathbf{F_1} \cdots \mathbf{F_i} \cdots \mathbf{F_n}$ here.

When the system response function is nonlinear, the Eq. (4) could be rewritten as

$$\mathbf{L_{non}^T} = \mathbf{D_{non}} \times \mathbf{F_{non}} \tag{5}$$

where $\mathbf{D_{non}}$ represents a group of color values of system nonlinear response, and $\mathbf{F_{non}}$ represents the system spectral radiance reconstruction matrix of nonlinear system. However, $\mathbf{F_{non}} \neq \mathbf{F_1} \neq \mathbf{F_i} \neq \mathbf{F_n}$, if the reconstruction methods are still the same as the condition of linearity data, large errors will occur.

The mean relative error (MRE) is used to describe the error of reconstructed spectrum here. It is defined as:

$$MRE = \frac{\left\| \mathbf{D_m} \cdot \mathbf{F_m} - \mathbf{L_0^T} \right\|_1}{\left\| \mathbf{L_0^T} \right\|_1} \tag{6}$$

where $\mathbf{D_m}$ represents the color value adopted in spectra information reconstruction, $\mathbf{F_m}$ represents the spectral radiance reconstruction matrix in the corresponding system.

In order to compare the differences in spectra reconstruction between linear and nonlinear data, the mean relative difference (MRD) is described as:

$$MRD = \frac{\|\mathbf{D_{non}} \cdot \mathbf{F_{non}} - \mathbf{D} \cdot \mathbf{F}\|_1}{\|\mathbf{D} \cdot \mathbf{F}\|_1} \qquad (7)$$

3.2 Color Difference of Reconstructed Spectral Information

Spectral information can be transformed into tristimulus value. Both measured spectral information in laboratory and reconstructed spectral information can be transformed into CIE 1931 tristimulus value, it means that color difference can be calculated. As the CIELAB and CIELUV color difference have good consistency with the visual color difference, they are used to evaluate the accuracy of spectral information reconstruction. The CIE L*a*b* and CIE L*u*v* color space are based on the CIE XYZ color space, and their corresponding color differences can be calculated as shown below:

$$\Delta E_{uv} = \sqrt{(\Delta L^*)^2 + (\Delta u^*)^2 + (\Delta v^*)^2} \qquad (8)$$

$$\Delta E_{ab} = \sqrt{(\Delta L^*)^2 + (\Delta a^*)^2 + (\Delta b^*)^2} \qquad (9)$$

where L^* is named as metric lightness, u^* and v^* are named as metric chromaticity in CIE L*u*v* color space, and a^* denotes the chromaticity in the red and green axis, b^* denotes the chromaticity in the yellow and blue axis.

4 Comparison Between Linear and Nonlinear Data in Spectrum Reconstruction

An experiment was performed to analyze the affection of nonlinearity. The experimental setup schematic is shown in Fig. 1. A CanonEOS600D camera was used to capture the image of different color patches. A spectral irradiance colorimeter (SPIC-200) was adopted to measure the target spectrum on the BOE BOD065D LED display. The measured spectral irradiance is shown in Fig. 2.

The linear response data adopts a TIFF format image, which comes from raw format data. The sRGB standard nonlinear response data adopts a PPM format image, which also comes from raw format data. The DCraw software is used to obtain different image formats with linear or sRGB standard nonlinear response.

A flat-field comparative calibration experiment was also conducted to test the response curve. A Labsphere integrating sphere with a 2 *m* diameter was adopted as a uniform flat-field source, the outlet diameter of which is 35 *cm*. The CanonEOS600D camera was used to image the uniform flat field. In order to obtain different input radiation energy, different exposure times and F numbers are selected. The system F number was set as F/6.3, F/10, F/14 and F/22 respectively. And the selected exposure times were

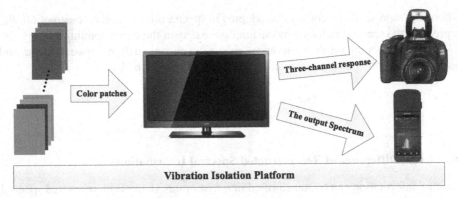

Fig. 1. Schematic diagram of experimental setup

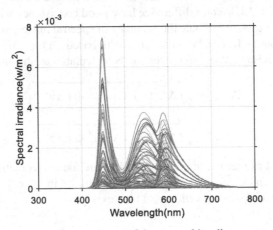

Fig. 2. Output spectrums of the spectral irradiance meter

13 s, 10 s, 6 s, 4 s, 2 s, 1 s, 1/3 s, 1/4 s, 1/8 s, 1/10 s, 1/15 s, 1/25 s, 1/30 s, 1/40 s and 1/50 s under each F number. Therefore, the imaging experiment was totally performed 60 times under different conditions. Comparative calibration response curves are shown in Fig. 3.

4.1 Differences of Linear and sRGB Data in Reconstruction Matrix

The reconstruction matrix is important for spectrum reconstruction, which is different from linear and nonlinear response data. The reconstruction matrix estimated by the OLS method is shown in Fig. 4. The curves in Fig. 5 and Fig. 6 show the data corresponding to the Wiener filter method, and the PCA method, respectively. We can see that the six matrices are substantially different. Especially, the differences in matrix are very large between linear and sRGB nonlinear data, leading to different reconstruction spectra.

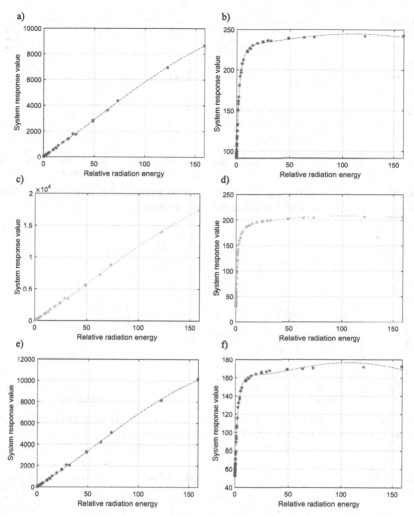

Fig. 3. Comparative calibration response curve, a) R-channel response curve corresponds to linearity TIFF format data, b) R-channel response curve corresponds to nonlinearity PPM format data, c) G-channel response curve corresponds to linearity TIFF format data, d) G-channel response curve corresponds to nonlinearity PPM format data, e) B-channel response curve corresponds to linearity TIFF format data, and f) B-channel response curve corresponds to nonlinearity PPM format data.

4.2 Differences of Reconstructed Spectrum Between Linear and sRGB Nonlinear Data

The reconstruction matrices mentioned above are used to reconstruct spectral information. The reconstructed spectral information corresponding to the 9-th color patch is shown in Fig. 7, Fig. 8 and Fig. 9. We can see that the difference of reconstructed spectra information between linear and sRGB standard nonlinear data is very obvious. The error of reconstruction data from sRGB standard nonlinear data is very large.

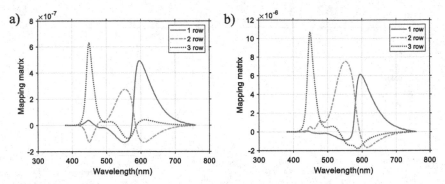

Fig. 4. Reconstruction matrix estimated by OLS method, a) Linear data from TIFF format image, and b) Nonlinear data from sRGB standard PPM format image.

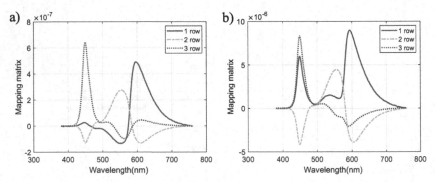

Fig. 5. Reconstruction matrix estimated by Wiener filter method, a) Linear data from TIFF format image, and b) Nonlinear data from sRGB standard PPM format image.

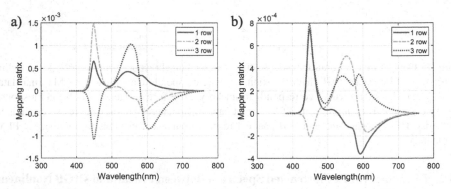

Fig. 6. Reconstruction matrix estimated by PCA method, a) Linear data from TIFF format image, and b) Nonlinear data from sRGB standard PPM format image.

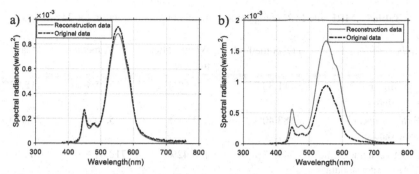

Fig. 7. Reconstructed spectral information based on OLS method, a) Linear data from TIFF format image, and b) Nonlinear data from sRGB standard PPM format image.

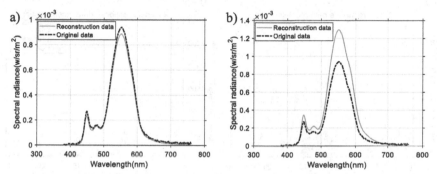

Fig. 8. Reconstructed spectral information based on Wiener filter method, a) Linear data from TIFF format image, and b) Nonlinear data from sRGB standard PPM format image

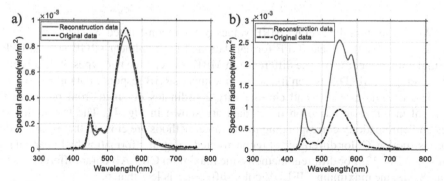

Fig. 9. Reconstructed spectral information based on PCA method, a) Linear data from TIFF format image, and b) Nonlinear data from sRGB standard PPM format image.

4.3 Error and Color Difference of Linear Data and sRGB Nonlinear Data

The mean relative errors (MRE) of different methods including the OLS methods, Wiener filter, and PCA are shown in Fig. 10. The MRE and MRD of spectral information reconstruction for 24 patches are summarized in Table 1 .

Table 1. MRE and MRD of spectral information reconstruction for 24 patches

Methods	OLS method	Wiener filter method	PCA method	Mean
MRE of linear response data	11.38%	11.52%	13.15%	12.02%
MRE of nonlinear response data	183.40%	232.31%	375.39%	263.70%
MRD between linear and nonlinear response data	349.63%	446.42%	712.01%	502.69%

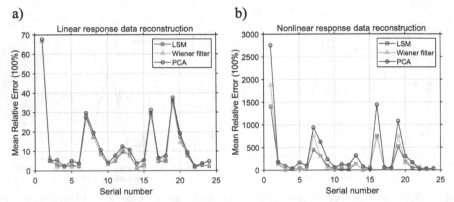

Fig. 10. MRE of reconstruction spectra, a) reconstruction from linear response data, and b) reconstruction from sRGB standard nonlinear response data.

We can see that the average MRE values of the reconstructed spectrum are 12.02% and 263.70%for the linear TIFF format data and the nonlinear sRGB standard PPM format data, respectively. The difference in MRE between the two types of data is huge. The average of MRD between linear and nonlinear sRGB response data is 502.69%.

The tristimulus value and chromaticity coordinates obtained from reconstructed spectral information based on linear data are shown in Fig. 11. The tristimulus values and chromaticity corresponding to the three methods are close to that of linear data reconstruction. Color difference of reconstructed spectral information by linear data are shown in Fig. 12. For different methods, the maximum CIELAB color difference is less than 8, and the maximum CIELUV color difference is less than 6.

Tristimulus value and chromaticity coordinates calculated from the reconstructed spectral information by sRGB standard nonlinear data are shown in Fig. 13. The reconstructed spectra using three methods all largely deviated from the original spectra. The color differences of reconstructed spectral information by nonlinear data are shown in Fig. 14. For the three reconstruction methods, the maximum LAB color difference is greater than 30, and the maximum LUV color difference is greater than 20.

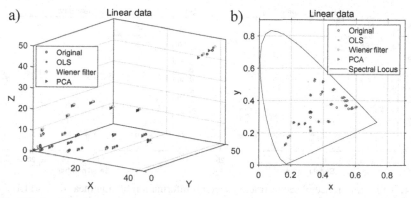

Fig. 11. Tristimulus value and chromaticity coordinates corresponding to reconstructed spectral information by linear data and different methods, a) tristimulus corresponding to reconstructed spectral information, and b) Chromaticity coordinates corresponding to reconstructed spectral information.

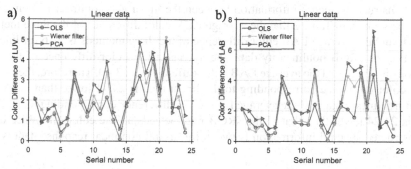

Fig. 12. Color difference of reconstructed spectral information by linear data a) LUV color difference, and b) LAB color difference.

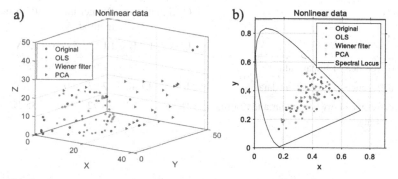

Fig. 13. Tristimulus value and chromaticity coordinates corresponding to reconstructed spectral information by nonlinear data, a) Tristimulus value corresponding to reconstructed spectral information, and b) chromaticity coordinates corresponding to reconstructed spectral information.

354   H. Chen et al.

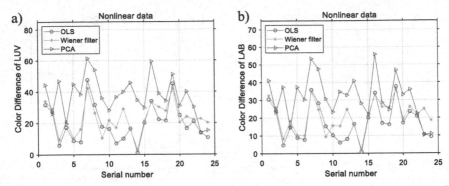

Fig. 14. Color difference of reconstructed spectral information by nonlinear data, a) LUV color difference, and b) LAB color difference.

The mean color difference of 24 patches corresponding to linear response data and sRGB nonlinear response data are shown in Table 2. We also give the color difference of the reconstructed spectral information between the linear and nonlinear response data. It can be seen from Table 2 that the average LUV color difference of the three methods is 2.04, and the average LAB color difference of the three methods is 2.16 for linearity data. For the sRGB nonlinearity data, the average LUV color difference of the three methods is 26.75, and the average LAB color difference is 23.40. Therefore, the average LUV color difference corresponding to the linear data is 24.71 lower than that of the sRGB nonlinear data, and the average LAB color difference corresponding to the linear data is 21.24 lower than that of the sRGB nonlinear data. The color difference of the reconstructed spectral information between linear and nonlinear response data is very huge.

Table 2. Mean color difference of spectral information reconstruction for 24 patches

Methods	OLS method		Wiener filter method		PCA method	
	LUV	LAB	LUV	LAB	LUV	LAB
Color difference of linear data	1.77	1.69	2.01	2.08	2.35	2.70
Color difference of Nonlinear data	19.85	17.42	22.93	20.90	37.47	31.89
Color difference between linear and nonlinear response data	18.08	15.73	20.92	18.82	35.12	29.19

4.4 Simulation Analysis of Error and Color Difference for Nonlinearity

Gamma transformation is implemented for the linear data to simulate the affection of nonlinearity. The MRE and color difference of the reconstruction spectra corresponding to different levels of nonlinearity are shown in Fig. 15, Fig. 16 and Fig. 17.

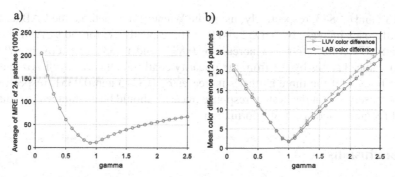

Fig. 15. Analysis of reconstruction spectra corresponding to different nonlinearity simulation using OLS method, a) MRE, and b) color difference

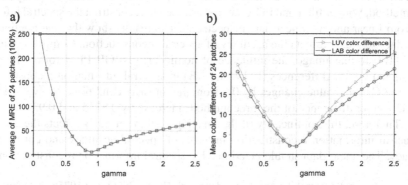

Fig. 16. Analysis of reconstruction spectra corresponding to different nonlinearity simulation using Wiener filter method, a) MRE, and b) color difference.

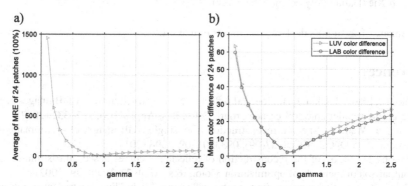

Fig. 17. Analysis of reconstruction spectra corresponding to different nonlinearity simulation using PCA method, a) MRE, and b) color difference.

We can see that the nonlinearity of system response seriously affected the accuracy of reconstruction spectral information. If the Gamma value changes by 0.1 from the linearity condition, the LAB and LUV color difference for the OLS method increase by 0.9132 and 0.9843, respectively; using the Wiener filter method, the LAB and LUV color difference increase by 0.6952 and 0.7876, respectively; for the PCA method, the LAB and LUV color difference increase by 0.8944 and 1.0333, respectively. When the Gamma value changes by 0.1 from the linearity condition, the average LAB and LUV color difference of the three methods increases by 0.8343 and 0.9351, respectively. It could be observed that the system response linearity should be guaranteed to reduce the error of reconstructed spectral information.

5 Conclusions

The imaging system response nonlinearity has an influence on spectral reconstruction based on the trichromatic imaging system. In this paper, the influence of nonlinearity on spectral reconstruction by trichromatic imaging system is theoretically analyzed, the OLS method, Wiener filter and PCA method are used to reconstruct the spectral information from linear and nonlinear data respectively. The results show that the nonlinearity of the data seriously affects the accuracy of spectral reconstruction. Compared with the linear TIFF format image, the influence of nonlinearity sRGB PPM format image is more than 17 color differences (LUV or LAB) in spectral information reconstruction. When the Gamma value changes by 0.1 from the linearity condition, the average LAB and LUV color difference of the three methods increase by 0.8345 and 0.9350, respectively. Therefore, the nonlinearity of the imaging system seriously affects the accuracy of spectral information reconstruction in terms of spectral accuracy and chromaticity accuracy. The linear data should be adopted in spectral information reconstruction.

Funding. National Natural Science Foundation of China (NSFC) (61975012), which was researched by Prof. Ningfang Liao (Beijing Institute of Technology); Basic Research Projects of Liaoning Provincial Department of Education (LJKFZ20220215), which was researched by Dr. Xufen Xie (Dalian Polytechnic University).

Disclosures. The authors declare no conflicts of interest.

References

1. Cao, B., Liao, N., Cheng, H.: Spectral reflectance reconstruction from RGB images based on weighting smaller color difference group. Color. Res. Appl. **42**(3), 327–332 (2017)
2. Liang, J., Wan, X.: Spectral reconstruction from single RGB images of trichromatic digital camera. Acta Optica Sinica. **37**(09), 0933001–0933008 (2017)
3. Dupont, D.: Study of the reconstruction of reflectance curves based on tristimulus values: comparison of methods of optimization. Color. Res. Appl. **27**(2), 88–99 (2002)
4. Zhang, X., Xu, H.: Reconstructing spectral reflectance by dividing spectral space and extending the principal components in principal component analysis. J. Opt. Soc. Am. A **25**(2), 371–378 (2008)
5. Shen, H.L., Xin, J.H., Shao, S.J.: Improved reflectance reconstruction for multispectral imaging by combining different techniques. Opt. Express **15**(9), 5531–5536 (2007)
6. Ayala, F., Echávarri, J.F., Renet, P.: Use of three tristimulus values from surface reflectance spectra to calculate the principal components for reconstructing these spectra by using only three eigenvectors. J. Opt. Soc. Am. **23**(8), 2020–2026 (2006)

7. Mohammadi, M., Nezamabadi, M., Berns, R.S., Taplin, L.A.: Spectral imaging target development based on hierarchical cluster analysis. In: Proceedings of the Color & Imaging Conference, pp. 59–64 (2004)

8. Shen, H.L., Xin, J.H.: Spectral characterization of a color scanner by adaptive estimation. J. Opt. Soc. Am. A **21**(7), 1125–1130 (2004)

9. Wu, G., Shen, X., Liu, Z., Yang, S., Zhu, M.: Reflectance spectra recovery from tristimulus values by extraction of color feature match. Opt. Quant. Electron. **48**(1), 1–13 (2016)

10. Jaaskelainen, T., Parkkinen, J., Toyooka, S.: Vector-subspace model for color representation. J. Opt. Soc. Am. A **7**(4), 725–730 (1990)

11. Hardeberg, J.Y., Schmitt, F., Brettel, H.: Multispectral image capture using a tunable filter. In: Proceedings of the SPIE, vol. 3963, pp. 77–88 (1999)

12. Haneishi, H., Hasegawa, T., Hosoi, A., Yokoyama, Y., Tsumura, N., Miyake, Y.: System design for accurately estimating the spectral reflectance of art paintings. Appl. Opt. **39**(35), 6621–6632 (2000)

13. Shen, H.L., Wan, H.J., Zhang, Z.C.: Estimating reflectance from multispectral camera responses based on partial least-squares regression. J. Electron. Imaging **19**(2), 020501-1-4 (2010)

14. Hardeberg, J.Y.: Acquisition and reproduction of colour images: colorimetric and multi-spectral approaches, A dissertation of Ecole Nationale Supérieure des Télécommunications, pp. 28–95 (1999)

15. Murakami, Y., Obi, T., Yamaguchi, M., Ohyama, N.: Nonlinear estimation of spectral reflectance based on Gaussian mixture distribution for color image reproduction. Appl. Opt. **41**(23), 4840–4847 (2002)

16. Li, C., Wan, X., Liang, J.: Spectral Reconstruction from trichromatic digital camera responses based on interim connection space for spectral data. Chin. J. Luminescence. **37**(12), 1571–1578 (2016)

17. Heikkinen, V., Jetsu, T., Parkkinen, J., Hauta-Kasari, M., Lee, S.D.: Regularized learning framework in the estimation of reflectance spectra from camera responses. J. Opt. Soc. Am. A **24**(9), 2673–2683 (2007)

18. Cohen, J.B., Kappauf, W.E.: Metameric color stimuli, fundamental metamers, and Wyszecki's metameric blacks. Am. J. Psychol. **95**(4), 537–564 (1982)

19. Cohen, J.B.: Color and color mixture: scalar and vector fundamentals. Color. Res. Appl. **13**(1), 5–39 (2010)

20. Zhao, Y., Berns, R.S.: Image based spectral reflectance reconstruction using matrix R method. Color. Res. Appl. **32**(5), 343–351 (2007)

21. Wang, J., Liao, N., Wu, W., Cao, B., Li, Y., Cheng, H.: Spectral reflectance reconstruction with nonlinear composite model of the metametric black. Spectrosc Spectr. Anal. **37**(03), 704–709 (2017)

22. Cohen, J.: Dependency of the spectral reflectance curves of the munsell color chips. Psychon. Sci. **1**(1–12), 369–370 (1964). https://doi.org/10.3758/BF03342963

23. Chen, Y., Xu, H., Zhang, X., Luo, M.R.: Study of spectral reconstruction based on digital camera. Acta Optica Sinica. **29**(05), 1416–1419 (2009)

24. Fairman, H.S., Brill, M.H.: The principal components of reflectances. Color. Res. Appl. **29**(2), 104–110 (2004)

25. Agahian, F., Amirshahi, S.A., Amirshahi, S.H.: Reconstruction of reflectance spectra using weighted principal component analysis. Color. Res. Appl. **33**(5), 360–371 (2008)

26. Wu, G., Liu, Z., Fang, E., Yu, H.: Reconstruction of spectral color information using weighted principal component analysis. Optik **126**, 1249–1253 (2015)

27. Ma, L., Qiu, X., Cong, Y.: Spectral image reconstruction through the PCA transform. In: Proceedings of the SPIE, vol. 9811, 98110C-1-6 (2015)

Applications of Image and Graphics

Adversarial Reinforcement Learning for Steering Cars from Virtual to Real World

Shiquan Lin, Yifan Li, and Yuchun Fang[✉]

School of Computer Engineering and Science, Shanghai University,
Shanghai 200444, China
{funterlin,ycfang}@shu.edu.cn

Abstract. A promising method to achieve autonomous driving is reinforcement learning which excels at sequential decision-making and control problems. Training reinforcement learning models in the virtual environment is appealing as it can provide abundant data at a lower cost and avoid unpredictable safety issues. But the visual reality gap between the virtual environment and the real world makes the vision-based model trained with a simulator hard to generalize to the real world. We proposed a domain-adversarial reinforcement learning method to bridge the reality gap in which a domain classifier that requires only unlabeled real-world data is introduced to help the alignment of visual features between two domains. The common semantic representation of images from different domains is learned when the domain classifier fails to classify the source domain of the feature. Thereafter the model generalizes well in the real world without any extra labeled data or processing. We train the proposed model in The Open Racing Car Simulator (TORCS) and validate its effectiveness and superiority on a real-world dataset containing images recorded in real-world driving with steering angle labels.

Keywords: Reinforcement learning · Adversarial learning ·
Autonomous driving

1 Introduction

Autonomous driving is promising nowadays which can not only ease our everyday life but also speed up transport to benefit the whole society. Autonomous driving usually involves a series of complex operations based on complex situations. The system should map the sensation to the operations. Developing an autonomous driving system is training the artificial intelligence model to control cars. But training such a competent model in a conventional supervised manner requires a massive resource, computation, and labeled data, which is expensive and inefficient. Reinforcement learning excels at sequential decision-making and control problems without expensive labeled data for training [15]. With rapidly developed deep learning, the reinforcement learning methods incorporating deep neural networks can handle complicated problems in a more complex environment.

W. Yongtian and W. Lifang (Eds.): IGTA 2023, CCIS 1910, pp. 361–372, 2024.
https://doi.org/10.1007/978-981-99-7549-5_26

Deep reinforcement learning has proved its superiority in playing video games at human-level or even above [10] and robotic-related tasks. So it is promising for autonomous driving with a lower cost. But the trial-and-error process in reinforcement learning in the real world may cause unpredictable consequences such as unaffordable damage to the cars or environment, and even harm to the people around.

Training reinforcement learning agent directly in the real world is impractical. Therefore most studies train reinforcement learning models in a virtual environment instead [1,11,12,17] as training the reinforcement learning model in the virtual environment is much easier. However, the virtual environment generated by the simulator must be the abstract of the real world due to the restriction of complexity. As a result, there is an inevitable inconsistency between the virtual environment and the real world, which results in the bad generalization of the model in the real world. The main sensation for autonomous driving is vision, the same with humans. So this work follows the previous studies [1,8,11,14,17] and focuses on the visual inputs. The key operation for autonomous is steering, which is closely related to safety and collision avoidance. Therefore, we study autonomous steering agent trained only in a virtual environment but also work well in the real world.

It is a great challenge to combat the inconsistency between the virtual environment and the real world for reinforcement learning on robotics-related problems. Applying the knowledge learned in the virtual environment to the real world is a case of transfer learning. [12] bridged the "reality gap" by randomizing the dynamics of the simulator during the training which results in a close level of performance of object pushing robotic arm to the one in simulation. [13] proposed using progressive networks to bridge the reality gap and transfer learned policies from simulation to the real world. It enables the reuse of everything from low-level visual features to high-level policies for transfer to new tasks. [11] proposed a realistic translation network that can convert non-realistic virtual image input into a realistic one with a similar scene structure to ensure the model trained in the virtual environment is workable in the real world. [17] proposed a novel framework of reinforcement learning with an image semantic segmentation network to make the whole model adaptable to reality.

In this paper, we proposed a domain-adversarial reinforcement learning method (DARL) to align the visual representation in the different scenes. So the reinforcement learning agent trained in a virtual environment can have a similar performance in the real world without any extra processing or labeled data. We introduce the domain classifier that requires only unlabeled real-world data for training, inspired by [4–6], to perform adversarial training. When the feature extracted from the different scenes can not be classified by the domain classifier, the representation describes the consistent scene structure. We train the outstanding deep reinforcement model Rainbow [7] to steer for driving safely in The Open Racing Car Simulator (TORCS) [16] with only visual inputs. The model is trained with the auxiliary domain classifier and images recorded in real-world driving in SullyChen's dataset [2] without its steering label. We evaluate the proposed DARL in real-world data with the steering angle labeled to demonstrate its effectiveness and superiority over the previous method. Our main contributions are listed below:

- We novelly introduce adversarial learning to bridge the reality gap between the virtual environment and the real world that hinder the generalization of reinforcement learning agent in the real world.
- Compared with the previous studies, our proposed framework neither relies on any other computer vision model nor requires any labeled data. Therefore, our autonomous driving agent does no extra processing while driving in the real world. Moreover, the performance will not be influenced by other computer vision methods or the quality of auxiliary data.
- Our proposed model outperforms the existing method by a large margin in the real-world dataset to prove its superiority. The feature visualization with the t-SNE method also validates the effectiveness of the introduced adversarial learning.

2   Method

The proposed DARL is composed of three modules shown in Fig. 1. The first is the feature extractor, containing three convolution layers, that takes the driving view images as input to calculate the state representation of the environment for action prediction. The second is the action prediction network, containing two streams with two noisy linear layers in each stream, that predicts driving actions based on the representation from the feature extractor. The third is the domain classifier, containing three linear layers after a gradient reversal layer, which determines which domain the images come from, the virtual environment or the real world. The feature extractor and the action prediction networks constitute the deep reinforcement learning model that can be trained with the reinforcement learning method. The feature extractor and the domain classifier form the adversaries trained in an adversarial manner. With adversarial learning, the learned representation should be able to cheat the domain classifier but still useful for proper steering. Because we expect that the feature is domain-irrelevant so that the model has identical performance in different domains.

2.1   Reinforcement Learning to Drive

We adopt the outstanding reinforcement learning model Rainbow [7] as it has shown its superiority in complex controlling problems like playing Atari Games. Rainbow gains its superiority by combining six independent improvements over Deep Q-Networks [10].

To train the agent with the reinforcement learning model, we define the Markov decision process model by defining their state set, actions set, and reward function.

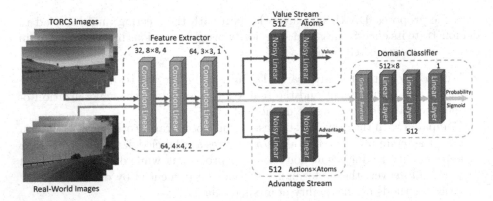

Fig. 1. The structure of the proposed domain-adversarial reinforcement learning model. The value stream and the advantage stream form the action prediction network.

State. The agent is learning to drive with the driving view images as visual input showing the scene in forwarding perspective. In each time step, the most recent four images are concatenated as input of the feature extractor. So the state is the feature of the four most recent views. It means the driving actions are based on not only the real-time view but also the historic view.

Action. Steering is consecutive action. But the basic method of Rainbow is Deep Q-learning which is designed for discrete action. To simplify the problem for feasibility, evaluation, and comparison with the existing works, we define three discrete actions following the previous study [11,17]: turn left, go straight, and turn right. In the virtual environment turning left and turning right are divided into three levels: slight, middle, and heavy. The details of actions are described in Sect. 3.2.

Reward. The reward function is what guides the behavior of the reinforcement learning agent. To guide the agent to drive safely, we define a penalty that is a fixed negative reward for collision including colliding with objects and running out of the track. To guide the agent's driving efficiency, we define a positive reward as a linear scale of the forward speed. To guide the agent to drive in the middle of the track, we define a negative reward as a linear scale of the distance to the middle line. In addition, to keep the car stable, we define a negative reward scales with the angle between the directions of the speed and the middle line. Formally, the reward function at time step t can be expressed by Eq. 1.

$$r_t = \begin{cases} \beta(v_t \times cos\,\alpha - v_t \times |sin\,\alpha| - distance_t), & no\ collision \\ \gamma, & collision \end{cases} \quad (1)$$

In Eq. 1, α is the angle between the directions of the speed and the middle line. So the $v_t \times cos\,\alpha$ represents the forward speed and $v_t \times |sin\,\alpha|$ represents the speed that causes the unstable driving. $distance_t$ represents the distance from the car to the middle line. β is a hyperparameter. γ is a negative reward to penalize the collision including running out of the track, which leads to the end of an episode.

The reinforcement learning agent can learn to drive based on the defined states set, actions set, and reward function in the virtual environment. Then we can transfer the learned driving policy to the real world for autonomous driving. The obstacle is the reality gap resulting from the difference in visual appearance or style between the virtual environment and the real world. So the agent has to learn the common semantics of the visual appearance.

2.2 Domain-Adversarial Learning Across Reality Gap

To bridge the reality gap, we introduce a domain classifier to be an adversary of the feature extractor inspired by [4–6]. It takes the feature from the feature extractor as input to make a binary prediction of the source domain of the feature. The objective of the domain classifier is binary cross-entropy that can be denoted as Eq. 2.

$$L_d(X, y) = \sum_{f_i \sim X} y_i log D(f_i) + \sum_{f_j \sim X} (1 - y_j) log(1 - D(f_j)) \tag{2}$$

In Eq. 2, X is the feature outputted by the feature extractor, y is the label of the source domain which is 1 when the source domain is the virtual environment and 0 when the source domain is the real world. So adversarial learning does not require any expensive data with task-related labels.

The introduced domain classifier estimates the difference between the distribution of two datasets. In the process of training, the domain classifier improves its ability to classify the source domain of the feature. Meanwhile, the feature extractor is trained as an adversary to learn the representation which can not reflect the source domain. We expect the learned representation to be domain-irrelevant but task-related. So the agent sees two domains as the same and drives well in both domains. The objective of adversarial learning can be denoted as Eq. 3.

$$\min_F \max_D L(D, F) = \mathbb{E}_{x_v \sim p_v} L_d(F(x_v), 1) + \mathbb{E}_{x_r \sim p_r} L_d(F(x_r), 0)$$
$$= \mathbb{E}_{x_v \sim p_v} log D(F(x_v)) + \mathbb{E}_{x_r \sim p_r} log(1 - D(F(x_r))) \tag{3}$$

In Eq. 3, p_v is the distribution of data from the virtual environment, p_r is the distribution of data from the real world, F is the feature extractor and D is the domain classifier.

2.3 Domain-Adversarial Reinforcement Learning

To incorporate adversarial learning in the reinforcement learning model, we separate the deep Q-network into two networks: all of the convolution layers as the feature extractor and all of the linear layers as the action prediction network. After the adversarial training of the feature extractor and the domain classifier, the feature from the two domains follows nearly the same distribution. Also guided by the information from action prediction, the feature is driving-related, which enables the agent to drive based only on the visual images in the real world.

To implement the domain-adversarial reinforcement learning, we optimized the feature extractor and the domain classifier in the opposite direction as the adversaries. Specifically, we add a gradient reversal layer between the feature extractor and the domain classifier, so the gradient backpropagated from the domain classifier be multiplied by a negative factor $-\alpha$. That means the gradient descending optimization of the feature extractor is in the opposite direction. Formally, denote the parameters of the feature extractor as θ_{feat}, the parameters of the action prediction network as θ_{act}, and the parameters of the domain classifier as θ_{cls}. Denote the loss of action prediction as L_{act} and the loss of domain classification as L_{cls}. The optimization can be expressed as:

$$\theta_{act} \leftarrow \theta_{act} - \eta \frac{\partial L_{act}}{\partial \theta_{act}} \tag{4}$$

$$\theta_{cls} \leftarrow \theta_{cls} - \eta \frac{\partial L_{cls}}{\partial \theta_{cls}} \tag{5}$$

$$\theta_{feat} \leftarrow \theta_{feat} - \eta(\frac{\partial L_{act}}{\partial \theta_{feat}} - \alpha \frac{\partial L_{cls}}{\partial \theta_{feat}}) \tag{6}$$

Algorithm 1. Training Process

1: Initialize virtual environment E, training set S, feature extractor F action prediction network C, domain classifier D;
2: **while** M is not convergent **do**
3:     sample a batch of images x_r from dataset S;
4:     sample a batch of images x_v from virtual environment E;
5:     feed forward calculation: $f_r = F(x_r)$ and $f_v = F(x_v)$;
6:     feed f_v and f_r forward in C and D respectively, calculate the action prediction loss L_{act} and domain classification loss L_{cls};
7:     optimized the parameters of F, C and D as Eq. 4, 5, 6;
8: **end while**

More explicitly, the process of training the proposed DARL model is described in the Algorithm 1.

3 Experiment

3.1 Dateset

Virtual Environment. We adopt The Open Racing Car Simulator (TORCS) [16] as the virtual environment to learn driving policy. TORCS is a highly portable multi-platform car racing simulation. It is used as an ordinary car racing game, also as an AI racing game, and as a research platform. It features many different cars, tracks, and opponents to race against, which provides sufficient diversity for learning to drive. Moreover its graphic features lighting, smoke, skid marks, and glowing brake disks. The simulation features a simple damage model, collisions, tire and wheel properties (springs, dampers, stiffness, etc.), and aerodynamics (ground effect, spoilers, etc.). So TORCS provides a realistic environment where the agent can learn the driving policy that can directly apply to real-world driving. The images from the TORCS environment are shown in Fig. 2.

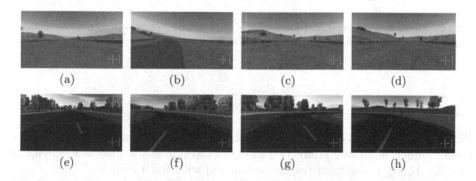

(a)   (b)   (c)   (d)

(e)   (f)   (g)   (h)

Fig. 2. Images from TORCS

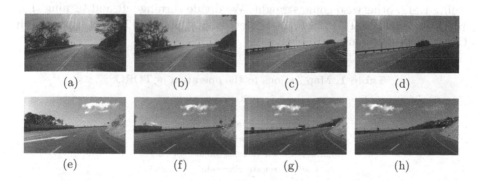

(a)   (b)   (c)   (d)

(e)   (f)   (g)   (h)

Fig. 3. Images from the SullyChen Dataset

Real World Dataset. We adapt SullyChen's dataset [2] which contains about 100k images recorded when driving around Rancho Palos Verdes and San Pedro California with the steering angle. The samples are shown in Fig. 3. We divide the data into the training set and test set according to the record time. The training set is recorded in 2018 with about 63k images and the test set is recorded in 2017 with about 45k images. The distribution of steering angle in the training set, the test set, and a set of samples from TORCS are shown in Fig. 4. The distribution is noticeably different, which indicates the difficulty of the task.

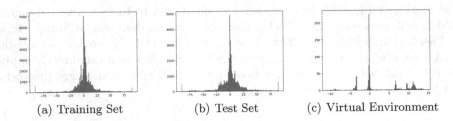

(a) Training Set   (b) Test Set   (c) Virtual Environment

Fig. 4. Steering angle distribution of data collections, x-axis represents the steering angle and y-axis represents the number of samples.

3.2   Settings

We transform the RGB images into gray-scale images to save memory for the replay buffer. Previous study [17] also indicates that the gray-scale image in TORCS brings stability of training compared with RGB images.

The real-world images from [2] are labeled with the steering angle. As we simplify the actions to turning left, going straight, and turning right, we also transfer the steering angle into actions. Specifically, we transfer the steering angle less than $-15°$ into turning left and transfer the one greater than $15°$ into turning right, otherwise going straight. We divide turning left and turning right into three levels in TORCS for a better driving policy. The setting values in TORCS for actions are in Table 1.

Table 1. Map Actions to the operation in TORCS.

Action	Operation in TORCS	Value
Go straight	no operation	–
slight left	set steering value	+0.1
middle left	set steering value	+0.2
heavy left	set steering value	+0.5
slight right	set steering value	−0.1
middle right	set steering value	−0.2
heavy right	set steering value	−0.5

In all experiments, we adopt the Adam optimizer. For the data from the virtual environment, the learning rate is set to be 6.25×10^{-5} and the batch size is 32. For the real-world data, the learning rate is 3×10^{-4}. The α for gradient reversal is 1.

We set up three experiments to demonstrate the effectiveness of the proposed method. The first is to train the feature extractor and the action prediction network of the DARL as a supervised model in a supervised manner with the training set of real-world data and evaluate it on the test set. The second is to train the proposed model as we describe above and evaluate it on the test set. The third is to train the DARL without a domain classifier and evaluate it on the test set. We also compare the results with some existing methods. Results are listed in Table 2.

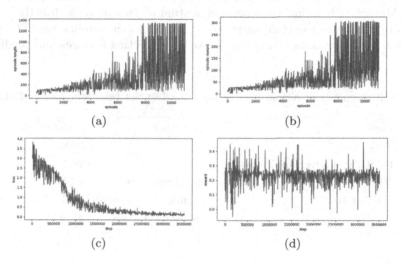

Fig. 5. Training curves of (a) episode length, (b) episode reward, (c) step loss and (d) step reward.

3.3 Result and Analysis

Qualitative Analysis. The training curves of the domain-adversarial reinforcement learning model are shown in Fig. 5. The episode reward grows rapidly after enough trial-and-error epochs, the episode length also grows to 1400 from less than 100 at the beginning. That indicates that the agent has learned to drive farther safely. The curve of step loss shows the effectiveness of the learning in the virtual environment and the convergence of the model.

Quantitative Analysis. The Accuracy of Action Prediction is listed in Table 2. As shown in the table, supervised learning achieves the best result with massive labeled data. The reinforcement learning trained in TORCS without adversarial learning performs poorly in the test set as the visual appearance is quite different between the virtual environment and the real world. The Realistic Translation Network (RTN) [11] improves the performance with the image translation as it translates the images from the virtual environment into the real-world style. The quality of the realistic images relies not only on the translation model but also on the quality dataset, which can hinder the generalization of the model. PSPNet-RL [17] achieves better performance by learning image segmentation. They adopted PSPNet [18], which is trained on extra dataset Cityscape [3] and also the segmentation images in TORCS gained by hacking source code. Our method achieves the best result among the existing comparable methods and outperforms them by a large margin. The superiority comes from the flexible alignment of features, which does not rely on any other auxiliary method or data. Moreover, learning the common feature of two domain directly require less computation in the training process and also in the application. The agent does not need any extra computation except extracting features and predicting actions.

Table 2. Accuracy of Action Predition on the Test Set from SullyChen's Dataset

Method	Transfering	Accuracy (%)
Supervised	–	52.8
DARL w/o adversarial learning	–	28.4
RTN	image translation	43.4
PSPNet-RL	semantic segmentation	36.6
DARL	adversarial training	**48.5**

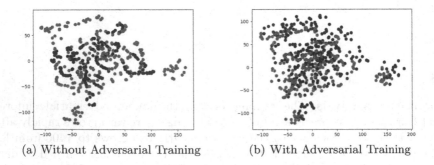

(a) Without Adversarial Training   (b) With Adversarial Training

Fig. 6. Visualization of the feature of samples, the red dots represent the samples from the real world and the blue ones represent the samples from the virtual environment. (Color figure online)

Visualization of Feature. To validate the aligned feature from two domains, we visualize the feature learned with or without adversarial learning with the t-SNE method [9] in Fig. 6. In the visualization of feature distribution, it is obvious that the distribution does not match well without adversarial learning and becomes close after introducing adversarial learning.

4   Conclusion

In this paper, we proposed a domain-adversarial reinforcement learning method to develop an autonomous steering agent based on only visual input for autonomous driving. The model can be trained in the virtual environment at a low cost and generalized well in the real world. We achieve this by aligning the visual feature between two domains. Compared to the previous studies, our proposed model works more directly without any extra process or relies on other methods. Suffering less restriction from other auxiliary methods, our model achieves better performance. The best performance is still achieved by supervised learning methods. In the future, more domain adaptation methods and better reinforcement learning methods will be further explored for outperforming the supervised methods without massive expensive labeled data.

References

1. Bojarski, M., et al.: End to end learning for self-driving cars. arXiv preprint arXiv:1604.07316 (2016)
2. Chen, S.: Autopilot-tensorflow, vol. 1, no. 5, p. 6 (2016). https://github.com/SullyChen/Autopilot-TensorFlow
3. Cordts, M., et al.: The cityscapes dataset for semantic urban scene understanding. In: Proceedings of the IEEE Conference on Computer Vision and Pattern Recognition, pp. 3213–3223 (2016)
4. Ganin, Y., Lempitsky, V.: Unsupervised domain adaptation by backpropagation. In: International Conference on Machine Learning, pp. 1180 1189. PMLR (2015)
5. Ganin, Y., Ustinova, E., Ajakan, H., Germain, P., Larochelle, H., Laviolette, F., Marchand, M., Lempitsky, V.: Domain-adversarial training of neural networks. J. Mach. Learn. Res. **17**(1), 2096–2130 (2016)
6. Goodfellow, I., et al.: Generative adversarial nets. In: Advances in Neural Information Processing Systems, vol. 27 (2014)
7. Hessel, M., et al.: Rainbow: combining improvements in deep reinforcement learning. In: Thirty-Second AAAI Conference on Artificial Intelligence (2018)
8. Islam, M.K., Yeasmin, M.N., Kaushal, C., Al Amin, M., Islam, M.R., Showrov, M.I.H.: Comparative analysis of steering angle prediction for automated object using deep neural network. In: 2021 9th International Conference on Reliability, Infocom Technologies and Optimization (Trends and Future Directions)(ICRITO), pp. 1–7. IEEE (2021)
9. Van der Maaten, L., Hinton, G.: Visualizing data using t-SNE. J. Mach. Learn. Res. **9**(11) (2008)
10. Mnih, V., et al.: Human-level control through deep reinforcement learning. Nature **518**(7540), 529–533 (2015)

11. Pan, X., You, Y., Wang, Z., Lu, C.: Virtual to real reinforcement learning for autonomous driving. In: Proceedings of the British Machine Vision Conference (2017)
12. Peng, X.B., Andrychowicz, M., Zaremba, W., Abbeel, P.: Sim-to-real transfer of robotic control with dynamics randomization. In: 2018 IEEE International Conference on Robotics and Automation (ICRA), pp. 3803–3810. IEEE (2018)
13. Rusu, A.A., Večerík, M., Rothörl, T., Heess, N., Pascanu, R., Hadsell, R.: Sim-to-real robot learning from pixels with progressive nets. In: Conference on Robot Learning, pp. 262–270. PMLR (2017)
14. Shen, Y., Zheng, L., Shu, M., Li, W., Goldstein, T., Lin, M.: Gradient-free adversarial training against image corruption for learning-based steering. In: Advances in Neural Information Processing Systems, vol. 34 (2021)
15. Sutton, R.S., Barto, A.G.: Reinforcement Learning: An Introduction. MIT Press, Cambridge (2018)
16. Wymann, B., Espié, E., Guionneau, C., Dimitrakakis, C., Coulom, R., Sumner, A.: TORCS, the open racing car simulator, vol. 4, no. 6, p. 2 (2000). http://torcs.sourceforge.net
17. Xu, N., Tan, B., Kong, B.: Autonomous driving in reality with reinforcement learning and image translation. arXiv preprint arXiv:1801.05299 (2018)
18. Zhao, H., Shi, J., Qi, X., Wang, X., Jia, J.: Pyramid scene parsing network. In: Proceedings of the IEEE Conference on Computer Vision and Pattern Recognition, pp. 2881–2890 (2017)

Efficient Multimodal-Contribution-Aware N-pair Network for Focal Liver Lesions

Xiao Han[1], Xibin Jia[1], Gaoyuan Yu[1], Luo Wang[1(✉)], Zhenghan Yang[2],
and Dawei Yang[2]

[1] Faculty of Information Technology, Beijing University of Technology, Beijing 100124, China
wangluo@bjut.edu.cn

[2] Department of Radiology, Beijing Friendship Hospital, Capital Medical University,
Beijing 100050, China

Abstract. Magnetic resonance imaging (MRI) is currently the main non-invasive method for detecting focal liver lesions (FLLs) as it can provide rich information from multiple modals. Although deep learning has made significant progress in medical image diagnosis, medical image datasets rarely contain large scale labelled data which often leads to overfitting and poor model generalization. In order to make full use of the multimodal MRI under few-shot scenarios, we propose an Efficient Multimodal-Contribution-Aware N-pair (EMCAN) network, which constructs a lightweight and efficient feature extractor to enhance representation of features. To improve the separability of the features of this network, we propose the multi-class N-pair loss. Experimental results show that our method outperforms conventional deep learning models in terms of diagnostic accuracy and provides more accurate reference for clinical diagnosis.

Keywords: focal liver lesions · multimodal · few-shot · efficient multimodal-contribution-aware n-pair network · MRI

1 Introduction

The liver is an important part of the human body. Liver cancer is also one of the most common cancers worldwide and primary liver cancer is the second leading cause of cancer-related death [1]. Liver diseases can be divided into focal liver lesions (FLLs) and diffuse lesions based on the location and mechanism of disease [2]. Accurate diagnosis of FLLs is important for early detection and further treatment of liver cancer. However, the variety and complexity of FLLs, especially rare malignant FLLs, pose a challenge in the clinical diagnostic process. Therefore, it is an extremely challenging task to make an accurate diagnosis and qualitative diagnosis of the extent of lesions in FLLs.

Magnetic resonance imaging (MRI) is currently the main diagnostic tool used domestically and internationally for examining liver diseases. MRI can use multiple sequence scans, with high image quality and soft tissue resolution, which can clearly display the tissue structure of lesions, surrounding liver parenchyma, blood vessels, and bile duct system. This technique has advantages in the diagnosis of FLLs [3], and is considered

© The Author(s), under exclusive license to Springer Nature Singapore Pte Ltd. 2023
W. Yongtian and W. Lifang (Eds.): IGTA 2023, CCIS 1910, pp. 373–387, 2023.
https://doi.org/10.1007/978-981-99-7549-5_27

an indispensable clinical diagnostic, detection, and qualitative tool. Due to the different pathological features reflected by different modal sequences, multimodal MRI can provide rich imaging information for further evaluation of liver cancer.

However, medical imaging data involves personal privacy issues and high professional requirements for annotators, and the annotation process is time-consuming and labor-intensive, which makes it difficult to collect large-scale data for training deep neural networks. Therefore, medical MRI imaging data often exhibits the characteristics of multimodal and small data volume. According to the Vapnik-Chervonenkis (VC) dimension theory [4], a hypothesis space with a higher dimension has stronger learning ability. But when the number of annotated data used for training is insufficient, the network is prone to overfitting and poor generalization performance. Moreover, when dealing with FLLs with multiple disease types and complex symptoms, neither the subjective diagnostic experience of doctors nor traditional deep learning algorithms can achieve good diagnostic results.

Moreover, in the field of multimodal medical image classification and diagnosis, the commonly used methods for clinical multimodal image fusion are feature concatenation [5] and shared network parameter training [6]. Nevertheless, the approach of sharing network parameters frequently ignores the proprietary properties carried in different modals. And concatenation method is difficult to update the parameters of multiple feature extraction network, which can easily lead to overfitting and difficulty in model convergence. Thus, improving diagnostic performance on multimodal MRI data with small data volumes is also a major challenge.

To deal with these challenges, in this paper, given a limited sample size in a multimodal MRI dataset, we will establish an effective and lightweight deep neural network model that can qualitatively diagnose various types of FLLs by integrating the characteristic information of different modals. Inspired by the experience of doctors in clinical diagnosis, who focus on different modals for different diseases, we propose an Efficient Multimodal-Contribution-Aware N-pair (EMCAN) network that is suitable for few-shot medical multi-classification scenarios. The specific contributions of this research are as follows:

- We use the Modality Grouping Convolution (MGC) module to extract features within each modal and design an Efficient Multimodal Contribution Aware (EMCA) block based on the attention mechanism. These two parts are combined to construct an efficient and lightweight framework to complete the feature extraction and fusion of multimodal medical images.
- Building upon the aforementioned framework, we introduce the idea of non-parametric metric learning to enhance the separability of various class samples in the feature space without increasing model complexity and parameters. This improves the model's performance in multi-classification diagnosis.
- We construct a few-shot FLLs multi-classification dataset based on clinical image data provided by a third-class hospital. Based on this dataset, we validate the effectiveness of our method by comparing its diagnostic performance with that of other deep classification models. Experiments of module effectiveness evaluation are also conducted to prove the necessity of each module.

2 Related Works

2.1 MRI Applied to the Diagnosis of FLLs

The liver is the largest digestive and metabolic organ in the human body and is one of the most important organs for maintaining good health [1]. Focal Liver Lesions (FLLs), which are common form of liver diseases [2], are divided into benign lesions and malignant lesions. Benign focal lesions mainly include Hemangioma (HEM), Focal Nodular Hyperplasia (FNH), Hepatocellular Adenoma (HCA), liver abscess (ABSCESS), and liver cyst (CYST), while malignant lesions mainly include Hepatocellular Carcinoma (HCC), Intrahepatic Cholangiocarcinoma (ICC), and Metastatic Tumor (MET) [3]. Therefore, accurate qualitative and quantitative diagnosis of FLLs is a challenging task, which is of great significance for the early detection and diagnosis of liver cancer and further treatment.

Clinical diagnosis has shown that Magnetic Resonance Imaging (MRI) has become the most important tool for non-invasive diagnosis of FLLs in current clinical practice due to its non-radiation and its superior advantages in terms of detection and qualitative accuracy [7].

In recent years, deep learning has made remarkable progress in various fields of artificial intelligence [8–10], especially in emerging cross-disciplinary applications such as "intelligent healthcare", which have attracted widespread attention. Compared to traditional manual diagnosis relying on clinical experience of doctors, intelligent analysis of medical images using deep learning techniques can automatically learn potential knowledge from large-scale image data, capture easily overlooked details, and assist doctors in image reading, thereby improving the accuracy and efficiency of non-invasive diagnosis.

2.2 Multimodal Medical Imaging Diagnosis

MRI can obtain multimodal images of the same tissue through different scanning methods, which can reflect the current lesion situation from different perspectives. Therefore, medical image diagnosis based on multimodal fusion has received increasing attention in recent years [11–13]. Researchers have processed multimodal image data through data fusion, feature fusion, or decision fusion, and have achieved certain results in lesion qualitative diagnosis, lesion segmentation, and other aspects. Xie et al. [14] propose TMME framework for discriminate between benign and malignant lung nodules, which uses three independent network to extract features from three enhanced CT modals and fuses them at the decision layer. Zhou et al. [10] use Linear Correlation Block to learn the correlation between modals. He et al. [13] use multi-scale attention modules to extract local and global features, and region-guided attention modules to extract features from OCT images. Jia et al. [15] propose Multimodality-Contribution-Aware TripNet (MACT) focusing on important modal channels and suppressing the influence of non-important modals on the final diagnosis. It uses Multimodal Adaptive Weighting Module to calculate the contribution of multiple modals to HCC grading tasks.

The above research results demonstrate that multimodal fusion technology has made great progress in various medical image diagnosis tasks. Most multimodal fusion diagnosis methods calculate the features of each modal or the fusion features of multiple modals through complex network and attention modules. Nevertheless, when facing medical few-shot diagnosis tasks, too many parameters can easily lead to overfitting. Therefore, it is worth exploring more effectively method to calculate the representations of each modal and multimodal image fusion while maintaining a low-complexity network.

2.3 Metric Learning

The limited number of medical image datasets, due to the constraints of data collection, makes it inevitable to result in overfitting of prediction results and poor generalization for deep learning training. Metric learning can design metric losses to optimize the feature space, which can improve the consistency of feature representations among the same class samples and enhance the separability of features. Thus, metric losses can effectively mitigate the overfitting caused by the small amount of data and improve the generalization of the model.

Matching Network [16] calculates the similarity between query set samples and support set samples using cosine distance after obtaining the embedding vector that aggregates contextual information. Prototypical Network [17] computes the mean embedding vector of the same class as the prototype of current class and uses the Euclidean distance to measure the similarity between the query set and the support set class prototypes for classification. The triplet loss [18], which is commonly used as a metric learning loss, can narrow the distance between samples of the same class while widening the distance between samples of different classes, and it is suited to address few shot problems. It has been widely applied in many fields such as face recognition, person re-identification and medical diagnosis. Nevertheless, triplet loss can only optimize samples from two classes, which may cause instability and slow convergence when applied to multi-classification problems.

3 Method

3.1 Overview

MRI can reflect liver lesions from multiple angles through different scanning and imaging methods. In this paper, we propose an Efficient Multimodal-Contribution-Aware N-pair (EMCAN) network which can improve the diagnostic accuracy through efficient use of the rich information in multimodal MRI. It can also reduce the complexity of the network, and is more suitable for few-shot scenarios of medical imaging. The general structure of the network is shown in Fig. 1.

In order to make the input data more compact and reduce the computational complexity, as well as to facilitate the interaction between multimodal information, we adjust the multimodal MRI slices of each patient to a uniform size and concatenate them along the channel dimension to obtain a 3D matrix as an input sample.

First, in EMCAN network, the multimodal fusion features are extracted efficiently by Efficient Multimodal Contribution Aware network which consists of MGC and several EMCA block. We use MGC module to extract features for each mode independently,

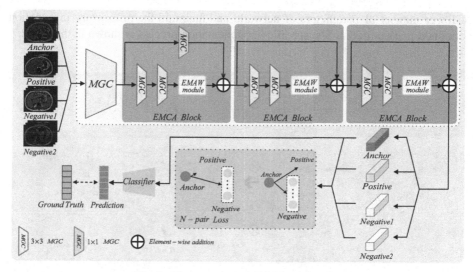

Fig. 1. The structure of EMCAN network

preventing the loss of proprietary information carried by each mode by interfering with each other in the early stage of feature extraction. And then, obtained features are fed into the EMCA block, which calculates the contribution of each modal to the diagnosis results based on the interaction of information between modals. Then, the features are weighted according to the modals contribution to obtain multimodal fusion features.

Then, in order to optimize the structure of the feature space and improve the representation of features, referring to the design of metric learning, multi-class N-pair loss is computed using cosine similarity between N-pair embedding vectors. Multi-class N-pair loss can optimize the distribution of multiple class features simultaneously, and can also overcome the slow convergence and poor local optima which are disadvantages presenting in the conventional deep metric learning framework.

Finally, the extracted features are fed into a classifier that outputs class probabilities. Both the cross-entropy loss and the multi-class N-pair loss are used to update the network parameters to optimize the multi-class feature space.

In the next two subsections, we will introduce EMCA block and multi-class N-pair loss in detail respectively.

3.2 Efficient Multimodal Contribution Aware Block

In this subsection, EMCA block is put forward to adaptively calculate the modals' contribution to the diagnosis after efficiently extracting the proprietary information of each modal, and fuse the multimodal features according to the contribution. In this subsection, we will present the two important parts of this block, MGC module and Efficient Multimodal Adaptive Weighting Module (EMAW) module, separately.

Modality Grouping Convolution Module. For multimodal medical image few-shot diagnosis tasks, we utilize the MGC to fully utilize multimodal data under the premise of lower number of parameters of network, and maintain the proprietary information contained in each modal. The specific implementation process is shown in the Fig. 2.

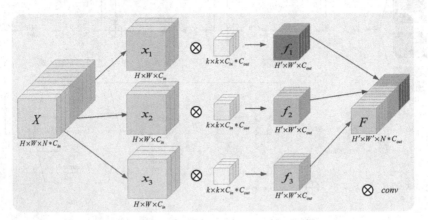

Fig. 2. The process of Modality Grouping Convolution

For the input data $X \in R^{H \times W \times N*C_{in}}$, where H and W denote the height and width of a single slice, C_{in} and C_{out} denote the number of input and output channels of each modal respectively, and N is the number of modals. * denote the scalar multiplication. The input data are grouped according to the number of modals N. Each group of modal data x_i ($i \in 1, 2, \cdots, N$) is convolved in the same convolution operation using different convolution kernels $kernel_i$, which are operated on data x_i to obtain the feature f_i. Then we concatenate f_i along the channel direction to obtain the final output feature $F \in R^{H' \times W' \times N*C_{out}}$. The calculation process is shown in Eq. (1) and Eq. (2).

$$f_i = concat\left[\sum_{j=1}^{C_{in}} conv\left(x_{i,j}, kernel_{i,j}\right)\right], f_i \in R^{H' \times W' \times C_{out}} \tag{1}$$

$$F = concat[f_1, f_2, ..., f_N] \tag{2}$$

When the convolution operation is performed using the same $k \times k$ size convolution kernel, the number of parameters required for the conventional convolution operation is $(C_{in} * N) \times k \times k \times (C_{out} * N)$. However, for MGC, the number of parameters can be reduced to $(C_{in} \times k \times k \times C_{out}) * N$. It effectively reduces the complexity of the model and the risk of overfitting while avoiding the mutual interference of information between each modal, and is more suitable for the task of classification and diagnosis of small samples in medical image.

Efficient Multimodal Adaptive Weighting Module. Considering that different modals reflect different pathological characteristics of lesions, in order to give more accurate diagnosis, doctors will comprehensively evaluate the information reflected by multiple modals that play important roles in diagnosis. Therefore, EMAW module for multimodal fusion features is designed by combining the efficient multimodal attention mechanism for inter-modal information interaction (EMAW-IM) and efficient multimodal attention mechanism for cross-modal information interaction (EMAW-CM). The specific structure is shown in Fig. 3.

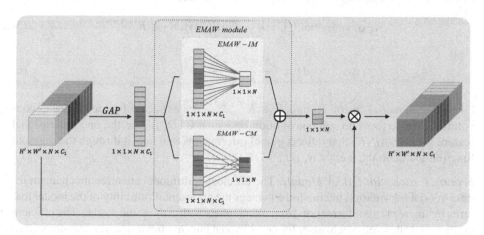

Fig. 3. The structure of EMCA Block

EMAW-IM. Since the same scanning method is used for collecting the same modal of images, there is consistency in the representation among the images of the same modal. Therefore, we use an efficient self-attention mechanism to weight different channels of data for the same modal. To deal with more diverse data formats and reduce the number of learnable network parameters, we design an adaptive strategy to determine the size of the one-dimensional convolution kernel k_1 and the sliding stride s. The specific attention weight calculation process is shown in Eq. (3) and Eq. (4), where $C1D_{k_1,s}()$ represents the adaptive one-dimensional convolution process and N represents the number of modals included in the current feature and C' represents the number of channels for each modal.

$$w_{IM} = Sigmoid\left(C1D_{k_1,s}(GAP(F))\right), w_{IM} \in R^{1 \times 1 \times N} \tag{3}$$

$$k_1, s = (N * C')/N \tag{4}$$

For the multimodal fusion feature $F \in R^{H' \times W' \times N * C'}$ extracted by the MGC, we first obtain a one-dimensional feature vector that reflects global information by performing a global average pooling (GAP) along the channel dimension. Then, we use the adaptive convolution operation $C1D_{k_1,s}()$ and the sigmoid function to obtain the weight w_{IM}. By weighting the multimodal feature F, we achieve information interaction within each modal and enhance the representation ability of modal features.

EMAW-CM. As different modals of medical images are obtained under specific scanning parameters or contrast agents, the feature maps generated by different modals exhibit diversity and complementarity. Therefore, in this chapter, we propose to use the complementary information between the target modal feature and its adjacent modal features to jointly compute the weight of the current target modal, in order to capture cross-modal interactions with a small number of parameters. The specific calculation method is shown in Eq. (5) and Eq. (6), where $C1D_{k,D}()$ represents the dilated convolution operation with a fixed kernel size k, and D is the adaptive dilation rate.

$$w_{CM} = Sigmoid\left(C1D_{k,D}(GAP(F))\right), w_2 \in R^{1 \times 1 \times N} \qquad (5)$$

$$D = \lceil \frac{N * C' - N}{K - 1} \rceil + 1 \qquad (6)$$

For the multimodal fusion feature $F \in R^{H' \times W' \times N * C'}$ extracted by modal group convolution, we perform dilated convolution operation $C1D_{k,D}()$ on the one-dimensional feature vector $GAP(F)$ that reflects global information, and map it through the Sigmoid function to obtain the weight w_{CM}.

Feature Fusion with EMAW Module. The efficient multimodal attention mechanism for intra-modal information interaction enhances the representation ability of the modal features by aggregating information from all channels within the same modal. The efficient multimodal attention mechanism for cross-modal information interaction captures complementary information between the target modal and its adjacent modals, with a small number of convolution parameters. It calculates the weight for the target modal by integrating the contributions of all modals, and enhances the corresponding modal features accordingly. This approach improves the diagnostic performance and the robustness of the model. The calculation process of EMCA Block is shown in Eq. (7).

$$F' = F \otimes_m Sigmoid(C1D_{k_1,s}(GAP(F)) + C1D_{k,D}(GAP(F))) \qquad (7)$$

3.3 Multi-class N-pair Loss

Triplet loss in the field of metric learning is often used to mitigate the problem of overfitting and poor generalization caused by the small sample size.

Although triplet loss has demonstrated its superiority in many fields, it has certain shortcomings when optimizing the feature space for multi-classification tasks. The triplet loss can only select two types of samples for optimization, so when there are many categories to be classified in the dataset, it is easy to encounter the problem of deteriorating the distance between other category samples while optimizing the current selected category sample. In addition, triplet loss has issues with instability and slow convergence. To address these issues and avoid large computational overhead, this paper uses the multi-class N-pair loss to optimize the feature selection and calculation process, as shown in the Fig. 4

After obtaining the one-dimensional embedding vector computed by the feature extractor, two features are randomly selected from each class in a batch to form a subset S with the feature size of $2M$ where M represents the number of categories. Then, as shown in Fig. 4, for each anchor feature f_i in S, another positive feature f_i^+ in the same class can be selected from S, and $(M-1)$ negative feature f_j^+ can be selected by choosing one feature from each other class. This avoids the large computational cost of pushing

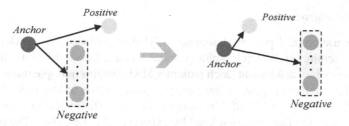

Fig. 4. Schematic diagram of multi-class N-pair loss

away all non-class samples and the specific calculation process is shown in the Eq. (8). The distance function used here is the cosine distance.

$$L_{Metric}(\{f_i, f_i^+\}_{i=1}^M) = \frac{1}{N} \sum_{i=1}^{M} log(1 + \sum_{j \neq i} exp(f_i^T f_j^+ - f_i^T f_i^+)) \qquad (8)$$

When facing a multi-classification problem, using the multi-class N-pair loss is more able to consider the distance between all class samples, making the optimization more holistic compared to the triplet encoding loss. Therefore, in the multi-classification few-shot diagnosis task of FLLs, multi-class N-pair loss is used to enhance the diagnostic accuracy of the model for complex representations and a variety of liver focal lesions.

3.4 Final Loss

The final loss is a linear combination of multi-class cross-entropy loss and multi-class N-pair loss. The multi-class cross-entropy loss and the final loss function used in this research task are shown in Eq. (9) and Eq. (10).

$$L_{CE} = - \sum_{i=1}^{n} y_i log(p_i) \qquad (9)$$

$$L_{total} = \alpha L_{CE} + (1 - \alpha) L_{Metric} \qquad (10)$$

In Eq. 9, y denotes the one-hot label encoding of sample x category, n denotes the number of categories, and p_i denotes the probability that the sample belongs to category i. L_{CE} is the multi-categorical cross-entropy loss between the prediction result and the ground truth of the sample. In Eq. 10, L_{Metric} is multi-class N-pair loss, L_{total} is the final loss and α is the weighting factor.

4 Experiments

In order to evaluate the effectiveness of EMCAN for the diagnosis of FLLs, we construct a multimodal MRI medical dataset with the help of the Radiology Department of Beijing Friendship Hospital. Next, comparative experiments and module effectiveness evaluation experiments are designed to evaluate the diagnostic performance of EMCAN on the FLLs dataset.

4.1 Data Pre-processing

This study use clinical patient abdominal MRI data provided by the Department of Radiology, Beijing Friendship Hospital, Capital Medical University. Since the scanning sequences vary for each patient, each patient's MRI contains multiple different modals. Based on this batch of image data, this paper constructs a liver lesion multi-classification dataset. The dataset consists of 310 samples in total. The collection, screening, and annotation of image data are completed by experienced radiologists. The pathological labels include the lesion regions annotated by radiologists and six common liver lesion category labels, as shown in Fig. 5.

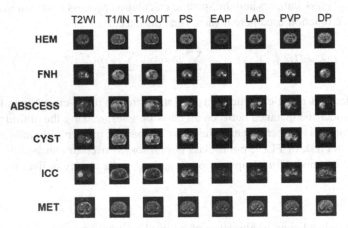

Fig. 5. Types of FLLs and the composition of MRI modal

To consider the potential contribution of partial liver background information in discriminating focal lesions, we use the entire liver cross-sectional 2D slice with the largest lesion area in each modal. To ensure the consistency of input size across all modal sequences, this study adjust the size of all modal slices to 128 in width and height.

Besides, to increase the diversity, geometric transformation data augmentation methods are conducted to expand the dataset to eight times the original size in order to simulate the possible forms of clinical cases for the original data.

4.2 Comparative Experiments

In order to evaluate the effectiveness of EMCAN network, this experiment compare it with mainstream deep learning frameworks, including ResNet [9], SENet [19], MACT [15] that have been applied in medical image diagnosis, as well as the attention mechanism model ECANet [20] that has been applied in natural image domain.

We perform 5-fold cross-validation experiments on the training data of FLLs. The hyperparameters that achieve the highest average F1 score on the 5-fold validation set are selected as the overall training parameters. Then, the final FLLs diagnosis model is trained using the selected hyperparameters and the entire training data, and test on the testing data. The training and testing processes of the overall model are repeated 5 times, and the average diagnostic metrics of the model from the 5 experiments are used to evaluate its performance.

During training, EMCAN's the loss consists of multi-class N-pair loss and multi-class cross-entropy loss, with weighting coefficient $\alpha = 0.5$, while the loss functions of other methods are set to multi-class cross-entropy loss, and the backbone network used is ResNet18. Finally, the diagnostic performance of each network model on the six categories of liver lesion diagnosis in the testing data is shown in Table 1:

Table 1. Results of qualitative diagnostic tests on the FLLs Dataset

Model	Paras	Accuracy (%)	Sensitivity (%)	Precision (%)	F1 score
Resnet	0.275M	61.03 ± 8.33	74.00 ± 8.00	67.33 ± 11.62	0.70 ± 0.11
SENet	0.280M	62.56 ± 3.84	67.17 ± 9.71	65.20 ± 3.60	0.72 ± 0.06
ECANet	0.278M	66.67 ± 4.29	69.83 ± 9.01	63.50 ± 9.32	0.75 ± 0.07
MCAT	0.280M	68.21 ± 5.28	74.50 ± 9.27	74.33 ± 10.41	0.81 ± 0.06
EMCAN	**0.064M**	**75.38 ± 4.76**	**77.06 ± 5.89**	**71.21 ± 3.11**	**0.82 ± 0.05**

It can be seen from the experimental results that the proposed EMCAN network achieves better diagnostic performance in FLLs diagnosis tasks compared to other methods, which diagnostic accuracy rate reached 75.38%. Meanwhile, this indicates that introducing multi-class N-pair loss to optimize the feature space and EMCA block to weighted features can help improve the overall diagnostic performance of the model in multi-class tasks with a small number of samples.

In terms of the number of parameters, the parameters of EMCAN network are about one third of the backbone network ResNet18. However, its diagnostic accuracy has a significant improvement compared with all method in Table 1 above. This further illustrates that applying lightweight computing frameworks with lower computational complexity and feature space optimization are beneficial to improve classification diagnostic performance with only a slight increase in parameters.

Visualization of Results. To verify the discriminability of the multimodal weighted features under the constraint of multi-class N-pair loss and to demonstrate that the EMCAN network can achieve optimal feature extraction and diagnostic performance with few parameters, a two-dimensional feature embedding space obtained by optimizing the EMCAN is shown in Fig. 6.

According to the visualization results of the feature embedding space before and after training, it can be found that under the joint constraint of EMCA block and multi-class N-pair loss, the distribution of the six types of FLLs samples in the feature space is clearly separable.

In addition, the confusion matrix of the test set diagnostic results is shown in Fig. 7. It can be found that the diagnostic accuracy of Abscess, HEM, and CYST reaches 83.33%, 92.72%, and 83.33%, respectively, which is similar to the sample distribution in the feature space.

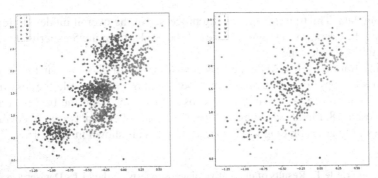

Fig. 6. Feature distribution of training set (left) and test set (right) samples. I denotes ICC, II denotes FNH, III denotes Abscess, IV denotes HEM, V denotes CYST, and VI denotes MET

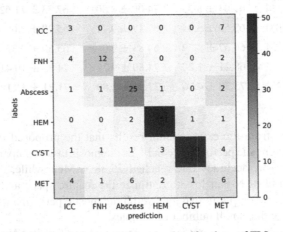

Fig. 7. Confusion matrix for six classifications of FLLs

In summary, EMCAN network adopted in this paper can achieve considerable diagnostic performance in the diagnosis of benign and malignant focal lesions, with the qualitative diagnosis of benign lesions, the qualitative diagnosis of two types of malignant tumors with more complex appearances and less obvious pathological signs still needs further study.

4.3 Further Discussions

In order to verify the influence of different multimodal attention mechanisms and metric loss functions on diagnostic performance, a comparative experiment is designed based on the FLLs diagnostic task with Resnet18 as the basic network framework in the intersection of computer science and medicine. The experimental results are shown in the Table 2, where MAWM [15] represents the addition of the Multimodal Adaptive Weighted Module using channel attention. EMAW represents the addition of the Efficient Multimodal Adaptive Weighted Module, Triplet represents the optimization method using the Triplet Loss, and the margin value in the loss function is set to 0.2.

N-pair represents the optimization method using the multi-class N-pair loss, where the weighting coefficient α in the loss function is set to 0.2.

Table 2. Result of FLLs dataset lesion task with different module

Module	Accuracy (%)	Sensitivity (%)	Precision (%)	F1 score
MAWM + Triplet	68.21 ± 5.28	74.50 ± 9.27	74.33 ± 10.41	0.81 ± 0.06
MAWM + N-pair	70.77 ± 2.05	77.22 ± 7.54	76.00 ± 8.79	0.80 ± 0.03
EMAW + Triplet	71.28 ± 5.48	81.75 ± 6.30	74.50 ± 6.78	0.83 ± 0.03
EMAW + N-pair	75.38 ± 4.76	77.06 ± 5.89	71.21 ± 3.11	0.82 ± 0.05

From the comparison between "MAWM + Triplet" and "EMAW + Triplet", it can be seen that the diagnostic model integrated with EMAW has improvements of 3.07%, 7.25%, 0.17%, and 0.02% in accuracy, sensitivity, precision, and F1 score, respectively. The comparison between "MAWM + N-pair" and "EMAW + N-pair" also yields the same conclusion, indicating that the lightweight multimodal attention calculation method is more suitable for few-shot medical multimodal image diagnosis scenarios.

In addition, by comparing the results of the two groups of experiments "MAWM + Triplet" and "MAWM + N-pair", and "EMAW + Triplet" and "EMAW + N-pair", it can be found that using the multi-class N-pair loss for multi-classification has a significant performance improvement, with diagnostic accuracy improved by 2.56% and 4.1%, respectively. This indicates that the multi-class N-pair loss is more suitable for optimizing the feature space of multi-classification scenarios, and can further improve the diagnostic performance of the classifier from a global perspective by enhancing the separability between multiple categories.

5 Conclusion

This paper proposes an Efficient Multimodal-Contribution-Aware N-pair (EMCAN) network for the diagnosis of FLLs using multi-modal MRI. EMCAN first employs Modality Grouping Convolution (MGC) to independently extract features from each modality. And then, we introduce the idea of multi-class metric learning into a network with Efficient Multimodal Contribution Aware (EMCA) block, which simulates the multimodal sequence diagnosis experience of doctors and improves the diagnostic performance of the model for medical small-sample multi-classification. The final loss consists of multi-class N-pair loss and multi-class cross-entropy loss. The multi-class N-pair loss can optimize the structure of the feature space based on the difference in distance between different classes of samples. Experimental results on a FLLs dataset show that EMCAN network performs well in improving the diagnostic performance of FLLs compared to traditional neural network models based on attention mechanisms. More experiments are also implemented to prove the effectiveness of the EMCA block and the multi-class metric learning constraints. EMCAN network provides a feasible solution for medical small-sample multi-classification scenarios involving multiple modalities.

Acknowledgments. This work is supported by The National Natural Science Foundation of China under Grant 82071876 and 62171298.

References

1. Xiao, J., et al.: Global liver disease burdens and research trends: analysis from a Chinese perspective. J. Hepatol. **71**(1), 212–221 (2019)
2. Galanski, M., Jrdens, S., Weidemann, J.: Diagnosis and differential diagnosis of benign liver tumors and tumor-like lesions. Chirurg **79**, 707–721 (2008)
3. Xie, L., Guang, Y., Ding, H., Cai, A., Huang, Y.: Diagnostic value of contrast-enhanced ultrasound, computed tomography and magnetic resonance imaging for focal liver lesions: a meta-analysis. Ultrasound Med. Biol. **37**(6), 854–861 (2011)
4. Zhou, W., et al.: Prediction of microvascular invasion of hepatocellular carcinoma based on contrast-enhanced MR and 3D convolutional neural networks. Front. Oncol. **11**, 588010 (2021)
5. Zhang, Y., et al.: Deep learning with 3D convolutional neural network for noninvasive prediction of microvascular invasion in hepatocellular carcinoma. J. Magn. Reson. Imaging **54**(1), 134–143 (2021)
6. Vapnik, V.N.: The Nature of Statistical Learning Theory. Springer, New York (1995)
7. Matos, A.P., Velloni, F., Ramalho, M., AlObaidy, M., Rajapaksha, A., Semelka, R.C.: Focal liver lesions: Practical magnetic resonance imaging approach. World J. Hepatol. **7**(16), 1987 (2015)
8. Krizhevsky, A., Sutskever, I., Hinton, G.E.: Imagenet classification with deep convolutional neural networks. Commun. ACM **60**(6), 84–90 (2017)
9. He, K., Zhang, X., Ren, S., Sun, J.: Deep residual learning for image recognition. In: Proceedings of the IEEE Conference on Computer Vision and Pattern Recognition, pp. 770–778 (2016)
10. Yang, D., Jia, X., Xiao, Y., Wang, X., Wang, Z., Yang, Z.: Non-invasive evaluation of the pathologic grade of hepatocellular carcinoma using MCF-3DCNN: a pilot study. BioMed Res. Int. **2019** (2019)
11. Zhou, Q., et al.: Grading of hepatocellular carcinoma using 3D SE-DenseNet in dynamic enhanced MR images. Comput. Biol. Med. **107**, 47–57 (2019)
12. Zhou, T., Canu, S., Vera, P., Ruan, S.: 3D medical multi-modal segmentation network guided by multi-source correlation constraint. In: 2020 25th International Conference on Pattern Recognition (ICPR), pp. 10243–10250 (2021). IEEE
13. He, X., Deng, Y., Fang, L., Peng, Q.: Multi-modal retinal image classification with modality-specific attention network. IEEE Trans. Med. Imaging **40**(6), 1591–1602 (2021)
14. Xie, Y., Xia, Y., Zhang, J., Feng, D.D., Fulham, M., Cai, W.: Transferable multi-model ensemble for benign-malignant lung nodule classification on chest CT. In: Descoteaux, M., Maier-Hein, L., Franz, A., Jannin, P., Collins, D.L., Duchesne, S. (eds.) MICCAI 2017. LNCS, vol. 10435, pp. 656–664. Springer, Cham (2017). https://doi.org/10.1007/978-3-319-66179-7_75
15. Jia, X., Sun, Z., Mi, Q., Yang, Z., Yang, D.: A Multimodality-contribution-aware TripNet for histologic grading of hepatocellular carcinoma. IEEE/ACM Trans. Comput. Biol. Bioinf. **19**(4), 2003–2016 (2021)
16. Vinyals, O., et al.: Matching networks for one shot learning. In: Advances in Neural Information Processing Systems, vol. 29 (2016)
17. Snell, J., Swersky, K., Zemel, R.: Prototypical networks for few-shot learning. In: Advances in Neural Information Processing Systems, vol. 30 (2017)

18. Weinberger, K.Q., Saul, L.K.: Distance metric learning for large margin nearest neighbour classification. J. Mach. Learn. Res. **10**(2) (2009)
19. Hu, J., Shen, L., Sun, G.: Squeeze-and-excitation networks. In: Proceedings of the IEEE Conference on Computer Vision and Pattern Recognition, pp. 7132–7141 (2018)
20. Wang, Q., Wu, B., Zhu, P., Li, P., Zuo, W., Hu, Q.: ECA-Net: efficient channel attention for deep convolutional neural networks. In: Proceedings of the IEEE/CVF Conference on Computer Vision and Pattern Recognition, pp. 11534–11542 (2020)

Lung Nodule Classification Based on SE-ResNet152 and Stratified Sampling

Jiancheng Li, Junying Gan, Lu Cao$^{(\boxtimes)}$, and Xuexia Xu

Department of Intelligent Manufacturing, WuYi University, Jiang Men 529000, China
caolu20001742@163.com

Abstract. Lung nodules, an early indication of lung cancer, are crucial for its treatment. Existing studies primarily focus on improving model structures, neglecting the issue of data imbalance in lung nodule classification. In this work, we propose a multiple-stage stratified sampling (MS-SS) to address the issue of data imbalance. This approach aims to achieve data balance while preserving the original data distribution structure to the maximum extent. Additionally, we introduce the SE-ResNet152 model combined with transfer learning to handle lung nodule classification, enabling feature recalibration through the SE module. To evaluate the proposed method, experiments are conducted on the Luna16 dataset. The results demonstrate a remarkable F1-Score of 96.358% on the test set, confirming the effectiveness of our approach in accurately classifying lung nodules.

Keyword: Lung nodule classification · SE-ResNet152 · Downsampling strategy · Stratified sampling · Imbalanced classification

1 Introduction

Lung cancer is currently the leading cause of cancer-related deaths and poses a serious threat to human health, with approximately 350 deaths from lung cancer occurring daily [1]. Early detection of lung cancer is crucial for effective treatment, highlighting the importance of large-scale screening for early-stage lung cancer. Lung nodules, as one of the early manifestations of lung cancer, play a significant role in screening. Lung nodules are defined as round or oval lesions on chest X-rays or CT scans with a diameter of less than three centimeters. Distinguishing between lung nodules and non-nodules requires experienced healthcare professionals, but the presence of numerous rounded shadows on chest X-rays or CT scans makes this task time-consuming and labor-intensive. Furthermore, the clinical experience of individual doctors varies, leading to inconsistent diagnostic outcomes. The use of computer-aided systems to assist doctors in the diagnosis of lung nodules has become a mainstream trend, as it can effectively improve diagnostic efficiency.

Computer-aided lung nodule classification techniques can be broadly categorized into traditional classification methods [4] and deep learning methods. In recent years, deep learning has demonstrated remarkable feature learning capabilities and has been extensively employed in various tasks [14, 15], including lung nodule classification.

W. Yongtian and W. Lifang (Eds.): IGTA 2023, CCIS 1910, pp. 388–398, 2023.
https://doi.org/10.1007/978-981-99-7549-5_28

Convolutional neural networks (CNNs) have become the mainstream technology for recent lung nodule classification tasks, with researchers either improving existing CNN architectures or utilizing multiple CNNs to achieve better classification performance. Some studies have used specific CNN architectures for lung nodule classification, such as 3D AlexNet and modified VGG16 [9, 10]. FractalNet was proposed as a network specifically designed for lung nodule classification [2]. Many studies have explored the use of multiple CNNs for feature extraction or have designed novel classification models by combining various CNN architectures to achieve better classification results. For example, researchers like [21] utilized both AlexNet and ResNet for feature extraction, while Ahmed H.A. et al. combined NiN and CNN to create a new classification model [5]. Mkindu H. et al. reduced the inference computation of network architecture by integrating feature maps from the beginning to the end of the network using CSPNet and minimized the information path between lower and higher-level features using PANet. They proposed combining a 3D version of ResNet with PANet and CSPNet for feature extraction [7], which yielded promising classification results. Additionally, there have been studies that combine traditional classification methods with CNNs. For example, [3] used ResNet50 as a feature extractor and SVM as a classifier in a hybrid strategy for lung nodule classification. While these methods have achieved significant improvements in lung nodule classification, the scarcity of lung nodule data remains a challenge, with only 1351 sample available in the Luna16 dataset. This limitation hinders the exploration of data-driven deep learning approaches. Consequently, many researchers have started to address the data scarcity issue using transfer learning methods. [10] applied transfer learning to classic CNN architectures, and Shah G. et al. utilized pre-trained VGG16 and VGG19 for classification [8]. Moreover, the attention mechanism has gained popularity in recent years, and some studies have incorporated attention mechanisms into CNNs to enhance model performance [19].

Most of the existing studies on lung nodule classification have focused on improving classification performance through classifier or feature extraction enhancements, with limited improvements at the data level. Lung nodule dataset exhibits extreme class imbalance, and most methods employ traditional random down sampling techniques to balance the data, which can easily affect the distribution of the sampled. In our study, we combine a stratified sampling approach to down sample the data, ensuring that the sampled data represents the distribution of the original dataset to the maximum extent. Previous studies have demonstrated that CNNs indeed exhibit promising performance in lung nodule classification tasks. Hence, we attempt to use a convolutional network that can improve classification performance in the lung nodule task. Specifically, we employ the SE-ResNet152 model [18], which has better feature extraction capabilities. The SE module can be inserted into various network architectures and allows for feature recalibration, selectively emphasizing informative features and suppressing less useful ones using global information. This helps to capture better features from lung nodule images. We pretrain the SE-ResNet152 model on the ImageNet large-scale dataset and further fine-tune it on the lung nodule classification task.

2   Method

2.1   Overall Architecture

As shown in Fig. 1, we first transform the three-dimensional data into two-dimensional images using the coordinates and category information of the lesions in the cases. Considering the significant difference in the number of lung nodule and non-nodule images, we perform oversampling on the lung nodule images and down sampling on the non-nodule images to achieve a relatively balanced distribution of the two classes. In particular, to preserve the distribution structure of the data, we employ stratified sampling instead of traditional random down sampling, as it may disrupt the data distribution. Additionally, to enhance the sensitivity of channel features and improve classification performance, we utilize the SE-ResNet152 model, which incorporates the SE module. This enables the model to better handle the task of lung nodule classification.

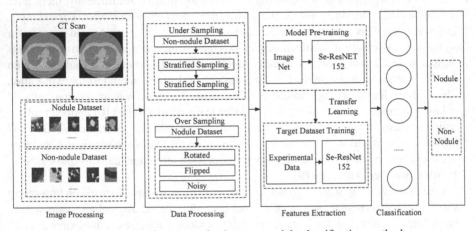

Fig. 1. Overall flowchart of pulmonary nodule classification method.

2.2   Se-ResNet152

Jie Hu et al. proposed a novel architectural unit called the SE-Block, which consists of two parts: Squeeze and Excitation. The SE-Block adaptively recalibrates channel-wise feature responses by selectively emphasizing informative features and suppressing less useful features using global information. They integrated the SE-Block into advanced networks such as VGG, ResNet, and Inception, and demonstrated its ability to improve network performance across various tasks [18]. The architecture of the SE-ResNet152 model, shown in Fig. 2, follows the structure of ResNet152 but incorporates an SE module in each residual module.

To balance performance improvement and increased model complexity, the SE module uses global average pooling in the squeeze stage, followed by two fully connected layers and channel scaling operations in the excitation stage. Specifically, the global pooling operation captures the global features of an input image, and the subsequent fully connected layers capture complex inter-channel correlations. The global features are compressed into a single channel using dimensionality reduction through a fully connected layer activated by the ReLU function. Then, another fully connected layer increases the dimensionality, followed by activation using the sigmoid function for adaptive recalibration.

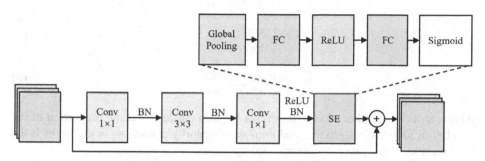

Fig. 2. SE-ResNet152 Block.

2.3 Stratified Sampling

In the Luna16 dataset, there exists a severe class imbalance between nodules (minority class) and non-nodules (majority class). To ensure effective model training, it is imperative to address this issue by down sampling the non-nodules, thereby achieving a more balanced representation. Traditional down sampling methods typically employ random down sampling techniques. However, when the majority class data exhibits a clustered structure, random down sampling tends to capture samples predominantly from a single cluster, thereby limiting the extraction of valuable structural information from the majority class samples.

Stratified sampling is a systematic approach to selecting samples from a population based on a predefined rule. In our study, we employ stratified sampling to address the issue of data imbalance in lung nodule classification. The process involves dividing the original data into blocks according to a specified rule, allowing us to explore the structural information within the data. We then perform independent and random sampling from these different data blocks. This sampling strategy ensures that the obtained sample set retains the distribution structure of the original data to a certain extent, as depicted in Fig. 3.

The process of the stratified sampling method can be described as follows. First, the data is divided into multiple subclusters C_i $(i = 1, 2...n)$ using clustering techniques. Then, according to the relationship between sample variance and mean value [17], samples are extracted from each subcluster $DataSet_j$ $(i = 1, 2...m)$ in a certain proportion. Specifically, we use the variance δ^2 and mean value μ to measure the deviation between the data. When the variance is large, it indicates a relatively dispersed distribution of samples within the cluster, and more samples need to be extracted as representatives of the current cluster to preserve the structural feature information of the original dataset to the maximum extent. Conversely, when the variance is small, it indicates a relatively tight distribution of samples within the cluster, and only a few sample points need to be extracted to maintain the structural feature information of the original data. The specific calculation formula is:

$$\mu_i = \frac{1}{n_i} \sum\nolimits_{x_i \in c_i} x_i \tag{1}$$

$$\sigma_i^2 = \frac{1}{n_i} \sum\nolimits_{x_i \in c_i} (x_i - \mu_i) \tag{2}$$

$$\alpha_i = |P| \times \frac{\omega_i \times \sigma_i}{\sum_{i=1}^{k} \omega_i \times \sigma_i} \tag{3}$$

where, α_i is the number of samples drawn by each cluster, ω_i is the proportion of the number of samples in C_i to the total number of majority classes, $\omega_i = n_i / |p|$, $|p|$ is the total number of samples after downsampling.

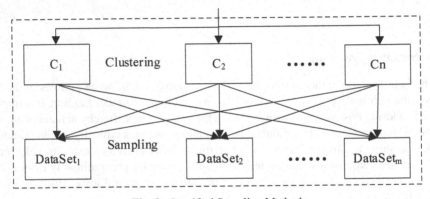

Fig. 3. Stratified Sampling Method.

When applying the stratified sampling method for dataset downsampling, we employ three different approaches. Firstly, we utilize the K-means++ clustering method [12] with $m = 1$, as illustrated in Fig. 3, to obtain the classification results of the data after the initial stratified sampling, denoted as K-means++ Stratified Sampling (KSS). Similarly, we also employ the DBSCAN clustering method [13] following the same process as KSS, resulting in DBSCAN Stratified Sampling (DSS). Considering the strengths and weaknesses of both clustering methods, we combine K-means++ and DBSCAN. Specifically, we conduct the first stratified sampling using the K-means++ method with $m = 10$, obtaining sub-samples $DataSet_1$, $DataSet_2$,... $DataSet_{10}$. Subsequently, we perform the second stratified sampling using the DBSCAN method with $m = 1$ on each sub-sample $DataSet_j$ $(i = 1,2...10)$. Finally, we merge the samples $DataSet_{j1}$ obtained from each sub-sample $DataSet_j$ to obtain the final sample, referred to as Multiple-Stage Stratified Sampling (MS-SS).

2.4 Transfer Learning

In medical imaging research, the scarcity of medical image data is a common challenge. This is often due to the limited number of occurrences of certain diseases, making it difficult to collect sufficient data, or the high cost and complexity of annotating these diseases. As a result, transfer learning has gained increasing attention. It allows models to leverage prior knowledge obtained from large existing datasets and quickly improve their performance on specific tasks by transferring this knowledge to related datasets [16]. Similarly, in the Luna16 dataset, there is a scarcity of nodule data, and the large number of non-nodules leads to a highly complex data distribution. Therefore, transfer learning methods are needed to enhance the performance of models in lung nodule classification tasks.

The specific workflow of transfer learning is depicted in Fig. 1. We use the ImageNet dataset [22] for pre-training the model because ImageNet contains a rich collection of images. Initially, the SE-ResNet152 model is selected and pre-trained on the ImageNet dataset. The network model parameters are then frozen, and the model is further trained on the training set of the Luna16 dataset. Through transfer learning, the performance of the network model in classification tasks can be significantly improved, enabling better handling of the task.

3 Experiments and Result

3.1 Dataset

The experiment utilized the Luna16 dataset, which comprises 888 cases of CT data and 551,065 candidate nodule information (coordinates and category labels). The CT data is stored in the mhd and raw formats, while the candidate nodule information is stored in Excel format. To accommodate the SE-ResNet152, a 2D network model that requires three-channel 2D images as input, the CT data needed to be transformed into image format, specifically the PNG format.

Initially, based on the candidate nodule coordinates, a 48x48x48 cubic region was generated with the coordinates as the center. Subsequently, a 48 × 48 central candidate nodule image was extracted. The images were categorized into two classes: nodules and non-nodules, based on their label values (0 or 1). The experiment obtained a total of 1,351 lung nodule images and 549,717 non-nodule images as the raw data. Figure 4 displays some examples of these data.

In the obtained image data, there is a significant imbalance between the lung nodule and non-nodule classes. Directly training the model on the original data can easily lead to a bias towards the non-nodule class, making it difficult for the model to effectively learn. Therefore, we performed oversampling and downsampling on the original data to bring the two classes to a similar quantity level.

Initially, the original data was divided into training and test sets. Subsequently, over-sampling and downsampling operations were conducted on the training set. For over-sampling, techniques such as rotation, flipping, and noise addition were employed. For downsampling, the methods of Random Sampling (RS), K-means Stratified Sampling (KSS), DBSCAN Stratified Sampling (DSS), and Multiple-Stage Stratified Sampling

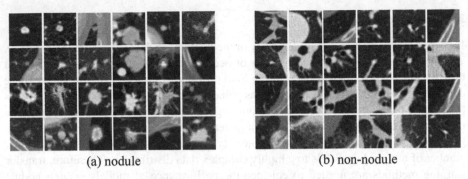

(a) nodule   (b) non-nodule

Fig. 4. Some samples from the Luna16.

(MS-SS) were utilized. As a result, a total of 13,510 lung nodule images and 40,530 non-nodule images were obtained.

3.2 Experimental Setting

During the stratified sampling process, Kmeans++ clustering was performed with 400 clusters. For DBSCAN, the Eps-neighborhood parameter was set to 5.3, and the minimum number of points for a cluster was set to 3. The dataset was divided into an 80:20 ratio for training and testing, respectively. To ensure the effective utilization of all data, a five-fold cross-validation method was applied to the training set. The loss function used was cross-entropy, and the weights were updated using the stochastic gradient descent algorithm with a learning rate of 0.01. The implementation was carried out using the PyTorch deep learning framework, and the computations were performed on a single GeForce GTX 3090 GPU.

3.3 Experiment Metrics

To address the issue of data imbalance in the lung nodule dataset, evaluating the proposed methods using recall and precision metrics can yield better results. In order to provide a comprehensive evaluation of the downsampling methods, the F1 score is used to assess the performance of the four downsampling methods. Additionally, specificity and accuracy are also employed. The relevant calculation formula is as follows:

$$Accuracy = \frac{TP + TN}{TP + FP + TN + FP} \tag{4}$$

$$Precision = \frac{TP}{TP + FP} \tag{5}$$

$$Recall = \frac{TP}{TP + FN} \tag{6}$$

$$Specificity = \frac{TN}{TN + FN} \tag{7}$$

$$F1 - score = \frac{2 \times Precision \times Recall}{Precision + Recall} \tag{8}$$

where *TP*, *TN*, *FP* and *FN* are true positive, true negative, false positive, and false negative values, respectively.

3.4 Experiment Result

Firstly, to evaluate the impact of different downsampling methods on the classification results of the SE-ResNet152 model, RS, KSS, DSS, and MS-SS were applied to the training set for downsampling. The resulting from each method was then fed into the model for training. The F1 values corresponding to each downsampling method were depicted in Fig. 5.

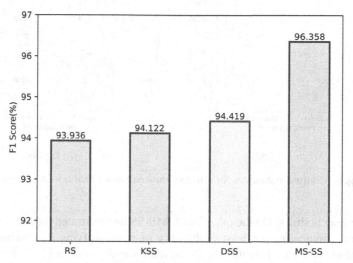

Fig. 5. Comparing F1 score of different downsampling methods on the test set

As shown in Fig. 5, when using RS for downsampling, the F1 score is 93.936%, which serves as the baseline for the entire experiment. Subsequently, when employing stratified sampling methods as downsampling techniques, specifically using K-means and DBSCAN as clustering methods, there is a slight improvement in F1 scores, with increases of 0.186% and 0.483% relative to the baseline, respectively. To better leverage the advantages of clustering methods, we utilized K-means as the clustering method in the first round of stratified sampling and DBSCAN in the second round. This led to a significant enhancement in the classification performance, achieving an F1 score of 96.358%, representing a 2.422% improvement relative to the baseline.

To further evaluate the effectiveness of the proposed methods, we employed a confusion matrix to assess the classification performance of lung nodules when using different downsampling techniques, as depicted in Fig. 6. Among the four downsampling methods, DSS exhibited the lowest FN (False Negative) rate, indicating a minimal probability

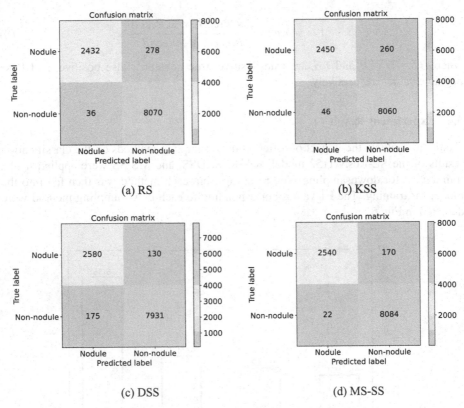

(a) RS

(b) KSS

(c) DSS

(d) MS-SS

Fig. 6. Confusion matrices for different downsampling methods on the test set

of missing lung nodules. On the other hand, MS-SS demonstrated the lowest FP (False Positive) rate, indicating the least probability of misclassifying non-nodules as lung nodules. Moreover, based on the confusion matrix and formulas (4–7), we computed accuracy, precision, recall, and F1 scores, as presented in Table 1.

Then, we compared the results of our proposed methods with some representative works in the field, as presented in Table 1. These works were based on the Luna16 dataset. Among them, [20] demonstrated good overall performance, achieving an F1 score of 93.900%. It also achieved high accuracy, precision, recall, and specificity, with values of 92.810%, 91.880%, 92.370%, and 93.190%, respectively. When using only RS for downsampling, our proposed methods surpassed [20] in terms of accuracy, precision, and specificity, but fell behind in terms of recall. However, when utilizing the MS-SS method, our proposed methods outperformed [20] in all metrics. Even though [21] achieved a recall rate of 95.000%, our DSS method was able to achieve a comparable recall rate while also showing improvements in other aspects. These results indicate that our proposed methods exhibit promising performance in addressing the task of lung nodule classification.

Table 1. Comparing the test results of different network architectures on the original dataset.

Reference	Accuracy	Precision	Recall	Specificity	F1 score
Kaya,A. [4]	88.800%	×	88.410%	94.120%	×
Ahmed,H.A.,et al. [5]	×	85.000%	85.000%	×	85.000%
Bansal, G., et al. [6]	83.330%	90.000%	87.100%	89.660%	88.520%
Shah, G., et al. [8]	95.000%	×	84.000%	97.000%	×
Lai K D., et al. [19]	×	93.000%	66.000%	84.000%	77.208%
Naik A., et al. [21]	94.300%	×	95.200	91.110	×
Reddy N S, et al. [20]	92.810%	91.880%	92.370%	93.190%	93.900%
RS	97.097%	98.541%	89.742%	96.670%	93.936%
KSS	97.171%	98.157%	90.406%	96.875%	94.122%
DSS	97.180%	93.648%	95.203%	98.387%	94.419%
MS-SS	98.225%	99.141%	93.727%	97.940%	96.358%

4 Conclusion

In this work, we proposed an effective method for lung nodule classification. Specifically, we introduced the MS-SS downsampling method to address the issue of data imbalance in medical image data by downsampling non-nodule samples. Additionally, we employed the Se-ResNet152 model, which has the capability to capture better features of lung nodules, for the classification task. We validated his method on the LUNA16 lung nodule dataset and achieved impressive performance in terms of accuracy, precision, recall, specificity, and F1 score, reaching values of 98.225%, 99.141%, 93.727%, 97.940%, and 96.358%, respectively. These results demonstrate promising performance of our proposed method in the task of lung nodule classification.

Acknowledgements. This work was supported by the Jiangmen Basic and Theoretical Science Research Science and Technology Plan Project (NO.2022JC01022 and NO.[2023]111).

References

1. Siegel, R.L., Miller, K.D., Wagle, N.S., Jemal, A.: Cancer statistics, 2023. Ca Cancer J. Clin. **73**(1), 17–48 (2023)
2. Naik, A., Edla, D.R., Kuppili, V.: Lung nodule classification on computed tomography images using fractalnet. Wireless Pers. Commun. **119**, 1209–1229 (2021)
3. Bhatt, S.D., Soni, H.B., Kher, H.R., et al.: Automated system for lung nodule classification based on ResNet50 and SVM. In: 2022 3rd International Conference on Issues and Challenges in Intelligent Computing Techniques (ICICT), pp. 1–5. IEEE (2022)
4. Kaya, A.: Cascaded classifiers and stacking methods for classification of pulmonary nodule characteristics. Comput. Methods Programs Biomed. **166**, 77–89 (2018)

5. Ahmed, H.A., Mahmood, S.A.: A deep learning technique for lung nodule classification based on false positive reduction. J. Zankoy Sulaimani **21**(1), 107–116 (2019)
6. Bansal, G., Chamola, V., Narang, P., et al.: Deep3dscan: deep residual network and morphological descriptor based framework for-lung cancer classification and 3D segmentation. IET Image Proc. **14**(7), 1240–1247 (2020)
7. Mkindu, H., Wu, L., Zhao, Y., et al.: Lung nodule classification of CT images based on the deep learning algorithms. In: 2021 5th International Conference on Imaging, Signal Processing and Communications (ICISPC), pp. 30–34. IEEE (2021)
8. Shah, G., Thammasudjarit, R., Thakkinstian, A., et al.: Nodulenet: a lung nodule classification using deep learning. Ramathibodi Med. J. **43**(4), 11–19 (2020)
9. Gupta, P., Shukla, A.P.: Improving accuracy of lung nodule classification using AlexNet model. In: 2021 International Conference on Innovative Computing, Intelligent Communication and Smart Electrical Systems (ICSES), pp. 1–6. IEEE (2021)
10. Saleh, A.Y., Rosdi, R.A.: Lung nodules classification using convolutional neural network with transfer learning. In: Wah, Y.B., Berry, M.W., Mohamed, A., Al-Jumeily, D. (eds.) Data Science and Emerging Technologies: Proceedings of DaSET 2022. LNDECT, vol. 165, pp. 253–265. Springer, Singapore (2023) https://doi.org/10.1007/978-981-99-0741-0_18
11. Anjoy, S., De, P., Mandal, S.: Identification of lung cancer nodules from CT images using 2D convolutional neural networks. In: Das, A.K., Nayak, J., Naik, B., Vimal, S., Pelusi, D. (eds.) Computational In-telligence in Pattern Recognition. CIPR 2022. LNNS, vol. 480, pp. 133–140. Springer, Singapore (2022). https://doi.org/10.1007/978-981-19-3089-8_13
12. Arthur, D., Vassilvitskii, S.: K-means++: The advantages of careful seeding. Technical report, Stanford (2006)
13. Ester, M., Kriegel, H.P., Sander, J., et al.: A density-based algorithm for discovering clusters in large spatial databases with noise. In: kdd, vol. 96, pp. 226–231 (1996)
14. Gao, C., Wang, Z., Wang, W., et al.: MRI Brain Tumor Classification Based on Efficientnet with Non-rigid Transformations. In: Image and Graphics Technologies and Applications: 17th Chinese Conference, IGTA 2022, Beijing, China, April 23–24, 2022, Revised Selected Papers. pp. 292–303. Springer (2022)
15. Chen, M., Yuan, G., Zhou, H., Cheng, R., Xu, L., Tan, C.: Classification of solar radio spectrum based on VGG16 transfer learning. In: Wang, Y., Song, W. (eds.) IGTA 2021. CCIS, vol. 1480, pp. 35–48. Springer, Singapore (2021). https://doi.org/10.1007/978-981-16-7189-0_4
16. Zhuang, F., Qi, Z., Duan, K., et al.: A comprehensive survey on transfer learning. Proc. IEEE **109**(1), 43–76 (2020)
17. Xinyue, W., Liping, J.: Stratified sampling based ensemble classification for imbalanced data. J. Shenzhen Univ. (Sci. Eng.) **36**(1), 24–32 (2019)
18. Hu, J., Shen, L., Sun, G.: Squeeze-and-excitation networks. In: Proceedings of the IEEE Conference on Computer Vision and Pattern Recognition, pp. 7132–7141 (2018)
19. Lai, K.D., Le, T.H., Nguyen, T.T.: Image classification of lung nodules by requiring the integration of attention mechanism into ResNet model. In: 2022 14th International Conference on Knowledge and Systems Engineering (KSE), pp. 1–5. IEEE (2022)
20. Reddy, N.S., Khanaa, V.: Intelligent deep learning algorithm for lung cancer detection and classification. Bull. Electr. Eng. Inform. **12**(3), 1747–1754 (2023)
21. Naik, A., Edla, D.R., Dharavath, R.: A deep feature concatenation approach for lung nodule classification. In: Misra, R., Shyamasundar, R.K., Chaturvedi, A., Omer, R. (eds.) ICMLBDA 2021. LNNS, vol. 256, pp. 213–226. Springer, Cham (2022). https://doi.org/10.1007/978-3-030-82469-3_19
22. Deng, J., Dong, W., Socher, R., Li, L.J., Li, K., Fei-Fei, L.: ImageNet: a large-scale hierarchical image database. In: 2009 IEEE Conference on Computer Vision and Pattern Recognition, pp. 248–255. IEEE (2009)

Fusing CNN and Transformer for Diabetic Retinopathy Image Grading

Haitao Yao, Ke Pan, Lijun He, and Jianxin Zhang[✉]

School of Computer Science and Engineering, Dalian Minzu University, Dalian
116600, China
jxzhang0411@163.com

Abstract. Convolutional neural networks (CNN) are widely used for
diabetic retinopathy (DR) aided diagnosis, but the CNN approach suffers from insufficient global feature extraction capability. In this paper,
a DR grading method based on the fusion of CNN and Transformer
network is proposed to assist doctors in implementing DR image diagnosis. The proposed uses a dual-branch network architecture, utilizing the
lightweight EfficientNet model in CNN to better extract local features
from retinal images by balancing network depth, width and resolution.
Meanwhile, in another branch, the Swin Transformer with good translation invariance and hierarchy is introduced, thus capturing global features of DR images with the powerful global modeling ability. Then, the
local and global features of the dual-branch are fused at the end of the
network to achieve a more robust DR image representation. The method
achieves 86.14% DR grading accuracy on the Aptos_sigmaX10 dataset,
an improvement of 2.99% and 1.09% compared to using only CNN or
Transformer, respectively.

Keywords: Network fusion · EfficientNet · Swin Transformer ·
Diabetic retinopathy

1 Introduction

As an incurable chronic disease, diabetes will not only cause blood glucose
metabolism problems, but also cause chronic damage to eyes, kidneys, heart
and other organs. Diabetic Retinopathy (DR) is a typical set of lesions caused
by damage to the microvasculature of the retina as a result of diabetes [1]. The
DR proportion of adult diabetes patients accounts for more than 40% of the
total number of diabetes patients, which is one of the most common causes of
adult blindness [2]. DR is not clinically evident in the early stages of the disease,
and by the time it is detected it has already produced severe retinal disease.
As there are still no good clinical treatment options for patients with advanced
DR, early prevention of retinopathy has become very important [3]. At present,
the diagnosis of DR relies mainly on the recognition of professional ophthalmologists, but as the diagnosis of retinal images is a difficult and time-consuming
task, there is an urgent need for computer-aided retinal image diagnosis [4].

W. Yongtian and W. Lifang (Eds.): IGTA 2023, CCIS 1910, pp. 399–412, 2024.
https://doi.org/10.1007/978-981-99-7549-5_29

With the development of deep learning technology and its outstanding performance in various fields, researchers have attempted to introduce deep learning methods represented by CNN into DR image assisted diagnosis. Among them, Pratt et al. [5] proposed the use of multilayer convolutional neural network (CNN) for five classification prediction of DR images, which greatly improved the accuracy of computer processing of DR image classification task and demonstrated the effectiveness of using deep learning for DR classification. On this basis, Dekhil et al. [6] proposed a network model with five convolutional layers to further improve DR image grading accuracy through image preprocessing and network lightweighting. To enhance the network's ability to extract features from retinal images, Torre et al. [7] propose an interpretable classifier. The method uses convolution to adapt the network architecture so that the receptive field is as close as possible to the original image size, and the classification results are interpreted by assigning a score to each point in the hidden and input spaces. The method also incorporates information from binocular retinal images. With the wide application of attention mechanism on deep learning, Zhou et al. [8] proposed a DR image grading network based on the attention mechanism to enable more attention to be paid to the information of lesions in the retina during grading, To detect small lesions in retinal images, Gu et al. [9] instead proposed a network based on a multi-channel attentional selection mechanism. The method introduces sorting losses to optimise the amount of information in each layer of the channel, and improves the accuracy of classification by combining fine-grained classification methods with multi-channel attentional acquisition of local features. In addition, to overcome the problem that the cross-entropy loss function is sensitive to noisy data and hyperparameter changes, Islam et al. [10] proposed a two-stage comparison method having a supervised comparison loss function, which also achieved better performance in DR grading.

Although CNNs have shown good results in DR image grading tasks, CNN methods also suffer from a lack of ability to capture global features [11]. With the rapid development of the Transformer model based on the self-attention [12] mechanism, researchers have also attempted to introduce the Transformer into DR image analysis, taking advantage of its strengths in global feature modeling to complete DR image classification prediction [13]. Based on the above content, this article aims to consider a scheme that can balance global and local modeling for DR image classification. More specifically, we propose a dual branch DR image classification method that combines CNN and Transformer, as shown in Fig. 1, to improve task performance by combining the advantages of CNN and Transformer. The method takes the form of a typical dual-branch network architecture, with a lightweight EfficientNet [14] model architecture as the CNN branch, which has a good balance of network depth, width and image resolution, allowing it to effectively extract local features from retinal images. In the other branch, the Swin Transformer [15] model is used, which uses a sliding window mechanism in the local window to process the image, giving the network excellent translation invariance and multi-level feature representation, able to consider global features of the DR image while taking into account local features. Finally, at the end of the two-branch network, local and global features are fused to obtain a more robust representation of the DR image. The method achieved an accuracy of 86.14% on the DR dataset Aptos-sigmaX10, achieving better performance compared to the CNN and Transformer methods.

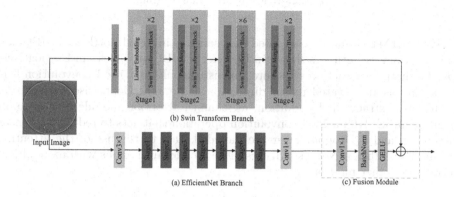

Fig. 1. CNN-Swin Transformer Network Structure.

2   Method

First, the principles of the EfficientNet and Swin Transformer models associated with this paper are presented in Sec. 2.1 and Sec. 2.2, then, a description of the specific model structure of this paper is given in Sec. 2.3, and the data pre-processing method is described in Sec. 2.4

2.1   EfficientNet

In CNNs, performance was usually optimised by adjusting the width and depth of the network model as well as the resolution of the images. Although this approach is simple and effective, it undoubtedly incurs further computational overhead. In order to achieve performance improvement while ensuring the portability of the model, EfficientNet [14] has brought a new approach that achieves a good balance between velocity and accuracy. EfficienctNet uses a composite scaling approach, where the network width w, network depth d, and image resolution r are scaled uniformly by defining the parameter φ, achieving a high-precision and efficient balance through optimization of w, d, and r. With this in mind, EfficientNet is based on a baseline network structure, which can be scaled to generate a series of networks of different sizes by adjusting w, d and r. Reducing the number of parameters and computation while maintaining the performance benefits of the network.

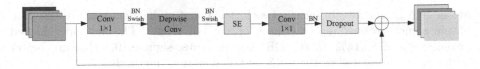

Fig. 2. MBConv structure diagram.

EfficientNet is mainly composed of a series of inverted bottleneck MBConv. The MBConv structure is shown in Fig. 2. The MBConv block, an EfficientNet-specific feature extraction structure, consists mainly of a 1×1 convolution kernel acting as an elevated tensor dimension and a $k \times k$ Depthwise Convolution for feature extraction. In addition, an channel attention module Squeeze-and-Excitation(SE) [16], a 1×1 convolution operation that acts to reduce the tensor dimension and a Dropout layer are included. Due to the use of the attention mechanism, EfficientNet also focuses more on relevant regions with more object detail than other models.

2.2 Swin Transformer

Transformer is a model based on a self-attentive mechanism that was originally applied to the field of natural language processing with advanced results. Subsequently, Dosovitskiy [17] et al. introduced the Transformer to the field of computer vision, proposing the Vision Transformer (ViT). ViT extracts image features by stacking Transformer blocks, which do not require convolution operations, and also performs well on computer vision tasks. ViT's high computational volume is not suitable for the application. Swin Transformer [15] proposes a feature pyramid network architecture based on multi-scale hierarchical design, and designs a shift window to construct a multi-headed attention module, as shown in Fig. 3. This operation of paying attention in the local window enhances the Transformer's ability to focus on finer local information. Also, this approach has enabled Swin Transformer to achieve higher accuracy and faster computational efficiency, achieving advanced results in multiple vision tasks.

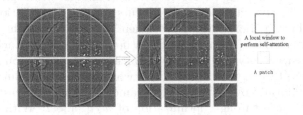

Fig. 3. Shifted Window.

Swin Transformer blocks are the most important component of the Swin Transformer. Swin blocks differ from ViT blocks in that they change the standard

Multi-Head Self-Attention (MSA) in ViT to Shifted Windows Multi-Head Self-Attention (W-MSA/SW-MSA), and by iteratively stacking Swin Transformer blocks, they not only improve the feature extraction of image blocks, but also establish dependencies between features of adjacent image blocks [18].

2.3 Overall Architecture

To more accurately detect DR patients, this paper proposes a deep learning dual-branch network model based on CNN and Transformer fusion from a model fusion perspective, enabling the network to make full use of both global and local features to achieve higher image classification results than both, providing ophthalmologists with better medical aid diagnostic references. The structure of the proposed fusion network model is shown in Fig. 1 and consists mainly of two branches, the CNN branch (a) and the Transformer branch (b), as well as a feature fusion module (c) for tensor adjustment.

In Fig. 1(a), the CNN model is chosen as EfficientNet-B4. The EfficientNet network is more effective in feature extraction by using a self-attentive module to focus on relevant regions with more informative features. EfficientNetB0-B7 is implemented by scaling adjustments on top of EfficientNet-B0. The network structure and parameters of the EfficienctNet-B4 model, which was mainly used for the experiments, are shown in Table 1 for an input image resolution of 224×224 RGB images.

Table 1. The structure of EfficientNet-B4.

Stage	Operator	Resolution	Channels	Layers
1	Conv3 × 3	224 × 224	48	1
2	MBConv1, k3 × 3	112 × 112	24	2
3	MBConv6, k3 × 3	112 × 112	32	4
4	MBConv6, k5 × 5	56 × 56	56	4
5	MBConv6, k3 × 3	28 × 28	112	6
6	MBConv6, k5 × 5	14 × 14	160	6
7	MBConv6, k5 × 5	14 × 14	272	8
8	MBConv6, k3 × 3	7 × 7	448	2
9	Conv1 × 1 & Pooling & FC	7 × 7	1792	1

In Fig. 1(b), the Transformer model is chosen as swin-T. The Swin Transformer architecture is used, where the input RGB image (size $4 \times 4 \times 3$) is first processed into non-overlapping image blocks by Patch Partition, and then the image blocks are processed into feature dimension 48 ($4 \times 4 \times 3$). After processing, each image block has a dimension of $\frac{H}{4} \times \frac{W}{4} \times 48$. After linear transformation by Linear Embedding to expand the tensor dimension to an arbitrary size, the tensor is fed into the Swin blocks of the hierarchy to learn the image features to obtain the complete image information. The tensor is first passed through a Linear Embedding layer, except for Stage 1, where a Patch Merging layer is applied to the feature map. The Patch Merging layer takes the small patches and combines them into one large patch to increase the field of perception and obtain more feature information from the image.

The feature fusion module corresponding to Fig. 1(c) contains mainly a 1×1 convolution of size, a BatchNorm layer and a GELU activation function, which serves to adapt the features to be fused. The CNN branch outputs a feature image with dimension $7 \times 7 \times 1792$ for an RGB image with input 224×224 and $7 \times 7 \times 768$ for the Transformer branch. The fusion method was chosen by adjusting the tensor to the same $7 \times 7 \times 768$ and then performing the fusion operation to obtain information with both local and global features of the image for DR grading.

In addition, the adopted classifier consists of a global average pooling layer and a fully connected layer, and is converted to classification probabilities using the Softmax function.

2.4   Data Preprocessing

Due to the different contrast of retinal images in the dataset, as well as the presence of black areas in most of the images, in addition to the problem of image blurring caused by differences in shooting height and angle, etc., which can affect the grading accuracy to a certain extent, data pre-processing of the DR images in the data is necessary for this reason.

Firstly, considering the large amount of black area noise present in the original DR image, the image was cropped to the maximum rectangle to obtain the effective image area. As the size specification of the cropped image is not uniform, the image is processed to a uniform size (pixels) after rounding the effective area of the retina using the binary method of circular cropping.

As in Eq. (1), based on the height and width of the image, the value of the binary method of locating the coordinates of the image centroid can be calculated.

$$\begin{cases} x = \frac{width}{2} \\ y = \frac{height}{2} \end{cases} \tag{1}$$

Based on the centre coordinates of the circle, the circle is drawn with the minimum height and width as the radius, as in Eq. (2), then a blank image of the same size as the original image is drawn, and the pixel values of the circular part of the original image are overlaid with this area in the blank image, resulting in a binary method circular cropped image.

$$radius = \frac{\min\left(width, height\right)}{2} \tag{2}$$

Thereafter, a Gaussian filter smoothing function is used to suppress other noise in the retinal image. Specifically, a Gaussian function is used as a template to do a convolution operation with the input image and a weighted average of the image pixel values. The expression for the two-dimensional Gaussian function is given in Eq. (3):

$$G(x,y) = \frac{1}{\sqrt{2\Pi\sigma^2}}e^{-\frac{x^2+y^2}{2\sigma}}$$

(3)

where x^2, y^2 represent the distance between the central pixel and the other pixel points in the field. σ represents the standard deviation. $G(x,y)$ indicates the weight of the calculated pixel point. When the size of the window template is $(2k+1) \times (2k+1)$ its value per pixel is calculated by Eq. (4)

$$H_{i,j} = \frac{1}{\sqrt{2\Pi\sigma^2}}e^{-\frac{(i-k-1)^2+(j-k-1)^2}{2\sigma^2}}$$

(4)

where i, j denote the coordinates of the ranks in the convolution kernel and k denotes the size of the convolution kernel.

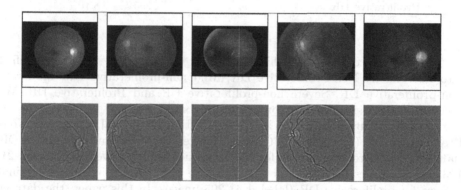

Fig. 4. Comparison chart before and after image pre-processing.

The resulting image in Fig. 4 shows the image in the dataset after image pre-processing. As can be seen from the figure, the retinal image features are enhanced to some extent after processing the cropped image by the Gaussian filter function. In addition, image enhancement strategies such as random level flipping and image rotation are used simultaneously to increase the generalisability of the network and to improve the training efficiency of the network.

3   Experiment Preparation

In Sect. 3.1 the dataset used in this experiment is first introduced, followed by Sect. 3.2 which describes the setup used in this experiment, and in Sect. 3.3 which describes the evaluation metrics used in this paper.

3.1   Dataset

The DR dataset Aptos_sigmaX10, publicly available on the Kaggle website[1] was used, which was filmed and provided by technicians at the Aravind Eye Hospital and examined and classified by specialist clinicians according to the actual degree of lesion.

Table 2. Distribution of the number of images in the Aptos dataset

Degree of lesion	Category labels	Number	Percentage
Non-Proliferative DR	0	1805	49.30%
Mild non-proliferative DR	1	370	10.10%
Moderate non-proliferative DR	2	999	27.30%
Severe non-proliferative DR	3	193	5.30%
Proliferative DR	4	295	8.10%

The dataset contains 3662 high-resolution colour retinal images, classified into five classes: Non-Proliferative DR, Mild non-proliferative DR, Moderate non-proliferative DR, Severe non-proliferative DR and Proliferative DR. We train in five classifications according to this scale. For the training data set the data distribution is shown in Table 2, with 1805 retinal images for Non-Proliferative DR (labeled 0), 370 retinal images for Mild non-proliferative DR (labeled 1), 999 retinal images for Moderate non-proliferative DR (labeled 2), 193 retinal images for Severe non-proliferative DR (labeled 3) and 295 retinal images for proliferative DR (labeled 4) 295 images. In this paper, the dataset was divided into a training set, a validation set and a test set in the ratio of 8:1:1 for model evaluation.

3.2   Implementation Details

The experiments were conducted in Ubuntu 20.04.2 on an Intel(R) Core(TM) i7-9700 CPU, RTX 2080 Ti GPU with 12 GB of video memory, and CUDA version is 11.4. The Transformer branch uses the officially published pre-trained weights for network initialization, and the CNN branch does not use migration learning for initialization. The model was trained using the AdamW [19] optimizer with a base learning rate set to $1e-4$. The batch size was set to 16 and the number of training epochs to 100.

3.3   Evaluation Metrics

The DR image grading evaluation criteria used in the experiments were Confusion matrix. The confusion matrix can be used to reflect the relationship between

---

[1] Dataset courtesy of http://www.kaggle.com.

the predicted and true values, it mainly includes: TP (True Positive), FN (False Negative), FP (False Positive), TN (True Negative). Besides, precision, accuracy, and recall coefficient are also used to evaluate the fusion model.

$$Precision = \frac{TP}{TP + FP} \tag{5}$$

$$Accuracy = \frac{TP + TN}{TP + TN + FP + FN} \tag{6}$$

$$Recall = \frac{TP}{TP + FN} \tag{7}$$

4 Experiment

To validate the effectiveness of the proposed method of grading diabetic retinopathy fusing CNN and Transformer, multiple sets of experimental tests were used on the dataset Aptos_sigmaX10.

4.1 Comparison of Different EfficientNet Models

The first set of experiments were selection experiments for different EfficientNet models. According to the results in Fig. 5, the EfficientNet-B4 model showed the best results with better feature extraction in the same DR dataset, chieving a grading accuracy of 83.15%, so in the subsequent use of EfficientNet-B4 for network fusion.

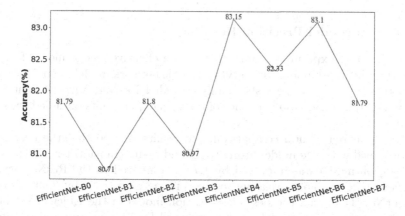

Fig. 5. Comparison of the grading effects of the EfficientNet series models.

4.2   Comparison of Different Swin Transformer Models

In addition to the ablation experiments carried out on EfficientNet, the same experiments was carried out using Swin Transformer for the dataset Aptos_sigmaX10, the results of which are shown in Fig. 6. The experimental results show that among the three Swin Transformer models, Swin-tiny can achieve the best accuracy results with a grading prediction accuracy of 85.06%. Therefore, we subsequently chose Swin-tiny as a complementary model to the global features of EfficientNet-B4.

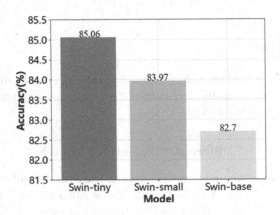

Fig. 6. Comparison of the grading effects of the Swin series models.

4.3   Fusion Model Precision Results

The third set of experiments aims to test the effectiveness of model fusion by comparing the fused model with a typical single network model in an experiment. The networks used for the tests mainly included ResNet, Vit, EfficientNet-B4 and Swin-tiny and the results of the comparison experiments obtained are shown in Table 3.

After an experimental comparison, the results showed that the best results were obtained with the model fusing CNN and Swin Transformer. The accuracy of the fusion model was improved by 1.74% compared to the ResNet network, and even more by 3.53% relative to the ViT network, and by 2.99% over the EfficientNet-B4 model, the best classification model in the EfficientNet family. In addition, the fusion model can be improved by 1.07% compared to the best performing Swin-tiny model in the Swin Transformer range. The results of the fusion model are not only higher than the accuracy of the EfficientNet model, but also higher than the accuracy of the Swin Transformer model, which proves the effectiveness of the fusion model of EfficientNet and Swin Transformer. it

Table 3. Comparative analysis table of the validity of the fusion model.

Models	Accuracy (%)
ResNet50 [20]	84.40%
ViT	82.61%
EfficientNet-B4	83.15%
Swin-tiny	85.06%
Ours	86.14%

can complement the global feature extraction ability of EfficientNet to a certain extent, and further improve the local feature extraction ability of the Swin Transformer model.

In addition, the confusion matrix results for the fusion model test results are given in Fig. 7. The figure shows that the fusion model correctly classified 179 of the 181 images non-Proliferative DR in the test set, 26 of the 37 images with mild non-proliferative DR, 88 of the 100 images with moderate non-proliferative DR, 7 of the 20 images with severe non-proliferative DR and 17 of the 30 images with proliferative DR. The best prediction results for non-Proliferative DR and the worst prediction results for severe non-proliferative DR may be due to the relatively large proportion of non-Proliferative DR images in the dataset, resulting in the model learning more information about that category during training; Additionally 50% of the severe non-proliferative lesions were misclassified as moderate non-proliferative lesions, mainly due to the small number of severe non-proliferative lesions in the dataset and the similarity of lesion information between moderate and severe non-proliferative lesions, such that a large number of images of severe non-proliferative lesions were judged as moderate non-proliferative lesions.

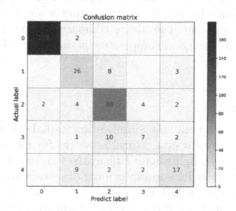

Fig. 7. Confusion Matrix for fusion model test results.

4.4 Comparison Results with Other Models

To further validate the validity of the model, the fusion model was compared with models proposed by other researchers on the dataset Aptos_sigmaX10 and the experimental results are shown in Table 4.

Table 4. Compared experimental results with other models model.

Reference	Year	Method	Accuracy (%)
Dekhil O et al. [6]	2019	Five-layer CNN	77%
Li et al. [21]	2019	CANet	83.20%
Yu et al. [22]	2021	Vision Transformer	85.50%
Islam M R et al. [10]	2022	Xception+CLAHE+t-SNE	84.36%
Ours	2023	EfFicientNet+Swin Transformer	86.14%

As shown in Table 4, the proposed fusion model achieved 86.14% graded accuracy on this dataset, outperforming better than the results of the other four models. A 9.14% improvement in grading accuracy compared to the five-layer convolutional network model proposed by Dekhil et al. [6], Relative to the cross-disease attention network CANet proposed by Li et al. [21], this method uses the disease-specific attention module and the disease-dependent attention module to selectively learn useful features of the disease, achieving an accuracy of 83.20%, but still 2.94% lower than the proposed method, Comparing the two-stage comparison method with a supervised comparison loss function proposed by Islam et al. [10] also yields an accuracy gain of 1.78%. Furthermore, Yu et al. [22] attempted to use Vit for retinal disease classification tasks and achieve 85.50% accuracy performance by pre-training the Transformer model in a large fundus image database and then fine-tuning it in a downstream retinal disease classification task, but the results of this paper's method still outperformed it by 0.64%. Taken together, the above comparative experimental results can effectively demonstrate the good competitive performance of the proposed fusion model.

5   Conclusion

Diabetic retinopathy is a common complication in diabetic patients. To address the shortcomings of convolutional neural networks for DR image grading, a DR grading method that fuses lightweight EfficientNet and Swin Transformer models is proposed to assist physicians in performing diagnosis, so as to better capture global and local features of DR images to improve the discriminative properties of the overall features. In future work, we will explore convolutional neural networks and Transformer architectures that are more suitable for this medical task and explore more effective fusion methods, such as feature interaction and combination in the middle of a dual-branch structure.

Acknowledgements. This work was supported in part by the Applied Basic Research Project of Liaoning Province under Grant 2023JH2/101300191, and the Young and Middle-aged Talents Program of the National Civil Affairs Commission.

References

1. Chen, C., Wu, S.Q., Wang, Y.F., et al.: Correlation between the duration of diabetes mellitus and diabetic retinopathy. China Mod. Phys. **58**(11), 77–80 (2020)
2. Yunlan, F.X.: Mechanism of NLRP3/IL-1β pathway in proliferative diabetic retinopathy. Int. J. Ophthalmol. **19**(09), 1559–1562 (2019)
3. Selvachandran, G., Quek, S.G., Paramesran, R., et al.: Developments in the detection of diabetic retinopathy: a state-of-the-art review of computer-aided diagnosis and machine learning methods. Artif. Intell. Rev. **56**(2), 915–964 (2023)
4. Lachurej, J., Deorankar, A.V., Lachure, S., et al.: Diabetic retinopathy using morphological operations and machine learning. In: IEEE International Advance Computing Conference (IACC), pp. 617–622 (2015)
5. Pratt, H., Coenen, F., Broadbent, D.M., et al.: Convolutional neural networks for diabetic retinopathy. Procedia Comput. Sci. **90**, 200–205 (2016)
6. Dekhil, O., Naglah, A., Shaban, M., et al.: Deep learning based method for computer aided diagnosis of diabetic retinopathy. In: 2019 IEEE International Conference on Imaging Systems and Techniques (IST), pp. 1–4. IEEE (2019)
7. de La Torre, J., Valls, A., Puig, D.: A deep learning interpretable classifier for diabetic retinopathy disease grading. Neurocomputing **396**, 465–476 (2020)
8. Zhou, Y., He, X., Huang, L., et al.: Collaborative learning of semi-supervised segmentation and classification for medical image. In: Proceedings of the IEEE/CVF Conference on Computer Vision and Pattern Recognition, pp. 2079–2088 (2019)
9. Gu, T.F., Hao, P.Y., Bai, C.W., et al.: Grading diabetic retinopathy in combination with multichannel attention. Chin. J. Graph. Arts **26**(07), 1726–1736 (2021)
10. Islam, M.R., Abdulrazak, L.F., Nahiduzzaman, M., et al.: Applying supervised contrastive learning for the detection of diabetic retinopathy and its severity levels from fundus images. Comput. Biol. Med. **146**, 105602 (2022)
11. Chen, H., Li, C., Wang, G., et al.: GasHis-transformer: a multi-scale visual transformer approach for gastric histopathological image detection. Pattern Recogn. **130**, 108827 (2022)
12. Vaswani, A., Shazeer, N., Parmar, N., et al.: Attention is all you need. In: Advances in Neural Information Processing Systems, vol. 30 (2017)
13. Tsiknakis, N., Theodoropoulos, D., Manikis, G., et al.: Deep learning for diabetic retinopathy detection and classification based on fundus images: a review. Comput. Biol. Med. **135**, 104599 (2021)
14. Tan, M., Le, Q.: EfficientNet: rethinking model scaling for convolutional neural networks. In: International Conference on Machine Learning, pp. 6105–6114. PMLR (2019)
15. Liu, Z., Lin, Y., Cao, Y., et al.: Swin transformer: hierarchical vision transformer using shifted windows. In: Proceedings of the IEEE/CVF International Conference on Computer Vision, pp. 10012–10022 (2021)
16. Hu, J., Shen, L., Sun, G.: Squeeze-and-excitation networks. In: Proceedings of the IEEE Conference on Computer Vision and Pattern Recognition, pp. 7132–7141 (2018)
17. Dosovitskiy, A., Beyer, L., Kolesnikov, A., et al.: An image is worth 16×16 words: transformers for image recognition at scale. arXiv preprint arXiv:2010.11929 (2020)

18. Liang, J., Cao, J., Sun, G., et al.: SwinIR: image restoration using swin transformer. In: Proceedings of the IEEE/CVF International Conference on Computer Vision, pp. 1833–1844 (2021)
19. Loshchilov, I., Hutter, F.: Decoupled weight decay regularization. arXiv preprint arXiv:1711.05101 (2017)
20. He, K., Zhang, X., Ren, S., et al.: Deep residual learning for image recognition. In: Proceedings of the IEEE Conference on Computer Vision and Pattern Recognition, pp. 770–778 (2016)
21. Li, X., Hu, X., Yu, L., et al.: CANet: cross-disease attention network for joint diabetic retinopathy and diabetic macular edema grading. IEEE Trans. Med. Imaging **39**(5), 1483–1493 (2019)
22. Yu, S., et al.: MIL-VT: multiple instance learning enhanced vision transformer for fundus image classification. In: de Bruijne, M., et al. (eds.) MICCAI 2021, Part VIII. LNCS, vol. 12908, pp. 45–54. Springer, Cham (2021). https://doi.org/10.1007/978-3-030-87237-3_5

Cross-modal Domain Adaptive Instance Segmentation in SAR Images via Instance-aware Adaptation

Xiao Cheng[1]([✉]), Chunbo Zhu[2], Lijie Yuan[3], and Suhua Zhao[4]

[1] Institute of Remote Sensing Satellite, CAST, Beijing, China
`gau1855@163.com`
[2] Image Processing Center, School of Astroautics, Beihang University, Beijing, China
[3] Tianjin Zhuocheng Technology Development Co., LTD., Tianjin, China
[4] China Shield Tunnelling Engineering Co., Ltd., Tianjin, China
`sy1915228@buaa.edu.cn`

Abstract. Synthetic Aperture Radar (SAR) images are valuable assets in remote sensing and earth observation due to the imaging ability in all-weather and all-time scenarios. However, acquiring and labeling SAR images can be challenging and expensive. Therefore, the domain adaptation (DA) from easily available optical image data to SAR image data is a significant motivation in SAR image interpretation. In this paper, a novel cross-modal DA approach from optical to SAR is introduced, namely CDA-SAR. It is pre-trained on easily obtained optical remote sensing images and achieves cross-modal instance segmentation in SAR images via unsupervised domain adaptation (UDA). The proposed UDA method contains sample-level and feature-level adaptation strategies to perform style-transferring and feature alignment in the latent space, respectively. The proposed domain adaptive approach is validated to be universal to various CNN-based instance segmentation models. Experimental results prove CDA-SAR achieves more than 280% performance improvement on HRSID dataset than that without DA. Furthermore, it shows robustness in complex background interference and multi-scale object distribution scenes in SAR images.

Keywords: Domain adaptation · Instance segmentation · SAR images · Cross-modal

1 Introduction

As an all-weather imaging method, SAR has played an important role in the field of remote sensing and earth observation. As the high-resolution and vast extent characteristics of SAR images, object detection with SAR images has a unique advantage on marine safety monitoring and marine resources development compared to other remote sensing methods. However, due to the difficulty in obtaining SAR images and the high cost of labeling, the interpretation model for SAR images has become an urgent problem. Therefore, it is of great benefit to studying cross-domain SAR image interpretation

W. Yongtian and W. Lifang (Eds.): IGTA 2023, CCIS 1910, pp. 413–424, 2023.
https://doi.org/10.1007/978-981-99-7549-5_30

based on transfer learning. In recent years, unsupervised domain adaptation (UDA) is proposed to address this issue. In such works, a model trained on a source domain dataset with pixel-level segmentation annotations is adapted for an unlabeled target domain. A popular domain adaptation choice is to align the image style and feature representations of different domains [1, 2]. A majority of recent methods [3–6] explore semantic-level adaptation such as category-level and instance-level alignment. Another effective approach, which employs GAN [7] architectures, is to minimize the accuracy of domain prediction. Instance segmentation is of great significance for SAR images, which combines semantic segmentation and object detection. On the basis of realizing the localization of the instance, each pixel of the input image is divided into semantically interpretable categories, and an instance mask of fine description is formed. As a more complex method of interpretation, it has a finer description and perception of objects.

In this paper, we present a novel unsupervised domain adaptation method that leverages a large-scale optical remote sensing dataset as the source domain to improve the interpretation of SAR image targets. Our proposed cross-modal domain adaptive instance segmentation method, illustrated in Fig. 1, performs domain adaptation on cross-domain images from the sample-level and feature-level, respectively. On the one hand, the domain adaptation at the sample level is mainly to approximate the low-level features such as texture and color of the SAR image. On the other hand, the domain adaptation at the feature level is mainly to optimize the classifier for the failure of the classifier for features in the latent space of the high-dimensional feature distribution. The two adaptation modules are performed together to achieve model adaptation on real SAR target domain images.

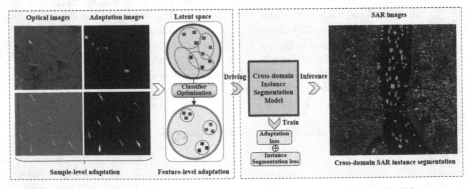

Fig. 1. The proposed cross-domain instance segmentation from optical to SAR images.

In view of the large difference in feature distributions between SAR images and optical images, a domain adaptation strategy based on target prototype alignment is proposed in this paper. Across the source and target domains, the target prototypes are extracted and aligned according to different modal targets. Furthermore, the measurement and aggregation of modal similarity are explored, and a reasonable mathematical model is designed to extract representative modal features. Moreover, several methods of modal similarity measurement are compared to realize domain adaptation task at model level effectively.

The main contributions of this paper are summarized as follows.

1) This paper proposes a cross-modal domain adaptation method for SAR instance segmentation, which supports transferring the model trained on optical images to SAR images. 2) The proposed sample-level and feature-level adaptation modules can collaboratively migrate SAR image features to reduce classifier bias since the large domain gap between optical and SAR images. 3) The experimental results on HRSID validate the effectiveness of the proposed method, which achieves competitive performance in instance segmentation tasks.

2 Related Work

2.1 Domain Adaptive Object Detection

In the domain adaptation problem, the source domain and the target domain often belong to the same type of task, but the distribution is different. From the adaptation manner, the UDA approaches can be mainly divided into image-level and feature-level methods. The image-level adaptation refers to changing the appearance of images such that images from the source domain and the target domain are more visually similar. These methods [8, 9] usually transfer the color, texture, illumination and other stylization factors of images from one domain to another. The feature-level transferring refers to matching the extracted feature distributions between the source and target domain. Zhao et al. [10] proposes a geometry-consisency constraint for domain adaptation in remote sensing images. In terms of object detection, Domain Adaptive Faster R-CNN [11] is a pioneering work of domain adaptation at the model level. It takes Faster R-CNN as the basic framework, adds a discriminator branch on the basis, and attaches to the feature map and candidate regions output by the feature extraction network. Huang et al. present Mask Scoring R-CNN [12] to improve instance segmentation performance by prioritizing more accurate mask predictions during COCO AP evaluation. Diversify and Match [13] uses CycleGAN [14] in the source domain and Generate multiple intermediate domain images between the target domains and share a label with the source domain to complete data enhancement. There are also few-shot UDA methods [15] and weakly-supervised methods [16] for cross-domain object detection. However, the cross-modality domain adaptation is still a challenging problem remaining unsettled.

2.2 Instance Segmentation in SAR Images

The traditional SAR object detection algorithm is mainly composed of spectral residual (SR) [17], constant false alarm rate (CFAR) [18] and improved algorithms derived therefrom. As the first attempt of instance segmentation applied on CNN, Mask R-CNN [19] adds a mask branch to predict the segmentation mask for each region of interest (RoI), paralleling the classification and regression branch in Faster R-CNN. Cascade Mask R-CNN [20] proposed a multi-stage detection architecture for both training and inference stages. Recently, cross-domain SAR instance detection are also investigated. Hybrid Task Cascade [21] improves Cascade Mask R-CNN with a joint multi-stage processing. Jeong et al. [22] leverage label-rich electro-optical images gradually instilling cross-domain knowledge. However, cross-domain instance segmentation from optical image to SAR image is challenging since the large domain gap. Wang et al. [23] proposes a few-shot SAR ship detection method based on metric leanring. Zhu et al. [24] combine the content of the optics and the style of the SAR and incorporates multiscale features in backbone and improves performance in ship instance segmentation.

However, current UDA methods for SAR instance detection lack the simulation of SAR image representation. In this paper, we leverage the domain adaptation from sample-level and feature-level concurrently, and an instance-level contrastive loss is designed for reducing the domain gap between the source optical and the target SAR images.

3   Method

This paper introduces a cross-domain instance segmentation method named CDA-SAR. It consists of a Sample-level Image Transfer (SIT) module and a Feature-level Domain Adaptation (FDA) module, which supports cross-domain instance segmentation in SAR images. The detail of CDA-SAR is introduced in the following chapters.

3.1   Problem Setting

Given a source domain dataset with images and instance-level annotations $\{x_S, y_S | x_S \in X_S, y_S \in Y_S\}$, and a target domain with only images $\{x_T | x_T \in X_T\}$. The goal is to train a model that can produce the instance-level predictions $\{\hat{y}_T\}$ of the target domain images.

3.2   Sample-level Image Transfer

Due to the large domain gap between optical and SAR images, the classifier may exhibit bias on the target domain due to the large intra-class variance across different domains. Therefore, a siamese generative-adversarial network called GeminiGAN is proposed in this for image style transfer from optical to SAR. As depicted in Fig. 2, on the basis of CycleGAN, GeminiGAN consists of siamese-adversarial branch and siamese-generative branch to support adversarial-generative training. Specifically, the annotation of instance mask x_M from the source optical domain image is also used as supervision in the generation of cross-domain samples x_S'. In this way, the network can focus on instances when generating the SAR-style samples in the target domain, reducing background interference such as sea clutter and terrain.

Beyond CycleGAN, the proposed GeminiGAN also take the instance mask from the source optical domain annotation as the input. Concretely, the generator G_{TS}, G_{ST} and G_{SM} are used to build a siamese architecture. In this way, when the transferred image is generated, the overall style of the image and the instance-wise style can be considered simultaneously. In siamese-adversarial network, the source domain image x_S is transferred to SAR-style x_T'. In the meantime, the instance-wise mask x_M is also transferred to x_M'. Likewise, in siamese-generative network, G_{ST} outputs the reconstructed source

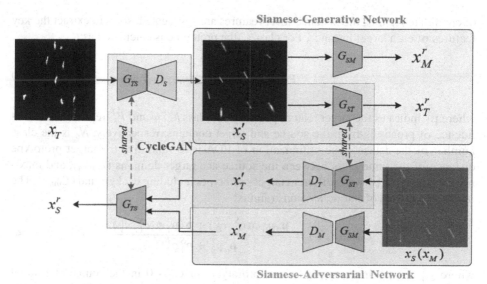

Fig. 2. The proposed sample-level image transfer module. Through the proposed siamese generative network and siamese adversarial network, the source domain image x_S can be transferred to x_S^r that approximates the real SAR images x_T.

domain image x_S^r. G_{SM} outputs the reconstructed instance mask x_M^r. The optimization goal of GeminiGAN is defined as:

$$
\begin{aligned}
\mathcal{L}_{Gemini}(G_{TS}, G_{ST}, G_{SM}) = \\
\mathcal{L}_{GAN}(G_{TS}, D_S, T, S) + \mathcal{L}_{GAN}(G_{ST}, D_T, S, T) + \lambda\mathcal{L}_{cyc}(G_{TS}, G_{ST}, G_{SM})
\end{aligned} \quad (1)
$$

where $\mathcal{L}_{GAN}$ represents the primal GAN loss and $\mathcal{L}_{cyc}$ is the cycle-consistency loss. λ is a constant coefficient that balances the instance branch. Since GeminiGAN expands the CycleGAN architecture, in terms of cycle-consistency, GeminiGAN considers the distribution of three generators, i.e., G_{TS}, G_{ST} and G_{SM}. Thus the objective of SIT is:

$$
\begin{aligned}
\mathcal{L}_{SIT}(G_{TS}, G_{ST}, G_{SM}) = \\
+ E_{y \sim P_{data}(s)}\big[\|G_{TS}(G_{ST}(s)) - s\|_1\big] \\
+ E_{t,m \sim P_{data}(t,m)}\big[\|G_{ST}(G_{TS}(t, m)) - t\|_1\big] \\
E_{t,m \sim P_{data}(t,m)}\big[\|G_{SM}(G_{TS}(t, m)) - m\|_1\big]
\end{aligned} \quad (2)
$$

3.3 Feature-level Domain Adaptation

Considering the inner feature inconformity in the latent space across optical and SAR images, we propose a feature-level adaptation method based on instance-level contrastive learning. Since the modal-variance between optical and SAR images, the adaptation includes the measurement of modal similarity and the aggregation of different modes of the same class. By constructing an incidence matrix that considers the location and size of candidate regions, the instance-level features are aggregated, so as to extract the key features of each target instance. For class k, the prototype is calculated as:

$$\mathbf{p}_k = \frac{\sum_{i=1}^{N_c} \tilde{c}_{ik} \cdot \tilde{F}_i^T}{\sum_{i=1}^{N_c} \tilde{c}_{ik}} \tag{3}$$

where $\mathbf{p}_k$ indicates the target feature prototype of class k. $\tilde{c}_{ik}$ and $\tilde{F}_i^T$ represent the confidence of proposals from the source and target domains, respectively. N_c is the class number of the dataset. The optimization of FDA is to minimize the target prototype distance of the same class between the source and target domains ($\mathcal{L}_{intra}$), and maximize the distance between different target prototypes including background ($\mathcal{L}_{inter}$). The optimization goal of intra-class constraint is:

$$\mathcal{L}_{intra}(S, T) = \frac{\mathbf{p}_0^S \mathbf{p}_0^T \phi(c_0^S, c_0^T) + \mathbf{p}_1^S \mathbf{p}_1^T \phi(c_1^S, c_1^T)}{\mathbf{p}_0^S \mathbf{p}_0^T + \mathbf{p}_1^S \mathbf{p}_1^T} \tag{4}$$

where $\mathbf{p}_0^S$ and $\mathbf{p}_0^T$ indicate the feature prototype for class 0 in the source and target domains, respectively. The optimization goal of inter-class constraint is defined as:

$$\mathcal{L}_{inter}(D, D') = \max(0, m - \phi(c_0^D, c_1^{D'})) \tag{5}$$

Thus the objective of FDA is defined as the unifying of $\mathcal{L}_{intra}$ and $\mathcal{L}_{inter}$:

$$\mathcal{L}_{FDA} = \mathcal{L}_{intra}(S, T) + \frac{1}{2}(\mathcal{L}_{inter}(S, S) + \mathcal{L}_{inter}(T, T)) \tag{6}$$

The model is trained in a two-step way. Firstly, the source-domain images are transferred to the SAR-style according to Eq. (2). Secondly, the cross-domain instance segmentation is trained via transferred images by optimizing Eq. (6).

3.4 Cross-domain Instance Segmentation

The proposed DA method is model-independent, which means it can be embedded in a variety of target detection and segmentation models based on neural networks. This paper focuses on instance segmentation, a refined target location approach to construct a cross-domain SAR instance segmentation model with the proposed hierarchical domain adaptation mechanisms on the basis of Cascade Mask R-CNN architectures.

Concretely, the instance segmentation task can be decoupled to a detection task and a segmentation task. The domain adaptation loss function is optimized together with the classification regression loss of the candidate region, and the classification regression and segmentation loss of R-CNN. The loss function of the whole network can be expressed as:

$$\mathcal{L}_{CDA-SAR} = \mathcal{L}_{cls}^{RPN} + \mathcal{L}_{loc}^{RPN} + \mathcal{L}_{cls}^{RCNN} + \mathcal{L}_{loc}^{RCNN} + \mathcal{L}_{mask}^{RCNN} + \mathcal{L}_{FDA} \tag{7}$$

where $\mathcal{L}_{cls}^{RPN}$ and $\mathcal{L}_{loc}^{RPN}$ represent the classification loss and localization loss for RPN. $\mathcal{L}_{cls}^{RCNN}$ and $\mathcal{L}_{loc}^{RCNN}$ indicate the corresponding loss for R-CNN architecture. While $\mathcal{L}_{mask}^{RCNN}$ is the instance-wise loss for instance segmentation task.

4 Experiments

4.1 Datasets and Evaluation Metrics

Datasets. LEVIR [25] is a large-scale optical remote-sensing object detection dataset that contains more than 22,000 images. We construct a subset called LEVIR-ship, which contrain 1491 images with newly annotated instance segmentation annotations. The High-Resolution SAR Images Dataset for Ship Detection and Instance Segmentation (HRSID) [26] has 5604 cropped SAR images and 16951 ships from 136 panoramic SAR imageries with a resolution ranging from 1 m to 5 m. We randomly select the same number images as the LEVIR-ship for experiment. In our implementation, LEVIR-ship is used as the source domain and the HRSID is used as the target domain.

Metrics. According to MS COCO standards, we take AP50, AP75 in different IoU threshold, and APs, APm, APl for different target scales to characterize the performance, which are in all respects for detection with bounding boxes and segmentation with masks. For sample-level transfer, the Fréchet Inception Distance (FID) [27] and Kernel Inception Distance (KID) [28] are used to evaluate the distance between the transferred images and real images.

4.2 Implementation Details

The proposed method was implemented using the PyTorch toolbox and MMDetection [29], and all experiments were conducted on four NVIDIA 2080Ti GPUs for 12 training epochs. The initial learning rate was set to 0.001 and decreased by 0.1 after 8 and 11 epochs. SGD [30] was used as the optimizer, and the momentum and weight decay were set to 0.9 and 0.0001, respectively.

4.3 Performance Comparison for SAR Ship Instance Segmentation

To investigate the instance segmentation efficiency on SAR images, we compare the proposed method with various instance segmentation models including Mask R-CNN [19], Mask Scoring R-CNN [12], Cascade Mask R-CNN [20] and Hybrid Task Cascade [21] to achieve cross-domain instance segmentation. Please note that the training data is transferred images by the proposed GeminiGAN. As seen in Table 1, the proposed CDA-SAR model outperforms all other models with respect to AP, AP50 and AP75. In detail, CDA-SAR achieves 56.5 AP, which is the highest among all models.

Overall, the CDA-SAR model achieves state-of-the-art performance with competitive detection accuracy, location precision, and small target detection capability. In terms of the APs metric, which measures the average precision for small targets, the CDA-SAR model achieves the highest 58.7%. This indicates that the CDA-SAR model has solider small target detection capability, which is highly effective in SAR images. Figure 3 displays a representative SAR scene with multi-scale ship targets and complex cartographic background. The proposed CDA-SAR shows superior ability in reducing false-alarm and error detection rate. Figure 4 shows the results of the proposed CDA-SAR in multiple scenes including sea surface, harbor and complex background areas, which demonstrate the generalization of the proposed method.

Table 1. Cross-domain instance segmentation on HRSID dataset. The proposed domain adaptation method can be embedded into various instance segmentation models. The best results are marked in bold.

Model	Metric					
	AP	AP50	AP75	APs	APm	APl
Mask R-CNN	54.2	85.1	64.8	56.3	52.6	4.4
Mask Scoring R-CNN	54.3	84.7	64.6	55.8	**55.7**	2.4
Cascade Mask R-CNN	53.7	84.3	64.2	55.7	53.4	3.7
Hybrid Task Cascade	54.2	85.0	64.8	55.6	54.3	**4.9**
CDA-SAR (Ours)	**56.5**	**88.4**	**67.9**	**58.7**	54.1	4.2

Mask R-CNN   Cascade Mask R-CNN   CDA-SAR (Ours)

Fig. 3. Qualitative comparison between different instance segmentation methods. The proposed CDA-SAR achieves more robust performance with lower false-alarm and error detection rate.

Table 2 presents the test results on the real SAR image dataset HRSID, using the transferred image data generated by CycleGAN and GeminiGAN at the sample level. The transferred image data was used to train the models, and the results deminstrate that the simulated data generated by GeminiGAN is closer to the distribution of real SAR image data than CycleGAN, with respect to the trained model achieves higher performance.

In detail, without domain adaptation, the model performance on HRSID is only 9.0% AP. With the proposed sample-level adaptation, i.e., GeminiGAN, the AP was dramatically improved to 26.3%, and the performance on various sizes of targets are improved synchronously in terms of APs, APm and APl. These results validate the necessity of sample-level domain adaptation methods in cross-domain ship instance segmentation tasks.

The second part of Table 2 shows the cooperativity of sample-level and feature-level domain adaptation. Under the joint training conditions of GeminiGAN and FDA, the model achieved a performance improvement of over 280% in AP (from 9.0% to 34.3%), and the segmentation performance of different scale targets was greatly improved.

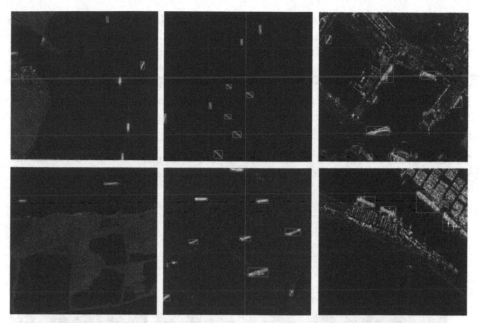

Fig. 4. Qualitative visualizations of cross-domain ship instance segmentation of CDA-SAR in various scenes.

Ablation study on the instance-level contrastive learning approach demonstrate the effectiveness of intra-class aggregation and inter-class separation.

Table 2. Impact of various domain adaptation method on the cross-domain instance segmentation performance in HRSID.

Domain Adaptation		Metric					
Sample-level	Feature-level	AP	AP50	AP75	APs	APm	APl
None	None	9.0	24.1	4.7	9.0	12.3	0.2
CycleGAN	None	25.8	49.7	24.6	26.0	32.6	2.4
GeminiGAN	None	26.3	49.8	25.6	26.7	32.4	2.2
GeminiGAN	FDA-intra	33.5	61.9	33.8	35.5	29.6	3.2
GeminiGAN	FDA-inter	32.7	60.5	33.8	35.0	30.8	3.1
GeminiGAN	FDA	**34.3**	**62.5**	**35.4**	**36.4**	**32.6**	**4.3**

4.4 Ablation Study on Sample-level Transfer

To investigate the sample-transfer efficiency from the source optical images to target SAR style, we evaluate the FID and KID on the source optical image, transferred image by

CycleGAN and transferred image by GeminiGAN in Table 3. The experimental results demonstrate the transferred images by the proposed GeminiGAN achieve the best performance in both FID and KID, which indicates the superior image-style transfer ability from optical image to SAR image of the proposed GeminiGAN. Figure 5 displays the qualitative transferred image samples from CycleGAN and GeminiGAN, respectively. It can be seen that GeminiGAN achieves style transfer results that are more similar to SAR images, validating the transfer efficiency from optical image to SAR style.

Table 3. Quality assessment of the transferred image. Quantization results in both FID and KID prove that the proposed GeminiGAN achieves better approximation of SAR image.

Source domain images	FID ↓	KID × 100 ↓
Optical image (source domain)	162.11	13.01
CycleGAN	102.06	6.94
GeminiGAN	**74.65**	**4.08**

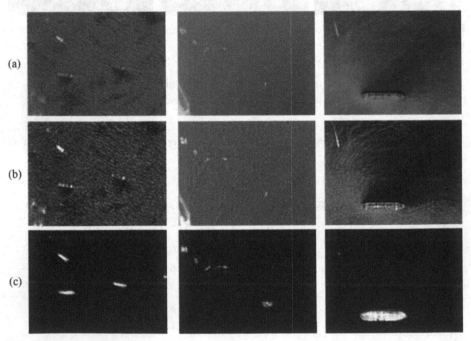

Fig. 5. Image transfer result by sample-level domain adaptation. (a) Source-domain optical images; (b) CycleGAN results; (c) GeminiGAN results.

5   Conclusion

This paper presents CDA-SAR, focusing on cross-domain and cross-modality instance segmentation from optical to SAR images. Specific to the challenging instance segmentation task, we propose a hierarchical domain adaptation method using large-scale, easily accessible optical dataset as the source domain, and addresses SAR instance segmentation without annotation in SAR images. The proposed method reduces the domain differences between the optical and SAR images at both the sample level and the feature level. Experimental results in HRSID validate the effectiveness of CDA-SAR. Our future work will further explore cross-domain unsupervised domain adaptation methods under low-sample conditions.

References

1. Zhang, Y., Qiu, Z., Yao, T., et al.: Fully convolutional adaptation networks for semantic segmentation. In: Proceedings of the IEEE/CVF Conference on Computer Vision and Pattern Recognition, pp. 6810–6818, June 2018
2. Tsai, Y., Hung, W., Schulter, S., et al.: Learning to adapt structured output space for semantic segmentation. In: Proceedings of the IEEE/CVF Conference on Computer Vision and Pattern Recognition, pp. 7472–7481, June 2018
3. Wang, Z., Yu, M., Wei, Y., et al.: Differential treatment for stuff and things: a simple unsupervised domain adaptation method for semantic segmentation. In: Proceedings of the IEEE/CVF Conference on Computer Vision and Pattern Recognition (CVPR), pp. 12632–12641, June 2020
4. Lv, F., Liang, T., Chen, X., et al.: Cross-domain semantic segmentation via domain-invariant interactive relation transfer. In: Proceedings of the IEEE/CVF Conference on Computer Vision and Pattern Recognition (CVPR), pp. 4333–4342, June 2020
5. Wang, H., Shen, T., Zhang, W., et al.: Classes matter: a fine-grained adversarial approach to cross-domain semantic segmentation (2020). arXiv:2007.09222
6. Yuan, B., Zhao, D.P., Shao, S., et al.: Birds of a feather flock together: category-divergence guidance for domain adaptive segmentation. IEEE Trans. Image Process. **31**, 2878–2892 (2022)
7. Goodfellow, I.J., Pouget-Abadie, J., Mirza, M., et al.: Generative adversarial nets. In: Proceedings of the NIPS, pp. 1–9 (2014)
8. Li, Y., Yuan, L., Vasconcelos, N.: Bidirectional learning for domain adaptation of semantic segmentation. In: Proceedings of the IEEE/CVF Conference on Computer Vision and Pattern Recognition (CVPR), pp. 6929–6938, June 2019
9. Wu, Z., et al.: DCAN: dual channel-wise alignment networks for unsupervised scene adaptation. In: Ferrari, V., Hebert, M., Sminchisescu, C., Weiss, Y. (eds.) Computer Vision – ECCV 2018. ECCV 2018. LNCS, vol. 11209, pp. 518–534. Springer, Cham (2018). https://doi.org/10.1007/978-3-030-01228-1_32
10. Zhao, D.P., Yuan, B., Gao, Y., et al.: UGCNet: an unsupervised semantic segmentation network embedded with geometry consistency for remote-sensing images. IEEE Geosci. Remote Sens. Lett. **19**, 1–5 (2022)
11. Chen, Y.H., Wen, L., Christos, S., et al.: Domain adaptive faster R-CNN for object detection in the wild. In: 2018 IEEE/CVF Conference on Computer Vision and Pattern Recognition, pp. 3339–3348 (2018)
12. Huang, Z.J., Huang, L.C., Gong, Y.C., et al.: Mask scoring R-CNN. In: 2019 IEEE/CVF Conference on Computer Vision and Pattern Recognition (CVPR), pp. 6402–6411 (2019)

13. Kim, T., Jeong, M., Kim, S., et al.: Diversify and match: a domain adaptive representation learning paradigm for object detection. In: 2019 IEEE/CVF Conference on Computer Vision and Pattern Recognition (CVPR), pp. 12448–12457 (2019)

14. Zhu, J.-Y., Park, T., Isola, P., et al.: Unpaired image-to-image translation using cycle-consistent adversarial networks. In: Proceedings of the IEEE International Conference on Computer Vision (ICCV), pp. 2242–2251, October 2017

15. Wang, T., Zhang, X.P., Yuan, L., et al.: Few-shot adaptive faster R-CNN. In: 2019 IEEE/CVF Conference on Computer Vision and Pattern Recognition (CVPR), pp. 7166–7175 (2019)

16. Inoue, N., Furuta, R., Yamasaki, T., et al.: Cross-domain weakly-supervised object detection through progressive domain adaptation. In: 2018 IEEE/CVF Conference on Computer Vision and Pattern Recognition, pp. 5001–5009 (2018)

17. Hou, X.D., Zhang, L.Q.: Saliency detection: a spectral residual approach. In: 2007 IEEE Conference on Computer Vision and Pattern Recognition, pp. 1–8 (2007)

18. Robey, F., Fuhrmann, D., Kelly, E.J., et al.: A CFAR adaptive matched filter detector. IEEE Trans. Aerosp. Electron. Syst. **28**, 208–216 (1992)

19. He, K., Gkioxari, G., Dollár, P., et al.: Mask R-CNN. IEEE Trans. Pattern Anal. Mach. Intell. **42**, 386–397 (2017)

20. Cai, Z.W., Nuno, V.: Cascade R-CNN: delving into high quality object detection. In: 2018 IEEE/CVF Conference on Computer Vision and Pattern Recognition, pp. 6154–6162 (2017)

21. Chen, K., Ouyang, W., Loy, C.C.: Hybrid task cascade for instance segmentation. In: IEEE Conference on Computer Vision and Pattern Recognition (CVPR), pp. 4974–4983 (2019)

22. Jeong, S., Kim, Y., Kim, S., et al.: Enriching SAR ship detection via multistage domain alignment. IEEE Geosci. Remote Sens. Lett. **19**, 1–5 (2022)

23. Wang, X., Zhou, H.J., Chen, Z., et al.: Few-Shot SAR ship image detection using two-stage cross-domain transfer learning. In: IGARSS 2022 - 2022 IEEE International Geoscience and Remote Sensing Symposium, pp. 2195–2198 (2022)

24. Zhu, C., Zhao, D., Qi, J., et al.: Cross-domain transfer for ship instance segmentation in SAR images. In: 2021 IEEE International Geoscience and Remote Sensing Symposium IGARSS, pp. 2206–2209 (2021)

25. Zou, Z., Shi, Z.: Random access memories: a new paradigm for target detection in high resolution aerial remote sensing images. IEEE Trans. Image Process. 1100–1111 (2018)

26. Wei, S., Zeng, X., Qu, Q., et al.: HRSID: a high-resolution SAR images dataset for ship detection and instance segmentation. IEEE Access (2020)

27. Heusel, M., Ramsauer, H., Unterthiner, T., et al.: GANs trained by a two time-scale update rule converge to a local Nash equilibrium. In: NIPS (2017)

28. Binkowski, M., Sutherland, D.J., Arbel, M., et al.: Demystifying MMD GANs. ArXiv, abs/1801.01401 (2018)

29. Chen, K., Wang, J., Pang, J., et al.: MMDetection: Open MMLab Detection Toolbox and Benchmark. arXiv 2019, arXiv:1906.07155

30. Bottou, L.: Large-scale machine learning with stochastic gradient descent. In: Lechevallier, Y., Saporta, G. (eds.) Proceedings of COMPSTAT'2010, pp. 177–186. Physica-Verlag HD, Heidelberg (2010). https://doi.org/10.1007/978-3-7908-2604-3_16

Application of Computer Vision Technology in Collaborative Control of the "Zhurong" Mars Rover

Jia Wang[1], Guolin Hu[1(✉)], Dafei Li[1], Saijin Wang[1], Shaojin Han[1], Xin Li[1], Xiaohui Liu[1], Ziqing Cheng[1(✉)], Hui Zhang[1], Zhao Huang[1], Ximing He[1], and Xiaoxue Wang[1,2]

[1] Beijing Aerospace Control Center, Beijing 100094, China
`masterhgl@sina.com, 303241844@qq.com, heximing15@nudt.edu.cn`
[2] Key Laboratory of Science and Technology on Aerospace Flight Dynamics, Beijing 100094, China

Abstract. The "Zhurong" Mars rover successfully landed on the surface of Mars on May 22, 2021, and began its inspection and exploration. Currently, it has traveled 1921 m and achieved a series of important scientific discoveries. Due to objective difficulties such as harsh terrain conditions, insufficient energy, and limited communication, the "Zhurong" Mars rover adopts a collaborative control mode of "semi intelligent on board autonomous + ground teleoperation". Computer vision technology is the key core technology supporting the collaborative control of the rover. In the enter descent landing stage and Mars surface roving, computer vision technology has broken through key technologies, such as rapid localization of the lander, terrain analysis of landing areas, three-dimensional terrain reconstruction, terrain classification, navigation and positioning, path planning, and simulation verification, solved the problem of long-term efficient mobile technology of the rover, and significantly expanded the detection range of the Mars rover, robustly guaranteeing the efficient and stable inspection and long-term survival of the Mars rover. This paper elaborates on the aforementioned technologies and their special on-orbit applications.

Keywords: Zhurong · collaborative control · navigation and positioning · 3D-reconstruction · path planning · simulation verification

1 Introduction

China's first Mars landing rover was launched at Wenchang Space Launch Center in Hainan on July 23, 2020 [1]. After more than 10 months of flight and survey around Mars, it successfully entered and crossed the Mars atmosphere on May 15, 2021, and landed safely in the pre-selected landing area south of Utopia Planitia [2, 3]. On May 22, 2021, China's first Mars rover, the "Zhurong", drove onto the Mars surface and began conducting its inspection and exploration mission after completing imaging of the landing platform. On June 12, 2021, the National Space Administration released panoramic views of the landing site, Martian terrain, and other images, marking the successful completion of China's first Mars exploration mission and becoming the second country in the world to successfully land and conduct inspections on the Martian surface [4, 5].

Guided by remote sensing data, the "Zhurong" Mars rover has maintained an efficient mobile detection mode [6], traveling southward to trace the boundary zone between the ancient oceans and land. As of May 18, 2022, the rover had been working on the surface of Mars for approximately 360 sols, traveling a total of 1921 m [7]. Together with the orbiter, the rover collected scientific data with different perceptual scales and accuracy for five major scientific objectives [8]. The discovery of the "Zhurong" Mars rover filled the gap in the observational evidence of liquid water at low latitudes on Mars [9]. The rover endured a sun outage lasted 50 days, conducted relay communication experiments with the Mars Express orbiter [10], and was the first to interact with human probes on other planets. Currently, the "Zhurong" Mars rover is dormant.

The "Zhurong" Mars rover adopts a collaborative control mode of "semi intelligent on board autonomous + ground teleoperation". Ground teleoperation combines the performance of the rover and information obtained from perception, illumination, ephemeris, energy, temperature, and position to develop a mission-level exploration plan for the rover. Behavior planning was performed under various global and capability constraints, and the rover could be ultimately controlled to complete the inspection and exploration task through a command sequence [11]. Computer vision technology is an important core technology supporting the remote operation of the "Zhurong" Mars rover. During the enter descent landing stage and Mars surface roving, the problem of long-distance, efficient mobile technology was solved, and the detection range of the Mars rover was significantly expanded [1], providing a strong guarantee for efficient, robust patrol survey and long-term survival of Mars rover.

Based on the characteristics of the first Mars exploration mission, this article first briefly introduces the control mode of the "Zhurong" Mars rover and then introduces key technologies and methods, such as high-precision landing point positioning from coarse to fine, absolute positioning of the rover, 3D reconstruction and terrain classification, hierarchical path planning and simulation verification. Finally, the practical on-orbit application of these computer vision technologies was demonstrated.

2   Collaborative Control of the Rover

Compared with lunar surface missions, Mars exploration missions detect distant targets and dynamically changing environments, resulting in significant differences in operational control between Mars and lunar rovers. The primary challenges include poor terrain conditions, insufficient energy, and limited communication [10]. The distribution density of rocks on the Mars surface is approximately twice that on the Moon, and various rugged terrains exits. The soil has a hard surface layer and a loose inner layer caused by weathering and has a certain degree of visual deception [12]. The intensity of illumination on the Mars surface is only 1/5 of that on the Moon [13], even in clear weather, the optical depth does not exceed 0.5, and there are unpredictable long periods of sand and dust weather, which can last for up to one year in severe cases, and the optical depth is close to 10 [14]. Therefore, a Mars rover faces the treatment of insufficient energy throughout its entire mission cycle. Communication conditions on Mars are severely limited, resulting in delays in uploading commands, astral space occlusion, and low data transmission rates [15]. Constrained by its Martian orbit, the Mars rover communicates periodically with the orbiter. In the relay orbit, communication between devices occurs twice a day, and in the later stage of the remote sensing orbit, daily inter satellite communication is reduced to one or no communication [16]. Therefore, it is extremely important to obtain as much scientific exploration data as possible and plan the working sequence and driving route of the Mars rover reasonably and efficiently while meeting the constraints of the time-varying environment on the surface of Mars and the working ability of the rover [16].

The "Zhurong" rover adopts a collaborative control mode. Based on the telemetry, image, and detection data transmitted from the relay communication, the rover behavior evaluation of the rover on the previous sol day and the remote reconstruction of the current surface environment were conducted by ground crew, and the task planning for the next sol day was completed. Finally, all control sequences of the next sol day were uploaded using an uplink. Compared with the "Yutu 2" lunar rover, the "Zhurong" rover has significantly improved autonomous control ability [17]. To improve the mobility, active suspension Mars surface mobile technology [18] was adopted for the first time, which has a variety of special functions such as crawling, wheel lifting, crab walking, etc. A vision based long-distance mobility scheme was designed, breaking the limitation of traditional mobility schemes that cannot move more than 10 m at a time [10]. An autonomous sleep-reboot system was designed to address the energy security issues of the Mars rover after encountering dust and sand. We designed periodic work templates based on local time on Mars, antenna autonomous tracking and communication based on ephemeris and orbiter orbit, and other functions to achieve autonomous work under unmanned conditions and solve the long-term autonomous survival problem in non-communication situations, including sun outage [10].

3 Computer Vision Technology

Computer vision technology played a crucial role during the inspection and exploration process of the "Zhurong" Mars rover, which was mainly reflected in four aspects: lander localization, rover localization, 3D terrain reconstruction and classification, path planning and simulation verification.

3.1 Lander Localization

The Tianwen-1 probe was equipped with a Guidance Navigation and Control (GNC) optical sensor at the bottom, with a vertical downward viewing angle facing the Martian surface. During the entry, descent and landing (EDL) process, the Martian surface sequence was imaged [19]. However, owing to the limitations of communication transmission data, the ground cannot quickly receive a large number of descent images as landing point localization data. After determining the data transmission priority according to the requirements of the Tianwen-1 mission, only one descent image can be received during the initial landing stage, with a low imaging height (approximately 100 m) and a small coverage field of view [20]. Therefore, in the early landing stage of the "Zhurong" spacecraft, it is very difficult to use traditional methods to match the descent image with the high-resolution orbital Digital Orthophoto Map (DOM) of the landing area for lander localization. After landing, the stereo Navigation Terrain Cameras (NaTeCams) of the "Zhurong" Mars rover captured images of the land area at a nearly horizontal pitch angle (-5°) on the landing platform, and all data were transmitted to the ground [20]. Compared with the descent image, a 360° panorama has a larger range of characteristics, that is, the topological relationship between mud volcano, meteorite crater, sand dune and other landforms around the landing site, and the camera's internal and installation parameters were accurately calibrated on the ground, which could be used for space resection with multi-image to calculate the precise position of the lander [21]. Figure 1 shows the method flow for the rapid localization of the lander.

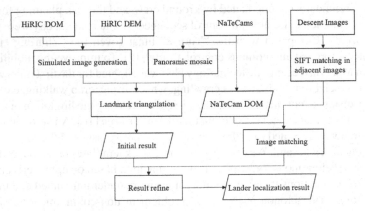

Fig. 1. Flowchart for localization of the lander based on coarse to fine strategy.

3.2 Rover Localization

After the initial landing on the Martian surface (the "Zhurong" Mars rover was not separated from the lander), the "Tianwen-1" landing patrol assembly first uses the precise positioning results (longitude, latitude and height) of the lander to establish a landing coordinate system (LCS) ($O - XYZ$). The origin is the landing point, with the positive X-axis following the local due north direction and the positive Z-axis pointing towards the center of the Martian. The positive Y-axis, along with the positive X-axis and positive Z-axis, forms a right-hand coordinate system [21, 22]; therefore, this LCS is uniquely determined and remains unchanged. Next, based on the geometric installation relationship between the "Zhurong" Mars rover and the landing platform, the working coordinate system (WCS) ($W_n - XYZ$) of the rover is established using the LCS as a reference, pointing to the same coordinate system as the LCS, with the origin being a certain waypoint of the rover, and n being the current working coordinate system serial number. Subsequently, the onboard inertial navigation system, odometer equipment, and vision-based positioning methods are all based on the current WCS to determine the relative position of the waypoints in the WCS.

The localization of the waypoints of the "Zhurong" rover adopts a combination of "onboard autonomy + ground correction" [11]. Positioning methods for ground correction are based on image matching, including cross-site relative visual localization and absolute localization based on DOM matching [21]. The former serves as a standard method during the remote operation mission of the Mars rover to ensure continuous positioning of all stations. The latter is an additional method used when the terrain on the Martian surface exhibits distinct characteristics. Therefore, through a series of transformations of the waypoints, WCSs, and LCS, the absolute localization of the rover can be obtained, and the corresponding implementation process is shown in Fig. 2.

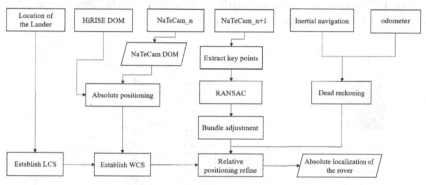

Fig. 2. Flowchart for rover localization [21].

3.3 3D Reconstruction and Terrain Classification

After completing the "landing group photo", the "Zhurong" Mars rover adopts a long-distance movement mode, expanding its daily movement distance from 10 m to approximately 20 m [11]. Compared to the Chang'e mission, the ground requires the use of NaTeCams to construct a larger range of three-dimensional terrain. For distant targets (usually 7 m away), the measurement error of the same point in adjacent images will significantly increase, leading to an obvious "burrs" phenomenon during data fusion. After analysis, this phenomenon is mainly caused by the measurement error of the mast yaw angle. In this case, the measurement error of the mast yaw angle causes a misalignment when adjacent stereo images are connected to point clouds [22]. Therefore, in the three-dimensional reconstruction of terrain, this study constructs a closed block adjustment model using the homonymous feature points between adjacent images, regards the mast yaw angle as the initial value, and achieves an overall calculation of the camera's relative pose through the overall least-squares adjustment, thereby avoiding the measurement error of the mast yaw angle [22, 23].

Unlike the high-vacuum and rigid (time-invariant) environment on the lunar surface, the Martian surface exhibits time-varying characteristics such as the atmosphere, wind field, sand, and dust. Long-term weathering can easily cause the outer surface to become soft, making the terrain somewhat deceptive. The "Zhurong" Mars rover landed in the Northern hemisphere of Mars, where there are mostly plains filled with lava at lower altitudes [24]. Lava flow will make the Martian surface irregular, making it more difficult for the rover to pass through; and particles with lower packing density and cohesion adhere to the surface of Mars, resulting in a loose state of the igneous soil, which makes it easy for the rover to slip while traveling on the surface of Mars [25]. Therefore, it is not sufficient to analyze only the geometric features of Martian terrain when evaluating its passability. It is also necessary to use computer vision methods to recognize the non-geometric features of ground types, namely, terrain classification. Non-geometric obstacles are difficult to distinguish, but they have a direct impact on the safe driving of Mars rovers. This study uses a deep learning method and deep convolutional neural networks (CNNs) to design a terrain attribute classifier for NaTeCams images [26]. The implementation process is illustrated in Fig. 3.

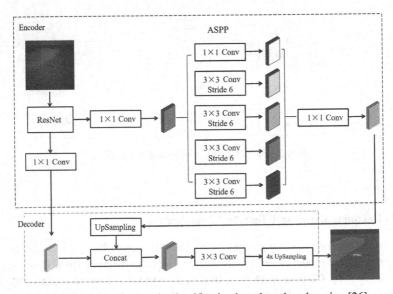

Fig. 3. Flowchart for terrain classification based on deep learning [26].

This classification model is based on DeepLab v3 + implementation. During the encoding process, ResNet is used as the basic network to extract input image features, before the input NaTeCams images features are extracted through multiple interval hole convolutions in the ASPP module, effectively avoiding information loss during feature extraction. When decoding, we connect the low-level features extracted from ResNet with the features extracted from ASPP, and finally add a sampling process to gradually restore the original size segmentation results. After sufficient training, the terrain classifier can achieve pixel-level segmentation.

3.4 Path Planning and Simulation Validation

The "Zhurong" rover pioneered the use of a multi-site mobility planning method that combines "ground long-range static planning and autonomous dynamic obstacle avoidance planning" [10, 11]. Through single planning, the rover is controlled to complete multiple, single movements of no more than 10 m, resulting in a significant improvement in the rover's control ability compared to the "Yutu&2" rover, with the maximum range of a single movement being increased to 40 m [17], effectively improving the efficiency of Mars rover inspection and exploration. As shown in Fig. 4, when conducting static planning on the ground, a perception method combining "orbiter DOM and NaTeCams images" is used, and a hierarchical planning strategy is adopted. First, based on the high resolution orbiter DOM, global planning is performed to determine the direction of the rover from its current position to the detection target; and based on local images of the NaTeCams, local planning is carried out to determine the specific movement strategy of the Mars rover for a single move. This plan reassesses the current Martian surface environment based on sensor information to ensure the rationality and safety of the rover's travel trajectory.

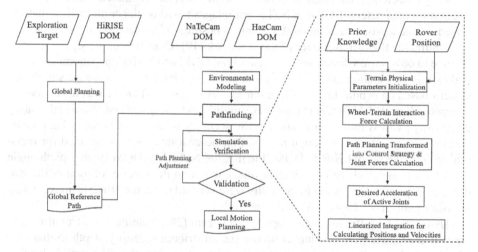

Fig. 4. Flowchart for layered path planning and simulation validation.

Considering that the ground does not have the conditions for real-time monitoring and control of the rover's movement and the risk of terrain is greater, the rover is prone to slipping [27], posing great challenges to its movement. Therefore, it is necessary to verify the local path planning strategy. In this study, we designed a simulation verification method based on dynamics modeling [8]. Because it not only considers the mechanical effects of various components, such as the vehicle body and wheels during the rover's movement process, but also the mechanical effects of the wheels and soil during the movement process [25], it can more accurately model the rover's movement process, thereby further reducing movement risk.

4 On-Orbit Implementation and Applications

Teleoperation is a crucial supporting technology for Mars rovers to conduct patrols and scientific explorations after soft landing on the Martian surface. Computer vision, as the primary means of obtaining landing environment information, plays an extremely important role. By obtaining Martian surface images and a series of processing and analysis technologies, it guarantees the implementation of scientific exploration missions and the safe driving of Mars rovers. The engineering goal of "efficient movement and detection" is achieved. This chapter provides a detailed introduction to the application of computer vision technology in the "Zhurong" Mars rover.

4.1 Lander Localization and Terrain Analysis of the Landing Area

The 12 left NaTeCam images captured at the top of landing platform with a pitch angle of -5° were used to generate a 360° panorama with image stitching, from which the candidate landmarks were also selected [19]. These eight image coordinates of candidate landmarks in the original NaTeCam images were obtained using the stitching transformation parameters. Each landmark azimuth angle was also calculated with the exterior orientation parameters (EOPs) of NaTeCam images based on the collinearity equation. Based on the least-squares method, the initial position of the lander can be calculated by minimizing the azimuth error of the landmark [19]. Considering the significant difference in observation directions between orbital DOM and NaTeCam panorama, which makes it is very challenging to find the corresponding landmarks, an image simulation system based on orbital Digital Elevation Model (DEM) and DOM was introduced to generate simulated NaTeCam images at multiple view angles. The simulated images effectively assisted in the verification of the accuracy of the corresponding landmarks. Guided by the initial localization results, four descent images were selected for registration with the orbital HiRIC DOM. Finally, the NaTeCam DOM (with a pitch angle of -30°) was matched with the descent image to obtain the precise location of the lander. Subsequently, the localization results were verified using the HiRISE image with a measurement error of approximately 3 m [20].

Using the ArcGIS plugin developed by the team [28], quantitative calculations and statistical analysis were conducted on the size, distribution density, depth-to-diameter ratio, and other aspects of the impact crater morphology near the "Tianwen-1" landing area to provide data support for scientific target selection and mission planning. Figure 5a shows the landing point of "Tianwen-1" as the center point and surrounding 20 × 20 km^2, the bottom image shows the rendering of CTX DOM overlaid with the fusion DEM of HiRIC and MOLA, indicating that the landing area is generally relatively flat. Figure 5b and 5c show the gradient map of this range and the kernel density map of the crater distribution within the impact crater radius of 1 km. Compared to the due south direction, the impact craters on the north side of "Zhurong" were denser and mostly clustered secondary craters. Moreover, scientists speculate that the southern area of the landing site is the boundary zone between the ancient sea and the ancient land, with more abundant geological features and higher scientific research value [4]. Therefore, "Zhurong" is travelling southward, gradually approaching the direction of the highland-lowland boundary (HLB) and the suspected shorelines [6]. The yellow areas or curves in Fig. 5d represent the four selected scientific exploration objects from near to far, and the white arrows represent the overall planned travel [6, 29].

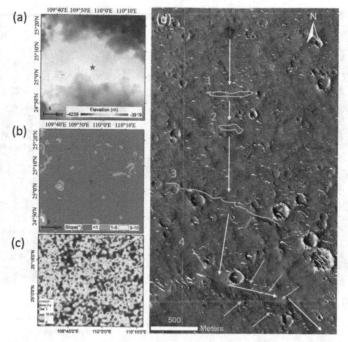

Fig. 5. Terrain analysis and driving direction planning of the landing area: (a) DEM; (b) slope; (c) crater kernel density; (d) detection targets and direction of travel.

4.2 Rover Localization and Error Evaluation

So far the "Zhurong" Mars rover, has moved 205 times in total. Continuous relative localization was performed for all stations using the localization method described in Sect. 3.2. Five absolute localization were conducted on July 2, 2021, July 24, 2021, August 20, 2021, January 19, 2022 and April 14, 2022 [22]. In the relative localization stage, owing to the generally small difference in yaw angles between adjacent stations (<30°) and relatively flat terrain at each waypoint (pitch angle and rolling angle basically <3°), using the least squares method to calculate the relative position can usually achieve stable convergence results. In addition, compared with the lunar surface, the terrain features observed in the Martian surface image were more abundant, and there was almost no significant difference in the illumination of adjacent waypoints. According to statistics, approximately 90% of the connection points could be determined through automatic matching. Only when the characteristics of the Martian surface were not obvious, it was necessary to use artificial selection of connection points for auxiliary positioning. In the absolute localization process, sand dunes, craters, and rocks in the NaTeCam images were used as the homonymous feature points to associate with the

HiRISE image to correct the cumulative error in relative localization caused by long-distance movement.

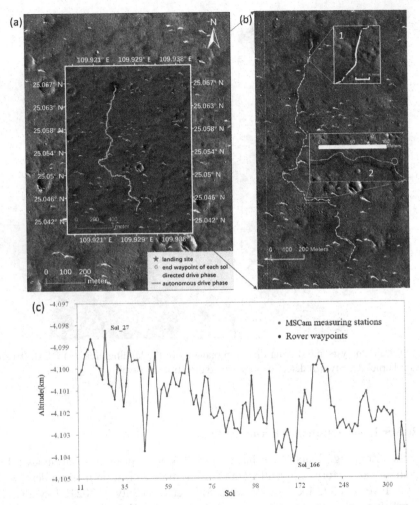

Fig. 6. Rover localization results and elevation changes of the moving path of the "Zhurong" Mars rover: (a) traverse map; (b) partial enlarge of (a); (c) elevation changes.

Figure 6a shows the driving route map of the "Zhurong" Mars rover, where the positions of each waypoint are the result of relative localization. Absolute localization was performed at 5 waypoints that underwent a 360°panorama (as marked in red in Fig. 6b), and the corrected localization of the rover almost completely coincided with the rut. The two enlarged views in Fig. 6b illustrate a significant slip of the rover as it passes through the "rough terrain". Figure 6c shows the vertical profile of the "Zhurong" Mars rover traversal, where vertical coordinates are the elevation from the HiRIC DEM with 3.5 m resolution [6]. Along the traversal, the lowest location is close to Sol. 166, and the highest location is close to Sol. 27, with a maximum elevation difference of 6 m.

4.3 3D Reconstruction and Terrain Classification

Before conducting path planning on the ground, the NaTeCam images were processed procedurally to generate DEM, DOM, and other terrain products with an accuracy of 0.02 m per pixel within a radius of approximately 30 m, for subsequent two consecutive (blind walking + autonomous obstacle avoidance) path planning. According to the theoretical formula for three-dimensional reconstruction accuracy of stereo images given in [30], the relationship between the measurement accuracy and distance of feature points in the camera system can be obtained. By substituting the relevant parameters of the NaTeCam, the following conclusions can be drawn: (1) the feature points are within a range of 3 m, and the reconstruction accuracy is 3.4 mm; (2) the feature points are within a range of 25 m and the reconstruction accuracy is 20 cm [22]. High-precision 3D reconstruction technology effectively guarantees tasks such as the departure of the rover, path planning, scientific target point coordinate measurement, and terrain evaluation of WiFi camera release positions [11, 22].

From the perspective of path planning accessibility, six terrain classifications were conducted on the NaTeCam images based on the terrain characteristics of the landing area of the "Zhurong" Mars rover, namely large rocks, sand, body and sky, textureless soil, small rocks and bedrocks, as shown in Fig. 7a. Using approximately 400 NaTeCam images from the first Sol. 150 after landing, a set of terrain type labels was manually annotated, and their proportions are shown in Fig. 7b. During the training process, the model was weighted based on the weights of different categories to ensure improved training results. To enhance robustness, all images were randomly translated and rotated. Finally, 15% of the images were randomly selected as the validation set and the rest were used as the training set. Figure 7c shows some of the terrain segmentation results. It can be seen that the constructed terrain classifier can accurately classify the Martian surface, providing data support for obstacle avoidance and path planning of the Mars rover.

Combining the point cloud depth information obtained by stereo matching of the image texture to generate RGBD data as network input can effectively remove false alarms during the segmentation process. Two indicators, Dice and IoU [31], were used to evaluate the classification performance of the model, and a comparison is shown in Table 1.

4.4 Path Planning and Simulation Verification

After the ground completes the telepresence reconstruction, a traffic obstacle map is generated after considering terrain slope, elevation difference, terrain category, and vehicle obstacle crossing ability [32]. The path endpoint was selected based on global planning. To maximize the inspection and exploration results within the design life cycle, a relay movement mode of "blind walking + autonomous obstacle avoidance" was designed, which not only expands the movement range of each sol day [11], but also effectively verifies the autonomous control ability of the Mars rover. The former adopts an improved heuristic A* search algorithm, which uses a secondary search strategy to

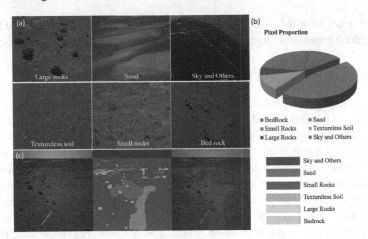

Fig. 7. Display of terrain classification results: (a) defined six individual types of terrain; (b) their pixel proportion; (c) segmentation results.

Table 1. Comparison of classification accuracy between two types of inputs.

type	Dice	IoU
image	85.4	76.2
image + depth	91.6	83.8

achieve an optimal planning path on a single search [33]. For the first time, a dynamic modeling method was used to verify the planning strategy, further improving the correctness of the planning strategy. The latter only needs to specify the location of the moving endpoint by the ground, and the Mars rover recognizes obstacles and plans paths through autonomous environmental perception, and drives to the target position through autonomous navigation control [17].

Figure 8 shows the simulation verification of the planned path by the ground operators, evaluating the visual position and telemetry attitude as true values. The green and red lines in Fig. 8a represent the centerline of the planned path and the dynamic simulation path of the vehicle body, respectively. Figure 8b shows a partial magnification of the movement process in Fig. 8a. Figure 8c and 8d show the slip ratio and wheel sinkage, respectively. Among them, the attitude accuracy is 1°, the position accuracy is 12%, the overall slip rate is less than 0.15, and the wheel sinkage is about 15 mm. This is consistent with the slip rate of the "Zhurong" wheel analyzed in [8] (less than 0.2), which verifies the correctness of the simulation model. Furthermore, owing to the limited mileage and range of the "Zhurong" Mars rover, the current experience area is mostly small rocks, so the mechanical properties of the Martian soil are relatively consistent, and the rover has only experienced mild wheel slippage.

To accurately evaluate the movement effect of the "Zhurong" Mars rover, this article only conducted preliminary statistics on the movement situation under 114 "blind walking" mode control. The visual location results were used as the actual position of the rover, and the planning strategy compared. The median error was smaller than the mean error, indicating that in the vast majority of cases, the use of "blind walking" mode to control the movement of the rover has achieved a predetermined position and orientation. Most of the significant deviations occurred in the "rough" areas where the "Zhurong" rover conducted multiple scientific explorations, marked as positions 1 and 2 in Fig. 6b. In these places, there were significant differences between the captured rut images and the localization results.

The on-orbit movement indicates that (1) the mechanical properties of the volcanic soil indeed have an impact on the wheel slippage, and (2) the slope of local terrain is also one of the factors causing slip. When the slope is relatively gentle, the longitudinal and lateral slip of the Mars rover are more balanced, and as the slope gradually increased, the longitudinal slip rate demonstrated an increasing trend, while the lateral slip rate remained relatively stable, and the sliding behavior of the Mars rover gradually became dominated by longitudinal slip. This conclusion was consistent with the ground verification situation mentioned in [25].

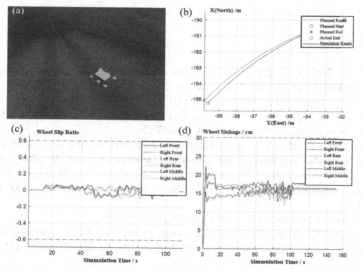

Fig. 8. Simulation and verification of the path planning strategy: (a) the simulated and planned traversal, with the terrain map built from NaTeCam images; (b) the comparison values between simulation and planned; (c) the simulation of wheel slip rate; (d) the simulation of wheel sinkage.

5 Conclusions

The Tianwen-1 Mars exploration mission set the pace of China's deep-space exploration and greatly promoted the development of China's space science, especially planetary science. On April 24, 2023, the National Space Administration and the Chinese Academy of Sciences jointly released the first global image map of Martian exploration, which provides a better basic map for Martian exploration and scientific research [34]. The "Zhurong" Mars rover has been heading south towards potential coastal areas, conducting in-situ exploration of multiple rocky targets along the way, and obtaining the first direct in-situ exploration data to support the existence of ancient oceans in the northern plains of Mars [35], deepening our understanding of the habitability and preservation of life traces on Mars.

During this period, computer vision technology has played an integral role in supporting the "Zhurong" Mars rover to safely travel on the Martian surface, effectively work longer, and achieve fruitful scientific results. This article discusses in detail the application of computer vision technology in the collaborative control of the "Zhurong" Mars rover and shows the actual processing results and application situation on-orbit. With further advancement in China's manned lunar landing, lunar exploration phase IV, and planetary exploration engineering tasks, computer vision technology will have a broader application space.

Acknowledgments. This study was supported by National Natural Science Foundation of China (grant No. 41771488).

References

1. Chen, J.X., Xing, Y., Li, Z.P., et al.: Autonomous environment perception and obstacle avoidance technologies of Zhurong Mars rover (in Chinese). Sci. Sin. Tech. **2022**(52), 1186–1197 (2022). https://doi.org/10.1360/SST-2022-0045
2. Wu, X., Liu, Y., Zhang, C., et al.: Geological characteristics of China's Tianwen-1 landing site at Utopia Planitia, Mars. Icarus **370**, 114657 (2021)
3. Zhao, J., Xiao, Z., Huang, J., et al.: Geological characteristics and targets of high scientific interest in the Zhurong landing region on Mars. Geophys. Res. Lett. **48**, e94903 (2021)
4. Zhang, R.Q, Geng, Y., Sun, Z.Z., et al.: Technical innovation of the Tianwen-1 mission. Acta Aeronaut. et Astronaut. Sinica **43**, 326689 (2022). https://doi.org/10.7527/S1000-6893.2021.26689
5. http://www.gov.cn/xinwen/2021-06/12/content_5617394.htm
6. Liu, J.J., Li, C.L., Zhang, R.Q., et al.: Geomorphic contexts and science focus of the Zhurong landing site on Mars. Nat. Astron. **6**, 65–71 (2021). https://doi.org/10.1038/s41550-021-01519-5
7. https://mp.weixin.qq.com/s/DY38UK-f5Uy8US8o6hrsTg
8. Ding, L., Zhou, R.Y., Yu, T.Y., et al.: Surface characteristics of the Zhurong Mars rover traverse at Utopia Planitia. Nat. Geosci. **15**, 171–176 (2022). https://doi.org/10.1038/s41561-022-00905-6
9. Qin, X.G, et al.: Modern water at low latitudes on Mars: potential evidence from dune surfaces. Sci. Adv. **9**, eadd8868 (2023)
10. Sun, Z.Z., Chen, B.C., Jia, Y., et al.: The Tianwen-1 roving exploration technology for the Martian surface (in Chinese). Sci. Sin. Tech. **2022**(52), 214–225 (2022). https://doi.org/10.1360/SST-2021-0487
11. Zhang, H., et al.: Teleoperation technology of Zhurong Mars rover (in Chinese). J. Deep Space Explor. **8**(6), 582–591 (2021)
12. Chhaniyara, S., et al.: Terrain trafficability analysis and soil mechanical property identification for planetary rovers: a survey. J. Terramech. **49**(2), 115–128 (2012)

13. Haberle, R.M., Leovy, C.B., Pollack, J.B.: Some effects of global dust storms on the atmospheric circulation of Mars. ICurr Alzheimer Resus **1982**(50), 322–367 (1982)
14. Montabone, L., Forget, F., Millour, E., et al.: Eight-year climatology of dust optical depth on Mars. ICurr. Alzheimer Resus **2015**(251), 65–95 (2015)
15. Jia, Y., et al.: Overview on development of planetary rover technology (in Chinese). J. Deep Space Explor. **7**(5), 419–427 (2020)
16. He, T.: Research on mission planning method of Mars rover under complex constraints. JiLin University China (2022)
17. Xing, Y., et al.: Development of autonomous sensing and control technology for extraterrestrial mobile exploration unmanned systems (in Chinese). Aerosp. Control Appl. **47**(6), 01–08 (2021). https://doi.org/10.3969/j.issn.1674-1579
18. Pan, D., Chen, Z., Yuan, B.F., et al.: Sinkage mechanism and extrication strategy of Mars rover (in Chinese). ROBOT **44**(1), 2–8 (2022). https://doi.org/10.13973/j.cnki.robot.210258
19. Wan, W.H., et al.: Visual localization of the Tianwen-1 lander using orbital, descent and rover images. Remote Sens. **13**(17), 3439 (2021)
20. Yan, Y.Z., Zhang, J.L., Qi, C., et al.: Fast and precise localization of Tianwen-1 Mars rover landing site (in Chinese). Chin. Sci. Bull. **2022**(67), 204–211 (2022). https://doi.org/10.1360/TB-2021-0541
21. Wang, J., et al.: High precision localization of Zhurong rover based on multi-source images (in Chinese). J. Deep Space Explor. **9**(1), 62–71 (2022)
22. Ma, Y.Q., Peng, S., Zhang, J.L., et al.: Precise visual localization and terrain reconstruction for China's Zhurong Mars rover on orbit (in Chinese). Chin. Sci. Bull. **2022**(67), 2790–2801 (2022). https://doi.org/10.1360/TB-2021-1273
23. Ma, Y.Q., et al.: Prediction of terrain occlusion in Chang'e-4 mission. Measurement **152**, 107368 (2020)
24. Gu, M.: Mars environment simulation technology (in Chinese). Equipment Environ. Eng. **18**(9), 35–42 (2021)
25. Zhang, T.Y.: Research on slip behavior of mars rover for on-orbit application. JiLin University China (2022)
26. Cheng, Z.Q., et al.: Automatic classification method for mars surface terrain based on deep learning. In: China Engineering Science and Technology Forum: Deep Space Exploration Science and Technology and Applications, 2021, Shenzhen (2021)
27. Leger, P.C., et al.: Mars exploration rover surface operations: driving spirit at Gusev crater. In: 2005 IEEE International Conference on Systems, Man and Cybernetics, vol. 2, pp. 1815-1822. IEEE (2005)
28. Liu, Z.Q., et al.: A global database and statistical analyses of (4) vesta craters. Icarus **311**, 242–257 (2018)
29. Jiang, C.S., et al.: Initial results of the meteorological data from the first 325 sols of the Tianwen-1 mission. Sci. Rep. **13**, 3325 (2023). https://doi.org/10.1038/s41598-023-30513-2
30. Zhang, J.Q., Pan, L., Wang, S.G.: Photogrammetry (in Chinese). 2nd ed., pp. 54–72. Wuhan University Press, Wuhan (2009)
31. Long, J., Shelhamer, E., Darrell, T.: Fully convolutional networks for semantic segmentation. In Proceedings of the IEEE Conference on Computer Vision and Pattern Recognition, pp. 3431–3440 (2015)
32. Wang, Y.X., Wan, W.H., Gou, S., et al.: Vision based decision support for rover path planning in the Chang'e-4 mission. Remote Sens. **12**(4), 624 (2020)
33. Peng, S., Jia, Y.: Improved A* algorithm in global path planning of lunar rover (in Chinese). Spacecraft Eng. **19**(4), 80–85 (2010)
34. https://www.cas.cn/sygz/202305/t20230511_4886796.shtml
35. http://www.xinhuanet.com/tech/20230522/aa1c66d3c126490c9bdd8ae290ac5013/c.html

ME-GraphSAGE: Minority Class Feature Enhanced GraphSAGE for Automatic Labeling of Coronary Arteries

Yang Ding[1], Tianyu Fu[2]([✉]), Sigeng Chen[1], Deqiang Xiao[1], Jingfan Fan[1], Hong Song[3], Yang Yu[4], and Jian Yang[1]

[1] Beijing Engineering Research Center of Mixed Reality and Advanced Display, School of Optics and Photoics, Beijing Institute of Technology, Beijing, China
[2] School of Medical Technology, Beijing Institute of Technology, Beijing, China
fty0718@163.com
[3] School of Computer Science and Technology, Beijing Institute of Technology, Beijing, China
[4] Department of Cardiac Surgery, Beijing Anzhen Hospital, Capital Medical University, Beijing, China

Abstract. Automatic labeling of coronary artery segments improves efficiency in the diagnosis and treatment of coronary artery disease, but faces challenges due to the class imbalance between main and side branches. State-of-the-art methods primarily focus on position-direction and pixel features, which leads to suboptimal performance when dealing with bifurcated segments. In this paper, we propose a minority class feature enhanced GraphSAGE (ME-GraphSAGE), which alleviates class imbalance by generating minority class nodes. We extract bifurcation features from Digital Subtraction Angiography (DSA) images taken from four commonly observed views of coronary arteries. These features, along with other relevant ones, are fed into ME-GraphSAGE to enhance the accuracy of segment labeling in bifurcated regions. By combining the results from the four views, a higher-level sixteen-segment-based coronary labeling is obtained. Our method is evaluated on a dataset of 205 coronary DSA sequences. The experimental results show that ME-GraphSAGE significantly outperforms state-of-the-art methods in labeling coronary artery branches.

Keywords: coronary artery labeling · minority class feature enhanced GraphSAGE · bifurcation features · DSA

1 Introduction

Coronary artery disease (CAD) is a major cause of mortality worldwide [1, 2]. DSA is the gold standard for CAD diagnosis [3]. Manual diagnosis of complex CAD using DSA images is a time-consuming process for clinicians. Automatic segment labeling of the

This work was supported by the National Science Foundation Program of China (62271057), Beijing Municipal Science and Technology Project (211100003521021), Beijing Natural Science Foundation (JQ22030).

coronary artery tree extracted from DSA images can assist clinicians in swiftly assessing the severity and type of lesions, ultimately facilitating the formulation of an appropriate surgical plan [4]. Subsequently, automatic identification of anatomical branches can provide valuable information for the generation of SYNTAX score [5] and visualization of lesion diagnostic results.

The sixteen-segment-based standard of coronary arteries is shown in Fig. 1 (a). The left main (LM) and intermediate (RI) are labeled, the left anterior descending (LAD), left circumflex (LCX) and right coronary artery (RCA) are separated into proximal, middle and distal segments respectively, the obtuse marginal (OM), posterior left ventricular (PLV), diagonal artery (D), right posterolateral branch (PLB), and right posterior descending branch (PDA) are classified in detail. In the clinic, the sixteen-segment-based standard of coronary arteries is commonly used for the SYNTAX score. Generally, LM, LAD, LCX and RCA are treated as main branches, and the other branches are treated as side branches.

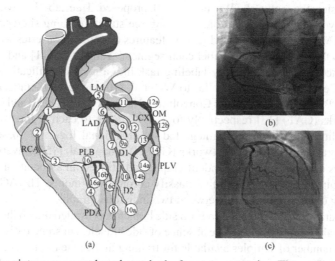

Fig. 1. (a) The sixteen-segment-based standard of coronary arteries. The coronary artery tree consists of two components: left domain and right domain. The left domain originates from LM/5 and bifurcates into LAD, LCX and RI/12. LAD is separated into proximal (6), middle (7) and distal (8) segments, D is from LAD and is divided into first diagonal (9), first diagonal a (9a), second diagonal (10) and second diagonal a (10a). LCX is separated into proximal (11), middle (13) and distal (14b) segments, OM and PLV are from LCX and are divided into obtuse marginal a (12a), obtuse marginal b (12b), left posterolateral (14) and left posterolateral a (14a). The right domain originates from RCA, which is separated into proximal (1), middle (2) and distal (3) segments. PLB and PDA are from RCA and are divided into posterolateral (16), posterolateral a (16a), posterolateral b (16b), posterolateral c (16c) and posterior descending (4). (b) The example of coronary arteries in R-LAO, segment 1, 2 and 3 are clear and segment 16, 16a, 16b and 16c are overlapping. (c) The example of coronary arteries in L-RAO, segment 5, 11, 13, 14b, 12a, and 12b are clear and segment 6, 7 and 8 are overlapping.

There are various methods for pixel-level semantic segmentation, such as using end-to-end attention residual U-Net [6] or progressive perceptual learning [7] to label each pixel of coronary arteries. However, their models focused only on segmenting main branches, while neglecting side branches. As a result, their clinical applicability is limited. In addition, these methods which rely on intensity and semantic features, have difficulty in accurately segmenting and labeling each branch due to the weak greyscale information of the DSA image and the semantic similarity among different branches.

Several segment-level classification methods have been developed to assign labels to arterial segments by exploiting topological features of the coronary artery tree. Traditional methods typically build a 3D coronary tree model to identify the main branches by registration and then label the side branches [8, 9]. However, building a universal coronary artery model is difficult because of the significant individual variability inherited in human anatomy. Moreover, the traditional method is not robust enough due to the lack of data-driven.

Learning-based methods extract features of coronary arteries and classify arterial segments using the network. Wu et al. [10] proposed TreeLab-Net, which consists of a multilayer perceptron and a bidirectional tree-structured long short-term memory (BITreeLSTM). The position and direction features of coronary arteries were extracted and fed into the TreeLab-Net to label each segment. Yang et al. [11] and Hampe et al. [12] converted the coronary artery labeling task into a node classification task on the graph. They extracted features similar to Wu et al. [10] and used them as input for the Conditional Partial Residual Graph Convolution Network (CPR-GCN) and Graph Attention Networks (GAT) [13] respectively to assign a label to each segment. To enhance interpretability, Zhou et al. [14] integrated the traditional logic rule-based approach with gated graph convolutional networks (GGCN). Zhao et al. [15] converted coronary DSA images into multiple independent graphs and utilized an association graph-based graph matching network (AGMN) to classify coronary segments. The AGMN learned the mapping of arterial branches between two individual graphs.

The accuracy of previous methods on side branches is limited due to the class imbalance in a small training dataset. The absence of side branches in some individuals results in a smaller number of samples available for training in the side branch compared to the main branch. This makes it challenging for the network to learn the features of minority class side branches. The state-of-the-art methods only extract the position-direction features and pixel features. This approach often leads to incorrect classifications on the main and side branches at the bifurcation as well as on the side branches of adjacent bifurcations due to the presence of similar features. In addition, obtaining sixteen-segment-based information of coronary arteries from a single view DSA image is challenging due to the overlap of arterial segments in 2D images, as shown in Fig. 1 (b) and (c). Thus, the state-of-the-art methods do not classify LAD, LCX, and RCA into proximal, middle and distal segments, nor do they classify side branches in detail. The segment rule of this level cannot be used to accurately assess lesion severity and determine complex lesion types.

Based on the above analysis, a minority class feature enhanced GraphSAGE (ME-GraphSAGE) is proposed to address the class imbalance between the main branch and side branch and improve the classification accuracy of side branches. In the proposed method, the minority class feature enhanced module is constructed to generate minority class side branch nodes and establish links between synthetic nodes and real nodes. The angle and coordinate information of the bifurcated vessels are extracted as bifurcation features for the accurate classification of the arterial segments at the bifurcation. This is because bifurcation features can reduce the similarity of the main and side branches at the bifurcation as well as the side branches of adjacent bifurcations in the feature space. To overcome the limited clinical applicability of existing methods' segment rule, we have chosen DSA images of left coronary left-anterior oblique (L-LAO), left coronary right-anterior oblique (L-RAO), right coronary left-anterior oblique (R-LAO), and right coronary right-anterior oblique (R-RAO) from the common imaging positions used by clinicians, and label the proximal, middle and distal segments of LAD, LCX, RCA and their side branches in detail. Combining the information from the four views, sixteen-segment-based information of coronary arteries with a higher level is obtained.

In summary, the contributions are as follows:

1) We construct a minority class feature enhanced module in GraphSAGE to address the class imbalance between the main branch and side branch. The network's ability to classify minority class side branches is enhanced by generating corresponding branch nodes and establishing links between synthetic and real nodes in the module.
2) To solve the misclassification of arterial segments at bifurcation with similar position-direction and pixel features, we propose extracting the angle and coordinate information of bifurcated vessels as bifurcation features to reduce their similarity in the feature space and improve their classification accuracy.
3) We propose a strategy to achieve sixteen-segment-based coronary labeling with a higher level than existing methods. The DSA images of L-LAO, L-RAO, R-LAO and R-RAO are selected for labeling LM, the proximal, middle and distal segments of LAD, LCX, RCA and the side branches on them. Then, the information from the four views is combined, providing a basis for the clinical diagnosis of complex CAD and the generation of SYNTAX score reports.

2   Methods

In this section, we describe the process of labeling coronary artery segments of DSA images based on minority class feature enhanced GraphSAGE in detail. As shown in Fig. 2, our method first extracts the centerline of the coronary arteries and identifies the key points. Then, the coronary segments and their connections are converted into nodes and edges on the graph, and the position-direction features, pixel features and bifurcation features of the artery are extracted. Finally, they are fed into the ME-GraphSAGE to obtain the labeling results for coronary segments.

2.1   Graph Generation

The coronary artery tree of DSA images is first segmented using the UNet [16]. Then the segmented results are dilated to preserve the connectivity and topology of the coronary arteries and the centerline is extracted by refinement. The distance from the centerline to the vessel boundary is measured as the radius of the vessel. We first iterate through all the points on the centerline to detect the endpoints with degree 1 and bifurcation points with degree 3. Then incorrectly detected points are removed and the separation points with degree 2 are added to obtain the key points. As shown in Fig. 1(b), the coronary artery is separated into several arterial segments by the key points. The segments with diameters less than D_{thre} and lengths less than L_{thre} are deleted because of non-clinically significant. In addition, the catheter is stored as auxiliary information for clinical diagnosis.

The coronary centerline is converted into graph structure, where the nodes represent the key points and the edges represent the arterial segments connecting the key points. However, our network aims at labeling arterial segments by node classification, not to label key points. Therefore, the nodes and edges on the graph are interconverted to obtain the final graph $G(V, E)$, where V is the set of nodes, representing arterial segments, and E is the set of edges, representing key points. The arterial graph is shown in Fig. 2(c).

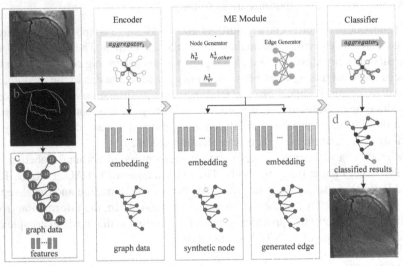

Fig. 2. (a) original DSA image. (b) centerline extraction and key point detection. (c) generated graph data and extracted features. (d) results of node classification. (e) segment labeling result rendered based on node classification and centerline. Encoder aggregates first-order information of the current node and its neighboring nodes to generate embeddings. Node Generator generates embedding for new samples from the minority classes. Edge Generator establishes links between the synthetic and real nodes. Classifier aggregates the second-order information of the current node and its neighboring nodes to classify nodes.

2.2 Feature Extraction

We extract the features of coronary arteries in Euclidean space by representing the point on the centerline as $p = (x, y)$. The start point of the coronary artery tree is taken as the origin, noted as $p_0 = (x_0, y_0)$. The endpoint of the coronary segment which is close to the origin on the centerline is taken as the start point $p_{s,j} = (x_{s,j}, y_{s,j})$, the other is taken as the end point $p_{e,j} = (x_{e,j}, y_{e,j})$, j is the index of each segment.

According to clinical experience, the relative position and growth direction of each coronary segment are essentially fixed in DSA images taken at common imaging positions. Thus, the distance and direction vectors of each coronary segment are calculated as $Dist_j$ and $Direct_j$ to define a position-direction feature vector as follows:

$$Dist_j = \frac{1}{n}\sum_{i=1}^{n}\sqrt{(x_{i,j} - x_0)^2 + (y_{i,j} - y_0)^2} \tag{1}$$

$$Direct_j = CONCAT(\frac{1}{n}\sum_{i=1}^{n}(p_{i,j} - p_0), \frac{1}{n}\sum_{i=1}^{n}(p_{i,j} - p_{s,j})) \tag{2}$$

$$Vec_j^{Dist,Direct} = CONCAT(Dist_j, Direct_j) \tag{3}$$

where $p_{i,j}$ is the point on the coronary segment j, n is the number of centerline points. $Vec_j^{Dist,Direct}$ denotes the position-direction feature vector of coronary segment j.

We represent the number of pixels from origin to the start point of the coronary segment on the centerline as $Num_{locat,j}$, the length and diameter of the coronary segment, expressed in number of pixels as $Num_{len,j}$ and $Num_{dia,j}$. The tortuosity $Tort_j$ is calculated by $Num_{len,j}$ and used together with preceding pixel information to construct pixel feature vector of coronary segment j which is represented as Vec_j^{pix}:

$$Tort_j = \frac{Num_{len,j}}{\sqrt{(x_{e,j} - x_{s,j})^2 + (y_{e,j} - y_{s,j})^2}} \tag{4}$$

$$Vec_j^{pix} = CONCAT(Num_{locat,j}, Num_{len,j}, Num_{dia,j}, Tort_j) \tag{5}$$

To solve the misclassification of the main and side branches at the bifurcation as well as the side branches of adjacent bifurcations, we concatenate the angle of bifurcation vessels $Angle_{adj,j}$ and the average of Y-coordinate of bifurcation vessels $Y_{ave,j}$ to define a bifurcation feature as follows:

$$Angle_{adj,j} = cos^{-1}(\frac{(p_{e,j} - p_{s,j}) \cdot (p_{e,j'} - p_{s,j'})}{\sqrt{(x_{e,j} - x_{s,j})^2 + (y_{e,j} - y_{s,j})^2} \times \sqrt{(x_{e,j'} - x_{s,j'})^2 + (y_{e,j'} - y_{s,j'})^2}})/90 \tag{6}$$

$$Y_{ave,j} = \frac{1}{n}\sum_{i=1}^{n}y_{i,j} \tag{7}$$

$$Vec_j^{Bif} = CONCAT(Angle_{adj,j}, Y_{ave,j}) \tag{8}$$

where j, j' are the index of the coronary segments at the same bifurcation, i.e., $p_{s,j} = p_{s,j'}$.

Since Eq. 6 has the same result on the main and side branches at the bifurcation, the following rules are formulated to distinguish them: If the degree of the bifurcated arterial segment is 2, it is regarded as a side branch, $Angle_{adj,j}$ is recorded as the Eq. 6; if the degree of the bifurcated arterial segment is greater than 2, it is regarded as a main branch, $Angle_{adj,j}$ is recorded as 0. In addition, the coronary segment without bifurcation is regarded as a main branch, $Angle_{adj,j}$ is recorded as 0. Since the bifurcation angles of the side branches at adjacent bifurcations are very similar and their relative positions on the Y-coordinate are highly variable, the average value of the Y-coordinate of coronary segments are added to discriminate them as the Eq. 7. The above feature vectors are normalized and combined to define the final feature vector Vec_j. The final feature vectors of all segments are concatenated to obtain the feature matrix as follows:

$$Vec_j = CONCAT(Vec_j^{Dist,Direct}, Vec_j^{pix}, Vec_j^{Bif}) \qquad (9)$$

$$F_N = CONCAT(Vec_1, \cdots, Vec_N) \qquad (10)$$

where N is the number of coronary segments, F_N is the feature matrix to be added to the graph, as shown in Fig. 2 (c).

2.3 Minority Classes Feature Enhanced GraphSAGE

Encoder
We use a GraphSAGE block in the encoder. GraphSAGE is an inductive learning framework that can learn multiple local topological relationships and make predictions in new graph structures [17], which is compatible with our node classification task on independent graphs. For a node, the convolution layer in GraphSAGE aggregates the feature vector of its neighbors and concatenates the feature vector of current node with the aggregated feature to generate its embedding as follows:

$$h_{Nei(v)}^1 \leftarrow AGGREGATE_1(\{F_N[v, :], \forall u \in Nei(v)\}) \qquad (11)$$

$$h_v^1 \leftarrow \sigma(W^1 \cdot CONCAT(F_N[v, :], h_{Nei(v)}^1)) \qquad (12)$$

where $v \in V_N$ represents the node in the graph, $F_N[v, :]$ is the feature vector of node v, $Nei(v)$ is the neighborhood function of node v. W^1 is the weight parameter, σ refers to the activation function such as ReLU, and h_v^1 denotes the embedding of the node v. Higher-order neighborhood features can be aggregated by increasing the number of convolution layers in the GraphSAGE block, but too many layers will lead to overfitting of the graph network. In summary, we set the number of convolutional layers of GraphSAGE block in the encoder module to 1.

Minority Classes Feature Enhanced Block
The number and type of main branches are relatively fixed in each individual, while most individuals have only a small number of side branches growing on the coronary arteries, and the type of these side branches varies greatly. There is a class imbalance between the main and side branch, which makes the network less able to classify minority classes of side branches. Misclassification of side branches leads to an incorrect assessment of the severity of the lesions on them, which affects the clinician's judgement of complex lesion types such as trifurcation and bifurcation lesions. This also affects the calculation of the SYNTAX score. To balance the class distribution, we add a minority class feature enhanced module consisting of node generator and edge generator to the network.

In the synthetic node generation stage, we extract the output of each minority class node of the encoder and concatenate the embedding belonging to the same minority class node to get its embedding matrix. The SMOTE strategy is used to generate new embedding for each minority class from its embedding matrix [18]. The basic idea of SMOTE is to interpolate each minority class node with other nodes of the same class in the embedding space:

$$h_{v'}^1 = (1 - \delta) \cdot h_v^1 + \delta \cdot h_{v,other}^1 \tag{13}$$

where h_v^1, $h_{v,other}^1$ are embedding belonging to the same minority class, δ is the interpolation factor which is taken as 0.5 in this paper, and $h_{v'}^1$ is the synthetic node embedding. In this way, the labeled synthetic node $V_{N'}$ is obtained, N' is the number of synthetic nodes.

We apple SMOTE to each minority class to generate synthetic nodes randomly embedded into graphs without this class of nodes to obtain the extended node $V_{N|N'}$. Then the embedding of the synthetic nodes and the embedding of the real nodes are concatenated together:

$$H_{N|N'}^1 = CONCAT(H_N^1, H_{N'}^1) \tag{14}$$

where H_N^1 is the embedding matrix of the real node V_N output by encoder, H_N^1 is the embedding matrix of the synthetic node $V_{N'}$ output by node generator, and $H_{N|N'}^1$ is the augmented embedding matrix of the extended node $V_{N|N'}$.

However, the synthetic nodes are isolated from the raw graph G because they have no links. Therefore, an edge generator is proposed that predicts the neighbor information for the nodes by their embedding:

$$E_{k,l} = softmax(\sigma(h_k^1 \cdot S \cdot h_l^1)) \tag{15}$$

where k, l represent the nodes in $V_{N|N'}$, h_k and h_l are the embedding of node k and l, S is the parameter matrix for predicting the link between node k and l, σ refers to the linear layer, and $E_{k,l}$ is the prediction of the link between k and l.

Then the link predictions of all nodes are concatenated to generate a new adjacency matrix $A_{N|N'}$. In this paper, $Loss_{edge}$ is used to optimize edge generator on real nodes and existing edges:

$$Loss_{edge} = ||A_N - A_{N|N'}[v, v]||_F^2 \tag{16}$$

where A_N is the adjacency matrix obtained through the connectivity of the real nodes in G, $A_{N|N'}[v, v]$ is the predicted links among the real nodes in V_N. The neighbor information of the synthetic nodes predicted by the edge generator is added to the original adjacency matrix A_N to obtain the augmented adjacency matrix $\tilde{A}_{N|N'}$ as the input of the Classifier:

$$\tilde{A}_{N|N'} = \begin{bmatrix} A_N & A_{N|N'}[V_N, V_{N'}] \\ A_{N|N'}[V_N, V_{N'}] & A_{N|N'}[V_{N'}, V_{N'}] \end{bmatrix} \tag{17}$$

where $A_{N|N'}[V_N, V_{N'}]$ and $A_{N|N'}[V_N, V_{N'}]$ represent the link predictions of the real nodes and the synthetic nodes, $A_{N|N'}[V_{N'}, V_{N'}]$ represents the link predictions among the synthetic nodes.

Classifier

In the Classifier module, we use another GraphSAGE block and a linear layer, the number of the convolution layers of this block is set to 1. The augmented embedding matrix $H^1_{N|N'}$ and the augmented adjacency matrix $\tilde{A}_{N|N'}$ are fed into the classifier, the output of the classifier can be calculated in a simplified way as follows:

$$P_v = soft\max(\sigma\left(W^2 \cdot CONCAT\left(H^1_{N|N'}[v,:], H^1_{N|N''}, \cdot\tilde{A}_{N|N''}[:, v]\right)\right)) \tag{18}$$

where $H^1_{N|N'}[v,:], \tilde{A}_{N|N'}[:, v], P_v$ represent the embedding, adjacency and probability distribution on class labels for node v in $V_{N|N'}$. W^2 is the weight parameter. During the test, we take the class with the highest probability as the predicted result of the node. Cross-entropy loss is used as the loss function of the final classification result denoted by $Loss_{node}$.

3 Experiments and Results

3.1 Dataset, Evaluation Metrics and Parameters

In this study, we use a private dataset of 205 DSA sequences collected from Beijing Anzhen Hospital, Capital Medical University for training and testing. The frame completely filled with contrast agent in each sequence is selected and resampled to 512 × 512. 205 DSA images are acquired, including 56 from the L-LAO view, 66 from the L-RAO view, 40 from the R-LAO view, and 43 from the R-RAO view. 70% of the images are randomly selected for training, while the remaining 30% were used for testing. All images are annotated under the guidance of experts. In practice, clinicians diagnose left domain coronary lesions by looking at LAD and its side branches through the L-LAO view and LCX and its side branches through the L-RAO view. Therefore, LAD and OM are annotated as segment 5, 6, 7 and 9, 9a, 10, 10a in detail in the images of L-LAO, RI, LCX, D and PLV are annotated as segment 12, 11, 13, 14b, 12a, 12b and 14, 14a in detail in the images of L-RAO. Similarly, for the images of the right domain coronary, RCA is annotated as segment 1, 2, 3 in detail in the images of R-LAO, PLB and PDA are annotated as segment 4 and 16, 16a, 16b, 16c in detail in the images of R-RAO.

All coronary artery segments are evaluated by predicted label and ground truth label. The accuracy of each segment is calculated by precision, recall, and F1-score:

$$PRE = \frac{1}{N} \sum_{c=1}^{C} \frac{TP_c}{TP_c + FP_c} \times N_c \tag{19}$$

$$REC = \frac{1}{N} \sum_{c=1}^{C} \frac{TN_c}{TN_c + FN_c} \times N_c \tag{20}$$

$$F1 = \frac{1}{N} \sum_{c=1}^{C} \frac{TP_c}{TP_c + \frac{1}{2}(FP_c + FN_c)} \times N_c \qquad (21)$$

where TP_c, TN_c, FP_c and FN_c are true positive, true negative, false positive and false negative in the predicted results. C is the total number of coronary segment classes and c is the index of each class. N is the total number of coronary segments and N_c is the number of coronary segments with class c.

In this study, the dimension of the embedding output from the convolution layer of GraphSAGE block in encoder and classifier is set to 64. In the minority class feature enhanced module, only minority class side branch nodes are generated, and the number of synthetic nodes is one times the number of existing minority class samples. The dropout is set to 0.1, the learning rate is set to 0.001, the mode is trained 1000 epochs using Adam optimizer with NVIDIA RTX 3090 GPU, and each mini-batch contains only one graph. The loss function of ME-GraphSAGE $Loss_{total}$ is calculated by combining $Loss_{node}$ and $Loss_{edge}$:

$$Loss_{total} = \theta Loss_{node} + (1 - \theta) Loss_{edge} \qquad (22)$$

where θ is the scaling parameter and is set to 0.95.

3.2 Comparison with Existing Methods

We conduct experiments using the Conditional Partial Residual GCN proposed by Yang et al. [7] and Graph Attention Networks used by Hampe et al. [8] and compare them with our approach, the results are shown in Table 1, Table 2 and Table 3. Our method has the highest overall accuracy on the four views, with precession of 0.959, recall of 0.961, and F1-socre of 0.956 in the L-LAO view, and with precession of 0.950, recall of 0.957, and F1-score of 0.948 in the L-RAO view. Because of the simple structure of the right domain coronary, only F1-score is recorded, which is 1 in the R-LAO view and 0.949 in the R-RAO view.

We first compare the results on the main branches. All methods achieve higher than 0.95 F1-score for LM, which is due to the diameter and length characteristics of LM clearly distinguishing it from other coronary segments. RCA is 100% classified by all methods due to the simple vascular structure of the right domain coronary and the unique tortuosity characteristic of RCA. CPR-GCN and GAT perform almost equally on LAD in the L-LAO view, but not as well as our method. For LCX in the L-RAO view, CPR-GCN and GAT perform well on both proximal segment 11 and middle segment 13, especially GAT has the highest F1-score of the three methods at 0.970 on segment 11. However, CPR-GCN and GAT are less effective on distal segment 14b, because 14b and PLV have similar position-direction features and pixel features, increasing the difficulty for the network to recognize them, as shown in the L-RAO Samples in Fig. 3. Our method extracts the bifurcation features to reduce the similarity between 14b and PLV in the feature space, and achieves 100% accuracy on 14b.

The results on the side branches are then considered. Both CPR-GCN and GAT outperform our method for OM in the L-RAO view. In particular, GAT achieves 100%

Table 1. Comparison of CPR-GCN, GAT and ME-GraphSAGE in the L-LAO view.

Method		CPR-GCN			GAT			ME-GraphSAGE		
Metric		PRE	REC	F1	PRE	REC	F1	PRE	REC	F1
LM	5	0.956	0.956	0.956	0.956	0.956	0.956	**1.000**	**1.000**	**1.000**
LAD	6	0.927	0.898	0.886	0.934	0.891	0.898	**1.000**	**1.000**	**1.000**
	7	0.902	0.956	0.906	0.913	0.927	0.900	**0.967**	**1.000**	**0.979**
	8	0.927	1.000	0.949	0.847	1.000	0.891	**0.949**	1.000	**0.963**
LCX	-	0.833	0.833	0.833	0.892	0.852	0.862	**0.941**	**0.901**	**0.911**
D	9	0.720	0.823	0.749	0.852	0.882	0.862	**0.937**	**0.937**	**0.937**
	9a	0.399	0.399	0.399	0.799	0.799	0.799	0.799	0.799	0.799
	10	0.499	0.499	0.499	0.499	0.499	0.499	**0.749**	**0.749**	**0.749**
	10a	0	0	0	0.199	0.199	0.199	**0.666**	**0.666**	**0.666**
OM	-	0.666	0.666	0.666	0.666	0.666	0.666	**0.833**	**0.833**	**0.833**
CATH	-	0.956	0.956	0.956	1.000	1.000	1.000	1.000	1.000	1.000
All	-	0.872	0.874	0.858	0.896	0.884	0.874	**0.959**	**0.961**	**0.956**

Table 2. Comparison of CPR-GCN, GAT and ME-GraphSAGE in the L-RAO view.

Method		CPR-GCN			GAT			ME-GraphSAGE		
Metric		PRE	REC	F1	PRE	REC	F1	PRE	REC	F1
LM	5	1.000	0.972	0.981	1.000	0.972	0.981	1.000	**1.000**	**1.000**
LAD	–	0.749	0.944	0.820	0.666	0.777	0.711	**0.972**	**0.972**	**0.962**
LCX	11	0.935	**0.981**	0.951	0.981	0.972	**0.970**	1.000	0.944	0.962
	13	0.953	0.981	0.959	0.953	0.824	0.866	**0.972**	**1.000**	**0.984**
	14b	0.722	0.944	0.787	0.768	0.944	0.814	**1.000**	**1.000**	**1.000**
D	–	0	0	0	0	0	0	**0.916**	**1.000**	**0.944**
OM	12a	0.866	0.866	0.866	**1.000**	**1.000**	**1.000**	0.799	0.799	0.799
	12b	0.857	0.857	0.857	**1.000**	**1.000**	**1.000**	0.857	0.857	0.857
PLV	14	0.416	0.416	0.416	0.541	0.583	0.555	**0.861**	**1.000**	**0.902**
	14a	0	0	0	0	0	0	**0.499**	**0.499**	**0.499**
RI	12	0	0	0	0.599	**1.000**	0.733	**0.799**	0.799	**0.799**
CATH	–	0.944	0.944	0.944	0.944	0.944	0.944	**1.000**	**1.000**	**1.000**
All	–	0.816	0.859	0.828	0.853	0.865	0.846	**0.950**	**0.957**	**0.948**

accuracy on 12a and 12b because the attention mechanism assigns different weight parameters to each neighboring node during aggregation, which optimizes the embedding update of the network. For PLV in the L-RAO view, RI and D in the L-LAO view, the performance of CPR-GCN and GAT is terrible. This is due to a severe class imbalance problem caused by a small percentage of segment 12, 9a, 10a, and 14a in the training sample. Our method alleviates the class imbalance and perform well on these segments. Segment 16b and 16c in the R-RAO view are challenging for all methods. These segments originate from the same position on segment 16 and share similar features, making it difficult for even experienced clinicians to differentiate them from a single frame of DSA images, as shown in the R-RAO examples in Fig. 3. Although the selected main and side branches are only classified in detail in the fixed view, our method is still effective for other segments in this view.

Table 3. Comparison of CPR-GCN, GAT and ME-GraphSAGE in the R-LAO and R-RAO view.

View		R-LAO			R-RAO		
Method		CPR-GCN	GAT	ME-GraphSAGE	CPR-GCN	GAT	ME-GraphSAGE
Metric		F1	F1	F1	F1	F1	F1
RCA	1	1.000	1.000	1.000	1.000	1.000	1.000
	2	1.000	1.000	1.000			
	3	1.000	1.000	1.000			
PDA	4	0.111	1.000	1.000	0.988	0.971	0.979
PLB	16	0.666	1.000	1.000	**0.988**	0.971	0.979
	16a				**0.949**	0.899	0.899
	16b				0.533	0.783	**0.799**
	16c				0.466	0.466	**0.883**
CATH	-	1.000	1.000	1.000	1.000	1.000	1.000
All	-	0.888	**1.000**	**1.000**	0.869	0.883	**0.949**

3.3 Ablation Study

Extensive experiments are conducted to verify the effectiveness of the bifurcation feature and the minority class feature enhanced module. We use GraphSAGE, which is the backbone of our network, and extract the position-direction features and pixel features to construct a baseline method. All experimental results are derived from the modifications of the baseline method. Because the left domain coronary has rich vascular information and its results are more convincing, ablation experiments in this study are performed only on the data from L-LAO view and L-RAO view.

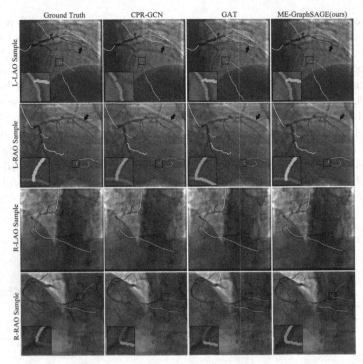

Fig. 3. Comparison of labeling results of CPR-GCN, GAT and ME-GraphSAGE methods in L-LAO, L-RAO, R-LAO and R-RAO views. Different colors represent different categories of segments. The red box and red arrow show contrast between correct and incorrect labels.

3.4 Bifurcation Features

According to clinical experience, the relative position, growth direction and pixel information of arterial segments are the basis for their identification. Therefore, most existing methods extract the position-direction features and pixel features of coronary arteries as input to the graph network. However, the main and side branches at the bifurcation as well as the side branches of adjacent bifurcations have a high similarity in position-direction and pixel features, resulting in misclassification by the network. The first two columns of the experimental results of L-LAO and L-RAO in Table 4 show that the bifurcation features enhance the performance on the main and side branches at the bifurcation, such as segment 14 and 14b, and on the side branches of adjacent bifurcations, such as segment 9, 9a, 10 and 10a.

Minority Class Feature Enhanced

To address the bad performance of minority class side branches caused by class imbalance between the main and side branch, a minority class feature enhanced module is added to GraphSAGE. The minority class feature enhanced module can increase the number of minority class nodes in the training process, which enhances the feature learning efficiency and classification ability of the network for minority class nodes. From the experimental results in the first and third columns of L-LAO and L-RAO in

Table 4. Results of ablation for some modules of our method in the L-LAO and L-RAO views. Bifurcation features and minority class feature enhanced module are key components of our method.

View		L-LAO				L-RAO			
Method		SAGE	SAGE + BF	SAGE + ME	SAGE + ME + BF (ours)	SAGE	SAGE + BF	SAGE + ME	SAGE + ME + BF (ours)
Metric		F1	F1	F1	F1	F1	F1	F1	F1
LM	5	1.000	1.000	1.000	1.000	0.981	1.000	0.981	1.000
LAD	6	0.959	0.985	0.985	**1.000**	0.944	0.925	0.962	0.962
	7	0.926	0.974	0.956	**0.979**				
	8	**0.978**	0.963	0.963	0.963				
LCX	11	0.970	0.911	0.970	0.911	0.955	0.955	0.936	**0.962**
	13					0.956	0.984	0.947	**0.984**
	14b					0.888	1.000	0.925	1.000
D	9	0.744	0.937	0.906	0.937	0.944	0.944	0.944	0.944
	9a	0	0.733	0.666	**0.799**				
	10	0.499	0.624	0.749	0.749				
	10a	0	0.333	0	**0.666**				
OM	12a	0.833	0.833	0.833	0.833	0.799	0.799	**0.911**	0.799
	12b					1.000	0.857	1.000	0.857
PLV	14	–	–	–	–	0.694	0.861	0.788	**0.902**
	14a					0	0	0	**0.499**
RI	12	–	–	–	–	0.599	0.599	0.799	0.799
CATH		1.000	1.000	1.000	1.000	0.944	1.000	0.944	1.000
All		0.907	0.945	0.945	**0.956**	0.900	0.924	0.925	**0.948**

Table 4, it can be concluded that the extended network enhances the classification performance of minority class side branches with an F1-score improvement of 0.666 for segment 9a, 0.250 for segment 10, and 0.200 for segment 12.

Bifurcation Features and Minority Class Feature Enhanced

The bifurcation features and the minority class feature enhanced module focus on the different fields in the accuracy improvement. The bifurcation feature focuses on both the main branch and side branch, which can improve the accuracy of both. The minority class feature enhanced module only focuses on the information of the side branch, which aims to enhance the classification ability of the network for minority class side branches. Both are added to the baseline method in this study can complement each other and further enhance the effect of labeling coronary arteries. Considering the first and third columns of the experimental results of L-LAO and L-RAO in Table 4, the bifurcation feature and the minority class feature enhanced module improve the overall F1-score by 0.049 for L-LAO and by 0.048 for L-RAO. In particular, these two components significantly improve the accuracy for minority class side branches such as segment 9a, 10a and 14a.

4   Conclusion

In this study, we propose the ME-GraphSAGE network for automated segment labeling of coronary arteries. Specifically, the proposed bifurcation features in this paper play a crucial role in identifying segments at coronary bifurcations. To improve the classification accuracy of side branches, we introduce a module that enhances the features of the minority class. We conducted experiments on our private dataset consisting of 205 DSA sequences. The results demonstrate that our approach achieves sixteen-segment-based coronary labeling at a higher level than existing methods, which meets the segment labeling standard of the SYNTAX score. Combining automated segment labeling of coronary arteries with lesion identification enables the rapid generation of SYNTAX score reports, thereby facilitating clinical diagnosis of complex CAD. Furthermore, the accurate result of coronary artery labeling aids clinicians in formulating appropriate surgical plans, leading to improved hemodynamic reconstruction rates and reduced complications, with wide application prospects.

References

1. World Health Organization (WHO). Cardiovascular diseases (CVDs). https://www.who.int/news-room/fact-sheets/detail/cardiovascular-diseases-(cvds)
2. Libby, P., Theroux, P.: Pathophysiology of coronary artery disease. Circulation **111**, 3481–3488 (2005)
3. Yang, J., Wang, Y., Tang, S., Zhou, S., Liu, Y., Chen, W.: Multiresolution elastic registration of X-ray angiography images using thin-plate spline. IEEE Trans. Nucl. Sci. **54**, 152–166 (2007)
4. Taggart, D.P.: PCI or CABG in coronary artery disease? Lancet **373**(9670), 1150–1152 (2009)
5. Neumann, F.-J., et al.: 2018 ESC/EACTS Guidelines on myocardial revascularization. Eur. Heart J. **40**, 87–165 (2019)
6. Xian, Z., Wang, X., Yan, S., Yang, D., Chen, J., Peng, C.: Main coronary vessel segmentation using deep learning in smart medical. Math. Probl. Eng. **2020**, 1–9 (2020)
7. Zhang, H., Gao, Z., Zhang, D., Hau, W.K., Zhang, H.: Progressive perception learning for main coronary segmentation in X-ray angiography. IEEE Trans. Med. Imaging **42**, 864–879 (2023)
8. Yang, G., et al.: Automatic coronary artery tree labeling in coronary computed tomographic angiography datasets. Comput. Cardiol. **20**, 109–112 (2011)
9. Cao, Q., et al.: Automatic identification of coronary tree anatomy in coronary computed tomography angiography. Int. J. Cardiovasc. Imaging **33**, 1809–1819 (2017)
10. Wu, D., et al.: Automated anatomical labeling of coronary arteries via bidirectional tree LSTMs. Int. J. CARS. **14**, 271–280 (2019)
11. Yang, H., Zhen, X., Chi, Y., Zhang, L., Hua, X.-S.: CPR-GCN: conditional partial-residual graph convolutional network in automated anatomical labeling of coronary arteries. In: 2020 IEEE/CVF Conference on Computer Vision and Pattern Recognition (CVPR), pp. 3802–3810. IEEE, Seattle, WA, USA (2020)

12. Hampe, N., Wolterink, J.M., Collet, C., Planken, R.N., Išgum, I.: Graph attention networks for segment labeling in coronary artery trees. In: Medical Imaging 2021: Image Processing, pp. 410–416. SPIE, Online Only, United States (2021)
13. Veličković, P., Cucurull, G., Casanova, A., Romero, A., Liò, P., Bengio, Y.: Graph attention networks. In: Proceedings of the ICLR. pp. 1–12 (2018)
14. Zhou, C.: A hybrid approach for coronary artery anatomical labeling in cardiac CT angiography. J. Phys.: Conf. Ser. **1642**, 12–20 (2020)
15. Zhao, C., et al.: AGMN: association graph-based graph matching network for coronary artery semantic labeling on invasive coronary angiograms. arXiv preprint arXiv:2301.04733 (2023)
16. Ronneberger, O., Fischer, P., Brox, T.: U-net: Convolutional networks for biomedical image segmentation. In: Navab, N., Hornegger, J., Wells, W.M., Frangi, A.F. (eds.) MICCAI 2015. LNCS, vol. 9351, pp. 234–241. Springer, Cham (2015). https://doi.org/10.1007/978-3-319-24574-4_28
17. Hamilton, W., Ying, Z., Leskovec, J.: Inductive representation learning on large graphs. In: NIPS, pp. 1024–1034 (2017)
18. Zhao, T., Zhang, X., Wang, S.: GraphSMOTE: imbalanced node classification on graphs with graph neural networks. In: Proceedings of the 14th ACM International Conference on Web Search and Data Mining, pp. 833–841. ACM, Virtual Event Israel (2021)

LR-SARNET: A Lightweight and Robust Network for Multi-scale and Multi-scene SAR Ship Detection

Shibo Chang, Xiongjun Fu[✉], Jian Dong[✉], and Hao Chang

School of Integrated Circuits and Electronics, Beijing Institute of Technology, Beijing 100081, China

{fuxiongjun,radarvincent}@bit.edu.cn

Abstract. SAR Ship image has the characteristics of complex background, blurred target edge and scale difference, which makes the target detection difficult. This article builds a lightweight and robust network for multi-scale and multi-scene SAR ship detection (LR-SARNET). Firstly, with the goal to minimize the computational complexity of the model, a lightweight backbone feature extraction network (CGNet) is designed to generate sufficiently redundant feature maps with low computational cost. Secondly, a linear feature fusion module (ENECK) is designed to efficiently fuse deep local feature maps. Finally, the extremely efficient spatial pyramid (EESP) is integrated into the target detection head, which expands the receptive field of the network. The experiment on SSDD and HRSID dataset proves that our algorithm has strong robustness and excellent generalization performance.

Keywords: Ship detection · SAR image · Intensive object detection · Anchor-free mechanism · Small target detection

1 Introduction

The ocean encompasses 71% of the earth's surface area, offering abundant resources and ample room for human activity. The protection and development of the ocean is a strategic point for all countries in the world. In recent years, the development and application of synthetic aperture radar (SAR) have received more and more attention. SAR technology is a critical component of satellite remote sensing. Compared with other remote sensing systems, it is less interfered by natural conditions such as atmosphere and clouds, and can work all day and all day in complex working environments. Therefore, the use of SAR ship images detection has obvious advantages, which is more conducive to protecting marine resources and maintaining the order of territorial waters.

There are numerous challenges in the field of SAR ship images detection, such as complicated background, small ship scale relative to the background, rich ship categories, and large differences in scale characteristics. Traditional SAR ship image identification algorithms are examined primarily from four perspectives: model, statistics, structure, and transformation. The four most widely used traditional methods are transformation [1], saliency [2], superpixel [3], and constant false alarm rate (CFAR) [4]. The above algorithms seriously depend on the applicability of clutter statistical distribution model. The algorithm is complex, the model robustness is poor, and the detection speed cannot meet the actual needs.

In recent years, with the rapid development of high-performance computing equipment, the deep learning technology has made steady progress, achieving excellent performance in optical image detection, and subsequently transitioned to SAR ship image detection. The convolution neural network learns the edge features and local features of the target by superimposing convolution layers with high depth and width, and has good detection performance. Existing target detection algorithms can be classified into two categories:

(1) Two-stage detection algorithms based on candidate box: the algorithm generates a region proposal that may contain the object to be discovered at first. And then using a convolutional neural network to classifies and locates the prediction box, which has a modest detection speed but a high accuracy. R-CNN series is the representative of the two-stage algorithm for target detection
(2) Single-stage detection algorithms based on regression: Single-stage detection methods transform object detection into a regression problem. The network architecture is simple because there is no need to generates the region proposal. Specifically, it can be divided into anchor-based and anchor-free architectures. The anchor-based methods learn to classify objects and regress their positions using anchor boxes. Compared to two-stage algorithms, they have significant speed advantages but rely more on manual design, resulting in lower efficiency during training and inference. Typical algorithms in this category include YOLOv3 [5], SSD [6], YOLOv4 [7], YOLOv7, etc. Anchor-free detection algorithms directly detect the center and boundary information of objects, decoupling object classification and position regression into two sub-networks. This enables efficient training and inference without the need for a series of hyperparameter designs of anchor boxes. Anchor-free detection algorithms are rapidly developing, and current mainstream frameworks include CenterNet [8], FCOS [9], YOLOX [10], among others.

Because of its unique imaging mechanism, SAR ship images have the characteristics of complex background, blurred target edges and multi-scale differences. Due to the different characteristics of SAR images and optical images, the detection algorithm based on optical image design cannot been directly used to SAR ship image detections. Nowadays, there are also researches devoted to improve the detection algorithm by focus on SAR image characteristics Tang et al. [11] improved the detection of SAR images in noisy environments by denoising them, and achieved good results. Jiang et al. [12] proposed YOLOv4-light, using Non-Subsampled Laplacian Pyramid (NSLP), reducing the model complexity and achieving good detection results. Lin et al. [13] proposed the Feature Pyramid Network (FPN). FPN can extract feature for each scale of the image, it is able to produce multi-scale feature representations, and all levels of the feature map have strong semantic information. Zhang et al. [14] proposed a balanced Feature Pyramid Network (B-FPN), further balance of feature information at different scales. Sun et al. [15] proposed an anchor-free detection method for ship target detection in SAR images, using Fully Convolutional One-Stage (FCOS) as the basic network, avoiding all hyperparameters related to anchor frames and highly sensitive to the final detection results. Chang et al. [16] proposed the self-balancing position attention, effectively balance the detection accuracy and speed.

The above algorithms have achieved some excellent results, but through research, it is found that there are still the following problems in SAR ship image detection:

(1) Currently, the algorithms used in optical images are generally applied for partial optimization, and there is no dedicated detection network design for the SAR images. Many modules in the network have low-cost performance, which limits the performance of detection.
(2) When the model is deployed to the edge equipment for practical application, not only the complexity and calculation speed of the model should be considered, but also the performance stability of the model. The anchor box with manually modified parameters remains the foundation of the mainstream approach, this kind of model not only has large amount of calculation and poor generalization ability, but also has unstable actual detection effect.

To address the above problems, this paper proposes a lightweight and robust network for multi-scale and multi-scene SAR ship detection (LR-SARNet) through enhanced feature information learning by analyzing the characteristics of SAR images, which balances the detection speed and practical performance through clever structural design. It performed exceptionally well in SSDD and HRSID dataset testing. Our primary contributions include the following:

(1) LR-SARNet constructs an efficient lightweight feature extraction backbone network (CGNet), which uses the FOCUS network to improve the detection effect, and uses the residual structure GhostBottle. By CGNet, LR-SARNet ensures the quality of feature maps while greatly reducing the network parameters.
(2) Given the characteristics of SAR target blur and complex background, LR-SARNet introduces the channel and the spatial attention mechanism into the linear feature fusion network, which improves the network's ability to characterize the target, improves the network's detection accuracy.
(3) We proposed the multi-scale target detector (EESPHead). It obtains the receptive fields of different scales through the depth-separable dilated convolution pyramid and extracts the spatial hierarchical features of the target. Achieves efficient localization of targets at different scales.

2 Methods

According to the application requirements of practical SAR target detection and SAR image characteristics, this paper proposes a lightweight and robust network for multi-scale and multi-scene SAR ship detection (LR-SARNet). It includes three modules: the lightweight backbone network (CGNet), the linear feature fusion network E-NECK, and the multi-scale target detection head EESPHead. The architecture of LR-SARNET proposed in this paper is shown in Fig. 1.

The input image is feature extracted by the lightweight backbone CGNet, and ENECK uses a lightweight linear structure to efficiently fuse the deep detail features and

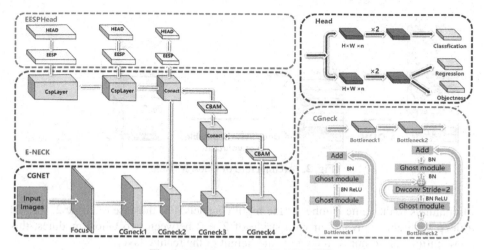

Fig. 1. Architecture of LR-SARNET.

shallow contour features of the input feature map, using an attention mechanism to make the network more focused on the target, and finally the output results are detected by the multi-scale target detection head. The structure of CGNeck, the fundamental module in CGNet, is shown in the bottom right block diagram, and the structure of head is shown in the top right block diagram, GIoU loss for Regression, BCE loss for Classification, and objectness. Detailed information will be described in the following subsections.

2.1 Lightweight Backbone-CGNet

The anchor-free target detection network uses CSPDarkNet53 as the backbone feature extraction network. Although the detection accuracy of the network is high, the model is too complex resulting in low inference speed.

According to the characteristics of SAR targets, we took inspiration from the lightweight detection network GhostNet to design a feature extraction network CGNet. As shown in bottom-left corner of Fig. 1, CGNet is composed of FOCUS and CGNECK. FOCUS takes pixel separated values from the image, obtains four independent feature layers, and stacks them. The input channel is expanded four times, and the image information is concentrated on the channel, which can reduce the information loss caused by downsampling and extract features more fully.

CGNeck is consists of two bottleneck structures with step size 1 and step size 2, each containing two stacked Ghost modules. The Ghost module performs 1×1 convolution on the input to obtain x1 and condenses the necessary features for obtaining input features. Afterwards, $x1$ is subjected to depth-separable convolution to obtain $x2$. $x2$ is the similar feature map (Ghost) of $x1$. Finally, $x1$ and $x2$ are stacked on the channel and output, and the architecture of Ghost Module is shown in Fig. 2.

For the stride of 1, the neck consists of two Ghost Modules connected in series, where the first Ghost Module expands the number of channels to twice the number of channels of the original feature map, and the second Ghost Module reduces the number

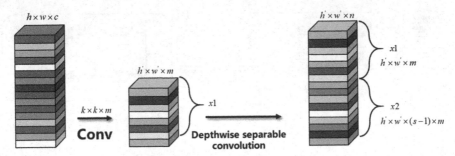

Fig. 2. Architecture of Ghost Module.

of channels to the same number as the input channels. For the case of stride 2, we add a deep separable convolution with stride of 2 × 2 between two Ghost modules, this convolution can compress the width and height of the feature layer.

Compared with regular convolution, the Ghost module in CGNeck uses depthwise separable convolution, it can improve the computational performance and reduce the parameters number of network, and computational costs, depthwise separable convolution. Depthwise separable convolution decomposes the standardized convolution into depthwise convolution and pointwise convolution. The architecture of Depthwise separable convolution is as shown in Fig. 3. In depth convolution, a single filter is applied to each input channel, a 1 × 1 convolution is performed point by point within each channel, and a new feature map is generated by combining the outputs of different depth convolutions.

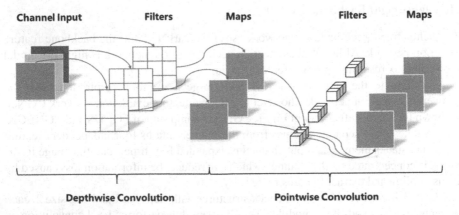

Fig. 3. Architecture of Depthwise separable convolution.

2.2 Enhanced Feature Fusion Network-ENECK

The classification and localization of targets depend on the semantic information and perceptual field of the extracted feature maps. The feature maps extracted by the deep layer network have larger perceptual fields, less geographical information and more semantic information, which are more suitable for the recognition and localization of small targets, while the feature maps extracted by the shallow layer network contain more target contour information and are more suitable for the recognition and localization of large targets. Therefore, using an effective feature fusion module to fuse the feature maps of each layer can improve the classification and localization accuracy of the network for targets.

$$F' = M_c(F) \otimes F \tag{1}$$

$$F'' = M_s(F') \otimes F' \tag{2}$$

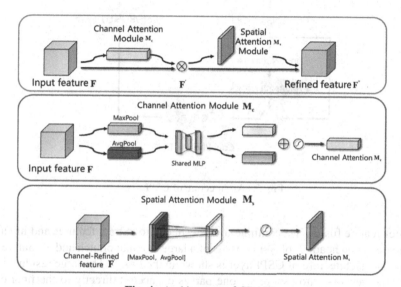

Fig. 4. Architecture of CBAM.

Given the real-time detection application requirements, LR-SARNet adopts a linear fusion structure integrated with the CBAM attention mechanism and residual module CSPLayer, which makes the network portable, efficient and easy to deploy. The CBAM attention mechanism, a lightweight module used between feature extraction layers, mixes cross-channel information and spatial information together to extract information features, which increases the representational power of the overall network: focusing on important features, suppressing unnecessary features, avoiding identifying complex backgrounds as targets, and improving model accuracy. The CBAM attention mechanism applies the Channel and the Spatial Attention Module, and the Channel Attention Module focuses on the target category information in the input picture. The spatial Attention Module focuses on the target location information in the input picture, and CBAM's structure is shown in Fig. 4. The method comprises the following steps of performing global maximum pooling and means value pooling on an input feature map according to a channel; performing pooling on two one-dimensional vectors through a Share MLP module to obtain two results activated by a ReLU activation function, adding the two outputs results element by element, generating one-dimensional channel attention $M_c \in R^{C \times 1 \times 1}$, which is multiplied by the input elements to obtain the characteristic map F'; Secondly, use the global maximum pooling and mean pooling of F', and then splice and convolute the two two-dimensional vectors generated by pooling, and use a sigmoid activation function to generate two-dimensional spatial attention $M_s \in R^{1 \times H \times W}$, which is multiplied F' by the elements to obtain the final feature map F''.

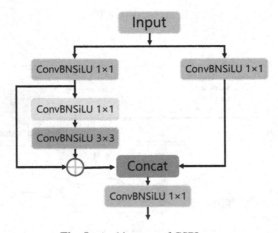

Fig. 5. Architecture of CSPLayer.

After feature fusion, we continue to use csplayer to extract features and input them into the detection head. Csplayer consists of a large residual branch and a small residual branch. The architecture of CSPLayer is shown in the Fig. 5. The large residual branch divides the network into two parts, one part is connected directly to the final output, and the other part is processed by the small residual branch. The main part of the small residual branch includes a 1×1 convolution and a 3×3 convolution, and the residual part is concatenated with the tail of the main part. Csplayer structure improves the accuracy of detection by increasing the depth of csplayer, alleviates the problem of gradient disappearance, ensures the effectiveness of features, and prevents network overfitting.

2.3 Multi-scale Object Detection Head—EESPHEAD

SAR targets have the characteristics of multi-scale and sparseness. The spatial information reflected by multi-scale targets on the feature map is quite different, and the targets are relatively sparse, which increases the difficulty of detection. The EESP module has a small number of parameters, which can improve the receptive field of the network and obtain the spatial information of the feature map. Therefore, we input the features into the EESP module first, and then use the detection head for detection.

The structure of the EESP module is shown in the Fig. 6. The input features are divided into four groups by group point-by-point convolution. The dilation rates of each group of feature channels are 3, 5, 7, 9, and the depthwise separable convolution kernel is 3 × 3. The network extracts the representative features of the target from different effective receptive fields and obtains the spatial scale information of the target. Then the hierarchical feature fusion (HFF) method is used to fuse the feature map to solve the mesh effect caused by dilates convolution. Finally, concat the fused features. EESP module can efficiently extract spatial features from SAR images. EESP module is facilitates to multi-scale detection, and can improves the small targets detection performance, only with low additional parameters.

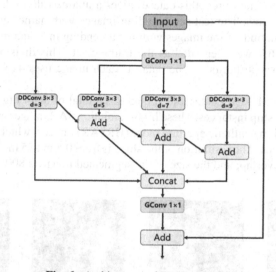

Fig. 6. Architecture of EESP module.

Finally, decouple head (YOLO HEAD) is used to obtain the bounding box position and object class information. It uses a positive and negative sample allocation strategy (SimOTA algorithm) to calculate the training and prediction losses. First, the network determines the center of the target ground-truth box through feature extraction and downsampling operations, defines the regions in the center as the candidate region, calculates the Regression and Classification loss of each target ground-truth box, and sums the 10 samples with the largest IoU of each target ground-truth box. The number of true samples dynamic_K of the target ground-truth box is determined, and the samples with the minimum loss dynamic_K of each target ground-truth box are taken as positive samples, thereby calculating a loss training supervision model. The SimOTA algorithm makes module have faster operation speed, and avoids additional hyperparameter design.

464   S. Chang et al.

3 Experiments

3.1 Datasets and Setting

We use SSDD dataset [18] and High-Resolution SAR Image Dataset (HRSID) dataset to test the performance of our model. The image samples in the SSDD and HRSID datasets are shown in Fig. 7.

SSDD dataset: The SSDD dataset is a public dataset in the field of SAR ship images detection. It contains 1160 SAR images and 2456 ships. The dataset covers a variety of scenes such as nearshore and deep sea; A variety of sea conditions; Multiple radar polarization conditions; Multi-scale difference; Multi-object ship targets. To unify the individual algorithm measures, this dataset gives a unique rule to divide the training, validation and test sets: The test set including images with names ending in 1 and 9, the validation set including the images with names ending in 8, and images with names ending in 2,3,4,5,6,7 were regarded as the training set. This division can ensure the consistency of the distribution of the dataset. Each image uses 416 × 416 pixels for training and testing.

HRSID dataset: HRSID dataset [19] contains a total of 5604 high-resolution SAR images and 16951 ship instances. These high-resolution SAR images are segmented into 5604 high-resolution synthetic aperture radar (HRSAR) images, which contain a total of 16951 ship instances. The resolution of the ships is from 0.5 m to 5 m. The segmentation is based on 25% overlap, and the size of the segmented image is 800 × 800 pixels.

Samples of ships in the SSDD datasets.

Samples of ships in the HRSID datasets.

Fig. 7. Samples of ships in the SSDD and HRSID datasets.

3.2 Evaluation Index

In order to evaluate the model intuitively and quantitatively, we use precision, recall, mAP, F1 and model parameter indicators to analyze different detection algorithms. The

IoU threshold of mAP is set to 0.5, and the confidence threshold of precision, recall, and F1 is set to 0.3. The calculation formula is as follows:

$$\text{Precision} = \frac{TP}{TP+FP} \tag{3}$$

$$\text{Recall} = \frac{TP}{TP+FN} \tag{4}$$

$$F1 = 2\frac{\text{Precision}\times\text{Recall}}{\text{Precision}+\text{Recall}} \tag{5}$$

$$\text{mAP} = \int_0^1 P(\text{R})d\text{R} \tag{6}$$

Params reflects the complexity of the model and is a very important parameter when evaluating the model. Params determine the minimum amount of video memory required for a model to be deployed on hardware.

FLOPS is the computation amount of the model, which evaluates the inference running time of the network and represents the computational time complexity. FLOPS determines the minimum amount of GPU computing power required for the model to be deployed in hardware.

3.3 Experimental Results and Analysis

3.3.1 Ablation Experiment

We validated the effectiveness of design modules through four ablation experiments, and the experimental results were evaluated under the optimal weights. The specific content of the ablation experiment is as follows:

1. Use the basic lightweight network YOLOX.
2. Use our designed CGNet to replace the backbone network, leaving the rest unchanged.
3. Use our designed CGNet to replace the backbone network, ENECK to replace the feature fusion network, and keep the other parts unchanged.
4. Use LR - SARNET.

Table 1. COMPARISON OF SHIP TESTING INDICATORS ON SSDD (IoU = 0.5).

Backbone	Neck	Head	mAP (%)	P (%)	R (%)	F1	Params (M)	Flops (GMac)	Runtime (ms)
CsPDarknet	FPN	YOLO-head	93.85	94.23	92.67	0.93	5.06	6.45	16.33
CGNet	FPN	YOLO-head	95.53	92.02	94.75	0.93	3.67	2.41	27.86
CGNet	ENECK	YOLO-head	95.62	94.45	93.59	0.94	3.59	2.28	19.97
CGNet	ENECK	EESP Head	**96.32**	**94.57**	**95.60**	**0.95**	3.59	2.31	19.35

1. CGNet: Use CGNet to replace the backbone network and the results are shown in the Table 1. The amount of model parameters is reduced by one third, the amount of model calculation is reduced by two thirds, and F1 is almost unchanged. Compared to CsPDarknet, CGNet generates equivalent feature maps in a more lightweight structure, while increasing mAP by 1.68%.
2. ENECK: Compared to the traditional feature pyramid fusion structure (FPN), ENECK uses a lightweight linear structure, resulting in a further reduction of 0.08M in model parameters and only 0.13 GMac in computational complexity.
3. EESPHead: EESP structure can better capture the spatial context information of targets, improve the multi-scale detection performance. The parameter quantity remains almost unchanged, with mAP reaching 96.32%, F1 increasing by 1%, precision reaching 94.57%, recall reaching 95.60%, and computational complexity only increasing by 0.03 GMAc. The model performance is stable.

3.3.2 Comparison With the State-of-the-Art Methods

Table 2. Comparison with the state-of-the-art methods (SSDD dataset).

Networks	mAP (%)	Precision (%)	Recall (%)	F1	Params (M)	Flops (G)	Runtime (ms)
Faster-RCNN [21]	78.6	73.1	88.5	0.78	136.7	57.7	30.2
YOLOv3 [5]	95.0	90.7	94.7	0.92	61.5	49.6	10.4
YOLOv4 [7]	96.1	93.6	94.0	0.93	64.0	29.9	12.9
YOLOv7	93.6	93.6	84.9	0.89	37.2	22.1	21.5
FCOS [9]	88.7	94.4	85.6	0.89	50.8	69.8	25.9
CenterNet [8]	93.5	93.3	94.5	0.93	32.7	23.1	21.5
YOLOX-tiny	93.8	94.2	92.7	0.93	5.0	6.4	16.3
SSD [6]	94.0	92.0	88.0	0.90	23.6	57.8	19.8
LR-SARNet	**96.3**	**94.6**	**95.6**	**0.95**	**3.6**	**2.3**	19.3

In order to evaluate the performance of the model more objectively, we conduct experiments on SSDD datasets and compare with the existing state-of-the-art methods.

1) SSDD: The experimental evaluations performed on this dataset are shown in Table 2, the results show that our approach achieves state-of-the-art performance, Compared with Faster-RCNN, YOLOv3 [5], SSD [6], YOLOv4 [7], YOLOv7, FCOS [9], CenterNet [8] and YOLOX-tiny, mAP increases by 17.7%, 1.3%, 2.3%, 0.2%, 2.7%, 7.6%, 0.8%, 2.5%. At the same time, LR-SARNet has the lowest time and space complexity, and its Runtime is also competitive.

The PR curve is a curve made with precision and recall as variables, where recall is the horizontal axis and precision is the vertical axis. The larger the curve coverage area, the better the performance of the model. A comparison chart of the PR curve of the

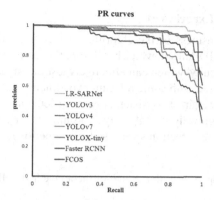

Fig. 8. The PR curves.

state-of-the-art method and LR-SARNet is shown in the Fig. 8, LR-SARNet (the yellow line) performs the best, which proves the excellent performance of the algorithm.

We choose the multi-scale target in offshore scene for algorithm comparison. It can be seen from the Fig. 9 that when facing multi-scale targets, other algorithms mostly have different degrees of missed detection, while LR-SARNet realizes the accurate detection of dense multi-scale targets and provides high confidence. Experiments on SSDD datasets preliminarily prove that LR-SARNet has excellent robustness.

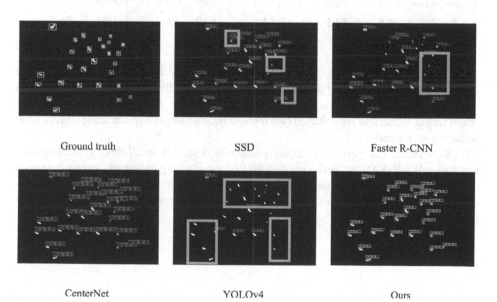

Fig. 9. Comparison with the state-of-the-art methods. (Green box is ground truth, blue box is missed targets, orange box is our results) (Color figure online).

3.3.3 Generalization Experiment

In order to test the robustness of the algorithm, we conducted further generalization experiments on the HRSID dataset, which has a complex background, many small targets, and high detection difficulty, which can effectively test the robustness of the algorithm. The algorithm is compared with some relevant experiments, and the experimental environment configuration remained consistent. From the detection results shown in Table 3, LR-SARNet achieves lightweight while outperforming existing advanced methods, with mAP up to 90.8% and the detection speed is also competitive.

Table 3. Comparison with the state-of-the-art methods (HRSID dataset).

Networks	mAP(%)	Precision(%)	Recall(%)	F1	Params(M)	Flops(G)	Runtime(ms)
Faster R-CNN [21]	78.2	88.8	77.5	0.83	60.1	181.9	56.1
SSD [6]	88.8	87.4	85.3	0.86	60.4	182.6	57.6
YOLOv4 [7]	87.2	90.6	84.0	0.87	64.3	110.5	26.0
RetinaNet	82.5	69.8	83.8	0.76	55.1	175.4	55.0
FCOS [9]	86.6	91.9	79.5	0.85	50.8	170.6	50.9
CenterNet [8]	81.8	87.4	84.5	0.85	20.2	63.3	55.0
CenterNet++	82.2	82.2	87.3	0.85	20.3	64.9	54.5
LR-SARNET	**90.8**	**94.5**	**84.6**	**0.89**	**3.6**	**8.4**	36.6

The overall recognition effect of LR-SARNet on the HRSID dataset is shown in Fig. 10. We selected three typical scenarios from the HRSID dataset results, including offshore multi-scale target scene, complex land interference scene, and canal-dense small target scene, and we selected two representative images in each scene to verify the accuracy of the model.

LR-SARNet can perform extremely accurate detection in all three typical scenarios. Overall, LR-SARNet performs excellently, maintaining extremely strong detection performance in multi-scale and complex scene environments, effectively alleviating several SAR ship detection problems, and demonstrating strong robustness and excellent generalization ability.

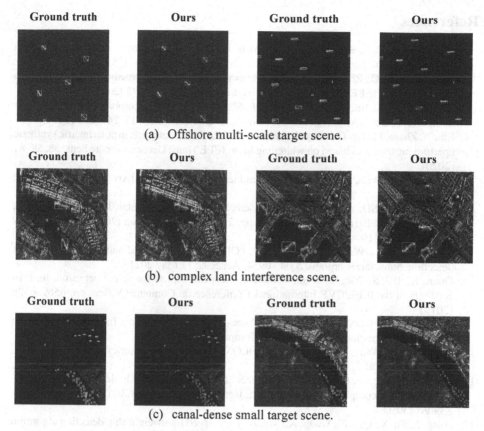

(a) Offshore multi-scale target scene.

(b) complex land interference scene.

(c) canal-dense small target scene.

Fig. 10. Comparison with the state-of-the-art methods.

4 Conclusion

SAR ship image detection plays an important role in maritime safety and marine management. Considering the SAR ship image characteristics such as the complex background interference, large differences in multi-scale features, and blurred ship features, we propose a lightweight robust algorithm for multi-scale and multi-scene SAR ship detection. A lightweight backbone feature extraction network is designed and the Enhanced Feature Fusion Network (ENECK) is used to extract the target semantic features, suppress the complex background effects, and improve the multi-scale detection, especially the small ship detection performance. In terms of detection results, LR-SARNet is more conducive to deployment to the end and has excellent detection performance compared with other advanced algorithms. Although there are still some unsatisfactory detection performances, we will explore the transformer framework for SAR target detection in the future, exploit the global field of view potential of transformers, combine it with CNN using local field of view, and achieve more accurate and stable SAR target detection algorithms with the help of image super-resolution reconstruction techniques.

References

1. Schwegmann, C.P., Kleynhans, W., Salmon, B.P.: Synthetic aperture radar ship detection using Haar-like features. IEEE Geosci. Remote Sens. Lett. **14**, 154–158 (2017)
2. Yang, M., Guo, C., Zhong, H., Yin, H.: A curvature-based saliency method for ship detection in SAR images. IEEE Geosci. Remote Sens. Lett. 18, 1590--1594 (2020)
3. Lin, H., Chen, H., Jin, K., Zeng, L., Yang, J.: Ship detection with superpixel-level fisher vector in high-resolution SAR images. IEEE Geosci. Remote Sens. Lett. **17**, 247–251 (2020)
4. Liu, T., Zhang, J., Gao, G., Yang, J., Marino, A.: CFAR Ship detection in polarimetric synthetic aperture radar images based on whitening filter. IEEE Trans. Geosci. Remote Sens. **58**, 58–81 (2020)
5. Redmon, J., Farhadi, A.: YOLOV3: an incremental improvement. arXiv preprint arXiv:1804. 02767 (2018)
6. Liu, W., et al.: SSD: single shot multibox detector. In: Leibe, B., Matas, J., Sebe, N., Welling, M. (eds.) ECCV 2016. LNCS, vol. 9905, pp. 21–37. Springer, Cham (2016). https://doi.org/10.1007/978-3-319-46448-0_2
7. Bochkovskiy, A., Wang, C., Liao, H.M.: YOLOv4: optimal speed and accuracy of object detection. https://arxiv.org/abs/2004.10934. Accessed 12 May 2021
8. Duan, K., Bai, S., Xie, L., et al.: CenterNet: keypoint triplets for object detection. In: Proceedings of the IEEE/CVF International Conference on Computer Vision, pp. 6569–6578 (2019)
9. Tian, Z., et al.: FCOS: fully convolutional one-stage object detection. In: Proceedings of the IEEE/CVF International Conference on Computer Vision (2019)
10. Ge, Z., Liu, S., Wang, F., Li, Z., Sun, J.: YOLOX: exceeding YOLO series in 2021. arXiv2021. arXiv:2107.08430
11. Tang, G., Zhuge, Y., Claramunt, C., Men, S.: N-YOLO: a SAR ship detection using noise-classifying and complete-target extraction. Remote Sens. **13**, 871 (2021). https://doi.org/10.3390/rs1305087
12. Jiang, J., Fu, X., Qin, R., Wang, X., Ma, Z.: High-speed lightweight ship detection algorithm based on YOLOV4-TINY for three-channels RGB SAR image. Remote Sens. **13**, 1909 (2021). https://doi.org/10.3390/rs13101909
13. Lin, T.Y., Dollár, P., Girshick, R., He, K., Hariharan, B., Belongie, S.: Feature pyramid networks for object detection. In: Proceedings of the IEEE Conference on Computer Vision and Pattern Recognition (CVPR), Honolulu, HI, USA, 21–26 July 2017, pp. 936–944 (2017)
14. Zhang, T., Zhang, X., Shi, J., Wei, S., Wang, J., Li, J.: Balanced feature pyramid network for ship detection in synthetic aperture radar images. In: Proceedings of the IEEE Radar Conference, pp. 1–5 (2020)
15. Sun, Z., et al.: An improved oriented ship detection method in high-resolution SAR image based on YOLOv5. In: 2022 Photonics & Electromagnetics Research Symposium (PIERS). IEEE (2022)
16. Chang, H., et al.: SPANet: a self-balancing position attention network for anchor-free SAR ship detection. In: IEEE Journal of Selected Topics in Applied Earth Observations and Remote Sensing (2023). https://doi.org/10.1109/JSTARS.2023.3283669
17. Han, K., et al.: GhostNet: more features from cheap operations. In: Proceedings of the IEEE/CVF Conference on Computer Vision and Pattern Recognition (2020)
18. Li, J., Qu, C., Shao, J.: Ship detection in SAR images based on an improved faster R-CNN. In: 2017 SAR in Big Data Era: Models, Methods and Applications (BIGSARDATA), Beijing, China, pp. 1–6 (2017). https://doi.org/10.1109/BIGSARDATA.2017.8124934
19. Wei, S., Zeng, X., Qu, Q., Wang, M., Su, H., Shi, J.: HRSID: a high-resolution SAR images dataset for ship detection and instance segmentation. IEEE Access **8**, 120234–120254 (2020). https://doi.org/10.1109/ACCESS.2020.3005861

20. Chang, Y.-L., Anagaw, A., Chang, L., Wang, Y.C., Hsiao, C.-Y., Lee, W.-H.: Ship detection based on YOLOv2 for SAR imagery. Remote Sens. **11**, 786 (2019). https://doi.org/10.3390/rs11070786
21. Ren, S., He, K., Girshick, R., Sun, J.: Faster r-CNN: towards real-time object detection with region proposal networks. In: Proceedings of the International Conference on Neural Information Processing Systems (NIPS), Montreal, QC, Canada, 7–12 December 2015, pp. 91–99 (2015)
22. Wei, S., et al.: Precise and robust ship detection for high-resolution SAR imagery based on HR-SDNet. Remote Sens. **12**, 167 (2020). https://doi.org/10.3390/rs12010167

A Coverless Image Steganography Method Based on Feature Matrix Mapping

Li Li[1], Chao Yang[1(✉)], and Jie Chen[2]

[1] Department of Electronic and Communication Engineering, Beijing Electronic Science and Technology Institute, Beijing 100070, China
yc19980403@163.com
[2] Department of Cyberspace Security, Beijing Electronic Science and Technology Institute, Beijing 100070, China

Abstract. To address the challenge that the current coverless image steganography (CIS) method requires more cover images and more information, a coverless image steganography method based on feature matrix mapping is proposed. In this paper, the low-frequency component of the Discrete Wavelet Transform (DWT) is used as the image eigenvalue, and a robust feature sequence is obtained by comparing the size of the main and minor diagonal blocks with the eigenvalues of other blocks. This paper proposes a feature matrix mapping rule to obtain the mapping matrix of the cover image and the secret information through the feature matrix mapping. The transmission of secret information is achieved through the cover image and the mapping matrix, which solves the problem of large transmission overhead and the need for more cover images and additional information. Experimental results show that this scheme has certain advantages in terms of the number of mapped images and additional information required, and has better security against most image attacks.

Keywords: Coverless image steganography · Discrete Wavelet Transform · Feature matrix mapping

1 Introduction

With the development of the Internet and cloud computing, more and more data is being transmitted over networks, and people do not want data to be stolen by unauthorized parties while they are transmitting it. Currently, there are two main ways to protect data transmitted in the channel: encryption and information hiding [1]. The main purpose of information hiding is different from that of encryption, as the former aims to hide the information itself for covert transmission, while the latter aims to protect it from being stolen by unauthorized parties by increasing the confidentiality of the information. In recent years, information-hiding techniques have received increasing attention along with the widespread use of digital media such as voice, images and video. Steganography and digital watermarking are important techniques for using digital media for information hiding [2]. In steganography, secret information is embedded in a conventional medium, such as text, images or audio, making the existence of the secret information undetectable to anyone other than the recipient.

W. Yongtian and W. Lifang (Eds.): IGTA 2023, CCIS 1910, pp. 472–488, 2023.
https://doi.org/10.1007/978-981-99-7549-5_34

Images as a digital medium are transmitted in large numbers over networks, providing great convenience for the transmission of secret information using steganography. Traditional image-based steganography methods fall into two main categories: spatial domain-based methods and transform domain-based methods [3]. Spatial domain-based methods embed the secret information directly into the cover image by changing the pixel values; this method has a large embedding capacity but is less robust. Transform domain-based methods mainly include Discrete Cosine Transform (DCT) [4], Discrete Wavelet Transform (DWT) [5] and Discrete Fourier Transform (DFT) [6], which have improved robustness compared to spatial domain-based methods. However, these traditional image steganography techniques can also modify the cover image while hiding information, which is easily detected by steganalysis algorithms.

Coverless image steganography (CIS) is a newer form of steganography that solves the disadvantage of used steganography schemes which are easy to be detected by steganalysis algorithms. CIS hides secret information by generating a cover or establishing a mapping rule between the cover and the information [7]. Coverless image steganography can be divided into texture synthesis-based steganography methods and mapping rule-based steganography methods.

Texture synthesis-based coverless steganography is a classical image steganography technique, which mainly uses texture synthesis to generate images to hide secret information, and texture synthesis coverless steganography ensures the security and concealment of secret information. Xu et al. proposed a reversible steganography algorithm based on texture deformation [9], which reversibly deforms the stego image containing the secret information to synthesize a different marble texture. By embedding the location information in the texture image, the secret information can be extracted and the extraction process is a reversible reduction process, but the algorithm is less robust. Qin et al. proposed a coverless image steganography technique based on generative adversarial networks [10], which encodes the secret information into the cover image and uses adversarial to optimize the quality of the stego image and thus can better avoid the steganography analysis tools. The texture-based coverless steganography method is less robust and the synthesized stego images may be detected as anomalous by the human eye.

The coverless image steganography method based on mapping rules establishes the relationship between secret information and the sequence of cover image features. Since it does not modify the image, it greatly improves security. Zhou et al. first proposed a coverless image steganography method based on an index table created by the image [12], which divides each image into nine blocks and calculates the feature sequence based on the relationship between the mean values of pixels in adjacent blocks, thus allowing the use of one image to represent an 8-bit feature sequence. Zhang et al. proposed a coverless image steganography algorithm that maps robust feature sequences to secret information through mapping rules [13], which can effectively resist detection by steganalysis algorithms and is more robust because its feature sequences consist of DC coefficient relationships between neighboring blocks. Kadhim et al. propose a scheme that divides the cover image into multiple non-overlapping blocks, indirectly hiding the secret data blocks in the sub-bands of the DT-CWT coefficient of the selected cover block [14]. Liu et al. proposed an image mapping rule-based steganography method for coverless images that compares DWT coefficients between blocks in a sawtooth scan to generate feature sequences [15]. Because the DWT transform extracts more stable low-frequency signals from the image, the algorithm is robust to most image attacks. Yang et al. proposed a coverless image steganography method based on the highest valid bits of the image [16]. The value of the highest bit of the image pixel value is used as a criterion to achieve the concealment of secret information. This scheme relies on a pre-agreed sequence for mapping and suffers from the problem of requiring a large amount of additional information. Liu et al. proposed a method that uses a single cover image [17]. The ring statistics are extracted from the image to generate the feature sequence, which makes it more robust. The method also introduces a chaotic system to map one image to multiple secret messages using different scrambling features, which greatly reduces the number of cover images and increases the difficulty of steganalysis, but requires more additional information and the computational overhead of the information hiding phase is relatively high.

The existing mapping rule-based CIS methods still have some challenges in terms of steganography and robustness, such as the need for multiple cover images and a large amount of additional information as support for information extraction. To improve the performance of the mapping-based CIS method, this paper proposes a coverless image-hiding method based on feature matrix mapping, which aims to overcome the problem of needing more cover images and additional information in the existing methods, and further improve the stealth and robustness of information hiding.

2 Feature Matrix Mapping Rules

This section illustrates the feature matrix mapping rules proposed in this paper by introducing both the construction of the feature matrix and the feature matrix mapping.

2.1 Feature Matrix

The feature matrix is constructed from feature sequences based on the size of the secret information and is the bridge between the secret information and the cover image to establish a mapping relationship. The feature sequence is a sequence of fixed length obtained from the cover image and is a sequence of features related to the cover image based on the inherent features of the image (such as pixel values, luminance values and texture features), with different sequences corresponding to the cover image or a part of the cover image. As the cover image may be subject to attacks such as noise attacks, luminance attacks, edge cropping and contrast transformations during transmission, the feature extraction algorithm requires strong robustness to ensure that the feature sequence acquired remains unchanged after the image has been attacked.

In this paper, the cover image is processed using the Discrete Wavelet Transform (DWT). The values of the low-frequency component of the cover image are used as the eigenvalues, and the eigenvalues are used to obtain the feature sequence. The Discrete Wavelet Transform is widely used for data pre-processing, downscaling and feature extraction. The image is decomposed into four images of 1/4 the size of the original image after the discrete wavelet transform, containing one low-frequency image and three high-frequency images, where the low-frequency component contains most of the energy of the original image, while the high-frequency component contains the detailed information of the image, as shown in Fig. 1. The low-low sub-band corresponds to the smoothed part of the original image. This part of the signal is highly stable, resistant to interference and less affected by image attacks, and is suitable for feature extraction of the images in this paper.

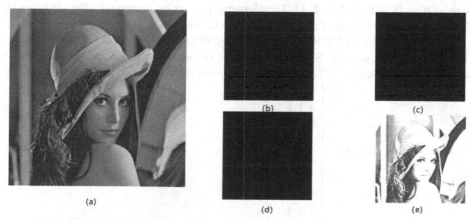

(a) original image (b) High-High sub-band (c)High-Low sub-band (d)Low-High sub-band (e)Low-Low sub-band

Fig. 1. Image after discrete wavelet transform.

1	1	2	8
8	2	7	3
7	6	3	4
5	6	5	4

Fig. 2. Image block classification rules

The first step in constructing the feature matrix is to chunk the image, dividing the blocks into two parts, the main and secondary diagonal blocks, and the other blocks. Then, the eigenvalues of the main and minor diagonal blocks are arranged by size, and the eigenvalues of the other blocks are also arranged by size, and the two parts of the eigenvalues are compared one by one to obtain the feature sequence. If the eigenvalue of the diagonal block is greater than the eigenvalue of the other blocks, the element value of the feature sequence is 1. If not, the element value of the feature sequence is 0. Finally, the secret information is converted into binary numbers in the form of segments of length l, where l is the number of bits in the segment, resulting in n binary information segments of length l. Using n as the number of rows of the matrix l as the number of columns of the matrix, the elements in the feature sequence are selected in order from the feature sequence to form the feature matrix X. Take Fig. 2 as an example, there are 8 blocks of white for the main and minor diagonal blocks and 8 blocks of black for the other blocks. The eigenvalues of the white blocks are listed in order of size as $A = \{8, 7, 6, 5, 4, 3, 2, 1\}$ and the eigenvalues of the black blocks are listed in order of size as $B = \{8, 7, 6, 5, 4, 3, 2, 1\}$. The elements in A are compared with the elements in B one by one to obtain the feature sequence, which is

$\{0111111100111111000111110000111100000111000000110000000100000000\}$

There are 64 bits in total. Suppose the secret message is divided into 8 binary message segments of length 4. The first 32 elements of the feature sequence are selected to

form the feature matrix as
$$\begin{bmatrix} 0 & 1 & 1 & 1 \\ 1 & 1 & 1 & 1 \\ 0 & 0 & 1 & 1 \\ 1 & 1 & 1 & 1 \\ 0 & 0 & 0 & 1 \\ 1 & 1 & 1 & 1 \\ 0 & 0 & 0 & 0 \\ 1 & 1 & 1 & 1 \end{bmatrix}.$$

2.2 Feature Matrix Mapping

The existing CIS methods for mapping are broadly based on creating index tables, creating mapping relationships between secret information and image fragments by prior agreement, and matching secret information by scrambling image features with seed keys and specific systems. Both the index table approach and the cross-referencing approach have some computational overhead. The prior agreement approach usually comes with some additional information, and the prior agreement approach requires the agreement information to be changed periodically to ensure better security. The use of different seed keys and a specific system to permute the same sequence of features to produce a different sequence to match the secret message is very informative and has a certain computational overhead. In this paper, we propose a method for mapping secret messages using matrix transformation, which reduces the amount of information transmission and does not require additional information. The specific approach is shown in Fig. 3:

$$\begin{bmatrix} x_{11} & x_{12} & \cdots & x_{1l} \\ x_{21} & x_{22} & \cdots & x_{2l} \\ \vdots & \vdots & \vdots & \vdots \\ x_{n1} & x_{n2} & \cdots & x_{nl} \end{bmatrix} \times \begin{bmatrix} d_{11} & d_{12} & \cdots & d_{1l} \\ d_{21} & d_{22} & \cdots & d_{2l} \\ \vdots & \vdots & \vdots & \vdots \\ d_{l1} & d_{l2} & \cdots & d_{ll} \end{bmatrix} = \begin{bmatrix} s_{11} & s_{12} & \cdots & s_{1l} \\ s_{21} & s_{22} & \cdots & s_{2l} \\ \vdots & \vdots & \vdots & \vdots \\ s_{n1} & s_{n2} & \cdots & s_{nl} \end{bmatrix}$$

Fig. 3. Mapping method

$[x_1, x_2, ..., x_n]^T$ is the feature matrix X, $X \in R^{n \times l}$, $[d_1, d_2, ..., d_l]^T$ is the mapping matrix D, $D \in R^{l \times l}$ $[s_1, s_2, ..., s_n]^T$ is the secret information matrix S, $S \in R^{n \times l}$ where n is the number of segments into which the secret information is divided and l is the length of each segment $(n > l)$. The mapping matrix D reflects the mapping between the feature matrix X and the secret information matrix S.

The information to be transmitted by the sender is the cover image and the mapping matrix D. The receiver constructs the feature matrix X from the cover image and solves the secret information matrix S from the feature matrix X and the mapping matrix D. The size of the mapping matrix D is smaller than the secret information matrix S and no additional information is required to solve the secret information matrix.

The feature matrix mapping rule proposed in this paper involves the multiplication of matrices and therefore requires that the feature matrix X has full column rank. The mapping approach depicted in Fig. 3 is valid only if the feature matrix X has column full rank. Since the value of each element of the feature matrix X is based on the cover image, it is not guaranteed that the feature matrix X constructed from any of the cover images will be column full rank. Therefore, Singular Value Decomposition (SVD) is introduced to satisfy the requirement of column full rank of the matrix. Taking the eigenmatrix X as an example, the singular value decomposition of X is

$$X = U \sum V^T \tag{1}$$

where U is a left singular matrix, $U \in R^{n \times n}$, $\sum$ is a singular value matrix, $\sum \in R^{n \times l}$ and V is a right singular value matrix, $V \in R^{l \times l}$. Both U and V are orthogonal matrices. Extracting U' from the first l column of U to replace the eigenfrequency vector X to satisfy the column full rank requirement. The final mapping rule is shown in Fig. 4, where $[u_1', u_2', ..., u_n']^T$ represents the matrix U', $U' \in R^{n \times l}$;

$$\begin{bmatrix} u_{11}' & u_{12}' & \cdots & u_{1l}' \\ u_{21}' & u_{22}' & \cdots & u_{2l}' \\ \vdots & \vdots & \vdots & \vdots \\ u_{n1}' & u_{n2}' & \cdots & u_{nl}' \end{bmatrix} \times \begin{bmatrix} d_{11} & d_{12} & \cdots & d_{1l} \\ d_{21} & d_{22} & \cdots & d_{2l} \\ \vdots & \vdots & \vdots & \vdots \\ d_{l1} & d_{l2} & \cdots & d_{ll} \end{bmatrix} = \begin{bmatrix} s_{11} & s_{12} & \cdots & s_{1l} \\ s_{21} & s_{22} & \cdots & s_{2l} \\ \vdots & \vdots & \vdots & \vdots \\ s_{n1} & s_{n2} & \cdots & s_{nl} \end{bmatrix}$$

Fig. 4. Mapping rules

3 CIS Scheme Based on Feature Matrix

The flow of the scheme is shown in Fig. 5, which consists of an information-hiding phase for the sender and an information-extraction phase for the receiver. The sender first divides the secret information into n binary information segments of length l and forms the secret information matrix S, then selects the cover image from the image database to obtain the feature sequence, selects the elements of the feature sequence according to the size of the secret information to construct the feature matrix X, and obtains the mapping matrix D through matrix mapping, and finally sends the cover image,n and the mapping matrix D to the receiver. After obtaining the cover image,n and the mapping matrix, the receiver obtains the feature matrix X based on the cover image and n, and finally obtains the secret information matrix S through the feature matrix X and the mapping matrix D, and recovers the secret information based on the secret information matrix S.

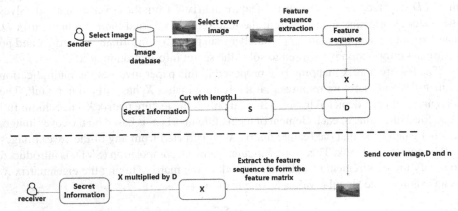

Fig. 5. Flowchart of the proposed CIS

3.1   Information Hiding Phase

Feature Sequence Acquisition
In this paper, DWT is applied to an image to obtain a feature sequence using the low-frequency component of the image as the feature. The steps for obtaining the feature sequences are as follows.

Step 1. To improve the image's resistance to scaling, normalize all images to the size of $N \times N$ and divide the normalized image into blocks of M and each block of B_i has the size of $\frac{N}{\sqrt{M}} \times \frac{N}{\sqrt{M}}$.

$$B_i = \{B_1, B_2, ..., B_M\}, 0 < i \leq M, i \in Z \tag{2}$$

Step 2. Each block B_i is transformed to YUV color space, the Y channel is selected as the object of DWT transform, each block B_i is DWT transformed and the value of the low-frequency component of LL_i is extracted.

$$LL_i = DWT^2(B_i) \tag{3}$$

B_i denotes the block after image segmentation,LL_i denotes the value of the low-frequency component of each block after the DWT transform. DWT^2 denotes the two-dimensional transform.

Step 3. Extract the values of the low-frequency component of the main and minor diagonal blocks together at m and arrange them in order of size as LL_d, extract the values of the low-frequency component of the other blocks and arrange them in order of size as LL_o.

Step 4. The elements in LL_d are compared to the elements in LL_o one by one in order, with elements in LL_d greater than those in LL_o being taken as 1 and 0 otherwise, as follows

$$fs_{ij} = \begin{cases} 1 \ if \ LL_d > LL_o \\ 0 if \ LL_d \leq LL_o \end{cases} \tag{4}$$

where $0 < d \leq m, 0 < o \leq M - m$.

Information Mapping

Information mapping is the process of constructing a feature matrix using feature sequence and establishing a mapping relationship between the secret message and the cover image based on the feature matrix, in the following steps.

Step 1. Divide the secret message s of length L into binary segments of n of length l:

$$n = \begin{cases} L/l \ if \ L\%l = 0 \\ \lfloor L/l \rfloor \ otherwise \end{cases} \tag{5}$$

where $\lfloor \cdot \rfloor$ indicates a downward rounding symbol. If L is not divisible by l, the last segment is complemented by 0 to the length l. The secret message segment can be represented as a matrix $S = [S_1, S_2, ..., S_n]^T$.

Step 2. Obtaining the feature sequence of the cover image according to 3.1.1, constructing a feature matrix X by selecting $n \times l$ bits among the $m \times (M - m)$-bit feature sequence.

Step 3. Decompose the eigenmatrix X into singular values, select the left singular matrix U and select the first l columns of U to obtain the matrix U'.

Step 4. According to Sect. 2.2, find the mapping matrix D. Place the number of complementary zeros from Step1 in a binary form of length l in the last row of the matrix D. If there are no complementary zeros, then no information is added.

Step5. Send the cover image,n and the mapping matrix D to the receiver.

3.2 Information Extraction Phase

The receiver recovers the secret information based on the received cover image,n and the matrix D in the following steps.

Step 1. First, extract the last row of the matrix D to obtain the complementary 0 information.

Step 2. Normalize all images to the size of $N \times N$ and divide the normalized image into M blocks, each with the size of $\frac{N}{\sqrt{M}} \times \frac{N}{\sqrt{M}}$.

Step 3. Each block B_i is transformed to YUV color space, the Y channel is selected as the object of DWT transformation, and each block B_i is DWT transformed to extract the values of the low-frequency component of it LL_i.

Step 4. Extract the values of the low-frequency component of the main and minor diagonal blocks together at m and arrange them in size as LL_d, extract the values of the low-frequency component of the other blocks and arrange them in size as LL_o.

Step 5. The elements in LL_d are compared with the elements in LL_o one by one in order, with elements in LL_d greater than those in LL_o being taken as 1 and 0 otherwise.

Step 6. Construct the feature matrix X by selecting the elements of the feature sequence from n.

Step 7. Decompose the eigenmatrix X into singular values, select the left singular matrix U, and select the first l columns of U to obtain the matrix U'.

Step 8. Remove the last row of the matrix D, get the matrix S according to $U' \times D = S$, delete the complementary zeros in the matrix S according to the complementary zeros information extracted from Step1 in Sect. 3.2, and finally restore the secret information.

4 Experimental Results and Analysis

All experiments in this paper were performed on MATLAB 2021a. The dataset used consists of the INRIA Holidays dataset, which contains 1491 high-resolution, unclassified images, and the web dataset, which contains a total of 500 web images and images taken or intercepted by the author at different resolutions and with no fixed categories. The experimental parameters were set as follows: $N = 512, M = 25, l = 8$, the secret message was divided into 10 segments and the wavelet function type was set to $db1$. The analysis of the experiment consists of the following four parts: analysis of robustness, analysis of capacity, analysis of imperceptibility and analysis of security. Considering that robustness is the most important influencing factor, we discuss the impact of geometric attacks on robustness in Sect. 4.1, in addition to experimental comparisons with the literature [13], literature [15] and literature [17].

4.1 Analysis of Robustness

Robustness is an important performance index in CIS, reflecting the ability of covert information to resist attacks during transmission. Robustness was tested using the INRIA Holidays dataset and the web image dataset. Several types of attacks were applied to the cover images, as shown in Table 1.

In the experiments, the robustness RB is calculated as the difference between the original covert message and the recovered covert message under various attacks. RB Larger index better robustness of the steganography scheme. RB is defined as

$$RB = \frac{\sum_1^L f(b_i, b_i')}{L} \times 100\% \tag{6}$$

where L is the length of the secret message, b_i represents the i bit of information extracted from the unattacked cover image, b_i' represents the i bit of information extracted from the attacked cover image, and the function $f(\cdot)$ represents the following:

$$f(b_i, b_i') = \begin{cases} 1 \ if \ b_i = b_i' \\ 0 \ otherwise \end{cases} \tag{7}$$

The comparison results are shown in Tables 2 and 3. Table 2 shows the robustness against literature [13], literature [15] and literature [23] in the INRIA Holidays dataset. The results in the table show that the overall robustness of this scheme is stronger than that of literature literature [13], literature [15] and literature [23], and it still has a high success rate in recovering the secret information under the compression, noise and filtering attacks. The success rate of recovering the secret information under the geometric attack is significantly higher than that of the literature [13] and literature [15].

Table 3 shows a comparison with the literature [17] under the web dataset. From the comparison results, it can be seen that the overall robustness of this scheme is stronger than that of the literature [17] for attacks other than geometric attacks. The robustness against rotate 90° and 180° attacks and flip attacks is better than that of [17], while the robustness against other geometric attacks is lower than that of [17]. The reason for this result lies in the way of feature extraction. The feature extraction of this scheme is to divide the image into identical blocks, put the blocks on the main and minor diagonals together to calculate the values of their DWT low-frequency component separately, and put the other blocks to calculate the values of their DWT low-frequency component separately, and then compare the two sets of data sequentially one by one to obtain the feature sequence, which has the advantage that the rotate 90°, 180° attacks and flip attacks do not have an impact on the acquired feature sequences, while the values of the low-frequency component of some blocks change when the cover image is cropped causing changes in the acquired feature sequences, resulting in incorrect extraction of secret information. The scheme in the literature [17] divides the image into concentric rings so that the feature sequence is minimally affected when the image is subjected to geometric attacks so that its performance is more stable under rotation attacks at different angles as well as cropping attacks.

Table 1. Types of attacks

Attack type	Parameters
Rotation (RT)	50, 70, 90, 135, 180
Edge cropping (EC)	{10%, 20%}
Flipping (FL)	{Horizontal, Vertical}
JPEG compression (JPEG)	Quality factor = {50, 70, 90}
Gauss noise (GN)	Mean = 0; variance = {0.001, 0.005}
Salt and pepper noise (SN)	Mean = 0; variance = {0.001, 0.005}
Speckle noise (SPN)	Mean = 0; variance = {0.001, 0.005}
Gauss filtering (GF)	window = {3 × 3, 5 × 5}
Median filtering (MF)	window = {3 × 3, 5 × 5}
Average filtering (AF)	window = {3 × 3, 5 × 5}
Gamma transform (GT)	$\gamma = \{0.8, 1.2\}$

Table 2. Robustness of the INRIA Holidays dataset compared to the schemes in the literature [13, 15] and[23]

Attack	Literature [13]	Literature [15]	Literature [23]	ours
JPEG 50	93.0%	97.0%	100.0%	99.7%
JPEG 70	98.0%	100.0%	100.0%	99.9%
JPEG 90	99.0%	99.0%	100.0%	99.9%
GN 0.001	100.0%	100.0%	98.7%	99.3%
GN 0.005	92.0%	96.0%	97.0%	98.6%
SN 0.001	98.0%	100.0%	99.0%	99.9%
SN 0.005	92.0%	99.0%	99.0%	99.5%
SPN 0.001	93.0%	96.0%	100.0%	99.7%
SPN 0.005	87.0%	93.0%	99.0%	99.6%
MF 3X3	100.0%	100.0%	100.0%	99.9%
MF 5X5	99.0%	100.0%	100.0%	99.2%
GF 3X3	100.0%	100.0%	99.0%	99.4%
GF 5X5	100.0%	100.0%	99.0%	99.2%
EC 10%	26.0%	46.0%	45.0%	58.8%
EC 20%	18.0%	21.0%	32.0%	41.4%
RT 10	4.0%	8.0%	56.0%	57.1%
RT 30	0.0%	1.0%	48.0%	41.5%
RT 50	0.0%	0.0%	48.0%	50.0%

4.2 Analysis of Hidden Capacity

The hidden capacity of existing mapping rule-based steganography schemes for coverless images is determined by the length of the feature sequence. The larger the length of the feature sequence, the larger the hidden capacity. Accordingly, the number of images required to hide a fixed length of secret information is reduced.

Evaluate the hidden capacity of the CIS by calculating the number of cover images needed to acquire the desired feature sequence for a fixed feature sequence length

$$hc = \frac{T}{N_{CI}} \tag{8}$$

where,T indicates the length of the feature sequence,N_{CI} indicates the number of cover images required, and hc is larger, indicating a larger hidden capacity. The results are shown in Table 4.

As shown in Table 4, compared with the schemes proposed in [13] and [15], this scheme significantly reduces the number of cover images while ensuring sufficient capacity, compared with [17] the hidden capacity of the scheme proposed in this paper is improved, which is related to the length of the specified feature sequence, both schemes

Table 3. Robustness of the web dataset compared to the scheme in the literature [17]

Attack	Literature [17]	ours
JPEG 50	99.0%	99.9%
JPEG 70	99.3%	99.7%
JPEG 90	99.5%	99.9%
GN 0.001	99.0%	99.9%
GN 0.005	98.1%	98.8%
SN 0.001	99.3%	99.9%
SN 0.005	98.9%	99.3%
SPN 0.001	99.4%	99.8%
SPN 0.005	99.2%	99.1%
MF 3X3	98.1%	99.9%
MF 5X5	96.6%	99.3%
GF 3X3	98.7%	99.9%
GF 5X5	98.8%	99.5%
AF 3X3	97.5%	99.9%
AF 5X5	95.6%	99.2%
EC 10%	99.6%	65.3%
EC 20%	96.4%	57.5%
RT 50	97.3%	64.7%
RT 70	96.7%	62.4%
RT 90	95.9%	99.2%
RT 135	95.2%	60.5%
RT 180	94.9%	98.9%
FL horizontal	95.9%	96.2%
FL vertical	97.1%	96.9%
GT 0.8	96.7%	99.6%
GT 1.2	97.2%	99.8%

Table 4. Comparison of hidden capacities

Methods	Literature [13]	Literature [15]	Literature [17]	ours
T	15	15	32	160
N_{CI}	215	215	1	1
hc	4.58×10^{-4}	4.58×10^{-4}	3.2×10	1.6×100

can use one image to satisfy the feature sequence requirement of the whole algorithm. However, the difference is that [17] uses LTCS to map secret information into feature sequences by different keys, which are keyed to different keys, and the keys cannot be selected, and the eligible keys are screened out through a trial process, which requires higher computational ability. This scheme calculates the mapping relationship between the secret information and the feature matrix through a matrix operation, and the time required in this part of information mapping will be significantly reduced.

4.3 Analysis of Imperceptibility

Peak Signal Noise Ratio (PSNR) is normally used to analyse the distortion of a stego image and is measured in dB. The larger the value, the less distorted the stego image. The PSNR is calculated as follows

$$PSNR = 10 \log_{10} \left(\frac{255^2}{MSE} \right) \tag{9}$$

Mean Squared Error (MSE) is used to measure the similarity between the cover image and the stego image, and the MSE is calculated as follows

$$MSE = \frac{1}{WH} \sum_{x=1}^{W} \sum_{y=1}^{H} \left(I_{xy} - I'_{xy} \right)^2 \tag{10}$$

where W is the image width, H is the image height, x and y are the coordinates of the cover image. I_{xy} and I'_{xy} denote the pixel values of the cover image and the stego image at the coordinates (x, y), respectively. In the proposed scheme, the stego image is not modified when the secret information is hidden. In other words, the cover image is identical to the stego image, hence $I_{xy} - I'_{xy} = 0, MSE = 0, PSNR = \infty$.

The Structural Similarity Index (SSIM) measures the similarity between the cover image and the stego image. Its value ranges from -1 to $+1$. SSIM is equal to 1 when the cover image is the same as the stego image, which is the best value for SSIM. SSIM is expressed as follows.

$$SSIM \left(I, I' \right) = \frac{(2\mu_I \mu_{I'} + C_1)(2\sigma_{II'} + C_2)}{\left(\mu_I^2 + \mu_{I'}^2 + C_1 \right)\left(\sigma_I^2 + \sigma_{I'}^2 + C_2 \right)} \tag{11}$$

$$C_1 = (sc_1 D)^2 \tag{12}$$

$$C_2 = (sc_2 D)^2 \tag{13}$$

where μ is the average luminance, σ is the standard deviation of the signal contrast, sc_1 and sc_2 are stabilisation parameters with default values of 0.01 and 0.03, and D is the maximum value of the pixel value, here $C_1 = 2.55, C_2 = 7.65$.

The generic image quality index (Qi) is another important parameter to measure the similarity between the cover image and the stego image. When the cover image and the stego image are identical, Qi can be obtained as the optimum value of 1. Qi is expressed as follows:

$$Qi = \frac{4\sigma_{II'}\overline{I}\overline{I'}}{\left(\sigma_I^2 + \sigma_{I'}^2\right)\left[\overline{I}^2 + \overline{I'}^2\right]} \tag{14}$$

$\overline{I}$ and $\overline{I'}$ represent the mean luminance of the cover and stego images, $\sigma_{II'}$ is the covariance, and σ_I and $\sigma_{I'}$ are the standard deviations of the cover and stego images.

The proposed scheme in this paper is CIS, which does not modify the cover image compared to traditional steganography, so the values of PNSR, SSIM, Qi are optimally achieved to be ∞, 1, 1. Table 5 shows the comparison between this paper and the traditional steganography literature [11].

Table 5. The PNSR,SSIM and Qi comparison of literature [11] and ours

Methods	PSNR(dB)	SSIM	Qi
ours	∞	1	1
Literature [11]	49.17727	0.78914	0.99797

4.4 Analysis of Security

The security of a steganography scheme can be measured using steganalysis tools. In addition to resistance to steganalysis tools, the security of the solution itself is also an important aspect.

1. Resistance to steganalysis. Traditional steganography algorithms make some modifications to the cover image to hide the secret information, and the modified cover image can be a breakthrough for steganalysis tools. The existing steganalysis tools usually achieve steganalysis by detecting the modification traces of the stego image. The method proposed in this paper is a coverless image steganography method, which establishes a mapping relationship between the secret information and the cover image without modifying the cover image. Therefore, it can fundamentally resist existing steganalysis tools.

2. The security of the scheme itself. The information that can be intercepted by an attacker is the transmission image, the mapping matrix D and n. Without knowledge of the steganography method, the attacker cannot decipher the secret information; under the means of brute force cracking, the feature matrix X has $n \times l$ elements, i.e.X has $2^{n \times l}$ possibilities, the number of elements of the feature matrix X is the same as the length of the secret information, and as the length of the secret information grows, the workload of brute force cracking rises geometrically, taking $n \times l = 80$ as an example, assuming that the brute force cracking computational ability of X is 10 billion times/second, and the time to crack the feature matrix is 14 billion years. The above analysis shows that the attacker needs to be able to crack the secret message by obtaining

the following conditions: firstly, the mapping matrix D, secondly, the transmission image, thirdly, understanding the meaning of n, the composition of the feature matrix X and the composition of the matrix U', and fourthly, understanding the relationship between the matrices U', D and S.

In summary, the method proposed in this paper is resistant to existing steganalysis tools. On the other hand, the solution proposed in this paper is also inherently highly secure.

5 Summary

This paper proposes a coverless image steganography method based on feature matrix mapping, where the transmission of secret information is achieved through the cover image and the mapping matrix. The mapping matrix is obtained from the constructed cover image feature matrix and the secret information, and the mapping matrix contains the mapping relationship between the image feature matrix and the secret information matrix. In the information hiding phase, the scheme is resistant to existing steganalysis tools as no modifications are made to the cover image. It also increases the hidden capacity, as one cover image is sufficient for hiding the secret message, reducing the requirement for the number of cover images while not requiring additional information to recover the secret message. Experimental and theoretical results show that this scheme not only has good resistance to detection and steganalysis, but also has strong robustness to most image attacks, but has some limitations in terms of resistance to geometric attacks. Future work will focus on improving the robustness against geometric attacks.

Acknowledgments. This work is supported by the Key technologies and systems for password on-demand services in the cloud environment (2017YFB0801803); "High-precision" Discipline Construction Project in Beijing Universities (20210093Z0401); Fundamental Research Funds for the Central Universities (Grant Number: 328202244).

References

1. Kadhim, I.J., Premaratne, P., Vial, P.J.: Adaptive image steganography based on edge detection over dual-tree complex wavelet transform. In: Huang, D.-S., Gromiha, M.M., Han, K., Hussain, A. (eds.) ICIC 2018. LNCS (LNAI), vol. 10956, pp. 544–550. Springer, Cham (2018). https://doi.org/10.1007/978-3-319-95957-3_57
2. Joseph, P., Vishnukumar, S.: A study on steganographic techniques. In: Global Conference on Communication Technologies, GCCT 2015, pp. 206–210. IEEE (2015)
3. Khare, P., Singh, J., Tiwari, M.: Digital image steganography. J. EngRes. Stud. **2**, 101–104 (2011)
4. Huang, F., Huang, J., Shi, Y.Q.: New channel selection rule for JPEG steganography. IEEE Trans. Inf. Forensics Security. **7**, 1181–1191 (2012)
5. Zhiwei, K., Jing, L., Yigang, H.: Steganography based on wavelet transform and modulus function. J. Syst Eng. Electrons. **18**, 628–632 (2007)
6. McKeon, R.T.: Strange Fourier steganography in movies. In: Proceedings of the ICEIT, DeKalb, Illinois, USA, IEEE, pp. 178–182 (2007)

7. Chen, X., Sun, H., Tobe, Y., Zhou, Z., Sun, X.: Coverless information hiding method based on the Chinese mathematical expression. In: Huang, Z., Sun, X., Luo, J., Wang, J. (eds.) ICCCS 2015. LNCS, vol. 9483, pp. 133–143. Springer, Cham (2015). https://doi.org/10.1007/978-3-319-27051-7_12

8. Otori, H., Kuriyama, S.: Data-embeddable texture synthesis. In: Proceedings of the International Symposium on Smart Graphics, Kyoto, Japan, pp. 146–157 (2007)

9. Xu, J., Mao, X., Jin, X., et al.: Hidden message in a deformation-based texture. Vis. Comput. **31**, 1653–1669 (2015)

10. Qin, J., Wang, J., Tan, Y., Huang, H., Xiang, X., He, Z.: Coverless image steganography based on generative adversarial network. Mathematics **8**, 1394 (2020)

11. Patwari, B., Nandi, U., Ghosal, S.K.: Image steganography based on difference of Gaussians edge detection. Multimed. Tools Appl. 1–21 (2023)

12. Zhou, Z., Sun, H., Harit, R., Chen, X., Sun, X.: Coverless image steganography without embedding. In: Huang, Z., Sun, X., Luo, J., Wang, J. (eds.) ICCCS 2015. LNCS, vol. 9483, pp. 123–132. Springer, Cham (2015). https://doi.org/10.1007/978-3-319-27051-7_11

13. Zhang, X., Peng, F., Long, M.: Robust coverless image steganography based on DCT and LDA topic classification. IEEE Trans. Multimedia **20**, 3223–3238 (2018)

14. Kadhim, I.J., Premaratne, P., Vial, P.J.: High capacity adaptive image steganography with cover region selection using dual-tree complex wavelet transform - ScienceDirect. Cogn. Syst. Res. **60**, 20–32 (2020)

15. Liu, Q., et al.: Coverless steganography based on image retrieval of DenseNet features and DWT sequence mapping. Knowl.-Based Syst. **192**, 105375 (2019)

16. Yang, L., Deng, H., Dang, X.: A novel coverless information hiding method based on the most ppSignificant bit of the cover image. IEEE Access. **8**, 108579–108591 (2020)

17. Liu, X., Li, Z., Ma, J., Zhang, W., Zhang, J., Ding, Y.: Robust coverless steganography using limited mapping images. J. King Saud Univ. - Comput. Inf. Sci. **34**, 4472–4482 (2022)

18. Jegou, H., Douze, M., Schmid, C.: Hamming embedding and weak geometric consistency for large scale image search. In: Forsyth, D., Torr, P., Zisserman, A. (eds.) ECCV 2008. LNCS, vol. 5302, pp. 304–317. Springer, Heidelberg (2008). https://doi.org/10.1007/978-3-540-88682-2_24

19. Yuan, C., Xia, Z., Sun, X.: Coverless image steganography based on SIFT and BOF. J. Internet Technol. **18**, 435–442 (2017)

20. Zhou, Z., Cao, Y., Wang, M., et al.: Faster-RCNN based robust coverless information hiding system in cloud environment. IEEE Access **7**, 179891–179897 (2019)

21. Zou, L., Sun, J., Gao, M., et al.: A novel coverless information hiding method based on the average pixel value of the sub-images. Multimed. Tools Appl. **78**, 7965–7980 (2019)

22. Chen, X., Zhang, Z., Qiu, A., Xia, Z., Xiong, N.N.: A novel coverless steganography method based on image selection and StarGAN. IEEE Trans. Netw. Sci. Eng. **9**, 219–230 (2022)

23. Kulkarni, T., Debnath, S., Kumar, J., et al.: DCT based robust coverless information hiding scheme with high capacity. In: 2023 7th International Conference on Trends in Electronics and Informatics (ICOEI). IEEE, pp. 358--364 (2023)

24. Luo, Y., Qin, J., Xiang, X., Tan, Y.: Coverless image steganography based on multi-object recognition. IEEE Trans. Circ. Syst. Video Technol. **31**, 2779–2791 (2021)

25. Li, Q.i., Wang, X., Wang, X., Ma, B., Wang, C., Shi, Y.: An encrypted coverless information hiding method based on generative models. Inf. Sci. **553**, 19--30 (2021)

26. Xie, G., Ren, J., Marshall, S., et al.: A novel gradient-guided post-processing method for adaptive image steganography. Sig. Process. **203**, 108813 (2023)

27. Dong, T., et al.: Robust coverless information hiding based on image classification (in Chinese). J. Appl. Sci.**39**, 893–905 (2021)

28. Zhou, Z., et al.: Generative steganography method based on auto-generation of contours (in Chinese). J. Commun.**42**, 144–154 (2021)

29. Zhang, Z., Ni, J., Yao, Y., Gong, L., Wang, Y., Wu, G.: Text coverless information hiding method based on synonyms expansion and label delivery mechanism (in Chinese). J. Commun. **42**, 173–183 (2021)
30. Wang, Y., Wu, B.: An intelligent search method of mapping relation for coverless information hiding (in Chinese). J. Cyber Secur.**5**, 48–61 (2020)

Design and Implementation of a Digital Star Map Simulation Module

Chenghua Cao$^{(\boxtimes)}$, Xiaoyong Wang, and Yu Wang

Beijing Institute of Space Mechanics & Electricity, Beijing 100094, China
1806804825@qq.com

Abstract. Based on the stellar longitude, latitude, and visual magnitude brightness information obtained from the Smithsonian astrophysical observatory star catalog (SAO) and using the conversion relationship between the three coordinate systems and the conversion relationship between star visual magnitude brightness and image grayscale, a digital star map simulation module is built using hybrid programming of Visual C# and MATLAB. The generated star images are compared with known star images generation software such as the Sky Map, which verifies the accuracy of the generated image. Besides it supports the configuration of custom input parameters, and can simulate background noise, star position noise, star magnitude noise and missing of stars. The custom generation simulation of stars and pseudo-stars can provide support for various applications with starry sky as the background, such as star map recognition, space target positioning, space target motion trajectory detection, space target motion feature detection, and space situational awareness in the simulation stage.

Keywords: star simulation · hybrid programming · star simulator

1 Introduction

With the gradual enhancement of human's ability to enter space, more and more space craft are launched into space to perform various functions. At the same time, higher and higher requirements are placed on the autonomous navigation ability of spacecraft. The navigation system is an indispensable and important equipment for the spacecraft and plays an important role in the flight activities of the spacecraft [1]. The astronomical navigation system is an autonomous navigation system with high-precision attitude, positioning and orientation. As a high-precision spacecraft attitude measurement device, the star sensor is playing an increasingly important role [2]. Due to the high cost of testing and experimenting star sensors in orbit, simulation experiments on the ground become necessary. Conducting star sensor experiments is necessary to establish an accurate star map simulation system. It is the premise and foundation of operations such as background space target detection [3, 4], and the generation of digital images is an important part of star map simulation [5].

The present star map simulation software source code is hard to obtain, the functions is limited, and usually the graphical user interface (GUI) is hard to configure as needed in practical. The disadvantages above are handled by designing and implementing of a new digital star map simulation module. The idea of mixed programming is adopted to realize the simulation system of star image simulation, which combines the flexible graphical user interface design ability of Visual C# and the image processing and computing ability of MATLAB. This module can be used to develop star map recognition, space target detection and other requirements based on this system.

2 Principle and Method of Star Map Simulation

This section introduces the algorithm flow of the star chart simulation system in detail, which mainly includes the following steps: star table acquisition and preprocessing, the Visual Studio simulation system interface obtains user input parameters and initializes them, calls MATLAB functions, and passes the obtained parameters to the function, MATLAB transforms star coordinates to generate a simulated star map. The simulation system interface displays the generated star map on the visual interface. The program algorithm flow is shown in Fig. 1.

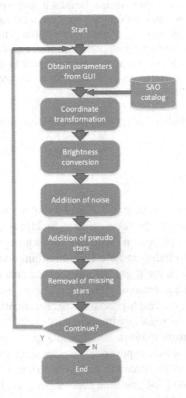

Fig. 1. Flow of the star simulation program

2.1 Acquisition and Preprocessing of SAO Catalog

Commonly used star catalogs include the SAO star catalog of the Smithsonian Observatory in the United States, Hipparcos star catalog, and Henry Draper Catalogue (HD). The SAO star catalog contains more than 200,000 stars information [6]. This paper uses the SAO star catalog as the data source. It contains 30 fields, a lot of field information is not needed, so the star number (name), longitude (LII, The Galactic Longitude), latitude (BII, The Galactic Latitude), visual magnitude (Vmag, the visual magnitude) is taken. The information of the four fields is sorted into a short table with smaller file size, which is convenient for program processing, and is sorted according to the apparent magnitude from small to large, which is convenient for searching and processing.

2.2 Coordinate System Transformation and Star simulation

The SAO star catalog stores the star's right ascension, ranging from 0° to 360°, the celestial equatorial equinox to the east is positive, and the declination, ranging from -90° to 90°, from the celestial equator to the north celestial pole is positive, the direction vector of the projection point of the star on the celestial sphere in the celestial space Cartesian coordinate system is:

$$\begin{bmatrix} U \\ V \\ W \end{bmatrix} = \begin{bmatrix} cos\alpha cos\delta \\ sin\alpha cos\delta \\ sin\delta \end{bmatrix} \tag{1}$$

The celestial space coordinate system can obtain the star sensor coordinate system through the sequential Euler rotation transformation of the three coordinate axes. Let the rotation matrix corresponding to the coordinate transformation be M, and M is obtained by multiplying the rotation matrices of the three coordinate axes, the transformation can be described as:

$$\begin{bmatrix} X \\ Y \\ Z \end{bmatrix} = M \begin{bmatrix} U \\ V \\ W \end{bmatrix} = M \begin{bmatrix} cos\alpha cos\delta \\ sin\alpha cos\delta \\ sin\delta \end{bmatrix} \tag{2}$$

The star sensor coordinate system to the charge coupled device (CCD) image plane coordinate system conforms to the principle of pinhole imaging, and the projection transformation formula can be obtained by using similar triangle formula.

$$\begin{bmatrix} x \\ y \end{bmatrix} = -f \begin{bmatrix} X/Z \\ Y/Z \end{bmatrix} \tag{3}$$

And:

$$f = \frac{N_x s}{2tan(FOV_x/2)} = \frac{N_y s}{2tan(FOV_y/2)} \tag{4}$$

In the formula, f is the focal length of the CCD camera system, N_x and N_y are the number of pixels in the x-axis and y-axis directions of the CCD detector, respectively, s

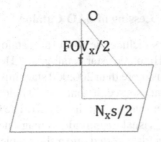

Fig. 2. Relationship between focal length, cell size and field of view angle

is the size of each pixel [7], and FOV_x and FOV_y are the size of the field of view in the x-axis and y-axis direction, as is shown in Fig. 2.

When formulas (2) and (4) are brought into formula (3), the final conversion relationship from the stellar coordinates to the CCD image plane coordinate system is:

$$\begin{bmatrix} x_i \\ y_i \end{bmatrix} = \frac{N \cdot s}{2tan(FOV/2)} \begin{bmatrix} \frac{cos\delta_i sin(\alpha_i-\alpha_0)}{sin\delta_0 sin\delta_i+cos\delta_0 cos\delta_i cos(\alpha_i-\alpha_0)} \\ \frac{cos\delta_0 sin\delta_i-sin\delta_0 cos\delta_i cos(\alpha_i-\alpha_0)}{sin\delta_0 sin\delta_i+cos\delta_0 cos\delta_i cos(\alpha_i-\alpha_0)} \end{bmatrix} \tag{5}$$

Among them, (x_i, y_i) is the coordinate of the i-th star in the image plane image coordinate system, the coordinate center is the center of the image, N is the number of pixels in the coordinate axis direction of the CCD detector, s is the size of each pixel, and FOV is angle of the field of view, α_i, δ_i are the coordinates of the i-th star, and α_0, δ_0 are the direction of the CCD boresight.

Let the radius of the circular field of view be R, α_0, δ_0 be the direction of the CCD boresight, and the star right ascension and declination coordinates is (α_i, δ_i) and the radius is R. In the circular field of view, the following inequalities can be obtained according to the spherical triangle formula, and the schematic diagram is shown in Fig. 3. In addition, it should be noted that since the right ascension is between 0° and 360°, when the calculated right ascension range is less than 0°, it is necessary to judge the right ascension plus 360° and then judge again. When the right ascension is greater than 360°, it should be subtracted by 360°.

$$\alpha_0 - \frac{R}{cos\delta_0} \le \alpha \le \alpha_0 + \frac{R}{cos\delta_0} \tag{6}$$

$$\delta_0 - R \le \delta \le \delta_0 + R \tag{7}$$

As shown in Fig. 4, the rectangular detector is inscribed inside the circular field of view. Since the stars located outside the rectangle and the inner area of the circle cannot be imaged on the detector, a second constraint needs to be added. The coordinate constraints on the detector need to satisfy the following inequalities.

$$-\frac{N_x}{2} \le x_i \le \frac{N_x}{2} \tag{8}$$

$$-\frac{N_y}{2} \le x_i \le \frac{N_y}{2} \tag{9}$$

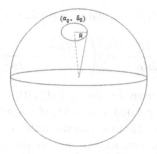

Fig. 3. Constraint of star imaging for circular field of view

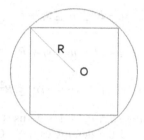

Fig. 4. Relationship between circular field of view and rectangle detector

The visual magnitude and image gray level of the stars in the star catalog can be converted by linear transformation [8] and exponential transformation [9], where the linear transformation adopts the following formula.

$$H_i = 255 - 10 \cdot (M_i - M_{min}) = 255 - 10 \cdot (M_i + 1.6) \tag{10}$$

Among them, 255 is the maximum value of 8bit quantization, and M_{min} is the visual magnitude of the brightest Sirius star in the star catalog, which is -1.6, and M_i is the visual magnitude of $star_i$, and H_i is the center brightness of $star_i$.

The exponential conversion formula is as follows.

$$H_i = \frac{255}{2.51^{M_i-5}} \tag{11}$$

However, after experimental comparison, it is found that in most cases, due to the difference in the brightness of the visual magnitudes in the field of view, the exponential conversion method makes the fainter stars almost invisible. Under the same parameter conditions more stars can be seen in the field of view with the linear conversion method.

The simulation system supports setting the variance of the Gaussian dispersion radius of the stars on the detector and the display radius R of the star point. The display radius R of the star point is the pixel range that participates in the calculation of the Gaussian dispersion pixel point around the $star_i$. The gray distribution of the star point uses two-dimensional Gaussian fitting distribution model, the center point x_i and y_i is the coordinates of the star, and the variance σ^2 is the Gaussian dispersion radius set by the user. The default setting is 1. The calculation formula is as follows.

$$I(m, n) = \frac{H_i}{2\pi\sigma^2} \cdot exp\left(-\frac{(x_m - x_i)^2 + (y_n - y_i)^2}{2\sigma^2}\right) \tag{12}$$

The maximum value is determined by formula (10), m and n are the range near the image coordinates of $star_i$ calculated by formula (5), and the following three conditions must be satisfied, among which (13), (14) are the search conditions, (15) is judgement of the calculation conditions, m, n are integers and are located within the valid coordinate range of the entire image, x_i and y_i is the coordinates of the star cand R is the display radius of the star point.

$$x_i - R \leq m \leq x_i + R \tag{13}$$

$$y_i - R \leq n \leq y_i + R \tag{14}$$

$$(m - x_i)^2 + (n - y_i)^2 \leq R^2 \tag{15}$$

The background noise of the starry sky image uses a mean value of 0, the noise variance is input by the user, and the default value is Gaussian white noise of 0.01. The position noise adopts a Gaussian distribution, the mean value is 0, the standard deviation is input by the user. The position noise is added to the ideal position of the image coordinate system calculated by the stars catalog, and the default value is 2 pixels. The visual magnitude noise obeys the Gaussian distribution with a mean value of 0, and the standard deviation can be configured as a noise with a default value of 0.1. Various noises can be added and configured simultaneously.

If "Missing Stars" function is selected, the specified number of stars will disappear, the default is 1 star missing. If "Pseudo Stars" function are selected, the specified number of pseudo stars of random brightness will be generated at random positions in the field of view. The default value is 1 pseudo star generated.

MATLAB library references MLApp (mlapp.tlb, Matlab Automation Server Type Library) and MWArray (MWArray.dll, MATLAB array wrapper classes for.NET) in Visual C# is added to support the capability of mixed programming, as shown in Fig. 5.

Fig. 5. Add reference library from MATLAB

The interface of the simulation system is shown in Fig. 6. The left side is the user parameter input area, including the detector limit magnitude, the CCD boresight point, the resolution of the generated star map image, the size of the CCD field of view, the detector pixel size, The setting or operation of the conversion relationship of magnitude and gray value, star point display radius, Gaussian spot dispersion radius variance, background noise, star point position noise, magnitude noise, missing stars, pseudo-stars and other parameters, the right side is the simulated starry sky image in the corresponding area of the corresponding area of the star map. After setting the user input parameters, click the start simulation button to preview the effect generated by the star map simulation in real time. The lower side is some information returned, and the "Save star map" button can save the generated star map for ease of use.

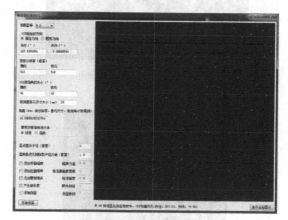

Fig. 6. GUI of star simulation module

3 Simulation Result Analysis

Setting the direction of the camera's boresight to the celestial coordinate position of Sirius (α Canis Major) with the brightest visual magnitude in the SAO table, that is, the right ascension is 227.2303061°, the declination is -8.89029581°, and the field of view is set to 40° in order to be able to display the constellation Canis Major where the entire Sirius is located, which is convenient for verifying the accuracy of the generated star map. The magnitude grayscale conversion relationship is set to linear, and the rest of the parameters are kept by the system default value. The star map generated by the simulation module is shown in Fig. 7. Sirius is in the center of the star map. It should be noted that the red line is added manually for the convenience of identification later. Using the Sky Map mobile app to query the location of Sirius, displaying it in the center of the screen, and taking a screenshot. The result is shown in the Fig. 8. As shown in Fig. 8, after detailed comparison, the images generated by the simulation system are consistent with the main stars, and the positions of the stars around the "wolf" body are also consistent with the Sky Map (the key points of former image match the latter through proper scaling value 1.7273 and moving), which verifies the accuracy of the simulation module.

Fig. 7. One image generated by star simulation module

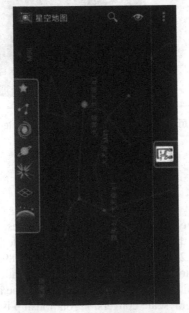

Fig. 8. Image of Sirius generated by Sky Map

4   Conclusion

The SAO star catalog is organized and preprocessed, and the conversion relationship between the celestial coordinates of the stars to the coordinates of the star sensor and the coordinates of the CCD image is deduced in detail. Taking advantage of the respective advantages of the two programming languages and using the mixed programming technology of Visual C# and MATLAB, a sky image generation module with arbitrarily configurable parameters is realized, which supports image background noise, star position noise, star magnitude noise, removal of missing stars, and addition of pseudo stars. The simulation is customized and compared with the results of Sky Map in detail, and the consistency of the results is verified, which proves the effectiveness of the simulation system. The simulation system can be applied to the star simulator system, which is of great significance to the research and testing of star sensors.

References

1. Zhang, G.: Star map recognition. National Defense Industry Press (2011). (in Chinese)
2. Nan, N., Cao, D., Zhang, H, et al.: A star map noise reduction algorithm based on space-time correlation. Space Recovery Remote Sens. **38**(1), 10 (2017). (in Chinese)
3. Luyao, H.A.N., Chan, T.A.N., Yunmeng, L.I.U., et al.: Research on the on-orbit real-time space target detection algorithm. Spacecraft Recovery Remote Sens. **42**(6), 122–131 (2021). (in Chinese)
4. Zhang, K., Zhou, F., Fu, D.: Research on space-based space target monitoring visible light remote sensor. Space Recovery Remote Sens. **26**(4), 5 (2005)
5. Xiang, L., Hongliang, Z., Yuanju, H.: Design and simulation of digital star map generation algorithm. Lab. Res. Explor. **37**(2), 120–123 (2018). (in Chinese)
6. Luo, L.: Research on star point extraction and star map recognition method based on star sensor. (in Chinese)
7. Zhang, R.: Design and implementation of star map recognition algorithm based on CCD star sensor. PLA University of Information Engineering (2007). (in Chinese)
8. Shuai, Z., Liu, Z., Xinlu, L.: Realization of simulated star map with noise. China. Opt. **7**(4), 581–587 (2016). (in Chinese)
9. Zhang, J., Lou, S., Ren, J.: A Simulation Generation method of space observation image. Electro-Opt. Control (11) (2014). (in Chinese)

Author Index

Printed in the United States
by Baker & Taylor Publisher Services